P9-AET-584

second edition

READINGS & CASES IN

INTERNATIONAL HUMAN

RESOURCE MANAGEMENT

Mark Mendenhall
University of Tennessee at Chattanooga

Gary Oddou
San Jose State University

SOUTH-WESTERN College Publishing

An International Thomson Publishing Company

Acquisitions Editor:	Randy G. Haubner
Developmental Editor:	Alice C. Denny
Production Editor:	Sharon L. Smith
Production Supplier:	Rebecca Gray
Cover Design:	Michael H. Stratton
Cover Photographer:	Photonica

GJ76BA
Copyright © 1995
by South-Western College Publishing
Cincinnati, Ohio

Library of Congress Cataloging-in-Publication Data

Readings and cases in international human resource manage-
    ment/ [edited by] Mark Mendenhall, Gary Oddou.—2nd ed.
        p.   cm.
    Includes bibliographical references and index.
    ISBN 0-538-84737-9
        1. Personnel management—Cross-cultural studies.
    2. Intercultural communication—Case studies. 3. International
    business enterprises—Personnel management—Cross-cultural
    studies. 4. Corporate culture—Cross-cultural studies.
    I. Mendenhall, Mark A. II. Oddou, Gary R. III. Title:
    International human resource management.
    HF5549.R3813   1995
    658.3—dc20   94-37700
                                                              CIP

ISBN: 0-538-84737-9

1 2 3 4 5 6 7 EB 0 9 8 7 6 5 4

Printed in the United States of America

I (T) P
International Thomson Publishing

South-Western College Publishing is an ITP Company. The ITP trademark is used under license.

Contributing Authors

NANCY J. ADLER
McGill University
CANADA

PAUL S. ADLER
*University of
Southern California*

RAE ANDRE
Northeastern University

AYAKO ASAKURA
JAPAN

PAUL BACDAYAN
University of Michigan

BARBARA BAKHTARI

SCHON BEECHLER
Columbia University

ALAN BERNSTEIN
Conservation Corporation
SOUTH AFRICA

ALLAN BIRD
*California Polytechnic
University, San Luis Obispo*

J. STEWART BLACK
*Thunderbird, The American
Graduate School of
International Management*

NAKIYE A.
BOYACIGILLER
San Jose State University

MARK C. BUTLER
San Diego State University

ROBERT E. COLE
University of Michigan

MARK CROWDER
Olan Mills, Inc.

WILLIAM H. DAVIDSON
*University of Southern
California*

C. BROOKLYN DERR
University of Utah/IMD
USA/SWITZERLAND

PETER J. DOWLING
University of Tasmania
AUSTRALIA

YVES DOZ
INSEAD
FRANCE

ROBERT W. EDER
Portland State University

GARETH EVANS

COLETTE A. FRAYNE
*California Polytechnic
University, San Luis Obispo*

J. MICHAEL GERINGER
*California Polytechnic
University, San Luis Obispo*

HAL B. GREGERSEN
Brigham Young University

MASAO HANAOKA
Daito Bunka University
JAPAN

ALAN HAWKINS
Brigham Young University

MARILYN HELMS
University of Tennessee,
Chattanooga

MARTIN HILB
University of St. Gallen
SWITZERLAND

SUSAN E. JACKSON
New York University

MERRICK L. JONES
University of Manchester
UNITED KINGDOM

HENRY W. LANE
University of Western Ontario
CANADA

PETER LAWRENCE
University of Loughborough
UNITED KINGDOM

PAUL LEMIEUX

MARK MENDENHALL
University of Tennessee,
Chattanooga

TOMASZ MROCZKOWSKI
American University

GARY ODDOU
San Jose State University

ASBJORN OSLAND
Lewis and Clark College

J. BONNER RITCHIE
Brigham Young University

WILLIAM ROOF
Science Applications
International Corporation

SUSAN SCHNEIDER
INSEAD
FRANCE

RANDALL S. SCHULER
New York University

JAMES. G. SCOVILLE
University of Minnesota

PAUL SPARROW
Manchester Business School
UNITED KINGDOM

SULLY TAYLOR
Portland State University

MARY B. TEAGARDEN
San Diego State University

DENICE E. WELCH
Monash University
AUSTRALIA

B. JOSEPH WHITE
University of Michigan

WARNER P.
WOODWORTH
Brigham Young University

LORNA L. WRIGHT
Queens University
CANADA

ALBERTO ZANZI
Suffolk University

Contents

READINGS AND CASES IN INTERNATIONAL HUMAN RESOURCE MANAGEMENT

The White Water Rapids of International Human Resource Management: An Introduction and Preface

Mark Mendenhall and
Gary Oddou

It is with gratitude that we undertake the second edition of this book, and the gratitude is for you, be you teacher or student, for your support of the first edition has motivated us to update the book to keep up with world events and new developments in international human resource management. In order to introduce this new, second edition, please consider how we introduced the first edition to you, back in 1991. The introduction began with the following observations:

> At the time of this writing . . . the world of politics and business had been turned upside down. The democratization movement in the People's Republic of China (PRC) was snuffed out by the bloody massacre at Tiananmen Square. Currently, the leadership of the People's Republic of China is looking to the past for economic and management models and is downplaying and slowly eradicating Western influences in the country's economy. Whether the capitalist-oriented free-trade zones in the PRC will go along with this is anyone's guess. What will happen in the go-go capitalist mecca of Hong Kong in 1997 is anyone's guess.

> Additionally, the Eastern Bloc nations have revolted against over forty years of Communist control, and long-suppressed democratic and capitalistic tendencies are flowering. East and West Germany are rapidly moving toward a political and economic reunification; Hungary and Poland are well on their way to reinstitutionalizing market systems into their economies; and even Romania has thrown off a narcissistic dictator and is wrestling with the social, economic, and political problems of remodeling a totalitarian nation into one more democratic.

> The European Economic Community (EEC) is moving toward integration on all fronts presently, though the Eastern bloc

Source: This article was written especially for this book.

1

nations' defection to democratic socialism and capitalism has thrown a stick in the spokes of the 1992 plan. Currently, no one knows how this will affect the EEC's plans—especially if West and East Germany reunify (as they seem to be doing with breathtaking speed). What will Europe really look like, be like, and act like, socially as well as in the business realm, when all barriers between the countries are eradicated? What are the economic threats and opportunities to countries and companies that want to do business there?

Even Japan, a country visualized by many in the Western world as being stable and conformist within its own boundaries, was rocked by political and business scandals that sent the monolithic ruling party (LDP) into a tailspin. Though the LDP managed to retain its power in the recent elections, the turmoil perhaps presages possible shifts and changes in the continental shelf of Japanese government and business policies. The cover of the April 23, 1990 edition of *Business Week* proclaims, "Suddenly, a series of shocks is buffeting the mighty Japanese economy. The stock market plunged 30%. The yen is weakening. Inflation and interest rates are both on the rise. Political leadership is weak. And now some strains are appearing in the nation's normally harmonious social structure. Japan has proved remarkably adaptable to adversity in the past. This time, it may be harder." Even Japan seems to be in the throes of social change.

Rereading our words of almost four years ago seems like reading ancient history. The PRC weathered the storm of Tiananmen Square and is currently employed in a vigorous effort, under the direction of Zhu Rongii, to restructure its economy towards a market system with federalized structures for banking, tax, and industry—albeit under a Communist political system and with public ownership (*Business Week*, January 31, 1994). The PRC seems to be back in business after the moral outrage of the West over Tiananmen Square. What will happen in Hong Kong in 1997 is still anyone's guess.

The re-unification of East and West Germany, long only a dream in the minds of many Germans, has occurred since the publication of the first edition, and the dream has become a hard-edged reality. Ethnic discontent, high unemployment, the need for retraining, and the albatross of non-competitive East German firms has challenged the acumen of Germany's policy makers. The EEC came to the house of integration with flowers, and upon seeing the face of integration, retreated from the doorstep. Integration looked much prettier from afar. Whether the relationship will blossom is now in question.

Japan, unlike China, continued into its descent into social change with more vigor, by kicking the LDP out of office. However, Hosokawa's coalition government was dealt a blow only days ago when its political reform package was voted down in the Diet. In reaction, the Tokyo Stock Exchange plunged. Japan continues to be in a recession. Pundits disagree on the long-term effects of the recession on the Japanese economy—no one can clearly see the meaning behind the tea leaves of the present in the Land of the Rising Sun. We will just have to wait and see what happens.

From an American standpoint the current issues of the day are violence, health-care, and North Korea. (Do the North Koreans have nuclear weapons or don't they? If they do, what should we do about it? If we do something about it, what will they do?) The North American Free Trade Act was an issue, but after its narrow passage it seems to have been relegated to the shelves of antiquity almost overnight. The future of the world is, indeed, not clear at all.

Thus, we reiterate what we wrote back in 1991. If this updated introduction seems outdated to you, owing to the changes that have taken place since its writing, then our point is proven all the more: We live in a world where the only thing we can count on is that change will take place.

The "White Water Rapids" of International Human Resources Management_____

Business leaders of the present—let alone the future—need to possess international business skills par excellence in order to survive the chaotic world of international business. It also goes without saying that human resource managers will face new, unforeseen obstacles. Peter Vaill uses the metaphor of "permanent white water" to describe the unpredictable, dynamic nature of doing business in the latter part of the twentieth century.

> Most managers are taught to think of themselves as paddling their canoes on calm, still lakes . . . They're led to believe that they should be pretty much able to go where they want, when they want, using the means that are under their control. Sure there will be temporary disruptions during changes of various sorts—periods when they will have to shoot the rapids in their canoes—but the disruptions will be temporary, and when things settle back down, they'll be back in a calm, still lake mode. But it has been my experience . . . that you never get out of the rapids! No sooner do you begin to digest one change than another one comes along to keep things unstuck. In fact, there are usually lots of changes going on at once. The feeling is one of continuous upset and chaos.[1]

This metaphor aptly illustrates the world of international business. As Vaill notes, in the world of international business "things are only very partially under control, yet the effective navigator of the rapids is not behaving randomly or aimlessly. Intelligence, experience, and skill

_____

[1] Peter Vaill, *Managing as a Performing Art: New Ideas for a World of Chaotic Change.* (San Francisco: Jossey-Bass, 1989) p. 2.

are being exercised, albeit in ways that we hardly know how to perceive, let alone describe" (p. 2). This book deals with the challenges that human resource managers will face in the 1990s and beyond. What will be the general nature of those challenges? Perhaps an example of a firm or individual would help illustrate these challenges; let us consider the case of Robin Earl.

Robin Earl's "White Water Rapids" _____

Robin is Director of Human Resources for BCN, a firm that among other things manufactures a line of semiconductors. BCN has been very successful in the last ten years. Sales have increased at an annual rate of 13 percent and profits have correspondingly grown.

BCN has had overseas sales offices for the last seven years, exporting its products from its local manufacturing operations to South America and Asia. Recently, BCN's top management has been mulling over the possibility of developing manufacturing capabilities in South America and Asia—and possibly even in Europe. Doing so would allow BCN to take advantage of cheaper labor rates and avoid export barriers. In addition, it could be more responsive to local demand for its products.

Robin was asked by the firm's CEO to prepare an analysis (due on his desk in two weeks) of the human resource impact such moves would have on the firm. As Robin sat down at her desk, she began to jot down ideas. She found herself somewhat baffled by this "international" angle of HRM, as she had no experience or training in managing human resources internationally. The following are some of her thoughts as she attempted to create an outline for her report.

I. How Will International Assignments Fit Into BCN's Business Strategy to Become a Multinational Firm?

Do we have a clearly focused business strategy for becoming a multinational firm? She made a mental note to call John Fukumoto, the V.P. of Finance to see how far the thinking of the top management team had progressed on that front. *How will the development of BCN's human resources fit into such a plan? I wonder why I am not on that planning team?* Robin wondered how she could insert herself into that process without being suspected of having ulterior motives.

What kind of perspective and experience should BCN's future top management have if they will be leading a true multinational firm? How will that experience be best obtained—through international assignments or by the use of consultants? Am I going to be responsible for educating management regarding international issues? If so, *it's the blind leading the blind,* she thought, for she would not even be sure how to evaluate the validity of an external consultant's proposals. *I could always hire experts to evaluate the bid proposals of consulting firms,* she thought, *but that would run into serious budget squeezes for my department.*

Will local managers—if we use local managers—desire to be promoted to U.S. headquarters? Will top management desire that? Fifteen years from now what will, and what should, BCN's top management look like: an Asian managing a South American plant and a mixture of South Americans, Asians, Europeans, and Americans at headquarters? The cost of hiring the numbers of new workers—not to mention well qualified managers—is not going to be loose change. I hope they aren't ignoring the cost of hiring well qualified managers and retaining them in their financial analyses, Robin thought. *How will we retain the best and the brightest? What do Asians want in rewards? What do South Americans want? Is a good salary enough or are other factors involved?*

II. Which Countries Have Cultures That Best Fit BCN's Needs?

Robin remembered reading a newspaper article that mentioned that one of the factors important to Japanese firms locating in the U.S. was finding compatible regional cultural norms. The Japanese liked the Southern U.S. culture because of its regard for interpersonal relations in business settings, tradition, and respect for elders and persons in positions of authority. *Which countries have educational systems that would best support the knowledge base that our personnel will need? Which countries have social systems that favor unions more than management? Which cultures within these regions are most favorable to American expatriates and their families? Most importantly, which cultures promote a strong work ethic?*

Which countries have governments that are stable and are not likely to change and upset the equilibrium of our workers' and managers' work schedules? What about the possibility of terrorism? Will I have to devise a terrorism-prevention training program? Which countries are friendly to us, not just businesswise but in their perceptions of Americans and their right to manage the local residents? I wonder how much kidnap insurance costs? Robin's mind began to wander. She envisioned herself in a small, boxlike hole covered with rusty, iron bars. When would her kidnappers give her water? Her reverie was broken by a more practical concern that flashed across her mind.

III. Should We Send Our Own Personnel Overseas or Hire Locally?

Which countries in Asia, South America, or Europe have qualified personnel to staff manufacturing operations from top to bottom? Do some countries have laws that require hiring a certain percentage of local workers? Robin remembered meeting a man once at a professional convention who had worked for a mining company in Africa. He reported having had to hire local workers for all positions below middle management level with the promise to phase out all Americans within ten years.

Can or should the subsidiary management come from BCN headquarters? If not, where would we find local managers to hire? The universities? Robin recalled reading once that in France the norm was to hire managers from the "Grand Ecoles" and not from the universities.

If we send our personnel, who should go? How long should their assignments be? How expensive will it be to house an American family at their accustomed standard of living in the new country? How should we select the Americans to send? Should we base our decisions on experience in the company, adaptability potential, or desire to relocate? What if nobody wants to go?

IV. How Will We Train Employees for Such Assignments?

How much training will they need before they go? Do they need language training or is English good enough? Robin thought that most business people around the world speak English, so maybe this was not really an issue. *Will the firm budget my department the resources necessary to do quality training or will I be left with a budget that will allow nothing more than bringing in a few local professors for a couple of hours each to do area briefings? Who can I call on to do the training?*

Robin felt somewhat relieved when she remembered reading about some cross-cultural training firms in the ad section of a HRM newsletter she reads. But her confidence ebbed when the following thought occurred to her: *How will I know if the training these external consultants provide is valid and helpful or just a dog and pony show? Can I, with my staff, develop our own training program? What kind of time and money will such an endeavor require?* As Robin began mentally planning a strategy to develop training programs with her staff, her mind switched to yet another problem.

V. What Are the Career Implications of Foreign Assignments?

Should the assignments be developmental or should slots simply be filled as they open up, regardless of whether or not the move will develop the employee? Robin was vaguely aware that companies such as IBM, CIBA-GEIGY, and Philips view international assignments as an integral part of their management development for senior posts. *If the assignment is developmental, what will we do when the employee returns?* Robin wondered if the company would give her authority to dictate what position returning managers should receive . . . She doubted they would give her that authority.

So, how will we reintegrate these employees into BCN's home operations? How will the HRM department keep informed of the needs, concerns, performance, and evaluation of the overseas employees? By phone? Telex? Fax? Site visits? Robin wondered whether she could justify trips to the Orient as site visits. They may be necessary but might be viewed by others as a new perk for the HRM department.

VI. How Productive Will the Cheap Labor Be?

If we do opt to set up in a country where the labor rates are inexpensive, can we introduce our management systems into the manufacturing plants? Will those systems be in harmony with the work culture of that country? I wonder if we will run into transfer of technology problems? Probably. Okay, so, how do we train local workers to understand how we do things at BCN? Will I have to design those training programs too?

I wonder if our managers will have to develop unique incentive systems to get their subordinates to work. No, probably, not . . . well, then again, maybe. After all, the people under me have different buttons that make them work harder—those buttons are not the same for everyone here in the U.S. Is it possible, Robin wondered, *for some cultures to have work norms that are antithetical to promotion and pay inducements? I think those would be universal motivators! Maybe this won't be a major problem. Maybe it will be more of a fine-tuning issue in terms of adapting our job design, incentive systems, and motivational techniques to the country where we decide to set up shop.* Then the thought occurred to her, *What about motivating and evaluating the Americans overseas?*

VII. How Should We Do Performance Evaluation?

Can we just use the same forms, procedures and, criteria, or is there something unique about a foreign assignment that requires unique performance evaluation systems? When should we evaluate people? Robin remembered reading in a professional newsletter that expatriate employees require at least six months to settle into their overseas assignments. *Would it be fair to evaluate employees before six months? When would it be valid? After eight, ten, or twelve months? This is getting very messy,* Robin sighed.

Should the criteria by which to judge performance in Asia and other places be relative to the country in question, or should we use the same evaluation criteria everywhere? The last thing Robin felt like doing was overseeing the development of a new performance evaluation system! *We can get by with our current one,* she mentally noted. *Who should do the evaluating? Headquarters, the regional subsidiary superiors, peers, or a mixture of superiors and subordinates? Should the criteria revolve around bottom-line figures or personnel objectives? If financial type performance criteria are emphasized, what happens if the dollar depreciates significantly against the local currency and wipes out the expatriate manager's cost savings and profits? How can the expatriate manager be evaluated, motivated, and rewarded under such conditions?*

What about nationality differences in performance evaluation? If an American manager is being evaluated by a Peruvian subsidiary manager, will the evaluation be fair or is there potential for some sort of cultural bias? What if the American manager is a woman? Will we be able to put together an attractive, but not too costly, compensation package for our expatriates? I wonder what such a package would look like.

VIII. Will the Unions Be Trouble?

Robin's thoughts were now racing between problems rapidly—the above question about the unions jumped into her consciousness unannounced. *I*

remember reading somewhere, she mused, *that in order to shut down a manufacturing facility in France (or was it West Germany or Sweden?) management
had to give the workers a full year's notice, retrain them, and then find them
new jobs!* She knew the top management of her firm would find such a
contingency troubling at best. *Well, maybe the Asian labor markets are less
unionized and won't be as problematic.* Then Robin recalled meeting a public relations spokeswoman for a toy firm at a party, and the nightmare
she had described.

It seems that the U.S. management of her company had pressured
the contract manufacturers in Hong Kong and the PRC to increase production dramatically in order to fill unforeseen demands during the
Christmas season. The press had gotten hold of cases where female
workers were working sixteen-hour days with no breaks; if they complained they were terminated on the spot. Also, some of the women
had miscarried. It was a public relations nightmare. *Maybe dealing with
unions wouldn't be all bad . . . maybe unions would protect us from question-
able ethical nightmares,* Robin thought. But then she thought of codetermination laws in countries like West Germany and worker's representatives sitting on the local boards of directors—that would not be easy
for American managers to stomach. And what about managing people
from other cultures? *We have a hard enough time in our California and
Texas plants, let alone overseas!*

As Robin put down her pen, the obvious complexity of the report
loomed before her. She had just scratched the surface of the basic
human resources issues of "going international" and there seemed to
be no end to the potential permutations around each problem. *This will
be no easy task,* she concluded. As she left her office and made her way
to the parking garage, she wondered, *Where can I go for help?*

The Aim of This Book

BCN's situation closely parallels the initial path on which virtually all
multinational firms have had to tread. Within this "international" context of business operations, many business decisions become critical.
While some of those decisions pertain to a firm's financial or physical
resources, the most neglected and perhaps most important decisions to
be made concern the management of the firm's international human
resources. One of the greatest problems is the lack of an international
perspective on the part of most American businesspeople. As a member of one culture, the businessperson tends to see life from that perspective, to judge events from that perspective, and to make decisions
based on that perspective. In an increasingly global business environment, such a perspective breeds failure.

This text has been developed to fill a void that has existed for too
long. Our principal objective is this: to sensitize the reader to the complex

human resource issues that exist in the international business environment. With this primary objective in mind, we have attempted to represent many parts of the world in the cases and readings. However, there has been no attempt to force-fit something into the book for the sake of regional or geographic representation. Our first concern was including in the book what we, our reviewers, and editors felt were the best available cases and readings in the international HRM field.

AACSB, Creativity, and Course Design

This book can be used in a variety of ways in human resource management courses. It can stand alone, if the instructor's preference is to teach predominately a case course. It can be used in tandem with other books in the Wadsworth International Business Series (*International Dimensions of Human Resource Management* by Peter J. Dowling and Randall S. Schuler or *International Dimensions of Organizational Behavior* by Nancy J. Adler) or as a supplement to them. Or it can be used as a main text in a human resource management course and supplemented with other readings and texts with which the instructor is comfortable.

Perhaps its most compelling use is that of helping to satisfy AACSB requirements in course offerings; it can be used with a traditional introductory text as a supplement in order to insert an international dimension into the course. This would facilitate matrixing into a traditional human resource management course an international dimension. However the text is used, we feel that it will spice up one's course, mainly because students find international problems fascinating and complex and unique, as we do.

The Instructor's Manual

Our second concern is to correct a problem that some of you had with the first edition; namely, that you wished that there were a teacher's manual to accompany the book. There actually was a teacher's manual available, but evidently that fact was not adequately communicated by us or by our previous publisher. So, to set the record straight, be assured that there IS a teacher's manual that accompanies this textbook, and it is available to all instructors who adopt the book for their courses. Please contact your South-Western College Publishing representative to order it.

Our third concern was to include a multiperspective view in the overall balance of cases and readings. In other words, we do not focus solely on any one country or on any one movement of operations (e.g., a U.S. firm moving overseas). To reiterate, we wanted as true a global perspective in our text as page length restrictions would allow. Finally, if we can begin to develop a sensitivity to the differences in human resource systems and broaden the student's and the manager's perspective on the appropriate management of human resources in a multinational context, then we will consider ourselves to have been successful. This book hopes to assist in making the following vision a reality.

> Peer into the executive suite of the year 2000 and see a completely different person. His undergraduate degree is in French literature, but he also has a joint M.B.A./engineering degree. He started in research and was quickly picked out as a potential CEO. He zigzagged from research to marketing to finance. He proved himself in Brazil by turning around a failing joint venture. He speaks Portuguese and French and is on a first-name basis with commerce ministers in half a dozen countries. Unlike his predecessor's predecessor, he isn't a drill sergeant. He is first among equals in five-person Office of the Chief Executive.[2]

Acknowledgements _____

We would like to thank all those who have contributed to this book. Many of the authors willingly sent us cases, articles, manuscripts in progress, and bibliographies that they had developed over the years. We regret that we could not include all the sources offered to us. Our thanks go primarily to two bastions of patience, perseverance, and professionalism: Alice Denny and Rebecca Gray. These two individuals literally made this book "happen." It is a rare pleasure to work with true professionals—Alice and Rebecca truly provided us with such an experience.

A special thanks goes to Terri Rieth, co-author of the instructor's manual, for her editing work and helpful suggestions, and to our wives, Janet and Jane, for putting up with our foolishness all these years over things international—they make all we accomplish possible and our gratitude to them is eternal.

MARK MENDENHALL
Signal Mountain, Tennessee

GARY ODDOU
San Jose, California

---

[2] A. Bennett, "Going Global: The Chief Executives in the Year 2000 Will Be Experienced Abroad," *Wall Street Journal*, February 27, 1989, A1, A4.

Part 1

CULTURE AND STRATEGY AND INTERNATIONAL HUMAN RESOURCE MANAGEMENT

Convergence or Divergence: Human Resource Practices and Policies for Competitive Advantage Worldwide

Reading 1.1
Paul Sparrow
Randall S. Schuler
Susan E. Jackson

Abstract

The world is becoming far more competitive and volatile than ever before, causing firms to seek to gain competitive advantage whenever and wherever possible. As traditional sources and means such as capital, technology or location become less significant as a basis for competitive advantage, firms are turning to more innovative sources. One of these is the management of human resources. Whilst traditionally regarded as a personnel department function, it is now being widely shared among managers and non-managers, personnel directors and line managers. As the management of human resources is seen increasingly in terms of competitive advantage, the question that arises is: What must we do to gain this advantage? Many of the most successful firms now have to operate globally, and this gives rise to a second question: Do firms in different parts of the globe practice human resource management (HRM) for competitive advantage differently? Because of their importance, these two questions form the primary focus of this investigation. Data from a worldwide respondent survey of chief executive officers and human resource managers from twelve countries are cluster analysed to identify country groupings across a range of human resource policies and practices that could be used for competitive advantage. Differences and similarities on fifteen dimensions of these policies and practices are statistically determined and the results interpreted in the light of relevant literature. This investigation concludes that there is indeed a convergence in the use of HRM for competitive advantage. However, in pursuing this convergence there are some clear divergences, nuances and specific themes in the areas of HRM that will take the fore and in the way in which specific aspects such as culture, work structuring, performance management and resourcing will be utilised. These patterns of HRM bear understanding and consideration in managing human resources in different parts of the world.

Introduction ————————————————————————————————

As firms pursue, aggressively, their short term and long term goals, they are realising that their success depends upon a successful global presence (Ghoshal and Bartlett, 1989). In turn, their success as global players is being seen increasingly as dependent upon international human resource management:

> . . . virtually any type of international problem, in the final analysis, is either created by people or must be solved by people. Hence, having the right people in the right place at the right time emerges as the key to a company's international growth. If we are successful in solving that problem, I am confident we can cope with all others (Duerr, 1986, p. 43).

In a comparative context, human resource management (HRM) is best considered as the range of policies which have strategic significance for the organisation (Brewster and Tyson, 1991) and are typically used to facilitate integration, employee commitment, flexibility and the quality of worklife as well as meeting broader business goals such as changing organisational values, structure, productivity and delivery mechanisms. Therefore, in order to explain the various "brands" of HRM on a worldwide basis in sufficient detail, any analysis must include ". . . subjects which have traditionally been the concern of personnel management and industrial relations . . . as well as . . . more innovative and strategic approaches to people management" (Brewster and Tyson, 1991, p. l).

This increasing reliance upon successful HRM as a key to gaining competitive advantage in the global arena is mirroring the same phenomenon that effective firms witnessed during the 1980s on the domestic scene. As technology and capital became commodities in domestic markets, the only thing left to really distinguish firms, and thereby allow them to gain competitive advantage, were skills in managing their human resources (Reich, 1990). Whilst attention has been devoted to international comparisons of production systems and management strategies for many years, the comparison of people management systems has until recently been overlooked (Brewster, Hegewisch and Lockart, 1991; Pieper, 1990). Yet in most business situations the technical solution to specific issues has been understood, whilst the associated implementation problems of how to change behaviour, improve performance, predict future performance and make the best use of available talents remain the most significant obstacles. Bournois and Metcalfe (1991) argue that in widening a firm's strategic focus beyond the confines of its national boundaries, the human element becomes paramount. Therefore in the global arena we find CEOs acknowledging the importance of the issue:

> . . . Limited human resources—not unreliable capital—are the biggest constraint when companies globalise. (Floris Maljers, CEO, Unilever, Bartlett and Ghoshal, 1992, p. 126).

Successful Global Human Resource Management

If long run as well as short run corporate goals are dependent upon successful global HRM, an interesting question is: What is successful global management of human resources? At the risk of oversimplifying, we argue that it is best defined as the possession of the skills and knowledge of formulating and implementing policies and practices that effectively integrate and cohere globally dispersed employees, while at the same time recognising and appreciating local differences that impact the effective utilisation of human resources.

This definition of the successful global management of human resources can be decomposed into two distinct components of international HRM. The first component represents the body of knowledge and action that multinational firms use in allocating, dispersing, developing and motivating their global workforce. The major HRM concerns tend to focus on expatriate assignment, payment schemes and repatriation (Black, Gregersen and Mendenhall, 1993; Dowling and Schuler, 1990). Concerns for third country and local nationals are reflected in issues relating to the management of global operations, such as who is going to run the various geographically dispersed operations? Thus relatively few individuals tend to be encompassed by this component of international HRM.

The second component represents the body of knowledge and action concerned with actually staffing and running the local operations. The topics and issues enacted at this level are essentially focused around an understanding of local differences relevant to attracting, utilising and motivating individuals (Adler, 1991; Poole, 1986; Punnett and Ricks, 1992).

As Ronen (1986) suggested, for global firms to be successful in managing their worldwide workforces, they need to have an understanding and sensitivity to several local environments. They must utilise local information and adapt it to a broader set of human resource policies that reflect the firm itself. Of the two components of successful global HRM, this appears to be the lesser developed. Consequently, the focus of this article is on providing a greater understanding of selected aspects of HRM on a worldwide, comparative, basis.

Human Resource Practices and Concepts for Gaining Competitive Advantage

Porter (1980) suggested the concept of gaining competitive advantage to firms wishing to engage in strategic activities that would be difficult for competitors to copy or imitate quickly. Schuler and MacMillan (1984) applied this concept to HRM. They, and others since (for example, Reich, 1990) have suggested that firms can use HRM to gain competitive advantage because it is difficult for competitors to duplicate. That is, while technology and capital can be acquired by almost anyone at any time, for a price, it is rather difficult to acquire a ready pool of highly qualified and highly motivated employees.

At the global level, firms can seize competitive advantage through the selection and use of human resource policies and practices. The most important questions to ask then are: What human resource policies and practices can firms consider using in their worldwide operations that might assist them in gaining competitive advantage? Are they likely to be the same across countries? Is there some uniformity that firms can pursue in their efforts to successfully manage their worldwide workforces? As Moss-Kanter (1991, p. 153) reported in her worldwide survey of 12,000 managers:

> . . . While the survey results indicate that the emergence of a global culture of management is more dream than reality, they also uncover the leaders of the dream. For the most part, traditional industrial enterprises—larger, older, publicly held manufacturing companies with long planning horizons—are leading the drive toward globalization.

Given the analysis by Moss-Kanter (1991) and Porter (1990), it seems reasonable to proceed on the basis that any understanding of comparative HRM would aid firms in seeking to develop and implement human resource policies and practices worldwide to gain competitive advantage.

Key Policies and Practices in Gaining Competitive Advantage

While there are several specific ways that firms can gain competitive advantage with HRM policies and practices, it is most useful to gather data on generalisable policies and practices that are consistently seen as central to the management of human resources. In order to provide a basis for international comparison, we elected to focus on five major groupings of HRM policies and practices identified in the literature (see Poole, 1990; Schuler, 1992; Walker, 1992). Broadly, these include: culture; organisation structure; performance management; resourcing; and communications and corporate responsibility.

Culture. The present study addresses two aspects of culture. The first is the problem of creating a culture of empowerment, of including all employees in the decision making and responsibility of the organisation. This aspect of HRM represents a significant trend in a number of U.S. and U.K. organisations (Lawler, 1991; Wickens, 1987). How important is it worldwide? The second aspect is the promotion of diversity management and the development of a culture of equality. These two practices are tied together by a policy of inclusion, of bringing everyone into the operation and treating them equally with respect.

Organisation Structure. Associated with the issue of culture is that of organisation structure. Organisation structure refers to the relationship among units and individuals in the organisation. It can be described as ranging from a hierarchical, mechanistic relationship to a flatter, horizontal and organic relationship (Burns & Stalker, 1961). Obviously, these represent rather contrasting approaches to structuring organisations. Although their impact on individuals has been explored, more investigation specifically related to comparative HR appears warranted. Are all countries pursuing strategies of reducing the number of vertical layers (delayering) with the same vigour?

Performance Management. Another important group of HRM policies and practices reflects those associated with performance management. This process links goal setting and rewards, coaching for performance, aspects of career development and performance evaluation and appraisal into an integrated process. As firms seek to "manage the most out of employees" they are turning their attention to issues associated with employee performance. Because of the nature of international competition, the specific concerns in performance management are with measuring and motivating customer service, quality, innovation and risk taking behaviour (Peters, 1992).

Resourcing. As important as motivating employees once they are employed are issues associated with obtaining the most appropriate individuals (external resourcing); training and developing them with regard to technology and business process change; and managing the size of the workforce through reductions, downsizing and skills reprofiling. Beer, et al. (1984) describe these issues as part of a human resource flow policy. Seen in aggregate, we also regard them as part of a total resourcing dimension to HRM, as discussed by a number of writers (Boam and Sparrow, 1992; Mitrani, Dalziel and Fitt, 1992; Torrington, Hall, Haylor and Myers, 1991).

Communication and Corporate Responsibility. The fifth and final group of HRM policies and practices to which we give consideration are those by which firms may seek to describe their philosophy of communication and corporate responsibility. These two aspects of HRM capture the flow and sharing of information, internal and external to the organisation (Daft, 1992). Both can be vital as firms seek to empower and include employees in the organisation; and, as they seek to recognise and incorporate aspects of the external environment such as the general quality of the labour force, legal regulations, or concerns about environmental quality and social responsibility.

In summary, while these five groupings of HRM policies and practices may not capture all the human resource policies and practices relevant to global firms seeking to gain competitive advantage, they represent some of the major contemporary policies and practices being considered by academics and organisations, and are, therefore, worthy of international comparison.

The current literature suggests that these five aspects of HRM policies and practices may have varying levels of effectiveness throughout the world (Moss-Kanter, 1991; Porter, 1990). Indeed, Whitley (1992a) notes that as organisations move towards greater integration there is increasing recognition of national differences in higher level business systems. Despite increasing internationalisation within many industries, national institutions remain quite distinct. The role of the state and financial sectors, national systems of education and training, and diverse national cultures, employment expectations and labour relations all create "national business recipes, "each effective in their particular context but not necessarily effective elsewhere. These different national business recipes carry with them a "dominant logic of action" that guides management practice. This logic of action is reflected in specific management structures, styles and decision-making processes, growth and diversification strategies, inter-company market relationships and market development (Hofstede, 1993).

The institutional argument against unconstrained globalisation and business integration runs broadly as follows. There are a number of different and equally successful ways of organising economic activities (and management) in a market economy (Whitley, 1992a). These different patterns of economic organisation tend to be a product of the particular institutional environments within the various nation states. The development and success of specific managerial structures and practices (such as HRM) can only be explained by giving due cognisance to the various institutional contexts worldwide. Not all management methods are transferable. The effectiveness therefore of any worldwide conceptualisation of HRM will very likely be constrained by the different institutional contexts for national practice.

Hypotheses and Expectations

Based on the work of Moss-Kanter (1991) and Hofstede (1993), two hypotheses are developed in direct relationship to the concept of convergence or divergence of human resource policies and practices. Moss-Kanter (1991) found in her worldwide survey of management practices and expectations that the results could be clustered, not necessarily according to geography but according to culture. Thus she coined the phrase "cultural allies" to signify results from several countries being identical (eg. U.S., U.K. and Australia) and "cultural islands" to signify results from individual countries being unique from other countries (e.g., Korea, Japan). Using her results and rationale, leads to these testable hypotheses:

> Hypothesis 1:
> In regards to using human resource policies and practices for competitive advantage, there will be cultural islands and cultural allies. The cultural islands will be Korea and Japan and the cultural allies will be Europe, North America, U.K. and Australia; and Latin America.

Our second hypothesis is more tentative, more exploratory than the first. Thus while we can propose cultural allies and islands to exist, given the existing literature we are unable to make specific predictions about how human resource policies and practices will differ across nations. While it might be argued that they will reflect national cultures (it might also be argued that they will reflect differences in local law, custom and union-management history), we have no guidance suggesting specific relationships between aspects of culture and specific human resource policies and practices. This research is intended to provide such information. Thus at this time, what we are able to offer is a second and somewhat exploratory hypothesis:

> Hypothesis 2:
> There will be differences in which human resource policies and practices are seen as important for gaining competitive advantage across nations.

Methodology ————————————————————————————

Questionnaire. To explore these hypotheses, we conducted secondary analyses on data obtained as part of a larger international survey conducted in 1991. This was a worldwide study of human resource policies and practices conducted by IBM and Towers Perrin. The survey data which forms the basis of the analysis in this paper has been published elsewhere (Towers Perrin, 1992). In developing the survey questionnaire, some of the authors of this paper were invited to incorporate policies and practices and then write survey items that represented the academic and practitioner research and literature through 1990. These items were reviewed for representation and agreement by a series of other academics and practitioners identified by the IBM Corporation.

A major topic addressed in one section of the questionnaire was "human resource concepts and practices for gaining competitive advantage." In this section, respondents were asked to indicate the degree of importance they attached to each item in their firm's attempt to gain competitive advantage through human resource policies and practices. They indicated this for the current year (1991) and for the year of 2000. For the purposes of this study, we have analysed the data for the year 2000. This allows us to consider the extent to which future plans and expectations within the firms surveyed are likely to converge.

The specific firms included were those identified jointly by IBM and Towers Perrin as being the most effective firms in highly competitive environments in each of several countries. Details of the sample are provided by Towers Perrin (1992). In summary, the following information is of relevance in order to raise attention to the nature of the sample and the limits to which the data may be generalised. Effective firms in highly competitive environments were identified for each country surveyed. Given the global nature of firms discussed in the introduction, major employers in one country were, in some cases, subsidiaries or divisions of firms headquartered in other countries. In all cases, Towers Perrin (1992) surveyed two executives from each firm. Invitation letters and questionnaires were mailed to respondents in Spring 1991. The respondents included the chief operating officers and the senior human resource officers (2,961 respondents or 81% of the sample). Of these respondents 22% were from firms that employed over 10,000 employees, 46% were from firms employing 1,000 to 10,000 employees and 32% were from firms employing less than 1,000 employees. The other 19% of the sample comprised leading academics, consultants and individuals from the business media. The total sample of respondents were located in twelve countries throughout the world (the figures in brackets denote the sample size for each country): Argentina (42), Brazil (159), Mexico (67), France (81), Germany (295), Italy (212), the United Kingdom (261), Canada (120), the United States (1,174), Australia (94), Japan (387) and Korea (69).

The strategy of gathering data from major employing organisations led to a natural bias in the sample towards those countries with significant numbers of large organisations (e.g., the United States, Japan, Germany and the United Kingdom). To overcome the potential bias this might introduce into the analysis, the statistical tests (as discussed later) used to establish significant differences between national samples are those that control for sample size. The analysis that follows then is primarily based upon responses from respondents in effective firms in highly competitive environments in twelve countries worldwide responding to surveys that were translated into the language of the representative country.

When survey responses are used for comparative analysis, there are a number of issues that have to be acknowledged. Different political, economic, social and cultural considerations lead to a reinterpretation of management agendas at a local level. For example, in carrying out the pilot studies for their surveys on European HRM, Brewster,

Hegewisch and Lockart (1991) noted that identical questions about specific HRM tools or issues were interpreted differently by respondents within their national cultural and legal context. For example, the issue of flexible working in Britain and Germany has been linked to demographic change and the need to reintegrate women into the labour market, whereas in France flexible working is seen as a response to general changes in life style and has little to do with female labour force participation. Another problem is that the actual level of rating is difficult to interpret. For example, a low rating to a particular item might reflect the fact that the firm does not think the issue critical because they do not have the competence or desire to pursue the issue, or it might reflect the fact that the firm is very good already in the area under question and so no longer thinks the issue critical (although it will still form part of their activity). Survey findings reflect a pot pourri of past cultural constraints and future expectations based on new practices. Surveys are also cross-sectional and only examine perceptions (current or future) at one point in time. The analysis in this paper is based on expectations and plans for the year 2000, and therefore should not be coloured by short term factors (such as economic problems) that might influence respondents. Nevertheless, ratings reflect current mindsets only and these may change over the next ten years as organisations implement the findings of the survey. The data are then not a guarantee of eventual action. Great care is needed in interpreting comparative survey results and where possible we support the survey findings by reference to other published work.

Having noted the methodological constraints of empirical survey work, we would point to the general dearth of large scale empirical data and the opportunities afforded by an analysis of the Towers Perrin worldwide data. The addition of new empirical data we believe outweighs possible limitations. The statistical analysis in this paper therefore uses the Towers Perrin (1992) survey data to shed light on hypotheses described above:

- is there any underlying pattern (i.e., statistical clusters of countries) in the national data on HRM policies and concepts?

- what is the nature of differences between countries or groups of countries across a range of HRM variables?

Statistical Analysis. We analysed the responses to 38 questions asked about various HRM practices and concepts. In the first analysis we used the cluster analysis . . . to ascertain whether there was any pattern in the anticipated HRM policies and concepts across the twelve countries included in the sample. . . .

Once the underlying clusters (or grouping of countries) were identified, the differences between the importance these clusters of countries attribute to various HRM policies and practices were analysed. In order to facilitate this analysis of difference, the 38 survey questions were reclassified (on a conceptual basis) into 15 underlying dimensions. These dimensions identify elements of culture change, structuring the organisation, performance management, resourcing, and communication and corporate responsibility. They, therefore, broadly correspond with current conceptualisations of strategic human resource management as discussed in the Introduction (see for example Schuler, 1992; Walker, 1992). Questions relating to each of the dimensions examined are listed in Figure 1. It is important to note here that we have grouped surveyed items on a logical basis rather than an empirical basis. . .

Figure 1: The Fifteen HRM Dependent Variables and the Questionnaire Items Combined to Create Them

---

CULTURE CHANGE VARIABLES:

(1) Promoting an Empowerment Culture
Facilitate full employee involvement
Require employees to self-monitor and improve
Promote employee empowerment through ownership

(2) Promoting Diversity and an Equality Culture
Promote corporate culture emphasising equality
Manage diversity through tailored programmes

ORGANIZATION STRUCTURE AND CONTROL VARIABLES:

(1) Emphasis on Flexible Organization/Work Practices
Require employee flexibility (i.e., jobs and location)
Flexible cross-functional teams/work groups
Flexible work arrangements
Utilize non-permanent workforce

(2) Emphasis on Centralisation and Vertical Hierarchy
Maintain specialised and directed workforce

(3) Emphasis on Utilising I.T. to Structure the Organization
Promote advanced technology for communications
Provide more access to information systems

(4) Emphasis on Horizontal Management
Increase spans of control and eliminate layers
Establish multiple and parallel career paths

PERFORMANCE/ PROCESS MANAGEMENT VARIABLES:

(1) Emphasis on Measuring and Promoting Customer Service
Reward employees for customer service/quality
Peer subordinate customer ratings

(2) Emphasis on Rewarding Innovation/Creativity
Reward employees for innovation and creativity
Opportunity includes autonomy, creative skills
Reward employees for enhancing skills/knowledge

(3) Link Between Pay and Individual Performance
Reward employees for business/productivity gains
Focus on merit philosophy, individual performance

(4) Shared Benefits, Risks and Pay for Team Performance
Implement pay systems promoting sharing
Flexible benefits
Share benefit risks and costs with employees

RESOURCING VARIABLES:

(1) Emphasis on External Resourcing
Emphasize quality university hiring programmes
Recruit and hire from non-traditional labour pools

(2) Emphasis on Internal Resourcing—Training & Careers
Identify high potential employees early
Emphasize management development/skills training
Require continuous training/retraining
Provide basic education and skills training

(3) Emphasis on Internal Resourcing—Managing Outflows
Provide flexible retirement opportunities
Develop innovative and flexible outplacement

COMMUNICATION/CORPORATE RESPONSIBILITY VARIABLES:

(1) Emphasis on Communication
Communicate business directions, problems and plans

(2) Emphasis on Corporate Responsibility
Active corporate involvement in public education
Ensure employees pursue good health aggressively
Offer personal/family assistance
Encourage/reward external volunteer activities
Provide full employment (life-time security)

Results

Hypothesis 1. The dendogram in Figure 2 shows the result of the successive fusions of countries, starting from the most similar. There are five resultant clusters of countries. The first cluster initially comprises the Anglo-Saxon business culture countries of the United Kingdom,

Figure 2: Rescaled Dendogram Showing the Average of the Twelve Countries

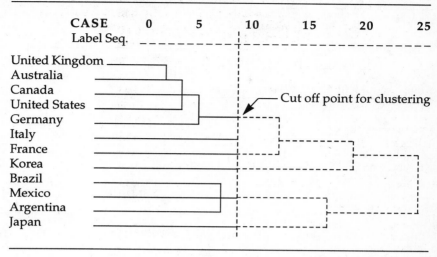

Australia, Canada, and the United States. These countries (the most similar) are subsequently joined by Germany and finally by Italy. The second cluster (a cultural island) consists solely of France. The third cluster is another cultural island consisting of Korea. The fourth cluster reveals another set of cultural allies comprising the South American or Latin countries of Brazil, Mexico, and Argentina, whilst the fifth cluster represents another cultural island consisting of Japan alone. These results, which are largely consistent with those we hypothesised, are discussed and interpreted later in this article primarily in relation to two other studies that have considered international patterns in business practice: the work of Hofstede (1980; 1993) on culture and the work of Moss-Kanter (1991) on attitudes toward change.

Three of the clusters only contained a single country. In order to complete the analysis of HRM differences between the other two clusters the United States was chosen to represent the Anglo-American cluster (as the largest sample contained within the cluster) and Brazil was chosen to represent the Latin American cluster on the same basis. The results are summarised in Table 1. Scores which are significantly[1] "higher" or "lower" (using the Standard Error of Difference in Proportions) than those of other countries on each variable are highlighted in the shaded boxes. In some cases, three grades of significant difference existed, i.e., higher, medium and lower.

---

[1] The term *significant differences, significant*, etc., refers to a statistical difference at the .05 level or lower.

Table 1: Summary of Differences in HRM between the Five Clusters of Countries

Survey Items	U.S. Anglo-Amer. Cluster	FRANCE	JAPAN	KOREA	BRAZIL S. American Cluster
Differences between the five clusters of countries on the Culture Change Variables					
Promoting Empowerment Culture	71.0% HIGHER	64.0%	52.7% LOWER	64.3%	78.7% HIGHER
Promoting Diversity and Equality Culture	53.0% HIGHER	36.5% LOWER	42.5% LOWER	49.5%	47.5%
Differences between the five clusters of countries on the Structuring Variables					
Emphasis on flexible work practices	59.8% HIGHER	39.8% LOWER	54.5%	53.3%	47.3% LOWER
Emphasis on centralisation and vertical hierarchy	6.0% LOWER	53.0% HIGHER	30.0% MEDIUM	51.0% HIGHER	10.0% LOWER
Emphasis on utilising IT to structure the organisation	50.0%	54.5%	46.0% LOWER	64.0% HIGHER	62.5% HIGHER
Emphasis on horizontal management	62.0%	55.5%	61.0%	58.5%	68.5%
Differences between the five clusters of countries on the Performance Management Variables					
Emphasis on measuring and promoting customer service	67.5% MEDIUM	82.0% HIGHER	50.0% LOWER	51.5% ·LOWER	66.5%
Emphasis on rewarding innovation/creativity	70.3%	62.7%	66.3%	67.3%	74.0%
Link between pay and individual performance	67.5%	64.5%	72.0%	70.0%	60.5%
Shared benefits, risks and pay for team performance	71.3% HIGHER	49.7%	40.1% LOWER	49.3%	60.7% MEDIUM
Differences between the five clusters of countries on the Resourcing Variables					
Emphasis on external resourcing	57.5%	50.0%	56.5%	42.0%	52.0%
Emphasis on training and careers	71.0%	60.7%	64.0% LOWER	81.5% HIGHER	73.3%
Emphasis on managing outflows	29.5% LOWER	40.5%	26.5% LOWER	34.0%	42.5% HIGHER
Differences between the five clusters of countries on the Communication and Corporate Responsibility Variables					
Emphasis on communication	85.0%	86.0%	83.0%	72.0%	81.0%
Emphasis on corporate responsibility	39.0%	28.6%	32.4%	37.4%	41.6%

Exploratory Differences on Hypothesis 2. In this section we outline those comparisons that resulted in significant differences regarding HRM practices to be used to gain competitive advantage. Interpretation and discussion of these differences is left until later in the paper. On the Cultural items Japan scores significantly lower on Promoting an Empowerment Culture compared to the Anglo-American representative United States and the Latin American representative Brazil whilst the United States scores significantly higher on Promoting Diversity and an Equality Culture compared to France and Japan.

On the Structuring items the United States scores significantly higher on Emphasis on Flexible Work Practices compared to France and Brazil. Nearly all the comparisons on the Emphasis on Centralisation and Vertical Hierarchy variable are significant. France and Korea score higher than Japan and Japan scores higher than the United States and Brazil. Variations on the Emphasis on Utilising I.T. to structure the organisation are less marked, but Japan scores significantly lower than Korea and Brazil and the United States scores lower than Brazil. No significant differences were found between the clusters on the Emphasis on Horizontal Management variable.

Less variation was found between the clusters on the **Performance Management** items. There were no significant differences on the Emphasis on Rewarding Innovation/Creativity and Link between Pay and Individual Performance variables. The extent to which emphasis was put on Customer Service and its measurement varied significantly. France placed significantly higher emphasis on customer service than the United States, whilst the United States placed more emphasis on customer service than Korea and Japan. The emphasis placed on Shared Benefits, Risks and Pay for Team Performance also varied significantly. The United States placed greater emphasis on this than Brazil, France, Korea and Japan. The Japanese score was also significantly lower than that for Brazil.

The **Resourcing** items yielded virtually no significant differences. Korea placed a higher Emphasis on Training and Career Management than Japan whilst Brazil placed greater Emphasis on Managing Outflows of staff than the United States and Japan.

Finally, there were no significant differences between the cluster country representatives in their emphasis on **Communication and Corporate Responsibility**.

Discussion and Summary

There are several ways in which we could discuss the results of this analysis of possible differences among firms from different nations as they seek to gain competitive advantage through their HRM practices. We could look at differences between countries across each of the fifteen dimensions of HRM that have been examined, or focus on overall country strategies (as reflected by the different priorities given to each area of HRM), or consider the relationship between cultural stereotypes of nations and the results obtained in this study. Each of these approaches provides complementary insights; therefore, we discuss the findings from all three angles.

Relationship to Cultural Stereotypes

It is useful to compare and contrast the results regarding our hypothesis (particularly the national clusters of countries) to other identified clusters of countries associated with cultural stereotypes (Adler, 1991; Hofstede, 1980; 1993; Phatak, 1992; Johnson and Golembiewski, 1992; and Laurent, 1991); or with studies on the management of change (Moss-Kanter, 1991). The Anglo-American cluster identified in this study contains very similar members to those identified in Moss-Kanter's (1991) study of 12,000 survey respondents worldwide. The United States, Australia, the United Kingdom and Canada were also grouped into a common cluster by Moss-Kanter (1991). There is an Anglo-American or Anglo-Saxon business culture that unites these countries. It is stereotyped in terms of openness and equality. This is reflected in the results on both the culture change items (particularly the "promoting diversity and equality" variable) on which the Anglo-American cluster scores significantly higher than for example France and Japan. Firms in the Anglo-American cluster see this cultural openness as one of their most important ways of gaining competitive advantage, reflecting the academic literature that describes future problems of demography in terms of the need to cope with diversity (Johnston and Packer, 1987). This cultural stereotype of openness and equality is also reflected in the results on the structuring items, where the Anglo-American cluster places a significantly higher emphasis on the criticality of flexible work practices and the lowest emphasis on the need for centralisation and vertical hierarchy. It is interesting to note that in Moss-Kanter's (1991) study, Germany formed part of a North European cluster of countries, and Italy formed part of a Latin cluster of countries. In contrast, our study suggests that where people management issues are concerned, the relative emphasis these countries expect to give in the year 2000 to the fifteen dimensions of HRM places them in the Anglo-American camp.

Our study indicated that Japan stands alone with a unique cluster of HRM emphases. This was also the case in Moss-Kanter's (1991) study which is why she called Japan a cultural island. It is interesting to note that although Japan faces even more severe demographic problems than the Anglo-American countries it does not place as high an emphasis on the cultural variables of empowerment, diversity and equality but places greater emphasis on centralisation and vertical hierarchy. Japan gave lowest importance for gaining competitive advantage to promoting empowerment, diversity and equality, reflecting the cultural importance given in Japan to respect for authority and its more homogeneous ethnic culture.

In Moss-Kanter's (1991) study France formed part of a North European cluster of countries. The only difference noted in this study is that Germany does not share the same pattern of HRM emphases as France. The results obtained for the French cluster also strongly reflect Hofstede's (1980) findings on culture. In Hofstede's analysis French managers have a higher Power distance score (68) in comparison for example with British managers (35). There are greater differences in formal power across management hierarchies in France and managers are more tolerant of such inequalities of power. French managers also have a higher Uncertainty avoidance score (86) in comparison to British managers (35) and might be expected to seek to eliminate uncertainty and ambiguity in their tasks. The way in which the manager-subordinate relationship enables them to do this nevertheless remains a delicate point in France (Poirson, 1993). The fear of face to face conflict, the way in which authority is conceived, and the mode of selection of senior managers all act as powerful cultural forces that make it difficult for French organisations to readily adopt Anglo-American management concepts (such as performance management). Rojot (1990) paints French corporate culture as one that creates situations in which subordinate managers seek more responsibility, but in fact remain passive, fear to commit themselves to specific objectives and mostly look for protection from above. Senior managers rule autocratically and see the organisation as an elite school in which they are the most intelligent and subordinates therefore cannot conceivably have valid ideas. French managers are therefore more possessive of their individual autonomy. Their reaction is: "I know my job, if I am controlled, this means they have no confidence in me" (Poirson, 1993). Even where Anglo-American concepts of HRM are adopted, they become ". . . the stake of a different game" (Rojot, 1990, p. 98).

Both our study and that of Moss-Kanter (1991) revealed Korea as another cultural island. The Korean results in our study reflect Korea's higher emphasis on protectionism, strong sense of corporate paternalism, preference for centralisation and greater optimism for the future, as noted by Moss-Kanter (1991). The utilisation of information technology to help do so appears consistent with the image of Korea as a nation that is respectful of authority and very hierarchically organised.

Recently, attention has been directed to the unique features of Latin America in terms of HRM (Baker, Smith, Weiner, 1992; Baker, Smith, Weiner and Jacobson, 1993; Nash, 1993). Moss-Kanter (1991) identified a Latin cluster of countries consisting of South American nations, Italy and Spain. Similarly, we found that the South American countries of Mexico, Argentina and Brazil clustered together. The one difference was that Italy seems to adopt an Anglo-American perspective on future

HRM practices for competitive advantage. Recent analyses of HRM in Italy and the European Latin countries (Camuffo and Costa, 1992; Filella, 1991) support this finding. The Latin cluster has many features similar to the Anglo-American cluster such as promotion of an empowerment culture, high decentralisation, high emphasis on using IT to support structuring in organisations, and a high desire to seek a sharing of benefits and risks in reward systems which may reflect the high levels of privatisation occurring in those countries. The Latin cluster differs from the Anglo-American cluster in that it places more value on the need to manage outflows from organisations and less emphasis on the need for flexible work practices.

National HRM Strategies

In this section we discuss the survey findings in relation to national patterns of HRM and draw upon other research to provide the necessary context to interpret the survey findings. Naturally, this section focuses on differences between countries. These differences should not be overstated, however, for balanced against these are the underlying convergences that are reducing many of these differences. These convergences will be discussed in the following section.

> . . . European-style class consciousness, a serious socialist movement . . . penetration of Marxist ideology in "old Europe" . . . have variously served to structure both the perception and reality of superior-subordinate and management-worker relations in industry (Lawrence, 1992, p. 12).

Lawrence (1992) argues that HRM is essentially an Anglo-Saxon construct that has been "grafted on"—but has not "taken root"—in continental Europe. Classic HRM functions such as recruitment, socialisation, training and development are determined by different conceptions of management in Europe, and underpinned by a related set of values. Historically, HRM has not had the same élan and in part has been socially and culturally by-passed. When compared with American (or indeed British) concepts of HRM, a European model needs to take account of a number of factors. The distinctions drawn between concepts of HRM prevalent in continental Europe as opposed to the Anglo-American model (Brewster and Hegewisch, 1993; Pieper, 1990) include more restricted employer autonomy, difficult hiring and firing decisions, lower geographic and professional employee mobility and a stronger link between type of education and career progression. There is an increased role of "social partners" in the employment relationship, a stronger role of trade unions influence in the setting of HRM policy, collective bargaining at the state and regional level and direct co-determination at the firm level. Finally there are higher levels of government intervention or support in many areas of HRM, a state role in education through public school and university systems, formal certification systems influencing personnel selection and careers and more comprehensive welfare policies.

It is therefore all the more interesting that Germany and Italy, as two continental European countries, actually fell within the Anglo-American cluster. However, a preliminary analysis of this cluster suggests that whilst the constituent members are all more alike each other than they are alike the other countries (France, Korea, Japan and so forth), there are still likely to be some significant differences in HRM practices within the cluster. Germany and Italy only "joined" the Anglo-American cluster towards the end of the mathematical forcing process (see Figure 2), and could be considered as worth separate investigation. A useful area for further investigation would be to investigate national pathways and statistical differences within the regional clusters.

The characteristics of French HRM (recently discussed by several authors such as Barsoux and Lawrence, 1990; Besse, 1992; Poirson, 1993; and Rojot, 1990) as revealed by our analysis supports many of the cultural distinctions drawn above. For example, the strong French educational élite, distinct cadres of management, and extremely rigid hierarchical approach to both performance and career management is reflected in the significantly lower rating given to a culture based on diversity and equality as well as a significantly higher emphasis given to centralisation and vertical hierarchy. However, the context within which HRM in France is practiced has changed considerably over the last ten years (Poirson, 1993; Rojot, 1990). Increased and globalised competition, the growth of multinational organisations, the shortening of product life-cycles, and the growing importance of product quality have all provided a new justification of managerial authority in France, and a new language amongst the employers' associations and bodies has legitimised a number of management and HRM practices, including performance management (Rojot, 1990). A 1987 survey by Hay France of 220 French organisations employing more than 65,000 managers found that 91% had a policy of fixing individual objectives for managers, 81% evaluated performance in relation to these objectives and 87% had an annual performance appraisal review meeting. This renewed fervour for and emphasis on objectives-based performance management is reflected in the French sample high rating for the need to emphasise the promotion and measurement of customer service.

Many of our findings reflect the existing competence and perceived priorities in the Japanese HRM system (see Aoki, 1988; Dore, 1986; and Koike, 1987) and reveal the unique approach to HRM created by its internal labour market. Japanese HRM has been characterised by hierarchical pyramid-type organisations with bureaucratic control. The Japanese respondents rated an emphasis on centralisation and vertical hierarchy as significantly more critical than the Anglo-American cluster (30% compared to 6%). However, the Korean and French samples placed an even greater emphasis on these issues. Performance in Japan is evaluated in the long term and there is a model of life-time employment. Skills are firm-specific and there is a reliance on in-house specific on-the-job training. Not surprisingly our Japanese sample rated the need to manage outflows from the organisation significantly lower than Brazil or France and placed a lower emphasis on training and development (linked to careers as opposed to jobs) given the existing high levels of informal on-the-job training.

Communication in Japan is more informal and relies on managerial networks. Promotion systems (particularly to senior management level) are more geared to an educational elite (Koike, 1987; Whitley, 1992b), female participation rates are low and there is a marked labour market segmentation between core (65% to 90%) employees and lower status, higher mobility, temporary workers. This is reflected in the survey finding that the Japanese sample provide a significantly lower rating to the criticality of promoting a culture that promotes diversity and equality (42% compared to 53% in the Anglo-American cluster).

Japanese wage differentials are based on hierarchy and have remained fairly stable, despite the pressures for change discussed later. Bonuses in Japan are not regarded as a reward or dividend of profit as in the Anglo-Saxon countries, but are taken more for granted and assumed to be part of regular earnings despite the fact they account for around 33% of nominal salaries (Aoki, 1988). They do not decrease even in difficult times (Sano, 1993). Jobs are also highly segmented. The survey data reflected this paradox with the Japanese sample giving a significantly lower rating to pay systems that share risks and benefits or reward team performance (40% compared to 71% in the Anglo-American cluster).

More recently a number of reviews have pointed to growing pressure for change in the Japanese model of HRM (see for example Sano, 1993; Sasajima, 1993; and Takahashi, 1990). Japanese organisations are facing a crisis and their traditional patterns of HRM are under structural pressure to change. Increasing difficulties are being faced in maintaining employment security and automatic pay increase systems. Demographic pressures have resulted in an aging workforce with an increasingly long length of service (Sano, 1993), creating fears about skills shortages and upward pressure on labour costs. Education levels have increased markedly, as have female participation and part time work (these pressures are also apparent in the U.S. and Europe). It is interesting to note that the Japanese sample provided the lowest rating to the importance of promoting an empowerment culture. This could be interpreted in two contrasting ways: a reflection of the fact that the Japanese HRM system already achieves this and so it is a lower priority for the future, or a recognition by Japanese managers that external pressures may interfere with their ability to maintain this type of culture.

Some authors have argued that in Japan new technology is being used increasingly to deskill jobs and combine business processes because productivity of more senior and skilled employees is falling. However, our survey data does not appear to reflect this concern. The

Japanese sample viewed the use of IT to structure the organisation as significantly less important compared to, for example, the Korean and Brazilian samples.

Wilkinson (1988) has noted that some features of the Korean labour system resemble those of the Japanese, such as the segmentation of the labour market (our data supported this with both countries rating the need to promote an empowerment culture or culture based on diversity and equality as low) and overall philosophy behind their reward systems (similarly supported by our analysis showing no significant differences between Korea and Japan on any of the four dimensions used to examine performance management). However, a number of writers have noted a number of striking differences between Japanese and Korean labour systems (Biggart, 1989; Chung and Lee, 1988; Deyo, 1989; Michell, 1988; Park, 1992; Sharma, 1991; Shin and Chin, 1989; Whitley, 1992b; Yoo and Lee, 1987). In relation to Japan, labour turnover in the manufacturing sector is high (Amsden, 1989) and managerial mobility is high (Biggart, 1989). This is perhaps reflected in our finding that Japan places a low emphasis on the importance of managing outflows from the organisation (27%) in comparison to Korea (34%), although the difference is not significant. Similarly, Michell (1988) reported lower employer commitment to employee welfare in Korea than Japan, mainly because its labour intensive industries (such as textiles) are following cost leadership strategies. Even in capital-intensive industries, lifelong employment is not seen as an ideal. Our analysis revealed that the Korean sample placed a significantly higher emphasis on work structuring through the use of IT and on centralisation and the vertical hierarchy. These are two dimensions of structure that are often associated with newly industrialising countries and their attempts to drive cost savings and improvements to the business process and productivity.

Attention has also been drawn to the greater scope for manager and owner discretion in Korea, more authoritarian and directive supervisory style focused on task performance as opposed to the facilitation of group performance (Parl, 1992; Whitley, 1992b), limited scope for supervisors to organise groups' work and lower levels of autonomy for workers in comparison to Japan (Deyo, 1989). We found only a marginally lower emphasis on the importance of horizontal management in Korea than in Japan and a more marked (but still insignificant) difference in the importance given to communication (72% in Korea, the lowest of all five clusters, compared to 83% in Japan). Perhaps reflecting a national desire to reduce this differential, recent moves towards democratisation and the atypical Korean trend towards greater unionisation (Park, 1992), the Korean sample placed higher importance on promoting an empowerment culture than did Japan (which as discussed previously may feel it has already achieved much in this area).

Recruitment decisions, whilst based on a university elite as in Japan, also differ in Korea. Shin and Chin (1989) argue that Korean selection and promotion decisions are more influenced by personal and regional networks and relationships than in Japan. Therefore, despite the acute labour shortages experienced in Korea since 1986 (Park, 1992) the lower level of formality in selection is reflected in our results, which show that in Korea only 42% of the sample felt that an emphasis on external resourcing was critical, compared to 57% of the Japanese sample, although again the difference was not significant. Amsden (1989) has also drawn attention to the high wages and fringe benefits (such as company housing, bonus payments and schooling for children) that characterise the Korean reward system. This is essentially a paternalistic system (without the Japanese guarantee of lifelong employment) in which loyalty is less directly incorporated into rewards systems than in Japan. However, as already noted, there were no significant differences between Japan and Korea on the four dimensions of performance management, although the Korean sample placed a lower emphasis on reward systems that share both benefits and risk or pay for team performance, but a higher emphasis on linking pay and individual performance, which seems to reflect the description of reward systems given by Amsden (1989).

Predictions About HRM Practices for Competitive Advantage

The comparison of differences thus far have been made using the data for the year 2000. These data were used for two primary reasons: First, using HRM to gain a competitive advantage takes time, thus historical data would not be as much use as data which reflects expectations and plans for the year 2000. Second, data for the year 2000 would enable us to assess the extent to which there is a convergence or divergence occurring worldwide in the practice of HRM.

In making predictions about HRM practices and policies for competitive advantage, it is necessary to establish the baseline from where we started. In this study, the baseline is 1991. If we look at these results in conjunction with the results for the year 2000 we not only have a better basis for prediction but also for comparison across the clusters. Table 2 shows the differences in the importance ratings from respondents for the 15 dimensions of HRM.

One clear pattern revealed by Table 2 is that the respondents in all the clusters rated all HRM items higher in the year 2000 than they did in the year 1991. This appears to be consistent with the academic and professional literature that suggests that the management of people is becoming a more significant force in organisations, particularly now that capital, technology and the like are readily available to everyone. It also reflects the points we made in the section on national strategies which showed that in France and Japan there are increasing pressures to adapt their highly nationalistic models of HRM. Another observation and prediction is that while people management is becoming

Table 2: Differences in HRM between the Five Clusters: Change from 1991-2000

Survey Items	U.S. Anglo-Amer. Cluster	FRANCE	JAPAN	KOREA	BRAZIL S. American Cluster
	Differences between the five clusters of countries on the Culture Change Variables				
Promoting Empowerment Culture	41-71 +31%	38-64 +26%	40-53 +13%	34-64 +30%	41-79 +38%
Promoting Diversity and Equality Culture	31-53 +22%	20-37 +17%	28-43 +13%	18-50 +32%	23-40 +25%
	Differences between the five clusters of countries on the Structuring Variables				
Emphasis on flexible work practices	26-60 +34%	24-40 +16%	32-55 +23%	15-54 +39%	17-47 +30%
Emphasis on centralisation and vertical hierarchy	0-6 0%	15-53 +38%	13-30 +17%	25-51 +26%	11-10 -1%
Emphasis on utilising IT to structure the organisation	16-50 +34%	19-55 +36%	21-46 +25%	23-64 +41%	21-63 42%
Emphasis on horizontal management	36-62 +34%	30-56 +26%	37-61 +24%	30-59 +29%	37-69 +32%
	Differences between the five clusters of countries on the Performance Management Variables				
Emphasis on measuring and promoting customer service	40-68 +28%	47-82 +35%	31-50 +19%	34-52 +18%	36-67 +31%
Emphasis on rewarding innovation/creativity	35-70 +35%	32-63 +31%	41-66 +25%	40-67 +27%	40-74 +34%
Link between pay and individual performance	52-68 +16%	42-65 +23%	44-72 +28%	45-70 +25%	48-61 +13%
Shared benefits, risks and pay for team performance	40-71 +31%	23-50 +27%	18-40 +22%	23-49 +26%	24-61 +37%
	Differences between the five clusters of countries on the Resourcing Variables				
Emphasis on external resourcing	24-58 +34%	37-50 +13%	41-57 +16%	40-42 +2%	23-52 +29%
Emphasis on training and careers	38-71 +33%	43-61 +18%	52-64 +12%	60-82 +22%	59-73 +14%
Emphasis on managing outflows	13-30 +17%	13-41 +28%	7-27 +20%	7-34 +27%	14-43 +29%
	Differences between the five clusters of countries on the Communication and Corporate Responsibility Variables				
Emphasis on communication	57-85 +28%	57-86 +29%	74-83 +9%	62-72 +10%	48-81 +33%
Emphasis on corporate responsibility	18-39 +21%	14-29 +15%	16-32 +16%	18-38 +20%	27-42 +15%

important in all the countries surveyed, the countries will continue to exhibit differences, both in degree and in kind. For example, when it comes to promoting an empowerment culture, the Japanese are increasing as are the French, but the Anglo-American cluster is increasing much more, (40-71% vs 40-53%).

When examining Table 2 it is important to keep these percentage differences in mind. They often provide explanatory evidence as to why the differences are indeed different. For the item "emphasis on communication" both Japan and Korea have small differences compared to the Anglo American cluster. However, an examination of the original percentage shows that both Japan and Korea had originally rated this item substantially higher than the Anglo American cluster. Is this suggesting that the Anglo American cluster is "playing catch-up"? Are we to assume that an understanding of future events is to be found in the Asian nations? Probably not. These differences more likely still reflect cultural and economic differences. Note that while Japan and Korea are geographical neighbours to the United States, overall their results are rather different. In fact, Australia is regarded by some as being in the Asia Pacific region, yet it falls into the Anglo-American cluster in the original analysis.

These observations about Table 2 being so noted, what other predictions about convergence can we offer concerning HRM practices and policies for competitive advantage?

1. The Culture Change dimensions: Firms in all clusters are seeing that it is likely to be useful to empower their employees more than today, and to promote a more diverse and egalitarian culture. As the world's workforce becomes more educated it is demanding more involvement and participation in workplace decisions and events. Task and knowledge, as well as employee needs and abilities, appear to be driving this trend in human resource practices. A related prediction here is that there will be continued examination of the role of the manager, with continued pressure for change in that role.

2. The Structuring dimensions: Following from the first prediction is the second: as the task and knowledge determine the involvement of employees and the role of the manager, they also impact the structure of the operation. In particular, they make it necessary for work practices to be more flexible to change as the skills and abilities needed to do them change. This removes the sole responsibility for decision making from the hierarchy to those in the know and those generally nearest the action.

3. The Performance Management dimensions: There is likely to be enhanced emphasis on obtaining performance and making performance a centre of attention. In particular, performance related to serving the customer would appear to be of most importance. This will be closely followed by an emphasis on the performance related to innovation, new products and services (of

course, designed with the customer in mind). To reinforce these emphases, remuneration schemes at both the individual and team level are likely to be implemented in significant numbers during this decade. There will be a greater sharing of risks and rewards. With the emphasis on promoting a culture of equality, this might also mean that greater sharing will occur at all levels of management and non-management employees.

4. The Resourcing dimensions: Flexibility will be desired and sought regarding all areas of the business. Just as there is likely to be more flexibility with regards to job assignments and decisions, there is likely to be more flexibility regarding staffing decisions, both at the entry and exit stages. That is, firms might be likely to seek greater use of part time or temporary workers to fill positions, and not bring them into full time employee status. Perhaps for the full time employees, firms will dedicate more resources to training and retraining. This will make the current workforce (the one that is more empowered and is making more decisions) more important to the organisation. Nevertheless, even this workforce may need to be replaced. Knowledge is doubling every seven years. To capture this, firms may need to be constantly incorporating new members and new ideas. This will demand constant change and adaptation by all. For some this may mean a need to exit the organisation. Consequently, firms will be equally concerned about managing the egress of employees. They will want to ensure that this is predictable and that employees with key skills, today and in the future, do not suddenly leave the firm.

5. The Communication and Corporate Responsibility dimensions: While organisations are likely to get more involved in community activities, particularly training and education, they are likely to still want employees to focus on the firm. Consequently, they will devote more resources to communicating and sharing the goals and objectives of the organisation with all employees. This will facilitate the empowerment of employees and help ensure that the decisions made by employees are as consistent with the needs of the business as those made by top management.

Conclusions _____

The function of managing people in organisations is perceived as important today for firms to gain competitive advantage. This level of importance, however, pales in comparison to the importance it is expected to have in the year 2000. While this is likely due to greater access organisations have to capital and technology, it is also likely due to a growing recognition that people do make a difference. Thus this relatively under-utilised resource called "people" is likely to receive greater attention from organisations throughout this decade, at least for firms seeking to be effective in highly competitive environments.

While "to receive greater attention" is likely to vary across firms, it is not expected to vary widely concerning several key themes or foci. These include the following: a greater emphasis on empowerment, equality, diversity management, flexibility in job design and assignment, flatter organisational structures, customer-based measures of performance and related remuneration schemes, flexibility in staffing decisions, training decisions and exiting decisions, and greater communication of the objectives and goals of the firm to all employees.

Finally, although the country clusters reported in this study did illustrate differences to these key themes, they also reflected similarity. The differences are probably better described as being more "in degree" than "in kind." Thus while it might be tempting to conclude that there is clearly a convergence rather than divergence in the practices and policies used by organisations to manage their human resources, this might be overstating the reality (as well as the complexity) of managing human resources effectively. Employees do reflect the larger society and culture from which they come to the organisation. From this they bring education and skill, attitudes toward work and organisation and general expectations about their role and responsibility in the organisation. The impact and relevance of these should not be understated. Thus while it may be tempting to conclude by using the term "convergence," it may be more an attempt to simplify reality prematurely.

References

Adler, N.J. (1991) *International dimensions of organisational behaviour.* Boston: PWS-Kent.

Amsden, A.H. (1989) *Asia's next giant.* Oxford: Oxford University Press.

Aoi, M. (1988) *Information, incentives and bargaining in the Japanese economy.* Cambridge: Cambridge University Press.

Baker, S., Smith, G., Weiner, E. and Jacobson, K. (1992) "Latin America: The big move to Free Markets," *Business Week,* June 15, 50-62.

Baker, S., Smith, G., and Weiner, E. (1993) "The Mexican worker." *Business Week,* April 19, 84-92.

Barsoux, J.L. and Lawrence, P. (1990) *Management in France.* London: Cassell Education Limited.

Bartlett, C.A. and Ghoshal, S. (1992) "What is a global manager?" *Harvard Business Review,* 70 (5): 124-32.

Beer, M., Spector, B., Lawrence, P.R., Mills, D.Q., and Walton, RE. (1984) *Managing Human Assets.* New York: The Free Press.

Besse, D. (1992) "Finding a new raison d'etre: Personnel management in France,", *Personnel Management,* 24(8), 40-3.

Biggart, N.W. (1989) "Institutionalised patrimonialism in Korean business." Program in East Asian culture and development research, *Working Paper No. 23, Institute of Governmental Affairs.* University of California: Davies.

Black, J.S., Gregersen, H.B. and Mendenhall, P. (1992) *Global Assignments.* San Francisco: Jossey-Bass.

Boam, R. and Sparrow, P.R. (1992) (eds.) *Designing and Achieving Competency.* London: McGraw-Hill.

Bournois, F. and Metcalfe, P. (1991) "HR management of executives in Europe: structures, policies and techniques." In C. Brewster and S. Tyson (eds.) *International Comparisons in Human Resource Management.* London: Pitman.

Brewster, C. and Hegewisch, A. (1993) "Personnel management in Europe: a continent of diversity," *Personnel Management,* 25 (1), 36-40.

Brewster, C., Hegewisch, A. and Lockhart, J.T. (1991) "Researching human resource management: methodology of the Price Waterhouse Cranfield Project on European trends," *Personnel Review,* 20 (6), 36-40.

Brewster, C. and Tyson, S. (1991) (eds.) *International Comparisons in Human Resource Management.* London: Pittman.

Burns, T. and Stalker, G.R. (1961) *The Management of Innovation.* London: Tavistock.

Camuffo, A. and Costa, G. (1992) "Strategic human resource management — Italian style." *Sloan Management Review,* 34 (2), 59-67.

Chung, K.H. and Lee, H.C. (1988) (eds.) *Korean Managerial Dynamics.* London: Praeger.

Daft, R.L. (1992) *Organization Theory and Design.* St. Paul, Minneapolis: West Publishing.

Deyo, F.C. (1989) *Beneath the Miracle: Labour Subordination in the New Asian Industrialism.* Berkeley, CA: University of California Press.

Dore, R.P. (1986) *Flexible Rigidities.* Stanford: Stanford University Press.

Duerr, M.G. (1986) "International business management: its four tasks," *Conference Board Record,* Oct., 43-7.

Dowling, P.J. and Schuler, R.S. (1990) *International Dimensions of Human Resource Management.* Boston: PWS-Kent.

Filella, J. (1991) "Is there a Latin model in the management of human resources?" *Personnel Review,* 20 (6), 14-23.

Ghoshal, S. and Bartlett, C.A. (1989) "The multinational corporation as an interorganisational network," *Academy of Management Review,* 15(4), 603-625.

Hofstede, G. (1980) *Culture's Consequences: International Differences in Work-Related Values.* London: Sage.

Hofstede, G. (1993) "Cultural constraints in management theories." *Academy of Management Executive,* 7 (1), 81-93.

Johnson, K.R. and Golembiewski, R.T. (1992) "National culture in organization development: a conceptual and empirical analysis," *International Journal of Human Resource Management*, 3 (1), 71-84.

Johnston, W.B. and Packer, A.E. (1987) *Workforce 2000: Work and Workers for the 21st Century.* Washington, D.C.: U.S. Govt. Printing Office.

Koike, K. (1987) "Human resource development and labour management relations." In K. Yamamura and Y. Yashuba (eds.) *The Political Economy of Japan. 2. The Domestic Transformation.* Stanford: Stanford University Press.

Lawrence, P. (1992) "Management development in Germany." In S. Tyson, P. Lawrence, P. Poirson, L. Manzolini and C.S. Vincente (eds.) *Human Resource Management in Europe: Strategic Issues and Cases.* London: Kogan Page.

Laurent, A. (1991) "Managing across cultures and national borders." In S.G. Makridakis (ed.) *Single Market Europe: Opportunities and Challenges for Business.* London: Jossey Bass.

Lawler, E.E. (1991) "The new plant approach: A second generation approach," *Organizational Dynamics*, Summer, 5-15.

Michell, T. (1988) *From a Developing to a Newly Industrialised Country: the Republic of Korea, 1961-82.* Geneva: International Labour Organisation.

Mitrani, A., Dalziel, M. and Fin, D. (1992) (eds.) *Competency-Based Human Resource Management.* London: Kogan Page.

Moss-Kanter, R. (1991) "Transcending business boundaries: 12,000 world managers view change," *Harvard Business Review*, 69 (3), 151-164.

Nash, N. (1993) "A new rush into Latin America," *The New York Times*, April 11, Sec. 3, 1-6.

Park, D.J. (1992) "Industrial relations in Korea," *International Journal of Human Resource Management*, 3 (1), 105-124.

Peters, T. (1992) *Liberation Management: Necessary Disorganisation for the NanosecondNineties.* London: Macmillan.

Phatak, A.V. (1992) *International Dimensions of Management.* Boston: PSW Kent.

Pieper, R. (1990) (ed.) *Human Resource Management: an International Comparison.* Berlin: de Gruyter.

Poirson, P. (1993) "The characteristics and dynamics of human resource management in France." In S. Tyson, P. Lawrence, P. Poirson, L. Manzolini and C.S. Vincente (eds.) *Human Resource Management in Europe: Strategic Issues and Cases.* London: Kogan Page.

Poole, M.J.F. (1986) *Industrial Relations: Origins and Patterns of National Diversity.* London: Routledge.

Poole, M.J.F. (1990) Editorial: "Human Resource management in an international perspective," *International Journal of Human Resource Management*, 1, 1-16.

Porter, M.E. (1980) *Competitive Strategy: Techniques for Analysing Industries and Competitors.* New York: Free Press.

Porter, M.E. (1990) *Competitive Advantage of Nations*. New York: Free Press.

Punnett, B.J. and Ricks, D.A. (1992) *International Business*. Boston: PWD-Kent.

Reich, R.B. (1990) "Who is us?," *Harvard Business Review*, 68 (1), 53-64.

Ronen, S. (1986) *Comparative and Multinational Management*. New York: Wiley and Sons.

Rojot, J. (1990) "Human resource management in France." In Pieper, R. (ed.) *Human Resource Management: an International Comparison*. Berlin: de Gruyter.

Sano, Y. (1993) "Changes and continued stability in Japanese HRM systems: choice in the share economy," *International Journal of Human Resource Management*, 4 (1), 11-28.

Sasajima, Y. (1993) "Changes in labour supply and their impacts on human resource management: the case of Japan," *International Journal of Human Resource Management*, 4 (1), 29-44.

Schuler, R.S. (1992) "Strategic human resource management: linking the people with the strategic needs of the business," *Organizational Dynamics*, 21 (1), 18-31.

Schuler, R.S. and MacMillan, I. (1984) "Creating competitive advantage through human resource management practices," *Human Resource Management*, 23, 241-55.

Sharma, B. (1991) "Industrialisation and strategy shifts in industrial relations: a comparative study of South Korea and Singapore." In C. Brewster and S. Tyson (eds.) *International Comparisons in Human Resource Management*. London: Pitman.

Shin, E.H. and Chin, S.W. (1989) "Social affinity among top managerial executives of large corporations in Korea," *Sociological Forum*, 4, 3-26.

Takahashi, Y. (1990) "Human resource management in Japan." In R. Pieper (ed.) *Human Resource Management: an International Comparison*. Berlin: de Gruyter.

Torrington, D., Hall, L., Haylor, I. and Myers, J. (1991) *Employee Resourcing*. Wimbledon: Institute of Personnel Management.

Towers Perrin (1992) *Priorities for Competitive Advantage: a Worldwide Human Resource Study*. London: Towers Perrin.

Walker, J. (1992) *Human resource strategy*. New York: McGraw-Hill.

Whitley, R. (1992a) (ed.) *European business systems: firms and markets in their national contexts*. London: Sage.

Whitley, R. (1992b) (ed.) *Business Systems in East Asia: Firms, Markets and Societies*. London: Sage.

Wickens, D. (1987) *The road to Nissan*. London: MacMillan.

Wilkinson, B. (1988) "A comparative analysis." In *Technological Change, Work Organisation and Pay: Lessons from Asia*. Geneva: International Labour Organisation.

Yoo, S. and Lee, S.M. (1987) "Management style and practice of Korean Chaebols," *California Management Review*, 29(4), 95-110.

The Link Between Business Strategy and International Human Resource Management Practices

Reading 1.2
Allan Bird and
Schon Beechler

Introduction

Research on international HRM has blossomed in recent years yet much of this research has been in the area of staffing. Reasons for focusing almost exclusively on this area, especially among practitioners, appear to stem from the high costs of making poor staffing decisions. Two issues which have been extensively researched are these: (1) staffing of parent country nationals vs. host or third country nationals; and (2) appropriate criteria for selecting expatriates. Some limited attention has also been directed at related expatriate issues, including compensation and type of training for expatriates.

In addition to research on expatriates, a few writers have examined the role of HRM in formulating and implementing business strategy at an international level. The focus of this work is on HRM's role in the formal design of business strategy, as well as its role as an enhancer of strategy, concentrating specifically on HRM's role in implementation.

In the general literature most work linking strategy and HRM has been prescriptive and focused on domestic settings, yet clear associations between strategy and human resource activities have been found. We can classify studies of linkages between human resource management practices and business strategy into two categories. The first group conceptualizes strategy-HRM linkages in a broad, macro perspective. These authors use one of a variety of strategic typologies and then relate specific strategies to general categories of HRM policy.

Source: This article was written especially for this book. Reprinted by permission of the authors.

Porter, for example, identifies two generic strategies: (1) overall cost leadership; and (2) differentiation. In his discussion of the skills, resources and organizational requirements needed for each strategy, Porter alludes to a strategy-manager match and considers some of the HRM policy implications that grow out of this match. A *cost leadership strategy* is based on the experience cost curve concept. This strategy places the company in a low-cost position where it can earn above-average returns despite strong competition. Under a cost leadership strategy, job requirements are those of establishing tight cost controls, making frequent reports, enforcing strict rules, and establishing incentives based on quantitative methods.

By contrast, a *differentiation strategy* is a strategy based on distinguishing the company's products or services from those of competitors. By providing unique and distinctive, non-price value, the company can insulate itself through customer loyalty. A differentiation strategy requires an emphasis on coordination, incentives based on qualitative methods, and the maintenance of quality and technological leadership.

Macro perspectives, such as Porter's, are useful in delineating possible strategy-human resources linkages, yet they lack specificity and fall short in their regard for the myriad details of HRM policy and practice. A remedy to this shortcoming is found in studies that have a micro perspective, attempting to trace relationships between strategy and individual HRM policies. Micro research, for example, proposes specific linkages between business strategies and selection practices or staffing and training practices that are likely to be found under different career systems. Mainstream HRM has adopted a micro perspective, attempting to trace relationships between strategy and individual HRM policies. Studies in this category often utilize one of the macro perspectives as a foundation for their more specific analyses.

However, while the existing research employing a macro perspective lacks specificity, studies in the second category of micro-focused approaches suffer a shortcoming of their own. They seek to identify linkages which extend from business strategy down to actual human resource policy applications; however, generally they focus only on a single function, failing to take into account how business strategy might influence other, related HRM functions.

Background _____

Both micro and macro approaches linking strategy and HRM fail to explicitly recognize the assumptions upon which they are predicated. There are two general assumptions which underlie all models connecting HRM practices and business strategy. First, it is assumed that the selection and mix of human resource practices are determined by the specific strategy a firm adopts, which is itself influenced by environmental constraints such as government regulations, competitor actions, etc. Second, it is assumed that firms achieving a tighter fit between alignment of environmental constraints, strategy requirements, and HRM practices will perform better than those that do not.

Failure to recognize these two assumptions has led researchers to ignore some of the complexities inherent in multinational firms. For example, consistency found between a parent company and its foreign subsidiaries with regard to business strategy and HRM policies has often been assumed. Differences between the environment of a parent organization and those of its foreign subsidiaries, however, may create strong pressures for the firm to modify its local operations in each country. This is particularly true with respect to HRM policies. Labor markets, union influence, worker skill level and skill variety, along with legal requirements relating to hiring, compensation, and dismissal practices are all likely to differ significantly from one country to the next.

The second contingency assumption specifies that effective performance is a result of the alignment of internal operations to the external environment. Given the potential cross-national variations cited above, multinational firms that achieve internal consistency (between parent and foreign subsidiary) would appear to run a high risk of misalignment with the external environment. Looking at these two assumptions together, the implication for multinational firms is one of competing pressures: internal pressures for consistency between strategy and HRM practices, and external pressures for consistency between HRM practices and the environment.

Recognition of competing pressures on HRM practices is a return to the well-documented dilemma of "standardization versus differentiation" that pervades debates of how to administer international operations. There is a dynamic tension between the need for the overseas affiliate to adapt to local conditions versus the need to integrate across the MNE as a whole. To date, most approaches have suggested that resolution of this dilemma is determined by the relative strength of the competing forces.

A Strategic Framework

We propose an alternative approach that focuses on the *extent to which a MNE firm requires consistency* between parent and subsidiary business strategy and between parent and subsidiary HRM practices. In doing so, we suggest that these twin needs for consistency are determined by (1) the strategies that firms adopt; and (2) the nature of the international competition in which they are involved. Internal and external pressures are filtered by two strategic choices that MNEs make. Firms decide on the strategy they will pursue and the domain within which they will pursue it.

The Environment-Business Strategy Match

One way of viewing the external environment of MNEs is to identify the nature of international competition in the industry in which a firm is involved. There are two types of industry competition. A *multidomestic* industry is one in which competition in a given country is essentially independent of competition in other countries. For example, the soft drink industry in Japan is not influenced by competition in the soft drink industry in China. Insurance and retailing are characteristic multidomestic industries. By contrast, an industry such as that of commercial aircraft manufacturing, involves competition where activities in one country have a significant influence on activities in another. For example, competition in the petroleum industry occurs across nations, with oil wells in one country, refineries and processing facilities in another, and various end-users located in those two countries as well as others. Industries of this type are labeled *global.*

Differences between the two types of competition are reflected in the varying demands for coordination that each imposes. Global industries exhibit greater coordination needs than do multidomestic industries. The need for coordination implies pressure for internal consistency.

While MNE environments can be classified into global versus multidomestic types, firms' strategic orientations can also be classified in terms of orientation with regard to two broad types: *cost leadership* and *product differentiation.* A cost leadership strategy, as alluded to earlier, seeks to achieve competitive advantage by being the least-cost producer of a product, while a product differentiation strategy seeks competitive advantage by providing unique value to a product.

Originally these two strategic archetypes were put forward as mutually exclusive. A firm could pursue a cost leadership strategy, for example, only at the exclusion of a product differentiation strategy. Indeed, "being stuck in the middle" was considered one the of the weakest positions a firm could occupy. However, recent research concludes that a single firm can successfully pursue both strategies.

Simultaneous efforts at cost leadership and product differentiation do not, however, suggest equal weighting between the two. Indeed, though changes in environmental pressures may encourage firms to adopt a combined strategy, organizational imprinting—locking into a particular view of the environment early in an organization's life—and the development of distinctive competencies within a firm may result in a persistent bias toward one or the other. For example, Sony and Matsushita both seek to compete on the basis of cost and product variety. Nevertheless, Sony's roots and corporate culture help maintain a preference for differentiation over cost. Similarly, when push comes to shove for Matsushita, the choice is in favor of cost.

Because the cost-differentiation distinction remains persistent in practice, it can be usefully employed in discussions if cost leadership and product differentiation are thought of as opposite ends of a continuum. Consequently, firms may locate themselves at any point along the continuum that reflects the mix of cost and differentiation strategies they are pursuing.

Since a strategy of cost leadership seeks to achieve competitive advantage by being the least-cost producer of a product, then this strategy requires a firm to focus on functional policies. Under a cost leadership strategy, internal operations of a firm command attention and the drive is for internal efficiency.

A product differentiation strategy, on the other hand, seeks competitive advantage through the ability of a firm to provide unique value to a product, one that will be more localized in terms of its appeal to a particular foreign market or segment. Using a strategy of differentiation, firms are less concerned with cost and more concerned with identifying what special value they are able to add. A differentiation strategy requires a firm to develop an external focus, to be intimately aware of what its customers desire.

When a MNE's strategic orientation is considered in combination with the type of international competition in which it is involved, we can map out the requirements for consistency. As shown in Figure 1, the four combinations of MNE strategic orientation and international competition exhibit their own unique requirements for consistency between the parent company and the overseas subsidiary.

Figure 1. The Pressures for Consistency Resulting from MNE Strategic Orientation and the Nature of International Competition

STRATEGIC ORIENTATION

	Cost	Differentiation
Multidomestic	• Strong pressure for consistency between parent & subsidiary strategy;	• Weak pressure for consistency between parent & subsidiary strategy;
	• Strong pressure for consistency with local external environments	• Strong pressure for consistency with local external environments
International Competition		
Global	• Strong pressure for consistency between parent & subsidiary strategy;	• Weak pressure for consistency between parent & subsidiary strategy;
	• Weak pressure for consistency with local external environments	• Weak pressure for consistency with local external environments

Pursuing a cost leadership strategy in an industry characterized by multidomestic competition generates the highest levels of stress on the parent-subsidiary relationship. The strategy of cost leadership, and its accompanying internal focus on efficiency, creates strong pressures for standardization in the business unit's strategy across countries. At the same time, the multidomestic nature of the industry provides strong encouragement for the firm to adapt to local conditions in order to compete with local and multinational competitors.

Firms pursuing a cost leadership strategy in an industry where competition is global, though experiencing strong pressures for internal consistency, will feel lower levels of pressure to conform to the myriad local external environments of its subsidiary operations. This is not to suggest that environmental constraints and pressures will be unimportant for MNEs in this quadrant. Rather, pressures will be lower relative to firms in the multidomestic-cost leadership quadrant which must respond to local competitor actions.

Pursuing a differentiation strategy in an industry characterized by multidomestic competition leads to low levels of stress on the parent-subsidiary relationship. The strategy of differentiation and its accompanying external focus aimed at providing unique value to its customers generate weaker pressures for standardization across countries. At the same time, the multidomestic nature of competition suggests that a firm should adapt to local conditions.

By contrast, a differentiation strategy in an industry where competition is global affords MNEs with the widest range of latitude in consistency requirements. Internal pressures for alignment of parent and subsidiary strategy are lower than for firms following a cost leadership strategy. Simultaneously, the global nature of the industry in which the MNE competes suggests that pressures to adapt to the local external environment will also be relatively weak.

Regardless of whether a firm competes in a multidomestic or global competitive environment, the efficiency orientation of a cost leadership strategy places greater emphasis on internal consistency than does a differentiation strategy. Second, localization pressures associated with a multidomestic competitive environment make it harder for MNEs to achieve consistency than in a global competitive environment. Therefore, consistency between parent and subsidiary business strategies will have a greater impact on firm performance in MNEs employing a cost leadership rather than a differentiation strategy. Moreover, firms competing in a multidomestic competitive environment will experience greater difficulty in achieving consistency between parent and subsidiary business strategies than firms competing in a global competitive environment.

The Business Strategy-HRM Strategy Match

If a MNE's performance is based on its capacity to internally align its operations in a way that allows it to match environmental constraints, then there must be a way to determine whether or not a firm is properly aligned with its environment. More than any other function within a MNE, the management of human resources is decentralized. With the exception of matters related to expatriates and international assignments, the vast majority of HRM affairs are handled at the level of the subsidiary. Consequently, a consideration of business strategy-HRM strategy linkages must necessarily shift attention away from a MNE's business strategy at the parent level and its position in international competition to a focus on how these two factors interact with subsidiary-level business strategy to influence the choice of HRM strategy.

At the subsidiary level, the requirement for internal consistency may be interpreted as the degree of integration with the parent company necessary for success. For example, due to strong pressures for internal consistency and relatively weak pressures for external consistency, we would expect subsidiaries of MNEs competing in global industries with a cost leadership strategy to be highly integrated with the parent. On the other hand, subsidiaries of MNEs pursuing a product differentiation strategy in multidomestic industries are more likely to be less integrated with the parent.

Human Resource Management Strategies

Business strategy determines how a firm competes in a given business. Firms select business strategies in accordance both with evaluations they make about the environment in which they wish to compete and the resources available within the firm. In order to develop and implement a business strategy, however, it is necessary to break it down into its various components or to develop functional strategies. These functional strategies are further decomposed into policies which, when implemented, become practice.

Policies can be thought of as decision rules. They are procedures that organization members are expected to follow. Practices, on the other hand, are less formal than policies and can be thought of as the actual decisions taken by organization members. Practices thus reflect those procedures that are actually carried out. In the international context, for example, a MNE may have a worldwide policy of equitable pay schemes for all of its employees, but how that policy is translated locally can vary from country to country. Thus, for a single firm, practices may differ across countries while the policy remains consistent.

Our framework predicts that if a firm's strategy is congruent with the external environment, firm performance will be higher than if its strategy does not match the environment. However, consistency between a plan (strategy) and the external environment is only a first step. It does not directly predict firm performance. Rather, firm performance is determined by the application of the plan, through the implementation of functional policies, including those contained in a HRM strategy.

A number of classification schemes have been suggested for categorizing HRM strategies. One widely used typology defines three types of HRM strategies. A *utilizer strategy* deploys the human resources of the firm as efficiently as possible through: (1) the acquisition and dismissal of personnel in accordance with the short-term needs of the firm; (2) the matching of employee skill to specific task requirements. An *accumulator strategy* builds up the human resources of the firm through: (1) the acquisition of personnel with large, latent potential; (2) the development of that latent potential over time in a manner consistent with the needs of the organization. A *facilitator strategy* is focused on new knowledge and new knowledge creation. It seeks to develop the human resources of the firm as effectively as possible through the acquisition of self-motivated personnel and the encouragement and support of personnel to develop, on their own, the skills and knowledge which they, the employees, believe are important.

Determination of the appropriate HRM strategy for a given subsidiary can be achieved by assessing the intersection of subsidiary's business strategy with its degree of integration with the parent. Appropriate combinations are shown in Figure 2.

Figure 2. The Implications for HRM Strategy of Subsidiary Strategic Orientation and Degree of Integration Between Subsidiary and MNE

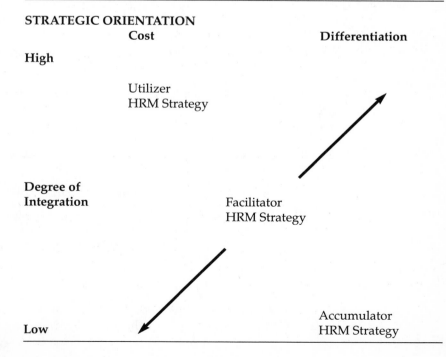

STRATEGIC ORIENTATION

Cost   **Differentiation**

High

Utilizer
HRM Strategy

**Degree of
Integration**

Facilitator
HRM Strategy

Accumulator
HRM Strategy

Low

Because a utilizer HRM strategy helps to maintain a lean workforce by acquiring or dismissing employees as and when skills are required, this strategy is more appropriate to a cost leadership business strategy. The utilizer strategy is effective not only because of its efficiency orientation, but also because of its high level of flexibility, making it easier to fit subsidiary human resources with the demands of the parent (high integration). With decreasing integration, the utilizer strategy may still remain somewhat effective. However, as pressures for local adaptation increase, the subsidiary is less able to implement a utilizer strategy, particularly if it is not in line with local norms and customs.

A facilitator strategy is appropriate in a wide range of circumstances because it can handle HRM demands along both dimensions. The facilitator is qualitatively different from the utilizer and the accumulator in that it seeks to support new knowledge creation. Complex and evolving human resource demands, resulting from strong pressures in opposing directions for both strategic orientation and integration, call for an evolutionary, learning orientation.

An accumulator HRM strategy facilitates the flexibility required under a differentiation strategy by providing an excess pool of employees with latent potential which can be tapped as needed. An effective accumulator strategy would be easiest to pursue under conditions of low need for integration with the parent. As the demand for integration rises, the accumulator strategy breaks down because of the increasing influence of the parent company which stem from its desire to exercise tighter control as a result of the subsidiary's increased centrality to the MNE's overall operations.

We would expect that those subsidiaries which match their HRM strategy to their combination of business strategy and degree of integration with the parent will perform better than those that do not. The following briefly summarizes the main ideas developed so far:

1. Among subsidiaries employing cost leadership business strategies and having a high degree of integration with the parent, those which adopt a utilizer HRM strategy will perform better than those that employ an accumulator or facilitator HRM strategy.

2. In subsidiaries employing product differentiation business strategies and having a low degree of integration with the parent, those which adopt an accumulator HRM strategy will perform better than those that employ a utilizer or facilitator HRM strategy.

3. Finally, for subsidiaries pursuing both cost leadership and differentiation strategies, those which adopt a facilitator HRM strategy will perform better than those that employ a utilizer or accumulator HRM strategy.

Consistency in Parent-Subsidiary HRM Strategy Alignment

Although HRM constitutes the most decentralized of all MNE functions, it is also true that the increasing globalization of MNEs has brought about an increased desire and need for greater coordination and consistency between parent and subsidiary. Application of the above framework in assessing HRM practices in both the parent and subsidiary provides a means by which to determine the extent to which the two are in alignment. Moreover, the relationships in Figure 1 indicate that the need for parent-subsidiary alignment of HRM activities may vary depending on the strategic orientation of the MNE and the nature of international competition for the industry in which it competes.

Firms pursuing a cost leadership strategy in industries characterized by multidomestic competition will strive for consistency in HRM activities. However, they will do so in the face of strong pressures to modify their practices from one country to the next. In such a situation, consistency between parent and subsidiary in the application of a utilizer HRM strategy may not only be difficult to carry out, but lead to a loss of local competitiveness as well. For example, pressure to adapt locally is usually amplified for HRM practices because labor, blue- and white-collar combined, represents an area where cost reductions may make a significant contribution to implementing a cost leadership strategy. Adapting to local labor conditions in an attempt to obtain cost advantages, however, may introduce greater disparity between parent and subsidiary with accompanying increases in the cost of monitoring and managing the overseas operation.

By contrast, firms employing a cost leadership strategy in industries typified by global industries will seek consistency in a more amenable context. While experiencing internal demands similar to those of cost leadership firms in multidomestic industries, they pursue consistency in a setting more willing to forgive a measure of local insensitivity. Aligning a utilizer HRM strategy in both parent and subsidiary may be more easily achieved. Additionally, firms in this quadrant are likely to achieve a higher degree of parent-subsidiary alignment than are firms in the other three.

We can conclude that firms employing a cost leadership/utilizer combination competing in industries characterized by global competition will achieve a higher degree of integration between parent and subsidiary than firms with similar combinations competing in industries characterized by multidomestic competition. Furthermore, firms employing a cost leadership/utilizer combination competing in industries characterized by global competition will perform better than firms with similar combinations competing in industries characterized by multidomestic competition.

MNEs with a differentiation strategy in industries characterized by multidomestic competition will experience relatively weak internal demands for parent-subsidiary consistency. Simultaneously, pressures on subsidiaries to be sensitive to local conditions make it difficult to achieve alignment between parent and subsidiary HRM practices. Unlike a utilizer HRM strategy, however, an accumulator HRM strategy is more appropriate since it emphasizes the accumulation of resources and possesses more organizational slack and latent human resources potential. The result is greater flexibility in human resource activities and less stringent requirements for consistency. Firms in this quadrant exhibit a lower degree of consistency than firms in the other three quadrants but this also means that consistency requirements may be less important.

Firms employing a differentiation/accumulator combination competing in industries characterized by multidomestic competition achieve a lower degree of integration between parent and subsidiary than firms with similar combinations competing in industries characterized by global competition. By contrast, firms employing a differentiation/accumulator match competing in industries characterized by multidomestic competition will perform better than firms with similar combinations competing in industries challenged by global competition.

Finally, MNEs with a product differentiation strategy in an industry where competition is global confront internal pressures for alignment that are lower than for firms with a cost leadership strategy. Simultaneously, the global nature of the industry in which these firms compete indicates that local external environment pressures are also weak. Alignment of parent and subsidiary HRM activities for firms in this quadrant is less critical to firm performance than for firms employing a cost leadership strategy. This leads to the conclusion that firms employing a differentiation/accumulator combination competing in industries characterized by global competition achieve a higher degree of integration between parent and subsidiary than firms with similar combinations competing in industries with multidomestic competition. Additionally, firms employing a differentiation/accumulator combination competing in industries characterized by global competition will perform better than firms with similar combinations competing in industries where competition is multidomestic.

Conclusion ───

This framework constitutes a model bridging macro and micro perspectives on the linkages between business strategy and HRM practice in MNEs. It concludes that there must be consistency between parent-level business strategy and subsidiary-level HRM strategy.

The framework also provides direction to HRM managers by clarifying the extent to which there is a need for consistency between parent and subsidiary in multinational operations. In doing so, it provides both a rationale and a means for them to sort through the dilemmas involved in trying to integrate parent and subsidiary operations.

Nissan Italia, S.P.A

Case 1.1
Ayako Asakura
Susan Schneider

One afternoon in late November, 1988, Mr. Sasaki, Director of Europe Group of Nissan Motor Co., was busy signing Christmas and New Years cards in his office at the headquarters in Tokyo. He felt the pile of cards were much higher than in the previous year. "This should be because of our recent development in Europe. Now we have Nissan Motor Iberia in Barcelona and Nissan Italy in Rome. And a factory in the U.K. has just started operation. It looks as if these two years have flown away, keeping us very busy with working for those projects."

Speaking to himself with a satisfied smile, Mr. Sasaki started to look back at Nissan's European operations. Though satisfied, he worries about the future development of, and some fundamental problems in Italy, wondering what lessons could be learned for other overseas operations and what were the implications for future globalization.

The Company

Nissan Motor Co., Ltd. was established in 1933. The company has always been strongly overseas oriented and set up its first plant outside Japan in Mexico as early as 1966. Even today it is the only Japanese automobile company that has its own manufacturing base in Europe.

This is not only because the company always has been second to Toyota in the domestic market. They recognized the necessity to be close to the market in order to better satisfy customer needs, to get integrated in and to contribute to the local economy. Therefore, Nissan is aiming at a whole process localization—to be an "insider" through all operations from R&D to sales.

Nissan has dramatically increased its presence in Europe these last few years. Several international economic and market environments have promoted this trend: yen appreciation, trade friction, increasing competition, and European common market integration. Reacting to those changes, Nissan has clearly positioned its strategy for internationalization and

Source: Ayako Asakura and Susan Schneider. "Nissan Italia, S.P.A." © 1989 INSEAD. All rights reserved.

further globalization. The company intends to go beyond export and partly overseas manufacturing, to exploit cost advantage, to establish various activities abroad and to integrate them horizontally.

Corporate Culture

Nissan does not have a strong corporate culture. Since it was established through mergers of some companies during the 1910s to the 1930s, Nissan has no clear founder. This is an obvious difference from the other Japanese overseas-oriented companies like Sony, Honda, or Matsushita, whose corporate cultures are directed or affected by the strong characteristics of the founders.

This gives freedom to the organization. People are not bound by a certain philosophy, policy, or image of the founder and hence the company. That the top management positions are totally open to all the employees helps create motivation.

On the other hand, absence of a strong philosophy or visible embodiment of the founder makes it difficult to unite the whole company, to provide a clear sense of direction, and to keep moving forward. This also causes weakness in the company's external image. Nissan has enjoyed a good reputation for its high technology, but it is declining, and other competitors are catching up. Apart from this, Nissan lacks a special image in the Japanese market.

Having recognized this point, in January, 1987, Nissan, for the first time, stated a clearly written "Corporate Philosophy." On the first page of the 1987 annual report, it says, "Nissan—growing and changing to meet the needs of today's customers." The company printed this on business cards and distributed them to every employee.

This statement is translated into the languages of each country where Nissan has plants, offices, or subsidiaries (Exhibit 1). The translation is not a literal one. It is aimed to express the core policy and objectives and rewritten so that the idea would be best implemented in each situation and cultural environment.

Policy Toward Overseas Operations

Nissan's policy toward overseas operations is not rigid. Taking many different situations into consideration, the company has a "clear end and loose means" policy. There is no standardized way. As far as it is in line with the realization of Nissan's objectives, it allows a certain amount of autonomy to each plant or subsidiary and lets each seek the best way, depending on the situation. For example, while the Mexico plant is run in a typical Japanese style, the American one in Smyrna, Tennessee, is

---

Exhibit 1. Profile of Nissan

Customer Satisfaction First

Corporate
Philosophy

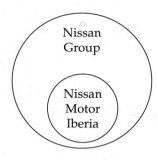

Globalization

Nissan
Group

Worldwide Activities
to Create and
Satisfy Customers'
Needs

Localization

Nissan
Motor
Iberia

Progress Towards
Future in Harmony
with Local Society

---

run in an American way with American top management. The British plant in Sunderland is run in a half-British, half-Japanese style.

This variety depends on many factors such as the location, form (green-field investment or joint venture), history, technological level, product, human resource availability, target market, and so on.

With its long history of overseas business and operations, the company points out two issues as keys to success. One is to be an insider in the markets wherever they are present. Another is to promote globalization of the headquarters in Japan. In order to understand the development and the situation of overseas operations of Nissan, there is a good example in Europe: Nissan Italia.

Nissan Italia, S.P.A. ————————————————————————

Nissan Italia is a distribution and after service (repair and part sales) company. Sixty-four percent of the share is owned by Nissan Motor Co. and the rest by Nissan Motor Iberia.

History

The company, named EBRO, was founded as a joint venture of an Italian company and Motor Iberia in February, 1978, for the commercial vehicle sales and after services.

In January 1988 Nissan Motor Co., purchased 49 percent of local share (the rest was owned by Nissan Motor Iberia) and changed its name to Nissan Italia S.P.A., and in March increased its share to 64 percent. Therefore Nissan Motor is now fully in control of Nissan Italia.

The mission given to Nissan Italia in the Nissan group is to cover a very protective Italian market from the sales and service side.

It is not, however, their first footing into the Italian market. Already in 1980 Nissan started a joint venture with Alfa Romeo. But it turned out to be very difficult to control the company because Nissan had only 50 percent of the shares and the personnel decisions were made by Italian managers and the company in Italy. Therefore Nissan could not take the initiative of the business, and annulled the joint venture in 1987. So it was after this experience that Nissan set up Nissan Italia as a new base for the Italian market. Now, Nissan Italia sells cars not only imported from Japan but also those produced by Nissan Motor Iberia in Spain and, from November, 1988, also those in a new factory in Sunderland, U.K.

Concerning parts supply, there are two routes: 73 percent (in 1987) are from Barcelona (the parts manufactured by Nissan Motor Iberia) and the rest from Nissan Motor Parts Center in Amsterdam (the parts imported from Japan).

Localization—Change to Nissan Italia

Based on Nissan's basic policy of clear end and loose means, and because of its evolution, Nissan Italia is a very Italian company. As seen in the organization (see Exhibit 2) and the communication, here Japanese have adjusted to the local way.

Even after March, 1988, when Nissan increased its share in the company, there has not been any drastic change. Mr. Arai, President of Nissan Italy, says,

> I did not give any speech to address the new president's declaration. This is not a change of that kind. I have been with them a while and nothing would suddenly change. The base of this company is Italy. Furthermore, without any formal words, the people understand Nissan's intention. In the meantime, maybe when we will move to the new office*, I will say a word.

It is obvious, however, that Nissan conveyed a clear message that it is going to be more seriously engaged in a longer-term development in the Italian market through this company. And there are also some other signals to show the company's determined will as seen below. From the part of the original company, this change is very well accepted because the company is given a chance to jump from a small business to a medium-sized one.

Present Situation

Organization. The organization remains very local. Although the board consists of three Spanish directors and four Japanese, in practice only the president and his assistant are Japanese and one director and

_____
*Nissan Italia is now going to have a new head office with warehouse facilities.

Exhibit 2. Nissan Motor Iberia Organization

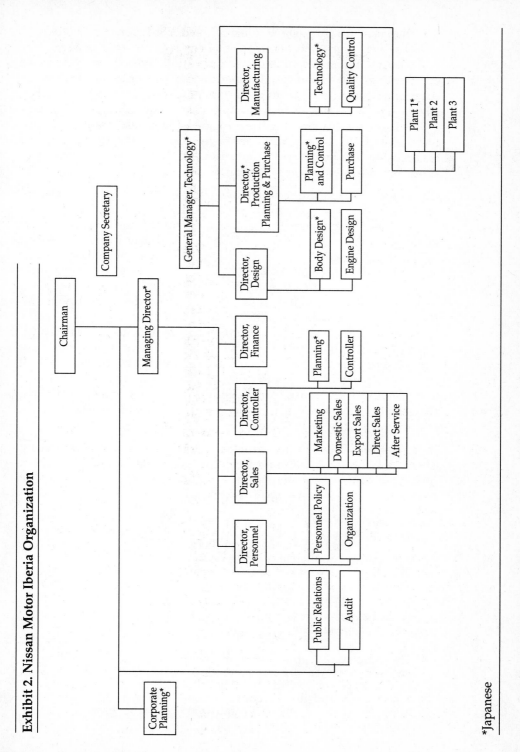

Chairman

Company Secretary

Managing Director*

Corporate Planning*

Public Relations

Audit

Director, Personnel

Personnel Policy

Organization

Director, Sales

Marketing

Domestic Sales

Export Sales

Direct Sales

After Service

Director, Controller

Planning*

Controller

Director, Finance

General Manager, Technology*

Director, Design

Body Design*

Engine Design

Director, Production Planning & Purchase

Planning* and Control

Purchase

Director, Manufacturing

Technology*

Quality Control

Plant 1*

Plant 2

Plant 3

*Japanese

one manager are Spanish (Exhibit 3). And Mr. Oyama, the Japanese assistant, was sent over only in September, 1988.

Mr. Arai, the president, is a veteran about Italy with his 18 years of experience as a government official in the Japanese Ministry of Foreign Affairs, as a businessman in a big Japanese trading company, and in Nissan. (He has been with Nissan since the joint venture with Alfa Romeo.)

This shows the organization is not a "Japanese managers with Italian subordinates" structure but is very open to the local people up to directors. The people are given responsibilities; for example, Italian staffs fly to Amsterdam or Japan for meetings.

Communication. Italian is always used in the company since the Spanish managers and both Japanese are fluent in Italian. But externally the official language is English. At the moment, the communication between the headquarters and Nissan Italia is mainly done in Japanese, but it will change as English is used more by both sides, that is, headquarters and the Italian staff. In order to improve communication efficiency and to increase the internationality of the company, English lessons for the Italian staff have been started, which will also help promote the open mentality of the organization.

The company has a very open atmosphere in spite of the individually separated office style. The door of the president's office is almost always kept open and people come in to talk with Mr. Arai. He says, "I don't like to use first name to call each other because it sounds to me too casual. But of course I don't mind other people doing so among themselves." And it is true that this is only a matter of his taste, and his relationships with the Italian employees seem very warm.

Japanization. There is no particular effort to Japanize the company. There have, however, naturally been some changes through the history of Nissan's increasing share and hence control in the company. Mr. Arai described the change so far as Phase 1.

> Up to now, Nissan has done everything it can to help this company: invest in the facilities, send the people; finance the capital; and introduce the passenger cars (before the company was dealing only in commercial vehicles). Phase 1 is the visible change from the top. Now in Phase 2 the company should change by itself based on these preparations.

> What I expect from them is to have the participation mentality and to propose their ideas voluntarily to the company.

> There are some variances among people's attitude depending on the department. The salespeople are quite participative and give their feedback from the field although they are paid on a salary basis and not on commissions. This is partly because sales results are, being quantitative and obvious, easier to use for control and motivation.

Exhibit 3. Nissan Italia

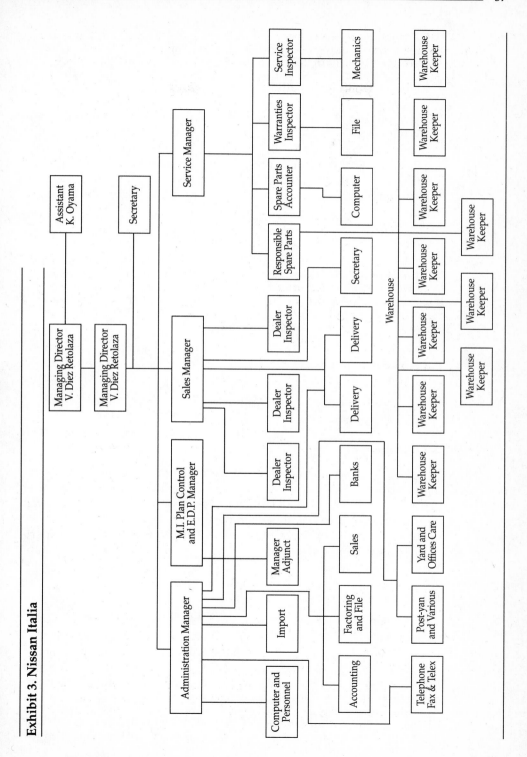

Compared to them, people in the office or in the warehouse are relatively passive and do not take the initiative. As their jobs are more difficult to evaluate objectively and quantitatively, this is understandable. But I would like them to change their working mind gradually.

Dealer Relationships. Dealer relationships in the case of sales network business are something equivalent to the supplier relationships in manufacturing. Nissan Italia's dealers are multifranchisers with contracts with several car manufacturers except Fiat. They sell various kinds of cars and being independent from Nissan, they are difficult to control. Mr. Arai says,

They are profit-oriented dealers. But I would like to change our relationships and develop a more longer-term one.

For this purpose, Nissan Italia makes efforts to improve communication with them, to make them understand Nissan's policy and product superiority and to ask for dealers' cooperation, for example, hold meetings, increase advertisement budget, and so on. And in the future, we would also like to have our own exclusive dealer network.

Perceived Problems

Working Style. Mr. Arai says, "Here the manager should give every instruction to get things done. You cannot expect the employees to act positively or manage voluntary activities like QC (quality circles). Especially the people in the workshop (repair and after service) who rarely do overtime."

Personnel. Labor mobility is also a big problem to the human resource management. The better a manager is, he tends to move to another company, and this makes it difficult to plan in-house training, to keep good people, and to accumulate expertise. "But on the other hand, we enjoy some merits of this mobility, too. That is, we can recruit experienced people from outside whenever necessary," says a Japanese manager with a bitter smile.

Expatriate Situation

Until September, 1988, Mr. Arai has been the only Japanese in the company, with Mr. Oyama coming to Rome sometimes for a long business trip.

Both of them do not seem to have any difficulty working and living here thanks to their language ability and personalities. Here some points are given by Mr. Arai as general comments about the expatriates' situation.

Inconvenience About Business Schedule. The difference of working hours, that is, the time lag and the difference in working hour length, causes the expatriates to work very long hours; for example, the early morning or late night telephone call to home, coming to the office on weekends, local holidays or during summer vacation, which is much longer here than in Japan.

Another thing is that they are expected to be attendants for Japanese managers or clients when they make a visit. They should play a role of "perfect" attendant: driver, interpreter, tourist guide, and shopping advisor all at the same time from morning to night. This is especially the case in big cities like Paris, London, or Rome.

Japanese Circle. In every city with more than a certain number of Japanese, there is a Japanese Association. So in Rome, but compared to Milan, where many companies locate, the Japanese population in Rome is small, and hence not many activities are going on in the Japanese circle.

According to Mr. Arai, "If you try to maintain a Japanese lifestyle or to stick together with Japanese, then you might have problems adjusting to the foreign life and people. But as far as you try to get accustomed to a new environment, there would be no problem."

And there are not many Japanese restaurants, either. "Anyway Rome is a bit different from other cities in terms of the food internationality. There are not many foreign food restaurants. For example, generally, fancy French restaurants are appreciated as the best cuisine and can be found in any big international city. But it seems that Italians mock French cooking, which damages the natural and original taste of the food with heavy sauce. People are just happy with their own Italian food," says Mr. Oyama, who also loves Italian food.

Children's Education. Last but not least, today perhaps the biggest issue for Japanese expatriates is the children's education.

Many foreign cities have a Japanese school with either a full-time or complementary staff depending on the Japanese population. However, since Japanese society is very education-conscious, many parents want their children to enter a good company meaning that they must enter a good university and before that a good high school. Therefore, at the critical age for high school or junior high school, many children (and their mothers) are sent back to Japan.

What is very interesting and shows a particular aspect of Japanese society is that this tendency is stronger for boys; there are many boys going back home to prepare for good universities while there are more girls going to local schools at various levels and staying abroad longer. Since the Japanese working world is still a rather male society with lifelong employment, it is thought that boys should equip themselves with a higher education for their own future happiness.

Back at Headquarters. Looking at the current situation in Nissan Italia, Mr. Sasaki is quite pleased with the evolution so far as the first phase. At the same time, however, he has realized some difficult problems. Most of them are not new; they come up more or less every time Nissan tries to develop business abroad. Therefore, to solve these problems would take a long time.

First, human resource management is of concern. As a whole, Nissan has kept the local identity of each subsidiary and retained almost all personnel. There seems to be no hostility or problem of adjustment. But there is a very fundamental difference among employees' working mentality, which has puzzled Japanese managers, namely, local staffs are not very participative and communication within the company (especially horizontal communication among functions and operations) is rather poor. Also high job mobility restrains them from accumulation of expertise and planning for human resource management.

"What can we do to motivate them and make them want to participate? Would the Japanese way of management with regard to motivation and incentive systems work?"

This first question leads to the second question, which is more fundamental. "How far could or should we reinforce Japanization in foreign subsidiaries? Where is the optimal balance?"

"And what is the role of Japanese expatriates and the headquarters?" Mr. Sasaki knows expatriates' frustration toward headquarters very well and recognizes the necessity of headquarter's globalization. "Expatriates' managers are sandwiched between demands from headquarters and the local subsidiary. They need our understanding and support in terms of money, people, technology, and human network and its mental support. But we cannot afford to respond to all of their needs because of shortages in resources, especially at this time of rapidly expanding overseas business. First of all, we should at least be better prepared to use English to facilitate communication between foreign subsidiaries. And more fundamentally, to raise good human resources able to cope with international operations. This will be a real long-term job."

And another question is how to train employees for globalization strategy? For example, now Nissan sends a few employees to business school, mostly in the United States. "Would we rather send someone to Europe, too, since our presence in Europe has very much increased? Then which school?"

The last question in his mind is about human resource management. How to respond to expatriates' problems both in the working situation and in the private life situation? How can headquarters support their job? How far should the company support them for their children's education or maintenance of houses they leave in Japan?

But, Mr. Sasaki was brought back to Nissan's policy at the end: clear end and loose means. "Maybe there is no right answer to be generalized, and we should try to think out each context."

The Anstrichehof Infrared Coating Corporation—AICC

Case 1.2
Alberto Zanzi
Paul Lemieux

"Well, I'm really not surprised," Ron Wheeler thought to himself as he looked in disgust at SwissAir's monitor. The "Arrivals" display video terminal read as follows:

11 MAR 1988   FLIGHT 402 - ZURICH 1 HOUR DELAY

It had been that kind of a day. More than the usual amount of bull at work, the Friday night traffic jam in the Sumner Tunnel, and now that he was finally inside the terminal, the flight from Zurich was late. If there was one thing he hated more than a trip to Logan Airport, it was a trip to pick up Dr. Buerlanger at Logan.

"I guess it comes with the territory," he sputtered barely under his breath. As executive vice president of AICC, he felt responsible to personally pick up the directors from AICC's parent company, Masseverk AG. The visits were becoming more frequent and more tense; this time Dr. Vogtgartener was also coming.

Ron found a corner table in the Skyway Lounge, ordered a Lite (an American beer!), and set out his workpapers in front of him. He had a right to be in such a foul mood. AICC was in major trouble. That trouble was traveling toward him at 1,100 miles per hour at 30,000 feet.

He sat back and thought about his beloved AICC. Started in 1968, its growth had been steady but not earthshaking. They actually shipped over $18 million worth of infrared products in 1986. Their current employment of 225 people was their highest level ever. AICC manufactured infrared band-pass filters and antireflection coatings for use in a wide variety of biochemical, military, and aerospace applications. AICC filters were on the job in communications satellites, blood analyzers, burglar alarms, and literally hundreds of other places. The growing worldwide market for commercial applications currently exceeded $250 million. Since the largest competitor only had 25 percent of the market, AICC's potential for continued growth was quite good.

Scource: Alberto Zanzi and Paul Lemieux. "The Anstrichehof Infrared Coating Corporation." Suffolk University, 1989. Reprinted by permission.

Ron marveled at the contrast to Masseverk AG, the parent firm. With 1986 revenues of over four billion Swiss francs ($2.8 billion), Masseverk was a significant force in European industry. Although over 60 percent of their production was military, their optics division, which included AICC, accounted for 12 percent of their total sales. AICC's president, currently a Dr. Mueller, reported directly to Dr. Buerlanger at the optics division headquarters in Zurich.

For the first five years after Masseverk had bought the company, AICC had lost money. Although they had managed to make a small profit last year, this year they barely broke even, and the trend at year end was down, with a bullet. To make things worse, all the good technical people were leaving just when the competition was getting tougher.

There was the memo from Dr. Buerlanger in front of him. As he began to reread it for the sixth time, he felt his ulcer kick up.

MEMORANDUM

TO: Dr. W. Mueller, Pres. AICC
CC: Mr. R. Wheeler, Exec. V.P.
FROM: Dr. J. Buerlanger, Mgr. Masseverk AG., Dir. AICC
SUBJECT: 1987 Performance

Needless to say we are extremely disappointed in your recently reported year end figures, especially after our repeated exhortations that you make improvements. We continue to fail to understand why your technical efficiency remains weak in spite of continued capital equipment investments on our part.

We thought it was sufficiently clear in our memo of 22 FEB 1986 that the new capital of nearly 3.8 Million SFr (2 Million US$) that we invested at that time was supposed to cure whatever was needed, and your predecessor readily agreed. It seems unlikely that the . . .

"Ladies and gentlemen! Your attention please! SwissAir Flight 402 from Zurich has been delayed one additional half hour."

"Waitress, another Lite, please. There goes any hope of making it home in time for the Celtics game. Now, where was I," he mused, as his agitation increased.

. . . seems unlikely that the present management team will ever reach the minimum level of success which Masseverk AG demands from all its subsidiary companies.

As some immediate and direct action on our part seems desirable, in fact unavoidable, I ask you to prepare in advance of our meeting on 12 MARCH 1988 at your location any defenses you wish to raise. Dr. Vogtgartener and myself have some thoughts on structural changes at AICC which may prove effective, but may not be your preference.

As always and best regards,

Dr. J. Buerlanger

Ron bottomed-up his second beer and wandered over to the plate glass windows overlooking the runway. A light rain was starting to fall. He allowed his mind to wander back to his early days at AICC. In retrospect, they were beginning to look like the good old days. "I'm starting to sound like my father," he thought wryly to himself.

When Ron started in 1973, proudly toting his new Suffolk M.B.A. under his arm (a nice supplement to his B.S. in chemistry from Northeastern), AICC hadn't been invented yet. It was a nice, fresh, American company, with a pleasantly high tech name, Infra-Tech. The founder, George Mason, was the man for all seasons, the life of the party, the perennial entrepreneur who was fully involved in everything and made everything work. Infra-Tech was vibrant, growing, alive, and exciting. Direct communication between employees was unhampered by rigid rules and regulations. Each employee felt a sense of involvement and contribution. People worked hard and derived satisfaction from their jobs. Productivity and creativity were high. Under Mason's informal style of leadership, the company flourished.

In the late 1970s, though, Infra-Tech started to lose its edge. Infrared technology was developing at a lightning pace. State-of-the-art equipment was expensive, and margins were slim. Infra-Tech's growth became stifled by lack of investment capital. They had good ideas, but they did not have the resources to bring those ideas to the market. Gradually, as the competition got the edge with better equipment, Infra-Tech tried to buy back its market share by cutting prices. Shortly after the margins disappeared, so did the cash. When Masseverk AG began looking for an American base for its infrared coating business in 1980, the match looked like a natural. The Swiss firm was a world recognized name in infrared technology; they would add their financial and technical strength to Infra-Tech. It had to be a winning combination.

Back in the lounge, Ron thought to himself how the vanishing foam on his beer was like his evaporating hopes over the AICC years. He had been a strong and early supporter of the buyout. But almost immediately things started to go wrong.

Dr. Buerlanger arrived with the contracts, the capital, and a new organization chart. George Mason was replaced with a Swiss national, who proceeded to alienate most of the Infra-Tech managers. By the end of the second year, most of the creative people had quit or been fired. Mason had run his firm in a loose, freewheeling manner, but he had encouraged close, frequent, and direct communication. No organization chart. No memo. No bull. Now all that was changed.

Dr. Buerlanger came from a different world. At Masseverk AG, where he had worked his whole long and successful career, company structure was hierarchical and very rigid. Employees were loyal and hardworking, and they knew their place. The working environment was strict and formal.

Wheeler was reminded of a meeting two years ago in Zurich. He recalled how he was out of sorts because all he could get with his meal was dark Swiss beer, no Lite. To his right, he had overhead Dr. Buerlanger make a comment to Dr. Vogtgartener under his breath about how the American's bad taste in beer was only surpassed by his childish impatience, disloyalty, and lack of organization. Dr. Buerlanger must have sensed Wheeler's attention because he turned his back slightly and continued in his native Suisse-Deutsche[1]:

Dr. B: Seriously, Herr Doctor, I cannot understand these Americans. They are bright, but they don't have any regard for the way things should be done. Everyone wants to be in charge. The technicians want to tell the scientists about ion exchange. The salesmen want to tell the supervisors how to run the plant. No one has any respect for order and control.

Dr. V: Believe me, I understand your disappointment. We have given them the opportunity to come here and learn from our success, but it is no use. They are hopelessly uncivilized. They carry their democratic ideas into the workplace; it is no surprise that the structure collapses.[2]

Dr. B: I would be content to deal with the EC [European Economic Community—ed.] countries; these are people I can understand. But the American market is too lucrative to ignore. I suppose we will have to continue to try to educate them to the correct way of doing things.

"Organization! Organization! Organization!" Wheeler thought over and over. "Ever since they have tried to make us an organization, we have stopped being an enterprise." Just that afternoon an angry exchange had taken place between Dave Howard, Manufacturing Manager, and Michael Steiner, Director of R&D. The stark contrast between now and Infra-Tech was foremost in Ron's mind as he recalled the scene in the corridor.

Howard: Where were you when Jonesie started up the 1500 Hi-Vac! He blew away almost $80,000 worth of germanium in two runs before Larry from QC shut him down!

Steiner: What do you mean "Where was I?" Where were you? You're the manufacturing manager, not me. Look on the wall in Wheeler's office next to manufacturing. That's you there, not me.

Howard: Listen, Mike. You know as well as I do that chart is Dr. B's little fantasy. You're the only one here who knows the right way to start up the 1500 Hi-Vac. We can't afford to foul up like this,

---

[1]Translated by the editor.

[2]Dr. Vogtgartener used the word *gefallenundversagenvollig,* a colloquialism which I have translated as "collapse." The literal meaning has a sense of total failure — ed.

or the Swiss will take their francs and go home. I got a kid in college and orthodontist bills to pay!

Steiner: Look Dave, it's nothing personal. But I've got to play it safe at least until I can get my résumé out on the street.

Howard: Well, do what you have to. But I'll tell you this much. This business is too complicated to run like the army. If we're gonna survive, we gotta learn to talk. And then we gotta learn to help each other out . . . not just hide behind the organization chart.

"Ladies and gentlemen! Your attention please! SwissAir Flight 402 from Zurich is now arriving at gate 12. Disembarking passengers can be met at the U.S. Customs exit in the lower lobby in approximately 30 minutes."

"Well, here they are. Buerlanger and Vogtgartener with another organization chart, and . . . ," thought Wheeler, "I don't even know if I'm on it!" The possibility of another president, the fourth in seven years, made Ron's ulcer kick up again. He pulled out the manilla folder which held tentative plans for a management leveraged buyout; he had been toying with the idea for six months, but it wasn't quite ready.

"Half an hour for customs? Waitress! I'll have another Lite, please."

Exhibit 1. Anstrichehof Infrared Coating Corporation Comparative Balance Sheet

	1981	1982	1983	1984	1985	1986	1987
Assets							
Current assets							
Cash	822,042	83,893	34,794	60,453	33,526	42,534	55,979
Accounts receivable	544,860	862,158	1,620,623	1,224,444	1,798,451	2,414,426	2,138,830
Inventories	363,029	641,220	1,772,533	1,988,948	1,508,320	1,813,490	1,757,092
Prepaid expenses	36,764	10,840	43,399	36,804	26,384	61,403	43,195
Total current assets	1,766,695	1,598,111	3,471,349	3,310,649	3,366,681	4,331,853	3,995,096
Equipment and Leaseholds, Net	1,610,522	4,119,974	3,686,767	3,598,186	3,543,186	3,589,534	3,995,455
Intangible Assets	92,340	81,262	58,774	30,028			
Total Assets	3,469,557	5,799,347	7,216,890	6,938,863	6,909,867	7,921,387	7,990,551
Liabilities & Equity							
Current Liabilities							
Notes Payable			1,100,000	2,600,000	2,100,000	1,750,000	3,400,000
Accounts payable accruals	256,122	719,511	1,763,529	1,607,329	548,434	1,564,220	614,781
Salaries, wages, taxes	139,864	42,610	69,871	48,805	59,592	134,536	127,568
Income taxes payable						450,288	
Deferred tax, current							10,710
Due to affiliates	36,802			589,210	2,000,000		92,141
Current portion, LTD				315,625	315,625	315,625	315,625
Total Current Liabilities	432,788	762,121	2,933,400	5,160,969	5,023,651	4,214,669	4,560,825
Deferred Taxes							4,590
Long Term Debt		2,525,000	2,525,000	2,209,375	1,893,750	1,578,127	1,262,502
Equity							
Capital	3,300,000	3,300,000	3,300,000	3,300,000	4,300,000	2,015,601	2,015,601
Retained earnings (deficit)	(263,231)	(787,774)	(1,541,510)	(3,731,481)	(4,307,534)	112,990	147,033
Total Equity	3,036,769	2,512,226	1,758,490	(431,481)	(7,534)	2,128,591	2,162,634
Total Liabilities	3,469,557	5,799,347	7,216,890	6,938,863	6,909,867	7,921,387	7,990,551

Exhibit 2. Anstrichehof Infrared Coating Corporation Comparative Statement of Income

	1981	1982	1983	1984	1985	1986	1987
Net Sales	2,305,046	6,101,116	8,456,087	8,888,253	14,795,246	18,275,256	17,916,961
Cost of Sales	1,601,356	4,822,067	6,817,782	8,749,517	12,583,515	13,747,058	13,906,623
	703,690	1,279,050	1,638,305	138,735	2,211,731	4,528,198	4,010,338
General, Administrative Expense	590,303	710,670	775,411	1,098,033	1,049,720	1,519,662	1,504,070
Selling Expense	161,408	547,316	646,117	742,743	634,106	873,087	961,367
Product Development	88,344	228,534	204,855	227,656	98,544	1,320,469	1,177,992
	840,055	1,486,520	1,626,383	2,068,432	1,782,370	3,713,218	3,643,429
Other Expense	126,865	317,072	765,658	260,274	1,005,414	250,756	306,566
Income Taxes						428,100	23,300
Earnings (Deficit)	(263,231)	(524,543)	(753,736)	(2,189,971)	(576,053)	136,125	37,043

Exhibit 3. Anstrichehof Infrared Coating Corporation Organization Chart

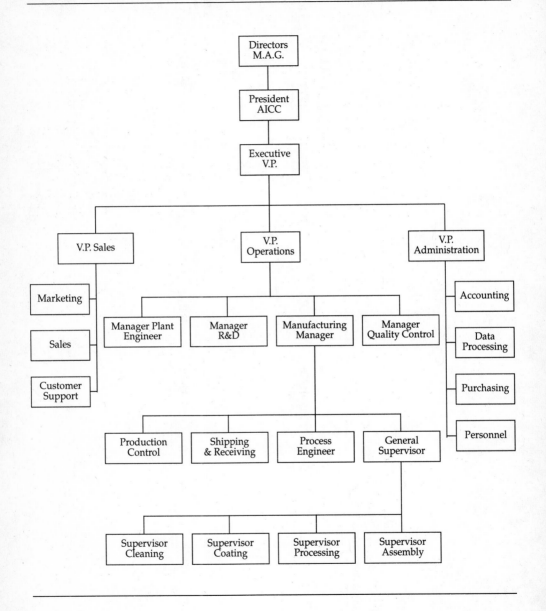

Part 2

INTERNATIONAL JOINT VENTURES

The Formation of an International Joint Venture: Davidson Instrument Panel

Reading 2.1
Randall S. Schuler
Susan E. Jackson
Peter J. Dowling
Denice E. Welch

"Ok, so you're thinking about manufacturing and selling your company's wares abroad, but you're more than a little daunted by the risks. Why not join forces with a foreign partner? That way, you can split the start-up costs and divide up any losses, not to mention gaining quicker international credibility, smoother distribution, and a better flow of information. Then again, maybe you'd rather not share your potential profits—or the secrets of your company's success—with anyone. That's fine. But don't be surprised if, after trying to crack a foreign market on your own, you develop a new enthusiasm for joint ventures" (Hyatt, 1988, p. 145).

Even without having first attempted to crack a foreign market on your own, you may be ready for an international joint venture (IJV). Such is the case with many U.S. firms today, especially since the advent of Europe 1992 and the events in Eastern Europe. In fact, there may be little real choice for firms that desire to expand globally. According to Nicholas Azonian, vice-president of finance at Nypro, an $85 million plastic injection-molding and industrial components manufacturer in Clinton, Massachusetts, with a presence in six countries and four international joint venture factories in the United States: "Without these foreign ventures, we'd be very limited in terms of our knowledge, our technology, our people, and our markets. We'd be a smaller company in every sense of the word" (Hyatt, 1989, p. 145).

Of course the benefits of IJVs are not limited to small companies. Sales of companies in which Corning Glass has a joint partnership are nearly 50 percent higher than the sales of its wholly owned businesses.

Source: Randall S. Schuler et al. "The Formation of an International Joint Venture: Davidson Instrument Panel." © 1991. *Human Resource Planning*, 14, 1991, pp51-60. Reprinted by permission.

Says Corning's CEO James Houghton of international opportunities and joint venture alliances:

> Alliances are the way to capture that window. By marrying one party's product to the other's distribution, or one party's manufacturing skill to the other's R&D, alliances are often quicker than expanding your business overseas—and cheaper than buying one (Stewart, 1990, p. 68).

With high failure rates and increasing competitiveness, launching an international joint venture offers little guarantee of success. Some of the most significant barriers to success involve people issues—issues relating to international human resource management. This article describes many of the issues associated with forming and managing IJVs and illustrates how one international joint venture is addressing many of them. Because this venture is in the early stages of formation, this article addresses only critical start-up barriers. This article addresses the international joint venture from the view of the U.S. partner, Davidson Instrument Panel.

Davidson Instrument Panel ——————————————————————————

Davidson Instrument Panel is one of 33 divisions of Textron, an $8 billion conglomerate headquartered in Providence, Rhode Island. Davidson Instrument Panel and its two sister divisions, Interior Trim and Exterior Trim, make up Davidson-Textron. All three divisions are component suppliers to the automotive OEMs (original equipment manufacturers). Davidson-Textron is the largest independent supplier of instrument panels for the U.S. automobile industry.

Originally begun as a maker of rubber products for drug sundries in Boston in the early 1850s, Davidson moved its operations to Dover, New Hampshire, in the 1950s. Its headquarters are now located in Portsmouth. A staff in Portsmouth of fewer than 50 oversees the operations of two manufacturing plants, one in Port Hope, Ontario, and the second in Farmington, New Hampshire. The 1,000-person operation in Port Hope is unionized, and the 900-person operation in Farmington is not.

The nature of the U.S. automobile industry has changed drastically during the past 20 years, and the effects have been felt by all of the Big Three auto makers. As the automobile industry has become globalized, success has turned on quality products that fit right and perform smoothly and reliably. But while quality has become a major concern to the auto industry so have cost and innovation. New products and new technology are vital to the success of the Big Three, but without cost reduction new products cannot be offered at competitive prices.

The characteristics of the auto industry are, of course, reflected in all companies supplying it. Davidson Instrument Panel is no exception. To succeed, they must adapt to the demands of the new environment.

Doing so will bring rewards, such as market share and even more important perhaps, an extensive, cooperative relationship with the Big Three. Essentially gone are the days of the multiple bidding system, where winning meant delivering at the lowest cost, with no assurance that the next year will be the same. Today, the automobile companies use sole sourcing for many of their supply needs. Accompanying this is a greater sense of shared destiny and mutual cooperation:

> The component suppliers are having to change with the times. The multinational car manufacturers increasingly want to deal with multinational suppliers, giving them responsibility for the design and development of sub-assemblies in return for single supplier status (*Financial Times*, March 1, 1990, p. 8).

Thus, it is not unusual to have design engineers from suppliers doing full engineering design of the components they will supply to their customers.

An important aspect of the new cooperative, sole sourcing arrangement adopted by the Big Three automotive makers is the willingness to conceptualize and form longer-term relationships. For Davidson Instrument Panel, this has meant the opportunity to establish an international joint venture. In the summer of 1989, Davidson agreed to establish an IJV to supply instrumental panels to a Ford Motor Company plant in Belgium beginning in 1992. They chose as their partner for this venture a British firm named Marley.

What seems like a good opportunity is not a guaranteed success, of course. U.S. studies estimate that the failure rate of IJVs is between 50 and 70 percent (Harrigan, 1986; Levine and Byrne, 1986). Because this IJV is in its early stages, evaluations of success would be premature. Probabilities of success can be estimated by comparing the actions of Davidson Instrument Panel with the recommendations of others and with the mistakes made by others in their early stages. These comparisons might offer guidance to firms seeking to go global through such alliances.

International Joint Ventures

Although there is no agreed-upon definition of an IJV, one definition is as follows:

> A separate legal organizational entity representing the partial holdings of two or more parent firms, in which the headquarters of at least one is located outside the country of operation of the joint venture. This entity is subject to the joint control of its parent firms, each of which is economically and legally independent of the other (Shenkar and Zeira, 1987a, p. 547).

The use of an international joint venture as a mode of international business operation is not a new phenomenon (Ohmae, 1989a,b,c), but economic growth in the past decade of global competition, coupled with shifts in trade dominance and the emergence of new markets, has contributed to the recent increasing use of international joint ventures. According to Peter Drucker, IJVs are likely to grow in importance in the 1990s:

> You will see a good deal of joint ventures, of strategic alliances, of cross-holdings across borders. Not because of cost, but because of information. Economists don't accept it, but it is one of the oldest experiences, that you cannot maintain market standing in a developed market unless you are in it as a producer. As an exporter, you will be out sooner or later, because you have to be in the market to have the information (Drucker, 1989, p. 23).

Reasons for Forming an IJV

Harrigan (1987a) argues that because a joint venture draws on the strengths of its owners, it should possess superior competitive abilities that allow its sponsors to enjoy synergies. If the venture's owners cannot cope with the demands of managing the joint venture successfully, Harrigan advises the owners would do better to use nonequity forms of cooperation, such as cross-marketing and/or cross-production, licensing, and research and development consortia. Some companies shun joint ventures, preferring 100 percent ownership to the drawbacks of loss of control and profits that can accompany shared ownership (Gomes-Casseres, 1989). However, there are many reasons why a firm, regardless of previous international experience, enters into an IJV arrangement. The most common reasons cited in the literature are:

- Host government insistence (Datta, 1988; Gomes-Casseres, 1989; Shenkar and Zeira, 1987b);

- To gain rapid market entry (Berlew, 1984; Morris and Hergert, 1987; Shenkar and Zeira, 1987b; Tichy, 1988);

- Increased economies of scale (Datta, 1988; Morris and Hergert, 1987; Roehl and Truitt, 1987);

- To gain local knowledge (Datta, 1988; Lasserre, 1983; O'Reilly, 1988) and local market image (Gomes-Casseres, 1989);

- To obtain vital raw materials (Shenkar and Zeira, 1987b) or technology (Gomes-Casseres, 1989);

- To spread the risks (Morris and Hergert, 1987; Shenkar and Zeira, 1987b);

- To improve competitive advantage in the face of increasing global competition; and

- Because globalization of markets forces cost-effective and efficient responses (Datta, 1988; Harrigan, 1987a and 1987b; Shenkar and Zeira, 1987b).

For many firms, several reasons apply. Some of these outcomes may be unanticipated but later recognized and welcomed, as was the case at Nypro. Nypro entered into a joint venture with Mitsui to operate a factory in Atlanta that could serve as a U.S. source for videocassette parts to Enplas, a Japanese concern. Enplas taught Nypro some lessons in both cost-saving management skills and quality control, according to Gordon Lankton, Nypro president and CEO:

> "Why did you reject this shipment?" Lankton would ask. "The label on the box," they would answer, "was crooked." "We eventually learned," says Lankton. Now, Nypro's Atlanta plant is its most productive, with sales per employee averaging $2,000. By comparison, most of Nypro's other nine plants hover around $1,250 (Hyatt, 1988, p. 148).

For Davidson Instrument Panel, gaining local knowledge, spreading risks, improving competitive advantage, and becoming more global are important reasons for their IJV. In addition, it is important for them to extend their relationship with the Ford Motor Company as much as possible. Being a sole source supplier means working with the customer as much as possible.

Failure in IJVs

IJV failure rates (50-70 percent) reflect the difficulty of establishing a successful IJV. Reasons for failure include:

- Partners cannot get along;

- Managers from disparate partners with the venture cannot later work together;

- Managers within the venture cannot work with the owners' managers;

- Partners simply renege on their promises;

- The markets disappear; and

- The technology involved does not prove to be as good as expected.

Failure rates are difficult to measure, however. Some of the difficulty in measuring success or failure rates is due to the fact that "joint ventures can be deemed successful in spite of poor financial performance, and conversely, they can be considered unsuccessful in spite of good financial performance" (Schaan, 1988, p. 5). The criteria for defining success or failure depend on the parent companies' expectations from and motives for establishing the joint venture. For example, financial performance may take second place to profits from fees for management or royalties for technology transfer.

It's a Marriage

Many writers compare the IJV to a marriage (Tichy, 1988). The analogy seems to spring from the factors that are necessary for success and the problems inherent in the IJV due to its contractual nature. To help manage an IJV for success, it is important to understand the joint venture process, which includes these five parts:

- Finding an appropriate partner;

- The courting and prenuptial process;

- Arranging the marriage deal;

- The launching of the venture and the honeymoon period; and

- Building a successful ongoing relationship.

Observers (Gomes-Casseres, 1987; Harrigan, 1986; Lyles, 1987) suggest that effective use of joint ventures requires managers to develop special liaison skills to cope with the mixed loyalties and conflicting goals that characterize shared ownership and shared decision making. Joint venture managers also need to have and to instill team-building values and receptivity to outsiders' ideas.

Increasingly, it is recognized that good joint venture marriages are not created with a handshake and a stroke of the pen. Instead of rushing headlong into a flurry of strategic partnering, savvy managers are now moving slowly into long-term relationships with their cross-national counterparts. They are purposefully trying to avoid many of the mistakes created by the kneejerk venturing behaviors of the early 1980s. One way to help make an IJV work is to establish equal partnerships. According to James Houghton, of Corning Glass, "To work alliances must be true marriages, not dates. A fifty-fifty deal usually works best because it commits both parties to success" (Stewart, 1990, p. 66). In addition, according to Gordon Lankton of Nypro, "Just finding a knowledgeable partner for a joint venture isn't enough, though. You have to make sure that partner's long-term goals are in sync with your own" (Hyatt, 1988, p. 145).

Critical Issues in Managing IJVs ————————————————————

There is consensus that the very nature of joint ventures contributes to their failure—they are a difficult and complex form of enterprise (see Shenkar and Zeira, 1987b, p. 30) and many companies initiate IJVs without fully recognizing and addressing the major issues they are likely to confront (Morris and Hergert, 1987). Success requires adept handling of three key issues. Below, we first describe each of these key issues. Then we discuss how Davidson is preparing to deal with them.

Control

Who actually controls the operation can depend on who is responsible for the day-to-day management of the IJV. Ownership distribution may matter less than how operating control and participation in decision making actually is apportioned (Harrigan, 1986). For a parent with minority ownership, for example, having the right to appoint key personnel can be used as a control mechanism (Schaan, 1988). Control can be achieved by appointing managers who are loyal to the parent company and its organizational ethos. Of course, loyalty to the parent cannot be guaranteed. "The ability to appoint the joint venture general manager increases the chances that the parents' interests will be observed, but it is no guarantee that the joint venture general manager will always accommodate that parent's preferences" (Schaan, 1988, p. 14).

Top managers will be expected to make decisions that deal with the simultaneous demands of the parents and their employees in the enterprise. At times, such decisions will, by necessity, meet the demands of some parties better than those of other parties. If the partners do not foresee such decisions, they may fail to build in control mechanisms to protect their interests. Weak control can also result if parent company managers spend too little time on the IJV, responding to problems only on an ad hoc basis. Finally, control-related failures are likely to occur if control practices are not re-evaluated and modified in response to changing circumstances.

Conflict

Business and cultural differences between IJV partners often create conflict. Working relationships must be established on trust. Because a joint venture is an inherently unstable relationship, it requires a delicate set of organizational and management processes to create trust and the ongoing capacity to collaborate. This means that the senior executives must be involved in designing management processes that provide effective ways to handle joint strategy formulation, create structural linkages, provide adequate day-to-day coordination and communication, and establish a win-win climate (Tichy, 1988).

Many of the misunderstandings and problems in IJVs are rooted in cultural differences (Datta, 1988). Differing approaches to managerial style are one area that can create problems. For example, one party may favor a participative managerial style, while the other believes in a more autocratic style of management. Another area that can be problematic is acceptance of risk-taking because one parent may be prepared to take more risks than the other. Such differences often make the process of decision making slow and frustrating. The resulting conflict can be dysfunctional, if not destructive. The big challenge here is how to work through top management disagreements and avoid deadlocks (Thomas, 1987).

Goals

The partners in an IJV often have differing goals. This is especially likely to be true when an IJV is formed as a solution for reconciling incongruent national interests. For example, a parent may be obliged to share ownership with a host government despite their preference for complete ownership and control. In such a case, the two partners are likely to be concerned with different constituencies, and business strategies may differ as a result. For example, the local partner may evaluate strategic choices based upon how effective they are likely to be in the local market, while the MNC parent would favor strategies that maintain their image and reputation in the global market (Gomes-Casseres, 1989). Cultural differences may also impact strategy. For example, Americans are alleged to have a short-term focus compared to the Japanese (Webster, 1989).

Differing levels of commitment from the two parents are yet another source of difficulty (Datta, 1988). The commitment of each partner reflects the project's importance to the partner. When there is an imbalance, the more committed partner may be frustrated by the other partner's apparent lack of concern. On the other hand, the less committed partner may feel frustrated by demands and time pressure exerted by the more committed partner. The level of commitment by the parties to the IJV can be a contributing factor to either success or failure (Bere, 1987).

Davidson's Preparation for the Critical Issues ──────────

The management at Davidson Instrument Panel has recognized the importance of these critical issues in their IJV. To begin, they were very careful in their selection of a partner. More than twenty-five years of licensing experience in Western Europe with four different licensees gave the company an opportunity to develop close relationships with at least four potential partners. From these they chose the one, Marley in England, with whom they had the most in common. This commonality includes:

- Both use a consensus style of management;

- Both are part of a larger organization that is relatively decentralized;

- Both have the desire to move to the Continent with a manufacturing presence;

- Both have similar views on how to grow the business;

- Both have similar philosophies on how to run a business and how to manage human resources;

- Both desire a fair and open relationship.

These several dimensions of commonality should help minimize difficulties that can arise due to differing goals and objectives.

Thus far the parents have already made several strategic decisions in their establishment of the IJV, including where to locate the new plant and who will be responsible for what functions. Davidson's preferences for how these decisions would be resolved were important influences on Davidson's selection of Marley as a partner. Being located in Europe, Marley gives Davidson knowledge of the market. But far more than this, it gives them functional fit and personal contacts. Whereas Marley understands the marketplace well, Davidson has expertise in manufacturing and administrative systems. Thus while Davidson supplies the technology and the systems, Marley supplies knowledge of the markets and the contacts needed to get the plant built.

Locating the Facility

The decision about where to locate the plant was an important decision and a very early test of the compatibility of the two parents. Together, the parents gathered extensive information and visited many sites. Of value here was Davidson's position as a division of a large conglomerate that could provide tax and legal guidance. Textron has an office in Brussels that provided this service. During the initial site selection process, Davidson collected information related to possible locations from the consulates of the nations located in the United States. According to Joe Paul, Vice President of Administration at Davidson Instrument Panel, the consulates provided extensive information about business conditions, and they provided names and telephone numbers of employment agencies, training centers, union officers, and local business organizations. Davidson also acquired information from DeutscheBank, the international banker for Textron.

The decision was made to locate in Born, The Netherlands. This decision was made after eliminating France, West Germany, and Belgium. These four nations were all possibilities because of their proximity to the Ford plant in Genk, Belgium, and because all four governments offer cash grants to firms locating in the coal region these four nations share. With relatively high unemployment, the governments of the four nations offer incentives to firms regardless of parent company nationality. The particular site in The Netherlands was selected because it is within thirty minutes of the Ford plant, a location that will facilitate compliance with Ford's just-in-time requirement.

According to Jonathan T. Hopkins, Vice President of Worldwide Business Development at Davidson Instrument Panel, the location was also selected in part because labor unions in the area indicated a willingness to consider accepting job flexibility and a relatively small number of job classifications. These features are important to both parents because they operate using principles of employee involvement and egalitarianism. Both parents want these principles to be reflected in the management style of the new plant in Born. Davidson's experience in running a unionized plant in Canada proved valuable to foreseeing some of these labor-related international issues.

Another important consideration was the availability of job applicants. The area now has a 15 percent unemployment rate. In addition, two government controlled firms are expected to privatize and down-size, thus increasing the pool of applicants with work experience. These considerations were deemed more favorable in The Netherlands than in the other three nations by both parents.

Human Resource Management: Unfolding Issues _____

As the establishment of the IJV between Davidson Instrument Panel and Marley continues over the next twelve months, six human resource management issues are likely to unfold (Shenkar and Zeira, 1990). In light of the shared goals and objectives of the two partners, the extent to which these issues are likely to become problem areas may be minimal. Nevertheless, the substance of the issues needs to be explicitly addressed (Lorange, 1986).

The Assignment of Managers

Since each partner may place differing priorities on the joint venture, it is possible for a partner to assign relatively weak management resources to the venture. To be successful, the assigned managerial resources should not only have relevant capabilities and be of adequate quality, but the overall blend of these human resources must have a cultural dimension. Recognizing the importance of key personnel appointments, the parents have agreed to collaborate in the selection of the general manager. They have already agreed on the search firm that will help them identify candidates, and they are now in the process of jointly deciding the final criteria to be used in the selection process. Although the selection criteria are not yet finalized, Davidson has expressed some desire to have a person with manufacturing experience in plastics who is from The Netherlands. Once this individual is selected (scheduled for early 1991), he or she will come to Davidson's headquarters in New Hampshire for several months. During this time, the individual will become familiar with Davidson's technology, manufacturing systems, and human resource management practices and philosophies.

Specific selection, performance appraisal, and compensation practices will be left to the discretion of the new general manager, but it is expected that this individual will adopt the Davidson-Marley philosophy of employee involvement, participation, job flexibility, egalitarianism, and teamwork. These are practices both parents adopted in their own operations to facilitate high quality. Davidson and Marley feel that local labor councils are flexible and open to these practices, but the task of actually negotiating specifics will be done by the IJV's management staff. At that point, control issues are likely to become very salient.

Transferability of Human Resources

Are the parents willing to transfer critical human resources to the new business venture? Given the long time frame of most joint ventures, strategic human resources sometimes have to be transferred from the parents on a net basis during the initial phase. In this case, because of the skills of the two partners, Davidson Instrument Panel is supplying the human resources relevant to the manufacturing systems and the administrative systems. Marley is responsible for actually building the plant, but Davidson is designing the interior of the facility to fit their technology. In addition, Davidson has already had to assign three design engineers from its facility in Walled Lake, Michigan, to be expatriates in Europe. These engineers work with fourteen contract designers recruited in Europe to design the components that will be manufactured in the plant. Marley has located a sales manager in The Netherlands and will supply the sales and marketing support to the company.

Davidson will also be supplying the new controller, who will install the administrative systems. Textron's accounting firm, which has offices in the United States and Europe, is also ready to provide assistance to the financial officer who will eventually be selected for the IJV. (Textron's accounting firm serves Davidson as well.) Davidson's accounting procedures will have to be adapted to the European environment, which will be done through the accounting office in Europe assisting the new financial officer. Over time, the remaining human resource management decisions will become the responsibility of the IJV as it begins to operate like an independent business organization.

Manager's Time-Spending Patterns

The IJV has to carry out a set of operating duties simultaneously with its development of new strategies. This raises the issue of the appropriate emphasis to give operating and strategic tasks. Sufficient human resources must be allocated for both strategic development and operating tasks. This situation is similar to that of an independent business organization in that the IJV must be able to draw sufficient human resources from the operating mode to further develop its strategy. If the parent organizations place strong demands for short-term results on the IJV, this might leave it with insufficient resources to staff for strategic self-renewal. In this case, the need for strategic planning and new business development is somewhat lessened due to the expected availability of a major customer, namely, Ford Motor Company. In addition, Marley's marketing expertise and knowledge of the

Continent will serve as a support mechanism that minimizes the time the new IJV needs to spend initially on longer-term issues. Over time, the balance between focusing on operations versus strategic planning will shift as the IJV becomes more independent and the short-term operating tasks become more manageable.

Human Resource Competency

Deciding how to judge how well IJV managers carry out their assignments will be another major challenge. It has been claimed that several joint ventures have failed because they have been inappropriately staffed (Lorange, 1986). Myopic, biased parent organizations may make poor selection decisions, or they may be tempted to use the IJV to offload surplus incompetent managers. Performance evaluation is therefore important. The long-term relationship and shared objectives between Davidson and Marley suggest that inappropriate staffing decisions are unlikely in this case. Further, the early decision to limit reliance on expatriates to the controller and three design engineers is likely to minimize the likelihood of problems arising from offloading surplus managers.

Management Loyalty Issues

Management of loyalty conflicts must be considered an integral part of the human resource management of IJVs. Assigned executives, the expatriates, are usually loyal to the IJV and are expected to stay with the IJV for a long period of time. If a conflict arises between parents and the IJV, they can be expected to side with the IJV. For Davidson and Marley, the assignments of the design engineers and the controller are primarily for startup purposes. Their loyalty may remain with Davidson because of the explicitly temporary nature of their assignments.

Career and Benefits Planning

A recent survey of expatriates found that 56 percent felt their overseas assignments were either immaterial or detrimental to their careers (*Wall Street Journal*, 1989), a finding that indicates the potential motivational problems any IJV may encounter. The motivation of executives assigned to an IJV can be enhanced by the creation of a clear linkage between the assignment and one's future career. Some assurance of job security may be needed to offset the perceived risks. Assignment to a joint venture, as with any overseas assignment, may make the manager's future career appear uncertain. In fact, if the parent company has not thought through this issue, the apparent uncertainty may be quite justified. Thus, parent organizations should offer career planning to counter the ambiguity and riskiness associated with an IJV assignment and to limit the potential for unsatisfying repatriation experiences.

Apart from career path disturbance, the assignment to an IJV post usually requires relocation to a foreign country, with all the disruption to family and social life that such a posting entails. Benefits packages must be designed to maintain the economic and social lifestyle of the manager so that the individual does not lose through the IJV assignment. In the present case, the number of expatriate employees involved is small, so these issues have not been considered major. They will become more significant with the assignment of the controller. At that time, Davidson's own experience with R&D expatriates and the experience of Textron will be helpful.

Lorange (1986) has argued that the IJVs must have their own, strong, fully fledged human resource management function. The person in charge must establish ways to work closely with each parent, particularly in the early years. The two major roles of the IJV's HRM function are (a) assign and motivate people via job skills, compatibility of styles, and communication compatibility and (b) manage human resources strategically so that the IJV is seen as a vehicle to produce not only financial rewards, but also managerial capabilities that can be used later in other strategic settings. To the extent an IJV is staffed with temporary managerial assignees, transferring people to an IJV every two years would not be likely to result in strategic continuity of management.

In addition to the two major roles noted by Lorange (1986), the new IJV will have to establish its own set of human resource practices, policies, and procedures. It will then use these immediately to staff the new operation. We are looking forward to tracking this process with the new general manager, before and after production has begun.

Summary

For an increasing number of U.S. firms, regardless of size and product, going global or international is no longer a choice. The world has become far too interconnected for many products and services to be offered within a domestic market context only. Faced with this reality, U.S. firms are seeking to establish their presence in the world market. Several large U.S. firms have already attained global presence. These companies entered the global arena early and are far wealthier than most U.S. firms. Their mode of entry into the global arena—through the direct establishment of their own subsidiaries—is an option that cannot be easily entertained today by most U.S. firms.

Consequently, many firms are considering entry into global markets via partnerships with firms outside the United States. Partnerships receiving much attention now are the international joint ventures (IJVs). This form of partnership, which some say is the only feasible vehicle for U.S. firms trying to enter foreign markets, can carry substantial risk. This potential risk comes from several sources, many of which are related to the quality of the relationship between the two partners, and many of which are related to a series of international human resource decisions. While the relationship between the two partners is established at the outset of the partnership, the series of international human resource decisions unfold over the life of the partnership.

References

Bere, J.F. "Global partnering: Making a good match." *Directors and Boards,* 1987, 11 (2), 16.

Berlew, F.K. "The joint venture—a way into foreign markets." *Harvard Business Review,* July-August 1984, 48-54.

Datta, D.K. "International joint ventures: A framework for analysis." *Journal of General Management,* 1989, 14 (2), 78-91.

Drucker, P.F. *The New Realities.* New York: Harper & Row, 1989.

Gomes-Casseres, B. "Joint venture instability: Is it a problem?" *Columbia Journal of World Business,* 1987, 22, (2), 97-102.

Gomes-Casseres, B. "Joint ventures in the face of global competition." *Sloan Management Review,* Spring 1989, 17-25.

Harrigan, K.R. *Managing for Joint Venture Success.* Boston, Mass.: Lexington Books, 1986.

Harrigan, K.R. "Managing Joint Ventures." *Management Review,* 1987a, 76 (2), 24-42.

Harrigan, K.R. "Strategic alliances: Their new role in global competition." *Columbia Journal of World Business,* 1987b, 22 (2), 67-69.

Hyatt, J. "The partnership route." *INC.,* December 1988, 145-148.

Lasserre, P. "Strategic assessment of international partnership in Asian countries." *Asia Pacific Journal of Management,* September 1983, 72-78.

Levine, J. B. and Byrne, J.A. "Corporate odd couples." *Business Week,* July 21, 1986, 100-105.

Lorange, P. "Human resource management in multinational cooperative ventures." *Human Resource Management,* 1986, 25, 133-148.

Lyles, M.A. "Common mistakes of joint venture experienced firms." *Columbia Journal of World Business,* 1987, 22 (2), 79-85.

Morris, D. and Hergert, M. "Trends in international collaborative agreements." *Columbia Journal of World Business,* 1987, 22 (2), 15-21.

Ohmae, K. "The global logic of strategic alliance." *Harvard Business Review,* March-April 1989a, 143-154.

Ohmae, K. "Managing in a borderless world." *Harvard Business Review,* May-June 1989b, 152-161.

Ohmae, K. "Planting for a global harvest." *Harvard Business Review,* July-August 1989c, 136-145.

O'Reilly, A.J.F. "Establishing successful joint ventures in developing nations: A CEO's perspective." *Columbia Journal of World Business,* 1988, 23 (1), 65-71.

Roehl, T.W. and Truitt, J.F. "Stormy open marriages are better: Evidence from US, Japanese and French cooperative ventures in commerical aircraft." *Columbia Journal of World Business,* 1987, 22 (2), 87-95.

Schaan, J.L. "How to control a joint venture even as a minority partner." *Journal of General Management,* 1988, 14 (1), 4-16.

Shenkar, O. and Zeira, Y. "Human resources management in international joint ventures: Direction for research." *Academy of Management Review,* 1987a, 12 (3), 546-557.

Shenkar, O. and Zeira, Y. "International joint ventures: Implications for organization development." *Personnel Review,* 1987b, 16 (1), 30-37.

Shenkar, O. and Zeira, Y. "International joint ventures: A tough test for HR." *Personnel,* January 1990, 26-31.

Stewart, T.A. "How to manage in the new era." *Fortune,* January 15, 1990, 58-72.

Thomas, T. "Keeping the friction out of joint ventures." *Business Review Weekly,* January 23, 1987, 57-59.

Tichy, N.M. "Setting the global human resource management agenda for the 1990s." *Human Resource Management,* 1988, 27 (1), 1-18.

Webster, D.R. "International joint ventures with Pacific Rim partners." *Business Horizon,* 1989, 32 (2), 65-71.

Challenges Facing General Managers of International Joint Ventures

Reading 2.2
Colette A. Frayne
J. Michael Geringer

Introduction

Driven by the fundamental changes which have occurred during the past decade, including trends toward internationalization of markets and competition as well as the increasing cost and complexity of technological developments, joint ventures have become an important element of many firms' international strategies (Harrigan, 1988; Moxon & Geringer, 1985; Perlmutter & Heenan, 1986). These ventures involve two or more legally distinct organizations (the parents), each of which actively participates in the decision making activities of the jointly-owned entity. It is considered to be an international joint venture (IJV) when at least one parent organization is headquartered outside the venture's country of operation, or if the venture has a significant level of operations in more than one country (Geringer & Hebert, 1989).

Although the frequency and strategic importance of IJVs have increased dramatically during the late 1980s and early 1990s (Geringer & Woodcock, 1989; Harrigan, 1988; Hergert & Morris, 1988), many IJVs have failed to achieve their performance objectives due to the unique challenges associated with managing these interfirm ventures (Geringer & Hebert, 1991; Holton, 1981; Harrigan, 1986; Pucik, 1988; Shenkar & Zeira, 1987). The challenge results from the presence of two or more parent organizations, which are often competitors as well as collaborators (Geringer, 1991; Hamel, 1990). This means that the IJV general manager (IJVGM) is placed in the unenviable position of balancing the frequently divergent or even opposing motivations, operating policies and cultures of the parents, as well as addressing the competitive requirements confronting the venture itself (Buckley & Casson, 1988; Frayne & Geringer,

---

Source: Reprinted by permission of the authors

1990a; Ganitsky & Watzke, 1990; Lynch, 1989; Sullivan & Peterson, 1982). The challenge of this task is compounded by the tendency to use these ventures in risky, uncertain settings (Anderson, 1990; Bleeke & Ernst, 1991), and by the fact that the IJVGM must operate across unfamiliar national and corporate cultures. As a result, it is understandable that a large proportion of IJV failures are attributable not to financial or technical problems, but rather to "cultural factors," such as conflicts in management styles, cultures, operational practices and degrees of control (Devlin & Bleackley, 1989; Dobkin, 1988; Ganitsky & Watzke, 1990; Geringer, 1988; Shenkar & Zeira, 1987). Indeed, these factors help explain why many IJVs begin to experience operational problems even after years of relatively stable performance.

The critical role of the IJVGM and its relationship to the venture's operations have been acknowledged in several prior studies (Bleeke & Ernst, 1991; Deloitte, Haskins & Sells, International, 1989; Geringer & Frayne, 1990; Lynch, 1989). Yet, despite the unique managerial challenges associated with this job, the academic and practitioner literatures have not focused on the role and required skills of the IJVGM. In particular, there has been essentially no discussion of variables associated with successful or unsuccessful IJVGM performance, or training programs which might enable IJVGMs to prepare for—and function better within—the complex environment of the IJV. The absence of such training programs may inhibit efforts to form IJVs which can successfully achieve the strategic objectives for which they were established.

The objective of this paper is two-fold: (1) to identify the role of the IJVGM and the key contextual issues associated with this role, and (2) to propose a comprehensive training program for developing the skills which IJVGMs require in order to function effectively within the IJV context. The next section of the paper, which discusses the IJVGM's role and contextual issues, is based on data collected in interviews with parent company executives and IJVGMs involved in forming and managing 42 developed country and 62 developing country IJVs. (Appendix A contains a summary of the methodology employed in collecting these data.) On the basis of these contextual issues, we then propose a four-part training program to prepare IJVGMs for functioning effectively within the IJV environment. This program consists of training in: (1) general contextual skills, (2) specific contextual skills, (3) interpersonal skills, and (4) self-management skills. The paper concludes with a discussion of implementation issues associated with the proposed training program.

The Role and Context of the IJVGM

Frequently, the job of the general manager (GM) has been equated with that of an organization's chief executive. Yet, the IJVGM position by its very nature is subordinate to the chief executive and represents more of a middle management type of position. As defined by Uyterhoeven (1972: p. 75), a middle-level GM is a "general manager who is responsible for a particular business unit at the intermediate level of the corporate hierarchy." The job of a middle-level GM differs significantly from top-level GM positions, and in many respects it is more difficult (Aguilar, 1988; Kotter, 1982).

The problems confronting the IJVGM have been well documented in several prior studies of joint ventures (Anderson, 1990; Geringer & Frayne, 1990; Harrigan, 1986; Janger, 1980; Lynch, 1989). The IJVGM's role typically differs from that of a GM in a subsidiary which is wholly-owned. Further, a strong argument can be made that the role of the IJVGM tends to be much more difficult than that of similar intracorporate positions, particularly due to the contextual challenges associated with the position, as will be discussed below. In fact, 88 percent of the IJVGMs and 86 percent of parent company executives participating in this study indicated that IJVGM skills were different from the general management skills required for similar positions in the parent firms' wholly-owned subsidiaries. Further, 78 percent of IJVGMs and 62 percent of parent company executives indicated that the requirements of the IJVGM position were *more* challenging than those of similar GM positions in the firms' non-joint venture businesses. None of the IJVGMs and only 4 percent of parent executives indicated that the IJVGM position was less challenging than similar non-joint venture positions.

IJVGMs are usually expatriates, especially for ventures in developing country contexts and when the venture is in an early stage of its life cycle. Although they tend to confront many of the same problems as any expatriate (Tung, 1981), there are substantive differences associated with the IJVGM position. As several of the participating executives remarked, the additional challenges of the IJVGM position are often not readily apparent, particularly for managers who have not previously been directly involved with one of these ventures. Respondents identified differences in terms of both the *degree* as well as the underlying *nature* of the challenges confronting the IJVGM. For example, role conflict, ambiguity and overload are inherent to the practice of management. However, for general managers of IJVs, the degree to which these factors are present is typically magnified (Geringer & Frayne, 1990; Lynch, 1989). Fundamental differences were also evident in terms of the nature of the challenges, including issues arising from the presence of two or more different parent organizations. Overall, the contextual challenges associated with the IJVGM's role include the following five issues: (1) the presence of multiple parent companies, (2) the existence of divided loyalties, (3) the need for operational independence despite limited preparation and support, (4) responsibility which exceeds authority, and (5) pressure for rapid action. This section addresses each of these issues individually.

1. The Presence of Multiple Parent Companies

Perhaps the most fundamentally different aspect of the IJVGM's context is the presence of two or more parent organizations which share both ownership and decision making in the IJV. The difficulties arising from multiple parents are sometimes ameliorated when one of the parents assumes a very dominant role over the venture (Deloitte, Haskins & Sells, International, 1989; Killing, 1983; Lynch, 1989). This may occur, for example, when there are highly asymmetric divisions of equity (e.g., 80/20) or when a parent assumes the role of a "sleeping" partner and therefore has essentially no active involvement in the IJV's operations. Yet, even situations such as these may eventually result in challenges for the IJVGM (Olk & Bussard, 1988). The root of the problem is that the different strategies, power bases, time perspectives, cultures and operating practices of the individual parent organizations typically result in substantive differences regarding their respective goals for the IJV as well as the means for achieving these goals (Blodgett, 1991; Ganitsky & Watzke, 1990; Geringer, 1988). Given the existence of small numbers of partner organizations and information asymmetry among these partners, there is potential for opportunistic behavior by one or more of the partners (or by the venture employees themselves) in an attempt to promote attainment of their own objectives, to the possible detriment of their partner(s). Indeed, parent company executives often disagree with the IJVGM regarding whether—or how—to clarify directions with their partner, and frequently attempt to manage the IJV as an extension of their other, wholly-owned operations. Therefore, in order for the IJV to function properly, IJVGMs must often devote substantial amounts of their time and energy toward ensuring effective coordination of and communication between these divergent partner organizations (Brown, Rugman & Verbeke, 1989; Geringer & Hebert, 1989).

    The challenges of being an effective manager in such an environment may be exacerbated by the manner in which IJVGM performance is evaluated. Only 9 percent of the IJVGMs in our sample reported that their performance was evaluated by parent firms exclusively using specific performance criteria. In contrast, for 42 percent of the IJVs, the parents reportedly did not employ *any* specific performance criteria for such evaluations. These results were consistent with Janger's (1980) finding that only 22 percent of his sample ventures used formal performance reviews to evaluate joint venture staff. Based on our interview data, the IJVGMs often did not know how well they were performing, nor did they receive clear indication regarding how to effectively run the IJV. Often, they were left with inconsistent expectations regarding what behaviors were required and had to rely on their own perceptions of what performance was expected. For some, it was not until they were replaced or the venture was dissolved that they realized they were not performing up to one or both of the parent companies' standards.

2. The Existence of Divided Loyalties

Due to the complexity resulting from multiple parents, IJVGMs must usually rely on the support, cooperation, or approval of a large number of people in order to achieve their goals. Yet, this task is exacerbated by the existence of divided loyalties, both of the IJVGM and of the other parent company and IJV personnel. For example, in attempting to respond to the conflicting demands of superiors within the parent firms, the IJVGM must simultaneously manage relationships with peers within one or another of the parent firms and who control critical resources. These peers often have more direct relationships—and more clearly defined career considerations—with the parent firm's senior managers, and less incentive to cooperate with the IJVGM on issues of pooled sales forces, corporate staff assistance, R&D or manufacturing assistance, and the like. Obtaining their support for the IJV is therefore a difficult proposition.

IJVGMs may also confront divided loyalties among their subordinates in the IJV itself, including the venture's managers, technical people, and other staff and line personnel. Because of their past experience and future prospects, these employees frequently exhibit strong allegiance to one or another of the parent firms—or to the host nation itself—rather than to the IJV. This situation may be exacerbated by the tendency for expatriate personnel to be paid according to home versus host country standards, which are often significantly higher than the compensation for local personnel performing similar roles. The IJVGM must not only recognize the possible existence of these divergent loyalties, but also find a means of focusing them effectively toward attainment of the venture's objectives. Success often requires balancing and tradeoffs. Yet, in the process of attempting to satisfy the demands of one set of relationships, the IJVGM may reduce his or her effectiveness in managing another. A common response of IJVGMs is to be reactive rather than proactive, and to address issues of a short term rather than a long term nature (Schaan & Beamish, 1988), which further limits their ability to achieve a consistent behavior pattern.

This tendency toward reactive management is exemplified by the case of a recently formed joint venture involving Japanese and American partners, and in which the IJVGM was appointed by the U.S. firm (Geringer & Miller, 1992). The Japanese partner's objective was to use the IJV to establish a base for learning about the North American market, while the U.S. firm wanted to learn about their partner's production techniques, particularly the "just-in-time" kanban system. Despite these objectives, the IJVGM vetoed repeated efforts by his subordinate managers (assigned from the Japanese partner) who wanted to ensure the effective execution of the kanban system in the IJV. The Japanese managers argued that the long term benefits would justify the additional costs. Yet, the IJVGM justified his short term, cost-focused decision as being a response to continued pressure by a U.S. appointee to the IJV's board to "get results," particularly in terms of keeping operating costs in line with the budgeted levels.

To further exacerbate such situations, the IJVGMs themselves often experience divided loyalties. In virtually every case, they are directly responsible for the performance of the IJV, and they have a fiduciary responsibility to ensure that the interests of each of the partners are protected. Yet, most IJVGMs, particularly those which are involved in the actual start-up of a venture, are appointed by and have been employed within one of the parent organizations. Their experience within that parent firm has often acculturated them to a particular way of thinking and acting, one which is peculiar to that parent organization. These values may be reinforced by the IJVGMs' personal and professional relationships within the parent as well as by their perceptions that, once the IJV posting is completed, their career path will involve a return to the parent firm. Since their position often involves postings far from parent firm headquarters, IJVGMs are more prone to being ignored and forgotten, which can be detrimental to future career development. Although extensive efforts at networking with headquarters personnel can help overcome such isolation, it is difficult to maintain and improve such critical interpersonal relationships while effectively and impartially managing the complexity of the IJV itself. Thus, the role of the IJVGM is fundamentally influenced by the potential for divided loyalties, both their own and those of individuals upon whom they are dependent.

3. Need for Operational Independence Despite Limited Preparation and Support

Despite the challenges described above, newly appointed IJVGMs typically have little in the way of guidelines or support systems to help them into their new jobs and they consequently encounter greater difficulty in being effective. For example, Kotter (1982: p. 172) found that effective GMs, "relied on more continuous, more informal, and more subtle methods to cope with their large and complex job demands." As a result, Kotter maintained that outsiders were often a risky choice for GM, regardless of their talent and track record. He argued that an outsider rarely has detailed knowledge of the business and organization, or good, solid relationships with the large number of people upon whom the GM is dependent.

Yet, by the job's very nature, the IJVGM is an outsider to at least one of the parent firms. In addition to being an outsider, factors such as geographic distance, time zone differences, staffing limitations, language differences and communication problems often make it more difficult for the IJVGM to obtain assistance. For an intracorporate position, the new GM may receive training to prepare him or her for the specific job, including lines of communication, plans for the business unit, policies, and the competitive and politico-legal environment. However, such training is seldom available for IJVGMs, particularly in the start-up phase of a venture involving two or more parent firms which embody disparate objectives, resources and policies. Since the parent firms themselves are often unsure of the exact form the IJV will assume (Deloitte, Haskins & Sells, International, 1989; Harrigan, 1986), providing appropriate training and other support to the new GM is often not possible. The barriers to providing such support are further increased by the existence of geographic and cultural differences associated with the IJV. These differences often require adaptation of policies and procedures for the requirements of the local context, yet these changes may thereby limit the usefulness of the organization's existing support infrastructure.

Given the constraints described above, the IJVGM often must be exceedingly entrepreneurial in order for the venture—and the IJVGM—to perform effectively. Especially at the start-up phase, and given the high costs associated with using expatriate personnel, there will generally be few specialists and supporting staff in the venture for the IJVGM to rely on for assistance on difficult issues. This situation may be perpetuated, since IJVs are often much smaller scale ventures than the parent company operations in which the IJVGM worked previously. Language and cultural differences, as well as infrastructure inadequacies in many developing country contexts which limit the number of qualified indigenous middle managers, serve to further inhibit access to and the effectiveness of relying on locally available support. The absence of adequate numbers of qualified middle managers may also inhibit the IJVGM's efforts to effectively utilize standard control and feedback systems. As a result, the IJVGM is forced to either obtain the requisite skills or information through other channels, despite the barriers of geography or time zone, or to operate on the basis of incomplete information or an inadequate resource base.

4. Responsibility Which Exceeds Authority

As noted above, the nature of the IJVGM role means that this manager assumes responsibility for the functioning and performance of the venture within an exceedingly complex operational context. However, the burden of this responsibility may be further increased due to the reality of limited authority which these managers are often able to wield. Although textbooks may state unconditionally that such an imbalance is wrong, having responsibility without a commensurate level of authority is another basic facet of most IJVGM positions. Indeed, particularly given the presence of divided loyalties among venture personnel, the existence of multiple partner firms, and the limited level of contextual training provided to most IJVGMs, these managers confront pressure to relinquish authority both up and down in the hierarchy.

For example, while formal controls may sometimes be relaxed and IJVGMs permitted to exercise more authority as the venture establishes a track record, it is not uncommon for each parent to attempt to exert a substantial amount of control over the IJVGM during the venture's initial stages (Schaan & Beamish, 1988). It is also common for parent firms to more closely monitor IJVs and further constrain IJVGMs' authority when the venture's objectives are not being fully attained. This phenomenon has been termed the "failure cycle" (Killing, 1983), since it can serve to further undermine the IJVGM's authority and may eventually destroy the manager's ability and perceived ability to manage the IJV operations effectively (Anderson, 1990). Nevertheless, IJVGMs are expected to function effectively—and relatively autonomously—despite limited levels of authority over the venture's often inadequate and divergent human and other resources.

5. Pressure for Rapid Action

New IJVGMs are also frequently hindered in their efforts to acclimatize to their positions. For instance, Kotter (1982: p. 139) recommends that, initially, a new GM usually needs to spend considerable time collecting information, establishing relationships, selecting a basic direction for his or her area of responsibilities, and developing an organization under him or her. During the first three to six months, demands from superiors to accomplish specific tasks, or to work on pet projects, can often be counterproductive. Indeed, Kotter maintains that anything that significantly directs attention away from agenda setting and network building may prove to be detrimental.

Yet, despite the desirability of the above acclimatization process, IJVGMs can seldom afford that luxury. For example, several studies have noted that a major impetus for IJV formation is rapid market entry and exploitation of products or technologies during the early stages of their life cycles (Contractor & Lorange, 1988; Geringer, 1988; Janger, 1980). These demands to undertake substantive action are further exacerbated by the limited time frame characterizing most IJVGM postings. In this study's sample, for example, the average length of an IJVGM's assignment ranged from 3 to 5 years. In confronting such a situation, the new IJVGM is thus under pressure to take quick and decisive action, within an environment characterized by complexity, inadequate information and nonexisting relationships.

Conclusions and Implications Regarding the IJVGM's Context

Given the challenging context described above, the IJVGM represents a critical variable to the effective control and performance of the IJV (Deloitte, Haskins & Sells, International, 1989; Frayne & Geringer, 1990a; Lynch, 1989). Their posting to the IJV was viewed by the vast majority of the IJVGMs as being of major importance to their personal and career development, as well as to implementation of the parents' strategy—particularly in terms of effective coordination and control of the parents' international operations. The importance of this position was further echoed in comments of the parent company executives, as well as by these firms' willingness to absorb the very high costs associated with the IJVGM position. For example, particularly for ventures in less developed countries and at the early stages of the venture's life cycle, the IJVGM is almost always an expatriate and the full cost of sending a senior expatriate and their family abroad was estimated by several of the participants at being over $1 million (U.S.) for an average four year assignment.

Despite the challenges of the position, the IJVGMs reported that they received essentially no advance preparation for their assignment, although the ability to balance conflicting goals and practices across different corporate and national cultures was identified as essential to successful IJV implementation and performance. In fact, less than 25 percent of the IJVGMs interviewed in this study received any specialized training or other preparation for their IJV assignment, despite the fact that less than 10 percent had any prior IJV experience. When queried as to why this situation occurred, several of the IJVGMs attributed it to the failure of their parent organizations to engage in planning for the assignment (or succession) of the IJVGM, as well as to the limited time frame which commonly resulted from this lack of planning. Even when specialized training *was* provided to IJVGMs, however, the programs were generally limited to a cursory overview of the local language and culture and they were usually administered over a relatively short period of time (i.e., one or two days' duration). Mechanisms for ensuring transfer of training, which is essential to maintain the benefits of training over time, were not emphasized nor incorporated into any of the training modules that the IJVGMs reported that they received. Several of the parent company executives rationalized that, because of the relatively limited number of IJVs which their firms were involved in, they had been unable to develop institutionalized support mechanisms for systematically acquiring and disseminating the requisite information and skills.

Although training programs were generally not administered to IJVGMs, the potential usefulness of such training programs was recognized by both the IJVGMs and the parent executives. In fact, over 85 percent of the IJVGMs and 80 percent of the parent company executives believed that development and delivery of specialized training programs would substantially improve IJVGM performance. Many of these respondents commented that, in the absence of training programs, it would typically be 12 to 18 months before the IJVGM could make substantive contributions to the management of the venture and attainment of the IJV's strategic objectives. In addition, both IJVGMs and parent executives noted that substantive undertakings were generally not forthcoming during the final 6 to 9 months of an IJVGM's assignment, as he or she began physically and mentally preparing for repatriation. Thus, in the absence of specialized training programs, IJVGMs on an average 4 year assignment would often have only $1\frac{1}{2}$ to 2 years in which they could perform effectively, and their effectiveness even during this time could be further hindered by the absence of adequate contextual or behavioral skills.

References

Aguilar, F.J. (1988). *General managers in action.* New York: Oxford University Press.

Anderson, E. (1990). Two firms, one frontier: On assessing joint venture performance. *Sloan Management Review,* Winter: 19-30.

Black, S., & Mendenhall, M. (1990). Cross-cultural training effectiveness: A review and theoretical framework for future research. *Academy of Management Review,* 15:113-136.

Bleeke, J. & Ernst, D. (1991). The way to win in cross-border alliances. *Harvard Business Review,* 69 (6): 127-135.

Blodgett, L.L. (1991). Toward a resource-based theory of bargaining power in international joint ventures. *Journal of Global Marketing,* 5 (1/2): 35-54.

Brown, L.T., Rugman, A.M. & Verbeke, A. (1989). Japanese joint ventures with Western multinationals: Synthesizing the economic and cultural explanations of failure. *Asia-Pacific Journal of Management,* 6 (2): 225-242.

Buckley, P. & Casson, M. (1988). The theory of cooperation in international business. In F. Contractor & P. Lorange (eds.), *Cooperative strategies in international business,* 31-54. Lexington, Mass.: Lexington Books.

Contractor, F. & Lorange, P. (1988). Why should firms cooperate? The strategy and economics basis for cooperative ventures. In F. Contractor & P. Lorange (eds.), *Cooperative strategies in international business,* 3-30. Lexington, MA: Lexington Books.

Deloitte, Haskins & Sells International (1989). *Teaming up for the Nineties — Can you survive without a partner?* New York: Deloitte, Haskins & Sells.

Devlin, G., & Bleackley, M. (1988). Strategic alliances—guidelines for success. Long Range Planning, 20 (3), 12-18.

Dobkin, J. (1988). *International technology joint ventures.* Stoneham, MA: Butterworth Legal Publishers.

Frayne, C.A. (1991). *Reducing Employee Absenteeism Through Self-Management Training.* Westport, Conn.: Quorum Books.

Frayne, C.A. & Geringer, J.M. (1990a). The strategic use of human resource management techniques as control mechanisms in international joint ventures. In G.R. Ferris & K.M. Rowland (eds.), *Research in Personnel and Human Resources Management,* Supplement Volume 2, 53-69, Greenwich, CN: JAI Press.

Frayne, C.A. & Geringer, J.M. (1990b). The relationship between self-management practices and performance of international joint venture general managers. *Proceedings of the Administrative Sciences Association of Canada*, 11 (9): 70-79.

Frayne, C.A. & Geringer, J.M. (1992). *A Self-Management Training Program for International Joint Venture General Managers.* Working paper, University of Western Ontario.

Frayne, C.A. & Latham, G.P. (1987). The application of social learning theory to employee self-management of attendance. *Journal of Applied Psychology*, 72: 387-392.

Ganitsky, J. & Watzke, G. (1990). Implications of different time perspectives for human resource management in international joint ventures. *Management International Review*, 30 (special issue): 37- 51.

Geringer, J.M. (1988). *Joint venture partner selection: Strategies for developed countries.* Westport, Conn.: Quorum Books.

Geringer, J.M. (1991). Strategic Determinants of Partner Selection Criteria in International Joint Ventures. *Journal of International Business Studies*, 22(1): 41-62.

Geringer, J.M. & Frayne, C.A. (1990). Human resource management and international joint venture control: A parent company perspective. *Management International Review*, 30 (Special issue): 103-120.

Geringer, J.M. & Hebert, L. (1989). Control and performance of international joint ventures. *Journal of International Business Studies*, 20(2): 235-254.

Geringer, J.M. & Hebert, L. (1991). Measuring Performance of International Joint Ventures. *Journal of International Business Studies*, 22(2): 249-263.

Geringer, J.M. & Miller, J. (1992). *Japanese-American Seating Inc.* (A). Case 9-92-G004, University of Western Ontario.

Geringer, J.M. & Woodcock, C.P. (1989). Ownership and control of Canadian joint ventures. *Business Quarterly*, Summer, 97-101.

Hamel, G.P. (1990). *Competitive collaboration: Learning, power and dependence in international strategic alliances.* Unpublished doctoral dissertation, University of Michigan.

Harrigan, K.R. (1986). *Managing for joint venture success.* Lexington, Mass.: Lexington Books.

Harrigan, K.R. (1988). Joint ventures and competitive strategy. *Strategic Management Journal*, 9 (2): 141-158.

Hergert, M. & Morris, D. (1988). Trends in international collaborative agreements. In F. Contractor & P. Lorange (eds.), *Cooperative strategies in international business*, 99-109, Lexington, Mass.: Lexington Books.

Holton, R.H. (1981). Making international joint ventures work. In L. Otterbeck (ed.), *The management of headquarters-subsidiary relations in multinational corporations*: 255-267. London: Gower.

Janger, A.R. (1980). *Organization of international joint ventures.* New York: Conference Board.

Killing, J.P. (1983). *Strategies for joint venture success.* New York: Praeger.

Kirkpatrick, D.L. (1967). Evaluation of training. In R.L. Craig (ed.), *Training and development handbook: A guide to human resource development:* 230-233. New York: McGraw-Hill.

Kotter, J.P. (1982). *The general managers.* New York: Free Press.

Lane, H.W. & DiStefano, J.J. (1988). *International Management Behavior.* Scarborough, Ontario: Nelson Canada.

Latham, G.P. & Frayne, C.A. (1989). Self-management training for increasing employee attendance: A follow-up and replication. *Journal of Applied Psychology,* 74: 411-416.

Latham, G.P., Saari, L.M., Pursell, E.D. & Campion, M.A. (1980). The situational interview. *Journal of Applied Psychology* 65: 422-427.

Lynch, R.P. (1989). *The practical guide to joint ventures and alliances.* New York: Wiley.

Mills, P. (1983). Self-management: Its control and relationship to other organizational properties. *Academy of Management Review,* 8: 445-453.

Moxon, R.W. & Geringer, J.M. (1985). Multinational ventures in the commercial aircraft industry. *Columbia Journal of World Business,* 20 (2): 55-62.

Olk, P. & Bussard, D. (1988). General manager succession in international joint ventures: Strategic management implications. Working paper 88-105. The Wharton School, University of Pennsylvania.

Perlmutter, H.V. & Heenan, D.A. (1986). Cooperate to compete globally. *Harvard Business Review,* 64 (2):136+.

Pucik, V. (1988). Strategic alliances with the Japanese: Implications for human resource management. In F.J. Contractor & P. Lorange (eds.), *Cooperative strategies in international business:* 487-498. Lexington, Mass.: Lexington.

Schaan, J.L. & Beamish, P.W. (1988). Joint venture general managers in LDCs. In F. Contractor & P. Lorange, (eds.), *Cooperative strategies in international business,* 279-299. Lexington, Mass.: Lexington Books.

Shenkar, O. & Zeira, Y. (1987). Human resources management in international joint ventures: Directions for research. *Academy of Management Review,* 12: 546-557.

Slocum, J. & Sims, H. Jr. (1980). A typology for integrating technology, organization and job design. *Human Relations,* 33:193-212.

Sullivan, J. & Peterson, R.B. (1982). Factors associated with trust in Japanese-American joint ventures. *Management International Review,* 30-40.

Thoreson, C.E. & Mahoney, M.J. (1974). *Behavioral self-control.* New York: Holt, Rinehart & Winston.

Tung, R.L. (1981). Selection and training of personnel for overseas assignments. *Columbia Journal of World Business,* 16 (1): 68-78.

Uyterhoeven, H.E.R. (1972). General managers in the middle. *Harvard Business Review,* 50 (2): 75-85.

Wexley, K. & Latham, G.P. (1981). *Developing and training human resources in organizations*. Glenview, Ill.: Scott Foresman.

Whetten, D. & Cameron, R. (1991). *Developing Management Skills*. New York: Harper Collins Publishers.

Young; G.R. & Bradford, S., Jr. (1977). *Joint ventures: Planning and action*. New York: Financial Executives Research Foundation.

Appendix

Details of Pilot Study Examining IJVGMs and Their Roles

To identify and develop appropriate training programs for IJVGMs, despite the limited existing literature on these topics, a pilot study was undertaken to examine IJVGMs and their roles. From a Statistics Canada database listing the population of two and three parent IJVs in manufacturing industries which were formed in Canada since 1981 and still in existence at the end of 1988, a sample of 48 ventures was randomly selected. The Canadian headquarters of each parent company, both domestic and foreign in origin, as well as the IJVGM were contacted. Participation was obtained from 101 managers involved with 42 JVs, including 41 current or prior IJVGMs and 60 parent company executives. Each parent company respondent had direct line responsibility for the IJV's operations, and virtually all had been intimately involved with the venture since its formation. Data on the IJVGM and his or her role were collected via a brief questionnaire, followed by in-person interviews to confirm and further probe responses. Questions addressed IJVGMs' managerial backgrounds, IJV responsibilities and performance. Respondents were also queried regarding the skills required for effective performance in IJVs, as well as potential IJVGM training needs.

A similar methodology was employed to examine these same issues, but in a developing country context. From public data sources on joint ventures in Indonesia, a sample of 100 IJVs in manufacturing industries and involving a developed country and a local firm were identified. Both the local and the foreign parent, as well as the IJVGM, were contacted for each of these ventures. Data were collected in semi-structured interviews from 107 executives involved in 62 IJVs, including 45 IJVGMs and 62 parent company executives. Each parent company respondent had direct line responsibility for the IJV's operations, and virtually all had been intimately involved with the venture since its formation.

Suji-INS K.K.

Case 2.1
William H. Davidson

Mike Flynn, president of the International Division of Information Network Services Corporation, was undecided as to how he could best approach several delicate issues with his Japanese joint venture partner. He needed to develop an agenda for his trip to Japan, scheduled for the following day. In many ways, he considered this trip of vital importance. For one thing, the problems to be discussed were likely to affect the long-term relationship between his company and the Japanese partner in the management of their joint venture. Moreover, this was his first trip to Japan in the capacity of president of the International Division, and he was anxious to make a good impression and to begin to build a personal relationship with senior executives of the Japanese firm.

Flynn had assumed the position of president several months previously in May of 1988. He was 40 years old and was considered to be one of the most promising executives in the company. After 2 years of military service followed by business school, he had joined a consulting company for several years prior to accepting a position with Information Network Services Corporation (INS). Prior to his promotion to the presidency of the International Division, he had served as managing director of INS's wholly owned subsidiary in Canada.

INS was a major provider of value added network (VAN) services in the United States. Its principal products included high-speed data communications (packet switching), data base management, transaction processing services, and a variety of industry-specific information services. The company's total sales for 1988 were roughly $250 million, and it had recently established successful presences in the United Kingdom and other European countries. International operations accounted for roughly 25 percent of the company's total sales, and the company's top management felt that international markets represented a major field for future growth.

The company's management recognized that in order to capitalize on the rapidly growing Japanese market, a direct presence was needed. By the mid-1980s, the company began to receive a number of inquiries

---

Source: William H. Davidson, "Suji-INS KK." © 1988. William Davidson School of Business, University of Southern California, Los Angeles, CA 90089. Reprinted by permission.

from major Japanese corporations concerning licensing possibilities. INS was particularly interested in the possibility of establishing a joint venture to provide VAN services.

The company, after 2 years of demanding negotiations, was successful in establishing a joint venture in Japan with Suji Company, a leading Japanese telecommunications equipment manufacturer. The arrangement was formalized in the summer of 1987.

Suji was one of the companies that approached INS initially to arrange a licensing agreement involving VAN technology and expertise. It appeared to be an attractive potential partner. Suji was a medium-sized telecommunication equipment vendor that was directly tied to one of the major Japanese industrial groups. The company had only limited sales to Nippon Telegraph and Telephone (NTT), the national telephone company. About half of its sales were exported, and the remainder went largely to other Japanese firms within the same industrial group. Suji had established a reputation for high quality, and its brands were well established.

In the mid-1980s, as the Japanese telecommunications market was deregulated, Suji began to explore opportunities in the telecommunication services market, particularly in paging and mobile phone services. Prior to deregulation, telephone and related services were monopoly markets served only by NTT. Under the terms of the 1984 New Telecommunications Law, other Japanese firms were permitted to offer these services to the general public. VAN services in particular could be initiated simply by notifying the Ministry of Posts and Telecommunications. The Ministry of International Trade and Industry had established several programs to provide incentives for new VAN services, including tax breaks and low-cost loans. Suji's management felt that VAN services would be a major growth area. Suji's management, after some investigation, concluded that the quickest and most efficient way to achieve entry into these markets was through either licensing or a joint venture with a leading U.S. company. Suji's management felt that timing was of particular importance, since its major competitors were also considering expansion into these markets. Suji's expression of interest to INS was timely, as INS had become increasingly interested in Japan. Suji was at first interested in a licensing arrangement, but INS, anxious to establish a permanent presence in Japan, wished to establish a joint venture.

The negotiations concerning this joint venture were difficult in part because it was the first experience of the kind for both companies. INS had virtually no prior experience in Japan, and for Suji this was the first joint venture with a foreign company, although it had engaged in licensing agreements with several U.S. and European firms.

The ownership of the joint venture was divided between the two companies, such that Suji owned two-thirds and INS one-third of its equity. Japanese law limited foreign ownership in telecom services vendors to one-third equity participation. In addition to a predetermined cash contribution, the agreement stipulated that INS was to provide network technology and the Japanese partner was to contribute facilities and network equipment. The joint venture was first to market data communication services and later was to introduce transaction processing services. The services were to be marketed under the joint brands of INS and Suji. The agreement also stipulated that both companies would have equal representation on the board of directors, with four people each, and that Suji would provide the entire personnel for the joint venture from top management down to production workers. Such a practice was quite common among foreign joint ventures in Japan, since given limited mobility among personnel in large corporations, recruiting would represent a major problem for foreign companies. The companies also agreed that the Japanese partner would nominate the president of the joint venture, subject to approval of the board, and the U.S. company would nominate a person for the position of executive vice president. INS also agreed to supply, for the time being, a technical director on a full-time basis.

INS had four members on the board: Flynn, Jack Rose (INS's nominee for executive vice president of the joint venture), and the chair and the president of INS. Representing the Japanese company were the president and executive vice president of Suji, and two senior executives of the joint venture, the president and vice president for finance.

By the fall of 1988, the venture had initiated tests of its data communication services, and a small sales organization had been built. Although the venture was progressing reasonably well, Flynn had become quite concerned over several issues that had come to his attention during the previous 2 months. The first and perhaps the most urgent of these was the selection of a new president for the joint venture.

The first president had died suddenly about 3 months before at the age of 68. He had been a managing director of the parent company and had been the chief representative in Suji's negotiations with INS. When the joint venture was established, it appeared only natural for him to assume the presidency; INS management had no objection.

About a month after his death, Suji, in accordance with the agreement, nominated Kenzo Satoh as the new president. Flynn, when he heard Satoh's qualifications, concluded that he was not suitable for the presidency of the joint venture. He became even more disturbed when he received further information about how he was selected from Jack Rose, the executive vice president of the joint venture.

Satoh had joined Suji 40 years previously upon graduating from Tokyo University. He had held a variety of positions in the Suji company, but during the previous 15 years, he had served almost exclusively in staff functions. He had been manager of Administrative Services at the company's major plant, manager of the General Affairs Department at the corporate headquarters, and personnel director. When he was promoted to that position, he was admitted to the company's board of directors. His responsibility was then expanded to include overseeing several service-oriented staff departments, including personnel, industrial relations, administrative services, and the legal department.

Flynn was concerned that Satoh had virtually no line experience and could not understand why Suji would propose such a person for the presidency of the joint venture, particularly when it was at a critical stage of development.

Even more disturbing to Mr. Flynn was the manner in which Satoh was selected. This first came to Mr. Flynn's attention when he received a letter from Rose, which included the following description:

> By now you have undoubtedly examined the background information forwarded to you regarding Mr. Satoh, nominated by our Japanese partner for the presidency of the joint venture.

> I have subsequently learned the manner in which Mr. Satoh was chosen for the position, which I am sure would be of great interest to you. I must point out at the outset that what I am going to describe, though shocking by our standards, is quite commonplace among Japanese corporations: in fact, it is well-accepted.

> Before describing the specific practice, I must give you a brief background of the Japanese personnel system. As you know, the major companies follow the so-called lifetime employment where all managerial personnel are recruited directly from universities, and they remain with the company until they reach their compulsory retirement age, which is typically around 57. Career advancement in the Japanese system comes slowly, primarily by seniority. Advancement to middle management is well-paced, highly predictable, and virtually assured for every college graduate. Competence and performance become important as they reach upper middle management and top management. Obviously, not everyone will be promoted automatically beyond middle management, but whatever the degree to which competence and qualifications are considered in career advancement, chronological age is the single most important factor.

> A select few within the ranks of upper-middle management will be promoted to top management positions, that is, they will be given memberships in the board of directors. In large Japanese companies, the board typically consists exclusively of full-time operating executives. Suji's board is no exception. Moreover, there is a clear-cut hierarchy among the members. The Suji board consists of the chair of the board, president, executive vice president, three managing directors, five ordinary directors, and two statutory auditors.

> Typically, ordinary directors have specific operating responsibilities such as head of a staff department, a plant, or a division. Managing directors are comparable to our group vice presidents. Each will have two or three functional or staff

groups or product divisions reporting to them. Japanese commercial law stipulates that the members are to be elected by stockholders for a 2-year term. Obviously, under the system described, the members are designated by the chair of the board or the president and serve at their pleasure. Stockholders have very little voice in the actual selection of the board members. Thus, in some cases, it is quite conceivable that board membership is considered as a reward for many years of faithful and loyal service.

As you are well aware, a Japanese corporation is well known for its paternalistic practices in return for lifetime service, and they do assume obligations, particularly for those in middle management or above, even after they reach their compulsory retirement age, not just during their working careers. Appropriate positions are generally found for them in the company's subsidiaries, related firms, or major suppliers where they can occupy positions commensurate to their last position in the parent corporation for several more years.

A similar practice applies to the board members. Though there is no compulsory retirement age for board members, the average tenure for board membership is usually around 6 years. This is particularly true for those who are ordinary or managing directors. Directorships being highly coveted positions, there must be regular turnover to allow others to be promoted to board membership. As a result, all but a fortunate few who are earmarked as heir apparent to the chair, presidency, or executive vice presidency must be "retired." Since most of these executives are in their late fifties or early sixties, they do not yet wish to retire. Moreover, even among major Japanese corporations, the compensation for top management positions is quite low compared with the U.S. standard, and pension plans being still quite inadequate, they will need respectable positions with a reasonable income upon leaving the company. Thus, it is common practice among Japanese corporations to transfer senior executives of the parent company to the chair or presidency of the company's subsidiaries or affiliated companies. Typically, these people will serve in these positions for several years before they retire. Suji had a dozen subsidiaries, and you might be interested in knowing that every top management position is held by those who have retired from the parent corporation. Such a system is well routinized.

Our friend, Mr. Satoh is clearly not the caliber that would qualify for further advancement in the parent company, and his position must be vacated for another person. Suji's top management must have decided that the presidency of the joint venture was the appropriate position for him to "retire" into. These are the circumstances under which Mr. Satoh has been nominated for our consideration.

When he read this letter, Flynn instructed Rose to indicate to the Suji management that Satoh was not acceptable. Not only did Flynn feel that Satoh lacked the qualifications and experience for the presidency, but he resented the fact that Suji was using the joint venture as a home to accommodate a retired executive. It would be justifiable for Suji to use one of its wholly owned subsidiaries for that purpose, but there was no reason why the joint venture should take him on. On the contrary, the joint venture needed dynamic leadership to establish a viable market position.

In his response to Rose, Flynn suggested as president another person, Takao Toray, marketing manager of the joint venture. Toray was 50 years old and had been transferred to the joint venture from Suji, where he had held a number of key marketing positions, including regional sales manager and assistant marketing director. Shortly after he was appointed to the latter position, Toray was sent to INS headquarters to become acquainted with the company's marketing operations. He spent roughly 3 months in the United States, during which time Flynn met him. Though he had not gone beyond a casual acquaintance, Flynn was much impressed by Toray. He appeared to be dynamic, highly motivated, and pragmatic. Moreover, Toray had a reasonable command of English. While communication was not easy, at least it was possible to have conversations on substantive matters. From what Flynn was able to gather, Toray impressed everyone he saw favorably and gained the confidence of not only the International Division staff but those in the corporate marketing group as well as sales executives in the field.

Flynn was aware that Toray was a little too young to be acceptable to Suji, but he felt that it was critical to press for his appointment for two reasons. First, he was far from convinced of the wisdom of adopting Japanese managerial practices blindly in the joint venture. Some of the Japanese executives he met in New York had told him of the pitfalls and weaknesses of Japanese management practices. He was disturbed over the fact that, as he was becoming familiar with the joint venture, he was finding that in every critical aspect such as organization structure, personnel practices, and decision making, the company was managed as though it were a Japanese company. Rose had had little success in introducing U.S. practices. Flynn had noticed in the past that the joint venture had been consistently slow in making decisions because it engaged in a typical Japanese group-oriented and consensus-based process. He also learned that control and reporting systems were virtually nonexistent. Flynn felt that INS's sophisticated planning and control system should be introduced. It had proved successful in the company's wholly owned European subsidiaries, and there seemed to be no reason why such a system could not improve the operating efficiency of the joint venture. He recalled from his Canadian experience that U.S. management practices, if judiciously applied, could give U.S. subsidiaries abroad a significant competitive advantage over local firms.

Second, Flynn felt that the rejection of Satoh and appointment of Toray might be important as a demonstration to the Japanese partner that Suji-INS was indeed a joint venture and not a subsidiary of the Japanese parent company. He was also concerned that INS had lost the initiative in the management of the joint venture. This move would help INS gain stronger influence over the management of the joint venture.

Rose conveyed an informal proposal along these lines to Suji management. Suji's reaction to Flynn's proposal was swift; they rejected it totally. Suji management was polite, but made it clear that they considered Flynn unfair in judging Mr. Satoh's suitability for the presidency without even having met him. They requested Rose to assure Flynn that their company, as majority owner, indeed had an important stake in the joint venture and certainly would not have recommended Satoh unless it had been convinced of his qualifications. Suji management also told Flynn, through Rose, that the selection of Toray was totally unacceptable because in the Japanese corporate system such a promotion was unheard of and would be detrimental not only to the joint venture but to Toray himself, who was believed to have a promising future in the company.

Flynn was surprised at the tone of Suji's response. He wondered whether it would be possible to establish an effective relationship with the Japanese company. Suji seemed determined to run the venture on their own terms.

Another related issue which concerned Flynn was the effectiveness of Rose as executive vice president. Flynn appreciated the difficulties he faced but began to question Rose's qualifications for his position and his ability to work with Japanese top management. During the last visit, for example, Rose had complained of his inability to integrate himself with the Japanese top management team. He indicated that he felt he was still very much an outsider to the company, not only because he was a foreigner but also because the Japanese executives, having come from the parent company, had known each other and in many cases had worked together for at least 20 years. He also indicated that none of the executives spoke English well enough to achieve effective communication beyond the most rudimentary level and that his Japanese was too limited to be of practical use. In fact, his secretary, hired specifically for him, was the only one with whom he could communicate easily. He also expressed frustration over the fact that his functions were very ill-defined and his experience and competence were not really being well utilized by the Japanese.

Flynn discovered after he assumed the presidency that Mr. Rose had been chosen for this assignment for his knowledge of Japan. Rose graduated from a midwestern university in 1973, and after enlisting in the Army was posted to Japan for 4 years. Upon returning home, he joined INS as a management trainee. In 1984, he became assistant district sales manager in California, Oregon, and Washington. When the company began to search for a candidate for executive vice president for the new joint venture, Rose's name came up as someone who was qualified and available for posting to Japan. Rose, although somewhat ambivalent about the new opportunity at first, soon became persuaded that this would represent a major challenge and opportunity.

Flynn was determined to get a first-hand view of the joint venture during his visit. He had many questions, and he wondered whether he had inherited a problem. He was scheduled to meet with Mr. Ohtomo, executive vice president of Suji Corporation, on the day following his arrival. Ohtomo, who had been with Suji for over 40 years, was the senior executive responsible for overseeing the joint venture. Flynn had not met Ohtomo, but he knew that Ohtomo had visited the United States and spoke English reasonably well. He wondered how best to approach and organize his meetings and discussions with Mr. Ohtomo. He also wondered if his planned stay of one week would be adequate to achieve his objectives. While practicing with chopsticks, he returned to reading *Theory Z*, a popular book on Japanese management, in the hope of gaining insight for the days ahead.

Caterpillar Inc. in Indonesia (A)

Case 2.2
J. Michael Geringer
Colette A. Frayne

In early September 1991, Mr. Richard Kahler, Managing Director of Caterpillar Inc.'s Indonesian subsidiary, P.T. Natra Raya (PTNR), was concerned about overstaffing in his recession-hit company. PTNR was a joint venture operation near Jakarta which assembled Caterpillar's earthmoving equipment for the Indonesian market. A booming Indonesian economy and a strong export market in the logging industry had led to a 50% increase in PTNR's revenues in 1990 versus 1989, and revenues had been projected to increase an additional 50% in 1991. To meet this increased demand and accommodate new business opportunities, PTNR had expanded its work force from 224 employees in 1989 to 339 by early 1991. Yet, unexpected economic developments early in 1991 had caused PTNR's sales to plummet. In contrast to projected full year sales of 985 units, only 315 units of equipment, mostly backlogged orders from 1990, had been sold through the end of August 1991. PTNR had received few new orders and a lengthy production pipeline had hindered volume cutbacks, causing PTNR's inventory to swell to over 700 units. PTNR was expected to record a substantial loss for 1991, the first loss since its startup days, rather than the record level of profits projected initially. Despite initiatives to utilize excess labor for other tasks, PTNR was overstaffed for current levels of demand. Mr. Kahler was concerned that retaining too many workers would inflate costs and damage PTNR's culture of discipline and hard work. Yet, dismissing the excess employees might generate problems, both within PTNR and with government agencies. Mr. Kahler wondered how he should address this dilemma.

Caterpillar Inc. and Its Indonesian Operations

Caterpillar Inc., based in Peoria, Illinois, was the world's leading manufacturer of earthmoving equipment, a position the company had

Source: © 1993 by J. Michael Geringer and Collette A. Frayne. Reprinted by permission of the authors.

maintained for several decades. With 1990 revenues of $11.4 billion and assets of $11.9 billion, Caterpillar's worldwide earthmoving equipment operations were more than twice the size of the industry's second largest firm, Komatsu of Japan. Caterpillar also was a major producer of diesel and natural gas engines. The company's Engine Division accounted for over 20% of Caterpillar's total revenues. The familiar "Hi-Way Yellow" color and distinctive "Cat" logo were found on all Caterpillar equipment and were recognized worldwide.

P.T. Natra Raya had been formed in 1982 as a joint venture between Caterpillar and P.T. Trakindo Utama, an Indonesian company which had been the exclusive agent for the sale and service of Caterpillar's products in Indonesia since the 1970s. One of over 50 facilities around the world which manufactured or assembled Caterpillar products, PTNR had begun production in 1984. Caterpillar's ownership stake in PTNR was 80%, while Trakindo's was 20%.

Indonesian Government Policy and the Earthmoving Equipment Industry

PTNR had been formed in response to the Government of Indonesia's efforts to create a domestic industry in small to mid-sized earthmoving and logging equipment. To assist in this effort, particularly given the economically inefficient levels of production which would be obtained initially, the government agreed at that time to license only two multinational entrants, Caterpillar and Komatsu. The government also agreed to provide a 20% tariff on all fully assembled imported equipment. Duties on components ranged from zero to very high levels, with the most common duty being 5% on "miscellaneous tractor parts."

The Indonesian government had recognized that, at least in its initial stages, the fledgling domestic earthmoving equipment industry would have to import most of its components. In order to retain their exclusivity, however, the two licensed manufacturers had to agree to an aggressive program aimed at achieving 100% local content by 1988. Subsequently, the government reevaluated Indonesia's market potential and domestic supply capabilities and agreed to relax this timetable by several years.

In addition to using licenses, the government controlled manufacturing and imports through a process of master lists. Master lists were an important tool in the government's "deletion" program approach to increasing local content. Once the government deemed that there was sufficient capability among domestic suppliers to produce a specific component, that component was deleted from the master list of goods allowed to be imported duty free. The decision regarding which parts would be deleted was determined through negotiations between the Government of Indonesia and individual firms or the industry's trade association. Master lists were updated twice a year, with the listed parts being subject to possible revision to a higher level of duty at each updating. Maintaining a positive attitude by the government toward the company and the emerging local industry was critical.

PTNR Strategy

PTNR was initially set up to produce track-type tractors, wheel-type loaders, and motor graders. Caterpillar diesel engines of up to 500 horsepower were also produced, both to power PTNR's equipment and for non-captive use. In 1987, PTNR acquired a local firm, P.T. Trigunautama Machinery Industries, and began to produce hydraulic excavators. In 1989, PTNR introduced a line of locally designed "Cat-powered" generating sets for producing standby electrical power.

Although Caterpillar and Komatsu had committed themselves to an aggressive schedule of increased local content, success was not to the level of the original government mandate. This may have contributed to the government's 1990 decision to license a third multinational, Hitachi of Japan, for local production of earthmoving equipment through an alliance with several local firms, including a leading local steel producer.

A multidisciplinary, internal company task force was established in 1989 to examine methods for PTNR to add local content to its product. Despite past efforts to increase productivity and domestic value added, PTNR's business of assembling completely knocked down kits (called "skidpacks") was inefficient. The components imported from Japan were expensive to assemble into skidpacks and to ship, due to their bulkiness and weight. The labor cost advantage that PTNR enjoyed over facilities in Japan and the United States was not sufficient to make up for these cost disadvantages. Without the 20% tariff protection, PTNR had no advantage over fully-assembled Caterpillar products imported from Japan. Faced with the potential of future government deregulation of the earthmoving equipment industry and decreases in the level of tariff barriers, an increase in PTNR's local content seemed necessary.

In light of increasing decentralization of responsibility in Caterpillar Inc., and given the changes in the competitive and supply conditions in Indonesia since the venture's formation, the task force recommended that PTNR aggressively increase local content, to reduce product cost by in-house production of key components. Consistent with this strategy, an analysis of the pros and cons of increased investment in local operations was conducted and this report was reviewed by Caterpillar's headquarters. The analysis of local market conditions projected continued strong demand and, in October of 1990, a formal proposal was made to expand the venture's business charter from one of "market access" to "regional manufacturing." This proposal included a recommendation for investment of $6.7 million in an expansion of PTNR's fabrication and assembly operations, including over 74,400 square feet of new facilities. In addition to doubling the throughput capacity of the assembly operation, the additional investment would enable increased fabrication of medium to large, low sophistication, and labor intensive components in order to substantially increase local content and take advantage of inexpensive local labor. PTNR would purchase raw materials such as steel, and then cut, bend, roll, and weld these materials to produce bulky components that were costly to import. Savings of $1.9 to $3.5 million per year were projected, particularly through the avoidance of costs such as freight, duty, and packaging. This proposal was accepted by both partners, and the expansion was scheduled to be completed by December 1991, with production due to commence by May 1992.

Manufacturing and Logistics

As shown in Exhibit 1, the relationship between Caterpillar and Trakindo was not limited to their joint venture operation: Trakindo was Caterpillar's sole dealer in Indonesia and therefore was also PTNR's sole customer as well as the customer for any equipment imported directly into Indonesia from Caterpillar's other operations. Virtually all items manufactured by PTNR were sold to Trakindo, which in turn sold them to final users. A fabrication subsidiary of Trakindo also supplied a small proportion of PTNR's parts. Trakindo was responsible for post-purchase servicing of all Caterpillar products, both those imported directly from abroad and those produced by PTNR.

PTNR's manufacturing facility was located on 25 acres of land on the outskirts of Bogor, a medium-sized city approximately an hour's drive from Jakarta on the island of Java. Skidpacks were ocean shipped in quantities (e.g., 4 or 6 units per order) based on demand and on efficient levels of packaging and shipping expenses. Crated skidpacks were stored in an outside yard until time for assembly, then brought inside to be unpacked, sorted, checked for damage or shortages of parts, and combined with locally sourced materials in preparation for assembly. As is common in such operations, particularly since several of PTNR's products had as many as 25,000 parts, many shipments had a degree of damage or discrepancy and the reconciliation and replacement process typically took about 10 days. Since many of PTNR's components were made of steel, equipment had to be assembled and painted or greased promptly or it would quickly rust in Indonesia's humid environment. Due to scheduling problems, missing parts, and delays with imports, parts and partially completed units typically required at least one anti-rust treatment before assembly and finishing activities could be concluded.

PTNR's factory was organized into a series of work stations, each dedicated to a different subassembly stage of the production process. Final assembly was conducted in batches on PTNR's site. The venture's engineering, manufacturing, and quality control personnel were responsible for ensuring that Caterpillar's international quality standards were maintained. Prior to shipping to a customer, the unit would be taken out of inventory and customized to incorporate individual

**Exhibit 1. Caterpillar Inc. in Indonesia.
Simplified Production Flow Chart for P.T. Natra Raya's Operations**

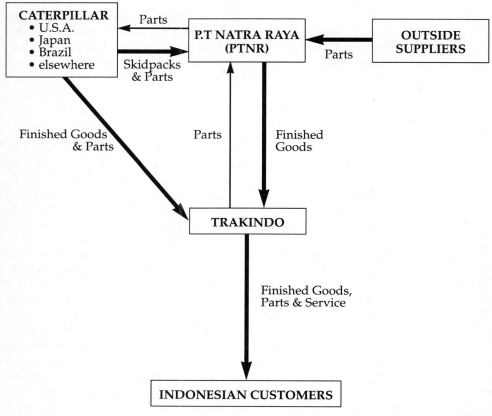

specifications and features; the equipment was cleaned, greased, and tested; and a finishing coat of paint and decals was applied. Overall, it took 6 to 9 months from the time PTNR ordered a skidpack until the point at which the unit was completed, plus any time an excess skidpack or work-in-progress might spend in inventory. Most of this time was consumed in waiting for the delivery of all of the component parts, with approximately 45 days' throughput time required in the factory once all necessary parts were available. Combined with the susceptibility of steel parts to rusting, which limited options for storing large quantities of parts, and with the high levels of working capital required for skidpack inventories, PTNR's ability to respond quickly to changes in market demand was limited.

The manufacturing and assembly operations performed "in-house" at PTNR, however, represented only a small part of the effort being made by Caterpillar and PTNR to develop an Indonesian supplier infrastructure. PTNR's assembly lines were directly supported by over 25 local suppliers. PTNR's technical personnel worked closely with these suppliers not only to ensure that they met Caterpillar's exacting specifications and quality standards, but also to enhance suppliers' cost effectiveness and delivery performance. Starting in 1988, several components produced by PTNR or its local suppliers were exported by PTNR to other Caterpillar operations. Most of these exports were lower technology and labor intensive items. The export of parts was viewed by PTNR's managers as an external confirmation of the company's success in achieving international standards of quality and cost.

PTNR's Marketing and Sales

By mid-1991, PTNR's product line included 12 basic models (see Exhibit 2), with prices for non-general or set equipment averaging around $100,000 apiece and ranging in price from $60,000 to $200,000. PTNR's generator sets ranged in price from approximately $30,000 to $40,000. Final demand for PTNR's products could be divided into four principal market segments, with the proportion of overall revenues indicated in brackets: logging (40%), construction (20%), agriculture (15%), and mining and oil exploration (15%). The demanding nature of the tasks being performed meant that the useful life for earthmoving equipment used in the logging sector tended to be relatively shorter, necessitating more frequent replacement than in other sectors. Caterpillar's larger earthmoving equipment, most of which was used in the mining industry and in heavy construction projects, was not produced in Indonesia. Instead, these larger units were imported from other subsidiaries, chiefly in the United States and Japan, and sold directly through Trakindo.

Trakindo generated twelve-month forecasts for Indonesian market demand, in consultation with Caterpillar marketing representatives in Jakarta. These forecasts were revised monthly to account for changing events. PTNR had no formal responsibility for market analysis; its orders for skidpacks and parts were made at least six months in advance of the projected sales date, based on sales projections developed by Trakindo. Under the joint venture agreement, however, Trakindo was only obligated to maintain an inventory equivalent to three months' worth of currently projected sales, and had no further obligation to purchase any specific quantity of units from PTNR based on prior or current sales projections. Since most of PTNR's demand tended to be very sensitive to business cycles, and due to the long order lead time, PTNR had to work very closely with Trakindo in order to anticipate customer trends and sales forecasts, and to identify economic events which might have an impact on PTNR's business.

Exhibit 2. Caterpillar Inc. in Indonesia.
P.T. Natra Raya Product Line

D7G TRACK-TYPE TRACTOR
Caterpillar 6-cylinder Diesel Engine Model 3306 DIT
  rated at 200 HP (149 kW) at 2000 rpm
Power Shift Transmission 3-Forward, 3-Reverse
Attachments: Bulldozers with A-blade or S-blade with tilt. Logging winch
  with mainline, hook and shackle. Ripper with three teeth.

D6H LOGGING SPECIAL TRACK-TYPE TRACTOR
Caterpillar 6-cylinder Diesel Engine Model 3306 DIT
  rated at 185 HP (138kW) at 1900 rpm
Power Shift Transmission 3-Forward, 3-Reverse
Attachments: Bulldozers with A-blade or S-blade with tilt. Logging winch
  with mainline, hook and shackle. Ripper with three teeth.

D6D HIGH PERFORMANCE TRACK-TYPE TRACTOR
Caterpillar 6-cylinder Diesel Engine Model 3306 DIT
  rated at 160 HP (119 kW) at 1900 rpm
Power Shift Transmission 3-Forward, 3-Reverse
Attachments: Bulldozers with A-blade or S-blade with tilt. Ripper with three teeth.

980C WHEEL-TYPE LOG LOADER
Caterpillar 6-cylinder Diesel Engine Model 3406 T
  rated at 270 HP (201 kW) at 2100 rpm
Power Shift Transmission 3-Forward, 3-Reverse
Attachments: Rock Bucket 5.25 cu.yd. (4.0 cu.m.)

966E WHEEL-TYPE LOADER
Caterpillar 6-cylinder Diesel Engine Model 3306 DIT
  rated at 216 HP (161 kW) at 2200 rpm
Power Shift Transmission 3-Forward, 3-Reverse
Attachments: General Purpose Bucket 4.25 cu.yd. (3.3 cu.m.).
  Third Hydraulic Valve for Log Forks

926E WHEEL-TYPE LOADER
Caterpillar 4-cylinder Diesel Engine Model 3204 DIT
  rated at 110 HP (82 kW) at 2400 rpm
Power Shift Transmission 3-Forward, 3-Reverse
General Purpose Bucket 2.25 cu.yd. (1.7 cu.m.)

120B MOTOR GRADER
Caterpillar 6-cylinder Diesel Engine Model 3306 PC
  rated at 125 HP (93 kW) at 2000 rpm
Direct Drive Transmission with Wet Clutch, 6-Forward, 4-Reverse

E200B HYDRAULIC EXCAVATOR
Caterpillar 6-cylinder Diesel Engine Model 3116 DIT
  rated at 118 HP (88 kW) at 1800 rpm
0.9 cu.m. Bucket

E110 HYDRAULIC EXCAVATOR
4-cylinder Diesel Engine Model 4D31-T
  rated at 74 HP (55 kW) at 1950 rpm
0.45 cu.m. Bucket

200 KW GENERATOR SET
Caterpillar 6-cylinder Diesel Engine Model 3306 ATAAC
200 kW Prime Power Generator; 220 kW Standby Generator

100 KW GENERATOR SET
Caterpillar 8-cylinder Diesel Engine Model 3208 DIT
100 kW Prime Power Generator; 110 kW Standby Generator

3208 MARINE ENGINE
Caterpillar 8-cylinder Diesel Engine Model 3208 DIT
320 BHP (238.5 kW) at 2800 rpm

Organizational and Management Structure

PTNR had a functionally-based organization structure (see Exhibit 3). Four of the seven departmental managers were expatriates from Caterpillar's U.S. operations, one was from Britain, and two were Indonesian. In addition, there were 15 division managers, all of whom were Indonesian nationals. All employees were located at the company's manufacturing facility.

Mr. Singgih held the role of President Director of PTNR, a position he had held since the venture was formed in 1982. Prior to joining PTNR, Mr. Singgih had been director of human resources for Trakindo since 1972. His activities were primarily focused on overseeing human resource management as well as managing relations with external organizations, particularly the Indonesian government and the industry's trade association. He also tried to assist newly-assigned managing directors in quickly acclimating to PTNR's context.

Mr. Kahler was PTNR's Managing Director. Although he had formal authority for all of the venture's day-to-day operations, Mr. Kahler solicited input and advice from Mr. Singgih on key issues. Both men got along quite well and they were able to communicate openly and directly on most issues. The strength of this relationship was important not only to the success of PTNR, but also to the quality of relationships with and among both Trakindo and Caterpillar.

PTNR had a five person Strategic Planning Council which developed and evaluated longer term plans. This Council met monthly and included Mr. Kahler (chairperson), Mr. Singgih, and PTNR's Business, Engineering and Systems, and Planning Managers.

Human Resource Management Systems

Effective management of human resources was viewed as a critical function by both of the partner companies as well as by PTNR's senior executives. Indeed, Mr. Singgih had made the management of PTNR's human resources his primary focus. He explained his focus as follows:

> Unless the people are managed well, no organization can be successful. I believe that the single most important task in PTNR

Exhibit 3. P.T. Natra Raya Organizational Chart, August 1991

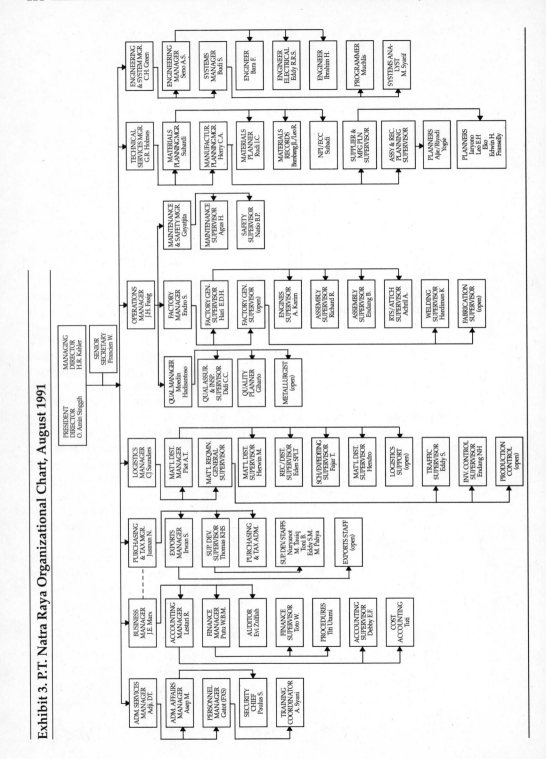

is to ensure that our employees and management are productive, team oriented, and committed to the venture. I have devoted myself to ensuring that we select the right people for this company, and that we take proper care of these people. It is the only way to ensure that we have a strong and healthy culture.

The human resource function was accorded equally high stature by Mr. Kahler. Upon his arrival at PTNR, Mr. Kahler had immediately established a Human Resource Council whose objective was to enhance the priority of human resource issues among PTNR's senior management, as well as to enable Mr. Kahler to better comprehend the functioning of the organization. This 5-person Council was comprised of Mr. Kahler, Mr. Singgih, and PTNR's Business, Administrative Services, and Operations Managers. The Council met monthly to discuss any issues, problems, or ideas for improved people management at PTNR.

PTNR had a very strong and supportive culture. Because most of PTNR's employees lived in Jakarta and its suburbs, an hour or more away from the plant, in some respects PTNR evidenced a commuter-type culture. Employees did not have much opportunity for social exchange after work because they boarded the company buses for a long ride home. However, a central dining area enabled employees and management to interact during meals and break periods. Since Indonesia was a predominantly Islamic nation, PTNR also had a common prayer room for the employees' daily worship. Morale at the plant was generally quite good, as was the relationship among the expatriate and local managers and employees. Turnover was only 2% per year and absenteeism had not been a problem.

PTNR's workforce was not unionized and any grievances which did arise were handled by the immediate supervisors and the Personnel Manager. Indonesia had a comprehensive system of labor laws and regulations which provided workers with many basic protections. A list of some of these laws is included in Exhibit 4. In general, most of PTNR's human resource systems were based on systems in use at Trakindo. The primary exception was the profit sharing system, which was adapted from a system used in Caterpillar.

Each year, PTNR attracted a large number of applications from the abundant Indonesian labor market. When possible, PTNR attempted to recruit from within when vacancies arose. For new hires, minimum qualifications included a high school diploma and satisfactory completion of a competency test in logic, language, and mechanical skills. Assessments were also made for quality, timeliness, and reasoning ability of the applicant. If they satisfied these basic requirements, applicants were then interviewed by the supervisors in the department where the position opening existed. Employees were also required to undergo a medical check-up. The final decision regarding hiring of an applicant was made by Mr. Singgih, after an in-person meeting at which Mr. Singgih discussed the importance of being a team player, as

Exhibit 4. Basic Indonesian Labor Laws

Indonesia has a comprehensive system of labor laws and regulations, which provide workers with the following basic protections:

Vacation Pay: Not less than two weeks of paid leave per year.

Maternity Leave: 3 months of paid maternity leave.

Public Holidays: 12 paid public holidays per year.

Hours of Work: 7 hours per day or 40 hours per week, with 1 half hour of rest for each 4 hours of work. Other regulations permit an 8-hour day, 5 days a week.

Overtime: Daily overtime at $1\frac{1}{2}$ times the normal hourly rate for the first hour, then 2 times the hourly rate for additional overtime, with overtime for scheduled rest days (including public holidays) at twice the hourly rate for the first 7 hours and 3 times the hourly rate for hours of overtime worked in excess of 7 hours on a holiday or rest day.

Sick Leave: An employee cannot be terminated if the employee is sick for less than 12 months, and an employee is entitled to receive sick pay as follows: First 3 months —100% of salary; second 3 months — 75% of salary; third 3 months — 50% of salary; fourth 3 months — 25% of salary.

Workplace Accidents: Employer provides all medical costs, including death benefits.

Social Insurance: A public fund compensates employees for sickness, pregnancy and death (to the extent not covered by the workplace accidents law, above); the employer contributes 5% of the employee's salary, the employee contributes 1% and the government contributes 2%.

Severance Pay: Statutory minimum severance pay consists of an amount equal to 1 month's wages for each year of service up to a maximum of four months' wages (though in practice, amounts usually exceed this statutory minimum). Severance pay is payable for all terminations including termination for cause, except in cases involving moral turpitude or serious criminal conduct.

Service Pay: In addition to severance pay, upon termination of employment the employee is entitled to receive service pay for long service, set at a minimum of 1 month's wage for service of 5 to 10 years, and an additional increment of 1 month's wage for each 5 year period, or portion thereof, up to 5 months' wages for over 25 years of service.

Wage Protection: Interest is assessed on unpaid wages (5% a day for the fourth through eighth day of delay, 1% a day thereafter up to a maximum of 50% of the wages due). Garnishment is limited to 20% of wages, and payment in kind is limited to 25% of wages.

well as his philosophy of achieving a disciplined, productive work-force. Commitment to the organization and hard work were the keys to PTNR's success and Mr. Singgih wanted to ensure that every new employee understood and espoused these values. Once hired, employees were placed on a 3 month probationary period, during which time an employee could be released if he or she was not fitting in. After the probationary period, employees became permanent members of PTNR's workforce, which meant that formal procedures would have to be initiated in order to lay off or terminate an employee.

Formal performance appraisals were conducted once a year for both management and non-management employees. Each employee would meet with their respective supervisor to discuss their performance, using a standardized performance appraisal form. At the end of the meeting, the employee would be asked to sign the form and this appraisal would subsequently be used as the basis for pay raises, promotional opportunities, and additional training. If the employee did not agree with the appraisal, this matter would be handled by the personnel manager. Performance appraisals were seen as an important tool for measuring and communicating performance standards, and the personnel department maintained complete records on each employee.

PTNR had sought to take advantage of the relatively low salary structure in Indonesia, but had made a management commitment to improve its relative salary competitiveness. One initiative involved PTNR's incentive compensation program. Each year, PTNR's business plan set performance targets related to profitability and other measures. If the company met its targets, then bonuses would be paid, in relation to the current salary structure. These bonuses served as important incentives for the workers, to help increase their motivation to perform. In 1990, all employees received bonuses averaging 8% of annual salaries, along with raises averaging 10%.

PTNR invested heavily in employee training and development. Cross-training programs were available and encouraged as a means of strengthening the skill set of the workforce, as well as to provide flexibility to departments in case of absenteeism or excess workload requirements. On-site language training in Japanese and English was also available to all employees. Caterpillar offered training in human resource management and supervisory skills for PTNR's management employees. Caterpillar also had a central training site in Singapore which was available to PTNR for providing a range of ongoing technical and management development courses.

PTNR's Financial and Market Performance

PTNR's overall objective was to be the leader in earthmoving equipment, diesel engines, and mobile power generating equipment in Indonesia. In terms of both overall revenues and units sold, PTNR was well on its way toward achieving this goal. Although year-to-year figures varied and comparison across individual product categories was difficult, Komatsu and Caterpillar brands were estimated to have achieved approximately equal shares of the Indonesian market in 1990. Other competitors had achieved limited success in competing for sales of these machines. Caterpillar machines and engines from PTNR were familiar sights throughout Indonesia's 13,500 islands. In addition, through this manufacturing operation and with the full cooperation of both Caterpillar and Indonesian suppliers, the local content of products made by PTNR had increased over time, assisting the Indonesian government in achieving its goals of increasing technology transfer and reducing the need for imports. Benefitting from rapid economic growth in Indonesia during the 1980s, particularly since 1986, and from the continued commitment of the partners, PTNR had achieved rapid increases in sales, production, and employment in recent years (see Exhibit 5). In 1990, on sales of approximately $63 million, PTNR had earned over $5 million in profit for its two shareholders. All of these earnings were added to accumulated retained earnings.

Recent Developments

The Indonesian economy grew rapidly from 1987 through 1990. In 1990, primarily through the use of overtime, PTNR had increased volume from the facility's stated capacity of 40 units per month to a level of approximately 60 units per month. Including a 200 unit order backlog, 1991 sales of PTNR's products were projected to be 1000 to 1200 units of equipment (plus additional sales of generator sets). PTNR's business plan for 1991 assumed the sale of 985 units. This sales volume

Exhibit 5. Caterpillar Inc. in Indonesia
P.T. Natra Raya Production and Employment, 1984-1991

Year	Engine Output	Equipment Output	Total Output	Number of Employees
		(units)	*(units)*	*(units)*
1984	—	66	66	88
1985	—	116	116	102
1986	—	147	147	107
1987	14	295	309	166
1988	16	504	520	189
1989	14	515	529	224
1990	148	624	772	297
1991 *(projected)*	268	985	1253	328

represented an increase of 62% compared to 1990, reaching nearly 85 units of equipment per month. Initial results in early 1991 had been consistent with projections, with PTNR receiving orders for nearly 100 machines and 30 generator sets during the first 6 weeks of the new year. In addition, PTNR was pursuing several new initiatives, including construction of the $6.7 million facility expansion to double production throughput capacity and to increase the level of domestic value-added through more in-house fabrication of parts, enlargement of the on-site painting facility, and addition of an outside storage yard.

To keep up with this continued rapid growth, Mr. Kahler and his management team had initiated a rapid expansion of PTNR's workforce. From June 1990 until February 1991, PTNR had been unable to hire and train personnel rapidly enough to satisfy ongoing production requirements, even though PTNR had added approximately 75 full-time workers. Many workers were earning an additional 50% to 100% of their salary each month in overtime pay, and a number of "casual" day laborers were brought in to help complete tasks with lower skill requirements. In late January of 1991, a second production shift was added in order to keep up with rising demand, and production peaked at nearly 100 units during February.

Despite strong market projections from Trakindo for 1991, several unanticipated economic developments early in the year began to concern Mr. Kahler. First, a change in Japanese government policy during early 1991 had produced a large and rapid decline in the level of Indonesian plywood exports to that nation, which had been the single largest market for these products. The logging industry was heavily influenced by the level of plywood export sales and, as a result of the rapid decline in plywood exports to Japan, demand from the logging sector for earthmoving equipment evaporated. A number of previous equipment orders were postponed or cancelled.

Problems associated with declining plywood exports were exacerbated by the Indonesian government's decision on February 27, 1991, to sharply reduce money supply in order to slow down an increasingly overheated economy and to keep inflation below 10% per year. It was not clear from statements by government spokespersons how long this monetary intervention would last. Nevertheless, in response to prime interest rates of 28% to 30% and limited availability of credit even at these high rates, companies quickly cut back on nonessential expenditures.

Also in early 1991, an increasingly persistent economic recession was lingering in many nations of the world, particularly in North America and Europe, a situation exacerbated by military conflict in Kuwait and Iraq. This recession, combined with declining plywood export demand and tight monetary policy, led to a rapid decline in the Indonesian market for earthmoving equipment. Beginning in late February, reports from Trakindo's salespeople became increasingly pessimistic. Virtually every week, Trakindo's sales projections were reduced and reduced again. The downward trend continued into mid-year, as customers delayed new orders or terminated prior ones in an effort to manage cash flows. The rush of orders received in late 1990 quickly slowed to a trickle. Mr. Kahler described the situation during 1991 and PTNR's response:

> We were essentially dependent upon Trakindo for our market intelligence, and they had been doing a superb job. The company had been on a steady upward curve since before my arrival in Jakarta in June of 1990. We also had a commitment from the partners to fund a major expansion of operations, and the new year brought further positive projections from Trakindo regarding market demand for the coming year.
>
> Around the end of February, the first pessimistic market reports began to filter in. We initially thought that the decline in orders would just be a short term phenomenon. The market had been quite strong over the prior year, and Trakindo's market reports did not suggest any sort of fundamental market shift. The nations of southeast Asia were growing rapidly and Indonesia's economy had been performing at a level equal to or above the average. All signs pointed to an expansion which could be maintained for several more years.
>
> In response to Trakindo's projections of continued growth, in January we moved from a single shift to a double shift production set-up. Thus, when the first market declines were reported by Trakindo, we decided to take advantage of what appeared to be a short breather by focusing our efforts on gaining control of quality and output in this new set-up and to reduce our large order backlog. By March, however, we realized that the decline in demand was stronger than it had first appeared. At least over the short term, we realized that there might indeed be a major change under way in terms of the level of market demand.
>
> Despite the market changes, we weren't sure how serious or long-lasting these developments would be. My predecessor and the other managers at PTNR explained that this type of market downturn had happened to PTNR before, most recently in 1986 when the rupiah underwent a major devaluation. The Indonesian market had achieved an impressive level of growth during the late 1980s, but it was still developing. Indonesia tends to be overly dependent on a few sectors, so it is not unusual for market fluctuations to appear and disappear with little warning. But in the past, the economy had quickly bounced back from such downturns and we wanted to make sure we did not overreact to what might essentially be an economic "hiccup."
>
> To be on the safe side, however, we quickly took several steps to respond to this continued decline in demand. In April, we cut back to a single production shift, except for a few items in

which we were seriously backlogged. This dropped our production volume to 60 units per month, from a peak of nearly 100 in February. We also scaled back our orders for skidpacks and parts, based on estimates from Trakindo on how many units would be needed 6 to 9 months in the future and on the level of inventory we would be building up between now and then. Despite cutting back on new orders, PTNR's inventory began to grow rapidly as skidpack orders, placed in late 1990 and early 1991 based on expected demand of 80 to 100 units per month, continued to arrive and work their way through the system. We tried to manage this flow by storing unneeded skidpacks in our outside storage lot.

Although still well above the level at which new orders were being received, we had little option but to maintain this production volume of about 60 units per month in order to reduce our order backlog and to complete assembly of the large number of skidpacks and partially-assembled machines which had been sitting in our lot waiting for one or a few missing parts. During 1990, demand had grown at a rate much greater than we—and our suppliers—were able to satisfy. By September of that year, we lacked adequate inventory to meet Trakindo's demands, and by the end of 1990 we had an order backlog of over 200 units. We may have lost some sales to Hitachi or Komatsu because we could not supply product quickly enough. We decided our only real option was to use the market slowdown as an opportunity to catch up with demand, rebuild inventory, and avoid any further losses to our competitors once the market finally began to rebound.

The inventory problem that began to arise around March was exacerbated by the situation at Trakindo. Under the joint venture agreement, Trakindo was required to maintain three months' worth of projected sales in inventory. This was required so that Trakindo could ensure rapid response time to customer orders, a key component of Caterpillar's worldwide commitment to customer service. When sales plummeted during March and April, and projections for May and June were revised sharply downward, their inventories relative to sales projections were excessive. Trakindo needed minimal additional inventory from us until their excess inventory was sold off, so they essentially turned off the order spigot at the very time that the scaled up level of skidpacks, pegged to Trakindo's earlier projections of robust market demand, had begun to arrive and work their way through PTNR's production system. Inventory at PTNR—skidpacks, partially assembled units, and finished goods—exploded. We were particularly overstocked on a few items. D6H tractors, for example, had recently been introduced for the logging industry, which was heavily impacted by the recession. The product simply backed up. Transportation diseconomies, tariffs, and high relative production costs prevented us from sending the skidpacks or completed units to other Caterpillar operations. We literally had acres of equipment parked on our production site.

At the same time we cut back to a single shift, we also imposed a hiring freeze, cut back our use of casual day laborers to virtually nil, and eliminated all non-critical overtime. Our intention was to keep our permanent workforce busy and even to let employment decline a bit through attrition, which would help to further reduce problems associated with overstaffing.

During this time, the market continued to decline—and rapidly! In the face of interest rates of over 30%, Trakindo's customers were delaying orders for new equipment and instead choosing to maintain their existing fleet of equipment until they had a better idea of how long the downturn would last. Even with only a single production shift, the absence of new sales meant that the order backlog was steadily declining. At the same time, arrival of previously ordered skidpacks and the completion of work-in-progress equipment caused our inventory levels to continue to swell.

By the end of May, although still receiving skidpacks ordered during our January and February production peak, it was apparent that we would not be able to keep all of our workers busy producing equipment for much longer. Based on Trakindo's projections and our own reading of the market, however, we were still hopeful that the market would begin to turn around soon. We began to pursue other options for keeping workers active. We initiated several activities which had been delayed during the hectic boom time, such as cleaning and repainting the factory, conducting maintenance on equipment, re-arranging work cells, and implementing inventory management programs. We also used this as an opportunity to implement extensive training and cross-training efforts, with programs particularly targeted toward increasing the skills of newer and poorer performing personnel. We allowed people to take their holidays early or to use unpaid leave to attend to personal issues, in order to reduce further the likelihood that people would just be standing around the plant without anything to do.

In addition, we set up task forces to investigate ways to increase asset utilization, to evaluate potential business opportunities, and to undertake departmental reviews of prospective cost savings. We also looked elsewhere for ways to cut costs, such as our decision to delay expansion of our office facilities.

As a result of these actions, we were successful in slashing nonessential costs and in getting operations in excellent condition. Our workforce was better trained than ever, but we were rapidly running out of work for them! We kept a large number of workers busy just keeping the rust under control on the hundreds of units of finished goods inventory which were sitting in our storage yard outside. But the reality was that production levels had to be cut, and they would have to decline further over the next few months.

Prospects deteriorated further during the summer months. Sales and new machine orders were almost non-existent and our backlog of orders had been eliminated. We had over 700 units in inventory—that's enough for over 2 years of sales at 1991 levels. On some models, the excess was much worse.

This month (September) we are finally beginning to benefit from our cutbacks in skidpack orders, a process which we began in March. Much smaller quantities of skidpacks are arriving at the plant, and we hope to begin eliminating some of our backlog of unassembled kits. Yet, even with only 20 to 25 skidpacks arriving per month during the next couple of months, without any additional new orders coming in, the situation doesn't seem likely to improve much in the near future. I feel that I have to make some decisions regarding this situation, and soon, particularly given the imminent prospect of literally dozens of workers being paid to essentially stand around doing nothing!

Options for Confronting the Employment Dilemma _____

Mr. Kahler felt compelled to take some immediate action to help stem the damage. In particular, despite initiatives to reduce employment through attrition and to utilize excess labor for other tasks, the diminished level of demand suggested that PTNR still had many more workers than it needed. Mr. Kahler's own rough estimates suggested that PTNR was currently overstaffed by at least 75 employees. To some extent, Mr. Kahler was concerned that having too many workers in the plant would inflate costs. Of greater concern was the prospect that such a high level of overstaffing might cause serious damage to the disciplined and hardworking culture which had been carefully cultivated in the plant since the company's formation. This concern appeared to be shared by Mr. Singgih, based on discussions between the two men during the past few weeks. In fact, Mr. Kahler thought that he was already beginning to see signs of such a decline in the employees' work ethic, as underutilized workers began to stand around the plant and, in some cases, be disruptive to other employees. Mr. Kahler commented:

Rumors had begun to circulate in the plant that some sort of labor cutback was going to be made. With further production decreases scheduled, at least over the near term, I was concerned that such problems would begin to increase exponentially. Dismissing some or all of the surplus workers might help to increase the level of work for the remaining employees, and might increase the motivation of these "survivors" to continue performing at high levels. This might also prove to be an opportunity for the company to dismiss several employees whose performance had continued to be lower than desired, despite our efforts to provide them with additional training and support.

Yet, terminating any or all of the surplus employees could also have serious implications for the operation. Despite the company's recent rapid growth, PTNR's culture was still very much one of "family." A decision to dismiss workers might harm morale among the employees and within our management team. Based on informal discussions with my functional managers and line supervisors, I knew that they were strongly committed to their work teams and wanted to avoid making any labor cutbacks. In addition, one of these supervisors told me that he had overheard an employee mentioning to his colleague over lunch, "I don't know why they (PTNR management) should consider eliminating our jobs. Why should the employees have to be the ones to suffer for mistakes made by management? We weren't the ones who wrongly predicted sales levels." I suspected that some of my managers might share such a perspective on workforce cutbacks.

Mr. Kahler also wondered what sort of impact a workforce reduction might have on PTNR's reputation in the local community. Indonesia had a very relationship-based society, one in which loyalty to family and friends was highly valued. How might a labor cutback by PTNR influence relations with local suppliers or customers? Would it put the company at a competitive disadvantage? In addition, although Indonesia suffered from high unemployment and PTNR had never experienced difficulty attracting qualified applicants, Mr. Kahler wondered whether a cutback might influence the company's ability to recruit good candidates in the future, particularly for skilled production or management positions. Would cutbacks now, regardless of how desirable they might be in the short term, hamper a quick and effective response by PTNR once demand *did* rebound? It was evident that customers had been maintaining existing, older units rather than purchasing new equipment. Mr. Kahler knew that customers would have to replace this worn-out equipment eventually. In order to avoid losing sales to competition, as had happened in late 1990, he wanted to be ready for the turnaround. The problem was forecasting when that turnaround would occur.

Finally, Mr. Kahler wondered how the Indonesian Ministry of Manpower and other government agencies might respond to a decision to reduce PTNR's workforce. By law, any proposal for substantial labor cutbacks had to be formally approved by the Ministry of Manpower. Given the current economic problems confronting the country, how would this ministry respond to such a proposal? Mr. Kahler did not wish to harm PTNR's relationships with the Indonesian government. As staffing reductions represented an operational issue, it was under the full authority of Mr. Kahler to decide how to resolve this issue. Yet, he had discussed the problem and options for addressing it with Mr. Singgih and the two men were in agreement that action was needed.

Mr. Kahler wondered how he should address this dilemma. If he chose to reduce the workforce, how large of a reduction should he seek, which workers should be targeted, and what should be the process for implementing reductions? Should he lay off the excess workers and then rehire them later, once demand improved, or should he just dismiss them? Or should he do nothing and merely wait out the slow demand period? The $6.7 million facility expansion, which was proceeding according to schedule, was expected to be completed by the end of the year and the equipment would be set up and ready to begin production by approximately April or May of 1992. If market demand increased sufficiently, this expansion was expected to create as many as 60 new positions in 1992. Mr. Kahler expected that many of these new positions could be staffed by excess personnel from current assembly operations and, at a cost of approximately $100 per month per employee, the financial cost of keeping these surplus workers on the payroll until the market improved and the expansion was completed would not be so large.

Mr. Joseph Smith, a Senior Vice President at Caterpillar, was scheduled to arrive in Jakarta next week for meetings with Mr. Kahler and the Chairman of Trakindo. Mr. Smith would certainly be interested in learning more about the difficulties confronting PTNR and what Mr. Kahler was planning to do about them. As he closed his briefcase and prepared for the long bus ride home, Mr. Kahler knew that he would have to make a decision soon.

Part 3

PERSONNEL SELECTION FOR OVERSEAS ASSIGNMENT

Pacific Basin Managers: A *Gaijin*, Not a Woman*

Reading 3.1
Nancy J. Adler

> It doesn't make any difference if I am blue, green, purple or a frog.
> If I have the best product at the best price, the Chinese will buy!

American female manager based in Hong Kong

About the single most uncontroversial, incontrovertible statement to make about women in international management is that there are very few of them. The evidence is both subjective and objective (Caulkin, 1977, p. 58). More strikingly, think how few female managers you have come across, either in your company or elsewhere, while working in Asia. As the international personnel vice president for a North American company, would you choose to send an American or Canadian woman to Asia as an expatriate manager? Would she succeed? Would it be fair to the company and the woman to send her to Asia? Would it be wise not to send her?

International commerce has become vital to North American prosperity. Robert Frederick, chairman of the National Foreign Trade Council, states that eighty percent of United States industry now faces international competition. Already by the beginning of this decade approximately seventy percent of all U.S. firms were conducting a portion of their business abroad (Thal and Cateora, 1979). Canada provides an even more dramatic example of the importance of international business. By 1980, over 500 Canadian-based companies had foreign subsidiaries, an increase of more than 43 percent in just six years (Dun and Bradstreet, 1980). Canadians import nearly one quarter of all the goods they consume and export a slightly larger percentage of their gross national product. Moreover, foreigners own more than half of Canada's manufacturing capacity (Dhawan et al., 1981).

Internationally, Pacific Rim business is the fastest growing in the world. Asian economies, most notably the "Four Tigers"—Hong Kong,

---

*A *gaijin* is a foreigner in Japan

Source: Nancy J. Adler. "Pacific Basin Managers: A *Gaijin*, Not a Woman." *Human Resource Management*, 26(2), 169-191. Copyright © 1987. Reprinted by permission of John Wiley & Sons, Inc.

Korea, Singapore, and Taiwan—have been among the most rapidly developing in recent economic history. At the same time, the People's Republic of China now commands the attention of Western economies, if for no other reason than the size of its potential market, while Japan continues to dominate global economic activity across a widening range of industries. To remain competitive, no major North American firm dare ignore Pacific Rim business.

Along with the globalization of business, stories describing women's changing role in society have gained prominence during the last decade. The United Nations' Decade of Women emphasized both what needs to be done for women to reach equality as well as the many changes now underway. Within this pattern of changes, what role do and will female managers play in Asia? Can women effectively manage in Asia? Can North American companies successfully send expatriate women to Japan? Korea? Hong Kong? And how will North American women manage in Singapore, Pakistan, India, Malaysia, Taiwan, Thailand, Indonesia, or the People's Republic of China?

One wonders if North American companies should respect Asian countries' apparent cultural norms and only send male managers overseas. Yet, with the increasing importance of international business, can North American firms afford to limit their personnel selection decisions to one gender? Women's role in international management has become one of the most important questions facing human resource managers of multinational firms. Due to the economic importance of Pacific Rim business and the apparent dearth of female managers, both local and expatriate, the question assumes particular importance. This article investigates the role of North American women working in Asia for North American firms. It begins by reviewing the context—the role of Asian women working within their own countries—and goes on to report the findings of a study investigating Canadian and American women's role as expatriate managers in Asia.

Do Asians Discriminate Against Women in Management? ————

All cultures differentiate male and female roles, expecting women to behave in certain ways, men in others; for women to fill certain roles and men others. In many cultures, the traditional female role supports attitudes and behaviors contradictory to those of a manager. Therefore women in many parts of the world have failed to aspire to become managers while men have blocked their pursuit of such careers. Asia is no exception. Few Asian women are managers; fewer still have achieved prominence. Using Canada and the United States as a point of comparison, let's look at the role women play as managers in a selection of Asian countries.

Already two decades ago in the United States, more than fifteen percent (15.8%) of working women held managerial and administrative positions, while in Canada almost ten percent (9.5%) held such positions (International Labor Office, 1970). By 1982, American women occupied over a quarter (27.9%) of all managerial and administrative positions (U.S. Dept. of Labor, 1982). Yet top management positions still elude women; even in the 1980s, American women only represent five percent of top executives (Trafford et al., 1984).

By comparison, the number of female managers in Asia remains infinitesimally small, especially those visible to the international business community. Female managers are almost nonexistent within the corporate structure and, more broadly, within the leadership ranks of the business sector. Women constitute less than one percent of the senior managers in Southeast Asian corporations (Singson, 1985, p. 4). But, our North American statistics, focusing primarily on major corporations, have missed some of the involvement of female entrepreneurs and women managing smaller and family-owned Asian companies. For example, Japan has more than 25,000 female company presidents, all of whom manage small to medium-sized firms; none are CEOs of multinationals (Steinhoff and Tanaka, 1986-1987). Similarly, a number of women control major family-owned firms in Thailand and Indonesia, while none hold top positions within corporate structures. Notwithstanding this overlooked involvement, neither the numbers nor the status of Asian women in management equals that of their male counterparts. Why? The following section reviews some of the cultural, legal, and economic dynamics explaining the role of women in management in six very different Asian countries: Indonesia, Japan, the People's Republic of China, India, Singapore, and the Philippines.

Indonesia

In Indonesia, only one in five women (20.8%) participates in the paid labor force, as compared with 60 percent in Sweden and 53 percent in the United States, 51 percent in Canada, 46.7 percent in Japan, and 45.5 percent in Australia (Sorrentino, 1983). This compares with a male labor force participation rate of over 70 percent in the United States (77%), Canada (78.3%), Sweden (74%), Japan (80%), and Australia (79%). While a few Indonesian women hold highly prestigious leadership positions, the vast majority remain outside of the corporate and managerial hierarchy.

As in most areas of the world, Indonesian managers come from the ranks of the educated. In Indonesia, only five percent of the total population has graduated from high school and fewer than one percent from academy or university (Indonesia, 1982, pp. 47, 67 as cited in Crockett, 1987). While the proportion of those educated is rising rapidly, and considerably faster for women than for men, women remain half as likely as men to be highly educated (Crockett, 1987). Not surprisingly, these highly educated women have the highest labor force participation rate, with government administration the second most common occupation after teaching in rural areas and sales in urban areas. Yet almost twice as many educated men as women hold such positions (Crockett, 1987). In the private sector, four times as many men as women hold managerial positions (Crockett, 1987).

Japan

Despite Japan's highly acclaimed advanced industrialization, private industry excludes women from most responsible managerial positions (Dahlby, 1977). In 1955, the proportion of professionals and managers in the entire female labor force was 3.5 percent, rising to only 8.5 percent by 1977 (Japan Census Bureau, 1977 as cited by Osako, 1978). By the 1980s, primarily due to women reentering the workforce after raising their families, the proportion of women working had risen to one of the world's highest, now constituting almost forty percent (39.7%) of the workforce (Women's Bureau, 1986), approximately on a par with Sweden (Hiroshi, 1982, p. 319; also see Cook, 1980). Yet, women continue to hold few managerial positions, especially in major corporations (see Steinhoff and Tanaka, 1986-1987). For example, the 1983 *Who's Who in Japanese Business,* covering the 1754 major companies listed in Japan's eight Stock Exchanges, included only 68 women among the 160,764 Japanese managers listed (Suzuki and Narapareddy, 1985). Moreover, fifty percent of all Japanese firms have no female managers, and that percent has remained constant since 1955 (Osako, 1978, p. 15). Of the Japanese women who have attained managerial status, almost all work for small and medium-sized businesses, not for multinational corporations. Despite recent legal changes, no major increase in the number of women in the latter category is predicted.

While cultural and legal constraints partially explain the role of women in Japanese management, the lifetime employment system explains their absence from major corporations. Culturally, a well-known Confucian saying states, "A woman is to obey her father as daughter, her husband as wife, and her son as aged mother" (Osako, 1978, p. 17). Not surprisingly, given this tradition, the Japanese have neither viewed women as authority figures nor as decision makers. Strong cultural norms have made it difficult for Japanese companies to send a woman on domestic or international business trips with a male colleague if not accompanied by a second man. Laws, including the Labor Standards Act, restrict certain positions to men, and preclude women from working overtime or at night in many professions. In general, Japanese society expects women to work until marriage, quit to raise children, and return, only as needed, to low level and part-time positions after age forty. Thus by 1985, women constituted seventy (70.7%) percent of all part-time workers (Women's Bureau, 1986). Clearly, in Japan, while the home has continued to be women's domain, the workplace remains the domain of men. Given this pattern, combined with major Japanese corporations' lifetime employment and promotion systems, most have not seen it as worthwhile to develop women for significant management positions. Major corporations generally place women on separate career paths from men, frequently treating them differently in wages, promotion, and retirement. Today, Japanese women seeking managerial careers often must take positions in foreign, rather than Japanese, firms (Kaminski and Paiz, 1984).

The People's Republic of China

Although one Chinese saying states that "Women hold up half of the world," numerous other traditional folk sayings and proverbs belittle women and disparage their leadership abilities. For example, when a woman becomes a leader, some Chinese say that it is like "a donkey taking the place of a horse which can only lead to trouble" (Croll, 1977, p. 596). Since the 1970s, the anti-Confucian and Lin Piao campaigns tried to create more favorable conditions for women by identifying obstacles to redefining women's role and improving their status (Jen-min jih pao, 1974). The media reported men's and women's groups "as coming to a new awareness of an old problem through the recognition of their ideological constraints originating in the Confucian principle of male supremacy" (Croll, 1977, p. 597). However, women are still under-represented in political and leadership positions, given unequal pay in rural areas, and following traditional courtship and marriage customs that maintain work-related gender differentiation and disproportionate shares of household work (Croll, 1977, p. 596; also see Davin, 1976). Given the rapidly changing political and economic environment in China and its increasing openness to international markets, it is difficult to assess the exact proportion of women currently holding managerial and executive positions. My own interviews with female Chinese managers in 1986 confirmed the continued pattern of placing women's primary responsibility in the home, with equality at work most accessible to those in lower positions and those whose children were grown up and thus beyond the need for daily maternal care.* Whereas physical labor knows few gender boundaries in the People's Republic of China, access to top managerial positions in industry and government remains the domain of men to a substantial degree.

India

While women have been guaranteed constitutional equality and occupied prominent positions in government since India's independence in 1947, only recently have they begun to take managerial positions in business organizations. A limited survey of thirty-three female executives

---

*Interviews were conducted in Tianjin with female managers from throughout the People's Republic of China in a management seminar jointly sponsored by the PRC's State Economic Commission and the U.S. Department of Commerce.

across a wide range of industries concluded that while Indian women have fewer opportunities for promotion than men, once promoted they perform as well as men in executive positions. However, while these Indian women believed that they could successfully combine the roles of wife and executive, some questioned the appropriateness of continuing to work with small children (Singh, 1980).

Singapore

Singapore has been one of the most rapidly developing "newly industrialized countries" in the Pacific Basin. To overcome critical human resource shortages, the government launched a major campaign in the early 1980s encouraging Singaporian women to rejoin the workforce, including supporting quality child care services, flexible work scheduling and incentives, training and retraining programs, and improved societal attitudes toward career women (Report of the Task Force on Female Participation in the Labor Force, 1985, pp. ii-iii). By 1983, Singaporian women constituted more than a third (35.5%) of the labor force and more than a sixth (17.8%) of the administrators and managers (up from 7% in 1980; Chan, 1987). Chan (1987) attributes the increases to prosperous economic conditions, the government's development policies encouraging women's participation in the workforce, and women's own career aspirations. While seeing Singapore's rapid growth as an enabling condition, she also notes the 1984 economic downturn's disproportionately adverse affect on women.

The Philippines

While women from prominent families clearly hold influential positions in Filipino political and economic life, the overall situation for women differs little from that in other Pacific Rim countries. The Philippine Labor Code prohibits discrimination against women with respect to rates of pay and conditions of employment (Foz, 1979). Yet, while women accounted for approximately a third of the labor force by 1976, less than three percent (2.7%) of the working women held administrative or managerial positions in government or business; a figure representing less than one percent of the total managerial positions (Ople, 1981). Their numbers have not increased. Philippine society still holds deeply rooted beliefs regarding the role of women at home and at work (Miralao, 1980). Social pressures in Philippine society, where both men and women frequently support strongly differentiated sex role stereotypes, make it difficult for a Filipina to choose a career instead of a family or to successfully combine marriage, career, and children (Dept. of Sociology, 1977; also see Castillo, 1977 and Gosselin, 1984).

Women in International Management _____

Given the culturally mandated scarcity of local female managers in most Asian countries, can North American companies successfully send female expatriate managers to Asia? More specifically, can Canadian and American companies send women to Japan, Korea, Hong Kong, the Philippines, the People's Republic of China, Singapore, Thailand, India, Pakistan, Malaysia, or Indonesia? Is the experience of local women—i.e., their relative absence from the managerial ranks—the best predictor of success, or the lack thereof, for expatriate women?

The following research study presents the story of a "noun," "woman," that appears to have gotten mixed up with an "adjective," "female" manager. It is the unfolding of a set of assumptions predicting how Asians would treat North American female managers based on North Americans' beliefs concerning Asians' treatment of their own women. The problem with the story, and with the set of assumptions, is that it has proven to be wrong. The assumptions fail to predict reality accurately.

The Study _____

This research on female managers in Asia is part of a four part study on the role of North American women as expatriate managers.* In the first part, 686 Canadian and American firms were surveyed to identify the number of women sent overseas as expatriate managers. The survey identified over thirteen thousand (13,338) expatriates, of whom 402, or 3%, were women—that is, 3.3% of American and 1.3% of Canadian expatriate managers are female. Overall, North American firms send thirty-two times as many male as female expatriate managers overseas (see Adler, 1984c and 1979).

Not surprisingly, larger companies send proportionately more women than do smaller companies, with financial institutions significantly leading other industries. However, the three percent, while significantly less than North American women represented in domestic management, should not be viewed as a poor showing, but rather as the beginning of a trend. The vast majority of North American female managers who have ever been sent abroad in expatriate status are currently overseas.

_____

*I would like to thank the Social Sciences of Humanities Research Council of Canada for their generous support of this research. A special thanks to Ellen Bessner and Blossom Shafer for their assistance in all phases of the research and to Dr. Homa Mahmoudi for her help, creativity, and professional insight in conducting the Asian interviews.

The second, third, and fourth parts of the study attempted to explain why so few North American women work as international managers. Each part was structured around one of the three most common "myths" about women in international management, that is:

- MYTH 1: Women do not want to be international managers.

- MYTH 2: Companies refuse to send women overseas.

- MYTH 3: Foreigners' prejudice against women renders them ineffective, even when interested and sent.

These beliefs were labelled "myths" because, while widely believed by both men and women, they had never been tested.

Women's Interest in International Careers

Are women less interested than men in pursuing international careers? The second part of the study tested this myth by surveying 1129 graduating MBAs from seven management schools in the United States, Canada, and Europe. The overwhelming result was an impressive case of no significant difference: male and female MBAs display equal interest, or disinterest, in pursuing international careers. Eighty-four percent of the MBAs said they would like an international assignment at some time during their careers. However, both males and females agreed that the opportunities were fewer for women than for men, and fewer for women pursuing international careers vs. domestic careers. While there may have been a difference in the past, today's male and female MBAs appear equally interested in international work and expatriate positions (see Adler, 1984b and 1986).

Corporate Resistance to Assigning Women Overseas

To test the corporate resistance "myth," personnel vice presidents and managers from sixty major North American multinationals were surveyed (see Adler, 1984a). Based on their responses, over half the companies (54%) hesitate to send women overseas. This is almost four times as many as those hesitating to select women for domestic assignments (54% as compared with 14%). Almost three-quarters believe foreigners are prejudiced against female managers (73%). Similarly, seventy percent believe that women, especially married women in dual-career marriages, would be reticent to accept a foreign assignment, if not totally uninterested. For certain locations, the personnel executives expressed concern about the women's physical safety, the hazards involved in travelling in underdeveloped countries, and, especially for single women, the isolation and potential loneliness. These results concur with those from a survey of 100 top managers in *Fortune* 500 firms operating overseas in which the majority believed that women face overwhelming resistance when seeking management positions in the international divisions of U.S. firms (Thal and Cateora, 1979).

Foreigners' Reactions to Female Expatriates

Why do three-quarters of the North American firms believe foreigners are prejudiced against expatriate women? Perhaps, due to their lack of experience, companies predict female expatriates' success, or the lack thereof, based on the role and treatment of local women within the particular foreign culture. Perhaps the scarcity of Asian women working as managers (substantiated by statistics cited in the prior section) has led North American companies to conclude that North American women would not receive the respect necessary to succeed in managerial and professional assignments. When interviewed, more than half of the international personnel executives declared that it would neither be fair to the woman nor the company to send a female manager to Asia when it could be predicted, based on the treatment of local women, that she would have difficulty succeeding. The fundamental question was, and remains, is this a valid basis for prediction?

Foreign Female Managers in Asia ————————————————————

To investigate the third myth, foreigners' prejudice against women rendering them ineffective as international managers, fifty-two female expatriate managers were interviewed while in Asia or after returning from Asia to North America. Due to multiple foreign postings, the fifty-two women represent sixty-one Asian assignments. The greatest number resided in Hong Kong (34%), followed by Japan (25%), Singapore (16%), the Philippines and Australia (5% each), Indonesia and Thailand (4% each), and at least one each in Korea, India, Taiwan, and the People's Republic of China. Since most of the women held regional responsibility, they worked throughout Asia, rather than just in their location of foreign residence. Of those working in Asia, financial institutions sent the vast majority (71%). Other industries sending more than two women to Asia included publishing (7%) and petroleum (6%). Those sending one or two women include: advertising, film distribution, service industries (including accounting, law, executive search, and computers), retail food, electronic appliances, pharmaceuticals, office equipment, sporting goods, and soaps and cosmetics.

On average, the female expatriates' assignments lasted two and a half years (29.7 months), ranging from six months to six years. Salaries in 1983, before benefits, varied from US $27,000 to US $54,000, and averaged US $34,500. The female expatriate managers supervised from zero to 25 subordinates, with the average falling below five (4.6). Their titles and levels in the organization varied considerably: some held very junior positions—"trainee" and assistant account manager—while others held quite senior positions—including one regional vice president. In no case did a female expatriate hold the company's number one position in the region or in any country.

Female Expatriates: Who Are They?

As the prior description indicates, the female expatriates were fairly junior within their organizations and careers. While their ages varied from 23 to 41 years old, the average female expatriate was under thirty (28.8). Nearly two-thirds (62%) were single, with only three having children. Five of the women married while overseas—all to other expatriates. While the women are considerably younger than the typical male expatriate manager, their age probably does not reflect any systematic discrimination for or against them. Rather, it is an artifact of the relatively high proportion of women sent by financial institutions—an industry that selects fairly junior managers for overseas assignments—and the relatively low proportion in manufacturing, where international assignees are generally quite senior (e.g., country or regional director).

The women were very well educated and quite internationally experienced. Almost all held graduate degrees, with MBAs the most common. Over three-quarters had extensive international interests and experience prior to their present company sending them overseas. For example, more than three-quarters (77%) had travelled internationally and almost two-thirds (61%) had had an international focus in their studies prior to joining the company. On average, the women spoke two and a half languages, with some speaking as many as six fluently. Based on subjective observation during the interviews, the women, as a group, had excellent social skills, and, by western standards, were very good looking.

The Decision to Go Overseas

How did the companies and the female managers decide on the overseas transfers? In the majority of cases, the female expatriates were "firsts," with only five women (10%) following another woman into the international position. Of the 90 percent who were "firsts," almost a quarter (22%) represented the first female manager the firm had ever expatriated anywhere; 14 percent were the first women sent to Asia, a quarter were the first sent to the particular country, and 20 percent were the first filling the specific position. Clearly, neither the women nor the companies had the luxury of role models; few could follow prior patterns. With the exception of a few major New York based financial institutions, both the women and the companies found themselves experimenting in hope of uncertain success.

The decision process leading the company to send a female manager to Asia could be described as one of mutual education. In more than four out of five cases (83%), the woman initially introduced the idea of an international assignment to her boss and company. For only six women (11%) did the company first suggest it to her, while for another three (6%) the suggestion was mutual.

Women used a number of strategies to "educate" their companies. Many women explored the possibility of an expatriate assignment during their original job interview and eliminated from consideration companies that were totally against the idea. In other cases, women informally introduced the idea to their bosses and continued informally mentioning it "at appropriate moments" until the company ultimately decided to offer them overseas positions. A few women formally applied for a number of expatriate positions prior to actually being selected. Some of the female managers described themselves as "strategizing their career" to be international, primarily by attempting to be in the right place at the right time. For example, one woman, who predicted that Hong Kong would be her firm's next major business center, arranged to assume responsibility for the Hong Kong desk in New York, while leaving the rest of Asia to a male colleague. The strategy paid off. Within a year, the company sent her, and not her male colleague, to Hong Kong. Overall, the women described themselves as needing to encourage their companies to consider the possibility of expatriating women in general and themselves in particular. In most cases, they described their companies as failing to recognize the possibility of expatriating women, not as having thoroughly considered the idea and having rejected it. In general, the obstacle was naiveté, not conscious rejection. Many women confronted numerous instances of corporate resistance prior to being sent. For example:

> *Malaysia.* According to one woman being considered for an assignment in Malaysia, "Management assumed that women don't have the physical stamina to survive in the tropics. They claimed I couldn't hack it."

> *Thailand.* "My company didn't want to send a woman to that 'horrible part of the world.' They think Bangkok is an excellent place to send single men, but not a woman. They said they would have trouble getting a work permit, which wasn't true."

> *Japan and Hong Kong.* "Everyone was more or less curious if it would work. My American boss tried to advise me, 'Don't be upset if it's difficult in Japan and Korea.' The American male manager in Tokyo was also hesitant. Finally the Chinese boss in Hong Kong said, 'We have to try!'"

> *Japan.* "Although I was the best qualified, I was not offered the position in Japan until the senior Japanese manager in Tokyo said, 'We are very flexible in Japan'; then they sent me."

While only true in a few cases, some women described severe company resistance to sending female managers abroad. For those women, it appeared that their firms offered them a position only after all potential male candidates for the post had turned it down. For example:

> *Thailand.* "Every advance in responsibility is because the Americans had no choice. I've never been chosen over someone else."

Japan. "They never would have considered me. But then the financial manager in Tokyo had a heart attack and they had to send someone. So they sent me, on a month's notice, as a temporary until they could find a man to fill the permanent position. It worked out and I stayed."

While most companies sent women in the same status as male expatriates, some showed their hesitation by offering temporary or travel assignments rather than true expatriate positions.

Hong Kong. "After offering me the job, they hesitated, 'Could a woman work with the Chinese?' So my job was defined as temporary, a one year position to train a Chinese man to replace me. I succeeded and became permanent."

Although this may appear to be a logically cautious strategy, in reality, it tends to create an unfortunate self-fulfilling prophecy. As a number of women reported, if the company is not convinced that you will succeed (and therefore, for example, offers you a temporary rather than a permanent position), it will communicate its lack of confidence to foreign colleagues and clients as a lack of commitment. The foreigners will then mirror the home company's behavior by also failing to take you seriously. Assignments can become very difficult or even fail altogether when the company's initial confidence and commitment are lacking. As one women in Indonesia said, "It is very important to clients that I am permanent. It increases trust, and that's critical."

Many women claimed that the most difficult hurdle in their international career involved getting sent overseas in the first place, not—as most had predicted—gaining the respect of foreigners and succeeding once there.

Did It Work? The Impact of Being Female

When describing their actual experience working in Asia, almost all (97%) of the North American women said it had been a success. While their descriptions are strictly subjective, a number of more objective indicators suggest that most assignments did, in fact, succeed. For example, most firms—after experimenting with their first female expatriate—decided to send other women overseas. Moreover, many companies promoted the women based on their overseas performance. In addition, many companies offered the women a second international assignment following the completion of the first one. In only two cases did women describe failure experiences: one in Australia and the other in Singapore. For the first woman, it was her second international posting, following a successful experience in Latin America and followed by an equally successful assignment in Singapore. For the second woman, the Singapore assignment was her only overseas posting.

Prior to the interviews, I had expected the women to describe a series of difficulties caused by their being female and a corresponding set of creative solutions to each difficulty. This was not the case. Almost half of the women (42%) reported that "being female" served more as an advantage than a disadvantage. Sixteen percent found "being female" to have both positive and negative effects, while another 22 percent saw it as "irrelevant" or neutral. Only one woman in five (20%) found it to be primarily negative.

Advantages. The women reported numerous professional advantages to being female. Most frequently, they described the advantage of being highly visible. Foreign clients were curious about them, wanted to meet them, and remembered them after the first meeting. It therefore appeared easier for the women than for their male colleagues to gain access to foreign clients' time and attention. Some examples of this high visibility, accessibility, and memorability include:

> *Japan.* "It's the visibility as an expat, and even more as a woman. I stick in their minds. I know I've gotten more business than my two male colleagues. They are extra interested in me."

> *Thailand.* "Being a woman is never a detriment. They remembered me better. Fantastic for a marketing position. It's better working with Asians than with the Dutch, British, or Americans."

> *India and Pakistan.* "In India and Pakistan, being a woman helps for marketing and client contact. I got in to see customers because they had never seen a female banker before. . . . Having a female banker adds value to the client."

The female managers also described the advantages of good interpersonal skills and their belief that men could talk more easily about a wider range of topics with women than with other men. For example:

> *Indonesia.* "I often take advantage of being a woman. I'm more supportive than my male colleagues. . . . They relax and talk more. And fifty percent of my effectiveness is based on volunteered information."

> *Korea.* "Women are better at treating men sensitively, and they just like you. One of my Korean clients told me, 'I really enjoyed the lunch and working with you.' "

In addition, many of the women described the higher status accorded women in Asia and that that status was not denied them as foreign female managers. They often felt that they received special treatment that their male colleagues did not receive. Clearly, it was always salient that they were women, but being a woman did not appear to be antithetical to being a manager.

> *Hong Kong.* "Single female expats travel easier and are treated better. Never hassled. No safety issues. Local offices take better

care of you. They meet you, take you through customs. . . . It's the combination of treating you like a lady and a professional."

Japan. "It's an advantage that attracts attention. They are interested in meeting a *gaijin*, a foreign woman. Women attract more clients. On calls to clients, they elevate me, give me more rank. If anything, the problem, for men and women, is youth, not gender."

Moreover, most of the women claimed benefits from a "halo effect." As they described, most of their foreign colleagues and counterparts had never met or previously worked with a female expatriate manager. At the same time, most of the foreign community was highly aware of how unusual it was for American and Canadian firms to send female managers to Asia. Hence, the Asians tended to assume that the women would not have been sent unless they were "the best," and therefore expected them to be "very, very good."

Japan. "Women are better at putting people at ease. It's easier for a woman to convince a man . . . The traditional woman's role . . . inspires confidence and trust, less suspicious, not threatening. They assumed I must be good if I was sent. They become friends."

Indonesia. "It's easier being a woman here than in any place in the world, including New York City. . . . I never get the comments I got in New York, like 'What is a nice woman like you doing in this job?' "

No impact. Other women found "being female" to have no impact whatsoever on their professional life. For the most part, these were women working primarily with the Chinese:

Hong Kong. "There's no difference. They respect professionalism . . . including in Japan There is no problem in Asia."

Hong Kong. "There are many expat and foreign women in top positions here. If you are good at what you do, they accept you. One Chinese woman told me, 'Americans are always watching you. One mistake and you are done. Chinese take a while to accept you and then stop testing you.' "

Hong Kong. "It doesn't make any difference if you are blue, green, purple or a frog. If you have the best product at the best price, they'll buy."

Disadvantages. The women also cited a number of disadvantages caused by being female. Interestingly enough, the majority of the disadvantages involved the women's relationship to their own home companies, not their relationships with Asian clients. As discussed earlier, a major problem involved difficulty obtaining the foreign assignment in the first place. A subsequent problem involved the home company limiting opportunities and job scope once overseas. More than half the female expatriates described difficulty in persuading their home companies to give them the latitude equivalent to that given their male colleagues, especially initially. Some companies, out of concern for the women's safety, limited their travel (and thus their region), excluding very remote, rural, and underdeveloped areas. Other companies, as mentioned previously, limited the duration of the women's assignments to six months or a year, rather than the more standard two to three years. For example:

> *Japan.* "My problem is overwhelmingly with Americans. They identify it as a male market . . . geisha girls . . ."

> *Thailand* (Petroleum company). "The Americans wouldn't let me on the drilling rigs, because they said there were no accommodations for a woman. Everyone blames it on something else. They gave me different work. They had me working on the sidelines, not planning and communicating with drilling people. It's the expat Americans, not the Thais, who'll go to someone else before they come to me."

Another disadvantage that some companies placed on the women was limiting them to work only internally with company employees, rather than externally with clients. The companies' often implicit assumption was that their own employees were somehow less prejudiced than were outsiders. Interestingly, women often found the opposite to be true: they faced more problems within their own organizations than externally with clients. As one American woman described:

> *Hong Kong.* "It was somewhat difficult internally. They feel threatened, hesitant to do what I say, resentful. They assume I don't have the credibility that a man would have. Perhaps it's harder internally than externally because client relationships are one-on-one and internally it's more of a group, or perhaps it's harder because they have to live with it longer internally, or perhaps it's because they fear that I'm setting a precedent or because they fear criticism from their peers."

Managing foreign clients' and colleagues' initial expectations proved difficult for many of the women. Some described initial meetings with Asians as tricky. Since most Asians previously had never met a North American expatriate woman holding a managerial position, there was considerable ambiguity as to who she was, her status, her level of expertise, authority, and responsibility, and therefore the appropriate form of address and demeanor toward her:

> *Hong Kong (Asia Region).* "It took extra time to establish credibility with the Japanese and Chinese. One Japanese manager said to me, 'When I first met you, I thought you would not be any good because you were a woman' . . . . The rest of Asia is OK."

People's Republic of China. "I speak Chinese, which is a plus. But they'd talk to the men, not to me. They'd assume that I, as a woman, have no authority. The Chinese only want to deal with top, top, top level people, and there is always a man at a higher level."

Since most of the North American women whom Asians had met previously had been male expatriate managers' wives or secretaries, the Asians naturally assumed that "she too is not a manager." Hence, as the women claimed, initial conversations often were directed at male colleagues, not toward the newly arrived female managers. Senior male colleagues, particularly those from the head office, became very important in redirecting the focus of early discussions back toward the women. If well done, old patterns were quickly broken and smooth ongoing work relationships established. If ignored or poorly managed, such challenges to credibility, authority, and responsibility became chronic and undermined the women's potential effectiveness.

The North American women clearly had more difficulty gaining respect from North American and European men working in Asia than from the Asians themselves. Some even suggested that the expatriate community in Asia has attracted many "very traditional" men who were not particularly open to the idea of women in management—whether at home or abroad. As three of the women described:

Singapore. "Colonial British don't accept women; very male. There are no women in their management levels. I got less reaction from the Chinese. The Chinese are only interested in if you can do the job."

Hong Kong. "British men . . . you must continually prove yourself. You can't go to lunch with U.K. expat company men. The senior U.K. guys become uncomfortable and the younger U.K. guys get confused as to lunch being a social or business occasion. So I hesitate inviting them. Interaction is just tenuous from both sides."

Hong Kong. "The older men had trouble imagining me with the bank in ten years."

As mentioned earlier, many women described the most difficult aspect of the foreign assignment as getting sent overseas in the first place. Overcoming resistance from North American head offices frequently proved more challenging than gaining foreign clients' and colleagues' respect and acceptance. In most cases, assumptions about Asians' prejudice against female expatriate managers appear to have been exaggerated. Predicted prejudice and reality did not match. Why? Perhaps foreigners are not as prejudiced as we think.

The *Gaijin* Syndrome ─────────────────────────────

Throughout the interviews, one pattern became particularly clear. First and foremost, foreigners are seen as foreigners. Similar to their male colleagues, female expatriates are seen as foreigners, not as locals. A woman who is a foreigner (*gaijin*) is not expected to act like the locals. Therefore, the rules governing the behavior of local women which limit their access to management and managerial responsibility, do not apply to foreign women. Whereas women are considered the "culture bearers" in almost all societies, foreign women in no way assume or are expected to assume that role. As one woman in Japan said, "The Japanese are very smart, they can tell that I am not Japanese and they do not expect me to act as a Japanese woman. They will allow and condone behavior from foreign women which would be absolutely unacceptable from their own women." Similarly, as Ranae Hyer, a Tokyo-based personnel vice president of the Bank of America's Asia Division, said,

> Being a foreigner is so weird to the Japanese that the marginal impact of being a woman is nothing. If I were a Japanese woman, I couldn't be doing what I'm doing here. But they know perfectly well that I'm not (Morgenthaler, 1978).

Many interviewees related similar examples of female expatriates' unique status as "foreign women" rather than as "women" per se. For example:

> *Japan and Korea.* "Japan and Korea are the hardest, but they know that I'm an American woman and they don't expect me to be like a Japanese or Korean woman. It's possible to be effective even in Japan and Korea, if you send a senior woman, with at least three to four years of experience, expecially if she's fluent in Japanese."

> *Japan.* "It's the novelty, especially in Japan, Korea, and Pakistan. All of the general managers met with me . . . It was much easier for me, especially in Osaka. They were charming. They didn't want me to feel bad. They thought I would come back if they gave me business. You see, they could separate me from the local women."

> *Pakistan.* "Will I have problems? No! There is a double standard between expats and local women. The Pakistanis test you, but you enter as a respected person."

> *Japan.* "I don't think the Japanese could work for a Japanese woman, . . . but they just block it out for foreigners."

> *Hong Kong.* "Hong Kong is very cosmopolitan. I'm seen as an expat, not as an Asian, even though I am an Asian American."

It appears that we may have mixed up the adjective and noun in predicting Asians' reactions to North American women. We expected the primary descriptor of female expatriate managers to be "woman," and predicted their success based on the success of the Asian women in each country. In fact, the primary descriptor is "foreign," and the best predictor of success is the success of other North Americans in the country. Asians see female expatriates as foreigners who happen to be women, not as women who happen to be foreigners. The difference is crucial. Given the ambiguity involved in sending women into new areas of the world, our assumptions of the greater salience of gender (male/female) over nationality (foreign/local) has led us to make inaccurate predictions as to their potential to succeed as managers.

Recommendations ————————————————————————————

It is clear from the experience of the women described and quoted in this article that North American female expatriates can succeed as managers in Asia. In considering expatriating them, both the companies and the women themselves should consider a number of aspects of the foreign assignment.

First, do not assume it will not work. Do not assume that foreigners will treat expatriate female managers the same way they treat their own women. Our assumptions about the salience of gender over nationality have led to totally inaccurate predictions. Therefore, do not confuse adjectives and nouns; do not use the success or failure of local women to predict that of foreign women. Similarly, do not confuse the role of the spouse with the role of a manager. While the single most common reason for male expatriates' failure and early return from an overseas assignment has been dissatisfaction of the spouse, this does not mean that women cannot cope in the overseas environment. The role of the spouse (whether male or female) is much more ambiguous and consequently the cross-cultural adjustment much more demanding than for the person in the role of the employee. While wives (female spouses) have had trouble adjusting, their situation is not analogous to that of female managers and therefore not predictive.

Second, do not assume that a woman will not want to go overseas. Ask her. While both single and married women need to balance private and professional life considerations, many are highly interested in taking overseas assignments. Based on the expressed attitudes of today's graduating MBAs, the number of women interested in working overseas will increase in the 1980s and 1990s, not decrease. Given that most expatriate packages have been designed to meet the needs of traditional families (working husband, non-working wife, and children), companies should be prepared to modify benefits packages to meet the demands of single status women and dual-career couples.

Such modifications might include increased lead time on announcing assignments, executive search services for the partner in dual-career couples, and payment for "staying connected"—including telephone and airfare expense—for those couples who choose to commute rather than relocating overseas.

Third, give a woman every opportunity to succeed. Send her in full status—not as a temporary or experimental expatriate—with the appropriate title to communicate the home company's commitment to her. Do not be surprised if foreign colleagues and clients direct their comments to the male managers rather than the new female expatriate in initial meetings, but do not accept such behavior. Redirect discussion, where appropriate, to the woman. Such behavior should not be interpreted as prejudice, but rather as the reaction to an ambiguous, atraditional situation.

The female expatriates had a number of suggestions for other women following in their footsteps. First, as they suggest, presume naïveté, not malice. Realize that sending women to Asia is new, perceived as risky, and still fairly poorly understood. In most cases, companies and foreigners are operating on untested assumptions, many of which are faulty, not out of a basis of prejudice. The most successful approach is to be gently persistent in educating the company to the possibility of sending a woman overseas. Second, given that expatriating women is perceived as risky, no woman will be sent if she is not seen as technically and professionally excellent. According to the women, it never hurts to arrange to be in the right place at the right time. And third, for single women, the issue of loneliness and for married women, the issue of managing a dual-career relationship, must be addressed. Contact with other expatriate women has proven helpful in both cases. For dual-career couples, most women considered it critical that they (1) discussed the possible international assignment with their husband long before it became a reality and (2) created options that would work for them as a couple. For most couples, that meant creating options that had never or rarely been tried in their particular company.

Global competition is and will continue to be intense in the 1980s and '90s. Companies need every advantage to win. The option of limiting the international area to one gender is an archaic luxury of the past. There is no doubt that the most successful North American companies will draw on both men and women to manage their international operations. The only question is how quickly and how effectively companies will manage the introduction of women into the worldwide managerial workforce.

References

Adler, N. J. "Do MBAs want international careers?" *International Journal of Intercultural Relations*, 1986, 10 (3), 277-300.

Adler, N. J. "Expecting international success: Female managers overseas." *Columbia Journal of World Business,* Fall 1984a, XIX (3), 79-85.

Adler, N. J. "Women as androgynous managers: A conceptualization of the potential for American women in international management." *International Journal of Intercultural Relations,* 1979, 3 (4), 407-435.

Adler, N. J. "Women do not want international careers: And other myths about international management." *Organizational Dynamics,* Autumn 1984b, XIII (2), 66-79.

Adler, N. J. "Women in international management: Where are they?" *California Management Review,* Summer 1984c, XXVI (4), 78-89.

Castillo, G. T. *The Filipino woman as manpower: The image and empirical reality.* Laguna, Philippines: University of the Philippines, 1977.

Caulkin, S. "Women in management." *Management Today,* February 1977, 80-83.

Chan, A. "Women managers in Singapore: Citizen for tomorrow's economy." In Adler, N. J. and Izraeli, D. (eds.), *Women in Management Worldwide.* Armonk, N.Y.: M. E. Sharpe, 1987 (in press).

Cook, A. H. *Working women in Japan: Discrimination, resistance and reform.* Ithaca, N.Y.: School of Labor and Industrial Relations, 1980.

Crockett, V. R. "Women in management in Indonesia." In Adler, N. J. and Izraeli, D. (eds.), *Women in Management Worldwide.* Armonk, N.Y.: M. E. Sharpe, 1987 (in press).

Croll, E. "A recent movement to redefine the role and status of women." *China Quarterly,* 1977, 69, 591-597.

Dahlby, T. "In Japan, women don't climb the corporate ladder." *New York Times.* September 1977, 18, section 3, 11.

Davin, D. *Women work: Women and the party in revolutionary China.* Great Britain: Oxford University Press, 1976, 53-69, 210-213.

Department of Sociology. *Stereotype, status, and satisfaction: The Filipina among Filipinos.* Quezon City, Philippines: University of the Philippines, 1977.

Dhawan, K. C., Etemad, H., and Wright, R. W. *International business: A Canadian perspective.* Reading, Mass.: Addison-Wesley, 1981.

Dunn & Bradstreet Canada Ltd., *Canadian Key Business Directory 1980.* Toronto: Dunn & Bradstreet Canada Ltd., 1980.

Foz, V. B. *The labor code of the Philippines and its implementing rules and regulations.* Quezon City, Philippines: Philippine Law Gazette, 1979.

Galenson, M. *Women and work: An international comparison.* ILR Paperback No. 13. Ithaca, N.Y.: N.Y. State School of Industrial and Labor Relations, Cornell University, 1973.

Gosselin, M. "Situation des femmes aux Philippines." *Communiqu'elles.* Janvier 1984, 11-12.

Hiroshi, T. "Working women in business corporations: The management viewpoint (Japan)." *Japan Quarterly,* July-September 1982, 29, 319-323.

Indonesia, Biro Pusat Statistik (Central Bureau of Statistics). Population of Indonesia Series S Number 2: Results of 1980 Population Census, 1982.

International Labor Office. "Statistical Information on Women's Participation in Economic Activity." Mimeographed. Geneva: ILO, 1970, Table VIII; as cited in Galenson, 1973, Table 4, 23.

Jen-min-jih-pao (Editorial), "Let All Women Rise Up," March 8, 1974.

Kaminski, M. and Paiz, J. "Japanese women in management: Where are they?" *Human Resource Management,* Fall 1984, 23 (3), 277-292.

Miralao, V. *Women and men in development: Findings from a pilot study.* Quezon City, Philippines: Institute of Philippine Culture, 1980.

Morgenthaler, E. "Women of the world: More U.S. firms put females in key posts in foreign countries." *Wall Street Journal,* March 16, 1978, 1, 27.

Ople, B. F. *Working managers, elites: The human spectrum of development.* Manila, Philippines: Institute of Labor and Management, 1981.

Osako, M. M. "Dilemmas of Japanese professional women." *Social Problems,* 1978, 26, 15-25.

Report of the Task Force on Female Participation in the Labor Force. National Productivity Council Committee on Productivity in the Manufacturing Sector, Singapore, January 1985.

Singh, D. "Women executives in India." *Management International Review,* August 1980, 20, 53-60.

Singson, E. R. "Women in executive positions." Paper presented at the 1985 Congress on Women in Decision Making, The Singapore Business and Professional Women's Association, September 1985, 22-23.

Sorrentino, C. "International comparisons of labor force participation, 1960-81. *Monthly Labor Review,* February 1983, 23-36.

Steinhoff, P. G. and Tanaka, K. "Women executives in Japan." *International Studies of Management and Organization,* Fall-Winter, 1986-87 (in press).

Suzuki, N. and Narapareddy, V. "Problems and prospects for the female corporate executives: A cross-cultural perspective." Working paper, University of Illinois at Urbana-Champaign, 1985.

Thal, N. L., and Cateora, P. R. "Opportunities for women in international business." *Business Horizons,* 22 (6), December 1979, 21-27.

Trafford, A., Avery, R., Thorton, J., Carey, J., Galloway, J., and Sanoff, A. "She's Come a Long Way Or Has She?" *U.S. News & World Report,* August 6,1984, 44- 51.

U.S. Department of Labor, Bureau of Labor Statistics "Current Population Survey." *In Employment and Training Report of the President,* Washington, D.C., 1982.

Women's Bureau, 1986. Fuin Rodo no Jitsujo, 1986 (The Actual Condition of Women Workers). Tokyo: Printing Office, Ministry of Finance, 1986.

The International Assignment Reconsidered

Reading 3.2
Nakiye A. Boyacigiller

Close to 41% of the major U.S. multinational corporations (MNCs) plan on reducing the number of U.S. nationals assigned overseas.[1] And yet, most MNCs see an increase in the international interaction most managers will be facing. Therein lies a paradox: Just when the need for international expertise is growing, U.S. MNCs are reducing the number of Americans sent overseas, thus depriving both the country and themselves of the opportunity to increase the international experience and knowledge base of our current and future managers.

The orientation most MNCs take toward international assignments needs to be reconsidered. U.S. MNCs must view expatriation as a strategic tool, a very different perspective from that traditionally used. Historically, firms sent managers and professionals overseas to fill positions on a seemingly ad hoc basis, paying little attention either to their selection and training or to the role they could play in the overall organization. Moreover, American firms frequently sent Americans overseas because of ethnocentric attitudes ("We have to assign Americans to key positions because foreigners can't be trusted to handle the job.") Both approaches created problems. Individuals sent overseas without adequate training often failed. Indiscriminate staffing with Americans created resentment among qualified local nationals.

Fortunately, a growing number of human resource professionals and researchers in this area are beginning to speak in terms of strategic international human resource management.[2] International assignments should be utilized to develop future managers with a global orientation and to manage key organizational and country linkages.

Consider two overseas branches of the same U.S.-owned international bank opened in 1975. Both grew to equal size as measured by loans, deposits, and employment. Yet the two branches use very different personnel staffing practices. In Branch A, only 7% of the professionals and managers are U.S. nationals, while in Branch B, U.S. nationals number close to 30%. Why the difference? Is it explained by location? Branch A is located in Copenhagen, Denmark, while Branch B is in Cairo, Egypt. Or can it be explained by internal organizational characteristics, such as the branches' complexity? The answer is both.

Source: Reprinted by permission of the author.

As suggested by the above example, there are a multitude of national and organizational characteristics that influence the relative utilization of U.S. and local nationals in overseas affiliates. Yet previous research in this area, while providing direction on the employee characteristics to emphasize in selection decisions, has not focused on organizational and national characteristics to consider when staffing overseas affiliates.

To fill this void in our knowledge of international staffing practices, a study was conducted of a major U.S. financial institution, here called ICB, to determine which organizational and environmental factors influence the use of U.S. nationals abroad.[3] ICB is structurally comprised of four regions: North America; Asia; Latin America and the Caribbean; and Europe, the Middle East and Africa. The present regional structure was established in 1974 to "decentralize [ICB's] approach to a coordinated global wholesale banking strategy."[4] The study includes all 84 foreign branches of ICB. Located in 43 different countries, the branches are wholly owned by ICB.

These ICB branches are involved in both wholesale (corporate) and retail (individual) banking to varying degrees. The Asian branches deal primarily in trade finance, while their European counterparts are mainly wholesale operations catering to large multinationals. In Latin America, much of the activity has been project lending and retail banking. The branches differ tremendously in size and scope of operations and the kind of businesses in which they engage. There are significant differences both across regions and within regions.

The study was designed to test the following hypotheses:

- *Political risk:* Greater levels of political risk will lead to a greater proportion of U.S. nationals in professional positions.

- *Cultural distance:* The greater the cultural distance between the host country and the U.S., the greater the proportion of U.S. nationals in professional positions.

- *Competition:* The greater the level of competition with other finance institutions, the greater the proportion of U.S. nationals in professional positions.

- *Interdependence:* The greater the interdependence between the branch and corporate headquarters, the greater the proportion of U. S. nationals in professional positions.

- *Complexity:* The more complex the branch operations, the greater the proportion of U.S. nationals in managerial and staff positions.

- *Cost:* The variance in the cost between a local national and an expatriate will not have an influence on the proportion of U.S. nationals in the branch.

Environmental (Country) Factors to Consider When Staffing Overseas Units _____

This research revealed three factors—political risk, cultural distance, and competition—to be particularly important in explaining the utilization of expatriates in a foreign unit.[5]

(1) Political Risk

What is the level of political risk in the country and how can it be managed? Conventional wisdom suggests that in countries where political risk is high, it is important to have a local profile, that is, to appear to act and look like a local firm. This approach would require minimal use of U.S. personnel.

Politically risky countries are often the most difficult for managers in corporate headquarters to understand. In addition, studies have shown that inherently volatile situations (like one of high political risk) are often accompanied by decisions based on judgments rather than specific structural arrangements to deal with the uncertainty.[6]

Yet how are these judgments to be made? The knowledge and insight a well-placed U.S. national can provide to corporate executives is crucial in environments where garnering the necessary information is problematic. Understanding how to interpret economic, political, and financial signals in an alien environment is difficult even when one is located in the country in question. When one is sitting thousands of miles away in an entirely different milieu, reaching erroneous conclusions is all too possible. Parent nationals located in overseas operations can be important conduits of information. This study found that ICB utilizes more expatriate managers in countries with high political risk ratings, as was hypothesized.

(2) Cultural Distance

Cultural distance refers to the extent that two cultures differ. Key dimensions of culture include such characteristics as how collectivistic or individualistic the culture is, how time is perceived, and how rigidly sex roles are defined. When two cultures differ significantly on these and other cultural dimensions, it is more difficult for individuals from these cultures to communicate and work well together. Strategically placed U.S. nationals play an important interpretative role between the host country culture and the U.S. headquarters offices. This bridging role is clearly evident in a Scandinavian manager's description of an MNC's operations in Japan:

> Nowadays there seems to be a tendency towards "over-Japanization" of the foreign company in Japan; i.e., the top management is, after initial stages of starting up business, staffed entirely with Japanese executives. It has been observed

that this can create serious problems particularly in the communication with the head office overseas. In one actual case,
the Japanese president of a joint venture company got so frustrated with this communication problem that he actually
resigned and returned to the large Japanese corporation he
originally came from. The occasional visitor from the head
office cannot possibly understand all the complexities of carrying out business in Japan, and what the Japanese executive in
the related case actually wanted was to have an able person
from the head office permanently stationed in Japan and with
whom he could discuss the various problems on the spot.[7]

My research found that the greater the cultural distance between
the host nation and the U.S., the greater the proportion of U.S. nationals in subsidiary management.

Competition

This research found the competition existing in the local environment
of the host country to lead to fewer U.S. nationals in the foreign
branches. There are two logical explanations as to why this would
occur. First, greater competition indicates a greater number of firms
(local and foreign) where local nationals are able to acquire banking
experience. With ample situations for training in finance and banking,
local nationals became more attractive to ICB.

Secondly, in a competitive market, local nationals are a critical
resource in garnering more local business. Local nationals often provide
critical links to local commerical communities, thus allowing the MNC
to gain new business. This is especially true, given that some countries
where competition was found to be the highest (e.g., Indonesia,
Bahrain, and Malaysia) are also countries where good contacts with
local government and business officials are very important.

Cost

Every CEO laments the high cost of sending Americans overseas on
assignment. Total expatriate compensation comes to about 2.5 times
the employee's U.S. base salary, when such expenses as cost-of-living
adjustments, tax equalization, housing, and education are included.[8]
Yet the cost of expatriation needs to be understood in a broader framework. First, thinking about cost in averages rather than focusing on
individual countries creates a fallacy. The cost of living varies greatly
across international borders, thus focusing on average costs can mask
real differences. For example, in 1983, the cost of a $36,000-a-year
American employee was $61,500 a year in Tokyo, $41,000 in Hong
Kong, $71,000 in Bahrain, and $36,000 in Argentina.

Secondly, MNCs need to address the cost issue within a broader
frame-work of what the company seeks to gain through overseas
assignments. If they use international assignments to develop future

upper-level managers with a global orientation and the ability to manage key organizational issues, then absolute cost must be viewed from a very different perspective. While costly in the short term, international assignments appear more useful when perceived as a long-term investment.

Still, one important caveat must be made regarding cost. It is always an important consideration when employees sent overseas fail. Previous research suggests that the reason many U.S. firms have not sent many Americans abroad is their high failure rates overseas.[9] Another study found that when compared to Japanese and European expatriates, American expatriates tend to have significantly larger failure rates (e.g., early returns due to lack of adaptation or ineffective job performance on the job).[10] The failures are not surprising given that assignments are often made hastily, with insufficient time and care paid to selection and training. Studies show that when choosing individuals for overseas sojourns, MNCs focus on technical and managerial competence, assuming that technically competent managers will automatically function effectively overseas. Unfortunately, this is often not the case. Characteristics such as adaptability, ethnocentrism, and the family's resistance to an international sojourn are often neglected and yet frequently lead to overseas failure.[11]

Characteristics of the Foreign Affiliate to Consider When Staffing

After considering the national factors, several characteristics of the overseas affiliate should be considered when deciding on an appropriate staffing policy. The most important are interdependence, complexity, and control mechanisms.

Interdependence

Subsidiaries of MNCs do not operate as closed systems. Typically, they have resource links to other subunits within the MNC as well as ties to firms and customers in host, home, and other countries. This interdependence with other organizations creates important implications for staffing. For example, if a foreign affiliate maintains a high level of interdependence with the U.S. headquarters, placing some U.S. expatriates in management positions facilitates intraorganizational communication and relations. Given significant interdependence with headquarters or other U.S. affiliates, U.S. nationals perform an important role in managing the uncertainty that derives from interdependence. This is clearly evident in the comments of the non-Swedish president of a Swedish joint venture on the appointment of a Swede to the position of production manager:

> It was absolutely necessary that Mr. X was appointed. Before he came we were never able to receive any attention from the product divisions when we needed faster deliveries for some reasons or when we needed special blueprints for our own production. As a result, we sometimes had serious production delays. He [Mr. X] has improved the situation a lot in many instances just by knowing whom to contact in Sweden.[12]

Alternatively, if the foreign affiliate has its most important resource ties within the host country, then parent country managers do not provide an equivalent benefit. Intracountry, as opposed to intercountry, interdependencies are best managed by local nationals.

Complexity

Most multinational corporations are comprised of units that differ widely in their levels of complexity. The complexity of an assembly plant in Western Europe is undoubtedly much lower than the complexity of an R&D lab in the same location. Controlling units that have disparate levels of complexity is difficult for MNCs. Complex tasks imply "an increase in information load, information diversity, or rate of information change."[13] Consequently, the amount of information processing necessary to control complex operations is much greater than the information processing required to control less complex units. Given that communication and control is facilitated among managers of the same nationality, it is not surprising that more complex units had more U.S. nationals assigned to them.[14]

Control Mechanisms: Socialization

Given ICB's decentralized approach to global banking strategy, the firm requires several specific control mechanisms to ensure that employees in foreign affiliates act in concert with the parent organization. As an ICB executive stated:

> If your major strength is a network of global operations, you must provide that network with a strong *esprit de corps*. As operations are decentralized, we cannot tell the branches what to do. Yet if a branch turns down the loan request of a person that is a key customer for our firm, just because that particular loan does not make sense for that particular branch . . . then the company will risk losing an important customer. Yet the more you decentralize the more you localize those decisions and risk that particular loan not be made. We must make sure that the customer is managed worldwide.

Three ways an organization can achieve control are bureaucratic rules, the use of hierarchy, and socialization. Of these, socialization is the most flexible and least obtrusive. Parent country nationals can provide an invaluable role in socializing local nationals into the MNC's ways of doing business. This is especially important in MNCs where increasing rules and standards may not be possible (because of high complexity and/or differentiation of operations) and increasing socialization may be the only mechanism for increasing control.

Conclusions: Consider Both ——————————————————————

Both organizational and country characteristics need to be taken into account when determining how to staff an overseas affiliate. First, and most important, one must assess the interdependencies between the subunit, the host government, local businesses, and corporate head-quarters. Complexity, political risk, and cultural distance increase the inherent difficulty of doing business in the foreign country and gener-ally require greater expatriate presence. In contrast, extensive local competition in the host country in turn increases the importance of local nationals as conduits to the local market.

International staffing decisions need to be tied to other strategic decisions. The emphasis during staffing should be on long-term orga-nizational development and management development and above all on long-term commitment to learning about international markets. If high-potential individuals are carefully selected and trained for over-seas positions, they will not only facilitate the maintenance of an inter-national network of operations in the short term but should be allowed to continue providing informational support upon their return to the U.S. The international education that future executives could acquire in these types of assignments cannot be replicated in any classroom.

Endnotes ——————————————————————————

1. Kobrin, S.J. *International Expertise in American Business: How to Learn to Play with the Kids on the Street.* New York: Institute of International Education, 1984.

2. See for example, Adler, N.J. and Ghadar, F. "Globalization and Human Resource Management." To be published in Alan Rugman (ed.), *Research in Global Strategic Management: A Canadian Perspective,* Volume One. Greenwich, Conn.: JAI Press, 1989.

3. For more detail, see Boyacigiller, N.A. "The role of expatriates in the management of interdependence, complexity and risk." Working paper 8703. San Jose State University, Department of Organization and Management.

4. An ICB internal document.

5. An expatriate refers to a parent country national assigned overseas; (e.g., an American IBM employee stationed in Japan for three years). A host national refers to a local national working for the multinational in his or her own country (e.g., a Japanese national working for IBM in Japan).

6. Leblebici, H. and Salancik, G.R. "Effects of environmental uncertainty on information and decision processes in banks." *Administrative Science Quarterly*, 1981, 578-596.

7. Delaryd, B. *The Japan Economic Journal*, May 30, 1972, 20.

8. "High cost of overseas staff." *World Business Weekly*, April 27, 1981, 4, 48.

9. Kobrin, S.J. "Expatriate reduction and strategic control in American multinational corporations." *Human Resource Management*, 1988, 27 (1), 63-76.

10. Tung, R.L. "Expatriate assignments: Enhancing success and minimizing failure." *The Academy of Management Executive*, 1987, 1, 2, 117-125.

11. Tung, R. L. "Selection and training of U.S., European, and Japanese multinational corporations." *California Management Review*, Fall 1982, 57-71.

12. Leksell, L. *Headquarter-Subsidiary Relationships in Multinational Corporations*. Stockholm School of Economics, 1981.

13. Campbell, D.J. Task complexity: A review and analysis. *Academy of Management Review*, 1988, 13 (1), 40-52.

14. On the challenges of managing a multicultural work force, see Adler, N.J. *International Dimensions of Organizational Behavior*. Boston, Mass.: Kent Publishing, 1986. For an in-depth study of the role of the manager, see Mintzberg, *The Nature of Managerial Work*. New York: Harper & Row, 1973.

Precision Measurement of Japan: A Small Foreign Company in the Japanese Labor Market

Case 3.1
James G. Scoville

Precision Measurement of Japan (PM-J) is a joint venture company between Takezawa Electric Company (TEC),* a Japanese electrical equipment manufacturing company, and Precision Management, Inc. (PMI), a Minnesota-based manufacturer of measurement devices. Major markets for these devices are chemical processes, pipelines, aircraft, and aerospace and power generation. As a multinational corporation, PMI is faced with the problem of penetrating the Japanese market before one of its Japanese competitors perfects the various gauges and shuts the U.S. company out of the Japanese market. In order to penetrate the Japanese market, PMI has entered into a business relationship with TEC thus forming a quasi-Japanese company, PM-J. This step was intended to increase PMI's credibility with the Japanese, and to forestall a Japanese competitor from using its protected domestic market to work out bugs, employ economies of scale, undercut PMI's pricing scheme, and generally take over the world instrument market. This would seriously, perhaps fatally, affect PMI's viability.

---

*All names have been changed. The company name is somewhat descriptive of its line of business; the employee names in Exhibit 2 are taken from a list of the 10 most common Japanese names collected by the Daihyaku Insurance Company. Christine Hoffman and Eliyahue Stein provided research assistance on this case.

I am also indebted to referees who commented on the case. One of their suggestions was a brief guide to pronunciation of the Japanese names in this case. In general, each vowel merits a syllable: thus, "Tah.Keh.zah.wah." The only exception is when "i" serves as a "y," as in the name of Keio ("Kayo") University. All "sh" combinations in this case are pronounced as in "shoe."

Source: This case was prepared by James G. Scoville (with the assistance of Christine Hoffman and Eliyahue Stein) as a basis for class discussion rather than to illustrate either effective or ineffective handling of an administrative situation. The U.S. Department of Education funded the preparation of this case under Grant #G00877027.

The Problem

The problem faced by his company, according to Joe Smith, President of PM-J, is that the Japanese instrument companies are becoming more visible and are developing broader product lines, which may directly affect PM-J's market share. Corporate PMI headquarters is genuinely concerned that the Japanese long-term plan is to capture and dominate the world instrument markets just as they have taken over camera, automobile, video recorder, and other high-tech markets. The instrument market could be the next Japanese strategic industry.

Currently, the Japanese tend to dominate only their domestic instrument markets, says Smith. This could change by working their familiar strategy. This is accomplished by closing the Japanese markets to foreign competition, acquiring volume and experience in domestic markets, and basing foreign marketing on that experience.

The usual Japanese strategy is to either (1) obtain licenses for advanced technology from other companies (usually from the United States) and then improve the technology and market it alone or (2) use some company's proven distribution to establish a market base and then go it alone. Both of these approaches save considerable time and expense to the Japanese company thus freeing resources and capital for quick and effective marketing of the new and/or improved technology. Smith reports that two competitors gained real substance in this manner.

After penetrating the foreign markets with this strategy, excellent service and responsiveness from the Japanese companies is generally reported. The Japanese will, no doubt, continue their patient, persistent way of presenting high-technology, high-performance products which are backed by quality service. Even though they gain market position slowly, says Smith, once the Japanese establish accounts, their outstanding customer relations and excellent service record often mean they keep the accounts; the non-Japanese are then in a position of lost accounts and a declining market share.

Objective

PMI wishes to establish a permanent position in the Japanese domestic market. Additionally, it would be preferable that any Japanese competition be retarded by PMI's establishment of a strong sales and manufacturing posture in Japan. To acquire and maintain a market share in the instrument industry, PMI must establish credibility as a viable company; this it sought to do by combining with TEC. By establishing PM-J, PMI is demonstrating a long-term commitment and significant investment in Japan. In its efforts to capture the Japanese market, PM-J is faced with two overriding questions:

1. Is it possible to hire a sufficient number of qualified sales engineers (preferably newly graduated) to increase sales, establish quality accounts, and achieve a reasonable profit growth?

2. In what manner might PM-J increase its market position and distribution in the Japanese market?

The answers to these questions are complicated by a variety of socioeconomic factors unique to Japan.

The Country

Japan has a small amount of inhabitable land located on a number of mountainous islands, with few natural resources but abundant human resources. Pressured by the need to import almost all raw materials, including 100% of all oil, the Japanese economy grew at phenomenal rates during the 1960s and 1970s. During this period, Japanese industrial products moved from a reputation as cheap and flimsy to a position known for quality and reliability. This achievement was attained in part through protective import practices and a coordinated industrial strategy featuring cooperation between major manufacturing groups and the government, especially through activities of the Ministry of International Trade and Industry (MITI).

The Company

Precision Measurement, Inc. was founded in the mid-1960s to produce a wide range of measurement and instrumentation equipment. Over the years, the company has remained at the forefront of this industry and continues to this day to pursue cutting-edge research. In recent years, the company's financial strength has been sustained by a classic "cash cow"—a gauge for measurement of flow and pressure. The success of this gauge relies on two factors: (1) very fine and precise machining of high-quality material to strict quality standards and (2) an ingenious application of elementary principles of physics. Neither of these constitutes a substantial barrier to Japanese competition: machining materials to high standard is straightforward; even the casewriter's late 1950s high school physics allows him to understand the way the gauge works!

Staffing Implications

To penetrate the Japanese domestic market, an optimal staffing pattern must be generated which would yield the desired sales capability.

Exhibit 1. Projected Staffing Patterns, 1985-1987

	April 1985	End 1985	End 1986	End 1987
Administration	5	5	5	5
Secretarial, clerical	5	5	5	5
Engineering				
Sales and marketing 3				
Engineering	8	11	13	15
Services group 3				
Production 2				
Production technicians	2	3	3	3
	20	24	26	28

(Manufacturing takes place in the U.S., with the gauge being modified to the customer's needs in Japan by production engineers and technicians.) PM-J's president supplied a table of desired staffing patterns from the beginning of 1985 through 1987, which focuses on their probable staffing needs (Exhibit 1). Although PM-J found it very difficult to hire the eight engineers who presently represent the company, it is now faced with the need to engage seven more in just two and one-half years.

Engineering Labor Markets in Japan ————————————————

The nature of Japanese labor markets, particularly for professionals and managers, directly affects attainability of the staffing patterns outlined by the company. Modern, large Japanese organizations generally hire people as they finish school for "lifetime employment." The employee then receives a traditional training, which consists of considerable job rotation, and general training, which develops broad skills; the employee, therefore, expects a pay system based primarily on length of service with the company rather than job-specific performance. Thus, PM-J's competitors would typically hire engineers on completion of university training and employ them until their early to mid-50s. Then, as is the practice with many managers, the senior employees are transferred to subsidiaries, client organizations, smaller plants, or less demanding jobs.

A small company, like PM-J, cannot easily compete in the labor market because it cannot guarantee its own survival for the career lifetime of the employees. Small organizations are more likely to go out of business and are, even if they survive, less likely to obtain a major share of the product market. This fact does little to instill confidence in the new graduate who expects lifetime employment as a condition of employment. The same weakness generally applies to foreign companies in Japan.

They often do not share a commitment to lifetime employment, traditional pay systems, or a long business presence in Japan. This image formed by some foreign companies that came to Japan and then laid off many people or totally withdrew is widespread among Japanese professionals.

PM-J has generally been unable to recruit the immediate post-graduate because it is both small and foreign. This has necessitated acquiring its engineering force in various ad hoc ways, predominantly relying on recommendations from its joint venture partner, TEC. While not optimal, it has at least allowed the company to develop a skeleton staff.

The first two columns of Exhibit 2 show the name and recruiting source of engineers currently employed by PM-J. The third and fourth columns show the salaries of these people (millions of yen per year) as compared with the average pay of employees of the same age and education in large companies in Japan. The final column shows each employee's job performance evaluation as reported by company president Smith. Exhibit 2 clearly demonstrates that PM-J's hiring pattern has strongly deviated from the stereotypical post-university hire/lifetime employment pattern of Japanese industry in general.

Alternatives to the Current Situation _____

Given the staffing and recruiting patterns of Japanese industries and the staffing dilemmas faced by PM-J, what alternative plans of action are available to a small, foreign company which will promote its stated objectives of expanded sales and increased market share? If PM-J is to predominate in the Japanese market, what alternatives to its current pattern of hiring mid-career engineers could move the company toward hiring newly graduated qualified engineers? Are there changes occurring in the Japanese labor culture which might benefit PM-J if the company recognizes and adapts the changes to fit its needs?

Attracting Younger Engineers _____

How might PM-J increase its hiring ratio of younger engineers directly out of school? Will it be as difficult to hire new graduates in the future as previous experience suggests? The latter situation seems to be loosening a bit as professors' influence in directing students has declined. Indeed, some students are more willing to consider employers other than just the very largest and more traditional Japanese companies. Furthermore, the typical lifetime employment pattern seems to be eroding as some younger professionals with relatively recent dates of hire move to new companies after only three or four years of employment. Organizations like The Recruit Center (a major recruiting and

Exhibit 2. Sales and Support Force, Spring 1985

Name	Source	Annual Pay Including Bonuses (million yen)	Average Pay at Large Companies* (million yen)	Performance Evaluation
Sato	Small company experience, recommended by the general manager of PM-J	9.5	9.7	55% effort rating; lower segment on performance
Suzuki	Formerly a representative for PM-J	7.3	5.8	80%
Takahashi	TEC (age: late 40s)	7.3	7.2	75–85%
Watanabe	Nihon Medical (age: early 50s), recommended by a classmate who is now a professor	9.5	9.5	Very high
Tanaka	Junior high school education plus 20 years in the instrumentation sales business; answered an ad in a trade journal			N/A
Ito	TEC (age: 32)	5.8	5.8	90%
Kobayashi	New university graduate	2.9	3.0	N/A
Saito	TEC (age: about 40)	6.3	6.3	Very high
Yamamoto	TEC (age: mid-40s)	8.4	7.8	Very high

*Equal to 18 months salary in the average large company, no housing or other allowances figured in. The extra six months' pay reflects the average level of bonuses in Japan. At present, large Japanese companies pay roughly two months' salary as a bonus three times a year (late spring, late summer, and at the Christmas-New Years season).

Source: Japan Institute of Labor Statistical Reports.

placement organization providing extensive published information on companies as prospective employers) and "headhunters" are supporting these changes in employment patterns by publicizing employment opportunities and company characteristics. Young professionals in engineering and other technical fields are beginning to rely on such data in making career decisions.

The advantages of this alternative, i.e., to employ personnel agencies, are straightforward. First, PM-J could more readily advertise the benefits and opportunities it is able to provide to career-minded professionals via the agencies and headhunters. Second, PM-J stands to gain credibility which the recruitment agencies and headhunters, as third parties, can confer as they present the company as a stable organization that demonstrates Japanese characteristics. Third, recruitment agents are financially motivated to match employers and employees; PM-J can capitalize on this by requesting younger, well-educated, technically qualified engineers who have a potentially longer career life with the company.

The principal disadvantages of personnel agencies are their high cost to the small organization, in terms of money and CEO time. Further caveats must be noted: Graduates of the best Japanese universities and engineering programs (University of Tokyo and Keio University) would probably not be interested in employment agencies because they would most likely be recruited by the large domestic companies via contacts with university professors. Likewise, headhunters would be less able to lure young new hires from large companies to work for a smaller foreign-based firm. Additionally, if PM-J accepted a large proportion of graduates from second-and third-tier universities, it would be unable to generate a level of credibility which a workforce of "better" educated employees from top-rated universities would confer.

Attracting Female Engineers ————————————————————

One intriguing labor market strategy might be to get women into PM-J's labor force as sales engineers. A growing number of women are enrolled in engineering programs at Japanese universities. Their employability, at least in principle, should be enhanced by equal opportunity legislation recently passed by the Diet (Japan's parliament). More distant observers, including some at the corporate offices of PMI, have occasionally brainstormed about job redesign and the use of women engineers; U.S.-based students may almost think this a natural option. Practical reaction at PM-J, however, stresses that the acceptability of women in many Japanese work roles is not immediately forthcoming, as the tale related in Exhibit 3 amply suggests. Moreover, it will be even longer in coming within the industrial setting where men are almost exclusively employed and where evening entertainment of customers is an expected job component.

Exhibit 3. Prospects for Female Engineers

The actual and potential roles of women in Japanese society and work life are undoubtedly changing. The increasing proportions of female students at universities is one index of this change and is directly related to PM-J's problems. Between 1970 and 1980, the female enrollment ratio more than doubled from 9.6 percent to 20.1 percent. In spite of this upsurge, the number of female engineering graduates in all fields remains very small; 1981 engineering graduates included 1,143 women as compared to 73,631 men.

Numbers alone fail to tell the full tale of how difficult it could be to employ women successfully in PM-J's sales engineering positions, where they would have to call on and entertain male customers. A recent event described in *Labor Trends in Japan*, 1983, may illuminate the employability of women in Japan today.

> A minor scandal erupted in 1983 with the publication of confidential employment guidelines of one of Japan's major bookselling chains employing 2,000 persons, over half of them women, in 28 outlets. The manual told office managers to guard against hiring certain types of women. Among these were women who wore glasses, short women (under 4 ft., 8 in.), ugly women and those with country bumpkin-like attributes. Educational criteria for exclusion included college drop-outs and graduates of four-year universities ("too head-strong"). Also to be avoided were potentially troublesome women including those who belong to political or religious organizations since they would not be able to easily change their way of thinking, those whose fathers are university professors or whose husbands are teachers or writers, and women who take an interest in legal affairs or who could otherwise be argumentative, such as those who belonged to school newspaper clubs. Another group which should not be hired, according to the manual, are women with complicated family situations or chronic illnesses. Lastly, presumably since their conduct might not be above suspicion, women who have changed jobs more than once, divorcées, single women renting their own apartments and women who respect "passionate artists" such as Van Gogh should be passed over. (*Labor Trends in Japan*, 1983)

Engineers vs. Salespeople ————————————————————————————

A variant on the idea of increasing the number of engineers at PM-J is to reduce the company's reliance on engineers by employing non-technically trained salespeople; the sales component of the engineers' positions would be eliminated or substantially decreased. After all, engineers don't do all the selling in the United States; rather, they provide technical backup and design work after the salesperson has made the pitch.

Perhaps it is feasible to explore hiring graduates of technical high schools and vocational schools for sales, following the example set when Tanaka was hired (Exhibit 2). This could be accomplished by multiple testing (less restricted in Japan than in the United States), and increased training to identify and qualify strong sales candidates. In fact, PMI in the United States and other organizations in Japan succeeded in using a combination of both occupations in marketing products.

By using non-engineering salespeople, PM-J could easily expand its labor force with younger employees. Unfortunately, the company is small and foreign; in reducing the perceived qualifications of its salesforce, it will suffer a further loss of credibility conferred on employees holding an engineering degree from a respected university.

Maintaining the Status Quo

Staying with the status quo is another strategy. PM-J could continue using mid-career people. Most of these employees have been recruited from the joint venture partner, TEC. This method is relatively inexpensive because the initial recruitment, selection, and training costs are absorbed by TEC since the engineers began employment there. An advantage of this method is that the engineers with 25 to 30 years' experience have far more business contacts than do fresh graduates. The principle disadvantage is that one cannot be certain that the TEC engineers are quality employees. After all, why should TEC give up its best people to PM-J and retain the marginal employees for its own use? It's quite conceivable that the joint venture could be receiving some of the less productive TEC personnel. This also perpetuates the current dilemma of a salesforce in its early to mid-50s, which does not assist the company's image, credibility, or ability to capture the difficult Japanese market.

A further complication in PM-J's reliance on TEC's transferred employees is that many mid-career professionals may be loyal to their previous employer; this will not result in a highly motivated salesforce which will be prepared to endeavor diligently to promote a new employer in the market.

Supplementing the Status Quo

Another strategic option is to supplement the status quo (hiring mid-career professional engineers) with headhunters and/or employment agencies such as The Recruit Center. Headhunters are more prevalent in the Japanese labor market recently, and many Japanese companies report some successes in employing their services. Even though such agencies and headhunters are quite expensive and time consuming, they do represent one means in filling gaps created by internal rotations of employees or vacancies resulting from terminated employees. Perhaps the most likely recruit from headhunting would be in the 28 to 30 year old range who is making a career move. Although not fresh from school, these engineers would still be relatively recent university graduates with respectively longer career lives ahead of them. This would tend to stabilize PM-J's engineering and salesforce turnover while simultaneously conferring the credibility to be gained from the honored university degree.

Toward an Appraisal of These Options

The likely success of these various strategies clearly depends on the prospective state of the Japanese engineer labor market. PM-J's hiring success will be *directly* enhanced by any developments which reduce the number of engineers absorbed by the rest of Japanese industry and by its ability to gain credibility as a stable "Japanese" company. *Indirect* effects are also possible.

For example, it's likely that any developments which loosen the supply of male engineers will make it even more difficult for female engineers to be accepted, especially in sales. Thus, a reliable forecast of engineering labor market conditions in Japan is central to any strategy recommendation to PM-J.

Future Labor Market Developments

Effects of an Aging Workforce

The Japanese labor force and population has aged in recent years, pressuring the social insurance and retirement systems, similar to the U.S. situation. This has led the government to explore postponing pension age from about 60 to about 65. The Japanese employment system for engineers (among other professions) initially moves employees in the 50 to 55 age range to secondary employment (within the firm) or to other employers.* Since the government has made early pension less likely, it seems that in coming years more men will seek longer second careers. As noted, this would dampen women's employability. It would also increase the availability of engineering resources to a company like PM-J.

The Decline of New Workers

The declining number of young people entering the labor market and the declining pool of new engineering graduates implies that small companies like PM-J are more likely to be squeezed out of the market. Based on present hiring patterns, 80 percent of the graduates of the top 10 Japanese engineering schools would be recruited and absorbed by a

---

*The age-related pay system (*nenko*), plus the common decline of productivity after a certain age implies that after that age older workers tend to become more and more expensive rapidly.

select group of employers consisting of the largest domestic and foreign organizations. This tightening of the youth market decreases the viability of a strategy aimed at hiring fresh graduates into small, foreign companies.

Foreign Product Competition and the Japanese Labor Market

One must consider the *labor market* effects of opening Japanese *product markets* to foreign competition. If Japan concedes to growing pressure from its allies to reduce import tariffs and trade barriers, who will be hit hardest? Which Japanese industries will be hurt by a policy of greater import penetration into Japan? First of all, it is not probable that agriculture will be hit heavily. Even though Japanese food prices are three to six times the world level, it's unlikely that the government would chance eroding its support base among small farmers. This is due to the fact that import restriction policies have supported the relatively large agricultural population who have in turn faithfully supported the incumbent government party, the Liberal Democrats, since the late 1940s.

Are import penetration liberalizations for non-agricultural products apt to affect big companies like Matsushita, Hitachi, or Asahi? These firms run the Japanese "economic miracle" and are closely tied to government policy through the coordinating activities of the Ministry of International Trade and Industry. Such an alliance between government and big business is likely to forestall serious import impacts on the key companies. Thus, won't any opening of Japanese markets to U.S. imports probably be designed to have the most impact on items produced by smaller businesses? As these smaller businesses cut back on employment; won't it have the effect of loosening the labor market exactly where PM-J is located (in terms of company size)?

Political considerations aside, it is also true that small-scale industry in Japan has much higher labor costs (relative to larger enterprises) than in the United States or Germany (another major trading country), as seen in Exhibit 4. Increased foreign product-market competition and a resulting loosening of the smaller-company labor market would increase a surviving small foreign company's ability to recruit and retain qualified employees.

To the extent that Japanese trade policy is liberalized, PM-J should be more successful on all fronts in trying to hire engineers in competition with Japanese firms. On the other hand, the staffing demands of other foreign firms which either expand or enter Japan as a result of this trade policy liberalization will have to be taken into account.

Product Market Issues _____

Having considered some major human resource dynamics affecting PM-J's penetration into the Japanese market, it is necessary to

Exhibit 4. Relative Labor Costs in Manufacturing by Size of Enterprise

Number of Employees	Japan 1985	USA (1977)	West Germany (1977)
1–9	136		N/A
10–49	129	102	97
50–99	124		101
100–499	108	92	102
500–999	97		99
1000 and more	100	100	100

Source: *Toward a More Vital Society,* Japan Federation of Employers Assns., 1985.

review what product market considerations are relevant to the company's success of PM-J in the Japanese market.

Standards are more frequently mentioned as problems or barriers by would-be American importers of technical equipment. Japanese standards are simply not the same as the United States' and are very difficult to understand or change. With respect to the "cash cow gauge," PM-J spent six or seven years on the standards acceptance process.

The biggest issue regarding the product market is the prospect for increased penetration of imports into the Japanese market. Japanese government policy on this is evolving. During the spring of 1985, as PM-J grappled with the strategic issues, Prime Minister Nakasone undertook his famous shopping trip, urging all Japanese to spend 25,000 additional yen on foreign goods. Whether this will help sell PM-J's product is doubtful since its principal applications are industrial. But if it becomes easier for foreign firms to bid on government jobs (pursuant to GATT agreements), PM-J might see a direct sales payoff in major government projects.

Issues from This Case _____

There are at least two preliminary issues for the student to address in this case.

First, is TEC doing its job? Are they providing qualified people to the joint venture, PM-J, or are they "dumping" marginal employees who are past their peak performance and on the downslide?

The second preliminary issue that the student should address is whether PM-J's pay scale is appropriate. Data in Exhibit 2 provide comparisons with big companies' pay levels.

The Longer-Run Labor Market Strategy Options

The student should identify the risks, benefits, and costs of various alternatives (including staffing options) against the backdrop of various "states of the world." Those states of the world will be dominated by the degree to which government policy changes so that PM-J (or more radically, a lot of foreign competition) is able to penetrate domestic markets in Japan. Some engineering labor market strategies will be higher risk and lower risk, with higher and lower costs and payoffs, depending on what one thinks will happen to the engineering labor market and PM-J's ability to penetrate the product market. Although Japanese government policies on foreign access to markets may dominate the scene, other things that will impinge upon the labor market should be considered:

- the aging population

- shortages of youth entering the labor force

- increased numbers of people (early to mid-50s) seeking longer second careers

- increased numbers of women seeking positions

- changing Japanese culture and labor markets

Considering the case as a whole, the basic issue can be starkly posed: How should PM-J attempt to recruit enough people to permit an effective penetration of the Japanese product market on which the survival not only of PM-J, but of its parent PMI, may depend?

——Recruiting a Manager for BRB, Israel ———————

Case 3.2
William Roof
Barbara Bakhtari

BRB Inc., a multinational electronics corporation, plans to establish a new subsidiary in Israel. The firm's base is in Los Angeles, California, with a second overseas headquarters in England. The U.S. office staffs and operates six North American divisions and three South American subsidiaries. The U.K. office is responsible for operations in Europe and Asia. The Israeli venture is the company's first business thrust in the turbulent Middle East.

During the past 10 years, BRB's phenomenal growth resulted largely from its ability to enter the market with new, technically advanced products ahead of the competition. The technology mainly responsible for BRB's recent growth is a special type of radar signal processing. With Fourier transforms, BRB's small, lightweight, and inexpensive radar systems outperform the competitions' larger systems in range, resolution, and price. It is this type of lightweight, portable radar technology that has enormous potential for Israel during conflicts with the Arab States.

BRB's human resource functions in the United States and Europe each boast a vice president. John Conners is the Vice President of Human Resources in the United States, and Francis O'Leary is the Vice President of Human Resources in the United Kingdom. Paul Lizfeld, the CEO of BRB, contacted the two vice presidents and told them to recruit a general manager for the Israeli operation. "I don't care who finds him, but he better be right for the job. I cannot afford to replace him in six months. Is that clear!" Lizfeld told them to look independently and then coordinate together to select the right person. They knew that their jobs could be in jeopardy with this task.

The two human resource operations were independent, and each was managed individually. Recruiting processes differed between U.S. and U.K. operations. Each had different organizational structures and corporate cultures. The only link between the two was Lizfeld's strong micromanagement style, which emphasized cost control.

Source: This article was written especially for this book.

U.S. Operations ————————————————————————

John Conners has worked for BRB for the past 20 years. He started with a degree in engineering and worked in the engineering department. After earning his M.B.A. in human resource management from UCLA, he transferred to the human resource department. Management felt that someone with an engineering background could hire the best technical employees for BRB. With BRB's high turnover rate, they felt that someone who could relate to the technical side of the business could better attract and screen the right people for the organization. BRB promoted Conners to vice president three years ago, after he hired the staffs for the subsidiaries in Peru and Brazil. Except for the general managers, they were all correct fits. Conners felt that the problem with the general managers was an inability to work with Lizfeld.

John Conners looked at many different strategies to determine how to begin recruiting for the Israeli position. He wanted to be sure he found the right person for the job. The first step in choosing the ideal candidate was to determine the selection criteria.

Conners defined the task in Israel to include control and management of BRB's Israeli operations. The GM must work with the Israeli government both directly and indirectly. The political unrest in Israel also requires the GM to conduct sensitive transactions with the Israeli government. This person would also work directly with Lizfeld, taking direction from him and reporting regularly to him.

As with many countries in the Middle East, Israel was in turmoil. Conners actually knew very little about the Israeli culture, but decided to ask different associates who had past dealings with Israel. He knew that the threat of war constantly hung over Israel. The country was also suffering from high inflation rates and troubled economics. Lately, he also learned that the country had become divided over certain political and cultural issues. The person accepting this job needed nerves of steel and extraordinary patience.

Conners decided the selection criteria that would be important for the candidate included technical skill, cultural empathy, a strong sense of politics, language ability, organizational abilities, and an adaptive and supportive family. He also felt that the GM would have to have the following characteristics: persuasiveness, ability to make decisions, resourcefulness, flexibility, and adaptability to new challenges. Now all he needed to do was find a person who had all these attributes.

He decided to begin his search for candidates within the organization. He knew this route had both advantages and disadvantages. Since BRB was still in the beginning stages of internationalization in Israel, a "home country" presence might prove to be very helpful. Lizfeld would appreciate this. The disadvantages would be many. It might be very difficult to find someone willing to relocate in Israel. The increased cost of living and the political unrest make it a tough package to sell. Conners knew of the "Israeli mentality." He also knew he would have to take care in sending someone who might either overpower the Israelis or break under their aggressive business style. Conners knew that Lizfeld wanted to have the home country atmosphere in Israel and planned to be very active in the management of Israeli operations.

The second option Conners had was to recruit from outside the company. The ideal candidate would have both domestic and international experience. Conners could recruit either by contacting an employment agency or by placing an ad in the *Wall Street Journal*. He thought he could find a person with the right qualifications, but he also knew it would be difficult to find someone Lizfeld liked outside the company. Conners had hired two managers for the South American offices, and Lizfeld had driven them over the edge within six months. Conners knew that he had to be extra careful. One more "unqualified" candidate might put his own job on the line.

Conners found three potential candidates for the Israeli position. One candidate, Joel Goldberg, was a recommendation from the headhunter Conners had commissioned. Goldberg had thirty-five years of electronics and radar experience. He had been CEO of Radar Developments Incorporated, a major electronics corporation in New York. Goldberg had taken control of Radar Developments Incorporated in 1981. By 1986, the company had tripled sales and increased profits fivefold. Goldberg had the technical knowledge to perform the job. He also had the necessary individual characteristics Conners felt would be important for this position. Goldberg had studied in Israel on a kibbutz for two years after college, spoke fluent Hebrew, and was a practicing Jew. He wanted to retire in Israel in a few years. Conners worried that Goldberg would not stay with the company long enough to establish a solid organization. Goldberg also liked running his own show, and that created a potential problem with Lizfeld.

The next candidate was Robert Kyle, Vice President of BRB's radar electronics department. Kyle had been with BRB for more than twenty years and headed two other international divisions for BRB in Japan and Canada. Kyle was familiar with the international process and the BRB corporate culture. Lizfeld had given him excellent reviews in the other two international positions. He had strong management skills and was highly respected both within the organization and in the industry. Kyle received his Ph.D. from MIT in electrical engineering and his M.B.A. from Dartmouth. He had the technical expertise and was familiar with the company and its procedures. Conners was afraid of Kyle's cultural acceptance in Israel since he did not speak the language and was not familiar with Israeli attitudes. He could require Kyle to participate in extensive cultural training, but Conners still had some reservations about sending a gentile to head operations in Israel.

The last candidate was Rochelle Cohen, an Israeli who relocated to the United States in 1982. She originally relocated to assist the head of the electronics division of Yassar Aircraft, an Israeli company that opened its first international office in 1978. Cohen did very well and brought Israeli thoroughness and assertiveness to the U.S. operations. She now wanted to move back to Israel to be with her family. Additionally, her fiancé recently relocated in Israel, and she wanted to return to marry and raise a family. Cohen had experience in the international circuit, having worked in the United States, United Kingdom, and Israel, but Conners was still worried about hiring her. Although she had the political knowledge and the proper connections in the Israeli government, the problems were her young age, lack of technical expertise, and sex.

Conners contacted O'Leary to see what progress he had made. Knowing the consequences that would come from this decision, Conners realized it was going to be a difficult one to make.

U.K. Operations ————————————————————————————————

Francis O'Leary reflected on his past eight years with BRB. His rise from the strife-torn east side of Belfast to BRB's corporate vice president for human resources was extraordinary. While most Irish business careers in large English firms peak at middle management, O'Leary's actually began at that point. He proved his capabilities through hard work, constant study, and an astute ability to judge the character and substance of people on first sight. His task of finding a suitable general manager for the new division in Israel offered a challenge he readily accepted.

O'Leary excelled at recruiting and hiring innovative employees who brought technical ideas with them to BRB. The management structure at BRB in England did not support internal growth of technology and innovation, so new ideas and technological advances were not rewarded with commensurate fiscal incentives. As such, turnover of experienced innovators forced O'Leary to recruit and hire innovation on a "rotating stock" basis. It was this success in hiring innovators that broke him from the shackles of middle management and thrust him to the top of the corporation. Four years ago, through a well-planned and well-executed recruiting program, O'Leary hired Rani Gilboa, a young Israeli engineer and former Israeli army officer. For Gilboa, the need for lightweight, inexpensive battlefield systems drove a desire to approach the problem from a new aspect: signal processing. After graduate study in this field, Gilboa sought and found a company that would support his concepts. That company was BRB. Gilboa's subsequent contributions to BRB's profits secured his and O'Leary's positions atop their respective disciplines within the firm.

Since that time, O'Leary had other successes hiring innovators from Israel. This stemmed largely from his tireless self-study of Israeli culture. With a feel for the Israeli people rivaling that of an "insider," O'Leary enjoyed success in pirating established innovators from Israeli firms. Now, he faced the task of recruiting and hiring a general manager for the newly established electronics division near Haifa.

Selecting the right manager would be more difficult than expected. With his knowledge of the Israeli culture, O'Leary knew intuitively that an Israeli should head the new division. Acceptance by the division's employees, ability to speak Hebrew, spousal support, and knowledge of Israeli government regulations and tax structures were vital to the success of the new division. Unfortunately, BRB's CEO preferred home country presence in the new division and directed O'Leary to recruit with that as the top priority. After O'Leary presented a strong case, however, the CEO agreed to review all candidates. Another potential problem arose when Lizfeld, the CEO, announced a hands-on management style with plans to participate actively in the management of the Israeli division. To O'Leary, this meant that Western values, along with the current innovative recruiting strategy practiced in England, would extend to Israel as well.

Until recently, O'Leary's recruiting for management positions concentrated on internal promotions. A known performer from within was a better bet than an outsider. When current employees could not meet the job requirements, O'Leary typically turned to newspapers as his primary source of candidates. The recent emergence of reputable executive placement services in England gave him an additional sourcing tool. At times, O'Leary had turned to social contacts, job centers, and the internal labor market as candidate sources, but the percentages of good leads from these were comparatively low .

After months of reading résumés, introductory letters, and job applications, three candidates emerged for the position in Israel. It was now up to O'Leary to decide the candidate he would recommend to Lizfeld.

Michael Flack worked for BRB for more than nineteen years. After graduating from Cambridge College with a degree in general engineering, Flack joined the company as a mechanical engineer. Initially, he worked in the mechanical design group of the radar division. After five years, BRB promoted Flack to engineering section manager. While in this position, he enjoyed various successes in radar miniaturization design. During his eleventh year, BRB again promoted Flack to department head in the manufacturing engineering group. Emphasis in this position shifted from design to production. During his seventeenth year, he became director of engineering design, where he was responsible for managing forty-three engineers' efforts in new-product design.

Flack had no international experience, and he was a reputed "tinkerer." He liked to spend time in the labs designing mechanical components along with his engineers. This generated tremendous esprit within his department but often resulted in inattention to his administrative responsibilities.

Rani Gilboa thought his friend Yair Shafrir was perfect for the position. Shafrir was currently vice-president of engineering at Elta

Electronics in Israel. Elta is one of Israel's top radar firms, with several products proven in actual combat during the last Arab-Israeli conflict. Shafrir received his degree in electrical engineering from the University of Jerusalem. He had spent his professional career in Israel, usually changing companies to accept promotions. He had been with four companies since graduating from the university nineteen years ago. Shafrir was a strong-willed, organized individual who took pride in his record of technical management accomplishments. He had been able to complete projects on schedule and within budget over 70 percent of the time, a rare feat for an Israeli company. This record resulted mainly from the force of his personal leadership and strength of will. With his entire career spent in Israeli companies, O'Leary had little doubt that Shafrir could manage BRB's new electronics division. Culturally, he was perfect for the job. O'Leary had concerns, however, about Paul Lizfeld's injection of Western culture through his active management plan. The obstinate Shafrir, with no international business experience, might resent the interference.

A well-placed advertisement in the *London Times'* employment section drew a number of responses. One of the three final candidates responded to the ad about four weeks after it appeared in the *Times*.

Harold Michaelson was an English citizen of Jewish faith. Michaelson's family fled Poland in 1938 when Harold's father insisted that the "Nazi madman" would never attack England, especially after Prime Minister Chamberlain's successful visit to Munich. Harold was born to the newly naturalized couple in 1940. Later, he attended college in the United States, where he earned both bachelor's and master's degrees in electrical engineering at Georgia Tech. After graduating, Harold spent two years with General Electric until his father's illness forced him to return to England. He accepted an engineering position with Marconi, and he has remained with that company. Shortly after his return, his father died. Michaelson continued to take care of his mother for the next year. Mrs. Michaelson had always dreamed of living in the Jewish homeland—a dream not shared by her husband. One year after his death, she joined her sister's family in Haifa. Harold had readily accepted a position with Marconi in Israel to work on the new Israeli defense fighter LAVI. Unfortunately, cancellation of the LAVI program also canceled his chances to work in Israel for Marconi. At the time of the interview, Harold was vice president of engineering for Marconi's air radio division. He was also the youngest vice president in the corporation. His background in engineering and administrative functions, coupled with his ability to speak Hebrew, made Harold a strong candidate for the position. During the interview, he mentioned his mother's failing health and her refusal to leave Israel. He intended, if selected, to take care of her there. O'Leary wondered if that was Harold's main reason for wanting to live in Israel. Would he still want to live and work there if he lost his mother? O'Leary was anxious to discuss his candidates with John Conners.

Part 4

MANAGING EXPATRIATE ASSIGNMENTS

A Practical but Theory-based Framework for Selecting Cross-Cultural Training Methods

Reading 4.1
J. Stewart Black
Mark Mendenhall

> Global citizenship is no longer just a nice phrase in the lexicon of rosy futurologists. It is every bit as real and concrete as measurable changes in GNP or trade flows (Ohmae, 1989, p. 154).

There is little debate that for executives in large multinational corporations (MNCs) today globalization is a daily reality. But what exactly is unique about the international environment that MNCs face compared to non-MNCs, what skills do executives need to successfully lead firms in this emerging global village, and how can appropriate training be designed to facilitate the acquisition of these new skills? These are not trivial questions.

One of the first issues that MNCs face that non-MNCs do not is the fact that if a firm operates in multiple countries, it must deal with multiple sources of sovereign authority. This involves working with different laws and legal systems or, in some cases, the lack of systematic legal structures and processes. Executives in positions at headquarters or at foreign subsidiaries must have the skills to understand the impact of various laws, tariffs, taxes, enforcement practices, and overarching legal systems and be able to work with host government officials in enacting and maintaining reasonable legislation across a wide variety of countries and cultures.

Second, MNCs must also operate in different markets with different cultures, histories, values, social systems, and languages, which often require not only product diversification but intraproduct differentiation by country. This requires managers who have a "sensitivity to local conditions" (Doz and Prahalad, 1986) and who can understand, work with,

Source: J. Stewart Black and Mark Mendenhall. "A Practical but Theory-based Framework for Selecting Cross-Cultural Training Methods." *Human Resource Management,* 28 (4), 1989, p511-539. Copyright © 1989. Reprinted by permission of John Wiley & Sons, Inc..

and direct people from various cultures. Third, different "countries offer different strategic opportunities for MNCs. . . . Differences in size, resource endowment, economic development, political regime, national development and industrial policies . . . play roles in differentiating the opportunities offered to MNCs by individual countries" (Doz and Prahalad, 1986, p. 56).

Despite the need for cross-cultural skills and the shortage of managers who possess these skills, most human resource decision makers do nothing in terms of cross-cultural training (CCT) for employees in general or for selected employees embarking on international assignments (Baker and Ivancevich, 1971; Black, 1988; Runzheimer, 1984; Tung, 1981). For example, 70 percent of U.S. expatriates and 90 percent of their families are sent overseas without any cross-cultural training (Baker and Ivancevich, 1971; Black, 1988; Black and Stephens, 1989; Runzheimer, 1984; Tung, 1981).

This is significant given that studies have found between 16 and 40 percent of all expatriate managers sent on foreign assignments return before they are supposed to because of poor performance or the inability of the employee and/or the family to effectively adjust to the foreign environment (Baker and Ivancevich, 1971; Black, 1988; Dunbar and Ehrlich, 1986; Tung, 1981). Other studies have found that negotiations between businesspeople of different cultures often fail because of problems related to cross-cultural differences (Black, 1987; Graham, 1984; Tung, 1984). The costs of failed cross-cultural encounters are high; for example, studies have estimated the cost of a failed expatriate assignment to be $50,000 to $150,000 (Copeland and Griggs, 1985; Harris and Moran 1979; Misa and Fabricatore, 1979). For a firm with hundreds of expatriate employees worldwide, the costs can easily reach into the tens of millions of dollars per year. In fact, Copeland and Griggs (1985) have estimated that the direct costs of failed expatriate assignments for U.S. corporations is over $2 billion a year, and this does not include unmeasured losses such as damaged corporate reputations or lost business opportunities. In addition, Lanier (1979) estimates that up to 50 percent of American expatriates who do not return early are nonetheless ineffective in their overseas jobs, or what she terms "brownouts." Given that the average compensation package for a U.S. expatriate is between $200,000 and $250,000 (Black, 1988; Copeland and Griggs, 1985), the costs of brownouts are staggering.

Cross-cultural training has long been advocated as a means of facilitating effective cross-cultural interactions (Brislin, 1981; Landis and Brislin, 1983; Bochner, 1982; Harris and Moran, 1979; Mendenhall, Dunbar, and Oddou, 1987; Tung, 1981). However, its use in American business organizations is not widespread. Various reasons have been cited by business organizations for the low use of cross-cultural training; the most prevalent being that such training is not thought to be necessary or effective, and thus, top management sees no need for the training (Baker and Ivancevich, 1971; Mendenhall and Oddou, 1985; Runzheimer, 1984; Schwind, 1985; Tung, 1981; Zeira, 1975). However, the fundamental reason behind the lack of training seems to lie in the same assumption that causes American corporations to look only at domestic track records and to ignore cross-cultural-related skills when selecting expatriate candidates. The assumption is that good management is good management, and therefore, an effective manager in New York or Los Angeles will do fine in Hong Kong or Tokyo (Miller, 1973). Consequently, based on this assumption, it is logical for HR decision makers to conclude that CCT would not be needed or justified.

An extensive review of the cross-cultural training literature, however, suggests that HR managers are mistaken in their assumptions that good management is good management, that a firm can simply select employees who have been successful in the U.S. for overseas assignments, and that cross-cultural training is not necessary or effective. Harvey (1982) argued that domestic track record is not a good predictor of whether or not an expatriate will return early from an overseas assignment. A simple example can illustrate the reason for this finding. Generally in the U.S., setting clear, realistic, and difficult goals with specific time lines and then rewarding individuals who achieve the goals on time would be considered a good management practice (see Locke and Latham, 1984, for a detailed review). People will be motivated if they believe they know what is expected, believe they can achieve the goal, and believe they will be rewarded for their efforts. However, in Japan such goal specificity would be contrary to cultural norms, and the rewarding of an individual for personal achievement can often result in decreased motivation on the part of the rewarded individual because he or she would not want to stand out from or above the group (Mendenhall and Oddou, 1986a). This is a work-related norm that would be counterintuitive to an American expatriate manager with no training regarding Japanese culture or management practices.

A review of the CCT literature and its effectiveness also strongly indicates that American managers are mistaken in their belief that CCT is not necessary or effective. In a recent review of the empirical literature, Black and Mendenhall (1990) examined the effectiveness of CCT relative to three outcomes: (1) cross-cultural skill development, (2) cross-cultural adjustment, and (3) job performance. Of the ten studies that examined the relationship between CCT and self-confidence concerning one's ability to function effectively in cross-cultural situations, nine found a positive relationship. Nineteen out of nineteen studies found a positive relationship between CCT and increased cross-cultural relational skills. Sixteen out of sixteen studies found a positive relationship between CCT and more accurate cross-cultural perceptions. Nine out of nine studies found a positive relationship between CCT and cross-cultural adjustment. Finally, eleven out of fifteen studies found a positive relationship between CCT and job performance in the cross-cultural situation. However, the review also found that most of the empirical work was not founded on a theoretical framework per se and that the literature lacked a systematic approach to the study of CCT effectiveness. It is possible that the lack of a systematic stream of research has allowed the belief that CCT is not effective enough to persist. Additionally, the lack of a theoretical framework has left managers with little means of deciding who would benefit most from training, or what training method would be most effective, or how to best design such training programs. Perhaps until managers are presented with a systematic yet practical means of addressing these questions, they will continue to resist the prescriptions from academics (or consultants) that CCT is necessary and effective.

The purpose of this paper is to begin to shed some light on a framework for CCT that would be both theoretically sound and useful in practice. Recently, scholars have argued that social learning theory (SLT) provides a solid theoretical basis for understanding cross-cultural learning, training, and adjustment (Black and Mendenhall, 1990; Church, 1982; David, 1976). This paper explores the utility of SLT as a framework for systematically examining four important questions: (1) how can the level of training rigor of specific cross-cultural training methods be determined, (2) who would benefit most from cross-cultural training, (3) what CCT methods are most appropriate in specific situations, and (4) what level of CCT rigor is needed for maximum positive results? A brief review of past typologies and frameworks of CCT is followed by a discussion of the major components of SLT. Finally, a new framework of cross-cultural training based on SLT is delineated and practical implications are explored.

Review of Past Frameworks ————————————————————————

Most of the writing in the cross-cultural training literature has focused on the discussion of different methods of training and general classifications of these methodologies, while less attention has been focused on the development of frameworks that would determine which training methods to utilize or the important contingency factors to consider in such determinations. The first part of this section summarizes a generally accepted typology of CCT methods, and the second part of the section reviews two recent frameworks that try to help managers determine which cross-cultural training methods to use in organizations.

Landis and Brislin (1983) have proposed a typology of cross-cultural training methods that has largely been accepted as a broad and integrative classification scheme of cross-cultural training methods. They developed the typology based on a broad review of the cross-cultural training literature. Their classification scheme is summarized in Exhibit 1.

Exhibit 1. Fundamental Cross-Cultural Training Methodologies

Information or Fact-Oriented Training: Trainees are presented with various facts about the country in which they are about to live via lectures, videotapes, and reading materials.

Attribution Training: The attribution approach focuses on explanations of behavior from the point of view of the native. The goal is to learn the cognitive standards by which the host-nationals process behavioral input so that the trainee can understand why the host-nationals behave as they do and adapt his or her own behavior to match the standards of behavior in the host country.

Cultural Awareness Training: The aim is to study the values, attitudes, and behaviors that are common in one's own culture so that the trainee better understands how culture impacts his or her own behavior. Once this is understood, it is assumed that he or she can better understand how culture affects human behavior in other countries .

Cognitive-Behavior Modification: The focus here is to assist trainees in linking what they find to be rewarding and punishing in their own subcultures (work, family, religion, etc.) and then to examine the reward and punishment structure in the host culture. Through an examination of the differences and similarities, strategies are developed to assist the trainee to obtain rewards—and avoid punishments—in the host culture.

Experiential Learning: The goal of this approach is to involve the trainees as active participants, to introduce the nature of life in another culture by actively experiencing that culture via field trips, complex role-plays, and cultural simulations.

Interaction Training: Here trainees interact with natives or returned expatriates in order to become more comfortable with host-nationals and to learn from the first-hand experience of the returned expatriates. The methods utilized can range from in-depth role plays to casual, informal discussions.

Source: Adapted from Landis and Brislin (1983).

Given the fragmented state of the literature, the development of a classification scheme for various cross-cultural training methodologies was an important step in improving an understanding of the area. However, managers responsible for training within corporations were often left without a means of determining which of the methodologies were most appropriate for specific training situations or which methods were more or less rigorous and effective. Recently, scholars have attempted to present means of making some of these determinations.

Tung's Framework of Training Method Selection

Tung (1982) presented a contingency framework for choosing an appropriate CCT method and its level of rigor. She argued that the two determining factors were the degree of interaction required in the host culture and the similarity between the individual's native culture and the new culture. The related training elements involved the content of the training and the rigor of the training. Essentially, Tung argued that if the expected interaction between the individual and members of the target or host culture was low, and the degree of dissimilarity between the individual's native culture and the host culture was low, then the content of the training should focus on task- and job-related issues as opposed to culture-related issues, and the level of rigor necessary for effective training should be relatively low. If there was a high level of expected interaction with host nationals and a large dissimilarity between the cultures, then the content of the training should focus on the new culture and on cross-cultural skill development, as well as on the new task, and the level of rigor of such training should be moderate to high.

While this framework does specify some criteria (i.e., degree of expected interaction and cultural similarity) for choosing CCT methods, the conclusions that the framework allows the user to make are rather general. Essentially, the framework suggests that the user emphasize task issues by utilizing training methods with relatively low levels of rigor and to emphasize culture learning, skill development, and task issues by utilizing a relatively high level of rigor. However, the framework does not help the user determine which specific training methods to use. In addition, the framework does not define what training "rigor" is and, therefore, does not help the user determine which specific training methods are more or less rigorous.

Mendenhall and Oddou's Framework for Selecting Training Methods

A more recent framework presented by Mendenhall and Oddou (1986b) moves beyond Tung's framework and provides more specificity. Like Tung, Mendenhall and Oddou acknowledge the importance of degree of expected interaction and similarity between the native and host cultures in determining the cross-cultural training method. In addition, Mendenhall and Oddou propose three key elements related to training. The first is the training method. Based on cross-cultural training typologies such as the one by Landis and Brislin (1983), Mendenhall and Oddou propose a three-part classification system and group specific training methods into low, medium, and high levels of rigor.

The framework presented by Mendenhall and Oddou is a significant improvement over the more general framework offered by Tung (1982). It provides a grouping of specific methods by level of rigor and also discusses the duration of training relative to the criteria of interaction and culture similarity. Despite these important improvements, the framework does not explain how the level of rigor of a specific CCT method or group of methods was determined and tells us little about the training and learning processes and, therefore, why the particular determinations are made. Also, the content of the training all seems to be "cultural" in nature and little integration of the individual's new job-related tasks and the new host culture is made. Finally, while both frameworks make intuitive sense, their theoretical grounding is never made explicit, and therefore, in the absence of empirical data to support the frameworks, it is difficult to evaluate their soundness for use and success in the real world.

The Need for a Theoretical Framework _____

Despite the plethora of work advocating the use of cross-cultural training in organizations, the empirical research in this area and even the conceptual work have been almost totally devoid of a theoretical framework (Adler, 1986; Black and Mendenhall, 1990; Roberts and Boyacigiller, 1982; Schollhammer, 1975). Bochner states that cross-cultural "research cannot be said to have been conducted with a great deal of theoretical sophistication. The tendency has been to use lengthy and diffuse questionnaires and/or interviews that generate masses of unrelated information" (1982, p. 16). A previous review of the empirical literature in cross-cultural training indicates that, in general, cross-cultural training seems to have a positive impact on skill development, adjustment, and performance (Black and Mendenhall, 1990); however, the lack of a theoretical framework leaves questions like why cross-cultural training is effective and which situations are best served by which specific training methods essentially unanswered. The purpose of this next section is to examine social learning theory as a theoretical framework that would begin to shed light on these questions.

Social Learning Theory

The potential of SLT to facilitate an understanding of the theoretical relationship between cross-cultural training and cross-cultural performance is significant (Church, 1982; David, 1976). Before discussing the particular relevance of SLT to cross-cultural training and its effectiveness, it is perhaps useful to briefly summarize the main points of the theory. SLT, as described by one of its leading authors (Bandura, 1977), argues that learning takes place both by the effect reinforcement has on behavior and by imitating or modeling the behavior of others and symbolically or vicariously making associations between behavior and consequence without direct, actual experience. As described by Bandura, SLT has four central elements: attention, retention, reproduction, and incentives (see Exhibit 2).

Attention. Before someone or something can be modeled, it must be noticed by the learner. Several factors have been found to influence the attention process of the subject or observer, including: (1) the status of the model, (2) the attractiveness of the model, (3) the similarity of the model,

Exhibit 2. Model of Social Learning Theory Process

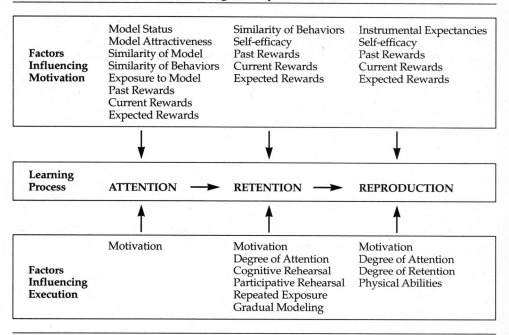

Factors Influencing Motivation	Model Status Model Attractiveness Similarity of Model Similarity of Behaviors Exposure to Model Past Rewards Current Rewards Expected Rewards	Similarity of Behaviors Self-efficacy Past Rewards Current Rewards Expected Rewards	Instrumental Expectancies Self-efficacy Past Rewards Current Rewards Expected Rewards
Learning Process	ATTENTION ⟶	RETENTION ⟶	REPRODUCTION
Factors Influencing Execution	Motivation	Motivation Degree of Attention Cognitive Rehearsal Participative Rehearsal Repeated Exposure Gradual Modeling	Motivation Degree of Attention Degree of Retention Physical Abilities

(4) the repeated availability of the model, and (5) past reinforcement for paying attention to the model (either actual or vicarious rewards).

Retention. Retention is the process by which the modeled behavior becomes encoded as a memory by the observer. Two representational systems are involved. The imaginal system is utilized during exposure to the framework. During exposure, images are associated on the basis of physical contiguity. These images are stored as "cognitive maps" which can later guide the observer in imitation. The second system is the verbal system. It represents the coded information in abbreviated verbal systems and groups similar patterns of behavior into larger integrated units. It should be noted that both the repeated modeling of a behavior and the repeated cognitive rehearsal of the modeled behavior serve to solidify the retention process.

Reproduction. The third major component of the modeling process involves the translation of the symbolic representations of the modeled stimuli into overt actions. As individuals try to imitate the modeled behavior, they check their performance against their memory of what was modeled. Actual reproduction of the modeled behavior, of course, can be inhibited by physical differences between the model and the person imitating the model, how well the model is observed, and how well the modeled behavior is retained.

Incentives and the Motivational Processes. The fourth major component of SLT involves the influence of incentives on the motivational processes of modeling behavior. Incentives have three primary sources. Incentives can come from the direct external environment, from vicarious association, and from the individual him- or herself. In turn, each of these different sources of incentives can affect several aspects of the learning process. Incentives can affect which models are observed and how much attention is paid to observed models. Incentives can influence the degree to which the modeled behavior is retained and rehearsed. Also, incentives can influence which learned behaviors are emitted. It is important to note that Bandura (1977) argued on the basis of empirical work that incentives play a much larger role in influencing what behavior is emitted as opposed to what behavior is learned. He concluded that individuals learn numerous behaviors which are not usually emitted because they are not positively rewarded. However, if the reward structure is changed, the behaviors are performed.

Expectancies. In relation to the motivational processes of learning, Bandura (1977) distinguishes between two types of expectancies. The first type of expectations Bandura calls "efficacy expectations." The individual's self-efficacy is the degree to which the individual believes he or she can successfully execute a particular behavior. This expectation is similar to the "effort to performance" expectancy proposed by Vroom (1964). In his view of the literature, Bandura (1977) found that higher levels of self-efficacy led individuals to persist at imitating modeled behavior longer and to be more willing to try to imitate novel behavior. The sources for increasing self-efficacy, in order of importance, including past experience ("I've done it or something like it before"), vicarious experience ("other people have done it"), and verbal persuasion ("people say I can do it").

In addition to efficacy expectations, Bandura (1977) argues that outcome expectations influence the modeling process. Outcome expectations are people's beliefs that the execution of certain behaviors will lead to desired outcomes. These expectations are similar to the "expectancy-of-performance-to-outcome" (instrumentality expectancies) proposed by Vroom (1964). Bandura concluded that in addition to the modeling processes of attention, retention, and reproduction, incentives influence what people learn and incentives and efficacy and outcome expectancies influence what learned behaviors are emitted.

Important Empirical Findings. Although a number of empirical findings are reviewed by Bandura (1977), several are important to summarize because of the insight they provide about fundamental elements in the learning process. The first finding is that gradual modeling is more effective than "one-shot" modeling, especially if the modeled behaviors are novel to the observer. Gradual modeling involves providing successive approximations of the final behavior to be modeled. This modeling process is more effective than modeling only the final behavior for several reasons: (1) observers pay more attention to models and modeled behaviors which are more familiar, (2) observers can more easily retain models which are more similar to cognitive maps already possessed, (3) observers have higher expectations of efficacy and outcome of behaviors which are more familiar, and (4) observers are more likely to be able to reproduce more familiar behaviors.

Second, Bandura argues that individuals can learn completely through symbolic modeling, that is, just by watching and rehearsing mentally. This symbolic learning process can be facilitated by the other variables discussed (attractiveness of the model, similarity of the model, etc.) and by having multiple models. Also, Bandura found that participative modeling is generally more effective than symbolic processes alone. Participative reproduction simply means that the observer actually practices (as opposed to only cognitive rehearsals) the modeled behavior. The external, and especially the internal, feedback processes serve to refine the observer's ability to reproduce the modeled behavior at a later time in the appropriate situation.

Social Learning Theory and Cross-Cultural Training ——————

Social learning theory provides a theoretical framework for systematically examining the level of rigor that specific CCT methods generally contain and for determining the appropriate cross-cultural training approach for specific training cases and situations. Based on the central variable of "modeling process" in SLT, the first part of this section explores a means of ranking specific cross-cultural training methods by the degree of rigor generally contained in the methods and examining two other factors that are related to the total rigor a training program might have. The second part of this section examines how SLT processes can provide a heuristic framework for deciding which CCT methods would be appropriate in specific situations. Throughout the second part of this section, we examine the practical implications of the framework for Mel Stephen's dilemma.

SLT and CCT Rigor

As was mentioned earlier, many of the past attempts to provide a means of choosing CCT methods have included the concept of training rigor but have not attempted to define what the term meant. Within the framework of SLT, rigor is essentially the degree of cognitive involvement of the learner or trainee. The modeling processes in SLT provide a useful means of not only defining rigor but also determining the relative degree of rigor that specific training methods generally have.

Within SLT, there are basically two modeling processes—symbolic and participative. Symbolic modeling simply involves observing modeled behaviors. However, this observation can have two forms. The first form consists of the learner or trainee hearing about the behavior and then translating those verbal messages into imagined images. Thus, the learner or trainee observes the behaviors in his or her mind. Cross-cultural training methods that generally exhibit this type of modeling process include verbal factual briefings, lectures, and books. The second form of symbolic modeling involves the trainee actually seeing visually the behavior being modeled. In this case, the trainee both sees and retains a cognitive image of the behavior and is more cognitively involved than when the symbolic modeling process only involves translating verbal messages into cognitive images. Specific CCT methods that generally exhibit this type of modeling include films, role modeling, demonstrations, and nonparticipative language training.

The second basic form of modeling is termed participative modeling. Participative modeling essentially means that in addition to observing the modeled behavior, the trainee also participates in modeling the behavior. This participation can take two forms. The first form involves "verbal" participation. In other words, the trainee participates in modeling the behavior by describing verbally what he or she would do. Cross-cultural training methods that generally exhibit this type of participative modeling include case studies and culture assimilators. The second form of participative modeling involves more physical participation in modeling the behaviors being learned. Cross-cultural training methods that generally require this type of participative modeling include role plays, interactive language training, field trips, and interactive simulations. Trainees are more cognitively involved when they must physically, as opposed to only verbally, participate in modeling the behaviors being taught.

In addition, rehearsal increases the level of cognitive involvement during symbolic or participative modeling. Rehearsal also has two basic forms. Cognitive rehearsal involves the mental rehearsal or practice of the modeled behavior (e.g., practicing eating with chop sticks in one's mind). Behavioral rehearsal involves actual physical practice of the modeled behavior. Because behavioral rehearsal involves both mental and physical processes, it is more cognitively engaging than cognitive rehearsal alone and, therefore, is more rigorous. By definition, symbolic modeling can utilize only cognitive rehearsal, while participative modeling can utilize either cognitive or behavioral rehearsal or both. Thus, the rigor of any specific CCT method could be enhanced through cognitive or behavioral rehearsal. Thus, by examining the modeling and rehearsal processes involved, the relative rigor of a specific CCT method can be approximated. Exhibit 3 provides an illustration of the relative ranking in terms of rigor for a set of specific and common CCT methods.

Exhibit 3. Modeling Processes, Rigor, & Training Methods

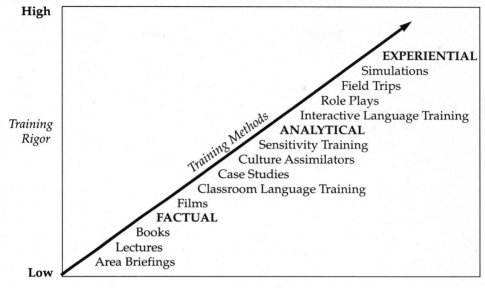

In determining the rigor of a CCT program, one would need to consider the rigor of the specific CCT method(s) utilized and the duration and intensity of the total CCT program. The duration and intensity of a CCT program is a function of the total hours of training and the time frame within which the training is conducted. Thus, all other things being equal, a training program that involved a total of 25 training hours over five days would be less rigorous than a program that involved 100 total hours over three weeks.

In general, the SLT literature and the CCT literature provide evidence to strongly suggest that the more rigorous the training the more effective the training will be in terms of the trainee being able to actually and appropriately execute the learned behaviors (Bandura, 1977; Black and Mendenhall, 1990; Tung, 1981). The basic explanation for this relationship is that rigor (i.e., cognitive involvement) increases the level of attention and retention, which in turn increases reproduction proficiency. As an example, Gudykunst, Hammer, and Wiseman (1977) found that a more rigorous CCT training program involving the "Contrast American" role play, "BaFa BaFa" cross-cultural training simulation, and field trips was significantly more effective for a sample of Navy personnel on overseas assignments in Japan than was CCT involving lectures on Japanese values and culture alone.

Important Situational Factors

In addition to providing a means of determining the general level of rigor of specific CCT methods, SLT also provides a framework for identifying situational factors that are important to consider in choosing appropriate CCT methods in specific situations. Social learning theory argues that the more novel the behaviors are that must be learned, the more difficult it is to attend to, retain, and reproduce them. In addition, SLT argues that the more frequently or accurately the learned behaviors are required to be reproduced in actual situations (as opposed to training situations), the greater the importance of the attention and retention processes during training. Thus, the greater the novelty of the behaviors to be learned and the greater the required level of reproduction, the higher the requisite levels of attention and retention needed, and the higher the level of the rigor of the training needed. These specific situational factors that are relevant to CCT are briefly discussed below.

Culture Novelty. Based on SLT and the arguments just made, the more novel the host culture is, the more difficult it will be for the individual to attend to and retain the various models of appropriate behavior (in the training situation as well as in the actual host culture). Thus, the more novel the host culture, the more assistance through rigorous training the individual will need in order to be aware of, retain, and appropriately reproduce the new behaviors appropriate in the foreign culture.

An important practical question is "How does one determine the degree of novelty in the host culture?" Once this question is answered, then the HR decision maker can begin to determine what the appropriate levels of CCT rigor and corresponding specific CCT methods are. While definitive decision rules are perhaps impossible to create, past cross-cultural research presents some rough guidelines (Haire, Ghiselli, and Porter, 1966; England and Lee, 1974; Hofstede, 1980). Information provided in Hofstede (1980) presents perhaps the most comprehensive yet simple means of estimating cultural novelty. Hofstede (1980) examined native employees in a U.S. multinational firm in 48 countries along four different scales (power distance, uncertainty avoidance, individualism, masculinity). A rough estimate of culture novelty can be obtained by calculating the absolute difference in scores on each one of the four scales between the employees of the target country and the American employees and then summing these differences. The larger the final number, the greater the culture novelty relative to the American culture. The work of Torbiorn (1982) also gives insight into the degree of cultural novelty. Torbiorn (1982) found that for Scandinavians the most difficult regions of the world to live and work in were: (1) Africa, (2) Middle East, (3) Far East, (4) South America, (5) Eastern Bloc, (6) Europe, (7) North America, and (8) Australia and New Zealand.

In addition to using Hofstede's (1980) results, one might estimate culture novelty by simply assessing whether the language of the host culture is different from that of the individual's home culture and whether learning the language will be a necessity for living and working in the host country. For example, even though Cantonese Chinese is the most common language of use in Hong Kong, English is still an official language and one can survive without Chinese language skills; however, survival would be more difficult without Spanish language skills in a country such as Chile (Kepler, Kepler, Gaither, and Gaither, 1983).

The next step in assessing the novelty of the target country and culture is to examine the previous experience of the specific individual candidate. Social learning theory would argue that the more experience the individual has had with a specific culture, even if that experience was in the distant past, the more the individual is able to recall and utilize those past experiences in coping with the present situation in the host culture. It should be mentioned that both the duration and intensity of the past experience serve to deepen what was retained from the experience and to facilitate later recall (Bandura, 1977). Thus, all things being equal, the Indonesian culture would be less novel for the candidate who lived there before than the candidate who had not. Likewise, all other things being equal, the candidate who had frequent and involved interactions with Indonesians during a three-year stay would find the culture less novel in a later visit than an individual who had infrequent and superficial interactions with Indonesians during a similar three-year stay. Thus, both the "quantity" and "quality" of an individual's previous experience must be examined. In addition, there is some empirical support that suggests that previous international experience, even if it is not in the host country's culture, reduces the novelty of the culture (Black, 1988). Based on SLT, one would expect that a candidate with previous experience in a country or region similar to the host country and culture would perceive less culture novelty, have an easier adjustment, and need less training than a candidate with previous experience in a totally different country or region, and that a candidate with frequent and involved previous interactions would need less training than a candidate with infrequent and superficial interactions. The following simple equation represents the basic assessment process: Net Culture Novelty = Objective Culture Novelty – (Quality + Quantity of an Individual's Previous Experience).

Degree of Interaction. The second situational factor in determining the degree of CCT rigor needed is the degree of expected interpersonal interaction between the individual and members of the host culture. The degree of interaction can be viewed in three ways. First, one can assess the degree of interaction through the relative frequency of interaction expected between the individual and members of the host culture. Also, one can assess the degree through the importance of the interactions. If one expects relatively few and mostly trivial interactions between the individual and members of the host culture, then the individual's ability to reproduce appropriate behaviors in the host culture is less important (and therefore, so would be the individual's attention and retention needs and the individual's need to get help to enhance attention, retention, and reproduction through rigorous training). If, on the other hand, one expects many and primarily important interactions between the individual and members of the host culture, then the individual's ability to reproduce appropriate behaviors is more important (and therefore, so would be the individual's need in getting help to enhance that ability).

In addition to the frequency and importance of the interactions, the nature of the interactions should also be assessed. Specific aspects of the nature of the interactions with host country nationals include the following:

1. how familiar or novel the interaction is;
2. the directionality of the interaction (one-way vs. two-way);
3. the type of the interaction (routine vs. unique);
4. the form of the interaction (face-to-face vs. other forms like mail);
5. the total duration of the cross-cultural interaction (e.g., one vs. five years); and
6. the format of the interaction (formal vs. informal).

Based on the communication literature (Jablin, Putnam, Roberts, and Porter, 1987), one would expect that novel, two-way, unique, face-to-face, long-term, and informal cross-cultural interactions would be more difficult than the opposite. The following equation represents the basic assessment of degree of interaction: Degree of Interaction = (Frequency of Interactions with Host Nationals) x (Importance of Interactions) x (Nature of Interactions).

Job Novelty. The third important situational factor involves the novelty of the new job and its related tasks. Based on precisely the same theoretical arguments that were presented concerning culture novelty, the more novel the tasks of the new job in the new culture, the more assistance the individual will need through rigorous training to produce the desired and necessary behaviors to be effective in the new job. Some scholars may reason that it is difficult to separate culture novelty from job novelty, arguing that if the culture is novel then to some degree the job will also be novel. Although culture novelty and job novelty are not independent of each other, there is both logical and empirical basis for separating the two issues. First, if there is little interaction between elements of the new culture and the job, and if the new job is very similar to the previous job, then it is quite possible to have a situation involving a novel culture but a nonnovel job. Likewise, it is possible to have a situation in which the new job is very different from the previous job but the host culture is similar to the individual's home culture. Recent empirical evidence suggests that individuals in international assignments adjust differentially to the culture and the job (Black, 1988; Black and Stephens, 1989), which suggests that while the novelty of the new job and culture can be linked they are not necessarily intertwined.

The question the HR decision maker must ask is "How novel is the new job and its tasks and responsibilities?" Although it is perhaps impossible to draw a definitive line between what would and would not be a novel job, Stewart's (1982) framework of job characteristics provides a useful means of determining where "job novelties" might occur. Based on Stewart's (1982) framework, the HR decision maker should first try to determine if the new *job demands* are similar to or different from those of previous jobs held by the candidate .

- Are performance standards the same?
- Is the degree of personal involvement required in the work unit the same?
- Are the types of tasks to be done similar?
- Are the bureaucratic procedures that must be followed similar?

Next the HR decision maker must determine how similar the new *job constraints* are.

- Are resource limitations the same?
- Are the legal restrictions similar?
- Are the technological limitations familiar?

Finally, the HR decision maker must determine the novelty of the new *job choices.*

- Is the freedom to decide how work gets done the same?
- Is the discretion about what work gets done similar?
- Is the freedom to decide who does which tasks the same?
- Are the choices about what work gets delegated similar?

If the HR decision maker examines the three job characteristics proposed by Stewart (1982), he or she should be able to make a rough estimate of the extent to which the new job is novel relative to a specific candidate. According to SLT, the more novel the new responsibilities and tasks, the more help the individual will need through rigorous training to learn and execute the desired and necessary behaviors.

The Family and CCT

The previous discussion has been presented as though the only person the HR decision maker needed to consider was the employee; however, research provides strong evidence to suggest that the candidate's family, especially the spouse, is also important to consider (Black, 1988; Black and Stephens, 1989; Harvey, 1986; Tung, 1981).

Culture Novelty. The process of determining the extent of training the family needs also begins with an assessment of culture novelty. The process of assessing the novelty of the culture obtained in relation to the candidate can be used for the family with two important qualifications. First, the final assessment of the host country's culture novelty must be made relative to the family's previous experience. Second, children under the age of about thirteen may need much less preparation than older children because they seem to have less difficulty adjusting to foreign cultures (Tung, 1984), and spouses must be given nearly as much consideration as the candidate is given because their adjustment or lack of adjustment can be a critical determinant of the candidate's success or failure in the foreign culture (Black, 1988; Black and Stephens, 1989; Tung, 1981).

Degree of Interaction. The spouse should also be given considerable attention concerning the degree of expected interaction in determining the level of CCT rigor needed to prepare him or her for living and functioning effectively in the foreign culture. The degree of expected interaction can be assessed in much the same manner as was suggested for the candidate (i.e., frequency and intensity). However, some important differences between candidates and spouses need to be considered. First, most spouses do not work in the host culture even if they worked before the foreign assignment (Stephens and Black, in press). Second, even if spouses are not required to interact with host country nationals, lack of the ability to interact can lead to feelings of isolation and loneliness, which in turn can be the primary cause of inadequate adjustment to the host culture and an early or premature return on the part of the entire family (Harvey, 1986; Tung, 1984; 1988). Consequently, even if the required degree of interaction between the spouse and host country nationals is low, the spouse will be better adjusted if he or she has the ability to interact effectively (Black and Stephens, 1989). Thus, it may be important to facilitate this ability through rigorous CCT even if the required degree of interaction does not seem to merit it.

Integrating Culture Novelty, Interaction, Job Novelty, and CCT Rigor

The theoretical reasoning behind the integration of culture novelty, interaction, and job novelty is relatively straightforward. The greater the culture novelty, required interaction, and job novelty, the greater the need for rigorous CCT. However, each of these three conditions is not "created equally." Research shows that adjusting to the culture and interacting with host country nationals is more difficult than doing the job (Black, 1988; Black and Stephens, 1989). This can be represented pictorially by a three-dimensional cube with a line running through the cube diagonally from the front left corner to the back right corner (see Exhibit 4).

**Exhibit 4. Integration of Cross-Cultural
Training Rigor and Main Contingency Factors**

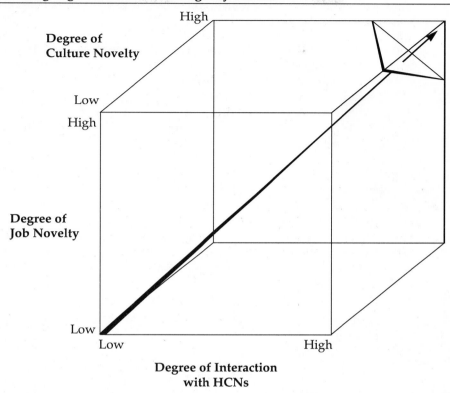

The vertical axis represents the dimension of job novelty, ranging from low to high novelty. The bottom horizontal axis represents the dimension of interaction, ranging from low to high required interaction. The top horizontal axis represents relative culture novelty, ranging from low to high novelty. The diagonal line, which runs from the front left corner to the back right corner, represents training methods and rigor, ranging from low to high rigor. Thus, a point can be plotted in the three-dimensional space by estimating the culture novelty, degree of required interaction, and job novelty of a specific impending cross-cultural assignment. The intersection of the plotted point and the diagonal line, and therefore the determination of the requisite level of rigor, can be determined by imagining a plane at a right angle to, and traveling on the same diagonal as the CCT rigor line. When the plane intersects the point plotted based on estimates relative to each of the three dimensions, it also intersects with a point on the diagonal line representing CCT rigor. That intersection provides a rough estimation of the CCT rigor required.

The plane is placed at a right angle because research has demonstrated that adjusting to a novel job in the work situation of an overseas assignment is easier than adjusting to the general culture or interacting with host nationals (Black, 1988; Black and Stephens, 1989). Thus, even in the case of a highly novel job but low culture novelty and low required interaction with host nationals, the highest level of CCT rigor is not required. By contrast, even if the level of job novelty is moderate, a high level of culture novelty and required interaction necessitates a high level of CCT rigor.

The content of the training would, of course, be a direct function of the three dimensions discussed. If the assessment indicates that there will be a high level of job novelty, then the CCT program should include content relative to the new behaviors that need to be learned to effectively perform the job. If there is a high degree of interaction required, then the CCT program should include in its content such topics as cross-cultural communication, interpersonal skills, perception, and ethnocentricity. If there is a high degree of culture novelty, then topics such as the host country's values, religious systems, political systems, social customs, and business practices should be included. The relative emphasis of the content would be a direct reflection of the relative low or high scores on each of the three dimensions.

Two Case Illustrations

Wave, one of the market leaders in the computer software industry, had just sealed a joint venture pact with one of Japan's largest designers and manufacturers of computers, Nippon Kankei. Wave, a Seattle-based company, agreed to send six Americans to work in Tokyo with fifteen of Nippon Kankei's best "high potential" software designers. The purpose of this effort was to train the Japanese designers in state-of-the-art software design while working on software applications for Nippon Kankei's products. Also, Nippon Kankei, through its distribution network, would market any products created by the joint venture research and development team to other computer manufacturers, distributers, and retailers as well. Wave would retain the copyright and share significantly in profits generated by the joint venture.

Wave retained complete managerial and creative control of the R & D team. The project manager was to be designated by Wave, and John Selby was selected and had agreed to go. John had vast experience in all aspects of the industry and had overseen four projects in the U.S. from the idea to the final product. The other five designers had limited managerial experience—they were pure designers. Nippon Kankei's management hoped that by rubbing shoulders and working jointly with these American designers their own staff would get "up to speed" in software design.

All of the designers agreed to relocate to Japan after feeling that their families' financial position and standard of living would not suffer because of the move. All of the designers were married. None of the designers indicated any reluctance on the part of their spouse concerning the three-year assignment; however, there were rumors that at least three of the wives were "less than thrilled" about disrupting their childrens' education and creating a new life in Japan.

What practical guidance concerning the cross-cultural training of this team of expatriates who are about to be sent to Japan can the framework we have discussed provide? The first step is to assess the culture novelty of the host country to which the team is being sent.

If Wave generalized Hofstede's (1980) research of Japanese who worked for an American multinational corporation to those Japanese who will be working with Wave's people in the joint venture, it would find the following: (1) Japanese have a much higher power distance (the degree workers accept power difference between managers and subordinates) of about 20 index points, (2) Americans are much more risk taking (53 index points on uncertainty avoidance), (3) Americans are much more individual and less group oriented than the Japanese (45 index points), and (4) Japanese accept traditional sex roles and have a higher work ethic than Americans (35 point differential). Hofstede's results suggest that not only does Japan have a culture quite different from American culture but it is one of the most different. The main language of Japan is also different. But to what degree will the expatriates from Wave need to speak Japanese? The ability of the Japanese assigned to the joint venture to read English is quite high, but their speaking and listening comprehension skills are marginal. Also, the American expatriates are likely to find it difficult to function effectively without Japanese language ability outside the workplace.

Next, Wave must assess the previous experience of the candidates. Unfortunately, though many had vacationed a time or two overseas, none of the candidates have lived or worked in Japan or have lived and worked outside the U.S. Thus, their previous experience would not reduce the culture novelty or the need for CCT. Based on all this information, it seems clear that the level of "culture novelty" that the Wave expatriates will experience will be quite high.

At first the degree of required interaction with Japanese workers for the American software designers would be fairly low, but would be much higher for John Selby, the project manager. However, the group-oriented nature of Japanese work organizations and the practice of consensus decision making increases the likelihood that all of Wave's expatriates will be interacting frequently with the Japanese. Additionally, the interactions are likely to be face-to-face, two-way, informal, and both routine and unique in nature over several years. Thus, while the degree of required interaction is likely to be higher for John Selby, it is still likely to be high for the other expatriates as well.

For Wave, on the surface it does not appear that the job novelty for the group of expatriates is very high. John Selby has managed four "start-up" projects before, and all the designers have had considerable experience in new product design. There are no new technical skills needed by the designers, and coming up with programs for new hardware systems is what they do for a living. Upon closer examination of the job demands, it seems that there is a high potential for performance standards, the tasks concerning training or working with Japanese, the way in which decisions get made, and the bureaucratic procedures that must be followed to all be different compared to their old jobs back in Seattle. Wave must also consider the novelty of job constraints. There is a high probability that resource limitations (e.g., communicating with colleagues and experts back at Wave), budgets, and legal restrictions are significantly different in Japan compared to Seattle. Finally, Wave needs to examine the novelty of job choices or discretion. Will the American designers be free to decide how to get work done (e.g., working hours) as they were in Seattle? Will John Selby be able to assign tasks and manage the team the same way he did back home? It is quite likely that all the members of the Wave team will need to make adjustments in order to work effectively with the Japanese. Wave's answers to these questions suggest that job choice novelty will be moderately high as well.

While there may be limits to Wave's budget, if it can, spouses should be included in the CCT program. This is because the novelty of the culture is high, and the ability to interact with shopkeepers, neighbors, banks, etc. greatly facilitates the spouse's ability to adjust to the new culture. As mentioned earlier, the spouse's adjustment is important because of the significance it has on expatriate adjustment (Black, 1988; Black and Stephens, 1989).

Thus, based on Exhibit 4, Wave needs to design or purchase a CCT program of fairly high rigor. The program should include some elements of symbolic modeling (both symbolic and observational) such as lectures, articles, books, and films on Japanese culture and business. But the CCT program should also include training methods that involve participative modeling as well. Specific methods might include case studies, culture assimilator exercises, interactive language study, role plays, and perhaps a premove visit to Japan. Additionally, the content of the training should include job, business, and general culture issues given the novelty of both task and culture. Obviously, a training program that includes all of these specific training methods will take time to execute. A reasonable estimate is that at least sixty hours of training will be needed. If time and scheduling constraints prevent all the training from occurring before departure to Japan, some follow-up training might be useful once the expatriates were settled in Japan.

A second case may provide further illustration of the practical implications of the framework presented. An academic association of management educators, primarily university and college business professors, was planning to hold a joint conference in Japan with Japanese business and business education leaders. The American professors were asked to submit professional papers on a wide range of business topics, and sixty were selected to participate in the international conference. The conference organizers decided to provide some type of CCT for the selected participants.

The designers of the training program had to first determine the culture novelty of Japan relative to the U.S. As has already been described, the work by Hofstede suggests that Japan is one of the most novel countries in relationship to America. However, the previous international experience of the selected participants in general or specifically in Japan were not known. Because participation in the training session could not be required, it was assumed that those who had the least amount of previous experience with Japan would be most likely to attend the training session. This, in fact, turned out to be the case. Thus, the degree of culture novelty was high.

Next the degree of interaction with host nationals had to be assessed. The design of the conference was such that there would be a mixture of formal, one-way interaction and informal, two-way interaction. The conference was scheduled to last only four days, so the duration of the interaction would be quite short but would involve frequent interactions during the four days. Although one of the purposes of the conference was to create better ties between the American and Japanese business scholars, the importance of the interactions was considered moderate. Also, the degree that the American scholars would need to know and utilize Japanese was small. It was expected that the Japanese participants would have a reasonable command of English since the entire program was to be conducted in English with very few sessions providing translators. Thus, the overall degree of interaction between the Americans and Japanese was expected to be low to moderate.

Finally, the job novelty for the American scholars had to be assessed. At first glance, the job novelty would seem quite low. In terms of presenting and listening to papers at an academic conference, this conference on paper looked quite similar to conferences held in the U.S. However, the demands of presenting research results to a culturally mixed audience (Japanese and Americans) were somewhat different from those of presenting to just an audience of American scholars. Overall, however, the job novelty for the American scholars was considered to be low to moderate.

Based on these assessments, Exhibit 4 would suggest the use of moderately rigorous training methods. Exhibit 3 indicates that moderate levels of training rigor consist of primarily symbolic modeling processes. Consequently, the training program was scheduled for a single day and included symbolic verbal modeling via (1) short lectures on specific aspects of Japan and Japanese culture that the American professors would likely encounter in their four-day stay, (2) a short video on the specific location of the conference, and (3) classroom language training focused on simple Japanese greetings and phrases. The training program also included some symbolic observational modeling via (1) demonstrations of such things as greetings and the exchanging of business cards and (2) role plays done for the training participants on presenting to a culturally mixed audience and on presenting using a translator.

Conclusion _____

A variety of implications can be derived from an SLT-based approach to CCT. The first three implications are related specifically to international or expatriate assignments. The next two implications are related to broader issues of good global development practices.

CCT Is a Necessity Not a Luxury

It is very clear from the research literature that the vast majority of senior executives do not support CCT programs for their employees who must work with foreign business people. The research literature is equally clear that American expatriates who work with foreigners without the benefit of CCT are less effective than those who have been trained. With so much at stake, from the success of business negotiations to the effective operation of overseas subsidiaries or joint ventures, there seems to be little reason not to invest time and money into training one's people who must work internationally. The training costs are small compared to the potential costs of early returns or business losses due to the lack of cross-cultural competency. As with any training intervention, unless top management support exists, the potential of a successful CCT program is low. HRM staff generally do not try to push through programs that are not sanctioned from on high; American senior executives need to start blessing the utilization of CCT programs—it's as simple as that.

It's a Family Affair

Of the few firms in the U.S. that do offer CCT to their expatriates, few offer such training to their spouses or other family members, despite the fact that research has demonstrated the impact that spouse and family adjustment can have on premature expatriate returns. A simple way to counteract this problem is to simply send spouses to the training sessions and to give them the same CCT the employee receives. While large portions of the training may be business related, much of it will be applicable to the nonworking spouse because cultural values and norms that affect business behavior also affect social behavior outside of the workplace. Also, knowing the challenges the employee will face at work may assist the spouse in offering support to the employee during the assignment. A more substantial effort would be to tailor a program that deals with the specific daily and cultural challenges that the spouse will face overseas. In some aspects, the spouse faces more challenges than does the employee. While the employee has his or her job and people at work, the spouse often has an empty house, no friends, and isolation with which to contend. Although much of the focus of this paper has centered on the employee and determining appropriate CCT methods for the employee, we have argued that these same assessment processes could be used to determine when it would be more or less critical to provide CCT for the spouse as well.

Avoid "Dog and Pony" Shows

Since many firms do not have the in-house expertise to design CCT programs, the use of external consultants and trainers is common. The lack of internal CCT expertise means that the ability of the HR staff to evaluate the quality and suitability of external CCT programs may be less than desired.

The framework presented in this paper provides HR decision makers with at least a rough template by which they can evaluate the quality, rigor, and appropriateness of training programs offered by consultants or universities. The decision maker could use the framework to evaluate consultants' bids or university programs in a more analytical fashion by comparing the training methodology to the various methods described in the paper. Next, by examining the various dimensions discussed, the decision maker could determine if he or she were buying more than was needed or whether the proposed training program would be inadequate and not sufficiently rigorous to meet the needs of the trainees in order to be more effective in their cross-cultural assignments.

CCT Is Not Just for Expatriates

Throughout this paper, much of the focus has been on expatriate employees; however, CCT is necessary for repatriated employees, for employees who go on short-term assignments, for good succession planning, and for general managerial development.

Just as the framework can be a guide for selecting or designing CCT for expatriates being sent overseas, it can also be used for selecting or designing training programs for employees returning to their home country after an international assignment. Although many managers would think that "coming home" would be "no big deal," Adler (1986) found that most managers found returning to the U.S. more difficult than adjusting to the foreign country.

In addition to CCT for employees being sent on or returning from long-term international assignments, the framework and theory presented suggests that employees sent on short-term assignments need CCT as well. The content of the training may need to be more focused and topic specific than for those headed for two-to-four-year assignments, as illustrated in the case of the American professors going to Japan for a four-day conference, but it is still necessary. Companies often send managers overseas for important tasks that take a relatively shorter period of time, yet fail to train these individuals as well. Sending someone to Korea to "explore business opportunities" or "work through the details of a joint venture agreement" require cross-cultural knowledge and skills. For example, Graham (1985) has demonstrated that Americans who do not understand Japanese negotiation tactics and their underlying values often utilize negotiation tactics and strategies that are counterproductive. The framework outlined in this paper regarding CCT methodology provides a means of determining the level of CCT rigor that is needed and specific methods that are appropriate.

The lack of CCT for international assignments can have a rather significant impact on succession planning for American firms. Consider the following scenario. U.S.A. MNC, Inc. does not provide CCT before international assignments. As a consequence, many good employees fail in their international assignments because they were not adequately prepared. Also, the firm does not provide CCT for returning expatriates or managers sent on short-term assignments. Some of these employees also fail because of inadequate preparation. Other bright employees notice this. Not wanting the same fate to befall them, the best and the brightest decline to accept international assignments. These best and brightest, who lack any in-depth international experience, then continue to move to the top of the firm. Once they make it to the top, one has to wonder how capable they will be at dealing with foreign competitors, with global markets, with international suppliers, with multicultural workforces, and so on.

In the introduction, we cited scholars who argue that corporations need to develop managers with the new skills, such as global visioning skills, multicultural relation skills, and so on, to effectively lead firms in the 1990s and into the twenty-first century. Consequently, developing these skills is a critical element of succession planning. At a macro level, the framework presented suggests that if managers in the future must deal with cultures different from their own, must tackle tasks quite novel from those in which they currently engage, and must be proficient in interacting with people from other cultures, then they must receive over the course of their career and development quite rigorous cross-cultural training. Thus, the framework can provide guidance concerning the level of CCT rigor and specific training methods, such as culture assimilators, necessary for a specific international assignment, but it can also suggest the level of CCT rigor and training methods, such as international assignments, needed to prepare individuals for general positions and responsibilities in the future.

Ethics and CCT

In addition to the "utilitarian" functions that CCT may serve, firms may want to consider the issue from a social responsibility or ethical perspective. The military trains its soldiers before sending them into battle, churches educate and train their missionaries before sending them out to proselytize, and governments train secret agents before they go under "deep" cover, but U.S. firms send employees overseas cold. Such a "sink-or-swim" approach would seem irresponsible and unreasonable to the military, clergy, or government, why then does it seem logical to the industrial sector? One must wonder if it is ethical to uproot an individual or a family, send them across the Pacific or Atlantic Oceans, and expect them to make their way skillfully through an alien business and social culture on their own. Perhaps American executives reason that the extraordinary compensation packages expatriates receive make the exchange a fair and ethical one. Living and working overseas involves adjustments and stress of a high magnitude. Placing individuals in such conditions without giving them the tools to manage these conditions seems not only economically costly to the firm, and personally costly to the individuals, but simply wrong. Ignorance is not held to be justifiable for failure domestically—why then should it be a justification for failure regarding international assignments? If U.S. firms are to successfully compete in what is becoming a global battleground, they must provide their soldiers with the weapons and ammunition necessary to wage effective and victorious campaigns.

References ————————————————————————————

Adler, N. *International dimensions of organizational behavior.* Boston, Mass.: Kent, 1986.

Baker, J. C. and Ivancevich, J. M. "The assignment of American executives abroad: systematic, haphazard, or chaotic?" *California Management Review,* 1971, 13, 39- 44.

Bandura, A. *Social learning theory.* Englewood Cliffs, N.J.: Prentice-Hall, 1977.

Black, J. S. "Japanese/American negotiations: The Japanese perspective." *Business and Economic Review,* 1987, 6 (1), 27-30.

Black, J. S. "Work role transitions: a study of American expatriate managers in Japan." *Journal of International Business Studies,* 1988, 19, 277-294.

Black, J. S. and Mendenhall, M. "Cross-culture training effectiveness: a review and theoretical framework for future research." *Academy of Management Review,* 1990, 15, 113-136.

Black, J. S. and Stephens, G. K. "The influence of the spouse on American expatriate adjustment and intent to stay in Pacific Rim assignments." *Journal of Management,* 1989, 15, 529-544.

Bouchner, S. *Culture in contact: Studies in cross-cultural interaction.* New York: Pergamon Press, 1982.

Brein, M. and David, K. H. "Intercultural communication and adjustment of the sojourner." *Psychology Bulletin,* 1971, 76, 215-230.

Brislin, R. W. *Cross-cultural encounters.* New York: Pergamon Press, 1981.

Church, A. T. "Sojourn adjustment." *Psychological Bulletin,* 1982, 91, 540-571.

Copeland, L. and Griggs, L. *Going international.* New York: Random House, 1985.

David, K. H. "The use of social learning theory in preventing intercultural adjustment problems." In Pedersen, P., Lonner, W. J., and Draguns, J. (eds.), *Counseling across cultures.* Honolulu, Hawaii: University of Hawaii Press, 1976.

Doz, Y. and Prahalad, C. K. "Controlled variety: a challenge for human resource management in the MNC." *Human Resource Management,* 1986, 25(1), 55-71.

Dunbar, E. and Ehrlich, M. "International practices, selection, training, and managing the international staff: a survey report." *The Project on International Human Resource.* Columbia University, Teachers College, 1986.

Early, P. C. "Intercultural training for managers: a comparison of documentary and interpersonal methods." *Academy of Management Journal,* 1987, 30, 685-698.

England, G. and Lee, R. "The relationship between managerial values and managerial success in the U.S., Japan, India, and Australia." *Journal of Applied Psychology,* 1974, 59, 411-419.

Graham, J. "The influence of culture on the process of business negotiations: an exploratory study." *Journal of International Business Studies,* Spring, 1985, 81-95.

Gudykunst, W. B., Hammer, M. R., and Wiseman, R. L. "An analysis of an integrated approach to cross-cultural training." *International Journal of Intercultural Relations,* 1977, 1, 99-110.

Haire, M., Ghiselli, E. E., and Porter, L. W. *Managerial thinking: An international study.* New York: Wiley, 1966.

Harris, P. and Morgan, R. T. *Managing cultural differences.* Houston: Gulf, 1979.

Harvey, M. C. "The other side of the foreign assignment: dealing with repatriation problems." *Columbia Journal of World Business,* Spring 1982, 53-59.

Harvey, M. C. "The executive family: an overlooked variable in international assignments." *Columbia Journal of World Business,* Spring 1985, 84-92.

Hofstede, G. *Culture's consequences: International differences in work related values.* Beverly Hills, Calif.: Sage.

Jablin, F. M., Putnam, L. L., Roberts, K. H., and Porter, L. W. *Handbook of organizational communication.* Beverly Hills, Calif.: Sage, 1987.

Kepler, J. Z., Kepler, P. J., Gaither, O. D., and Gaither, M. C. *Americans abroad.* New York: Praeger, 1983.

Latham, C. "Human resource training and development." *Annual Review of Psychology,* 1988, 39, 545-582.

Landis D. and Brislin, R. *Handbook on intercultural training.* Vol. 1. New York: Pergamon Press, 1983.

Lanier, A. R. "Selection and preparation for overseas transfers." *Personnel Journal,* 1979, 58, 160-163.

Locke, E. and Latham, G. *Goal setting: A motivational technique that works.* Englewood Cliffs, N.J.: Prentice-Hall, 1984.

Mendenhall, M. and Oddou, G. "The cognitive, psychological, and social contexts of Japanese management." *Asia Pacific Journal of Management,* 1986a, 4(1), 24-37.

Mendenhall, M. and Oddou, G. "Acculturation profiles of expatriate managers: implications for cross-cultural training programs." *Columbia Journal of World Business,* 1986b, 21, 73-79.

Mendenhall, M., Dunbar, E., and Oddou, G. "Expatriate selection, training, and career-pathing: a review and critique." *Human Resource Management,* 1987, 26, 331-345.

Mendenhall, M. and Oddou, G. "The dimensions of expatriate acculturation." *Academy of Management Review,* 1985, 10:39-47.

Miller, E. "The international selection decision: A study of managerial behavior in the selection decision process." *Academy of Management Journal,* 1973, 16, 234-252.

Misa, K. F. and Fabricatore, J.M. "Return on investment of overseas personnel." *Financial Executive,* April 1979, 42-46.

Ohmae, K. "Managing in a borderless world." *Harvard Business Review,* May-June, 1989, 152-161.

Roberts, K. H. and Boyacigiller, N. "Issues in cross national management research: the state of the art." Paper presented at the National Meeting of the Academy of Management, New York, 1982.

Runzheimer Executive Report 1984. "Expatriation/repatriation survey." No. 31. Rochester, Wisconsin.

Schollhammer, H. "Current research on international and comparative management issues." *Management International Review,* 1975, 15, 29-45.

Schwind, H.F. "The state of the art in cross-cultural management training." In Doktor, Robert (ed.), *International Human Resource Development Annual* (Vol. 1), 7-15, Alexandria, Va.: ASTD, 1985.

Stephens, G. K. and Black, J. S. "The impact of the spouse's career orientation on managers during international transfers." Forthcoming in *Journal of Management Studies.*

Stewart, R. *Choices for managers.* Englewood Cliffs, N.J.: Prentice-Hall, 1982.

Sundaram, A. "Unique aspects of MNCs: a top-down perspective." Working paper series. Amos Tuck School of Business Administration, Dartmouth College, 1990.

Torbion, I. *Living abroad.* New York: Wiley, 1982.

Tung, R. "Selecting and training of personnel for overseas assignments." *Columbia Journal of World Business,* 1981, 16:68-78.

Tung, R. *Key to Japan's economic strength: Human power.* Lexington, Mass.: Lexington Books, 1984.

Vroom, V. *Work and motivation.* New York: Wiley, 1964.

Zeira, Y. "Overlooked personnel problems in multinational corporations." *Columbia Journal of World Business,* 1975, 10(2), 96-103.

The Overseas Assignment: A Practical Look

Reading 4.2
Mark E. Mendenhall
Gary Oddou

John McNally, aged 38, is assistant to the vice president of marketing in a medium-sized firm in the electronics industry. He was recently approached by his boss about heading up the company's Far East operations. This position would offer John greater responsibility, decision-making authority, job autonomy, and a substantial increase in salary and perks. In many ways it would allow John the opportunity to do what he has always wanted to do—manage a sector of the firm that is unequivocally "his" from top to bottom. John's boss made it clear that this would be a great opportunity for him, and that it was his job to take or turn down because of his strong track record in the company.

How would John's wife, Nancy, and their two kids react to moving from the Bay Area to Tokyo? Like John, Nancy has never lived overseas. As John reached for the phone to call his wife, the initial excitement of the offer was tempered by a nagging doubt. It seemed so appealing on the surface, but he wondered what the down sides were to this move. Even knowing the down sides, could he really afford to turn it down? He began to dial, wondering if he could sort all of this out in the two weeks he was given to make the decision.

John McNally's experience is not different from that of most managers who have been approached about relocating overseas. Since most managers do not like to take leaps of faith in their careers, they sometimes feel as though they are stepping into the unknown in their family life, social life, and career path, when they accept overseas assignments. What does John need to learn in the next two weeks about the reality of international assignments before making his decision? More generally, what should every executive know before agreeing to an overseas assignment?

The Potential Failure of Expatriates ————————————————

It has been estimated that approximately 20 percent of personnel sent abroad return prematurely from an overseas assignment, so John has reason to be concerned.[1] Many others endure to the end of their assignments but find themselves ineffective in their jobs, unhappy in their social lives, and often close to a broken marriage. Why does this occur?

The main reason is called culture shock. This term covers anxieties about customs and security that appear when one must deal with a foreign culture. It manifests itself among expatriates in many ways: change in sexual drive, eating binges, bouts of depression, idiosyncratic nervous habits, manifestations of anger and aggression, substance abuse, alienation from others, homesickness, insomnia or oversleeping, lack of motivation at work, and impatience with family members.

The problems of expatriation are not limited to the overseas stay. Many expatriates report experiencing culture shock upon returning to the U.S. Culture shock can occur in many ways, but probably the most difficult for the expatriate is the shock of his or her new position. Returning managers nearly always experience less decision-making power, autonomy, and salary, and fewer perks upon return. No one seems to care that the expatriate spent three intriguing, eye-opening years in Venezuela, Japan, or wherever.

Even worse, however, is the estimate that about one-quarter of all American expatriates do not even gain a position in the firm upon return from a foreign assignment. One executive was told he had six months to find a place in the company or he would have to start looking elsewhere. He found a job in another firm. Some executives launch an informal in-house search and find positions within the firm. Some look elsewhere immediately. Others take demotions or find they must relocate or accept other constraints they had not expected to face.

Such consequences are traceable to the failure of organizations to anticipate problems and create policies to deal with them. With so much at risk, how can an executive know whether to accept the overseas assignment? Two areas must be considered: his or her personal cross-cultural adaptation skills; and his or her organization's philosophy and orientation toward an international assignment.

Cross-Cultural Adaptation Skills ————————————————

Research in expatriate adaptation clearly indicates that success in an overseas work assignment depends upon the possession of specific skills. These skills can be fit into one of three categories: personal skills, people skills, and perception skills.[2]

Personal Skills

Those techniques and attributes that facilitate the expatriate's mental and emotional well-being are personal skills. They can include meditation, prayer or other means of finding solitude, and physical exercise routines, all of which tend to decrease the executive's stress level. One's abilities to manage time, delegate, and manage his or her responsibilities are also personal skills.

People Skills

Effective interaction with others, particularly with foreigners, is another necessity for successful adaptation. The executive who desires or needs to communicate with others, is willing to try to speak the foreign language (even when not necessary), and doesn't worry about making linguistic mistakes is much more likely to be successful than the executive who is introverted, self-conscious, or otherwise not comfortable when interacting with foreigners.

Perception Skills

These skills deal with the cognitive processes that help the executive understand why foreigners behave the way they do. The willingness to make tentative conclusions from the first observation of different actions or attitudes is an important cognitive dimension. Managers have been taught to size things up quickly to make an equally quick decision. Perception skills also relate to one's consciousness of social cues and behaviors, one's attentiveness to them, and one's ability to imitate what he or she perceives.

The Firm's Philosophy About International Assignments ⎯⎯⎯⎯

Each firm looks at international assignments in a different way. The executive can understand this philosophy by looking at five elements, each of which will be discussed below.

The Strategic Importance of the International Assignment

Some overseas assignments are springboards to career growth within the firm. These positions usually are in overseas operations viewed by top management as keys to the firm's future performance. For example, a vice president of marketing for the Caribbean region does not carry the same clout as the vice president of marketing for the expanding markets in the Far East. The more strategic the overseas position, the greater the executive's visibility.

    Being key to a firm's future growth is not the only sign that an area is strategic, however. If the subsidiary is the cash cow of the European region, for example, there is a higher status level than if the position is in a dog or question-mark subsidiary in the same region.

If career advancement is your primary goal, you should not accept any overseas assignment unless you will get high visibility. If you have been with the firm for a relatively short time and don't know how valuable the various operations are, ask to look at the financial statements and talk to some of the old-timers. Don't be shy. It's *your* career.

The Degree of Integration of Human Resources Into Strategic Planning

Human-resource directors are not involved in strategic planning of MNCs, at least at the corporate level. At the strategic business unit (SBU) level some tying of human-resource issues with SBU international strategy exists, but the degree varies with each firm.[3] In the firms with the most integration, management training, selection, support, development, and other human-resource concerns are covered by formal policies created especially for the international needs of the SBU and based on valid information from the SBU's other functional areas.

An executive can get an indication of how formalized the worldwide human-resource-planning function is by the amount of lead time given before the expected departure. If lead times range from a few days to a couple of months, there is probably little to no international human-resource strategic planning. This lack of planning is a warning that the firm places relatively little value on international assignments in general. If the firm typically projects its worldwide needs several months to a year ahead of time, but only gives the executive a short amount of time to decide and leave, a forest-fire situation may exist. Either the previous expatriate failed and is returning home prematurely, or a sudden turn of events in an overseas operation requires immediate attention. In either case, the executive should be very cautious.

If very short lead times are typical of your firm, upper management probably places little real significance on overseas operations. It is doubtful that performing well overseas will enhance your career. Because chances for failure are great and the "out of sight, out of mind" syndrome must be considered, you should probably turn the offer down if you plan to advance in your present firm.

If another expatriate is returning home early, find out why. Is the work situation or the family situation the cause? If the work situation has been particularly difficult, what exactly is the problem and will you be able to solve it? Is the difficulty a perennial problem, typical of that assignment, or is it an emergency—open rebellion by the foreign employees, a political overthrow leading to a hostile government? Talk to the returning expatriate and get his or her perception of the problem. If it's the family situation, how different is your family from the one returning? Is yours more likely to adapt well?

The Amount of International Experience in Senior Management

A firm reveals how much value it places on overseas assignments by the amount of overseas experience its senior managers have. Some firms, such as AlCan of Canada, require their senior managers to have had overseas experience. But over two-thirds of senior managers in U.S. firms have had no real overseas experience.[4] Very little overseas experience at the senior level probably indicates that very little value is placed on such assignments.

However, one must be attentive to the trends within the firm. The expanding global market has many firms scrambling to take advantage of some of the opportunities abroad. If a firm is headed in such a direction, it probably will be looking for some of its best personnel to head up overseas operations.

Find out what the backgrounds of your senior managers are. Determine how much overseas experience they have, in which countries and in which assignments. It may be that value is placed on specific functional or geographical areas. If most of them have had European assignments, for example, then an assignment to South America might not be the plum you anticipated. But if senior managers have little overseas experience, beware. Executives who have not worked abroad do not really understand the difficulties involved or the growth that results from working abroad. With the added responsibility and independence usually experienced abroad, the executive typically develops more quickly than in the U.S. Unfortunately, the expatriate usually returns unappreciated and underutilized in the domestic operation.

The Validity of the Performance Evaluation Instrument and System

Valid performance evaluation is difficult enough to achieve in the U.S. Overseas assignments simply make a complex problem nearly impossible. What normally works in one culture might not in another. While delegating is generally considered a good management practice in the U.S., in some countries it is considered a management weakness. A motivational scheme based on job rotation might work in the U.S. but have disastrous consequences in countries where job specialization is mandated by law.

The distance from the corporate office to the overseas post can also create problems. The corporate office is almost always involved in the evaluation of the expatriate's performance. But how does someone in New York evaluate performance of someone in Peru? In such situations, the corporate personnel are forced to rely on global types of performance indicators: return on investment, cash flow, market share, and so forth. Situational factors that are outside the executive's control are usually not considered. Such factors can include devaluation of the domestic currency, runaway inflation, government-controlled work forces, political instability, and so on. These factors will have a definite effect on the overseas operation's performance.

Even if the executive overseas is not normally considered responsible for the total operation, performance evaluation problems can exist. For example, the comptroller of one of the largest electronic firms in the world once complained that in reality he, not the host national chief operating officer, was held responsible for maintaining the profit line of the overseas division he worked in. (He was the only U.S. citizen working in upper management in that division.) The ambiguity of the performance criteria can also cause problems. Expatriates are not always told how their performance will be evaluated, so they do not know where to expend their energy.

The more the evaluation is done by foreigners, the less control the expatriate has, since the evaluation can be culturally defined to a large extent. Similarly, the more the criteria are of the global type, the less control the expatriate has, particularly in countries where economic, social, political, and material resources are unstable.

Know before you leave what the performance evaluation system will consist of. Who will be evaluating you, and with how much validity can these individuals appraise your performance? If one or more of the evaluators will be from the foreign country, how much exposure have they had to Americans? Find out what their attitudes are through the grapevine. What will the criteria be, and are they ones over which you have a large degree of control? The more the criteria are of the global type (market share, profit status, ROI), the more likely it is that the corporate office's evaluation will count the most.

The less control you would have over the evaluation process and the results, the more suspicious you should be about the assignment.

The Degree of Formalization and Rigor of the Selection, Training and Overseas Support Systems

Selection. The vast majority of MNCs in the U.S. select their expatriates based on managerial or technical excellence. They assume that managing well in the U.S. takes the same characteristics as managing well in Amman, Jordan. This assumption is as false as the belief that managing one division in a firm is the same as managing another, and very different, division. Or they assume that the ability to solve a technical problem will lead to success in any environment. Technical competence has nothing to do with one's ability to adapt to a new environment, deal effectively with foreign coworkers, or perceive and if necessary imitate the foreign behavioral norms.

Furthermore, since the reason most often cited for early expatriate return is the spouse's inability to adapt, the selection procedure should include an appraisal of the spouse's likelihood to succeed overseas. The issue is further complicated when both spouses work. One of the two generally has to put a career on hold. In addition, families who have children in their middle and late teens often have more problems than those with younger children.

You should probably be flattered if you have been selected above others for an overseas assignment. It usually means you are admired for your technical or managerial competence. So the real assessment lies with you. Do you have the cross-cultural skills (personal, people, and perception skills) to adapt? How appealing is the assignment to your family? How likely are they to succeed? Are there support systems for them overseas?

Don't be afraid to turn the assignment down if you don't think you or your family will adapt. It is generally better to say "no thanks" up front rather than to return early from overseas with frayed nerves, an upset marriage, and a failure mark on your record.

Training. Firms vary in the type of training they offer executives. A few firms have an intensive, month-long training session, while others hand the executive a few brochures just before he or she boards the plane.

The content also differs widely. Those firms who understand that working abroad is more than solving a technical problem cover a much wider range of topics: foreign customs, thinking patterns, societal values, language, the organizational culture, environmental factors, support systems, and so forth. Other firms simply rely on the brochures they hand the executive to cover the necessary material. While brochures are sometimes quite informative, they do not treat factors that will directly facilitate adaptation.

When an executive is sent to a culture that closely resembles his or her own, information is probably sufficient. However, for the executive (and family) going to Malaysia or Japan, where the cultures differ significantly from the U.S., information might not be enough. Training should include role playing, culture confrontation, and behavioral situations. Only in behavioral situations is an individual forced to deal with the emotions that result from misunderstandings, frustration, and differences in customs and courtesies. The executive will confront these same emotions overseas. It is far better to try to understand and deal with them before leaving to reduce the amount of culture shock.

Finally, since the top reason for early returns is the spouse's inability to adapt, the wise firm will include the spouse and any other family members in their teens and older in the training. In fact, such training is actually more important for the spouse than it is for the executive. Although the executive changes job locations, often the exact nature of the job itself may not change drastically. It is the spouse who experiences extreme changes: a postponed career, a different language, different stores and shopping habits, a lack of friends and family upon which to rely, and so on.

An extensive cross-cultural training program reflects a firm's commitment to you and your success overseas. Chances are that such a firm also forecasts its worldwide human-resource needs months in advance and strategically values its overseas operations. If the training also includes your spouse and older family members, your probability of success abroad is much higher. If the assignment fits into your personal career plans, you should probably accept it.

On the other hand, if you are headed to Japan and are handed brochures as you are boarding the plane, you should probably hope there is one domestic stop before reaching the foreign country. If so, deplane and tell your firm you changed your mind.

Overseas Support Systems. Just as firms vary in their commitment to selection and training, they vary in their support of the executive and his or her family overseas. One executive of a large office-equipment multinational reported that his firm had a very organized support system overseas. The highest-ranking expatriate, as part of his job, was responsible for helping the other expatriates adjust. His duties included informal counseling, the sponsorship of monthly social gatherings to discuss problems and successes as expatriates, and the function of his spouse as a mentor to newly arrived spouses .

An organized effort such as this really helps. However, what if the executive and his or her family are the only ones at the foreign site? How do firms support them? The better ones encourage the executive to call corporate or division headquarters as often as needed. He or she must be able to ask questions for guidance, receive suggestions from other expatriates about difficulties the family is experiencing, or just have someone who will listen. This takes a great deal of pressure off the spouse.

A committed firm also informs the executive of any local support systems. For example, if the family is active in a religion, the firm should tell them about the nearest congregation of their faith. If the executive is a member of a club such as Rotary or Lion's, the firm can inform the executive of the nearest chapter. If another U.S.-owned firm or subsidiary in the area has expatriates, the two firms might have an understanding that encourages them to share information and otherwise help each other.

A firm can do many things to support its employees overseas. But some firms practice the "out of sight, out of mind" philosophy. One executive, for example, complained that calls to the home office were rarely returned. There were no organized social systems, no mentors to give advice, and no information about any local groups that might help ease his adjustment to the foreign country. The total experience put an extreme strain on his marriage and several times he vowed to return home. He finally sent his wife home with the children and remained overseas for the rest of the year.

If you are going to a distinctly different culture, don't leave without knowing what types of support you will find in the home office and overseas. Has your firm identified other expatriates that have recently been to your site, and encouraged you to call them as the need arises? Do you know what to expect once you arrive overseas? Are there other Americans? Has your firm identified support sources for you if there isn't an organized support system in your division? Is the system especially strong for spousal support, rather than being focused around your needs?

The stronger the support system, and the more it is directed toward spousal/family needs, the more likely you are to succeed overseas. If your firm cannot identify support resources and has no organized system overseas, think seriously about refusing the assignment if your location contrasts starkly with your home situation and your family is accompanying you. Don't build in failure.

What If I Am Stuck? _____

It may be that for political or other career reasons an overseas assignment just cannot be turned down. The organizational system may be full of red flags, but you are told that you must go anyway; you feel you have no choice. What can you do?

Prepare Yourself

There is no reason for anyone who will be living overseas to be ill-prepared for the experience. A list of books, articles, and other sources of information for the neophyte expatriate are given in the Reference section. In addition, various foreign-language packages can help prepare the expatriate linguistically for the overseas stay. If your firm has no language materials, talk to the foreign-language department of your local university.

In most cases, self-education will likely match the program most companies provide for their expatriates. The key is the executive's level of determination to be prepared for his or her overseas stay.

Keep Yourself in Touch

If your company has no program to keep you abreast of changes in the home office while you are away, create one. Consistent correspondence and phone calls to peers, superiors, and other significant players in the U.S. will inform them of your successes and progress, as well. Never assume that the corporate or division managers will try to watch your work by reading your reports. Realize that you will have to keep the communication lines open yourself .

Build Options Overseas

By the end of your stay you will have gained skills that most others in your profession do not have—how to operate, negotiate, and manage in one or more foreign countries. Despite your best efforts to stay in stay in touch with the home office, you may sense six months before your return that the home office will not have a suitable position for you upon your return. Begin your job search, both in-house and with other firms, at least a year before you are scheduled to return.

If you are willing to stay overseas, many companies who may be newcomers in the region might value your business skills. If you desire to return home, seek out firms who are either in the early stages of joint-venture development or trying to determine whether to export or set up operations in your country of expertise. They will likely view you as an important resource in their strategic planning efforts.

Never assume that you will have a position suitable to your experience guaranteed to you upon return. Use your overseas assignment to expand your skills and enhance your marketability, both domestically and internationally. Get involved in the activities of the expatriate community—they are one of the best sources of career opportunities.

Enjoy the Benefits of Personal Growth

Expatriates almost always say they would advise others to accept an overseas assignment. Their rationale is not that it really helped their careers, but that it expanded their minds. There is something about having to live in, adapt to, attempt to understand, and accept different behaviors and ways of thinking that broadens one's horizon.

A new culture can give you new lenses that highlight new dimensions of the human experience. Cultures tend to focus on certain aspects of life, and when you live and work in a culture that focuses on dimensions of life largely downplayed in the U.S., you can come to understand and value experiences and traditions previously unknown.

Revel in the Adventure

The overseas assignment can be a wonderful adventure if it is viewed as one. Modern conveniences and other artifacts of our society have taken much of the adventure out of life and made our existence much more predictable. Living overseas is perhaps one of the last great adventures for individuals and families. Taking this view makes the inevitable setbacks and barriers a little easier to deal with, creating a positive context for daily existence.

Living overseas is not easy. It takes much cognitive and emotional effort to learn the new culture, and some soul-searching at times when accepted behaviors abroad violate ethical or moral norms of one's value system. An executive must depend on others to accomplish things that were second nature in his or her own culture. These can be seen as negative aspects of living overseas or as positive challenges leading to the enrichment and refinement of one's personality. The choice really is up to the expatriate.

Notes _____

1. See Copeland, L. and Griggs, L. *Going International.* New York: Random House, 1985; Misa, K. F. and Fabricatore, J. M. "Return on Investment of Overseas Personnel." *Financial Executive,* 47(4), 42-46; Torbiorn, I. *Living Abroad: Personal Adjustment and Personnel Policy in the Overseas Setting.* New York: Wiley, 1982; Tung, R. L. "Selection and Training of Personnel for Overseas Assignments." *Columbia Journal of World Business,* 16(1), 68-78.

2. Mendenhall, M. and Oddou, G. "The Dimensions of Expatriate Acculturation: A Review." *Academy of Management Review,* 1985; 10, 39-47.

3. Miller, E., Beechler, S., Bhatt B., and Nath, R. "The Relationship Between the Global Strategic Planning Process and the Human Resource Management Function." *Human Resource Planning,* 9(1), 9-23.

4. Adler, N. *The International Dimensions of Organizational Behavior.* Boston: PWS Kent, 1986.

References _____

Adler, N. *The International Dimensions of Organizational Behavior.* Boston: PWS Kent, 1986.

Copeland, L. and Griggs, L. *Going International.* New York: Random House, 1985.

Gaylord, M. "Relocation and the Corporate Family." *Social Work,* May 1979, 186-191.

Hall, E. *The Silent Language.* Garden City, N.Y.: Doubleday, 1959.

Harris, P. R. and Moran, R. T. *Managing Cultural Differences.* Houston: Gulf, 1979.

Harvey, M. G. "The Executive Family: An Overlooked Variable in International Assignments." *Columbia Journal of World Business,* Spring 1985, 84-93.

Mendenhall, M. and Oddou, G. "The Dimensions of Expatriate Acculturation: A Review." *Academy of Management Review,* 1985, 10, 39-47.

Torbiorn, I. *Living Abroad: Personal Adjustment and Personnel Policy in the Overseas Setting.* New York: Wiley, 1982

Tullg, R. L. "Selection and Training of Personnel for Overseas Assignments." *Columbia Journal of World Business,* 16(1), 68-78.

Walker, E. J. "'Til Business us do Part?" *Harvard Business Review,* January-February 1976, 94-101.

Fred Bailey: An Innocent Abroad—A Case Study in Cross-Cultural Management

Case 4.1
J. Stewart Black

Fred gazed out the window of his twenty-fourth floor office at the tranquil beauty of the Imperial Palace amidst the hustle and bustle of downtown Tokyo. It had been only six months since Fred Bailey had arrived with his wife and two children for this three-year assignment as the director of Kline & Associates' Tokyo office. Kline & Associates was a large multinational consulting firm with offices in nineteen countries worldwide. Fred was now trying to decide if he should simply pack up and tell the home office that he was coming home or if he should try to somehow convince his wife and himself that they should stay and finish the assignment. Given how excited they all were about the assignment to begin with, it was a mystery to Fred how things had gotten to this point. As he watched the swans glide across the water in the moat that surrounds the Imperial Palace, Fred reflected on the past seven months.

Seven months ago, Dave Steiner, the managing partner of the main office in Boston, asked Fred to lunch to discuss business. To Fred's surprise, the business they discussed was not about the major project that he and his team had just finished, instead, it was about a very big promotion and career move. Fred was offered the position of managing director of the firm's relatively new Tokyo office, which had a staff of forty, including seven Americans. Most of the Americans in the Tokyo office were either associate consultants or research analysts. Fred would be in charge of the whole office and would report to a senior partner. Steiner implied to Fred that if this assignment went as well as his past projects, it would be the last step before becoming a partner in the firm.

When Fred told his wife about the unbelievable opportunity, he was shocked at her less than enthusiastic response. His wife Jennifer (or Jenny as Fred called her) thought that it would be rather difficult to have

---

Source: This case was written especially for this book.

the children live and go to school in a foreign country for three years, especially when Christine, the oldest, would be starting middle school next year. Besides, now that the kids were in school, Jenny was thinking about going back to work, at least part time. Jenny had a degree in fashion merchandising from a well-known private university and had worked as an assistant buyer for a large women's clothing store before having the two girls.

Fred explained that the career opportunity was just too good to pass up and that the company's overseas package would make living overseas terrific. The company would pay all the expenses to move whatever the Baileys wanted to take with them. The company had a very nice house in an expensive district of Tokyo that would be provided rent free, and the company would rent their house in Boston during their absence. Moreover, the firm would provide a car and driver, education expenses for the children to attend private schools, and a cost-of-living adjustment and overseas compensation that would nearly triple Fred's gross annual salary. After two days of consideration and discussion, Fred told Mr. Steiner he would accept the assignment.

The current Tokyo office managing director was a partner in the firm but had been in the new Tokyo office for less than a year when he was transferred to head up a long-established office in England. Because the transfer to England was taking place right away, Fred and his family had about three weeks to prepare for the move. Between transferring things at the office to Bob Newcome, who was being promoted to Fred's position, and getting furniture and the like ready to be moved, neither Fred nor his family had much time to really find out much about Japan, other than what was in the encyclopedia.

When the Baileys arrived in Japan, they were greeted at the airport by one of the young Japanese associate consultants and the senior American expatriate. Fred and his family were quite tired from the long trip, and the two-hour ride to Tokyo was a rather quiet one. After a few days of just settling in, Fred spent his first full day at the office.

Fred's first order of business was to have a general meeting with all the employees of associate consultant rank and higher. Although Fred didn't notice it at the time, all the Japanese staff sat together and all the Americans sat together. After Fred introduced himself and his general idea about the potential and future directions of the Tokyo office, he called on a few individuals to get their ideas about how the things for which they were responsible would likely fit into his overall plan. From the Americans, Fred got a mixture of opinions with specific reasons about why certain things might or might not fit well. From the Japanese, he got very vague answers. When Fred pushed to get more specific information, he was surprised to find that a couple of the Japanese simply made a sucking sound as they breathed and said that it was "difficult to say." Fred sensed the meeting was not achieving his objectives, so he thanked everyone for coming and said he looked forward to their all working together to make the Tokyo office the fastest growing office in the company.

After they had been in Japan about a month, Fred's wife complained to him about the difficulty she had getting certain everyday products like maple syrup, peanut butter, and good-quality beef. She said that when she could get it at one of the specialty stores it cost three and four times what it would cost in the States. She also complained that since the washer and dryer were much too small, she had to spend extra money by sending things out to be dry cleaned. On top of all that, unless she went to the American Club in downtown Tokyo, she never had anyone to talk to. After all, Fred was gone ten to 16 hours a day. Unfortunately, at the time Fred was preoccupied, thinking about a big upcoming meeting between his firm and a significant prospective client, a top 100 Japanese multinational company.

The next day, Fred, along with the lead American consultant for the potential contract, Ralph Webster, and one of the Japanese associate consultants, Kenichi Kurokawa, who spoke perfect English, met with a team from the Japanese firm. The Japanese team consisted of four members: the VP of administration, the director of international personnel, and two staff specialists. After shaking hands and a few awkward bows, Fred said that he knew the Japanese gentlemen were busy and he didn't want to waste their time so he would get right to the point. Fred then had the other American lay out their firm's proposal for the project and what the project would cost. After the presentation, Fred asked the Japanese what their reaction to the proposal was. The Japanese did not respond immediately, so Fred launched into his summary version of the proposal thinking that the translation might have been insufficient. But again the Japanese had only the vaguest of responses to his direct questions.

The recollection of the frustration of that meeting was enough to shake Fred back to reality. The reality was that in the five months since that first meeting little progress had been made and the contract between the firms was yet to be signed. "I can never seem to get a direct response from Japanese," he thought to himself. This feeling of frustration led him to remember a related incident that happened about a month after this first meeting with this client.

Fred had decided that the reason not much progress was being made with the client was that Fred and his group just didn't know enough about the client to package the proposal in a way that was appealing to the client. Consequently, he called in the senior American associated with the proposal, Ralph Webster, and asked him to develop a report on the client so that the proposal could be reevaluated and changed where necessary. Jointly, they decided that one of the more promising Japanese research associates, Tashiro Watanabe, would be the best person to take the lead on this report. To impress upon Tashiro the importance of this task and the great potential they saw in him, they decided to have the young Japanese associate meet with both Fred and Ralph. In the meeting, Fred had Ralph lay out the nature and importance of the task, at which point Fred leaned forward in his chair and said to Tashiro, "You can see that this is an important assignment and that we are placing a lot of confidence in you by giving it to you. We need the report by this time next week so that we can revise and represent our proposal. Can you do it?" After a somewhat pregnant pause, the Japanese responded hesitantly, "I'm not sure what to say." At that point, Fred smiled, got up from his chair and walked over to the young Japanese associate, extended his hand, and said, "Hey, there's nothing to say. We're just giving you the opportunity you deserve."

The day before the report was due, Fred asked Ralph how the report was coming. Ralph said that since he had heard nothing from Tashiro that everything was under control, but that he would double-check. Ralph later ran into one of the American research associates, John Maynard. Ralph knew that John was hired for Japan because of his language ability in Japanese and that, unlike any of the other Americans, John often went out after work with some of the Japanese research associates, including Tashiro. So, Ralph asked John if he knew how Tashiro was coming on the report. John then recounted that last night at the office Tashiro had asked if Americans sometimes fired employees for being late with reports. John had sensed that this was more than a hypothetical question and asked Tashiro why he wanted to know. Tashiro did not respond immediately, and since it was 8:30 in the evening, John suggested they go out for a drink. At first Tashiro resisted, but then John assured him that they would grab a drink at a nearby bar and come right back. At the bar, John got Tashiro to open up.

Tashiro explained the nature of the report that he had been requested to produce. Tashiro continued to explain that even though he had worked long into the night every night to complete the report it was just impossible and that he had doubted from the beginning whether he could complete the report in a week.

At this point, Ralph asked John, "Why didn't he say something in the first place?" Ralph didn't wait to hear whether or not John had an answer to his question. He headed straight to Tashiro's desk.

Ralph chewed Tashiro out and then went to Fred explaining that the report would not be ready and that Tashiro, from the start, didn't think it could be. "Then why didn't he say something?" Fred asked. No one had any answers, and the whole thing just left everyone more suspect and uncomfortable with one another.

There were other incidents, big and small, that had made especially the last two months frustrating, but Fred was too tired to remember them all. To Fred it seemed that working with Japanese both inside and outside the firm was like working with people from another planet. Fred felt he just couldn't communicate with them, and he could never figure out what they were thinking. It drove him crazy.

Then on top of all this, Jennifer laid a bombshell on him. She wanted to go home, and yesterday was not soon enough. Even though the kids seemed to be doing all right, Jennifer was tired of Japan—tired of being stared at, of not understanding anybody or being understood, of not being able to find what she wanted at the store, of not being able to drive and read the road signs, of not having anything to watch on television, of not being involved in anything. She wanted to go home and could not think of any reason why they shouldn't. After all, she reasoned they owed nothing to the company because the company had led them to believe this was just another assignment, like the two years they spent in San Francisco, and it was anything but that!

Fred looked out the window once more, wishing that somehow everything could be fixed, or turned back, or something. Down below the traffic was backed up. Though the traffic lights changed, the cars and trucks didn't seem to be moving. Fortunately, beneath the ground, one of the world's most advanced, efficient, and clean subway systems moved hundreds of thousands of people about the city and to their homes.

Catskill Roads

Case 4.2
J.B. Ritchie
Alan Hawkins

Introduction

Autumn had come early to the Catskills this year, and a fresh coating of leaves covered the floor of the yellow woods. Kathryn Hill-Baker rolled down her van window and the fresh, cool, mountain air that poured in seemed to ease the tension that had mounted over the past two hours. Kathryn's husband, Brian, was driving slower now as he looked for the turn-off to the lodge where they planned to stay for the weekend. As they left the crowded highways of metropolitan New York City two hours ago, they talked intensely about the future. But discussion slowed as they approached the mountains, and now Kathryn was lost in her own thoughts.

A few weeks ago four senior partners from Kathryn's New York City law firm had announced their plans to leave the firm and form their own. One of those partners was Kathryn's mentor, and he asked Kathryn to come with them and to assume the lucrative litigation practice with the new firm. If she accepted the offer, it would mean a substantial increase in salary and a tremendous career boost. However, she was currently involved with an enjoyable and challenging project with her present firm's largest client, a multinational pharmaceutical company that was establishing a new operation in Argentina.

But what was an important career decision for Kathryn became a critical family problem two days ago when Jim Collins called Brian into his office. Collins is an executive vice president at Universal Bank. He wanted Brian to go to Mexico City to pull Universal Bank (UB) through the coming crisis. During the oil boom years, UB's Mexico City office was one of its most profitable units. No one anticipated the severity of the economic collapse in Mexico, which sent banks with big Mexican loan portfolios reeling. UB was among the hardest hit—over four-hundred million dollars in loans outstanding to Mexico. A few smaller loans had already come due and were renegotiated to avoid default. But the next eighteen months would be critical as many big loans would come due and would almost certainly

---

Source: Reprinted by permission of the authors.

need to be refinanced. With domestic profits already squeezed by deregulated competition, UB couldn't afford losses in Mexico. Top management wanted a savvy manager to go to Mexico City to take the reins and they were personally involved in the selection process. Brian Baker, with his familiarity with the Mexican loan operations, his technical competence, his international experience, and his fluent Spanish, was the obvious choice.

Kathryn Hill-Baker ————————————————————

Kathryn, her husband Brian, and their two children currently live in an old but quaint house in a quiet New Jersey suburb. She was born while her family was abroad. Her father was a commissioned officer in the U.S. Marines. She was the fifth of six children in her family, the second one born in Japan. However, she was the only girl, and the family lavished her with affection. The Hills were very religious. Every morning the family would gather and read a brief passage from the Bible before breakfast. And every Sunday the family attended church services on the base.

Kathryn's family lived on a-military base near Tokyo until she was eight when her father was transferred to West Germany. They were only there two years. Her father retired from the military and took a management position with a large firm in Detroit that did a lot of contract work for the Defense Department. Through junior and senior high school, Kathryn excelled in both athletics and academics. She was a National Merit finalist and received a full-tuition scholarship to the University of Michigan where she was an English composition major. She also played on the junior varsity tennis team until her senior year. She graduated in the top five percent of the class.

Kathryn was initially attracted to Brian when they met during her senior year in an English literature class in which they studied Robert Frost poems. Over the summer, she gradually fell in love with a sensitive and warm man. He was different from her macho brothers and the guys she had usually dated in high school and college. Kathryn's family attended the wedding but her parents were upset that she was marrying outside her religious faith.

Brian Baker ————————————————————

Brian was born in Panama City where his father was a diplomat for the U.S. government. When he was five his family moved to Mexico City where his father became the head of the U.S. Consulate there. His father was a decorated World War II fighter pilot and his mother had been an army nurse.

After the war, Brian's father finished up his degree in Public Administration and International Relations at American University, while his mother worked for a VA hospital in Virginia. His father graduated summa cum laude and was offered a diplomatic position in Panama City. Brian was born two weeks after their arrival there. Despite the demands of a young baby, his mother was actively involved in UN efforts to upgrade health care in Panama. Brian's earliest memories were tagging along with his mother as she inspected hospitals in the more rural areas of Panama.

The family moved to Mexico City when Brian's father was promoted to an important consulate position there. Brian attended a private Catholic school and most of his companions were children of wealthy Mexican industrialists and government officials. Over the years he learned to speak Spanish as fluently as he spoke English.

Summers were the source of Brian's richest memories. When summer vacation began, Brian and his mother would fly to Vermont where his maternal grandparents lived. They usually spent about a month there. Then they would fly to Michigan and meet Brian's dad and spend another month or two at a summer cabin in northern Michigan owned by Brian's paternal grandparents. The cabin was right on a lake and Brian probably spent three-fourths of his waking hours in or on the water, swimming, sailing, water skiing, and fishing. In the evenings they barbequed on the beach, ate and watched the sun sink into the lake, painting the sky with streaks of warm colors.

When Brian was 16, his father suffered a mild stroke and decided to ease up and take a "cushy, state-side desk job." They moved to New York where Brian finished his senior year of high school. He was accepted to the honors program at the University of Michigan and decided to go there and live with his grandparents. He studied political science and journalism, planning to eventually go to law school. After graduating he worked for a year at a local insurance company before beginning his graduate work. He was disappointed when he was not admitted to the University of Michigan Law School. But he enjoyed his work at the insurance company and decided to apply to the business school and was accepted.

The summer before he began in the MBA program at Michigan, he took a couple of evening classes to sharpen his math skills. Just for fun he also took an English literature class, something he never seemed to have time for as an undergraduate. There he met an attractive English major, Kathryn Hill, who was attending summer school in order to graduate by fall. They often studied together at night in the library and then went to an ice cream parlor where they talked until it closed. They were married in August.

Work and Graduate School _____

After a honeymoon, Kathryn worked as a staff reporter for a Detroit newspaper and edited and typed student papers to earn extra income. Brian started the MBA Program at Michigan and although busy, they enjoyed their marriage and looked forward to starting their own family when Brian graduated. The only significant friction between them was a result of Kathryn's desire to attend Sunday services each week. Busy schedules didn't allow them much time together during the week, and they felt it was important to spend weekends together. Eventually, Kathryn decided to curtail her church attendance to every other week, and would spend the other weekends with Brian up at his grandparents' cabin.

Brian did well in school although he didn't "set the world on fire." His writing ability and hard work put him in the top third of his class. He received two good job offers, one with a small but respected brokerage firm, the second with a large multinational bank. Both offers would put the Bakers in New York City where Brian's parents lived. The brokerage firm offered more money, but the bank offered more exciting career opportunities. Brian hoped to go abroad in the future. Universal Bank had branch operations all over the world with many internationally assigned managers. Kathryn liked the idea of living in New York with its endless cultural opportunities. And there would be ample opportunities in the future to continue her career in journalism, if she wanted. They accepted UB's offer and moved to New York.

Universal Bank _____

Universal Bank was an established, somewhat conservative bank with a large portion of their business overseas. In an average year, UB earned nearly sixty percent of their revenues abroad. The year Brian began working the bank had revenues of nearly four billion dollars. The International Banking Division was run almost like a separate subsidiary and was the glamour division of the bank. However, they seldom hired entry level managers, preferring to take promising managers with good track records from the various domestic divisions. UB had strong footholds in most of the big cities in Europe and England. In recent years, they had gained ground in an increasingly competitive Far East market, where U.S. multinationals brought their capital and built many manufacturing facilities to escape the high labor cost in the U.S. During the start-up phase of a foreign operation, UB catered mostly to U.S. and other English-speaking industrialists doing business in a particular country. As they got to know the countries better and how local businesses operated, they would do more business with national firms.

The deregulation of the banking industry had strained UB's conservative management. Past strategy had been to put a UB branch "within two miles of nearly every resident and business in New York." As a result, UB owned the largest share of the deposit market in New York. However, recently several of UB's competitors had gone to an automated teller machine strategy with its significantly lower transaction costs. In addition, UB's competitors were rapidly expanding their product lines and services to attract the upper scale customers who were willing to pay a little more for what they really wanted. UB's philosophy had been to move deliberately and carefully into new product lines and services so as not to "overburden the standard customer who just wants a dependable bank in a convenient location." This strategy seemed now to have hurt UB. Profit margins slipped the last two years and their fixed assets-to-sales ratio was now, by a wide margin, the highest among New York banks.

Not surprisingly, a new top management team was installed in the late 1970s. They were young, brash and aggressive and determined to turn UB's domestic operations into a market-driven organization. They were depending on UB's healthy international operations to provide them the cash flow to put the domestic bank back up on its feet and in the race again.

New York _____

Brian began at UB as a loan officer in a branch handling mostly small corporate loans from steady customers with revolving accounts. Although the job did not really push his skills, he enjoyed the regular, close contact with his clients and took pride in the growth of their small businesses. He spent a lot of time out of the office with his clients trying to get a better feel for their unique needs and problems.

His track record after two years was good, and he was transferred to the central office downtown and asked to handle the accounts of some large multinational companies. But these big companies were just after the best prices and personal contact was lacking in the job. After a year he took a third position with a branch that did a good deal of loan business with Mexican and South American multinationals operating in New York City. Personal contact was more available in the job, and he enjoyed using his fluent Spanish again.

Kathryn had given birth to their first child shortly after they arrived in New York, and a second child followed only 18 months later. Homemaking was challenging to Kathryn. She had always been so active before, but now taking care of two small children kept her at home almost constantly. After the second child was born, Kathryn suffered a depression. She tried to hide it from Brian, hoping it would go away soon. But it only got worse and Brian started asking questions. Brian suggested some counseling but Kathryn did not like the idea. She tried to find part-time work as a journalist, but no one seemed interested. Instead, she applied to law school and was accepted at Columbia University. Although Brian was a little jealous, he encouraged Kathryn to go. They arranged for a babysitter in the afternoons and Kathryn studied at night and on weekends. Brian would get home about five o'clock and take care of the children and do the housework. Kathryn's mood improved, and Brian gained an appreciation for the rigors of domestic life.

However, leaving work at four o'clock every day did not help Brian's career. Although he got to work early and kept a fair client load, he was unable to drink with his colleagues after work, a regular activity in his unit. Brian's performance evaluations were still excellent but he did not have inclusion in the strong social network of the bank that was valuable for career progress. And because "he couldn't be counted on after four o'clock," he was seldom given the "plum accounts." But Kathryn was happier, and Brian sincerely liked his "daddy" role and the daily counterpoint it provided to the kinetic pace of work. In a few years the kids would be in school, and he could get back on track at work. The drawbacks were that money was tighter because of Kathryn's tuition, and quality time for Brian and Kathryn was limited.

Kathryn's grades her first year were good enough to get her on the law review. She graduated in the top ten percent of her class and accepted an offer to work for a medium-sized law firm that serviced many of the pharmaceutical companies in New York City. The children began school, so with Kathryn's extra income they purchased a small home in a suburb with an excellent school system. Kathryn worked 60-hour weeks and Brian took on some extra work and tried to get back into the social network now that he didn't need to be home at five o'clock every night. However, after about a year of both Kathryn and Brian working, Brian began to feel restless. He had been in the same unit almost five years and was risking career stagnation. He began to look at other positions. Although he was attracted to a possible international assignment, he didn't see quite how it could be managed with his current family situation.

It wasn't long after this, though, that a chance for an international assignment surfaced. UB was opening a branch in Buenos Aires, Argentina. Brian had done some loan work with several small Argentine firms operating in New York and had a pretty good feel for how they did business. With his fluent Spanish, he would be a good candidate to manage that new branch. When he casually mentioned the opening to Kathryn one night at dinner, she was concerned.

"How can we manage that? My work is going so well now, and with the house and all, it just doesn't seem to be the right time, Brian," she remarked.

"My chances are pretty slim, anyway," Brian replied. "They've been cutting back their international managers the last few years because they're just too expensive. It takes $100,000 just to move them, and maybe $300,000 a year for salary, bonus, benefits, and perks. It can be twice that much in some places where the cost of decent housing is so high, or where there's high inflation. Competition for these positions is stiff. And with all the money involved now, an executive-vice president has to make the selection decision. I doubt that they would search low enough in the ranks of the company to find me."

But Brian underestimated his credentials. When Bob Jasper, the Executive Vice-president for UB-International pulled Brian's name out of the computerized personnel planning system in the bank, he was interested and asked Brian to come talk to him. Their thirty-minute chat turned into a two hour lunch as they discussed Brian's background, his work experience, and plans for the new Buenos Aires unit. The British banks dominated among foreign banks in Argentina. Research had shown that times might be right to challenge the "stodgy British banks down there." Brian was honest about his family situation but he could hardly conceal his excitement about the prospects of such an assignment. He would have almost complete autonomy to formulate and implement a strategy for breaking into the Argentina market, as well as responsibility for getting the branch up and running.

Two weeks later Brian was back in Jasper's office.

"You're the man, Brian. We want you down there as soon as you can tie things up here—no more than six weeks. This is the break you need. You'll be in the limelight. This assignment can turn you into top management material."

Brian was nervous when he recounted his conservation with Jasper to Kathryn. He restrained his enthusiasm but still tried to highlight the positive aspects of the assignment.

"This kind of thing is really good for kids," he argued. "It gives them a better perspective of the world. We'll find them a good private school, and the bank said that they'd help in finding you a job somewhere. The bank pays for high class housing and maids. They'll fly us back once a year for a month-long vacation, and they pay for a two-week R&R leave every year as well. Jasper said that he'll bring us back in three years. This is a once-in-a-lifetime shot, Kathryn. I know it comes at a bad time for you with your work and all, but when we get back, I promise you that we'll settle in and you can pursue your career full steam!"

Kathryn wanted time to think. They continued to talk about it, usually until two or three in the morning. Kathryn wondered what she would do. Despite Brian's assurances, she was uncertain about the prospects of employment down there. She couldn't speak the language and knew little about the culture. Kathryn's firm told her that she could have her job back at any time, which made things easier, but still, the uncertainty was almost overwhelming. One night she phoned her parents to talk about it. Relations between Kathryn and her parents had become strained over the past few years. Although her parents would not actually come right out and say it, she knew that they felt she had "abandoned" Brian and the children when she went to law school and began working. Still, she wanted their input. They both encouraged Kathryn to go.

"Believe me, Kate," her father's voice boomed over the phone, "these kinds of opportunities come along only once. If you don't jump now, Brian may never get another chance."

That night, Kathryn informed Brian that she was willing to go. They had only four weeks to get their affairs settled and Brian was so busy at work that Kathryn had to do most of it herself while trying to wrap things up at work. The bank offered to pay for a week-long language and culture training program for Brian and Kathryn, but they simply didn't have the time to go. They stored the furniture, left the selling of the house to a real estate agent, packed their bags and were gone.

Argentina ─────────────────────────────────────

For the first 18 months in Buenos Aires Brian put in 16-hour days and traveled frequently. But it was just what he wanted: autonomy, challenge, responsibility, and excitement. The first few months he concentrated on putting together a good staff. Rather than bring down some Americans though, he hired away from other banks some local professionals who knew how business was done in Argentina and who had extensive contacts. And rather than target the big foreign multinationals, and compete head-on with the established British banks' bread and butter, he went after some middle- to large-sized domestic firms. Whereas English was usually the international language in business, Brian conducted all his business in Spanish. This meant he could usually deal directly with the president of the company rather than the designated English-speaking finance officer. His strategy was successful. The branch was soon profitable and growing rapidly.

His only major disappointment was that, contrary to Bob Jasper's "limelight" predictions, no one back in New York seemed to take notice of his accomplishments. Anonymity could be tolerated, but headquarters was painfully slow responding to any special requests. Of course, if his reports were late, he would get a call from some "knucklehead in the accounting department who thought Buenos Aires was another socialist state in the Caribbean."

Kathryn had a more difficult time adjusting to the move. The family spent the first two months in a hotel unable to find suitable housing within the bank's allotted housing allowances. Brian finally got someone in International Compensation back at headquarters to raise the allowance enough so they could afford a decent place to live. The children were sick much of the time the first few weeks.

Eventually they found a nice home to rent in a suburb of the city in a price range the bank would accept. But Kathryn hardly left the house the first few months. A maid did all the shopping and most of the housework. With the children in a private British school most of the day, Kathryn had more free time than ever before in her life. Much of it was consumed by Dickens' novels, which were enjoyable, but the loneliness grew more intense. Brian was concerned and hired a private Spanish tutor to come every day and help Kathryn learn the language, which the bank paid for. He also kept his eyes open for some kind of work for her. But women professionals were not well accepted in Argentina. After about a year there, he was able to pull some strings with a man who worked at the U.S. Embassy who had known Brian's father many years ago, and got her a position working with immigration cases, visas, and some sticky international licensing problems. Although apprehensive of her ability to speak the language, she was happy to be working and using some of her legal skills again. She quickly made some new friends.

At that point, things began to go well for the Bakers. Even though Brian still wasn't around much, Kathryn and the children took advantage of long school holidays to travel to scenic spots along Argentina's vast and beautiful coastline. Kathryn made close friends with some American women at work, and often they would travel together. Five years passed and no one seemed anxious to return to the United States.

Unfortunately, Brian's father's health had been deteriorating while Brian was in Argentina. Nevertheless, his death of a sudden stroke came as a shock to Brian. The family returned to New York for the funeral. While there, Brian dropped in to Jim Collins' office who had replaced Bob Jasper as Executive Vice President of UB International upon Jasper's retirement.

"It's good to get to meet you, Brian," Collins said. "You've done an outstanding job down there. You've put UB on the map in South America. As a matter of fact, we're thinking about opening a couple more branches in Chile and Brazil. If we do, I want you to move up and be a regional director for South America. I'll make you a senior vice president. You can still live in Buenos Aires if you want. Give it some thought, Brian."

Brian was flattered to finally be getting some recognition. Regional Director would be another exciting position. More importantly, Brian thought it was a signal from top management that he was being groomed for bigger things to come. Collins was a regional director in Europe prior to his promotion to Executive Vice-President at UB-International.

In addition, his family seemed genuinely happy. The children were receiving a superior education to what they would have received in the States. They had friends, and could speak the language. But they would soon be entering their teenage years and Kathryn was concerned that they might miss a crucial socialization period if they stayed abroad too much longer. If Brian took the Regional Director position, it would likely entail another five years of hard work. And Brian was concerned about the effect his long hours of work had on his marriage and his relationship with his children. He was also concerned about his mother, who was alone for the first time in her life. As her only child, Brian felt a responsibility to be closer to her now and help her adjust to his father's absence. It seemed clear to Brian and Kathryn that it was time to return to the States. Brian contacted Jim Collins and informed him of his plans to return in a few months when school let out for the summer. Collins was disappointed but said he would try to find a slot for him somewhere by the time he got back. With a feeling of pride for what they had accomplished during the last five and a half years, and anticipation for the future, the Bakers packed their bags and returned home to New York.

The Repatriation _____

Coming home wasn't easy. They left the warmth of Argentina and returned to the cold of winter in New York. There were no "Welcome Home" banners for Brian when he returned to work. In fact, he wondered if he was even in the right place. He hardly recognized anyone. Some major restructuring of the organization left Brian confused about strategic directions of the bank. The new (to Brian) top management team had replaced the old "knife-and-fork" banking culture with a lean, market-driven organization. But there were more serious problems. No clear position was available for Brian when he returned. Brian felt that he needed to get back into domestic operations if he was going to become top management material. But it soon became clear that no one was all that interested in taking him on board.

"These repatriates are out of touch with domestic operations now," was a frequently expressed opinion at the bank. "They walk around dazed for six months and when they finally come out of shock, they want to run the whole show. Overseas they had it all to themselves, but back here they forget we're a team."

Brian was assigned to work on a few projects at UB-International while he waited for some position to open up for him. He got involved with some of the sticky negotiations going on with refinancing some of the Mexican loans the bank had outstanding. But he felt more like a translator than a decision-maker. These projects hardly used the management skills he developed while abroad.

Meanwhile, the Baker children were having serious difficulties readjusting to American life. In terms of their education, they were well ahead of their peers in junior high. Socially though, they were perceived as odd, even stuffy, and had difficulty making friends. Brian felt responsible for the problems they were having and tried to compensate for it by taking the children to movies and spending a lot of time with them at night and on weekends. Although tired from work, Kathryn spent a good deal of time in the evenings talking with the children and helping them deal with their problems.

Kathryn was the only family member who seemed to be readjusting well. She went back to work full-time for the firm that she had worked for before they left for Argentina. They were delighted to have her back, and even paid for some legal update sessions at a nearby university. The firm had grown as some of their client companies had grown. One client company was now in the planning stages for a new manufacturing facility in Argentina. Kathryn become valuable in that process with her language ability, familiarity with local legal systems, and contacts. She traveled several times to Argentina on business and was very busy.

Brian was hoping that their return to the U.S. would give the family more time to spend with each other. He did spend more time with the children, but Kathryn's work didn't allow them to spend much time together as a couple. The five and a half years in Buenos Aires with Brian working 70-hour weeks had left their marriage strained. Their ability to communicate with each other, which played an important part of the happiness of their early years together, was rusty. But more importantly, they felt as if they were two separate persons traveling the same road, but in different directions, loosely coupled only by a son and a daughter. Brian and Kathryn were spending some time now with a marriage counselor, trying to repair some of the damage before it was too late.

After eight months of project work, Brian was still unable to find a suitable position at the bank. He was angry, frustrated, and wanted to quit. But the financial shock that accompanied their return to the States militated against that action right now. With the economy down, jobs were not easy to come by. Despite Kathryn's income, they were still struggling to meet their financial obligations. Real estate prices and interest rates had soared while they were gone and their new home required both incomes. Brian hung on, hoping that something would soon open up.

Then Brian ran across a friend he had gone to school with at Michigan. His friend mentioned an opening in the small New Jersey bank at which he had a revolving account. The vice-president of the bank was retiring next month. Although promotion opportunities were limited because the president was only a few years older than Brian and likely to remain in the number one slot for a long time, this kind of position would allow Brian to use his management skills again, and he would only have to work forty- to fifty-hour weeks. It was a stable position, and he could drive to work in ten minutes rather than commute two hours a day. He seriously considered applying for the position.

That's when Jim Collins called and asked Brian to go to Mexico City for eighteen months to handle the crucial negotiations coming up.

"You draw up the ticket," Collins told Brian, "and I'll sign it. Any guarantees you need, you name them, we'll do it. You've got my word that I'll bring you back in eighteen months as a senior vice-president anywhere you want to be. We're counting on you, Brian."

When Brian mentioned the offer to Kathryn, she was visibly shaken. Kathryn was still trying to decide whether she wanted to go with the new law firm or stay with the old one. And now this.

Brian called his mother and asked her to come stay with the kids for the weekend. Then he and Kathryn jumped in the van and headed for the Catskills to do some hard choosing.

Part 5

MANAGEMENT DEVELOPMENT

Management Development: An African Focus

Reading 5.1
Merrick L. Jones

Anyone interested in issues of Third World development is painfully aware of the complexities, contradictions, and cruel paradoxes involved. Recent events in Africa have thrown the issues into stark focus. Africa is a cockpit of turbulent change, where the transition from traditional societies to modern nation states confronts those involved with painful and complex puzzles. The myriad problems facing the continent are reflected daily in Western newspapers. Great human tragedies unfold as whole nations are devastated by droughts and other natural calamities. Famine, population growth, deforestation, the advancing deserts, civil wars, border disputes, military coups, political intrigues, one-party states, tribalism, guerrilla movements: the catalogue is reported with scant sympathy—indeed, it sometimes seems, with gleeful smugness. Meanwhile, the peoples of Africa struggle with the awful natural and man-made problems that confront them in building nation states within the arbitrary boundaries bequeathed to them by the departed colonial powers. No one can doubt that it will be a long and supremely difficult struggle. There have been, and will be, many failed experiments, many dead ends, many setbacks in the process. But one central reality seems inescapable: in coping with acute scarcity of resources and lack of developed infrastructure, great skills of management and organization will be imperative.

The question is: Will the importation of management concepts and practices from the industrialized West meet Africa's needs? Questions concerning the transferability across nations of management concepts and practices are complex and controversial. There is as yet no consensus about the nature of the arguments involved or about how empirical data can usefully be obtained and compared.

Onyemelukwe [1] considers the educational implications, asserting that "The belief is that whatever is not going well can always be rectified by training. The result is a staggering investment in foreign-orientated training schemes with little in the way of return in investment." And:

Source: Merrick L. Jones. "Management Development: An African Focus." *Journal of the Association for Management Education and Development,* 1986, 17(3), 202-216. Reprinted by permission.

Looking through courses and lectures on management organised in various parts of Africa by universities and institutes of management, one is faced with a galaxy of do-it-yourself kits and shorthand prescriptions. . . . it is the refusal of many authors and researchers in the field of management to give a significant place to social and cultural factors that limits the usefulness of their work.

In this paper I consider some of the issues in relation to an investigation of managerial thinking in one African country, Malawi. In particular, I focus on the data concerning the way Malawian managers think about their work, and implications for management education and training. Very briefly, the study involved 105 Malawian senior and middle-level managers from both the private and public sectors in a questionnaire survey designed to elicit their thinking on aspects of their work, especially their satisfactions and their relationships with subordinates. The questionnaire was based on an instrument used originally by Haire, Ghiselli, and Porter [2] in 14 countries, and subsequently in similar studies in many other parts of the world (including 3 African countries). In addition, 47 managers were involved in a semi-structured interviewing survey, which was intended to focus on similar issues and to provide insights on the contextual fabric of the Malawian manager's world. The aims of the study were:

1. to investigate managerial thinking about a limited number of important issues in a national context (Malawi);

2. to compare data from this investigation in a practical way with those produced by similar studies in other countries;

3. to examine factors in the Malawian context that might account for similarities and differences between the thinking of the Malawian managers and that of other managers;

4. to relate these findings to the education and training of managers in Malawi, and to consider their appropriateness; and

5. to consider possible areas for further investigation.

In this paper my intention is to focus mainly on item 4 above. Before considering the data from the study and their implications for the education and training of Malawian managers, it might be useful to present *very briefly*, some relevant information about the country.

Malawi is located in southern central Africa, bordering Zambia to the west, Tanzania to the north east, and Mozambique. By African standards it is not a big country, its area totaling 118,500 square kilometers, of which about one-fifth comprises the great lake that dominates the country, Lake Malawi. However, Malawi's population density is about four times as high as the African average, at 47 persons per square kilometer overall. At the time of the last population census, in 1982, Malawi's population stood at a little over 6.5 million.

In common with other nations in this part of Africa, Malawi has a turbulent history, experiencing long periods of stability and at other times the eruptions of migratory peoples entering the region from other population centers. Although the details of these movements are still being elaborated, it is clear that the great lake, the third biggest in Africa, has been a focal point for centuries in this part of the continent. In more recent times, the territory that now constitutes Malawi was subjected to the depredations of slave traders operating from the Indian Ocean coast, and to the influx of Ngoni peoples from the south, driven to their northward odyssey by the turmoil, in what is now the Republic of South Africa, caused by the rise of the great Zulu empire. Another powerful influence was the coming of European missionaries and explorers in the latter half of the nineteenth century. As the scramble for Africa divided the continent into spheres of influence for the European powers at the turn of the century, the area of the lake eventually became the British colony of Nyasaland.

Unlike other British colonies in Africa, Nyasaland offered no exploitable natural resources and did not attract large numbers of European settlers. Evidence suggests that Britain's attitude toward its colony of the lake was at least ambivalent, and possibly at times downright unenthusiastic. An attempt in 1953 to form a federation in central Africa consisting of Northern Rhodesia (now Zambia), Southern Rhodesia (now Zimbabwe), and Nyasaland was doomed to failure. The independent nation of Malawi emerged after a long and complex struggle that had its roots early in the present century, but developed as a significant movement during the 1950s.

The "wind of change" was then gathering strength in southern Africa, and the British colonies there were experiencing a common, if individually manifested, movement toward self-government. For Malawi the crucial moment came when Dr. H. K. Banda returned to Nyasaland, in July 1958, after having lived and practiced medicine in the USA, Europe, and Ghana for many years. From that day, events were set in train that led, with historical inevitability, to independence from Britain in July 1964 and, in 1966, to the status of a republic within the Commonwealth. Dr. Banda became President (and in 1971 was made the Life President) of the new Republic of Malawi. The story of Dr. Banada's apparently historic destiny in liberating the country of his birth from its colonial masters is extraordinary, and his continued dominance as leader of Malawi is an overwhelming factor in the nation's development. Since this reality forms a part of the national context in which Malawian organizations function and Malawian managers work, it may be useful to explore briefly the nature of Malawi's political milieu.

Since the 1960s we have observed the achievement of independence by most of Africa's former colonial territories. The dominant picture we in the West receive of Africa through our media is one of a continent in a turbulent transition, with national regimes apparently changing, sometimes violently, with bewildering frequency. Some states seem to have tried almost every conceivable form of government, from multiparty democracy to military dictatorship, in search of a suitable system. Malawi has been notably absent in reports of such developments. The overwhelmingly powerful and pervasive influence of the Life President on all facets of Malawian life is important, because we could expect that the consequences of such a situation would inevitably include the ways in which organizations operate and managers behave.

Turning to Malawi's economic position, the country is, in terms of per capita income, one of the world's poorest nations. At independence the country had a small industrial sector and a rudimentary economic infrastructure. Few exploitable mineral resources have been located in any quantity. The policies of the government since independence therefore have emphasized the development of agricultural, transport, and communications infrastructure. As a landlocked country, Malawi faces problems, sometimes acute, in routing its crucial agricultural exports and its imports. Problems of transporting goods great distances across difficult terrain are frequently aggravated by climatic conditions and guerrilla activity. Since Malawi's independence, the protracted war in Rhodesia (now Zimbabwe) and the continuing civil insurrection in Mozambique have presented intractable difficulties for Malawian administrators and businessmen.

Malawi, by African standards, enjoys a good climate for a variety of agricultural activities and is blessed with relatively productive soils. There has been impressive development in the production of a number of cash crops, including tobacco, tea, coffee, and sugar, which form the bulk of the country's exports. In addition, greater yields of subsistence crops, importantly maize, have been consistently achieved. Malawi is one of the few African countries that are largely self-sufficient in staple foodstuffs.

Although the industrial base remains modest in size, development in this sector also has been impressive. The following figures relating to paid employment in Malawi (1980) are relevant:

> Total in paid employment—294,707
> In professional, technical, and related posts—21,716 (7.4%)
> In managerial/administrative occupations—4,127 (1.5%).

These figures, supplied by the Manpower Planning Unit, Office of the President and Cabinet, relate to December 1980 and are the most recent available in this form. By 1983 (the latest figures available), the number of individuals in paid employment was approximately 387,000, over fifty percent of whom were engaged in agriculture.

Malawian Managers ————————————————————

It would be neither possible nor relevant to report in this paper the details of findings from the interviewing and questionnaire surveys. My intention is to put forward some fairly direct statements about Malawian managers and the organizations in which they work, and to consider their implications for management development. These statements appear to reflect as directly as possible the data produced by the investigation.

In general terms, management education and training have attracted some rather critical comments, and it may be useful to look very briefly at this wider context before we focus on the Malawian situation.

Safavi [3], reporting on a project involving the 57 countries and territories of Africa during a 4-year study of management education and development programs, paints a "gloomy picture" of "a number of areas of conflict between classroom and culture, between Western theory and African reality." A number of observers have similar concerns. Nyerere (cited by Onyemelukwe [1]) has observed that the training of African managers appears to have been designed to divorce them from the societies it is supposed to equip them to serve. Hofstede [4] claims that Western management theories, although widely taught, are not practiced by non-Western managers. Successful managers "perform a cultural transposition of ideas . . . there is no single formula for management development to be used in different cultures" (p. 380); there is a need to ascertain what constitutes "success" in a particular culture. Hyden [5] comments on the absurdity of what he calls "technique peddling" by Western management consultants in Africa, exemplified by bizarre attempts to undertake Organization Development (OD) consultancies (with their accompanying American individualistic, humanistic values) in African organizations: "The African personality is full and wholesome in a sense that does not tally with the demands of systematic rationality." Yet African managers "have been molded in a type of management thinking that makes them strangers in their own environment" (p. 159).

It is difficult to dispute the view that strategies and methods used to educate and train African managers have generally been based on Western theories and practices, with little, if any, consideration of the environments in which African organizations function. What can be done to change the situation? Simply asserting, as so many observers do, that management education and training must take cognizance of the environmental realities of Africa does not get us very far. Do the data from this study of Malawian senior and middle managers provide any pointers? It is perhaps appropriate to preface the discussion of the issues with two notes of caution.

First, it is important to avoid the common assumption that education and training can be relied upon to accomplish changes in human behavior and thinking. There is a line of reasoning (or rather, assumption) that:

TRAINING
(usually equated with classroom-based courses)
↓
INDIVIDUAL LEARNING
↓
IMPROVED INDIVIDUAL JOB PERFORMANCE
↓
IMPROVED ORGANIZATIONAL PERFORMANCE

At each level the assumption can be challenged, and experience indicates that, without positive managerial action, the training of individuals rarely leads to improved organizational performance. I am therefore conscious of the need to exercise caution in advancing ideas about the education and training of Malawian managers, especially since I believe that the causes of important aspects of their thinking are to be found in fundamental national sociocultural and political elements.

Second, there is at present no way of judging with any degree of accuracy the extent to which Malawian organizations and management have developed distinctive features. Malawi was a British colony, and is now a member of the Commonwealth. Its systems (for example, in education, communications, industry, commerce, technology, health care, public utility provision, and government organization) would be familiar to British expatriates and visitors. The major language of business and government is English. Most Malawian administrators and executives will have been trained on the Western model, many of them in Britain; and, as the data confirm, most have worked with expatriate (predominantly British) managers, often taking over from an expatriate boss. The study has shown that traditional modes of social and family organization still inhere in contemporary Malawi as fundamental aspects of the life of individuals, even those, such as managers, who have moved out of the rural subsistence economy to paid employment in the expanding urban sector. To ask the question "How Westernized are Malawian organizations and managers?" is not to anticipate a precise answer, but to realize that more research will be necessary before we can even begin to make useful judgments about this important issue.

Using the data from this study, supplemented by those from other relevant studies, I propose the following general statements about Malawian managers and the organizations in which they work, which may serve as a useful base for a discussion of relevant strategies for management education and training:

1. Malawian organizations function in an environment of acute resource scarcity, economic uncertainty, and highly centralized political power.

2. These organizations tend to retain the major characteristics of structures developed in the colonial era, namely, rather rigid bureaucratic, rulebound hierarchies.

3. Organizations tend to be viewed by society as a whole as having a wider mission than is generally understood in the West, being expected to provide socially desirable benefits such as employment, housing, transport, and assistance with important social rituals and ceremonies; considerations of profit maximization and efficiency may be viewed as secondary or incidental.

4. There is among Malawian workers a generally instrumental orientation toward work, involving high expectations of the benefits, to the worker and his extended family, that employment

brings, but less in the way of loyalty and commitment to the organization (or profession) that is said to typify the employer-employee relationship in the West.

5. There is in Malawian society an emphasis on prestige and status differences, creating relationships of dependency, which in organizations finds expression in wide differentials between organizational levels, particularly between managers and workers, extreme deference to and dependence upon one's boss, and a paternal, concerned, but strict style of management.

6. The collectivist values of Malawian society are reflected in organizations in the high regard managers have for their subordinates as people; in a view of workers as a network of people rather than as human resources; in an emphasis on maintaining relationships rather than on providing opportunities for individual development; in an emphasis on "highly ritualised interpersonal interactions which often place greater value on the observance of protocol than the accomplishment of work-related tasks" [6. p. 159]; in a desire by workers for a close relationship with the boss; and in a reluctance by managers either to accept individual blame for mistakes or to criticize individual subordinates in a direct manner.

7. Malawian managers tend to view their authority, professional competence, and information as personal possessions, rather than impersonal concomitants of their organizational role, and as a source of status and prestige.

8. This, coupled with the emphasis on the wide differential—in status, power, education, experience, and perceived ability—between managers and workers makes Malawian managers very reluctant to delegate authority, to share information, and to involve subordinates (who may be perceived as a potential source of threat) in decision-making processes.

9. Malawian managers regard security as an important factor in their work, to be reinforced by unchanging structures, detailed procedures, and close supervision of subordinates.

10. Malawian managers desire a good relationship with their boss, whom they perceive as a key figure, but frequently find this to be a problematic relationship because the boss manages them in a manner similar to that they employ with their own subordinates; this may find expression in dissatisfaction with their perceived opportunities for autonomy and self-actualization.

11. Individualistic (as opposed to universalistic) criteria tend to influence organizational behavior; hence, insecurity is increased because decisions cannot be consistently predicted, and blame for mistakes tends to be assigned on a personalized basis.

12. Malawian managers have constantly to be sensitive to political pressures and aware of developments that might affect them as power coalitions change.

13. Malawian managers tend to recognize their role in achieving

organizational performance (this, on the basis of our limited data, does not seem to apply to civil servants to the same degree), and to emphasize their individual professional or technical expertise rather than their "managerial" functions.

14. Malawian managers have a keen awareness of the necessity to acknowledge and manage their wider social obligations to extended family and kinship systems, and of the possible conflicts that may thereby exist in relation to their formal organizational roles.

15. Malawian managers often find their relationships with expatriate bosses and colleagues problematic and tend to view expatriate executives as lacking in the sensitivity they view as essential, especially in their dealings with workers.

The data from the study appear to confirm that the demands of formal organizations create tensions and conflicts for Malawian managers. It is well understood that the processes of industrialization on the Western model demand the utilization of technical and scientific knowledge, but it is perhaps less clearly recognized that the use of such knowledge depends somewhat on the acceptance of the values and "world view" that are its sociocultural foundation.

The data from this study provide several examples of the tensions and problems that can occur when Western management ideas and practices are transplanted into a non-Western environment. There is, for instance, the apparent contradiction that Malawi is a newly independent nation in the process of rapid change, a characteristic shared by all African states to a greater or lesser degree and likely to continue. Yet the organizations that are to be instrumental in bringing about and managing change are, as a number of commentators have observed, generally bureaucratic, rigid, and rule-bound. On the level of managerial motivation, there is another apparent contradiction: Malawian managers reflect in many aspects of their thinking African traditional, communalistic values, yet they stress the importance of their needs for autonomy and self-actualization at work (the individualistic focus more characteristic of Western societies).

Jenkins[1] and Rutherford,[2] in studies of Malawian managers, remark on the strong, expressed need for structure, guidelines, and clear direction (reflecting a preoccupation with security). This apparent acceptance of "universalistic" criteria for behavior in organizations is contrasted with the evidence that managers regularly bypass organizational structures and make decisions on the basis of "particularistic" (i.e., what the managers in the study referred to as "personalized") criteria.

1. Jenkins, C. "Management Problems and Management Education in Developing Economies: A Case Study of Malawi." Working paper. University of Aston, Management Centre, 1982.

2. Rutherford, P. "Attitudes of Malawian Managers: Some Recent Research." Unpublished paper. University of Malawi, 1981.

Education and Training of Malawian Managers _____

Organizational behavior is influenced by a complex set of interrelated factors. The Western notion of "rational" behavior is itself the product of such factors, but it is not automatically applicable in other contexts. What appears to a Western observer of African organizations to be "irrational," on closer examination can be seen to reflect a set of values that are different from, but no less valid than, those of the West. For this reason I take the view, in considering the education and training of Malawian managers, that it would be unrealistic and inappropriate to advance prescriptive proposals for changing the existing realities of Malawian organizational life.

The following propositions are intended rather to accept the socio-cultural, economic, and political realities and to suggest how Malawian managers might be assisted to be effective and, if they so desire, to change existing systems and practices:

1. Because the Malawian environment is less stable and predictable than is the case in the industrialized nations, "the probability of planned actions going wrong is high . . . margins of error are likely to be particularly large" [5. p. 157]. It is therefore important to recognize that the use of Western planning techniques cannot be assumed to guarantee any anticipated outcome. Malawian managers will need to reflect on experiences, since independence, of planning and its effectiveness, and to identify the particular factors that have influenced success or failure.

2. There is a need to acknowledge the collectivist values that inhere in contemporary Malawian society and to consider which Western management practices and techniques might tend to contradict them. For example, it is not difficult to understand why Western performance appraisal and Management by Objectives schemes may find intellectual acceptance by Malawian managers, yet fail in practice. Seddon [7] has observed that in many African societies it is a sign of weakness to admit incompetence or ignorance. Mistakes are believed to be beyond the control of individuals, and the maintenance of "face" is of crucial importance. There is a highly developed sensitivity to individual criticism, "the most powerful contingencies determining behavior (informally) are 'social evaluations'— pride and shame." In my study there was considerable evidence of a reluctance by managers to criticize individuals.

   In such circumstances, the use of Western practices for assessing individual performance appears to be inappropriate. For Malawian managers to have to learn such practices without a comprehensive analysis of their chances of success and their consequences in terms of Malawian values seems both impractical and wasteful.

3. Similar considerations apply to teaching Malawian managers about the benefits claimed, in the Western context, for delegation of authority, sharing of information, and a generally more

participative management style. In the situation I have described, such practices can be seen to contradict many Malawian social values, and have little chance at present of successful adoption. It is important, however, that Malawian managers clearly understand the consequences of their current management style, which (1) tends to push decisions upward in the organizational hierarchy; (2) involves managers in routine, trivial activities; (3) hinders the sharing of information within the organization, thus possibly reducing its capacity to anticipate and cope with change; (4) encourages highly dependent subordinate behavior; (5) reduces opportunities for subordinates to engage in more interesting work; and (6) on the evidence of my interview survey, appears to be a source of dissatisfaction for managers in terms of relationships with their bosses.

4. Malawian managers require highly developed political skills, both in monitoring developments that may affect them, as "particularistic" criteria influence decision makers inside and outside their employing organizations, and in their relationships with organizational superiors, colleagues, and subordinates. Such skills are not necessarily a major focus in Western management development strategies.

5. Malawian managers require well-developed diplomatic skills, particularly in two contexts. First, their bosses expect them to behave in a deferential manner, far more than is the case in Western views of such a relationship. It seems important that the implications of this type of relationship should be examined in relation to organizational performance. If managers are to be able to cope with change and to provide solutions to emerging problems, will their extreme deference to, and dependence on, more senior executives not inhibit them? Malawian managers expressed dissatisfaction with this relationship and wanted more opportunities (clearly delineated, nevertheless) for autonomy. They also wanted their bosses to behave in a more predictable (i.e., "universalistic") manner and to give them recognition for good performance. In such circumstances of dependency and unfulfilled expectations, Malawian managers need diplomatic and influencing abilities of a high order. Secondly, as we have seen, Malawian managers are often faced with demands from outside the organization, from extended family and kinship groups and (less frequently) from the Party. Such demands may well conflict with the manager's organizational role, and he will need to be skilled in explaining the demands and limitations under which he operates in the organization.

6. When Malawian managers are taught the paramount Western organizational values of effective and efficient use of scarce resources, it is important that they consciously consider and understand the implications of implementing these values in Malawian society, where there is a greater concern for social relationships than for performance, where there are social expectations about the role of organizations that are greater than is customary in the West, and where the notion of considering the individual as a "resource" is strange.

7. Malawian workers tend to have higher expectations about the organization's ability and willingness to accept a degree of responsibility for their welfare and development than is the case in the industrialized West. At the same time, there is a more instrumental attitude toward work, involving fewer considerations of loyalty to the organization. In these circumstances, managers could well consider the implications in terms of employee motivation. Western assumptions about the desirability of self-expression and fulfillment appear to be inappropriate, and uncritical teaching of Western motivation theories to Malawian managers needs to be challenged.

8. The managers in this study indicated that they derived considerable satisfaction from the use of their professional or technical competence, and were generally concerned about performance (this was decidedly less so in the case of the Malawian civil servants in the study). These strengths might be used in developing managers' understanding of their more directly managerial functions if it can be shown that job satisfaction can be enhanced when management work is viewed as requiring equally prestigious, admirable skills, and that effective performance is more likely when professional and technical expertise is reinforced by managerial capabilities.

9. Although the presence of expatriate managers will lessen in significance, it is at present an area of concern for many Malawian managers. Since it is not realistic to expect that expatriate executives will be selected primarily on the basis of their cultural sensitivity, it might be useful if Malawian managers were helped to understand more about the backgrounds, perspectives, and values of the expatriates. This may go some way in enabling Malawian managers to handle their relationships with expatriates effectively.

Strategies and Methods

Turning to considerations of appropriate methods for education and training of Malawian managers, I suggest that the foregoing discussion indicates that the following *outcomes* are priorities:

- In an environment of turbulent change, learning should become a conscious and continuous process for Malawian managers.

- Malawian managers should develop a profound awareness of, and sensitivity to, the sociocultural context in which they operate.

- They should also have a clear understanding of the implicit demands of Western management ideas and practices, and of the facets of Malawian society that might be congruent and incongruent with such demands (for example, deference and dependent relationships).

- There should be a deliberate and reasoned rejection of the uncritical adoption of Western (or other alien) organization and management theories.

- Managers and educators should acknowledge, analyze, and reflect upon the experience of Malawian organizations and develop from it indigenous explanatory concepts.

- Malawian managers should develop more confidence in the validity of their own experiences and their views on management (rather than deferring to outsiders).

When we consider how such outcomes might be achieved through education and training, several factors have to be borne in mind. First, just as Western management ideas must be critically examined in the light of Malawian sociocultural realities, Western notions concerning the education and training of managers have to be understood in terms of the assumptions they make about people and the values that influence them. Many current Western ideas about management development can be seen clearly to reflect values such as individual responsibility for self-actualization; learning as problem solving, involving puzzlement, perturbation, even discomfort for the learner; the value of self-discovered knowledge as opposed to prescribed knowledge; a view of the teacher-learner relationship as involving interdependence and assumed equality; development as involving risk and change for learners; a view of the professional as an individual of independent judgment, self-confident in his relationship with his employing organization; and an increasing degree of openness in relationships. Contrasted to this I have detailed Malawian values that might be expected to influence management education and training, including the collectivist (as opposed to Western individualist) nature of social relationships; greater awareness of hierarchical levels and deference to authority, which, according to Clarke[3], is expressed in the teacher-learner relationship by "a greater need (by the learner) for clear and unequivocal direction . . . and regular face-to-face contact"; education seen as a way to enhance status rather than for personal growth; learning viewed as a way of avoiding risk by acquiring additional information, to be hoarded and protected as a source of power; and training viewed as a threat rather than an opportunity for self-actualization if it involves an admission of ignorance or shortcomings.

In addition, managers indicated in the questionnaire survey that the most effective ways in which they had learned their managerial abilities were: by doing, by discussing real problems with colleagues, through training by the boss, by observing effective managers, and by analyzing their successes and failures.

This seems to suggest that approaches to management education and training in Malawi should include the following general criteria:

---

3. Clarke, R. "Independent Learning in an African Country, with Special Reference to the Certificate of Adult Studies in the University of Malawi." Ph.D. thesis. University of Manchester, Department of Adult and Higher Education, 1981, 240.

1. As Hyden [5] has noted: "For a manager to be effective he needs to be sensitive to and work in response to his proximate environment. Many African managers lack a grasp of how they can combine good management with effective response to their environment" (p. 59). People are intuitively and experientially aware of their environment, but it is suggested that managers need to be helped to develop a fuller understanding of and sensitivity to the sociocultural facets of their environment that affect their roles. This will involve teaching strategies that draw upon the experiences of managers and encourage them to reflect on the implications for future action.

2. It must be made clear in organizational policies that the organization accepts a substantial share of responsibility for the development of individuals, and that further education and training do not imply that a manager is incompetent or lacking in some area. It must be understood that management development does not involve a risk for the individual and that the learning environment will be supportive.

3. Learning strategies and methods should reflect the collectivist nature of Malawian society. This would imply that methods should be avoided that focus on individual performance (especially shortcomings). Small-group methods and other supportive techniques seem to be appropriate.

4. There needs to be an explicit focus on continuous learning from experience. Learning opportunities in the organization (such as deputizing for an absent boss, introduction of structural or technological change, launching of a new product, coping with unanticipated difficulties) should be identified and utilized. This will demand that attention be given to developing skills in analyzing successes and failures in a conscious, structured way.

5. Management education and training should help managers understand the processes of organizational change. As noted earlier, the structures of Malawian organizations tend predominantly to be rigidly bureaucratic (embodying security and stability in an environment of accelerating change). Managers need to understand the implications of such organizational patterns for the effective performance of the roles Malawian society expects organizations to undertake.

6. Managers should be trained in coaching skills, in order to be fully effective in developing subordinates. Organizations need to ensure that the job descriptions of managers include the coaching of subordinates as a priority function.

7. Management development strategies should include structured, on-the-job, developmental activities.

8. The group-oriented methods and problem-solving focus of Action Learning suggest that it might be worthwhile to experiment with this approach to management development. Revan's [8] notion of "comrades in adversity" may address the needs of Malawian managers for security and social interaction while

enabling them to identify real problems and to use their shared experience to develop solutions.

Conclusion —————————————————————————————

In the literature about the transfer of Western management concepts and practices, one can detect a developing dichotomy. Some writers assert that the imperatives of organizational life are so powerful, so pervasive, that the "culture of production" will sweep aside local variations in culture, values, and behavior. Others would claim, on the contrary, that in some countries the culture is so distinctive and so enduring that imported notions about organizations and their management will be radically modified or even rejected. The findings from the study of Malawian managers upon which this paper is based provide evidence that both tendencies are present. The "convergence-divergence" debate will continue as cross-cultural research adds to the stock of data for comparison.

For management educators this is inconvenient. It demands that strategies for management development should recognize the complex and distinctive realities of the contexts in which managers perform. The search for relevance will, I suspect, be a crucial task.

References —————————————————————————————

1. Onyemelukwe, C. *Man and Management in Contemporary Africa*. London: Longmans, 1973.

2. Haire, M., Ghiselli, E., and Porter, L. *Managerial Thinking: An International Study*. New York: Wiley, 1966.

3. Safavi, F. "A Model of Management Education in Africa." *Academy of Management Review*, 1981, 6(2), 319-331.

4. Hofstede, G. *Culture's Consequences: International Differences in Work-related Values*. London: Sage, 1980.

5. Hyden, G. *No Shortcuts to Progress: African Development Management in Perspective*. London: Heinemann, 1983.

6. Blunt, P., and Popoola, O. *Personnel Management in Africa*. London: Longmans, 1985.

7. Seddon, J. "The Development and Indigenisation of Third World Business: African Values in the Workplace." In Hammond, V. (ed.), *Current Research in Management*. London: Frances Pinter/ATM, 1985.

8. Revans, R. *The Origins and Growth of Action Learning*. Bromley: Chartwell-Bratt, 1982.

Management Development in Europe: A Study in Cultural Contrast

Reading 5.2
Peter Lawrence

Our starting point is that the management of human resources (HRM) is essentially an Anglo-Saxon construct. It has been "grafted on" rather than "taken root" in Continental Europe, where the classic HRM functions—recruitment, socialisation, training, development—are rather more determined by different conceptions of management, underpinned by related values. These same underlying beliefs and assumptions also colour the varied approaches which are taken to the making of managers in these countries. The purpose of this article is to throw the different European approaches to management development into sharp relief first by making the contrast with the American situation clear and then by drawing out the differences within Europe—most notably France and Germany.

Management's American Origins

Discussion of the origins of management is sometimes obscured by the fact that management is at the same time an activity, an idea, and a subject (Lawrence, 1986:2-5). As an activity, management has clearly existed for centuries. Past instances of the discriminant deployment of resources and the effective co-ordination of manpower abound, from the building of the pyramids to the organising of the army that Napoleon took to Moscow in 1812. But engaging *in* it is different from having an idea *of* it, and it is the latter which is the American *démarche*.

It was in the USA, that is, that the idea of management crystallised. Management was first identified and labelled in the USA, seen as a phenomenon that could be extrapolated, analysed, and made the subject of generalisation. The most potent cause of this development, no doubt,

Source: "Management Development in Europe: A Study in Cultural Contrast" by Peter Lawrence. *Human Resource Management Journal*, 3 (1), Autumn 1992. Published by IRS/PPL 18-20 Highbury Place, London, N5 1QP.

was the unusual circumstance of America from the end of the War of Independence (1783) until the last unclaimed land was distributed at Fort Sill, Oklahoma (1890): namely, a vast, empty continent was "filled in"—too much space and too many resources crossed with too few people and too little time. And the shortage of people betokened an even more acute shortage—of drive, entrepreneurialism, versatility, adaptability, and the opportunistic exploitation of circumstance and resource; that is to say, a shortage of (some of) the ingredients of management. And the sense of shortage led to a corresponding valuing, indeed valorisation, of these qualities.

It is a short step from the conceptualisation and valuation of management to the conviction that it is teachable: the Americans took this step. The world's first business school, at Wharton, Pennsylvania, was established in 1881 (cf. the London Business School established in 1965). Wharton was the first of many. By the 1950s business education, as we know from William Whyte's *Organisation Man* (1956), was not only a mass phenomenon but a mature one, inviting satirical treatment (management education has yet to become an object of satire in Europe).

The transition from a concept of management to the *teachability* of management itself expresses a variety of American values, with proactivity, a drive to efficiency, and equality of opportunity all playing a part. The American world view is active not contemplative, oriented to the here and now not the life thereafter, and above all to the conviction that man can and must shape his destiny. All this inclines an efficiency-conscious people to:

- be aware;

- work out how;

- formulate if possible;

- pass it on (teach).

So far we have argued for management's American origins, but in general terms. It is possible to go further and see the emergence of HRM and "management development" as pre-eminently American phenomena. There are a number of issues here. First is the general consideration that Americans, having invented management, espouse all its specialisms, techniques, and the "supporting cast" of business school teachable subjects. Thus the Americans invented mass production, marketing, and corporate strategy, just to take three lead examples. But more than this, the USA is the land par excellence of social science. While Britain, and to a lesser extent Continental Europe, discovered sociology in the 1960s and scrambled to establish sociology departments at universities, these had routinely existed in the USA for half a century. This tends to be obscured by the fact that it was the Europeans who produced all the "founding fathers"—Weber, Marx, Durkheim, Simmel, and so on—with the Americans making a systematic contribution to social theory only in the mid-twentieth century. But if Europe had the "officers" the USA had "enlisted men" in abundance. Indeed the inter-war period is something of a golden age in American empirical social science with a plethora of community studies, research on stratification systems, ethnic minorities, race relations, poverty, crime, and juvenile gangs.

This empirical outpouring did not end with the 1930s. When the Japanese bombed Pearl Harbor in December 1941 they unleashed not only an American military response but also a sociological one! A distinctive feature of the American war effort was its reflexive nature; it studied itself in the making. Americans wanted to understand the human and organisational dimensions of belligerence, and to profit from the understanding. It is sometimes said that the Second World War in the United Kingdom gave birth to operations research: in the United States it gave rise to group dynamics and leadership studies. In the post-war period the American preoccupation with people and groups enjoyed a new flowering. Consider that all the theories of motivation are American, so are virtually all the leadership studies, so is group dynamics, studies of supervisory effectiveness, informal organisation, work group behaviour, and much organisation theory and analysis. All this is a powerful thrust to the development of HRM, and to management as a teachable activity.

There is also an important facilitating factor. This is the absence in the USA alike of European-style class consciousness, a serious socialist movement, and any penetration of Marxist ideology. In "old Europe" these have variously served to structure both the perception and reality of superior-subordinate and management-worker relations in industry. But the American comes to these with an open mind. In the absence of any prestructuring these phenomena must be seen in their own terms, their own irreducible human and social terms. So that group dynamics, supervisory styles, context-specific leadership, and formal and informal systems have a greater relevance and immediacy.

One obvious manifestation of these tendencies is the American fascination with the organisation itself. Precisely because it is a man-made construct, "the organisation" is endlessly fascinating to Americans. Whereas the Germans, for example, see the organisation as a secondary consequence of engaging in manufacturing activity, in the American view the organisation is both primary and perfectable. Because people have made it, people can improve it, endlessly "tinker" with it (= OD) to get improvements in efficiency, effectiveness or enhanced interpersonal cooperation. Managerial leaders can be taught how the system works and thus be equipped to modify it.

Finally, the American concern with people—as individuals, in groups, as organisational members—is also heightened by American rejection of European élitism. As the land without monarchy, aristocracy or papacy, the USA is the society where people are primary, equal and important. People cannot be judged secondary to an idea, are less easily relegated to the status of role incumbents. So if people are primary, and equal, there must be a greater concern with their motivation, leadership, satisfactions and concerns, and with the dynamics of their cooperation.

For such reasons the USA is the country par excellence of HRM and formal management development, both in terms of practice and of the academic, research-driven underpinning. A major contention of this article is that these conditions and values, and therefore their results, are not replicated in Continental Europe in the same plenitude. But what of the "intermediate state," Britain?

HRM, Management Development and the British View of the Human Condition

There can be little doubt the HRM is "alive and well" in Britain. It is included on every conceivable management course from DMS to MBA, there is a flourishing Institute of Personnel Management which acts as a qualifying body as well as an interest group, and while it would probably be unrealistic to expect any staff function/department to enjoy the highest prestige, low esteem has traditionally been reserved for engineering (Gerstl and Hutton, 1966), design and production (Gill and Lockyer, 1978) rather than personnel. It must be equally clear that this is not because Britain shares with the USA any of the features or values explored above. Indeed, the only thing that Britain in this connection would appear to share with the USA is not being Continental European. So how is this parallel development of HRM in Britain to be explained?

It seems to this writer that the answer must lie in a number of intersecting negatives, but let us at least begin on a more positive note. For most of this century Britain has recognised that industry and management are not national strengths and there has been a corresponding tendency to "look up" to other countries whose superior economic performance was attributed in part to quality of management. For most of the twentieth century the USA has been the business role model. If you wanted to know how to do it you went to the USA to observe the professionals, and came back and did it in Britain—if you had the nerve and the trade unions would let you. This sustained British admiration of American business lasts at least until the 1970s, and is manifest in a number of shared enthusiasms—short termism, equity financing, mergers and acquisitions, financial planning, budgetary control, strategy, and management education. For all of these the enthusiasm evinced in Britain is observable, but later on less so than in the USA. So this standing of HRM and management development in Britain is in part a reflection of extended mid-century admiration for that dominant transatlantic economy. But there are other considerations.

A number of writers have identified an anti-industrial strain in British culture and society (Barnett, 1972; Wiener, 1981) and this anti-industrialism is also a well-worked theme in the "industrial novels" of the mid-nineteenth century, for example Disraeli's *Sybil* and Dickens's *Hard Times*. The essence of this genre is that industry is variously rejected as soulless, depersonalising, calculating, and overly-materialistic. Not an enterprise for the gentleman, or the intellectual, or for anyone with finer feelings. But note that the critique implies a plea for HRM, where the mission of personnel is to re-personalise a dreary and mechanistic operation. It also implies a vital need to teach managers "interpersonal skills," communication, leadership, and so on.

A similar thesis-antithesis may be perceived in the British undervaluation of *Technik*. Engineers have traditionally enjoyed lower standing in Britain than in Continental Europe (Hutton and Lawrence, 1981), the technical functions, including production, have lower relative status in British industry (Lawrence, 1980; Lockyer and Jones, 1980). Furthermore, the tendency in Britain has been to stereotype the engineer pejoratively as interpersonally inadequate, at ease only when communing with his machines. Here again the playing up of the human side of enterprise as a crucial managerial role is a very British response.

There are further antithetical elements. The persistence in Britain of subjective class consciousness renders communication (across class lines, in industry across authority lines) more problematic. Hence people, managers and supervisors, need to be coached in it, need to be made aware of the barriers by means of case studies and role plays. Or again the traditionally poor industrial relations in British industry are a stimulus to professional HRM. Poor industrial relations "flag up" a need for training—in communication again, in supervisory skills, in negotiation, and in being familiar with "the British system of industrial relations," a common course component. It also shapes the consciousness about the priorities to be included in management education, training and development processes. Furthermore, a number of elements already canvassed—anti-industrialism and class consciousness, aristocratic disdain and employee intransigence—all render motivation relatively more problematic than in other industrial societies. Once again, it is a challenge for management development.

Finally, this negatively induced concern with communication, negotiation, supervision and motivation in British industrial society is paralleled and sustained by a positive conviction. If there is one thing that "our glorious history" teaches us, it is that great men matter—from Clive to Churchill, from Wolf to Dowding. The British tendency to reject technology as depersonalising and administrative systems as mundane is matched by a valorisation of the human and individual. Human qualities, individual talents, creativity, social ease and political grasp are what matter; the ability to move others is decisive, leadership is at a premium. Again, it is a national inclination that works in favour of HRM. Personnel is the function charged with the selection, recruitment, and development of human talent, with "the care and feeding" of leaders. This is not a disposition that one finds, for instance, in matter-of-fact Sweden, or in the anti-heroic Netherlands.

We have deliberately spent some time exploring the differential underpinning of HRM and the nature of managerial priorities in the two key Anglo-Saxon countries as a backdrop to understanding Continental Europe. It is in fact because so many of the considerations explored in the British and American connection do not apply in mainland Europe, that HRM does not have the same élan there, indeed is in part socially and culturally by-passed. Let us begin with France.

Personnel Management and the Making of Managers in France ___

It should be said at the outset that the distinctions made in this article between countries are not of a "black and white" kind. In these discussions of the origin, standing, and nature of both the personnel function and role of management development we are dealing of course in matters of relative importance and national emphasis. With this qualification let us begin to situate the personnel function and French conceptions of management with a brief historical reference.

In the previous discussion of Britain it was suggested that part of the *raison d'être* for the personnel function was a need to civilise industry, to give manufacturing a human face. These arguments are not inapplicable to France but they are less important for that country. In the British case the humanising mission of personnel derives long term from the black imprint of the industrial revolution on the folk memory. Say "industry" to a British school child and he/she thinks of slums, squalor, and child labour in the cotton mills. All this applies rather less to France. In that country the industrial revolution started later than in Britain, and was far less comprehensive. France remained persistently if not predominantly rural until after the Second World War. It is generally agreed that industrialisation was only completed in France in the 1950s, part of the development connoted by the phrase *les trentes glorieuses*, the thirty years of growing prosperity after the Liberation. There are occasional French novels decrying the ills of industrialisation, but "the industry novel" is not a genre as in nineteenth century Britain. Or again the civilising mission of personnel, very obvious in the British case, is inappropriate in the case of France. In that society industry has been civilised from within by the quality and educational élan of the management élite, an idea that will be developed in the next section.

Another part of the *raison d'être* for the personnel function in general, and the management development activity in particular, is the conviction that industry has "special needs" in terms of the skills and capabilities of those who staff it. At the blue-collar level this simply means the development of craft skills and operating capabilities, but at management level there is an implicit distinction. This is that the skills of the manager (private sector, profit making) will need to differ somewhat from those of the administrator (public sector, non-profit making) where the former is historically recent and the latter, like the poor, has always been with us. The present writer has argued elsewhere (Lawrence, 1986:17-19) that the distinction is valid, that both the ambiance and values of public and private sector organisations differ, and that different capabilities are required by those who run them. But interestingly, this distinction is less salient for France, which country is distinguished by projecting a valorisation of public service models into the later twentieth century.

The heroes of French history have been authoritarian centralisers; one looks in vain for a Disraeli extending the franchise to industrial workers or for an Andrew Jackson articulating populist aspirations. In the French case the centralisers range from Cardinal Richelieu, Cardinal Mazarin and Louis XIV in the seventeenth century, through Robespierre's 1792-93 Committee of Public Safety during the Revolution and Napoleon shortly after, to Clemenceau and of course General de Gaulle in the twentieth century. And what these centralisers have done is to centralise power and decisions in the hands of a state bureaucracy, whether royal, revolutionary, imperial or presidential. In other words, France has long standing as a bureaucratic state. It is more bureaucratic than its neighbours, and bureaucratic forms are given more credence. Indeed it has been argued by Crozier (1963) that the French actually like bureaucracy, their individualism making them prefer the impersonal dictates of bureaucratic regulation to the willful direction of a physically present superior.

Historically, there is an interesting twist to this story. The Fourth Republic in France (1946-1958), from its inception until its transformation into the Fifth Republic with enhanced presidential power to the benefit of Charles de Gaulle, was unstable. Marked by too many political parties, unstable and fluctuating coalition governments and short-lived ministries, the Fourth Republic is viewed by the French as something rather shameful (although it presided over effective post-war reconstruction and growing prosperity, and enacted some desirable reforms) and there is a sense of national relief when de Gaulle comes to power. The interesting thing is that throughout the period 1946-1958 ministerial instability is compensated by bureaucratic continuity; it is the state service rather than a succession of short-lived premiers who ran France; the triumphs of the period are the triumphs of a technocratic civil service rather than those of parliamentarians. And the role of the state service raises its standing and even its esteem with the public at large.

The thrust of these remarks is that whereas in other countries management, coming later, felt a need to differentiate itself from civil administration, coming sooner, this dysjunction is much less in France.

There the state service enjoys higher prestige than in the Anglo-Saxon countries, is regarded as a suitable or at least plausible model for industrial organisation, with the result that the public sector v private sector distinction is much less marked. The relative closeness is furthered by the fact that senior posts in both the state service and in private industry are staffed by people with the same educational background, of which more in the next section. In addition, there is also mobility between the sectors, from public to private, whereby civil servants in mid-career may move to posts at or near the top in private industry; this institution is known as *pantouflage*. The result of this greater public sector v private sector closeness is a diminished role for management development, in a milieu less inclined to view the demands of industrial management as distinctive.

Management Development and French Understanding ————————

In the previous section we have explored "the outer edges" of management consciousness in France. It has been argued that industry in France did not in the twentieth century need to combat the negative image of early industrialisation, as was the case in Britain. That French industry was seen at an earlier stage than British as offering an appropriate career to intelligent and educated people, and therefore had less need to be "civilised" by a personnel function that would "respectably relate" it to the wider society. Furthermore, less discontinuity is perceived in France as between civil administration and industrial management, the standing of the former is high, and the two are linked by recruitment from a common educational source reinforced by some mobility from the state service into industry. What is more, profit-making companies in France differ less in terms of both organisational structure and *modus operandi* from the state bureaucracy. All these considerations imply a different and modified role for the personnel function in France and for the management development responsibility. But there is more.

Management development is less salient in France because in that country management is regarded more as a state of being than as the result of fashioned development processes within the company. It is or connotes an identity, more than an activity or set of capabilities. This is signalled in the term *cadres* by which managers are collectively known. This term was adopted in the 1930s, a period of troubled relations between organised labour and the *patronat* or class of business owners. With regard to these tensions the *cadres* were meant to be disinterested, impartial, distinct also from the owning class, devoted in technocratic style to the efficiency of the company. It is a solidaristic concept. It is an important label. Being a *cadre* cuts you off from other groupings, and automatically means you have things in common with all other people who are *cadres.* This solidarism is reinforced by the military ring (and origin) of the term, cf. *quadri* in Italian, though this is less widely used to designate managers in Italy than the ubiquitous *cadres* in France.

It is sometimes said that France has gone further towards making management a profession than have other industrial societies, and there is some truth in this. The reference here is not so much to professional excellence (though there is absolutely no suggestion that French managers are inferior) but again to self-identity. The entity *cadres* in France is not "fuzzy at the edges." One does not have debates in France as in Britain, about whether or not the foreman is part of junior management. In French companies people know who is, and who is not, a *cadre*, an understanding that is readily reflected in remarks such as *"en deux ans j´espere passer cadre"* (in a couple of years I hope to make it into the ranks of the *cadres*). This quasi professional unity is reinforced by other factors. The *cadres* have benefited much from the postwar economic development and rise in prosperity, the *trentes glorieuses* referred to earlier. The cadres are viewed if not exactly as the architects of this achievement then at least as those who presided over it and made it happen, and are thus further differentiated from the *patronat* (owners), many of whom were discredited by collaboration with the Nazis in the 1940-44 occupation period.

Or again *cadres* are treated separately by the state for the purposes of unemployment administration. They have for decades been the focus of attention by advertisers and especially advertisers of luxury and fashionable goods and services. This, of course, is not unknown in other countries, but there is a difference in France. This is that there the *cadres* have a stronger claim to be an educational and cultural élite as well as a disposable income élite. A further feature which is definitely French is that the *cadres* have been courted by the political parties in France. One speaks indeed of trying to capture the *cadres* vote (the nearest and much narrower equivalent in English, now discredited, would be going for the Yuppie vote).

But the most powerful factor acting upon the management development issue in France is that society's distinctive understanding of the management task. In France management is seen much more in ratiocinative terms, as being about analysis and rational decision. The qualities sought in *cadres* are correspondingly powers of analysis, synthesis, evaluation, and articulation. French management adverts are peppered with calls for such qualities as *la rigueur* and *l´esprit de synthèse* (Barsoux and Lawrence, 1990:47). There is a general "playing up" of these qualities at the expense of the Anglo-Saxon qualities of drive, pugnacity, self-starting, motivating communication.

In the French case, the demand is matched by the supply. France is unusual in having a two-tier system of higher education, where the "mere universities" are outclassed by the superior *grandes écoles*. From the standpoint of the able and ambitious, the system works like this. One attends a *lycée* (selective part of a secondary school), and works towards the *baccalaureat* exam, the equivalent of "A" levels in England or of *Abitur* in Germany, which is taken at the age of 18 and admits to university. But significant choices have already been made. There are different versions of the *baccalaureat* in the sense of different groupings of subjects and subject emphasis. Though there is an economics and business subjects *baccalaureat*, someone aiming at an eventual career in management would not take it! Instead the able and ambitious go for "bac C," the option that includes most maths and natural science, since these are thought to be the best test of intellectual and reasoning ability.

Having passed the bac one might go to university, but again the able and ambitious candidate, especially if male, will not do this (except for subjects such as medicine or computer science only offered at university). Instead our future manager will have his or her sight fixed on entry to one of the *grandes écoles.* To this end one enters an *école préparatoire* (known colloquially as a *prépa*) for an intensive two-year preparatory course. This is the most testing time in the aspirant's life, and (ex) *prépa* students speak routinely of working 70 and 80 hours a week. These labours culminate in taking the *concours,* nationally competitive exams that admit to the *grandes écoles.* This is the most important hurdle one ever has to scale; when it has been cleared, one is made for life. While the course at the typical *grande école* is not a rest cure and the final examination there is taken seriously, the system is "front end-loaded": it is getting in that is difficult and important, once there one is likely to succeed, educationally and occupationally.

The *grandes écoles* are élitist and exclusive. They admit not only on the basis of intense competition but also in small numbers—hundreds not thousands. There is no completely agreed list of the *grandes écoles,* but they are generally thought to number 140 to 160 or so establishments. Many are technical; engineering schools, both general technical and engineering subject specific. Others are commercial or business schools, known commonly as *Sup de Cos* (= *école supérieur de commerce*); and there are a few specialist schools such as the *Ecole Normale* which trains selective secondary school teachers. The *grandes écoles* are arranged in a prestige order that is clear to French people. The most prestigious of the engineering schools is the *Ecole Polytechnique;* the most prestigious of the *Sup de Cos* is HEC (*Haute Ecole de Commerce*), one of the three that are situated in Paris and known collectively as the *trois grandes parisiennes.*

The *grandes écoles* are the gateway to both management careeers and to higher posts in the state service. Not every *cadre* is *grande école* educated, but most are. They are massively overrepresented in the ranks of the chief executives: a 1990 *L´Expansion* survey of 100 chief executives found indeed that 28 of them came from the *Ecole Polytechnique* alone. Most name companies recruit exclusively from the *grandes écoles,* technical and commercial. To enter a company from the *grande école* means achieving *cadre* status early and being on what is known as the *voie royale* (royal road) to success. Non-*grande école* graduates who become *cadres* will variously do it at smaller, less renowned companies, it will take them longer; their career ceiling will be lower, and their *cadre* status will be tied to seniority and performance in the company that "ennobled" them. They will not possess "portable" credentials.

The thing to emphasise is that there is a high congruence between the French understanding of the essential nature of management on the one hand and the output of the education system on the other hand. From *lycée* to *grande école* the emphasis is on formal learning, the development of educated cleverness, numeracy, literacy and a stylish competence with the French language, together with a high level of formal reasoning ability and *culture générale*. All this fits very nicely in a milieu that conceives of management as being about ordering and deciding on the basis of analysis and synthesis, rather than about inter-personal manoeuvring, motivating, and implementing.

This is not to say that there is no "management development" of the graduates of the *grandes écoles* that companies recruit. But it tends to be more of a validating and grooming exercise. Young graduates are sent on assignments abroad, go out on fact-finding missions to the manufac-turing facilities in the provinces, or serve as an *attaché de direction* (PA to senior management). There is also a diagonal promotion route from research and development into general management; serving as the head of research units, or of planning, strategy, or development entities is all seen as an opportunity for the upwardly bound recruits to play their strengths and to cultivate the generalist label so important for progress into the higher ranks. Thus there is management development, but its role is modified by an assumtion that the important act of selec-tion has already taken place at the *concours* (entry to the *grandes écoles*) and been reaffirmed by *grande école* graduation. The task of management development is further simplified by the conviction that all the most important qualities the successful manager should possess are *already* in place and have been publicly certified by the education system.

So far in this article emphasis has been given to the deep-seated contrasts between the understanding of the nature of management in France and that existing in the Anglo-Saxon countries. These differ-ences, it has been suggested, have a profound impact upon the ways in which managers are made and upon the content of the knowledge transmitted to them. The thrust of the argument can be further elabo-rated if we now also bring into the picture an account of management development in another European country. At this point therefore it is worth looking briefly at the situation in Germany.

Management and Management Development in Germany ————

As with the previous analyses of Britain, America and France, it is worth beginning with a view of the general HRM scene before looking more closely at the conception of "management" and hence the way management might be learned. Germany offers a very interesting contrast with the USA and indeed is virtually a mirror image of the American norm. (Our discussion here refers to the personnel function in West Germany as it existed from 1949 to 1990; what are now called the New Federal States [East Germany] required separate treatment.) It should be said straight away that this does not imply any criticism of German personnel managers, they are not lacking in some way compared with their American and British counterparts. It is rather that a range of institutional factors have turned German personnel officers into a body of reactors, implementers, and law-enforcers. The first of these constraining factors is the force of law.

In Germany tradition, diffuse expectations, and custom and practice count for less, and the law counts for more. This reflects not only the relative newness of the (West) German state with its written constitution and Basic Law (1949) but also the much vaunted low tolerance for ambiguity (Hofstede, 1980). It is difficult to express such notions as "grey area" in German, and the German language in general does not lend itself to "fudging." More soberly a wider range of employment issues are legally regulated in Germany than in Britain, wage agreements have the force of law, and there is a system of labour courts. German personnel officers are much more concerned to do what the law commands, are more disposed to ask themselves in any exercise of discretion what it would look like in the labour court. It is not for nothing that the traditional qualification set of the German personnel manager is the equivalent of an LL.B plus a PhD in Law, although a small survey revealed the *de facto* range of qualifications to be somewhat wider (Lawrence, 1982: 31-3).

Second, there is the weighty matter of wage negotiations. In Germany wages are typically negotiated at a level above that of the individual company/employer between employers' associations and trade unions on a *Land* (state) by *Land* basis. This system does not in fact cover *all* German companies: smaller ones may not be members of the relevant employers' federation, and some very large ones, such as Siemens, may go it alone. With these exceptions German personnel managers seldom do what their British colleagues often do and their American colleagues invariably do—negotiate wages. But if they do not have authority, they do have responsibility. The wage agreements that emerge from the negotiations referred to above are in the form of endless pay scales, to which individual employees have to be fitted. This in turn necessitates complicated systems of job-grading, valid independently of particular job incumbents. All this is hard work, and it falls on personnel. So although the authority of initiative may be absent, the burden of implementation is very much present.

Third, there is the codetermination system, established in (West) Germany by law in the early 1950s, and in particular the institution of the elected *Betriebsrat* (works council). While there are clearly benefits to management from the German industrial democracy system of which the *Betriebsrat* is a central part, it does not serve to enhance the proactivity of the personnel function. Indeed the *Betriebsrat* decides some things in its own right, and is a watch-dog for all things that interest it. The personnel department in a sense services it, anticipates its concerns, provides up-front information, offers clarifications as demanded, and takes away critical issues raised in the *Betriebsrat* to "work on them" and provide "a management response." The other half of the equation is that this loss of proactivity by personnel in Germany tends to "free up" line management and particularly production managers.

The general drift of the arguments advanced in this section is to suggest that these several factors cast personnel management in Germany into a reactive mode, which, in turn, militates against an Anglo-Saxon style valorisation of the management development activity. But there is more. One of the earliest accounts of German management has as its major theme the idea that the German tradition venerated the entrepreneur and not the manager (Hartmann, 1959). Indeed the term manager came into use late, and was originally used to designate people running prize fights and road shows rather than industrial enterprises. It is also worth noting that the Germans never developed their own general-purpose term for manager, but simply say "manager" (with a capital M)—clearly indicative. Again tracing out these language peculiarities, the Germans cannot quite bring themselves to say "managerial" which should be *managerhaft* in German. Instead they say *unternchmerisch* (entrepreneurial) which has very positive connotations.

Management education of a general kind also came late to Germany. There is an undergraduate course that approximates to our first degree in management or business administration, the subject being called *Betriebswirtschaftslehre* or business economics. The interesting thing is that throughout most of the post-war era it was regarded as a bit inferior, something for second rate students. First rate people, on the other hand, did *Volkswirtschaft* or political economy, although it had less relevance for a career in management; industry followed the public estimation by hiring graduates in *Volkswirtschaft* on the grounds that they would be brighter. This state of affairs has now changed, but only in the 1980s, with *Betriebswirtschaftslehre* rising in esteem and increasing its enrolments substantially.

At the next level up, that of the MBA, Germany until very recently had nothing at all. The problem is compounded by the fact there are no Master's degrees in Germany anyway in the sense of a degree between the bachelor's and the doctor's (although some German universities call the first degree an MA to confuse foreigners!). In the last few years some MBA courses have sprung up in Germany, and revealingly some of them are franchised by universities in other countries (it is one of our invisible exports).

To round out this picture of management rejection it might be added that there is no equivalent in Germany of the BIM (British Institute of Management) nor any general management course/qualification akin to the DMS (Diploma in Management Studies). Germany does have an approximate equivalent of the IPM (Institute of Personnel Management) but it is a rather low profile affair compared with the British organisation: the present writer has interviewed personnel managers at patently respectable German companies who have not even heard of it.

This relatively weak concept of management, together with the belated emergence of general management education, does not, of course, bode well for management development. But there is another, and important element in this set of problems. The Germans typically have difficulty with the idea of management as something general, as something that can be viewed in the round, taken apart, and generalised about. When Germans look at a company they do not see a need for management: they see a variety of departments and functions requiring specialised knowledge and experience.

This specialist view of management also informs the German view of manager mobility. Germany is not a country where inter-company mobility is viewed as bad, as it is, for instance, in the Netherlands. But Germans expect that the mobility will take place within the same industry. In their view you cannot go from being, say, a purchasing officer in a machine tool company to an equivalent job in textiles: you would forfeit your expertise and have wasted the last ten years. The same sort of thinking informs mobility between functions. It simply does not make much sense, except for mobility between contiguous technical functions (design, production, maintenance, engineering, quality control). This specialist understanding of the management task is also perceptible in the organisation structure of German companies. These tend to be structured in big functional slabs with only a thin layer of general management at the top. Nor do German companies share the British predilection for breaking companies down into smaller units (profit centres) with generalist managers in charge of them.

All of the issues canvassed here militate against a flourishing management development activity in Germany. This does not, of course, mean that it is non-existent. It is often there in German companies but it is less widespread, less salient, more restrained by the reactive mode of the personnel function, and above all it gets away to a slow start because of the traditional German conviction that it is specialist knowledge (especially technical) and experience that are crucial.

Conclusions ——————————————————————————————

We have looked at Britain and the USA as a springboard for focussing on personnel and management development in France and Germany.

In neither of these countries is the Anglo-Saxon model to be found, albeit for different reasons in each case. There is no suggestion that this makes either the French or the Germans "worse managers" or "less professional." The non-universality of the Anglo-Saxon norm is attributable rather to two other considerations. First, these nation states have different configurations of institutions—educational, political, and economic—that impinge on management. Second, they exhibit different understandings of what management "is all about" and of the necessary qualities that managers should bring to it.

It is worth noting how much difference has surfaced from this simple line of inquiry: management development in two European countries. This result should be seen as salutory at a time when there is an increasing tendency towards rather facile "internationalism."

References

Barnett, Corelli. 1972. *The Collapse of British Power.* New York: William Morrow.

Barsoux, Jean-Louis and Peter Lawrence, 1990. *Management in France.* London: Cassell.

Crozier, Michel. 1963. *The Bureaucratic Phenomenon.* London: Tavistock Publications.

Gerstl, J.E. and S.P. Hutton. 1966. *Engineers: The Anatomy of a Profession.* London: Tavistock Press.

Gill, R.W.T. and K.G. Lockyer. 1978. *The Career Development of Production Managers in British Industry.* London: Report to the Joint CBI/BIM Advisory Panel on Management Education.

Hartmann, H. 1959. *Authority and Organization in German Management.* Princeton, NJ: Princeton University Press.

Hofstede, G. 1980. *Culture's Consequences.* Beverley Hills: Sage Publications.

Hutton, S.P. and P.A. Lawrence, 1981. *German Engineers: The Anatomy of a Profession.* London: Oxford University Press.

Lawrence, P.A. 1980. *Managers and Management in West Germany.* London: Croom Helm.

Lawrence, P.A. 1982. *Personnel Management in West Germany: Portrait of a Function.* Berlin: Report to Internationales Institut für Management und Verwaltung.

Lawrence, P.A. 1986. *Invitation to Management.* Oxford: Blackwell.

Lockyer, K.G. and S. Jones, 1980. "The Function Factor." *Management Today.* September, 5: 64.

Whyte, William H. 1956. *The Organisation Man.* New York: Simon & Schuster.

Wiener, Martin. 1981. *English Culture and the Decline of the Industrial Spirit. 1950-1980.* Cambridge: Cambridge University Press.

Internationalizing Managers: Expatriation and Other Strategies

Reading 5.3
Gary Oddou
C. Brooklyn Derr
Stewart Black

Internationalizing Managers

Japanese multinational corporations from the East are expanding their markets well beyond their borders, claiming a significant share of the global market in autos, computers, and consumer electronics since the 1970s. In so doing, they are sometimes encountering market areas that have traditionally been part of such European multinational corporations as Rhone-Poulenc, ABB, Nestlé, Siemens, Glaxo, Fiat, and many others. Simultaneously, many U.S., European, and Asian firms are expanding their primary markets internationally, thanks to the dissolution of the Soviet Union, the democratization and capitalization of Eastern Europe, the unification of Europe, and the opening of China and Malaysia.

The stakes are high. The potential for success is real, but so are the costs and risks. Multinational firms from all countries continue to make significant blunders as a result of cultural insensitivity or misjudgments. Toyota built a truck for the U.S. consumer, believing that there would be a market for a truck between three-quarter sized and full-sized trucks. Misjudging American taste for power and size, Toyota has been forced to reposition the truck and restrategize to market the truck.[1] Colgate Palmolive attempted to sell liquid cleaning products in Poland. They set the advertisement in the swimming pool of a "typical" resident, not anticipating that 99% of the Polish consumers could not relate to the image of a pool in their backyard.[2] AT&T fired high-ranking advertising executives over an ad that depicted Africans as a monkey.[3] With a great deal of international experience, it

Source: Gary Oddou, C. Brooklyn Derr, and Stewart Black, "Internationalizing Managers: Expatriation and Other Strategies." Selmer (ed.) *Expatriate Management* (Quorum Books, 1995). Reprinted with permission of the Greenwood Publishing Group, Inc., Westport, CT. © 1995.

is difficult to understand such blunders. This begs the important question: Can these and other leading multinational corporations develop culturally appropriate business strategies? Some believe that the key lies in the cultural savvy that a firm's decision-makers bring to the discussion—decision-makers who have had international experience and developed intercultural sensitivity. With such a background gained through their career development, such managers' strategic decisions are more likely to reflect invaluable knowledge about the social, political, economic, and legal systems of the firm's markets.[4]

This paper will explore the methods firms are currently using to internationalize their human resources, some of whom will become their future global leaders. To examine current trends, we will focus largely on how Japanese and European firms are approaching the challenge to internationalize their decision-makers. Given the similarities and differences found in our research, when feasible we will then attempt to generalize current trends to MNCs in general.

European Strategies

By and large, multinational corporations across Europe use a similar range of human resource development strategies.[5]

Traditionally, European firms have relied primarily on international assignments, not only to direct and coordinate their subsidiary networks but also to provide international career development experiences for selected employees.[6] This trend shows no signs of faltering. Ericsson, a Swedish telecommunications firm, regularly transfers teams of 30 to 100 engineers and managers from one foreign unit to another for one to two years.[7] The French chemical giant, Rhone-Poulenc, is developing strategies that coordinate international assignments with specific career development efforts. Volkswagen makes international assignments of new employees in their "firm-formative" stage to international posts to help them develop an international perspective.

With the development of the EC and the talk of the need for "Euromanagers," there is a strong belief that gaining international experience through international assignments will continue to be critical to the development of effective global leaders for European firms.

Japanese Strategies

As Japanese firms have begun to move beyond their borders through direct investment, they have experienced an increasing need to become aware of and work within the cultural systems of different countries. This need is especially crucial since many aspects of the Japanese style of doing business are not culturally transferable, including employee lifetime employment, attitudes toward authority, consensus decision-making, and Japanese career development practices.[8] Quite predictably, then, Japanese expansion internationally has been largely staffed by Japanese expatriates, rather than adopting other models of integration with and development of the host culture.[9] As a consequence, Japanese expatriates are typically assigned to their international posts for about five years, longer than either American or European expatriates.[10]

The "bamboo-ceiling" phenomenon for non-Japanese executives in Japanese firms, for example, has already become well known; even when a local national has a top position in the local subsidiary, some Japanese firms have a reputation for bypassing this individual when it comes to significant decision-making. Authority tends to become a privately held power, shared among a group of personal acquaintances who know each other, trust each other, and speak the same language— literally and metaphorically. So while Japanese firms continue to expand their business operations, their human resource strategy appears to remain constant: to control operations through strong links between Japanese expatriates and the Japanese home office. The personal cost of an expatriate assignment seems to be higher for the Japanese than for his European counterpart. Expatriate isolation is increased because many Japanese families remain in Japan so the children will maintain Japanese associations and follow Japanese academic programs. Without their families to increase the probability of their integration into the foreign culture, Japanese expatriate managers tend to remain more isolated from the host culture.[11]

Similarities and Differences in Strategies ————————————

Given these patterns of cultural similarities and differences in European and Japanese human resource practices, and logical extensions from these practices, we developed three major propositions about differences and similarities in Japanese and European strategies to internationalize their human resources:

1. Although probably for different reasons, the Japanese and Europeans will both continue to show a strong tendency to expatriate personnel to international posts.

2. The Japanese will expatriate their personnel for longer periods of time than the Europeans.

3. The Japanese will bring foreign nationals into their domestic operations/headquarters as a method of internationalizing their human resources less frequently than the Europeans.

Although these propositions were the principal focus of this study, other methods of internationalizing human resources were also investigated and will be discussed.

Methodology ——————————————————————————————————————

We sent questionnaires to human resources directors of 105 of Europe's most prominent multinational corporations, drawn from the "Business Associates" list of the International Institute for Management Development (IMD). Sixty-nine usable questionnaires were returned for an effective response rate of 66%. Of 100 questionnaires sent to Japanese MNCs, thirty-five usable surveys were returned for a 35% response rate.

In terms of industry representation, both samples were similar. The major industries represented include chemicals/pharmaceuticals, banking/financial, manufacturing, computer/electronics, and mining/petroleum/natural resources. In addition, a number of firms representing conglomerates responded from both groups, albeit somewhat more from the Japanese sample. Most of the European sample was represented by large MNCs originating from the following common language/culture groups: Anglo (England, Canada, Australia, and the United States), Germanic (Germany, Austria, and Switzerland), Scandinavian (Finland, Norway, Sweden, and Denmark), and Benelux (Holland, Belgium, Luxembourg) countries.

In both samples, approximately the same ratio of countries participated in one, two or three major markets outside the country of origin. In addition, 14 of the 69 European MNCs operate in four major markets outside their country of origin.

In terms of perceived competition, both sets of MNCs perceived themselves as being in "very" to "extremely" competitive business environments although more European firms report being in extremely competitive environments than do their Japanese counterparts.

In addition to demographic information, we asked respondents to identify the frequency and importance of two methods of internationalizing managers, the firm's future trends, the number of years expatriates remain in their assignments, and the percentage of foreign nationals in and qualified for local, regional, and corporate top management positions. We asked for responses to these questions on a 1-5 point Likert-type scale.

What We Found: Trends in Expatriation and Inpatriation ————————

First, both Japanese and European MNCs show a continuing strong tendency to expatriate personnel to international posts, as predicted. However, the Japanese clearly outpaced the European: $x=4.25$ (Japanese MNCs) to 3.62 (European MNCs). In terms of future trends in expatriation in their firms, 46% of the Japanese firms responded that expatriation would increase; only 8% predicted a decrease. Corresponding percentages for European multinational corporations were 49% for increased expatriation; however, 19% said they would expatriate fewer and 25% said the number would remain unchanged. The difference in mean frequency between Japanese and European respondents was significant.

Table 1. Differences in Importance of Expatriation in European and Japanese MNCs

	Europe	Japan	p. value
Importance of Expatriation	$x = 3.62^{1}$ (sd = .99)	$x = 4.25$ (sd = 1.1)	.02
% Expecting Increase	49%	46%	
% Expecting Decrease	19%	9%	
% Expecting No Change	25 %	37%	

[1] The scale is from 1 to 5, 1 = Not at All Important; 5 = Extremely Important.

Second, we also found as expected that the Japanese send their managerial and technical personnel for longer periods of time than the Europeans.

Line managers. All three levels of Japanese line managers (senior, middle and lower-level) were sent on international assignments for longer periods of time than their European counterparts (4.5 years v. 3.6 years). For middle management line positions, the difference was even greater (4.7 years for Japanese, 3.2 years for Europeans). This difference also existed for lower-level line managers (4.5 years for the Japanese respondents and 2.7 years for the European).

Technical Personnel. The length of time technical personnel were assigned to international posts paralleled the length of assignments of their managerial counterparts. The national differences were less pronounced, however. Japanese multinational corporations typically sent senior technical specialists on international assignments for 3.7 years compared to 2.7 years for the Europeans; mid-level Japanese technical specialists had typical assignments of 3.9 years for the Japanese as compared to 2.5 years for the European respondents. Junior technicians showed the widest gap: 3.6 years for those from Japanese multinational corporations and 2.1 years for those from European multinational corporations.

Third, we found that the Japanese companies bring foreign nationals into their domestic operations/headquarters less frequently than the Europeans. Frequency was measured on a 1-5 scale: 1 = never, 2 = seldom, . . . , 5 = extremely frequently. Although there was not a large mean difference in the frequency (2.2 for the Japanese and 2.83 for the European respondents), it was statistically significant. Even more interestingly, 80% of the Japanese respondents predicted a significant future

Table 2. Mean Differences in Length of Time on International Assignment by Line and Staff Positions (in years) in European and Japanese MNCs

| | Length of Time on International Assignment | | |
Line Management	Europe	Japan	p. value
Top Management	3.6[1] (sd = 1.6)	4.5 (sd = 1.1)	.02
Middle Management	3.2 (sd = 1.0)	4.7 (sd = 1.2)	.001
Lower Management	2.7 (sd = 1.3)	4.5 (sd = 1.2)	.001
Technical Staff			
Senior Level	2.7 (sd = 1.1)	3.7 (sd = 1.2)	.001
Mid Level	2.5 (sd = 1.2)	3.9 (sd = 1.3)	.001
Junior	2.1 (sd = 1.3)	3.6 (sd = 1.5)	.001

[1] The scale is from 1 to 5: 1 = Not at All Important; 5 = Extremely Important.

decrease in the number of foreigners that would be brought into their domestic headquarters positions. Only one Japanese firm predicted an increase. In significant contrast, 70% of the European firms said they would be increasing the number of foreign nationals brought into major corporate offices.

Internationalizing Senior Managers

One indication of how important a firm considers internationalizing its human resources is reflected in the amount and type of international experience of its senior executives. To examine this issue, we asked the European and Japanese firms to identify the percentage of the top 50 and top 200 line and staff managers who had extensive international business experience. This was intended as another measure of the degree to which the firms have internationalized their personnel. Although using absolute numbers represents different proportions of the firm's management (due to the differing size of the firms), they nevertheless can represent general tendencies.

First, approximately one-half of both Japanese and European firms indicated that their very senior line and staff managers (i.e., the top 200) have had extensive international experience. Of the top 50 *line* managers, the Japanese reported 45% had had extensive international experience while 67% of the European managers had. Of the top 50 *line* managers, however, the European multinational corporations reported 67% of these executives had international business experience while only 52% of the

---

**Table 3. Differences in European and Japanese MNCs'
Tendency to Bring Foreign Nationals into Domestic Operations**

	Europe	Japan	p. value
Mean Differences	2.83[1] (sd = 1.2)	2.2 (sd = 1.1)	.001
Percentage Expecting Increase	70%	3%	
Percentage Expecting Decrease	1%	80%	
Percentage Expecting No Change	20%	11%	

[1] The scale is from 1 to 5: 1 = Not at All Important; S = Extremely Important.

top 50 Japanese had had such experience. Findings for the top 50 and 200 *staff* managers were similar: 41% and 38% for the Japanese and European respectively. Looking only at the top 50 *staff* managers produced parallel findings: 53% of the Japanese had significant international experience as compared to 55% of the European respondents. For the top 200 *staff* managers, the percentage of those having had extensive international business experience decreased by about one half: 26% percent for the Japanese and 28% for the Europeans.

Second, in addition to looking at staff versus managerial employees, we also measured the percentages of different management and *staff* levels (i.e., senior, middle, and low) that had actually been expatriates. A small proportion of European and Japanese senior managers were reported as having at least one international assignment. Japanese respondents reported that 25% of the top 200 Japanese managers and 31% of the top 50 have had at least one international assignment. Figures for the European managers were 35% and 55%, respectively.

**Table 4. Differences Between European and Japanese
MNCs' Line and Staff's International Experience**

	Extensive Business Experience			One or More Int'l Assignments		
	Europe	Japan	p. value	Europe	Japan	p. value
Top 200 Line	46%	45%	NS	37%	26%	(.13)
Top 50 Line	66%	53%	(.11)	55%	31%	.01
Top 200 Staff	38%	41%	NS	29%	26%	(NS)
Top 50 Staff	56%	54%	NS	49%	30%	.05

Finally, we also asked respondents if candidates for the CEO position *had* to have international experience to be considered. This question was intended as a measure of genuine importance of international experience in a firm's most strategic decisions. No significant differences emerged between the two groups. On a 1 to 5 scale (1 = Always; 5 = Never), the mean response for Japanese firms was 2.94 while the mean for the European respondents was 2.5.

Internationalizing Subsidiary Management ————————————————

Another measure of the degree to which MNCs have internationalized is reflected in the percentage of foreign national v. corporate national subsidiary senior managers, and the percentage of foreign nationals qualified for top corporate positions. It can be argued that the more firms have developed foreign nationals to qualify for subsidiary and corporate senior management positions, the greater importance they place on internationalizing or globalizing their human resources.

First, we found that European firms generally appear somewhat more oriented toward internationalizing their key managers, foreign and domestic, than are the Japanese MNCs. Japanese multinational corporations reported that Japanese expatriate managers held 63% of the top subsidiary positions as compared to only 48% of the Europeans who held similar top-level subsidiary positions. In other words, more top foreign subsidiary posts were held by Japanese executives than by European executives in their respective firms. We found no real difference, however, in the percentage of local nationals who within their own countries were in positions of top subsidiary management: 47% of the Japanese held such posts while 50% of the Europeans held similar posts. Similarly, when we analyzed the nationality of third-country, regional managers, we found no statistical differences between European MNCs (34%) and Japanese MNCs (38%).

Second, when we asked respondents to identify the percentage of foreign nationals qualified to hold top subsidiary and corporate positions, significant differences emerged. Twenty-four percent of the Japanese firms reported that foreign nationals were qualified for top subsidiary management positions, while 49% of the European firms indicated that there were foreign nationals qualified for top subsidiary positions in their companies.

At the regional level, an even larger difference emerged. Japanese multinational corporations reported that only 5% of their foreign nationals were qualified for top regional positions in contrast to 38% of the European respondents. The most significant difference, however, was at the corporate senior management level. Japanese firms reported that only 0.2% of their foreign managers were qualified for such posts. In contrast, nearly 14% of the European firms stated that foreign managers were qualified for senior corporate management positions.

Table 5. Differences in Percentages of Foreign-Born Perceived to Be Qualified to Hold Top National, Regional and Corporate Posts

	Europe	Japan	p. value
Level of Post			
Top National	49%	24%	.002
Top Regional	38 %	5%	.12
Top Corporate	14%	.2%	.001

Conclusion

Although the samples in this research have been from European and Japanese MNCs, the larger and more important issue is the increasing strategic need for firms everywhere to internationalize their human resources and decide which methods to use in this internationalization process and their frequency of use. Based on the results of this research, we can offer the following tentative conclusions:

1. Different countries/cultures' perspectives on the usefulness of assignments, the time required to become effective in a new culture, and the level of integration desired will be some of the major determinants in methods selected to internationalize key human resources. For example, Japanese firms predict they will not only expatriate more than the European MNCs, but that they will expatriate their personnel for longer periods of time than European firms.

2. Nevertheless, despite the fact that Japanese firms will expatriate more frequently than their European counterparts, it seems clear from this research that expatriation will continue to be an important method used to develop future global leaders for both Japanese and European firms. In Europe, however, we found that this trend will in the future apply to younger and newer employees.

3. One of the trends that seems to be evident is that different countries will probably inpatriate (i.e., bring foreign nationals into corporate offices) at different rates and perhaps for different reasons.

Currently, neither Japanese nor European firms frequently bring foreign nationals into corporate headquarters positions, although Europeans do so more frequently than the Japanese. Both groups perceive this method as more important in the future than their current practice suggests, but they differ on how critical this will be. The Europeans definitely plan to increase the number of foreign nationals coming in to corporate offices, while the Japanese plan to decrease the number.

For some firms, inpatriation might reflect an increasing need for strategic control in operations that have evolved to the point that foreign nationals hold staff senior management positions. In order to maintain a consistent culture or overall perspective and integration of methods, the MNC might bring high potential foreign nationals into corporate domestic headquarters as a socialization tool.

Recommendations

What Can We Learn From European and Japanese MNCs?

With Japanese firms, their apparent philosophy toward integration might preclude serious attempts to inpatriate human resources from other countries and as a result, disallow foreign nationals into their senior management. This practice potentially can encourage unfriendly market reactions. More importantly, as MNC corporate decision-making will increasingly need to reflect a combined global integration and local market focus, firms must learn how to integrate those two needs. To be successful and survive long-term in today's global marketplace, a more open posture might be necessary than the Japanese currently reflect.

One Japanese firm, Nissan, is a good example of a more open approach.[12] It has a "clear end, loose means" approach to its operations. This kind of flexibility means that Nissan subsidiaries are less tied to corporate practices and policies (i.e., are less Japanese) and are allowed to discover the right mix of personnel and practices that will result in a successful local business operation. Nissan Italia, for example, has several powerful Italians (as opposed to figure heads) in its upper management structure. As a result, its way of operating better reflects the local culture than do most other Japanese MNCs in Italy. This kind of management adaptation may be necessary to gain acceptance in a culture that is quite protectionist.

European MNCs tend to exhibit more flexibility in their approach to internationalization, like Nissan. They are using a variety of means to integrate world-wide human resources in an attempt to create cogent and culturally-acceptable business strategies. Like Japan, one of the mainstays of integration appears to be the use of expatriation. However, European multinationals are experiencing some constraints in how freely they can and will be able to use this method in the future. Women in Scandinavian countries, for example, have for a long time been careerists and place greater importance on balancing work with personal and family needs than other European countries. This coupled with the high costs of expatriation and complications from dual-career couples means that European multinationals must balance international assignments with other globalization methods.

Alternatively, firms can do what Volkswagen has begun to do to avoid some of these problems. As stated in the beginning of this paper, they send new recruits on six-month to one-year assignments. Typically, at this age, recruits are single or usually without children. Volkswagen also wants to signal to its employees that international assignments are an integral part of the career development program for high potential employees. Further, it has determined that building an "international mind" occurs best when its employees' minds are still formative. Later in their careers, other international assignments are planned.

Another reported method of internationalizing both human resources and the firm's strategy is to organize more *international task forces/project teams*. For example, European pharmaceuticals like Ceiba-Geigy, Sandox, and Glaxo are centralizing their basic research but decentralizing their applications. To create a coordinated strategy, these firms regularly invite their scientists from various countries to discuss separate developments that potentially affect other units. From these types of meetings, more formal international project teams often develop.

Sponsoring more *international in-house seminars* is another method, increasingly popular in some firms. These seminars assemble international personnel within the company for exchanges of perspectives on various business strategies, global environmental changes, and other issues relevant to the performance of the firm. A variant of this method is *seminars with noncompany international personnel* from around the world. These courses are issues-centered rather than firm-centered. IMD and INSEAD in Europe, for example, typically have 15-20 different nationalities participating in a single course. Participants at such seminars often remark that the most valuable part of the seminar is not what the instructors had to present but the perspectives of other attendees on the global issues they are confronting and the strategies they are using. They also encounter first-hand the difficulties of cross-cultural communication, even though all may be speaking English. This is a potentially valuable tool of global socialization.

Whether this type of seminar requires being in the same physical location or can be done by video-teleconferencing is less important than the fact that the seminars are held. Obviously, though, being physically present where formal and informal discussions can occur is clearly advantageous.

A third option is that of encouraging and rewarding managers, scientists, and engineers who acquire and employ international perspectives. This can be a powerful way to integrate global perspectives. For example, an account manager one of the authors interviewed spent three years managing a Japanese subsidiary of the parent firm. From this challenging experience, he learned what "customer service" meant to the Japanese. When he returned to the parent firm, he made changes in how the parent firm—where the manufacturing was done—dealt with the Japanese subsidiary—the marketing and sales arm in Japan. The changes resulted in increased sales and improved U.S.-Japanese relationships among the personnel. The fact that the parent firm permitted the manager to make such changes was a very positive morale-builder for the executive. Although difficult to track and measure, such applications of what one learns from international experiences should also be more formally rewarded. Doing so sends a very loud and clear message to a firm's personnel that international experience, knowledge, and expertise is valued.

Such rewards can come in the form of formal recognition in meetings, company newsletters, or percentage bonuses of traceable increase in cost savings and/or sales. One of the most obvious incentives for an employee to gain and integrate his/her international experience is by witnessing increasing numbers of promotions to senior management positions given to those who have had and who have applied their international experience to the firm's procedures, policies, and strategies that are linked to the firm's success.

Forward-thinking firms will in the near future continue to expatriate and at younger ages, but they will also begin to investigate and better employ (1) cross-national task forces of all kinds, (2) extensive travel, including long business trips, (3) international management education seminars, (4) increased use of electronic means of communications, (5) networking internationally, and (6) hiring global competence externally. All of these methods will speed up the process of internationalizing company key managers in the 1990s.

There is little debate about the need for knowledgeable and skillful global leaders. The challenge for firms today is to determine how to get such leaders and then how to use them appropriately.

Endnotes

1. Armstrong, L., Miller, K., and Wood, D. (1993) Toyota's new pick-up: Oops. *Business Week,* Feb. 15, 37-38.

2. Schares, G. (1993) Colgate-Palmolive is really cleaning up in Poland; Sales are booming, but it's having to revisit Marketing 101. *Business Week,* March 15, 54-56.

3. *Wall Street Journal.* (1993) AT&T apologizes for racist drawing in worker magazine. Friday, September 17, B6.

4. Adler, N. & Bartholomew, S. (1992). Globalization and human resource management. In Rugman, A. & A. Verbeke (eds.) *Research in global strategic management: Corporate response to change.* Greenwich, Connecticut: JAI Press. Bartlett, C. & Ghoshall, S. (1989). *Managing across borders: The transnational solution.* Cambridge, MA: Harvard Business School Press. Cramer, J.A. Japanese management efficient school. *Nikusi Weekly,* May 15, 1991.

5. Oddou, G. & Derr, B. (1992). European MNCs: Strategies to internationalize managers. Paper presented at the third Conference on

International Personnel and Human Resource Management. Ashridge Management College; Berkhamsted, England.

6. Derr, B. & Oddou, G. (in press). Internationalizing managers: Speeding up the process. *European Management Journal.* Oddou, G. (1991). Managing your expatriates: What the successful firms do. *The Human Resource Planning Journal,* 14, 301-308.

7. Bartlett, C. & Ghoshall, S. (1989). *Managing across borders: The transnational solution.* Cambridge, MA: Harvard Business School Press.

8. Elmuti, D. & Kathalawa, Y. (1991). An investigation of the human resource management practices of Japanese subsidiaries in the Arabian Gulf region. *Journal of Applied Business Research,* 7, 82-88. Mortellaro, J. (1989). Business across a cultural void: Japan's management imperialism. *Business Marketing.* 74, 62-66. Negandi, A., Eshghi, G., & Yuen, E. (1985). The management practices of Japanese subsidiaries overseas. *California Management Review,* 27(4), 93-105.

9. Negandi, A., Eshghi, G., & Yuen, E. (1985). The management practices of Japanese subsidiaries overseas, *California Management Review,* 27(4), 93-105.

10. Tung, R. (1989). *The new expatriates: Managing human resources.* Cambridge, MA: Ballinger.

11. White, M. (1988). *The Japanese overseas.* New York: Free Press.

12. Akakura, A. & Schneider, S. (1991). Nissan Italia, S.P.A. In Mendenhall, M. and G. Oddou (eds.) *Readings and cases in international human resource management.* Boston: PWS-Kent.

Ciba-Geigy Management Development

Case 5.1
Yves Doz

On December 18,1981, Arnold Delage, soon to become Managing Director of Ciba-Geigy's French subsidiary, was looking forward to his dinner meeting in Basel, Switzerland (headquarters to Ciba-Geigy), with the top management of the parent company's Pharma Division. Together they were going to review candidates for the position of Sales and Marketing Manager for the French subsidiary's pharmaceutical business, an important position since this division accounted for nearly a quarter of total French sales and had shown rapid growth in recent years.

Until recently, Delage had been general manager of Ciba-Geigy's French Pharma Division and President of "Laboratories Ciba-Geigy," the pharmaceutical subsidiary of Ciba-Geigy in France, with sales of about Fr700 million. René Lamont, the current Managing Director of Ciba-Geigy France, was scheduled to retire effective at the end of the year, and Delage had been chosen by Ciba-Geigy's top management to succeed him, a selection announced in early December.

Delage had had a successful career with Ciba-Geigy. A Frenchman, he joined Esso-Africa upon graduation from INSEAD in 1965 and worked in Switzerland (Geneva) and in Madagascar, in sales and marketing positions. He was subsequently recruited by Ciba-Geigy and, after a year at Pharma Division's headquarters in Basel, was sent to Hong Kong in a sales and marketing management position. After four years in the Far East he was appointed Marketing Manager in Belgium, where he successfully launched a number of new pharmaceutical products. In 1973, he was promoted to Pharma Division Manager in Belgium, a position he held for three years. Delage was recalled to France in 1976 as Marketing Manager, where he successfully launched a new antirheumatic formulation (Voltarene) and, in 1979, was promoted to Pharma Division Manager. During the last two years he had considerably strengthened the management of the French Pharma division.

Delage's promotion to Managing Director of Ciba-Geigy France had opened the position of Pharma Division Manager within the

Source: This case was prepared by Yves Doz with the assistance of Ms. Martine van den Poel. © INSEAD, 1983. This case was adapted by Mark Mendenhall for this book in 1990 by permission from the author. Reprinted by permission.

French subsidiary. Jules Breton, an experienced manager recently hired from Sanofi (a major French pharmaceutical company where he had held the position of President and General Manager of one of its subsidiaries), was promoted to the post. The position of Pharma Marketing Manager therefore became vacant. Delage and Breton presented the candidacy of Pierre Dumont, a Frenchman who had recently been recruited from Specia (another French competitor) to head marketing and sales for the Geigy product line in France. Pharma Division headquarters in Basel had suggested several other candidates. Among them, their preference fell on Michel Malterre, a Swiss national from Montreux, currently heading Pharma marketing in West Africa and based in Abidjan, Ivory Coast.

Such decisions as the appointment of key executives in subsidiary companies were usually the result of joint agreement by divisional management in Basel and the local managing directors and were often debated at the highest levels within the company. A long-standing corporate commitment to human resource and management development ensured that such choices received considerable attention and that all relevant aspects were carefully weighed before a decision was reached.

The Company and Its Organization

Ciba-Geigy resulted from the 1970 merger between two long-standing Basel chemical companies: Ciba (created in 1884) and Geigy (created in 1758). Both companies were active competitors in certain business areas, e.g., dyestuffs, pharmaceuticals, industrial chemicals, and agro-chemicals. In other areas, their activities were complementary. Both were strong internationally, although Geigy had a stronger worldwide presence in agro-chemicals and Ciba a wider experience in pharmaceuticals.

The management styles and structures of the two companies, however, differed widely. Ciba was centrally managed by one person, Dr. Kappeli, its chairman. He relied on strong and entrepreneurial division managers to control Ciba's widely diversified activities. In contrast, Geigy had been reorganized in 1968 into a three-dimensional organizational structure where businesses, national subsidiaries, and corporate functions were managed by an Executive Committee regrouping Geigy's top management.

Following the merger, the Geigy structure was retained. By 1980-1981 the structure comprised the following units:

1. Divisional structure covering the seven main product areas: dyestuffs and chemicals, pharmaceuticals, agro-chemicals, plastics and additives, the Airwick consumer products group, the Ilford photographic products group, and the recently constituted electronic equipment products group

2. Geographic structure with 80 group companies organized in a loose administrative way into six main regions: North America, Western Europe, Latin America, Africa/Middle East, Eastern Europe, and Asia/Australia

3. Ten central corporate functions (legal, finance, technology, etc.) at group headquarters in Basel, Switzerland

In general, Ciba-Geigy had a policy of 100 percent ownership of group companies. As a rule, these group companies were responsible for all Ciba-Geigy activities in a given country, for making use of available opportunities for the local development of Ciba-Geigy's business, and for the overall financial results within their territories. The various product divisions and the Executive Committee (*Konzernleitung*) coordinated and integrated the group companies' activities.

Product divisions were responsible to the Executive Committee for the worldwide management of their businesses and their overall results. Research and development, production, and marketing of products were specific responsibilities of the divisions. Divisional plans and budgets for the group companies were discussed with headquarters' divisions in Basel and coordinated with group companies' managing directors. Major investment projects in the group companies were reviewed by the product divisions, which were also responsible for business development on a worldwide basis.

Divisional management also participated in establishing the organizational structure of, and in nominating candidates for top positions in, their corresponding divisions within group companies. Product divisions were managed through divisional management committees reflecting the main functions of a division.

Group companies combined all Ciba-Geigy's divisions and functions into one managerial entity in each country. The company believed that this structure allowed Ciba-Geigy to operate locally as a homogeneous unit, consolidate financial results across divisions, and optimize local financial resource utilization. In addition, central administrative functions could serve several local units more economically than if each division had to do so independently. Finally, relations with local government, industry and trade associations, and other national entities could be made more effective.

The group company Managing Director was responsible for the total activity of local units as well as for overall local financial results, but had to operate within the framework of policies and guidelines set from the center and harmonize plans between the various central units (divisions and central functions) and local requirements. The divisional heads within the group companies were administratively responsible to the Managing Director but were also functionally responsible to the corresponding division in Basel.

The *Executive Committee,* in Basel, had 10 members and was responsible for:

- Formulation and implementation of the group policy

- Approval of long-term objectives and strategies, and resource allocation decisions

- Approval of organizational structures and appointment of key managers within the product divisions, central functions, and group companies

- Creation of corporatewide uniform management systems and guidelines (especially for planning, resource allocation, and management information)

- Review of major integrated plans, budgets, and investment projects and decisions on their approval

- Control of the performance of the individual units and evaluation of the business and its results from a corporatewide perspective

Each member of the Executive Committee was overseeing, as a "patron," a number of countries and one or two divisions or central functions, so that all major units were covered. For example, the Executive Committee member responsible for the Pharma Division also was responsible for the plastics and additives division and the Southeast Asian and Chinese region. Another patron was responsible for the Airwick division, the finance function, Eastern Europe, and Latin America. The Executive Committee met as a group frequently, usually once a week.

The preparation and negotiation of decisions involving several divisions, group companies and/or central functions could be delegates to the Executive Committee to regional staffs. These provided an intermediate level between the group companies and the Executive Committee, since all 80 or so group companies could not effectively be supervised directly by the individual Executive Committee members.

Central services fell into two categories: Executive Committee staffs and corporate functions. They formulated, for the approval of the Executive Committee, opinions, guidelines, and procedures specific to their field, commented on functional plans and budgets to the heads of group companies, and participated in the nomination of group companies' functional executives. Central functions and staffs also placed their specific expertise at the service of group companies.

Two key Executive Committee staff functions were corporate planning and management development (the latter is described below in detail). Recently, planning had acquired more prominence with the redefinition of Ciba-Geigy's businesses into about 30 "corporate segments," and the establishment of a corporate strategic plan drawn from a bottom-up planning process at segment level rather than only at divisional level. The corporate planning staff at Ciba-Geigy employed only four people and was directly responsible to the Chair of the Executive Committee. Franz Hartmann, its Director, explained the changes in corporate strategy and in the way resources were allocated that had transpired over the past few years:

During the 1960s and early 1970s the resource allocation process in Ciba-Geigy was not very sophisticated. It was rather informal since there were no financial constraints. The real beginning of strategic planning occurred in 1974, in the sense of it being more than simple operational planning with a longer-term horizon. The 1974-1975 economic crisis was quite helpful to us, because it forced us to put more emphasis on actual strategic thinking and less on number pushing. We introduced a long-term strategic plan and conceded more flexibility in the process, emphasizing key issues and implementation through strategic projects and action plans. The strategic projects involved business entries and exits, new plant construction in foreign countries, etc. . . . In recent years, it became quite clear that the chemical industry was maturing. Some of our business-es were plagued by slow innovation and very intense competi-tion and, therefore, needed different strategies and different managers from those required by businesses that were still growing rapidly.

In 1980 we started to introduce portfolio approaches for the first time. We also faced a trend toward lower profitability and started a "turnaround" program. The program was not only designed to reduce inventories, cut personnel and cut costs but also to strengthen strategic planning and to allocate proper strategic roles and resources to each segment. This reflected the growing differentiation among our businesses and the need to account for different success factors in how and by whom they were managed. For example, the divisions are now moving from worldwide segment strategies to local portfolios. After the merger in 1970, we had needed to integrate operations central-ly. Now there is growing delegation in operational matters by the Executive Committee to divisions and group companies.

This segment approach questions the divisional structure. We will need to implement substructural changes to fit the seg-ments and reallocate functional responsibilities within divi-sions. We are also going to need better managers and more general managers. We are now recruiting MBAs and putting a lot of emphasis on young people and training, sending them abroad early in their careers to take up responsibility. In fact, we have been forced to look outside to find general managers for some of our new activities.

One implication of all this is that there is going to be a lot more internal competition within the firm. Changes are being made in the role of group company managers. Originally, they were mainly administrators and caretakers. The turn-around project has given them more control as they had to play a key role in cost cutting measures and had to make difficult tradeoffs among divisions within their companies on issues of employ-ment, investment, plant location, and so on. They are increas-ingly being asked to contribute to the planning dialogue between local and headquarter division management.

The Origins of Management Development at Ciba-Geigy ————

Leopold Luthi, a lawyer who joined Geigy in 1951, worked in line management positions in the Agchem division for over 15 years, and later became head of management development for Ciba-Geigy. He explained the early development of the management development (MD) function in the company as follows:

> After the 1968 reorganization which gave Geigy its three-dimensional structure a separate staff unit was created called "Executive Development" whose role was to assure a supply of qualified managers for top and line management positions. The unit was to report directly to the Executive Committee, and I was given responsibility for it. The idea was to make management development planning an automatic component of the yearly divisional and regional plans. At the beginning we overestimated the possibility of developing precise instruments of measurement and evaluation from which to derive the development potential. In fact, a formal system would not work. Line managers might comment quite differently on their people according to whether they evaluated current performance or future development potential. Then, in 1969, the merger with Ciba was announced and everything slowed down for a while.

From 1971 onward, the management development unit took shape and developed rapidly. According to Dr. Luthi:

> The units in Basel and abroad started to work on MD plans, we discussed these plans with them, and we started to present them to the chairman of the Executive Committee and to the unit's patron. One of the early issues was to get comparability of people and profiles on a lateral basis among the units. While in the late 1960s at Geigy, we dealt with only 400 people (200 executives and 200 potential executives); after the merger we had about 1,000 executives included in our MD program. At the beginning, the system we developed worked mainly with the executive group within each company where the immediate preoccupation with succession was the highest. We later expanded the process to reach those young men and women of high potential in the organization, and to increase the supply of them over time.

Management Development: Purposes and Functions in 1980-1981 ————————————

By 1980, the management development staff unit at corporate headquarters employed 14 people, roughly half of them working in management education, running and organizing in-house and external training courses, and the other half dealing with succession planning, recruitment, job rotations, MD plans, etc. (see Exhibit 1).

Exhibit 1. Management Development Staff Unit

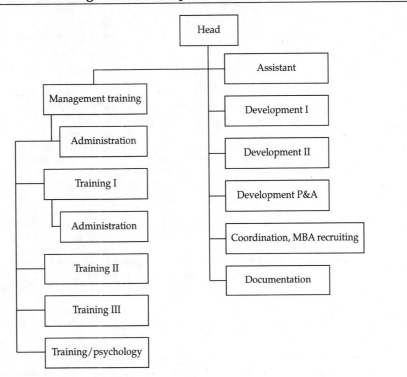

The Central Management Development program focused on some 2,100 employees (2 percent of total employment) of the company, the so-called executives and potential executives. In addition to slightly over 100 senior executives in top management positions, the executives occupied the 1,000 or so most senior management positions in Ciba-Geigy worldwide (400 in Basel and 600 abroad) including Directors, Deputy Directors, and Vice Directors of the parent company, and the top management positions within the group companies. The potential executives, numbering about 1,000, were employees at lower- and middle-management levels who in the opinion of their supervisors were likely to advance some day to an executive position. The final responsibility for appointments and selection to the list was with line management: the Executive Committee for executive appointments, and with the various group company, divisional, and central functional heads in the case of potential executives.

This corporate-wide management development program had several objectives:

1. Planning executive successions for the whole group on the basis of corporate, divisional, and group company MD planning reports

2. Identification of potential executives and planning their next development steps

3. Monitoring the quality and age structure of each unit's executive and potential executive population

4. Setting up career moves and job rotation for both executives and potential executives [During 1980, for example, 281 job rotations took place, mostly local, with a smaller number of international rotations between headquarters and group companies, as shown in Exhibit 2.]

5. Coordination of the moves of obsolete executives into new positions to give them new incentives and added motivation

6. The educational development of all executives and potential executives through internal (in-house) and external (business schools) management courses

As such the role of the MD unit was *conceptual* (policy and system development): *pedagogical* (assignment and coordination of management training activities): and *advisory* (to the Executive Committee). It follows that the three mainstays of Ciba-Geigy's MD program were the MD plans, its training programs, and its role in executive appointments.

Exhibit 2. Total Job Rotations, 1979-1980, and International Job Rotations, 1980

| | **Total** | | | | | |
| | | 1980 | | | 1979 | |
	Total	Local	Int'l	Total	Local	Int'l
Executives	96	76	20	66	51	15
Potential executives	185	154	31	181	156	25
Total	281	230	51	247	207	40

| | | **International** | | |
	Total	Headquarters to group company	Group company to headquarters	Group company to group company
Executives	20	3	8	9
Potential executives	31	14	5	12
Total	51	17	13	21

The MD Plans

Drawn up every two years by the heads of every group company and every division and function of the parent company, each MD plan showed the current executive positions in the organization, indicated future moves and candidates for job rotations, proposed internal successors and offered positions for outside candidates, showed potential executives, and defined action programs (see Exhibit 3 for examples). Upon receipt of an MD plan, the MD staff at headquarters would first discuss it with the unit head who wrote it, and then present it to the Chair of the Executive Committee and to the appropriate patrons. In the case of an MD plan for a group company, it would also be discussed with each corporate division or function as far as its corresponding local subunit was concerned. Dr. Luthi added:

> The way in which the various group companies are handling this question varies a great deal. In the United States and Italy, for example, the local group company's Executive Committee discusses the plan and then holds additional discussions with the various divisional management committees. The whole system permeates the group company. In Mexico they are now going to do a two-day human resource planning meeting in Cuernavaca. One day is going to deal with the strategic plan, and another day with implications in terms of the MD plan. That is good because they can couple the two systems very closely.

> Other countries do it with a lot more secrecy. They do not discuss this as a group, only face to face with the relevant managers. It is very important for us in Basel to have the confidence of line management. Therefore, we have to assure them that each unit's MD plan will be treated with appropriate confidentiality. . . .

> A critical element in the successful implementation of our objectives is the full commitment and backing of the Chair of the Executive Committee and its members. The general managers of large group companies come personally to Basel to discuss the management development plan with the Chairman of the Executive Committee, the patrons, and our staff. . . .

> Putting full responsibility for MD plans with line managers made the plan adaptive. Rather than try to forecast centrally what managerial profiles would be required, when and in what numbers, the process was designed to develop, cultivate and track a large inventory of diverse people, from which could be extracted those with the skills required for a particular position at any point in time.

Management Development in the Pharma Division _____

While some divisions were facing a slowdown in profitability and low growth prospects, the Pharma division was growing rapidly.

Exhibit 3.

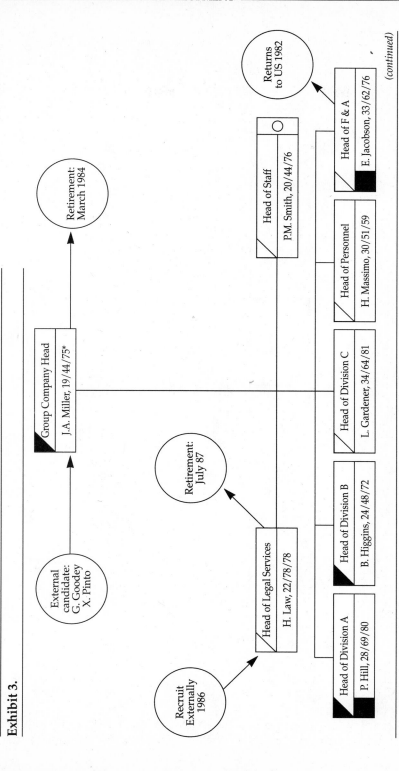

(continued)

Note: It is suggested that this chart show the top management organization and the succession situation for the company head and for any other key management positions not shown on the divisional/functional charts. The successor situation for the heads of divisions and functions is usually best shown on their respective charts.

*X/Y/Z figures, below names, mean: X, year of birth; Y, year when joined Ciba-Geigy (or the pre-merger companies), and Z, year when appointed to current position. Therefore, Mr. J. A. Miller was born in 1919, joined Ciba-Geigy in 1944, and has been head of the group company since 1975 (in the example given above).

Exhibit 3.

(continued)

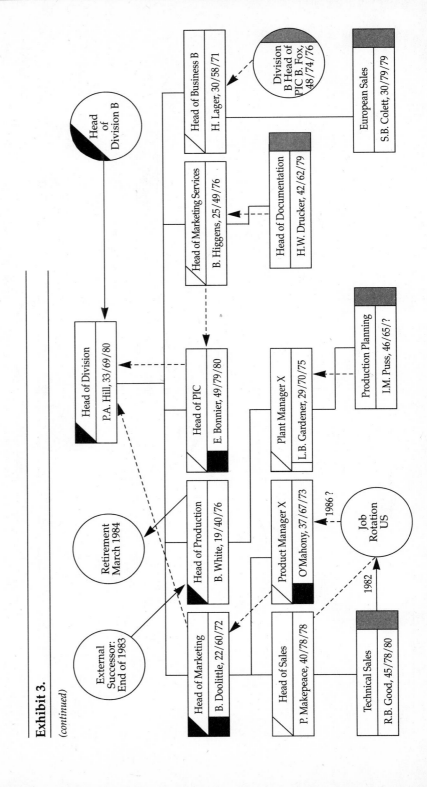

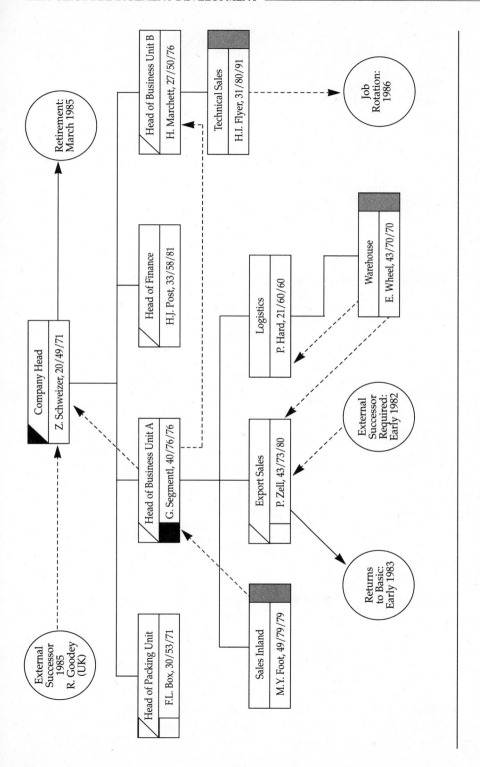

Divisional management was concerned that there would be a shortage of executives and potential executives to fill future positions. Alfred Steiner had been head of management development for the Pharma division for the past three years, and prior to that a member of the corporate MD staff for seven years. He explained the situation:

> Five years ago a new Pharma division head developed a strategy to branch out more broadly into the health care market, rather than stay exclusively in ethical pharmaceuticals. This diversification led divisional management to become overburdened and to the realization that what the division had as available potential executives was in no way sufficient to staff our needs for the next 5 to 10 years given the new growth targets. In fact, the division realized that it had too few potential executives even for current replacement alone.
>
> Part of the problem was that management development had not been taken seriously and that after the merger we had found ourselves with a top-heavy organization and no new people were recruited. The new division head realized that he couldn't cope with that problem and saw a need for an MD function within the Pharma division. Discussions took place with Dr. Luthi, since this was the first attempt at decentralizing a corporate function.
>
> When I first came to the Pharma division I soon realized that the secretary of the division's management committee had sat down over a weekend to get the MD plan done. The forms were filled in, but not taken very seriously. The official MD planning system was conceived as a corporate instrument with too-restrictive definitions for actual development purposes in critical stages. Potential executives were 35 to 40 years old, but by that age a career is almost over in development potential!
>
> Another problem is that the MD plan reflects today's organizational structure and does not project requirements into the future. The organization is changing constantly, you can't do tomorrow's succession planning based on an interpretation of today's structure. Therefore, it isn't a real plan: it remains a mere inventory, not an action program. But at least it shows us who are the potential executives and what they may become.

Steiner set out in 1978 with an action plan for management development in the Pharma division. Several goals were formulated such as achieving an even ratio between executives and potential executives, since currently the former far outnumbered the latter who would eventually be needed to fill an ever-increasing number of executive positions. He also initiated a program to recruit 40 young people each year, mainly MBAs, and put them on a fasttrack development. This was a major change from Ciba-Geigy's traditional recruitment policy. A study of the age structure in the Pharma division had revealed that only 24 percent of the potential executives were below age 35. Finally, systematic

MD planning was instituted that would account for different profiles of executives needed for the traditional drug business, new business sectors, and acquisitions (see Exhibit 4).

In total the MD unit in Pharma dealt with nearly 600 people, 330 executives and 250 potential executives on a worldwide basis, covering operations in over 60 countries. The MD action plan was specifically tailored to the needs of the Pharma division as Steiner remarked:

> Obviously, what we developed here would not apply to Ciba-Geigy as a whole since other divisions face different management development problems. But we were also in a Catch 22 situation because while the corporate turn-around rationalization plans placed an almost complete ban on recruitment, we were told to go ahead with our strategic recruitment program.

> The Pharma division is growing fast but competing head-on with other companies like Hoechst or MSD. If we want to compete successfully for executives, we have to offer salary levels comparable to those offered by our main competitors. Clearly we have a conflict between the salaries our division has to pay and those other divisions want to pay. Also, as a rule, the most profitable divisions believe that they should have a higher standard of living.

The Pharma Division in France

Pharma division operations in France had always been rather autonomous. In the old days, the French Pharma Division had been headed by Dr. Henri d' Encausses, a pharmacist and the Mayor of Gaillardon, a village in Southern France. He gladly entertained visiting executives from headquarters but carefully protected his autonomy. In this he had the implicit support of the company's Managing Director,

---

Exhibit 4. Pharma Division—Business, Structure, and Executive Assumptions

Type of Business	Future Business Structure	Types of Executives Required
Traditional drug business (3 pillars)	Same basic structure but trend toward more independent profit center units	Fewer functional managers, more entrepreneurs than in the past
New business sectors (e.g., antibiotics, OTC, generics)	Creation of self-contained business units	All-around managers, entrepreneurs
Acquisitions	Normally will remain independent units	All-around managers, entrepreneurs

Antoine Roux, who ran the French subsidiary quite successfully and kept headquarters at bay. Middle managers were caused to think that Basel was trying to influence the group company unduly. Since his thinking was often ahead of that in Basel, Roux maintained his advantage and kept the management of the French company close to his chest.

With the divisional reorganization which followed the merger, tensions grew between Roux and divisional and corporate management in Basel. He was replaced in 1977 by R. Lamont, a French-speaking Swiss national of English origin, who had been head of the French Pharma division since 1974. Lamont was succeeded in this role by Maitre Guillaume, a French lawyer, who was appointed at age 65, and retired in September 30, 1979, upon his replacement by Delage. Lamont was a skillful negotiator who did much to improve communications between headquarters and the French company.

Neither Lamont nor Guillaume had a strong feeling for management development. They did not have the necessary potential executives to fill new positions and let an enduring weakness develop in their supply of managers. At headquarters the situation was made difficult by a hiring freeze in the early 1970s that led to a scarcity 10 years later of promotable managers age 35 to 40. Following the merger, Ciba-Geigy had found itself with too many managers and with a commitment to its employees that no layoffs would result from it. Furthermore, some divisions, such as dyestuffs, faced shrinking markets and increasing competition. Pharma, alone, was growing rapidly in France from Fr250 million in sales in 1975, to over Fr700 million by 1981. When Delage came back to France in 1976, for instance, he was the only manager with a marketing background and a good knowledge of English. Lamont and Guillaume had satisfied corporate MD formal requirements by drawing up MD plans when requested, but concrete implementation actions rarely followed these plans, and little was done to recruit and develop potential managers.

Between 1976 and 1981, Delage strengthened the French Pharma Division considerably. First, he spent much time in the field improving the quality of the medical representatives' force by training, selection, and replacement. He then created two positions of product line managers—one for Ciba products, the other for Geigy's—to provide additional sales and marketing management competence and support. He also replaced several of the weaker product managers. By 1981, the Pharma organization in France (see Exhibit 5) was in much better shape.

The Choice of a New Marketing Manager

When Lamont retired, Delage was chosen to replace him in competition with a Swiss expatriate. Among many factors in the decision it was felt that national feelings in France would favor a Frenchman to

Exhibit 5. French Pharma Division—Sales and Marketing Structure, 1981

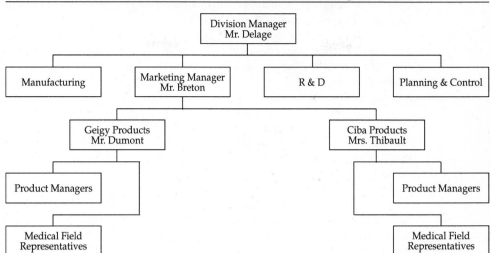

head the local group company. According to the manager of the European region in the Pharma division:

> Delage is a prototype of a successful career within Ciba-Geigy Pharma. He has been successful wherever he was. Delage is the type of person we really like. Among possible candidates he was closest to the ideal profile: a Frenchman to head the French group company, but with good experience of headquarters, several successful assignments abroad and a clear perspective on relationships with Basel. We want that type of person in key positions abroad. He already was an ideal division manager who understood the Ciba-Geigy philosophy well. There is nothing worse than having key people in group companies who know nobody in Basel, are not known to headquarters, and lack the company culture.

The major issue with Delage's appointment was that he had been division head in France for less than two years and, in reviewing the French MD plan, the Executive Committee had put a hold on him as recently as October 1981. Yet, since no other candidate came close to his profile, he was selected.

Finding a new Pharma division head to replace Delage was more difficult. In 1979, Delage proposed to hire Charles Mortier as Marketing Manager for Pharma-France. Nobody from the French Pharma division was well-qualified for the job, and the only candidate suggested by the corporate MD unit was a Swiss manager from Canada, Paul Aubert. Unfortunately, he came from another division and was not well-known to the Basel Pharma division management. Mortier had a good track record with a U.S. pharmaceutical company in France, where his career progression had been stifled, and he was a seasoned marketing and sales manager. After much discussion, his appointment was agreed to by all parties.

Yet, after a year with Ciba-Geigy, Mortier went back to his former employer. The unexpected dismissal of their marketing manager and a financially attractive offer had hired him back. Soon thereafter, the U.S. company introduced a product in direct competition to Ciba-Geigy's very successful Voltarene.

In the spring of 1980, Delage hired Jules Breton from Sanofi to become the new marketing manager.[1] Breton joined Ciba-Geigy by the late summer of 1980 and was more a general manager than a marketing specialist. Over a year later, with Delage's appointment as Managing Director, the opportunity to promote him as division head came. According to Mr. Steiner: "Breton was promoted; there was no better candidate. We are reluctant to go out on the market for division heads. Breton knew the French market and his people." The major difficulty was that Breton had only been with the company a very short time. He did not know headquarters or the Ciba-Geigy culture and was not well-known to headquarters' managers.

Breton and Delage then suggested Dumont as a replacement for Breton as marketing manager. Dumont had been recruited in March 1980 from Specia (a French competitor) to take responsibility for the marketing of the Geigy line of pharmaceutical products. He was a pharmacist (graduated in 1972) with an additional degree in political science (from "Science-Po" in Paris, 1974). In 1975, following military service, he had joined Boehringer-Ingelheim in Reims as product manager for over-the-counter (OTC) drugs. A year later, he joined a Specia subsidiary, overseeing two products which between them accounted for over 50 percent of the subsidiary's sales. In 1977 he became responsible for all product managers at Specia and was very successful. In 1979 he was offered to head a newly acquired market research subsidiary and to create, for the whole of Specia, a marketing "methodology" unit to advise and assist line managers. Seeing himself more as a line manager, he was not very pleased with the new position when he was approached by an executive placement firm on behalf of Ciba-Geigy in November 1979. Following interviews and discussions with Mortier and Delage, he decided to join Ciba-Geigy.

By the time Dumont came on board, in March 1980, Mortier had left the company, and for the next six months (until Breton actually arrived) the French Pharma Division had no marketing manager. Delage, in addition to his divisional management duties, concentrated most of his attention on the Ciba products, where rapid product line management turnover had created problems. Dumont was immediately given full responsibility for the Geigy product line with very little

---

[1] In the meantime. Delage had stepped back into the vacant marketing manager's role, spending about 60 percent of his time as division head on marketing and sales issues.

supervision. This included a marketing and sales force of about 120 people, supported by a service staff of more than 20 people. He handled them successfully, continuing the 20 percent per annum real rate of growth started under Delage. According to Dumont, the quality of the products, the commitment of management, and the financial means of Ciba-Geigy explained that continued success.

In less than one year, Dumont had created a good impression at headquarters. According to the Pharma European regional manager, Dr. Grunwald, "he attended meetings in Basel and left good impressions everywhere; he elicited positive feelings and was known within headquarters."

In spite of this positive view about Dumont among Pharma division management in Basel, headquarters routinely initiated a wider search for candidates. According to Mr. Steiner: "We were suggested 'why not go with Dumont?' by Delage and Breton. Our initial reaction was 'we do not really know Mr. Dumont, he has been in the company only a few months. Let us look at him. At first sight he is very young— he was born in 1948—but maybe we are getting old?' We then looked into who else we had. Delage knew all of them anyway."

Dumont had been very successful in France and knew both the techniques of marketing and the specific character of the French pharmaceutical markets extremely well. The French pharmaceutical market was considered to be one of the most difficult for foreign competitors, among European markets. France had some strong national competitors, such as Specia, with extensive positions on their domestic market but little international presence. Furthermore, prices were tightly controlled, and complex administrative and political procedures governed the registration of new drugs. In a price inelastic market, margins were slim. In 1981, the new Socialist government in France was about to initiate discussions with foreign pharmaceutical companies with the objective of granting price increases only to those which agreed to increase their local investment and employment levels.

Despite these difficulties the French market was important to Ciba-Geigy and one of the largest national markets for its pharmaceutical products. Among the group companies, France had had the most success with Voltarene, and this product now accounted for a substantial proportion of Ciba-Geigy's sales in France. Steiner and Grunwald drew up a profile of an ideal candidate. According to them, international exposure and headquarters experience were desirable characteristics that Dumont lacked. Together, they drew a more formalized profile to assess candidates. This blank profile would be sent to each senior manager within Ciba-Geigy who knew the candidate.

Steiner started to go through files of possible candidates from outside the French group company. On November 23, 1981, a first list of about 40 candidates was drawn from Steiner's files on 600 Pharma managers, worldwide. He then started to go through these, one by one.

The three main criteria used to pare the list were: suitability for the position, availability, and career development considerations. The requirement for full "perfect" fluency in French quickly eliminated all but 6 candidates. Only 3 of these could be considered as "genuine" candidates by Steiner and Grunwald. They were submitted to Delage.

Delage quickly brushed aside one candidate who looked perfect on paper but that he knew personally from his previous positions in the Pharma division and whom he did not consider suitable for the position. Another candidate turned out not to be available, having been in his current position only nine months and not being easily replaceable there. This left one possible candidate: Michel Malterre. Malterre, however, had been slotted to go to Greece in 1982 and was not, therefore, technically available.

Malterre, a French-speaking Swiss, born in 1944, was Marketing Manager for Pharma in West Africa. He had started with Ciba in 1970, two months before the merger, as a lawyer working on legal problems resulting from the merger. For the next two years he was legal assistant to the Pharma division's Manager for Planning, Information, and Control in Basel.

During the uprising of Bangladesh against Pakistan in 1971, the International Committee of the Red Cross (Geneva) asked Ciba-Geigy for Malterre's detachment on leave to Bangladesh, where he had worked with the Red Cross prior to his joining Ciba-Geigy. After four months spent organizing medical relief programs there, often flying in helicopters through combat zones, he returned to his job in Basel. The company's Executive Committee was interested in the value of lending executives to nonprofit organizations for humanitarian purposes and asked Malterre to make a detailed presentation of his experience upon his return.

In 1972-1973 Malterre was named product manager for anesthetics in Switzerland, after which he was appointed to the secretariat of the Chair of the Executive Committee. In 1978, he applied for a line job and was sent to the Ivory Coast to market Pharma products. By 1981 he had been quite successful in developing sales in Africa and had developed good relationships with local health officials and ministers. His MD plan called for his transfer to Greece at the end of 1982.

Headquarters executives were sensitive to various aspects of Malterre's career. According to Grunwald: "Malterre has worked in Pharma at corporate level and abroad. His big disadvantage is not to be French, but his mother tongue is French. He is well-experienced in the Ciba-Geigy organization and knows the French group company, since most products sold in French West Africa are made in France."

—— Amtar Oil Company* ——

Case 5.2
Lorna L. Wright
Henry W. Lane

Management Meeting (1978)—The Issue Discussed _____

Monday morning management meetings (see Exhibit 1 for an organization chart) were a tradition at Amtar Oil in Soronga. The manpower situation was of constant concern. Complicating the matter was uncertainty over the government's policy of gradually replacing foreign nationals with trained local managers and technicians. Was Amtar on the right path, or should it be doing something differently? If it did something differently, what should the changes be? Opinion was divided on the issue.

At every meeting the debate raged over whether to hire expatriate or local staff. Joe Thomas, Production Manager, always pressed to hire more expatriates. Dipo Jil, a Sorongan who was Amtar's Administration Coordinator, advocated more local hires.

Thomas: We are going to need more drillers and engineers if we're planning to increase production. I know a couple of people who would fit the bill. They've just come off a job in Iran. Shall I get in touch with them?

Jil: What about looking locally?

Thomas: There's no one here qualified. You know that.

Jil: What about our own people? Can we move more of them up?

Jamie Haliburton (Drilling Manager): None of them are sufficiently trained.

Thomas: I was hired to produce 23 million barrels of oil this year, not train a bunch of trainees. If you want me to do more training, our production is going to drop.

Haliburton: Right, Joe. And if I take someone off the drilling site to send for training, I lose two day's time that we'll never make up.

Jil: But wait a minute. Our contract stipulates an obligation to train.

Haliburton: We're spending $1 million on training now. What more do they want?

---

*Names of people, locations, agencies, and companies have been disguised.

Source: Western Business School case # 9-86-CO18 "Amtar Oil Company," written by Lorna L. Wright and Henry W. Kane, copyright © 1986, The University of Western Ontario.

Exhibit 1. Amtar Soronga Organization Chart (1978)

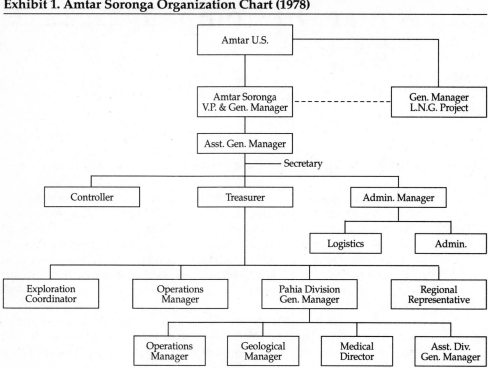

Ken Johnson (Accounting): I must admit I agree with Dipo. We have a moral obligation to be a good corporate citizen and help facilitate the development of our national employees.

Thomas: The government isn't serious about that. That's just to keep the newspapers happy. They're not going to go through with it. Just wait and see. Then we'll have wasted time and money for nothing. We need more expatriates in here who know the job and can produce.

Harry Leighton (Exploration Manager): Besides, we can't get the training department to do anything but push paper anyway.

Andy Petu (Finance Officer): One thing you haven't considered yet is what it costs to keep an expat here. We pay about $10,000 a month for each one, which is about ten times what a local costs us. It would pay us to invest in training now.

Harvey Clarke (Logistics Manager): Wait a minute. If we step up training, it's going to be expensive. Does anyone know if these costs will be covered under the contract?

Petu: Hmm. I'll have to look into that.

Jim Haines (Technical Manager): Well, we've got to do something. I can't operate either safely or efficiently with half-trained, inexperienced people. If we don't do something about the way we're conducting training now, we'll either have to bring in more expatriates or hire better locals. Whatever, let's get off our butts and do something.

Haliburton: Hold on there. We've been doing pretty well so far. It's only been six years since we first struck oil and we're already pulling in $20-30 million a year after cost recovery. I don't see that we have to change much.

Tom Jones (President, Amtar): That's the problem. Can we continue as we have with our employees or are we going to have to make a concentrated effort to fulfill the plan to replace expatriates with national employees? I wish I knew how serious the government was.

Background _____

In 1956, Jim Tarrant was chief geologist for the Gulf Coast division of PLESOP Corporation. He grew restless and, wanting more independence, established his own oil prospecting firm. From this chancy beginning, the company grew to be a multibillion dollar business by 1982. Impatience with government intervention in the oil and gas industry in the United States prompted Jim to expand internationally to seek less regulated environments. He found what was to be his greatest success in Soronga. Amtar Soronga soon dwarfed the American parent.

The venture started in 1968 with a production contract with SOROL-GA, the State oil company. Amtar bid for the drilling rights on land totalling 12,167 square kilometers. One property proved to be very rich. It was here that Amtar discovered Soronga's first major gas deposit and turned the company's main concentration from oil to gas.

Amtar's head office was in Kildona, the capital, but its main operating unit was on the island of Pahia. With over 2000 employees and $30 million in annual revenues, it would have qualified as a Fortune 500 company if it had been in the U.S. Headquarters in Oklahoma employed approximately 50 people and operated primarily as support for Amtar Soronga.

Start-Up _____

Amtar was a young company which had grown very quickly. It had been hard pressed to hire the manpower needed to keep pace with this expansion.

In the start-up phase, the top priority was for people who could explore, drill, and produce oil as quickly as possible. People were hired for their technical expertise. Then, as the company grew, they had to assume more management responsibilities. Paramount concern, however, was always production.

The bulk of Amtar employees were involved in the operations on Pahia. Bachelor quarters were built at the field site. An hour's helicopter ride away in Tava, a small town which was the provincial capital, the company built a complex for workers' families. It housed 150 families and included a clinic, fire station, community center with a restaurant, snack bar, swimming pool, and tennis courts, and paved streets.

The main office in Tava included logistics, accounting, and telecommunication departments, as well as the operational sections of engineering, drilling, and exploration. The much smaller office in Kildona existed primarily as a liaison between operations and the Sorongan government. Amtar Kildona took care of work permits and communicating any operating problems to SOROLGA. They also made sure that any changes in regulations were sent immediately to the field. Personal relations were important in Sorongan business and a primary function of the Kildona office was to maintain good relations with SOROLGA.

The Kildona office also provided information to Amtar's partners who provided funds and participated in planning but not in the day-to-day operations. Prospecting was a high risk, high capital business. Amtar's current profits were the result of more than a decade of capital and technology investment. Since financing a foreign operation was extremely expensive, Amtar, a small company, found it difficult to do alone. (For example, in the past five years, exploration and production costs for Amtar Soronga had been more than $1.5 billion.) Amtar had solved this problem by forming a six company joint venture with the stipulation that Amtar was sole operator.

Prospecting consisted of drilling wells at promising sites in the hopes of striking oil or gas. It usually took seven to ten wells before oil was found. These exploration wells were called wildcats. After three and a half years of geological and seismic work, the wildcat that found the prolific field was drilled. It had proved to contain over six trillion cubic feet of recoverable gas and 132 million barrels of recoverable crude oil.

The field was in a remote jungle far from any market. Working conditions were difficult. Supplies and materials had to be airlifted in or floated upriver on barges until roads could be built. A pipeline had to be constructed to bring the oil and gas to the coast. A gas liquefaction plant had to be built. This involved not only massive amounts of capital but new technology.

Pahia was an easy area to drill in, which also made it potentially dangerous. Most disasters happened in easy areas because workers would get careless. Also, the shallower the well, the faster something could happen. The higher volatility of gas, compared with oil, also increased the danger.

Since there was no market for liquid natural gas (LNG) in Soronga, the gas had to be exported. An agreement was negotiated with the

European Economic Community. Next, shipping contracts had to be developed. A new type of tanker was needed and had to be designed and built. Amtar was involved in all of this, plus much more. Liquefaction facilities, holding tanks, housing, recreational facilities, roads, etc. all had to be financed and constructed. The start-up phase was hectic and a large drain on both human and financial resources. Personnel often worked seven days a week.

There were 106 wells producing and six drilling rigs on site, and exploration continued along with production. Only a portion of the concession granted Amtar had been explored. Since Amtar would have to return some acreage on which it had not drilled to SOROLGA in 1980, the aim was to avoid giving back land with potential production.

Production Contracts _____

A Sorongan law stated that all minerals were owned by the government and people of Soronga and, therefore, mining should be done wherever possible by Sorongans themselves. Where not possible, the work could be contracted. All oil companies worked as contractors for SOROLGA. SOROLGA took on the general management functions and the oil companies worked closely with FCCD (government coordinating agency) in SOROLGA. FCCD was the liaison between the foreign companies and the Sorongan government. It provided help in obtaining necessary permits, facilitated needed imports, and oversaw company expenditures.

These operating contracts generally were limited to a term of thirty years. Under this system, Amtar was responsible for all exploration. It provided the funding until discoveries were made. When oil or gas was found, the costs were then recoverable from the revenues generated. All exploration and operating costs were included. To be cost recoverable, however, expenditures had to conform to government rules and regulations, and had to be preapproved by FCCD.

For example, one government decree stipulated that at different levels of expenditure only certain types of vendors were approved. For purchases of under $50,000, the small, weaker local firms had priority. Only if they were unable to supply the item would the oil company be allowed to seek another vendor from a different class. Also, they could not break a $100,000 purchase down into two lots of $50,000 to use a company with a cheaper price. If these rules were not followed, the expenses would not be recoverable. Training expenses also were recoverable if the training program had been approved initially by SOROLGA.

Once oil was struck, SOROLGA and Amtar shared the production resulting from the exploration. For oil production the proportions were 80/20 respectively for SOROLGA and Amtar, but for gas, a newer business for Soronga, the split was 65/35.

Soronganization _____

Soronga had gained independence from its colonial masters in 1958 and was trying to catch up with Western countries economically and technologically. To foster technology transfer, the government had embarked on a rapid process of replacing expatriates with national personnel. The Ministry of Labor issued a list of positions closed to expatriates and a schedule of when other positions would be closed, but this was negotiable on a company by company basis if there were extenuating circumstances.

A government decree in 1973 stated that oil companies with two years of commercial production should begin closing certain positions, starting with administration and personnel. This would be followed at the five year mark by closures of technical positions. (See Exhibit 2 for types of positions and length of time they could remain open.) The final step towards elimination of a position was relegating expatriates to the status of advisors. This could last for one year only. After that no expatriates would be allowed in those positions.

Since 1978, to facilitate orderly progress of turning over jobs to nationals in the oil industry, SOROLGA had been requiring all oil companies operating in partnership with it to submit five year plans of their organizational structure, job succession charts, and individual training. The organizational charts showed how the company planned to develop. The job succession charts showed who was holding the job at present and who was scheduled to take it over and when. The individual training charts showed the activities to prepare those scheduled to assume each position. Every employee had to be accounted for, which meant that the organizational charts often ran to eighty or ninety pages.

SOROLGA scrutinized these charts. If a company wanted to substitute another candidate for the one designated on the job succession chart, it had to justify the substitution. Lateral transfers of senior personnel were watched most carefully because SOROLGA was wary of companies trying to delay turning over positions to national employees.

Amtar, along with all other oil companies, prepared organizational charts, job succession charts, and individual training plans and presented them to SOROLGA every August. Discussions between SOROLGA and Amtar would follow in November. In December, there would be further discussion with MOM (Ministry of Oil and Mines). Final approval of an amended document might come the following February or March.

Each manager completed the charts for his or her own department. Because of the pressure of day-to-day operations, charts were usually ignored until the last minute and then there was a scramble to finish them on time. There was no overall corporate planning of chart preparation and the completed charts were not necessarily coordinated. Many managers had never thought about how to prepare a person to be Vice President of Exploration and Production, or to assume a position outside his department. There was little thought given to where someone would be six years from now. Managers resented the fact that each year it seemed they had to prepare the five year plan all over again. Not just an additional year to bring the plan up-to-date, but a complete, new plan.

Amtar felt it was unrealistic to be bound too tightly to the charts because many unexpected events could invalidate them. For example, a special project requiring expatriate expertise might be needed that hadn't been foreseen at the time the chart was made; someone might not respond as well to training as initially thought and, therefore, the employee's progress would not match that planned in the job succession chart; or it might become evident that someone needed broader experience in other departments before being promoted. These things were not always predictable.

Employment Passes

Employment passes for expatriates were issued on an annual basis. Extensions had to be approved every year. This could be a long process, usually taking about four months. A request would go to FCCD for its initial approval. Then it would go to MOM, which sponsored all employment passes and on to the Ministry of Labor. It was there that the actual employment passes were issued.

The employment passes then followed this chain back down again before reaching the oil company. The process could hit a snag at any stage. Each employment pass had to be followed carefully and shepherded through. Sometimes, even though a particular position was still approved for an expatriate, the particular candidate selected to fill it was unacceptable to FCCD and hard negotiating followed.

Under a new Minister of Labor, the government was taking a harder stance on the utilization of national employees. The timetable was being accelerated and fewer exceptions were being allowed.

There were two views about the replacement of expatriates by nationals. One was that the government was going to require 100 percent of a company's positions to be taken by Sorongans. The other, more prevalent view, was that the government wanted an orderly transfer of most positions to Sorongans when they were *well-trained and qualified;* recognizing the fact that foreign companies would always require some expatriate personnel to look after their interests, since they were required to invest substantial amounts of money.

Staffing

Amtar did not have any formal policies or procedures for recruiting either local or expatriate staff. Since the company had started up in a

Exhibit 2. Restricted Jobs List of Foreign Employees in Mining, Soronga

Group of Jobs	Job Title	Closed	Occupiable within a Specified Period	Open for an Unspecified Period
1	2	3	4	5
Board of Directors	1. Member			X
	2. Secretary			X
Management	1. Executive Jobs:			
	a. Representative			X
	b. President Director			X
	c. General Manager			X
	2. Senior and Junior Staff Jobs			
	a. within operational functions:			
	1. Director, Manager and Superintendent		3 to 5 years	
	2. Toolpusher		3 to 5 years	
	3. Chemical Engineer		3 to 5 years	
	4. Exploration Engineer		3 to 5 years	
	5. Geologist		3 to 5 years	
	6. Geophysicist		3 to 5 years	
	7. And other Senior Staff Jobs and such like		3 to 5 years	
	8. Supervisor		3 to 5 years	
	9. Driller		3 to 5 years	
	10. And other such like Junior Staff Jobs		3 to 5 years	
	b. in the services functions:			
	1. Director, Manager, Superintendent and Supervisor in:			X
	• Mechanical Engineering		2 to 4 years	X
	• Electrical Engineering		2 to 4 years	
	• Civil Engineering		2 to 4 years	
	• Logistics and		2 to 4 years	
	• Finance		2 to 4 years	

2. Director, Manager, Superintendent and Supervisor in:
   - Industrial Relations — X
   - Legal Affairs — X
   - Personnel Affairs — X
3. Auditor — 2 to 4 years
4. Treasurer — 2 to 4 years
5. Topographic Engineer — 2 to 4 years
6. Chief Cook — 2 to 4 years
7. And other such like Senior and Junior Staff Jobs — 2 to 4 years

Non-Staff

1. Non-Staff jobs:
   a. highly skilled/precision labor 1st, and 2nd class:
      1. Foreman — 1 to 2 years
      2. Mechanic — 1 to 2 years
      3. Machinist — 1 to 2 years
      4. Draftsman — 1 to 2 years
      5. Electrician — 1 to 2 years
      6. Welder — 1 to 2 years
      7. Machine and equipment operator — 1 to 2 years
      8. Cook — 1 to 2 years
      9. And other such like jobs — 1 to 2 years
   b. Skilled, semi-skilled and unskilled labor
      1. Clerk — X
      2. Typist — X
      3. Telephone Operator — X
      4. Plumber — X
      5. Carpenter — X
      6. Mess attendant — X
      7. And other such jobs. — X

Non-Industrial Occupations

Advisor, Consultant, — X
Teacher, Trainer and — X
Instructor — X

remote area, a large range of workers was needed. As well as drillers, geologists, and engineers, many support people were necessary, not just in logistics, accounting, and administration, but janitors, caterers, firemen, security guards, doctors, drivers, and maids. Amtar had built and supported a small town.

Gas technology was new to Soronga, and speed and efficiency were essential in the start-up phase, so most employees above the supervisory level were expatriates, experienced in the field. The expatriates were veterans from Vietnam as the war drew to a close, or hired from major oil companies such as Shell, Exxon, and Caltex. The latter usually brought their different policies and operating procedures with them.

Amtar was unable to offer its expatriate staff in Soronga long term job security. The head office in the U.S. was not large enough to absorb many employees and Amtar was uncertain how fast or how far the Sorongan government would go in requiring nationals to fill positions. Turnover of expatriates was therefore high.

Sorongan staff were needed quickly, so people were hired as available and qualifications were of minimal importance. Most of the workers were inexperienced and few had even finished high school. There were only three Sorongan engineers in the company.

The education system in Soronga had recently been expanded to encompass universal primary education and the resultant surge of students into the system stretched its capacity to the utmost. There was a shortage of trained teachers and classes were huge. The number of students entering university was limited by that system's capacity, so trained manpower was in short supply. There was keen competition among companies to obtain graduates to fill technical and management positions. An oil company competed not only with other oil companies, but with manufacturing, service, and mining companies.

People with experience were even scarcer than university graduates. Experience was important in the oil business, particularly in the technical areas, because each well site was unique. Principles learned in the classroom could never be applied exactly. Developing a feel for the situation was vital, and that only came with years of experience. Experience was even more critical on Pahia since it was a straightforward, easy operation. Many workers had no experience with technical problems. If something started to go wrong, they probably would not recognize the situation soon enough to prevent it, or to rectify it after the fact.

Experienced people working for other oil companies were coveted, but SOROLGA frowned on poaching. No one could be hired directly from another company. If someone was approached discretely and indicated an interest in changing jobs, he or she would first have to resign his or her present job and wait three months before applying for the new one. For special projects, Amtar often hired contractors for a specific term. At times there were as many people working on contract as there were actual Amtar employees.

In general, the working relationship between the Sorongans and the expatriates was good but there was tension. Comments such as "Just because we keep quiet, they think we are dumb," "We're not getting the best qualified expats," and "There are capable Sorongans passed over for a job just because their English is not so good" could be heard on the one side, and "We can't find qualified locals," "Sorongans don't have the drive to take responsibility," on the other side.

There were communication problems between the expatriates and the Sorongans because few expats spoke Sorongan and most of the Sorongan staff had limited English. There was also a communication problem between departments and between the head office in Kildona and the operating unit in Pahia. Lines of reporting and responsibility were not always clear.

Training

Since it was extremely difficult to fire anyone in Soronga, the training department became a dumping ground for unwanted personnel. Few had any background in training. Training directors came and went in rapid succession. In one three year period, there had been more than six.

There was no training policy. Training was offered piecemeal and on an emergency basis to equip people with the skills they needed to do their current job. When an expatriate's work permit expired, a Sorongan was put into the position to "sink or swim." There was no training offered to prepare an employee to move up in the company. Amtar could not use the head office in Oklahoma or other operations for training as the major oil companies could, because the head office was so small and the company had no other operations of any significant size.

The attitude to training was ambivalent. One the one hand, it was required to support the development of nationals, but on the other, time spent training was time taken away from production. There was great concern with operations and production. "Every barrel we lose through delay or machine breakdown is lost forever to us. Someone else will get it after our thirty years are up." The operating departments (exploration, drilling, and production) felt the training department did not understand its needs.

Training was provided at the request of individual managers. Once a certain type of training was requested, the training department would locate suitable courses. Sometimes a particular course was not available when needed. Or, it was inconvenient to release the designated person when the course was available.

Training courses varied widely in content. They included English for secretaries and drilling rig workers, Customs and Excises, mud technology, inventory control, and problem solving and decision making. (See Exhibit 3 for examples of the types of training given.) The training was

---

Exhibit 3. Monthly Activity Report Training Department March 1978

I. In-House Training
    1. Language Programs
        a. English for Logistics (80 employees—ongoing)
        b. English for support personnel (20 employees)
        c. English for Secretaries (28 employees—ongoing)
        d. English for Production (30 participants—ongoing)
        e. English for Logistics Warehouse (31 employees—ongoing)
        f. English for Fire and Safety (22 employees—ongoing)
        g. Word Processor Training (4 employees—1 month program)
    2. Technical Training
        a. Solar Generator Set Phase II (18 employees—7 hours)
        b. Electrical Safety (5 employees—ongoing program)
        c. First Aid (18 employees—15 hour program)
        d. Welding Up-grading (7 employees—52 hours)
        e. Basic Electronic (2 employees—3 hours a week)
        f. Architectural Design (2 employees—ongoing)
        g. Structural Design (1 employee—ongoing)
        h. Motor Control (9 employees—ongoing)
        i. Earthworks (6 employees—ongoing)
        j. Electrical Safety (8 employees—ongoing)
II. Vendor In-House
        a. Inventory Control (SEA Management at Wapatin and Tava)
        b. Typing (BKAS Business Services for 15 employees—3 weeks)
        c. Secretarial Course (BKAS Business Services for 43 employees)
III. Vendor
        a. Training Offices Course (SOROLGA—1 employee—3 weeks)
        b. Construction Seminar (Hako Construction Co., Kildona—2 employees—4 days)
        c. Water Treatment Course (Soronga Utilities, Letoro—1 employee—1 month)
        d. Problem Solving & Decision Making Certification (Kepner—Tregoe, Singapore—1 employee—3 weeks)
        e. Vibration Surveillance Course (Solar Turbine, Singapore—1 employee— 5 days)
        f. Design of Engineering Components, Structure and System for Corrosion Prevention and Control (SISIR, Singapore—1 employee—5 days)
        g. Stratigraphic Control for Hydrocarbon Accumulation Course (OGCI, Singapore—1 employee—5 days)
        h. Gas and Production Technology Courses (SORGAS, Kildona—1 employee— 2 months)
        i. Electronic, Instrumentation and Gas Technology Courses (SORGAS, Kildona—2 employees—7 months)
        j. Customs and Excises (Sorongan Management Institute, Kildona— 1 employee—3 weeks)
        k. Capital Asset Identification (SOROLGA, Kildona—2 employees—3 days)

conducted by in-house staff and by outside vendors, both in Soronga and abroad. It included on-the-job as well as formal classroom instructions.

Approximately $500,000–$1 million was allotted to training, but there were no guidelines as to content or the targeted participants. There were 2200 Sorongan employees in the company. A one week seminar would cost $1000, so even providing one week of training per year for 500 people would exhaust most of the budget with no great benefit for anyone.

Few records were kept of each individual's training. With the turnover in expatriate staff, it was not unknown for an individual to be sent on the same course twice.

A person could have taken forty training courses but they might not be related to the job, nor would they support a career plan. Courses could be an excuse for a holiday, or a reward for good behavior; only occasionally would they help the person do the job better.

Often the person might not have the qualifications necessary to take the training, or the training was given for the sake of training. For example, English classes were given for their own sake. Students were not grouped according to ability, nor was any thought given to whether the particular person actually needed English to do the job.

The Situation in 1982 ————————————————————————————————

The human resource situation and issues remained relatively unchanged to 1982 when George MacMillan, General Manager of the Pahia operation, became President of Amtar Soronga. George had been trying to convince others in the organization of the need to take the initiative on training and developing the national employees.

Amtar was at the point where it had to realize it was no longer a "cowboy outfit," but a large corporation that would have to plan its long range future. It would have to give systematic attention to its human resources. This realization stemmed from its maturing as a company and from government pressure. Expatriates were being hired with management experience rather than just operational experience. There also was continuing pressure to turn many positions over to Sorongans as fast as possible.

George remembered a recent meeting with FCCD, the Foreign Contractor Coordination Department of SOROLGA. Jipa Limbo, Amtar's Personnel Director, had faced Sar Pinto, the Director of FCCD. Pinto had held up two resumes; one of an expatriate for whom Amtar was requesting an employment pass extension, and one of a Sorongan.

"You're requesting an extension of employment pass for this man. Can you tell me any reason why the Sorongan isn't qualified to do the job? Look at them!" He pointed to the resumes. The American had four training courses listed. The Sorongan's list of courses covered three pages.

"How can you tell me that this man is less qualified than the American? You've been training him to take over the job. According to the job succession chart *you* prepared, he is scheduled to take it over now.

"I'm getting tired of Amtar never sticking to the organizational charts and job succession plans they prepare. Always you come back with excuses and more requests for employment pass extensions. I'm sorry. I can't accept this any longer. You're going to be losing more employment passes from now on. We're serious about using national personnel and it's time you realized it."

It was clear to George that it was time to do some systematic, long-range thinking. He reached for the memo pad to jot down a request for all his managers to put together their ideas on the best way to prepare Amtar for the future ahead of it. He wanted ideas for a development plan for the company: what it might cost, the scope, the time frame, and how it fit with the government's plans.

Part 6

CROSS-CULTURAL ISSUES IN PRODUCTIVITY AND QUALITY

Managing from Below

Reading 6.1
Warner P. Woodworth

This article provides a brief overview of the trend toward a bottom-up approach and then focuses in depth on a system of managerial democracy in Spain. Finally, the implications of such an approach for researchers and American managers are evaluated by discussing the problems and prospects of contemporary worker-managed enterprises.

Toward a System of Worker Participation in Management

The traditional form of labor-management relations in the United States has been the collective bargaining approach. Essentially an adversarial system growing out of earlier decades in this century, it has primarily consisted of fighting for bread-and-butter issues. More recently, new concerns have arisen which have broadened the agenda from wages to health and safety, job security, and so on. The latest thrust has been to institute a bargaining process which also emphasizes joint decision making and the social rights of workers.

Many firms have moved in the direction of work-place democracy, regardless of collective bargaining arrangements or unionization. Socio-technical strategies (Davis and Taylor, 1979; Hackman and Oldham, 1980) have attempted to give workers a voice in the redesign of their jobs. Autonomous work teams at Volvo (Gyllenhammar, 1977) and General Motors (Guest, 1979) have functioned to alter the traditionally exclusive domain of management to make production decisions. Especially since the late 1970s, mainstream U.S. industry has begun to experiment with a variety of innovations to involve workers, at least partially, in the managing of conventional firms (Lawler, 1978).

A more dramatic shift toward worker participation is occurring in some 6,000 American firms with a degree of employee ownership. In the past several years, a number of major airlines and trucking companies have given workers formal representation at the board-of-directors level in exchange for wage concessions. Although not state-mandated, as are the extensive systems of codetermination in Europe, the seeds of a broader, more fundamental change in power are being sown (Woodworth, 1984).

Source: Warner P. Woodworth. "Managing from Below."*Journal of Management*, 1986, 12(3), 391- 402. Reprinted by permission.

In the minds of most managers and organizational researchers, efforts to involve employee-owners are probably viewed as still somewhat experimental (Bernstein, 1980; Whyte and McCall, 1980). The bulk of worker participation efforts are clearly controlled and usually initiated by management (Conte and Tannenbaum, 1978; Hammer and Stern, 1980). The question of whether or not workers could actually run industry is debatable.

Internationally, some evidence is beginning to emerge that answers such a question affirmatively, or at least addresses its possibilities. The Mondragon system of nearly 90 worker-owned cooperatives sheds light on the possibility of a worker-managed economics. Drawing upon scant reports by other researchers and limited data of my own, a case is made for the potential of a bottom-up strategy for managing organizations.

The Mondragon Model _____

The Mondragon system consists of 89 small- to medium-sized industrial cooperatives in the Basque region of northern Spain. After several decades of severe unemployment in the town of Mondragon, the first small worker cooperative was established in 1956. Subsequently, other co-ops were created, all based on the practical need for jobs and on the democratic ideals of a labor-managed economy.

The cooperatives worked together in forming a support organization, Caja Laboral Popular (CLP) (The People's Savings Bank). It began to operate as a source of funding and expertise services in 1960. The CLP and the associations of cooperatives continued to grow and expand. By 1984, the CLP had over 300,000 individual depositors and assets of $1 billion. During the past decade, Mondragon has produced about 5% of the entire national output in certain consumer goods and comprises 14% of the total industrial output of the province of Guipuzcoa, where the Basque community is located (Bradley and Gelb, 1981).

General Structure

The cooperatives of Mondragon are all internally organized in basically the same way. The members of each cooperative are the ultimate authority. The general assembly of all members meets at least annually and is empowered to examine and approve the balance sheet and vote on organizational procedures. The assembly also elects those workers who are to serve on the supervisory board, which is a type of board of directors (Aranzadi, 1976).

The supervisory board appoints the managers who, in turn, are responsible to the board and through it to the general assembly. This indirect accountability of management has proved to be one of the strengths of the Mondragon cooperatives. It is important to note that managers can never be on the supervisory board. Management is directly responsible for administrative tasks.

The management council is an advisory and consultive body. The members of the council are usually managers, top executives, and outsiders with special expertise and skills.

The members of the cooperative also elect the social council, a body having wide prescriptive and advisory powers regarding all aspects of personnel management—work safety, social security, and wage levels. The watchdog council is the ultimate safeguard in ensuring the democratic running of the cooperatives' affairs. The general assembly elects three members to watch over the supervisory board and the two advisory councils and to inform cooperative members of any irregularities.

Exhibit 1 illustrates the organizational structure of the cooperative.

Membership

The Contract of Association states that "membership in the Associated Cooperative shall be voluntary and open to all persons who can render the services for which it was established, provided they agree to assume the responsibilities membership entails." This open-door policy ensures that all those who desire and qualify for membership can apply for it. Members who do decide to join and who have the needed skills or training pay an initial contribution in cash of approximately $3,000. This initial investment and the allocation of funds to the individuals' capital accounts make the workers owners of the cooperative.

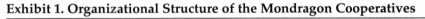

Exhibit 1. Organizational Structure of the Mondragon Cooperatives

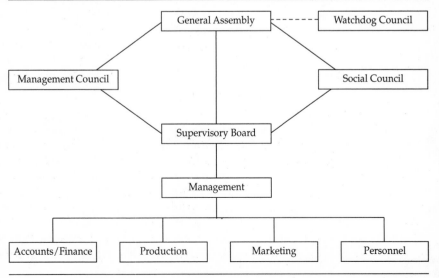

Decision Making

The major decisions of each cooperative are determined in annual meetings of the general assembly. Simple majority vote is sufficient in determining any policy, approval of a budget, admission of new members, or disciplining violators. Decisions are not determined by the number of shares a person has in the company, but rather on the basis of one person/one vote. This bottom-up structure of workers' control provides a network of participation channels and ensures the democratic sharing of organizational power. Power is not concentrated in an elite group of decision makers at the top, but remains with the membership as a whole.

Distribution of Wealth

The Mondragon system is unique in that money does not stay strictly within the cooperative. Under the Cooperative Law of Spain, it is permissible to form "second degree cooperatives," organizations that are not entirely worker-owned and controlled but which have associated cooperatives as institutional members. The Caja Laboral Popular is the primary second degree cooperative of the Mondragon system. It is designed to attract the savings of the local community and invest the money in the associated cooperatives. The bank provides computer services, conducts feasibility studies for new cooperatives, and loans up to 50% of the capital needed to launch a new business. Other bank support efforts include securing land for construction, designing new plants, and training workers as they launch their own businesses.

The initial capital contribution made by all new cooperators represents their capital share in the new enterprise. Thus, each new cooperative is financed in part by the capital contribution of its members and augmented by loans from the CLP. The employees' earning structure, being governed by solid principles and ideals of solidarity and equality, is different from that of a traditional firm. The maximum range of earnings is set at a 3 :1 ratio. In other words, the gross earnings of the highest paid managers cannot be more than three times that of the lowest paid worker-members.

Work Structures

Because the emphasis of Mondragon is on job creation and democratic control, work structures center on training and job security. For example, in the past the cooperatives' policy has been to send workers back to school to develop further expertise rather than lay them off during slow or bad times. Sometimes workers are temporarily sent to other cooperatives.

Nevertheless, cooperative factories that compete in markets have to organize their work efficiently. This has led to the division and diversification of work and the implementation of new technologies. Jobs center on teamwork rather than on assembly-line labor. The goal is to build a participatory organization by objectives rather than the traditional management by objectives. For instance, in a new furniture factory, all the work is planned by worker teams. A performance index is allocated to the entire team, which then decides how these gains should be distributed among members.

In 1977, several industrial cooperatives jointly established a research and development (R&D) center called Ikerlan in order to compete more efficiently with new technologies and products made elsewhere. Much time and money are devoted to the design of new components for existing products, to the study of competitors' products, and to keeping abreast of international developments.

Social Organization

Because Mondragon is not a communal system, work and social life are somewhat segregated. However, Mondragon is a complex of organizations, and its cooperative structure and ideals have had an important spillover effect on such social structures as education.

Education has been an important part of the Mondragon model from the beginning. The first cooperative firm was preceded by 13 years of education. Jose Maria Arizmendi, the visionary priest whose ideals significantly shaped the Mondragon system, continually repeated the words, "Knowledge is power; socializing knowledge implies the democratization of power."

The League for Education and Culture was organized years ago as a full-fledged cooperative with a general assembly and supervisory board designed to support the socio-economic system of Mondragon through education. There is great coordination between the educational system and the cooperatives. Students are trained in the skills needed by the cooperatives, and the students' training and research help shape the future. Students are not only trained technically but are also socialized regarding the ideals and functions of Mondragon.

The Results of Bottom-Up Management _____

In response to the query, "Can workers run industry?" the Mondragon experience suggests an affirmative answer. Out of the rubble of war and economic stagnation, over 25,000 jobs have been created. Starting with one co-op in 1956, there were eight by 1960, 60 by 1970, and today a total of 89 cooperative firms. Some of the worker-owned firms are fairly large, such as Ulgor, which has 3,400 members and six factories. It is the leading manufacturer of appliances in Spain, producing 300,000 refrigerators and 250,000 stoves a year. Some 25% of its products are marketed internationally. Other firms are smaller, ranging from agricultural equipment to steel construction, graphic arts, plastics, and robotics.

The worker cooperatives are supported by second-degree institutions such as the peoples' bank, a localized system of social security called Lagun Aro which provides welfare benefits and cooperative medical care, an R&D center, a technical school, and a college of engineering. An elementary cooperative educational system of 44 schools, day-care centers, 14 housing co-ops, some fifty cooperative supermarkets, and 7 agricultural co-ops round out the community structure for building an egalitarian society.

The track record of these cooperative businesses is impressive. Of 89 business start-ups thus far, there has not been a single failure, in contrast to the typical U.S. experience which suffers from a 50% failure rate in the first several years (Greene, 1985). Nor has the Mondragon system suffered massive layoffs during economic downturns. For instance, when the OPEC oil crisis hit in 1974, instead of losing their jobs as did their counterparts in traditional firms worldwide, Mondragon workers in hard-hit firms were simply transferred to the technical school for a few months to obtain new skills. Then they moved into other firms in the cooperative system which were experiencing growth, without losing a single day's pay in the process. In sharp contrast to most industries during that period, Mondragon increased employment by 7.5% while profits grew 26% and exports shot up 56% (Johnson and Whyte, 1977). Over the past decade, total cooperative sales have increased at a rate exceeding 25% annually, while industrial investment has grown 15% each year. Mondragon has a philosophy premised on Schumacher's *Small is Beautiful* (1973) logic, keeping the size of most firms well under 500 members. Such a scale seems to foster healthy interpersonal relationships and strong identification with the enterprise. An important result of this is that there has been only a one-day strike in the past 25 years of cooperative existence, and that was over job classifications in a large co-op. A labor relations climate such as this seems rather enviable when compared with the problems of distrust, alienation, and conflict which characterize all too many conventional firms.

References —————————————————————————————————————

Aranzadi, D. *Cooperativismo industrial como sistema.* Bilbao, Spain: Editorial Elexpuru Hnos., S.A. 1976.

Argyris, C. *Intervention theory and method: A behavioral science view.* Reading, Mass.: Addison-Wesley, 1970.

Argyris, C. and Schon, D. *Organizational learning.* Reading, Mass.: Addison-Wesley, 1978.

Beckard, R. *Organization development: Strategies and models.* Reading, Mass.: Addison-Wesley, 1969.

Bernstein, P. *Workplace democratization: Its internal dynamics.* New Brunswick, N.J.: Transaction Books, 1980.

Bradley, K. and Gelb, A. *Obstacles to a cooperative economy: Lessons from Mondragon.* London: London School of Economics and Political Science, 1981.

Braverman, H. *Labor and monopoly capitalism.* New York: Monthly Review Press, 1974.

Conte, M. and Tannenbaum, A.S. "Employee-owned companies: Is the difference measureable?" *Monthly Labor Review*, 1978 101, 23-28.

Dahl, R.A. "Procedural democracy." In Laslett, P. and Fishkin, J. (eds.), *Philosophy, politics and society* (5th series, pp. 97-133). New Haven, Conn.: Yale University Press, 1979.

Davis, L.E. and Taylor, J.C. *Design of jobs.* Santa Monica, Calif.: Goodyear, 1979.

Drucker, P. *Managing for results.* London: Pan Books, Ltd., 1964.

Edwards, R. *Contested terrain.* New York: Basic Books, 1979.

French, J.R.P., Jr. and Raven, B.H. "The bases of social power." In Cartwright, D. (ed.), *Studies in social power* (pp. 150-167). Ann Arbor: The University of Michigan, 1959.

Gorrono, I. *Experiencia co-operativa en el pais vasco.* Bilbao, Spain, 1975.

Greene, R. "Do you really want to be your own boss?" *Forbes*, October 21, 1985, 86-96.

Guest, R.H. "Quality of work life—Learning from Tarrytown." *Harvard Business Review*, 1979, 57, 76-87.

Gurdon, M.A. "Is employee ownership the answer to our economic woes?" *Management Review*, 1982, 71, 8-14.

Gyllenhammar, P.G. *People at work.* Reading, Mass.: Addison-Wesley, 1977.

Hackman, J.R. and Oldham, G.R. *Work redesign.* Reading, Mass.: Addison-Wesley, 1980.

Hammer, T. and Stern, R. "Employee ownership: Implications for the organizational distribution of power." *Academy of Management Journal*, 1980, 23, 78-100.

Harris, P.R. and Moran, R.T. *Managing cultural differences.* Houston: Gulf, 1979.

Hirschhorn, C. and Associates. *Cutting back: Retrenchment and redevelopment in human and community services.* San Francisco: Jossey-Bass, 1983.

Jackson, S.E. "Participation in decision-making as a strategy for reducing job related strain." *Journal of Applied Psychology*, 1983, 68, 3-19.

Johnson, A.G. and Whyte, W.F. "The Mondragon system of worker production cooperatives." *Industrial and Labor Relations Review*, 1977, 31(1), 18-30.

Kimberly, J.R. and Miles, R.H. (eds.). *The organizational life cycle.* San Francisco: Jossey-Bass, 1980.

Lawler, E.E., III. "The new plant revolution." *Organizational Dynamics*, 1978, 6(3) 3-12.

Likert, R. *The human organization.* New York: McGraw-Hill, 1967.

Locke, E. B. and Schweiger, D.M. "Participation in decision-making: One more look." In Staw, B. and Cummings, L.L. (eds.), *Research in organizational behavior* (Vol. 1, pp. 265-340). Greenwich, Conn.: JAL Press, 1979.

Long, R.J. "The effects of employee ownership in organizational identification, employee job attitudes, and organizational performance: A tentative framework and empirical findings." *Human Relations,* 1978, 31(1), 29-48.

Macy, B.A., Ledford, G.E., and Lawler, E.E., III. *The Bolivar quality of work experiment: 1972-1979.* New York: Wiley-Interscience, 1981.

McGregor, D. *The human side of enterprise.* New York: McGraw-Hill, 1960.

Meek, C. and Woodworth, W. "Employee ownership and industrial relations: The Rath case." *National Productivity Review,* 1982, 1(2), 151-163.

Olson, D.C. "Union experiences with worker ownership. *Wisconsin Law Review* 1982, 5, 729-823.

Ouchi, W.G. *Theory Z.* New York: Avon, 1981.

Peters, T.J. and Waterman, R.H., Jr. *In search of excellence.* New York: Harper & Row, 1982.

Schaaf, M. *Cooperatives at the crossroads.* Washington. D.C.: Exploratory Project for Economic Alternatives, 1977.

Schumacher, E.F. *Small is beautiful: Economic as if people mattered.* New York: Harper & Row, 1973.

Steiner, C. *Top management planning.* New York: MacMillan, 1969.

Strauss, G. "Workers' participation in management: An international perspective." In Staw, B. and Cummings, L.L. (eds.), *Research in organizational behavior* (Vol. 4, pp. 173-265). Greenwich, Conn.: JAI Press, 1982.

Tannenbaum, A.S., Kavcic, B., Rosner, M., Vianello, M., and Wieser, G. *Hierarchy in organizations.* San Francisco: Jossey-Bass, 1977.

Taylor, F.W. *The principles of scientific management.* New York: Norton, 1967. (Original work published 1911.)

Thomas, H. *The dynamics of social ownership.* Paper presented at the Third International Conference of the International Association for the Economics of Self-Management, Mexico City, August 1982.

Thomas, H. and Logan, C. *Mondragon: An economic analysis.* London: George Allen and Unwin, 1982.

Watzlawick, P., Weakland, J., and Fisch, R. *Change: Principles of problem formation and problem resolution.* New York: Norton, 1974.

Whetton, D.A. "Organizational decline: A neglected topic in organizational behavior." *Academy of Management Review,* 1980, 5, 577-588.

Whyte, W.F. and McCall, D. "Self-help economics." *Society,* 1980, 17(4), 22-28.

Woodworth, W. "Hard hats in the boardroom: New trends in workers' participation." In Ritchie, J.B. and Thompson, P. (eds.), *Organization and people* (pp. 403-413). St. Paul, Minn.: West, 1984.

Quality, Participation and Competitiveness

Reading 6.2
Robert E. Cole
Paul Bacdayan
B. Joseph White

Despite years of preaching from academics and repeated assertions of the benefits associated with participatory work practices, managers have been slow to embrace and incorporate these practices into everyday work routines in American corporations.[1] Why this is the case? Once we identify the obstacles, we can examine the role that a modern quality improvement focus plays in eliminating these obstacles.[2]

There are many different forms of employee participation.[3] By participation, we mean employee involvement in decision making that has three characteristics:

- It is *relatively formal*. It is part of official role behavior.

- It is *direct*. It involves individuals instead of, or in addition to, elected representatives .

- It is *relatively local and moderately open regarding decision-making access*. Workers have a strong input into most operational decisions directly affecting their work and will be delegated authority for some aspects of that work.

Though we will use the term "participation" (or "employee involvement"), work arrangements with such characteristics go by many names, such as "participative decision making" and "empowerment." Each has some distinctive nuance, but for our purposes they will be treated as the same.

The central puzzle is: "Why don't managers fully embrace participation?" Despite extensive exposure to ideas about participation and its alleged benefits, surveys of American firms show rather superficial participation: participatory techniques, while used in many companies, rarely affect large numbers of employees in any single company.[4] Comprehensive reviews of the effects of participatory practices often reveal modest short-run improvements with "a positive, often small effect on productivity, sometimes a zero or statistically insignificant effect, and almost never a negative effect."[5] These are modest claims indeed. Historical accounts suggest a long but on-again-off-again pattern of experimentation with participation. Thus, Tom Bailey's recent overview of employee participation in the United States concludes:

> There are many positive, even enthusiastic reports of the benefits of work reform and employee participation practices and to some extent these examples are supported by systematic research that also shows positive effects. Nevertheless, the diffusion of these practices has been slow and frustrating, and many efforts do not last.[6]

A variety of possible explanations may account for these outcomes. David Levine argues that the external environment of the firm is hostile to participation in the United States and it leads the market to discourage participation as well as related practices (e.g., encouraging employment security), "suggesting the need for public policies to overcome the current penalties suffered by initial adopters."[7] While these arguments may well be valid, they interact with internal inhibitors. Our own analysis of these internal factors attributes the low level of acceptance to the low level of managerial support—and that, in turn, to managers' perceptions of a weak connection between participation and improved productivity (or other desirable organization-level outcomes). Furthermore, an understanding of the internal factors leading managers not to support participation also can shed light on why workers don't give stronger support to participatory initiatives.

By examining the integration of participatory work practices with the modern quality paradigm, we highlight theoretically important and previously ignored relationships. These relationships promote desirable organization-level results, thereby heightening managerial support.

Strengths and Weaknesses of the Participation Tradition ——————

Table 1 provides an overview of the strengths and weaknesses of the participation tradition in terms of its contributions to individuals and groups on the one hand and to overall organizational objectives on the other. The extensive literature on participation treats its strengths (which are primarily at the individual and small group level) in great depth and can be summarized as follows:

- **Focus on Motivation**—The participation theme highlights the important relationship between human motivation and organizational outcomes. Its premise is that participation yields its best results when it is based on a voluntary act. The enactment of participation is said to lead to self-realization and human dignity.

**Table 1. Strengths and Weaknesses of the
Participative Tradition by Level of Analysis**

Level of Analysis	Strengths	Weaknesses
Individual/ Small Group	• focus on motivation	• lack of employee rewards
	• opportunity for goal agreement	• myopic emphasis on motivation
	• emphasis on interpersonal processes	
	• human capital development	
	• integrating interdependent tasks	
Department Managers	• release for higher-level activities	• absence of managerial rewards
		• absence of role for lower-level managers
System/ Organization/Society	• potential competitive advantage	• "flabbiness"
	• democratization	• absence of strategic context for group activities

- **Opportunity for Goal Agreement**—Participation provides a way of aligning individual and organizational objectives.

- **Emphasis on Interpersonal Processes**—Participation provides a heavy emphasis on human process skills like communications teamwork, and conflict resolution skills that improve the quality of decision making and enhance employee "buy-in."

- **Human Capital Development**—Participation stresses the importance of building individual and team competency through training. It thus encourages the development of human capital.

- **Integrating Interdependent Tasks**—Participation through team activity provides a strategy for integrating work involving highly interdependent tasks.

- **Release for Higher-Level Activities**—Participation releases managerial and technical personnel from firefighting activities by making lower-level employees responsible for maintaining and improving their work processes.

- **Potential Competitive Advantage**—Participation has the potential to unleash a great force through allowing all employees to make substantial contributions to improving work performance.

- **Democratization**—Notions of self-governance and self-determination underlie approaches to participation. Some individuals, particularly scholars and labor activists, see participation as a strong democratizing force that finally brings the benefits of political democracy to the workplace.

By contrast, the weaknesses of the participation tradition are primarily at the organization level. They are less commonly discussed, but they are critical because they diminish managerial and worker support for participation. The weaknesses can be summarized as follows:

- **Lack of Employee Rewards**—Employee rewards, including non-monetary enhancements such as employment security, are seldom specified. Without such assurances, individuals often will withhold commitment because they see participatory initiatives which lead to productivity gains threatening their economic security by lowering the demand for labor.

- **Myopic Emphasis on Motivation**—The overwhelming stress on the motivational benefits of participation tends to crowd out other necessary conditions for organizational success such as the improvement of operational processes. The simplistic idea that "if we could just get people motivated everything would turn out all right" is an implicit assumption of much American academic literature (perhaps a function of the domination of this literature by psychologists), not to speak of many American managers.

- **Absence of Managerial Rewards**—Managerial rewards (including power and status) for supporting participative work practices are seldom well-defined. Lower-level supervisors, and middle managers in particular, often see participatory initiatives as a threat to their traditional roles and prerogatives; they see little personal benefit in supporting them. Managerial promotion criteria typically have not been tied to success in introducing and leading participatory activities.

- **Absence of Role for Lower-Level Managers**—Looking at both the scholarly literature and practitioner experience, there is a lack of clarity about the operational requirements (integrating groups and participation into the existing managerial structure). As a consequence, participatory initiatives experience high resistance from supervisors and middle managers because their role is unclear.

- **"Flabbiness"**—Participation advocates are typically unclear about the nature of participative activities as they relate to actual work operations; the emphasis is on the process of participation per se, not the elements of a systematic work improvement methodology. It is often unclear just what one is supposed to be participating in. Consequently, firms tend not to sustain participatory efforts since managers do not see participation as tied to important organizational objectives. Participation comes to be seen as an end in itself.[8] Workers also perceive the irrelevance and similarly withhold their support. Under these conditions, the agenda of issues in which people can participate tends to dry up.

- **Absence of Strategic Context for Group Activities**—This is the final and critical factor. The workteam is portrayed as "context-less," that is, not embedded in the work flow and not tied to a customer. Given the lack of linkage to the work process, managerial support for participation fades because participation is seen as a peripheral activity, not linked to strategic objectives. In this context, participation comes to be seen more as a philosophy, a parallel work process (conducted apart from the main business activities of the enterprise), and as an end in itself rather than as a means to the end of increasing organizational effectiveness.

This list of weaknesses focuses heavily on what we believe are the major organizational forces driving change or inhibiting it. As can be seen in Table 1, the potential advantages identified as strengths of the participative tradition are canceled out at the organization level by the participatory tradition's flabbiness and the absence of strategic context for group activities. While the weaknesses are the sort of reasons that managers might give for not starting or for abandoning participation, and therefore merit attention, they are unfortunately not the reasons that researchers in the participatory tradition typically have addressed.

The majority of these weaknesses focus on managers' support for participation. Our intent in emphasizing this support is not to deny the need for employee cooperation and support (or union support, where relevant) in implementing participatory work practices. Rather, our intent is to assert that in most cases it is management, and only management, which can initiate such activities and command resources to consistently support them. Moreover, it is managers who are in a position to provide the resources that can secure worker commitment through providing such things as job security, recognition, and wages. But without benefits to managers and the organization as a whole, managerial support for participation is unlikely to be forthcoming, and if it is forthcoming, it is unlikely to be sustained.

A Brief Historical and Comparative Note ————————————

We can contrast Japan on the one hand with America and Europe on the other in terms of the historical relationship of participation to quality. Whereas the two traditions developed separately in America and Europe, they emerged after World War II as integrated practices in Japan. Known as total quality control (TQC), this approach stresses quality improvement through the efforts of all employees and all departments. This approach is distinctive and original in philosophy and scope.

The Japanese integration of quality and participation provides important organization-level benefits which, when coupled with individual- and group-level benefits, foster managerial support for participation. By the same token, the historic separation of the two traditions in America and Europe has weakened managerial support for participation and has stunted the development of both the quality and the participation movements. While the reasons for these different historical trajectories lie beyond the scope of this article, it relates to the unique development of Taylorism in the United States, driven in part by a large relatively uneducated immigrant labor force in the early 20th century. While Taylorism spread to both Europe and Japan, in Japan the participatory theme received an early hearing.[9]

Key Characteristics of the Modern Quality Paradigm————————

Table 2 lists the key characteristics of the modern quality approach as developed by the Japanese. Following is a brief overview of these characteristics:

- **The "Market-In" Principle**—"Market-in" is a major focus in Japanese quality improvement activities. It means bringing customer needs into every possible part of the organization, thereby heightening uncertainty. These activities include informing production workers or front-line service employees of warranty claims relevant to their work, informing a broad range of employees how customers use products and services, and educating as many as employees as possible on customer-desired product and service features. The market-in approach contrasts sharply with the reliance on specialized organization experts to process information about the environment and solve specific problems.

- **Quality as an Umbrella Theme**—Quality provides an overall theme for change in the organization, one that is more intrinsically appealing and less threatening than competing themes

---

Table 2. Characteristics of the Modern Quality Movement as It Evolved in Japan

---

- "Market-In" approach provides strong external customer orientation and uses internal customer chain as connection to final user

- Quality as an umbrella theme for organizing work

- Improved quality seen as strategy to strong competitive strategy

- All-employee, all-department involvement a pivotal strategy for improving quality of every business process

- Upstream prevention activities key to quality improvement

- Well-defined problem-solving methodology and training activities tied to continuous quality improvement

- Integration into control system of goals, plans and actions for continuous quality improvement

- Focus on cross-functional cooperation and information sharing

---

such as cost reduction or productivity improvement. It is hard to find anyone who is against quality, but cost reduction and productivity improvement often evoke fears of displacement. Quality by contrast is positive, unifying, and constructive.

- **Quality's Relationship to Costs and Productivity**—Japanese manufacturers (by which we especially mean large- and medium-sized firms) saw improved quality as flowing from the elimination of waste and rework in every business process; this definition contrasts with the traditional American view of improved quality through adding more product attributes and/or additional inspectors, thereby leading to added cost.

- **All-Employee, All-Department Involvement**—The Japanese extended the concept of quality improvement to include business processes beyond the shop floor (e.g., purchasing and design), thus broadening the scope of participation to include all employees and departments. In the typical manufacturing firm, employee involvement means that all employees, individually and in teams, are trained to engage in designing and redesigning their own work processes.

- **Upstream Prevention**—The Japanese also recognized that upstream prevention activities, particularly in the design phase, were the primary place where large-scale quality breakthroughs could take place. While to some extent this devalued the contributions of lower-level employees, it also made it clear that traditional efforts to blame lower-level personnel for poor quality were misplaced.

- **Problem Solving Methodology**—Japanese firms developed a simple yet powerful problem-solving methodology that was usable by workers with high school and even junior high school educations. This methodology is based on application of Shewhart's Plan, Do, Check, Act cycle (PDCA) and is used to improve the employees' own work processes. The methodology is backed up with training in a variety of problem-solving tools, including the Pareto and cause-and-effect diagrams. The solution to many problems was no longer the domain of the industrial engineering department. Simplified statistical tools became widely used among workers in all departments.

- **Integration with Control System**—The deployment of quality improvement efforts is carefully cascaded down through the organization, starting from a long-term plan, moving to the annual plan and then having each level (from managers down through worker quality circles) formulate quality improvement objectives that tie into these plans. Progress toward these plans is checked regularly through personal audits by top executives. By integrating quality into the control system in this way, middle managers and workers are made central to the execution of quality improvement and implicitly told that what they are doing is important. As Prof. Kano shows in the lead article in this issue, this policy management approach contrasts sharply with the traditional operation of MBO in the United States.

- **Cross-Functional Cooperation and Information Sharing—** Information about customer needs and expectations is critical to successful quality improvement because this information drives important processes such as goal setting, problem identification and problem solving. Japanese firms are less inclined to assign customer research to one highly specialized group and they tend to widely deploy the resultant information to as many organizational actors and departments as possible. Consider the example of Quality Function Deployment (QFD). QFD is a system for translating consumer requirements into appropriate company requirements at each stage from research and development through the intermediate stages to marketing/sales and distribution. From our point of view, however, QFD is important and successful because it involves a matrix of specified activities that brings members of different departments together regularly to solve problems. Through these discussions, customer needs and competitor information are widely shared throughout the organization. Key targets for quality, cost, and delivery (QCD) are typically set by cross-functional groups.

In sum, large Japanese firms—through wide sharing of customer information and the empowerment of decentralized work teams to act on that information—have implemented a system of broad-based, task-focused participation that yields quality gains.

Individual and Group Level Benefits of Quality-Participation Integration ————————————————

At the same time, the Japanese have realized important individual and group-level benefits from the integration of quality with participation which we can frame as improved *information processing* and improved *motivation*. These individual and group-level outcomes contribute indirectly to the organization-level outcomes of managerial support for participation.

First, from an information processing standpoint, comprehensive and grass-roots participation in problem solving allows firms to move the "distribution of intelligence" downward in the organization. Participation brings to bear increased information and capability in local problem solving without involving costly middle managers who then contribute to information distortion. As a consequence, participation can improve information processing and decision making, thereby increasing organizational effectiveness.[10]

Second, from an employee motivation standpoint, the market-in approach makes sense for two reasons. First, the process activities for meeting market requirements are based on the sound behavioral principle that those involved in work processes will more enthusiastically implement changes that they themselves have designed. In addition, quality—the act of satisfying the customer and therefore the market—

provides a powerful motivational theme around which to build employee involvement and commitment.

Organization-Level Benefits of Quality-Participation Integration _____

The organization-level interpretation of the benefits of merging quality with participation is the cornerstone of our answer to our original question about why managers haven't supported participation. Managers at all levels (and, to a lesser extent, workers) have lacked motivation to support extensive employee participation, particularly in the design of the routines that guide work. As we suggested earlier, the lack of organization-level benefits partly explains the low managerial support.

Just how does the Japanese approach of merging quality improvement with participation decrease the fear of changing routines and increase managerial support for participatory work practices? The answer requires a closer look at the synergy between participation and the "market-in" principle.

The idea that organizations might try to bring the market into the organization, and thus heighten uncertainty for many employees, runs counter to most social science (especially business strategy) thinking about organizations. Such thinking stresses uncertainty reduction as the normal criterion for organizational decision making. Buffers, which include inventories and specialized units to pre-process information from the environment, shield the bulk of organizational members from the direct forces of the environment.

The buffering approach to dealing with uncertainty probably captured a good deal of how Western firms have operated in the post-World War II period (and how many still do). Beyond the United States, buffering has been a common theme in the Swedish and German approach to group activity. Here, the strategy has been to buffer individual tasks from upstream and downstream pressures (with commensurate and expensive increases of in-process inventory). The idea was to avoid shutdowns when blockages occurred and/or to obtain a humane pace of work that gave workers more control and autonomy over their work environment. While the short-term benefits to workers and managers are clear, the long-term benefits to management and organization-level objectives are less obvious. Recognition of these problems is increasingly leading to the redesign of major Northern European companies. The model in Sweden for example is no longer Volvo with its buffered semi-autonomous work groups but Asea Brown Boveri (ABB) with its Project T50, which stresses decentralization, customer satisfaction, a learning organization, and reduced cycle time.[11]

In contrast to the traditional Western managerial approach to uncertainty, the modern Japanese manufacturer seeks to heighten the pressure for change that the environment exerts on all parts of the organization. The just-in-time system represents the most visible symbol of bringing market pressures into the firm, but the scope and depth of the market-in principle goes far beyond JIT. The "pull system" driving JIT initiates production as a reaction to present demand. But market-in provides far more comprehensive coverage of market characteristics, including anticipation of future demand and of multi-dimensional aspects of customer needs and expectations. Similarly, it widely distributes throughout the firm knowledge about other dynamic aspects of the firm's environment such as raw materials, suppliers, labor markets, regulatory environment, and so on.

The heightening of uncertainty associated with this approach is linked directly to a motivational strategy of involving all employees in the change process. The amount of business information on performance and environment that Japanese manufacturing firms distribute to employees, including those at the lowest levels, is staggeringly high compared to what occurs at most American firms. American managers often restrict sharing even elementary information on a unit's performance and environment.

Moreover, Japanese firms provide the necessary training to insure that employees understand the information being provided. Finally, Japanese managers empower employees to act on such information. By providing this framework in which employees are part of the improvement process, fear of changing existing routines is reduced. "Fearlessness" becomes an extraordinary asset as organizational environments become more uncertain in industry after industry. If the firm can better align itself with its environment and therefore better cope with rapidly changing circumstances, higher-level managers will be more inclined to support participation. One of the authors saw a dramatic visual representation of these themes at the Mazda Hiroshima transmission plant in 1988. A large banner hanging over the assembly line read: "Fear Established Concepts" (*Kyōfu Kisei Gainen*).

The Japanese focus on the customer and "market-in" ties work improvement efforts directly into internal and external customer satisfaction in a way that clearly benefits the company. But what about the workers? The reduced buffers certainly can contribute to more stressful work conditions. Janice Klein reports that when buffers were removed between and within work teams, American workers complained about their loss of team identity and individual freedom.[12]

The reduced buffers and the resultant tightened linkages, however, also have benefits for both workers and the firm. On the positive side, from the company's viewpoint, these practices make error more readily visible and subject to accountability. From the workers' side, customer satisfaction themes provide challenges to which they can relate, thereby reducing the seemingly arbitrary nature of managerial decision making. The emphasis on customer satisfaction tightens perceived connections among quality, job security and employee motivation. In short, employees can see a connection between their own job security and company goals like customer satisfaction and increased market share. These connections also provide an avenue for union cooperation in quality improvement initiatives.

Let us look now at the impact of market-in on management. Market-in increases managers' willingness to support participation in at least three ways. First, it increases participation's perceived utility to managers. The quality improvement methodology involves cascading customer satisfaction and other improvement goals down through the organization, assuring managers and executives that participation is controlled and directed towards important organizational outcomes (thereby also reducing management's fear of changing routines). Because market-in imposes customer requirements on the organization, it underscores the strategic importance of participation for the firm's prosperity and survival. Market-in also speeds response times and helps pinpoint quality problems, thereby reducing throughput time for business processes and insuring prompt delivery for internal and external customers. Managers are only too happy to reap the benefits associated with these activities.

A second way market-in promotes managerial support is by decreasing internal factionalism and increasing cohesion by focusing organizational activity on customer demands and competitor threats.

Third, market-in can enhance managerial commitment to participation through the creation of a common language of customer needs as well as methods and techniques designed to satisfy those needs. Given a common language, all employees regardless of status and department are better able to communicate with one another, and it becomes more credible for everyone to believe that all employees have valuable contributions to make. In the most fundamental sense, it is a common language that creates and sustains the existence of effective social groups and organizations.

The belief that all employees have a valuable contribution to make is important because the market-in approach depends on management's decentralization of decision making and problem-solving activities. Without an ability to make rapid on-the-spot decisions by those involved in the work process, market-in would be an organizational nightmare. There is no time for moving decisions up to higher-level superiors.

Notwithstanding the synergy between market-in and participation, there is no doubt that the focus on using the market as a driver, if not managed in a balanced fashion, can lead to excessive pressure on workers in the name of satisfying customers. Indeed, just this theme has emerged in Japan in recent years, particularly in the auto industry where long working hours have been associated with an excessive emphasis on meeting customer needs. In a rare example of joint positions, both the normally acquiescent Japan Autoworkers Union and the Chairman of the Japan Automobile Dealers Association, Kenichiro

Ueno, recently attributed the current economic problems of the Japanese domestic auto industry to the "excessive desire by manufacturers to maximize customer satisfaction." In particular, an overabundance of model and option variation greatly complicated the work process and created stressful work conditions.

Bringing It All Together

Let us return now to the weaknesses of the Western participation tradition (noted in Table 1), to show how a blending of participation with quality improvement addresses those weaknesses. The responses to the items below overcome the weaknesses at the system/organization level referred to in Table 1. In addition to providing employee rewards (described above), the blending secures managerial support providing an organizational context and focus for participation.

- **Addressing Flabbiness**—Recall that employees are typically unclear about the nature of participative activities as they relate to the work process, and they lack a systematic work improvement methodology. Linking participation to quality addresses all of these issues. The modern quality movement stresses continual quality improvement through better-designed work processes, and it has a well-defined problem-solving methodology. Participation is tied to the achievement of a publicly identified organizational objective: quality. This umbrella theme has intrinsic appeal to employees. At the same time, it has content and concreteness as opposed to the vagueness of the term "participation."

- **Addressing Absence of Strategic Context for Group Activities**—The second major problem with the participation tradition is that the work team is portrayed as context-less; the team is not embedded in the work flow and not linked to a customer. The linkage of participation with quality through a market-in approach insures a strong internal and external customer focus. It is possible to flowchart every work process and identify the process's immediate and/or ultimate customer. By giving the work team the responsibility for job design, the teams become an integral part of the work flow.

In sum, what the Japanese have shown us is that, taken separately, quality and participation are weak concepts with limited potential to transform the firm. But wedded, they are powerful in concept and consequences.

Conclusion

It is our contention that powerful interactive properties exist between a modern approach to quality and participation. This interaction arises because using quality as an umbrella theme for broad-based participation provides a plausible route to improving organizational performance. The connection of participation with organizational performance through quality can attract managerial support for participation, whereas participation alone attracts little support. To pursue participation without quality has proved ineffective, a recipe for failure in today's competitive markets. The most notable example in the U.S. were the failure of many quality circle programs in the early 1980s. These failures resulted from the lack of strong management support, which in turn derived from the flabbiness of the conventional participation concept and the absence of a linkage to the achievement of core business objectives. The linkage of participation with quality not only solves this problem, but the linking of the two can also operate as a significant motivating force for workers. Workers can benefit directly in terms of expanded responsibilities and skills and indirectly in union situations through negotiations to secure their fair share of organizational success.

Japanese and leading Western companies such as Motorola have demonstrated that participation, when framed as an avenue to the highly ranked corporate objectives of quality and waste reduction, becomes a credible organizational approach. This is not to say that we must precisely follow the Japanese formula nor that the particular Japanese way of combining quality with participation is without its problems. To the contrary, customer satisfaction, taken to an extreme, can be coercive and counterproductive. Indeed, in response to such problems some leaders in the Japanese quality movement recently have added to their traditional calls for customer satisfaction (CS), the new slogan CS + ES. That is to say, customer satisfaction must be combined with employee satisfaction. Such adjustments remind us that we should learn from the mistakes of the Japanese as well as their successes.

Finally, preliminary data analysis supports the view that the quality movement has become the major driving force for the participative movement in the United States. In their analysis of the 1987 national survey conducted by GAO, Lawler and associates found that quality accounted for the biggest reason that respondents (72%) gave for adopting employee involvement.[13] Moreover in analyzing this finding, Levine and Kruse discovered that those companies reporting that improving quality was their reason for initiating employee involvement had more success with employee involvement practices than those giving other reasons.[14] Quality was the most consistent correlate of organizational success as measured by increased productivity, worker satisfaction, customer service, competitiveness, employee quality of worklife, profitability and lower turnover and absenteeism. In short, initial data analysis supports our interpretation that linking employee participation initiatives to the quality initiative can yield strong positive results for the firm. We enhance managerial and worker acceptance by using quality to refocus participatory initiatives towards more organizational-level outcomes. In so doing, we increase the probability of bottom-line results for the firm. This, in turn, further increases managerial and worker acceptance thereby creating a "virtuous cycle."

Endnotes

1 . See, for example, Thomas Bailey, "Discretionary Effort and the Organization of Work: Employee Participation and Work Reform Since Hawthorne," paper prepared for the Sloan Foundation, August 1992.

2. For descriptions of the new quality paradigm, see Kaoru Ishikawa, *What is Quality Control* (Englewood Cliffs, N.J.: Prentice-Hall, 1985); Joseph Juran, *Juran on Leadership for Quality* (New York: The Free Press, 1989); and Shigeru Mizuno, *Company-Wide Total Quality Control* (Tokyo: Asian Productivity Organization, 1988).

3. For an overview of the various characteristics, see Peter Dachler and Bernhard Wilpert, "Conceptual Dimensions and Boundaries of Participation in Organizations: A Critical Evaluation," *Administrative Science Quarterly,* 23 (1978): 1-39.

4. Edward Lawler III, Gerald Ledford, Jr., and Susan Mohrman, *Employee Involvement in America* (Houston: American Productivity and Quality Center, 1989).

5. David Levine and Laura Tyson, "Participation, Productivity, and the Firm's Environment," in *Paying for Productivity* (Washington DC: Brookings Institution, 1990), pp. 203-204.

6. Bailey, op. cit., p. 51.

7. David Levine, "Public Policy Implications of Imperfections in the Market for Worker Participation," *Economic and Industrial Democracy,* 13 (1992): 183-206.

8. Edwin Locke and David Schweiger, "Participation in Decision-making: One More Look" in Barry Staw, ed., *Research in Organizational Behavior,* 1 (Greenwich, CT: JAI Press, 1979), pp. 265-339.

9. Robert E. Cole, *Work, Mobility & Participation* (Berkeley, CA: University of California Press, 1979), pp. 101-113.

10. Masahiko Aoki, *Information, Incentives, and Bargaining in the Japanese Economy* (Cambridge: Cambridge University Press, 1988).

11. John Stinesen, "T50 Seminarium med ABB: Kompetensutveckling Nyckelord For Ny Industriell Revolution," [T50 Seminar with ABB: Competence Development, a Key Term for the New Industrial Revolution] *Nya Verkstads Forum,* 1 (February 1992): 11-12.

12. Janice Klein, "The Human Costs of Manufacturing Reform," *Harvard Business Review,* 67(1984): 60-66.

13. Ibid.; Lawler et al., op. cit.

14. David Levine and Douglas Kruse, "Employee Involvement Efforts: Incidence, Correlates and Effects," unpublished manuscript, University of California, Berkeley, 1990.

Designed for Learning: A Tale of Two Auto Plants

Reading 6.3
Paul S. Adler
Robert E. Cole

A consensus is emerging that the hallmark of tomorrow's most effective organizations will be their capacity to learn. To survive in the competitive turbulence that is engulfing a growing number of industries, firms will need to pinpoint innovative practices rapidly, to communicate them to their employees and suppliers, and to stimulate further innovation.

However, there are two very different views on the organizational design most effective to support learning, particularly in labor-intensive production of relatively standardized products.[1] Proponents of the Japanese-inspired "lean production" model, such as the MIT researchers who contributed to *The Machine That Changed the World*, argue that organizational learning will be maximized in a system based on specialized work tasks supplemented by modest doses of job rotation and great discipline in the definition and implementation of detailed work procedures.[2] By contrast, European managers, union officials, and academics are engaged in a lively discussion on the possibility of a German-Scandinavian alternative.[3] Proponents of this "human-centered" model argue that organizational adaptability and learning is best served by greatly lengthened work cycles and a return to craftlike work forms that give teams substantial latitude in how they perform their tasks and authority over what have traditionally been higher-level management decisions.

Toyota is often credited with pioneering the key elements of the lean production model. In the United States, the best documented of Toyota's

The Toyota-GM joint venture, NUMMI, and Volvo's Uddevalla plant represent two different ways of organizing the labor-intensive production of standardized products, in this case, auto assembly. NUMMI is based on the Japanese "lean production" model, whereas Uddevalla has been called a "human-centered" model. Which model can best stimulate continuous improvement while maintaining worker morale? The authors argue that the answer is, emphatically, NUMMI.

plants is the Toyota-General Motors (GM) joint venture, the New United Motor Manufacturing, Inc. (NUMMI) plant in California. Volvo's Uddevalla plant exemplifies the human-centered alternative. It is one of Volvo's most innovative plants, radically extending the long-cycle and team autonomy concepts that shaped the famous Kalmar plant.[4]

In November 1992, Volvo announced that it would close the Uddevalla and Kalmar plants, but these plant closings should not close the debate over the significance of their innovations. The two plants are not being shut down due to poor performance. In fact, Kalmar operated at productivity and quality levels higher than those at Volvo's main Torslanda plant, and Uddevalla was already matching Torslanda in productivity. However, Volvo was operating at very low capacity utilization levels, and managers believed that shutting down the two smaller plants was an effective way to reduce total overhead. Although Volvo's innovations in work organization will continue in some of its truck and component plants, the closing of these two plants will end a remarkable twenty-five year period in which Volvo's efforts to humanize and democratize work inspired managers, union officials, and academics around the world. The concept of self-managing teams so popular in the United States today owes much to these two plants, as does the design of GM's Saturn plant. Whether the advocates of work reorganization within Volvo will be able to refocus their efforts on reforming Volvo's other facilities remains to be seen. Whatever the case, there is much to be learned from the Kalmar and Uddevalla experience.

Between us, we have studied firsthand a number of Toyota's Japanese plants, the NUMMI facility, and several Volvo facilities, including Uddevalla. In this article, we assess the relative merits of NUMMI and Uddevalla as organizations designed to support learning. In brief, we argue that, although elements of the Uddevalla approach do indeed promise a higher potential for *individual* learning, NUMMI is the more effective model for encouraging *organizational* learning. The NUMMI model thus assures a higher growth rate for productivity and manufacturing quality. Proponents of the Uddevalla model argue that the NUMMI model's purported technical strengths will be overshadowed by its lack of opportunities for personal development and that its regimentation will undercut worker motivation. We believe that this critique is misconceived and that the intense discipline created by NUMMI's job design creates not only world-class performance but also a highly motivating work environment.

First, we describe some of the key aspects of the two plants' organizational designs. Then, we compare their performance results and identify some technical factors that may contribute to these results. Finally, we closely examine the social factors and critique some popular misapprehensions about the sources of motivation and of organizational learning.

Comparing Organizational Designs ————————————————

NUMMI and Uddevalla are similar in several important respects. They are both truly committed to treating employees as their most important assets and to providing opportunities for employee growth. For both plants, governance is accomplished by a relatively strong partnership between union and management. Finally, they are both organized around production teams.

But the similarities give way to important differences when we examine the internal organizations more closely. The NUMMI and Uddevalla production teams are very different. At NUMMI, teams are composed of four or five workers under a team leader, and both team members and team leaders are hourly workers. Each team member performs a work cycle of about sixty seconds. In the final assembly department, the teams are linked in series, in a traditional "Fordist" assembly line pattern. Toyota's just-in-time inventory system ensures that this interdependence is very taut. Teams take on responsibilities not normally the province of line workers in U.S. auto plants, in particular for quality assurance, preventive maintenance, and internal job rotation schedules. They also define work methods and standards, but must satisfy managers and engineers that these methods and standards are optimal and that they are implemented identically across workers and shifts. Although such worker involvement in defining methods violates Frederick Taylor's principles of "scientific management," the resulting job designs are very Tayloristic in their narrow scope and gesture-by-gesture regimentation.

At Uddevalla, the break with Taylorism and Fordism was deliberate and radical. The plant's model evolved at a time when Volvo was experiencing a production capacity bottleneck in a protected market with no efficient Japanese competitors for its niche. In the mid-1980s, Volvo was selling everything it could make, and lack of productive capacity was the problem. The major constraint in breaking the capacity bottleneck was the tight Swedish labor market. The design of the Uddevalla plant was labor-market driven, not product-market driven. As one of the key managers involved in the plant design expressed it, "The problem we had was how could we make the plant attractive for Swedish workers to want to work in it."

In the newly designed plant, each of eight production teams took full responsibility for assembling the vehicle from the subsystems up—a work cycle of about two hours. The plant abolished the assembly line, as the eight teams worked in parallel. The teams were larger, ten people as opposed to four or five at NUMMI, and they had much broader responsibilities than at NUMMI. Because the work cycle was so long, Uddevalla teams paid much less attention than NUMMI teams to detailed, gesture-by-gesture standardization and instead focused on the more aggregated balance of tasks within the whole assembly cycle.

Not only did Uddevalla teams decide job rotation schedules, they also selected their own hires and decided on their own overtime schedules. At NUMMI, union representatives and managers jointly select team leaders based on objective tests, whereas at Uddevalla, teams selected their own leaders and often rotated the role.

Both organizations put great stock in worker training. NUMMI has invested considerable time and effort training workers in the principles and techniques of its production system, but it offers no pay premium for the accumulation of new skills. At Uddevalla, team members' pay increased with the accumulation of proved expertise.

Comparing Performance Results ————————————————

NUMMI took over the old GM plant in Fremont and hired about 85 percent of its workforce from the ranks of laid-off GM-Fremont workers. Pilot production began in December 1984, and by 1986, NUMMI was almost as productive as its sister Toyota plant in Takaoka and more productive than any other GM plant. Total hourly and salaried hours per vehicle averaged 20.8 at NUMMI in 1986, as opposed to 18.0 in Takaoka, 40.7 in the relatively comparable GM-Framingham plant, and 43.1 at the old GM-Fremont plant in 1978. Inventory levels averaged two days, which was significantly below U.S. auto industry averages, but still above the two-hour level prevailing in Takaoka, primarily due to difficulties in running true just-in-time inventory with suppliers in Japan and the U.S. midwest.[5]

More recent data indicate that this extraordinary performance was not merely a honeymoon phenomenon. According to a J.D. Power and Associates study of the number of problems per 100 vehicles experienced by customers within ninety days of purchase, NUMMI scored 116 in 1989, compared to an industry average of 148 for all cars sold in the United States. The number of problems went up in 1990 with the introduction of Geo Prizm and new domestic suppliers but then decreased to 93 in 1991 and to 83 in 1992 (when the industry average was 125 for all cars sold in the United States and the average for Asian nameplates was 105; for U.S. nameplates, 136; and for Europeans, 158).[6]

What of NUMMI's quality of worklife? Here, too, the indicators are very impressive:

- Absenteeism has held steady at about 3 percent.

- Participation in the suggestion program had increased to over 90 percent by 1991, and workers made over 10,000 suggestions that year, an average of about 5 suggestions per worker. The implementation rate for these suggestions was over 80 percent, which reflects as much or more on NUMMI's policy of encouraging involvement as on the quality of the suggestions themselves.

- Internal surveys of worker attitudes showed that the overall proportion of people describing themselves as satisfied or very satisfied with their job at NUMMI had increased from 76 percent in 1987 to 85 percent in 1989 to 90 percent in 1991.

How does this compare with the Uddevalla plant? Unfortunately, the data here are sketchy:

- According to a *New York Times* article, it took fifty hours to assemble a vehicle at Uddevalla as opposed to an average of twenty-two hours for Japanese plants in the United States.[7] When we visited the plant in the summer of 1991, the plant manager claimed that these data were old and that the plant had already reached the productivity of the Torslanda plant, which this *Times* article estimated at forty hours per vehicle. Even adjusting for the larger size of the vehicles produced at Uddevalla, the productivity differential would be substantial. (Unfortunately, we have no comparable quality data on Uddevalla's output.)

- Although absenteeism was half that of Volvo's main plant at Torslanda, it was still very high: sick leave absences averaged about 12 percent in 1990 and long-term disability about 10 percent, for a total of about 22 percent, compared to 3 percent absenteeism at NUMMI. Uddevalla workers benefited from much more generous sick leave provisions, and it is possible that NUMMI's strictness on absenteeism does not allow workers sufficient flexibility to balance work- and non-worklife. It is nevertheless clear that Uddevalla's worklife did not provide sufficient intrinsic satisfaction to overcome the long-standing Swedish tradition of high absenteeism rates.

- Turnover was high during Uddevalla's startup because some workers without industrial work experience did not accommodate to the pressures of the very demanding work in auto assembly. However, turnover settled at about 6 percent by 1991. This figure is comparable to NUMMI's, but turnover, like absenteeism, is influenced by many factors outside the plant's control.

- More telling, perhaps, was a 1992 survey of worker satisfaction across Volvo plants, which revealed that Uddevalla scored in a similar range to the very traditional Torslanda plant. This was a big disappointment to management, which could only argue that it was the reflection of the workers' high expectations. This argument has some merit, but such a score also suggests that craft-style production may have been idealized by Uddevalla's designers and oversold as a cure to the ills of modern labor.

Perhaps we too have succumbed to this idealized view because we think that Uddevalla, not NUMMI, would be the more desirable place to work. Uddevalla offers a much less regimented environment, more task variety, more autonomy, and a lot more team self-management. However, there is little doubt as to which production system is capable of delivering the greatest efficiency and quality: it is NUMMI.[8] In fact, one Volvo executive we interviewed stated flatly that Uddevalla would not have been built under today's circumstances, and it would be hard to find others at Volvo who would disagree. The context that produced Uddevalla has changed. The labor bottleneck has disappeared and efficient Japanese competitors are hurting Volvo in its export markets.

The question remains, Is the technical and economic superiority of the NUMMI system achieved at the expense of workers' well-being?

Interpreting the Results: Some Methodological Difficulties ———————

Critics of the lean production system argue that it does not provide a viable model for production organization. Two variants of the criticism have been articulated. One line of criticism argues that, in the lean system, workers are forced to work under excessive stress.[9] As a result, their motivation to ensure world-class quality and their participation in the *kaizen* (continuous improvement) process will eventually taper off, and the potential benefits of standardized, narrow jobs will be outweighed by the costs of worker disaffection. An alternative hypothesis assumes that workers will continue to participate in *kaizen* efforts frequently enough to ensure its productive superiority, but they will do so only out of fear of losing their jobs. Thus their bodies and minds are put under excessive stress, and many workers will quit their jobs exhausted after a few years, leaving society to pay the costs of this premature depreciation of our human resources.

Some observers have presented *prima facie* evidence for one or the other of these scenarios and jump to the conclusion that NUMMI's production system is just a new way of further intensifying work effort, a form of ultra Taylorism.[10] Kamata's description of his experience as a temporary worker in Toyota City in the early 1970s and Fucini and Fucini's description of the Mazda Flat Rock plant, for example, are cited as evidence supporting this characterization.[11] Parker and Slaughter have compiled an impressive dossier on the stress experienced by workers in some team concept plants.[12]

But it is not easy to draw strong conclusions from the anecdotal evidence available. Public debate and scholarly research both confront a number of methodological challenges in sorting out the relative merits of the alternative systems. First, many conceptions of the stressful, ergonomically unsound Japanese factory are based on old descriptions and images. In a recent systematic comparison of the Japanese and American auto industries, Richard Wokutch concluded that in spite of several significant weaknesses, safety and health conditions and practices in *large* Japanese auto firms were superior in many important respects to those in comparable American firms.[13]

Second, not all Japanese plants and transplants are identical. We should not assume that a practice found at one can be extrapolated to all. We should not assume that "good practices" at NUMMI are necessarily representative of all transplants or for that matter that they are even representative of all Toyota plants. Good case can be made that the Japanese have been forced to modify the harsher aspects of their production system to make them more compatible with the expectations of Western workers. In this article, we focus on the NUMMI version of the Japanese production model.

Third, problems observed at a plant at a given point in time may not be inherent in the underlying model. For example, Uddevalla experienced a high rate of turnover during its startup, but this was for reasons that are largely unrelated to the central debate. A fair assessment should assume that both approaches are capable of learning and evolution.

Fourth, it is important to avoid the frequent polemic device of shifting the point of comparison. From the worker's perspective, production systems at Japanese transplants like NUMMI are far from ideal, but the ideal is a rather remote comparison point, and we need to use realistic comparison points to make reasonable assessments.

Finally, if the debate is over the merits of alternative production system designs, we should filter out as much as possible other, unrelated aspects of management. Some Japanese transplants, for example, have been criticized for discriminatory employment practices and for the difficult relations between U.S. managers and Japanese shadow managers.[14] These management problems are often real and serious, but an alternative explanation is that these problems are symptomatic of Japanese firms' inexperience in international operations.[15] Some of these practices do indeed appear racist, but it is certainly racist to assume that they are inherent features of Japanese management.

Interpreting the Results: Technical Aspects ————————————————

To what then is NUMMI's productive superiority due? In particular, can this superiority be attributed to excessive stress imposed on workers? Our research suggests that the primary factor is NUMMI's effort to constantly improve the details of the production process. Such constant improvement is the key to productivity and quality in a product as standardized as an automobile. This constant improvement effort creates a certain level of stress, but as the worker attitude surveys show, the level is not so high as to degenerate into strain and distress.

Workers at both NUMMI and Uddevalla were encouraged to seek out improvements. And to help them, both groups received feedback on their task performance over their respective work cycles. But Toyota's standardized work system makes this feedback far more effective in sustaining improvement. At NUMMI, the work cycle is about sixty seconds long, and performance of the cycle is very standardized. Therefore, it is easy to identify problems, define improvement opportunities, and implement improved processes.

Uddevalla workers, too, had detailed information on their work cycle performance, but as this cycle was some two hours long, they had no way to track their task performance at a more detailed level. This problem was exacerbated by the craft model of work organization that encouraged Uddevalla workers to believe that they should have considerable latitude in how they performed each cycle.

Some proponents of the Uddevalla design principles argue that it offers a way around the line-balancing problems that limit the efficiency of traditional sequential assembly lines.[16] But NUMMI effectively resolves those problems through a combination of modest doses of worker flexibility (far less extensive than Uddevalla's) and aggressive efforts to reduce set-up times. The standardization of detailed work methods facilitates efforts to reduce set-up times. Moreover, as the variety of models produced in a given plant increases, it becomes increasingly difficult for workers to recall the right procedure for each job, and shorter cycle times with well-defined methods help assure quality. As a result, NUMMI's assembly line can handle a relatively broad range of product types with minimal disruption.

Could the semiautonomous work teams at Uddevalla have come to see shorter work cycles and formalized methods as a better way and adopted it autonomously? Although Uddevalla had a bonus system that encouraged work teams to improve performance continually, the teams had neither the focus on the kinds of microscopic *kaizen* opportunities that drive NUMMI performance (because of Uddevalla's long work cycle) nor the tools to capture these opportunities (because they lacked standardized work processes). To the contrary, in fall 1991, we were informed that there was no detailed documentation available to workers describing how to perform each work task and specifying how long it should take. One of the Uddevalla workers we interviewed argued, "You don't really need all that detail because you can feel it when the task isn't going right; you can feel the sticking points yourself." But workers at Uddevalla had no mechanism for identifying, testing, or diffusing the improvements that individual workers might make to eliminate these sticking points. The engineering staff from different work areas met to share new ideas. But without a well-documented, standardized process, it is hard to imagine how these people could have spotted improvement opportunities or shared them across the teams. You cannot sustain continual improvement in the production of products as standardized as automobiles without clear and detailed methods and standards.

Interpreting the Results: Human Aspects —————————————

The key points of contention in the debate over the human aspects of the competing models are work design and the broader plant governance process. Let us compare NUMMI and Uddevalla on these dimensions.

NUMMI's work organization follows what we have called the "democratic Taylorism" model.[17] As Frederick Taylor and modern industrial

engineering practice recommend, jobs are specialized and work processes are standardized to the extent justified by the repetitiveness of the
production task. But unlike traditional "despotic Taylorism," NUMMI's
methods and standards are not designed to squeeze more work out of
employees that management assumes are recalcitrant and irresponsible.
Instead, these methods and standards are determined by work teams
themselves: workers are taught how to time their own jobs with a stop-
watch, compare alternative procedures to determine the most efficient
one, document the standard procedure to ensure that everyone can
understand and implement it, and identify and propose improvements
in that procedure. At any given time, the task of standardized work
analysis might be delegated to a team leader or a team member, but
everyone understands the analysis process and can participate in it.

At Uddevalla, work teams were left to their own devices. In the very
early days of Uddevalla, managers gave workers the procedure documents from the Torslanda plant. But these procedures were not very well
designed, as Torslanda is a traditional plant where workers play no role
in defining procedures. As a result, the Uddevalla workers quickly dis-
carded them and, along with them, the very idea of detailed methods
and standards. In auto assembly operations, where competitiveness
hinges so greatly on efficiency and manufacturing quality, this management philosophy sounds more like abandonment than empowerment.

There is one aspect of work design where we believe Uddevalla had
the edge over NUMMI. Uddevalla's "pay for knowledge" system provided substantial incentives for workers to build a deeper and broader
knowledge base. The United Auto Workers (UAW) contract at NUMMI
does not allow such individualized pay systems. But here NUMMI is
behind the practices of Japanese assembly plants, which have an elabo-
rate system of skill grades as well as individual merit evaluations.[18]
These evaluations (*satei*) have been characterized by critics as a manipulative tool of management control.[19] Indeed, in the absence of a strong
union, such manipulative use seems likely, and there is indeed evidence
of such use in Japan. But if management wants workers to contribute
innovative ideas—to act as knowledge workers—then reward systems
will need to be redesigned to look more like those used for knowledge
workers, such as the skill-and-merit systems typically used to reward
engineers.[20] Clearly, if these systems are to be successful, they will need
to be implemented with the careful attention to equity that managers
usually show in dealing with knowledge workers.

The second key dimension of comparison is at the plant governance
level. Uddevalla had a democratic form of plant governance in which the
union played a strong role in shaping the plant's design and operating
policies.[21] NUMMI, too, has relatively democratic plant governance. The
union actively participates in a broad range of policy decisions that were
previously closely guarded management prerogatives. Union and management representatives jointly investigate all problems; management

has committed to advance consultation with the union on layoffs, schedule changes, and major investments; and management and the union jointly review any unusual or mitigating circumstances before employees are discharged or suspended. When workers objected to favoritism in the selection of team leaders, the union negotiated a selection process with an explicit set of criteria and a joint union-management selection committee.

Critics of NUMMI's system argue that the absence of firm, explicit contract language and the extent of informal, cooperative problem solving at NUMMI are symptomatic of a degeneration into "company unionism." We argue, to the contrary, that any democratization of plant governance inevitably must draw the union into greater partnership, and the Local leadership's effectiveness in representing worker interests in this new setting depends on management's commitment to cooperation as well as on the Local leaders' skills, the level of internal Local democracy, and the resources and guidance provided by the International. NUMMI's record in these areas is certainly not flawless, but nevertheless justifies strong optimism.[22]

But the critics' concerns can then be restated: Can the NUMMI model, with the corresponding UAW influence and involvement, be sustained? And can it diffuse to other parts of U.S. industry? The critics can advance two arguments for their skepticism. First, the pattern of industrial relations we observe in Japanese industry might suggest that "company unionism" is the more "natural" counterpart to the Japanese-style production system. Second, the current industrial relations climate in the United States and the prevailing hostility to unions and to union-management cooperation put severe pressure on cooperation at NUMMI and create barriers to the diffusion of this cooperative model.

Our hopes for the future of the NUMMI model are based on the evidence suggesting that firms or regions that can sustain the more democratic variant of the lean model are well positioned to outcompete those that cannot. While the evidence for both sides of this debate is sketchy, we believe that it supports the argument that in the absence of strong, independent unions, the Japanese-style production system risks sliding into a despotic and less productive mode:

- The institutionalization of strong worker "voice" seems to contribute significantly to NUMMI's world-class performance.[23]

- By contrast, in Toyota plants in Japan, worker voice is more muted and more often subordinated to corporate interests.[24] This situation contributes to the maintenance of difficult working conditions reflected in poor ergonomics, excessive overtime, and stressful pressures, especially in small subcontract firms. These difficult working conditions relative to other industries make it difficult to recruit new workers, thus undermining the viability of the Japanese variant of the Toyota production System.[25]

- Strong worker voice is difficult to sustain absent independent unions. In the United States, those nonunion plants that do afford workers a real voice often appear to do so as part of a union-avoidance strategy. Where these "progressive" personnel policies are due instead to the genuine humanism of the plant manager, the resulting employee relations system is fragile since workers can easily conclude that their influence is only accepted at the discretion of management and within the limits circumscribed by management.

To summarize this section, then, if we ask whether NUMMI provides as much scope as Uddevalla for the development of workers' human potential, our answer remains, unfortunately, no. But does it create an oppressive, alienating, stultifying work environment? The answer must be, emphatically, no.

If Uddevalla's productivity and quality potential were close to NUMMI's, then its human advantages would tip the scale in Uddevalla's favor. A small gap in productivity and quality could be overcome easily by judicious public policy support. The available evidence suggests, however, that: (1) Uddevalla was not within striking difference of NUMMI's productivity and quality, and (2) NUMMI's quality of worklife, although not ideal, is in the "acceptable" range as far as workers are concerned. We conclude that Uddevalla, if it had survived, would have had to evolve in dramatically new directions in order to qualify as a viable option.

Challenging Underlying Assumptions _____

The goal of Uddevalla's work organization was to create a "new profession of car-builder" based on "a model drawn from the system of craftsmen and guilds, with apprentices, journeymen, and masters."[26] The assumption underlying this approach is that a work organization based on narrow tasks and detailed standards is intrinsically dehumanizing. We believe that the NUMMI case shows this assumption to be wrong. NUMMI's approach to standardized work shows that Tayloristic efforts to define the technically optimal "one best way" are not necessarily weapons used by management to extract maximal effort from a recalcitrant workforce. In fact, there are three ways that the knowledge required to make improvements can be used: (1) by management, coercively forcing ever-higher levels of work intensity; (2) by workers, covertly using that knowledge to reduce their own work effort (back to the "soldiering" observed by Taylor!); and (3) by the joint efforts of workers, managers, and engineers to fuel a continuous improvement of efficiency and quality without intensifying work beyond workers' capacities. We believe that the NUMMI case demonstrates that the third option is possible. Practices in Japanese plants and in other "lean" transplants probably vary considerably in this respect, but NUMMI shows that continuous improvement does not have to be based on an escalating appropriation of workers' know-how.

The contrast between Uddevalla and NUMMI also leads us to challenge a second widely held assumption: that world class performance can be based only on very high intrinsic work satisfaction. It would be wonderful if we lived in a world where every job could be an opportunity for Maslovian self-actualization. But when products are fairly standard and mass produced, and when automation is still not cheap enough to eliminate labor-intensive methods of production, then efficiency requires narrowly specialized job assignments and formalized standard methods—a form of work organization that precludes the very high intrinsic work satisfaction that would, for example, stimulate workers to come in without pay on a day off to tackle a production problem. Is this equation merely the result of "corporate greed" as some critics contend? We think not: any community that needs such standardized goods will object to paying the exorbitant costs associated with an inefficient and poor-quality production organization.

As we have argued, the quality of worklife in such industries can be much improved by democratizing the work design and business governance processes. Clearly these changes leave work in the category of "instrumental necessity" rather than "self-actualization opportunity." NUMMI shows us, however, that even when work has a basically instrumental function for workers, it can be organized to sustain both a moderately high level of worker motivation and world-class performance.[27]

A third assumption built into the Uddevalla approach and one that underlies much of Western industry is that an increase in individual learning automatically leads to an increase in organizational learning. This is a fundamental fallacy. The Japanese model does not take organizational learning as a given; managers consciously work to create policies and practices that facilitate it.[28]

Uddevalla designed an extremely impressive range of personal learning opportunities for its employees. Workers spent the first sixteen months developing basic skills, then progressively learned all the jobs on their teams until they could build the entire car themselves. Then they went on to develop teacher competence, team spokesperson competence, and skills in other managerial and engineering areas. But this emphasis on individual learning had no counterpart in organizational learning. Team autonomy and decision decentralization were Uddevalla's central design objectives. As a consequence, little thought was given to how work groups might learn from one another to facilitate continuous improvement. Indeed, in an interview we conducted, the plant design project leader described how the planning team ignored the need for cross-group, organizational learning: "We didn't put much thought into how to learn from other groups. Our focus was on building jobs bigger—to lengthen and widen the job; that was what we were aiming for."

In contrast, the Japanese production model explicitly focuses on strategies for organizational learning. Standardization of work methods is a precondition for achieving this end—you cannot identify the sources of problems in a process you have not standardized. Standardization captures best practice and facilitates the diffusion of improvement ideas throughout the organization—you cannot diffuse what you have not standardized. And standardization stimulates improvement—every worker is now something of an industrial engineer. At NUMMI, the skill development strategies for individual workers are managed as a component of this process, rather than as a way of maximizing personal opportunities. As a result, training focuses on developing *deeper* knowledge, not only of the relatively narrow jobs but also of the logic of the production system, statistical process control, and problem-solving processes. Understanding a *broader* range of jobs—the focus of Uddevalla's skill development approach—is recognized as an important stimulus to *kaizen* efforts, but this broadening of skills builds on, rather than replaces, the standardized work process and the deepening of skills. Our study of NUMMI suggests that management may not be sufficiently attentive to the importance of planned skill broadening, but the sister Japanese plants systematically rotate workers through related departments over a period of years.

Conclusion

We have argued that NUMMI's combination of technical-economic and quality-of-worklife strengths makes its production system the most appropriate type for relatively repetitive, labor-intensive activities like auto assembly. It is worth asking whether this system will be undermined by the progressive automation of these activities, by changing worker expectations, and by the shift toward volatile markets, lower volumes, and greater product variety. Was Uddevalla simply ahead of its time?

At first sight, the recent innovations at Nissan's new Kyushu plant seem to support such speculation. In response to labor conditions—a tight Japanese labor market, the difficulty of attracting workers to auto assembly, and long-term projections of labor shortages—Nissan has eliminated the conveyer belt, has installed significantly more automation, and is using many of the ergonomic job designs that characterized Uddevalla.[29] Toyota's new Tahara plant embodies many similar innovations. Indeed, Japanese auto executives were among the most frequent visitors to Uddevalla.

But these new plant designs do not suggest that the Japanese are switching to an Uddevalla model. First, ergonomic work task designs are a distinguishing feature not of the Swedish model but of enlightened management faced with tight labor markets. Second, the work cycle has remained short and very standardized. Third, with lower volumes and greater product variety, the natural learning curve effect is even less reliable, and these plants will therefore pursue even more aggressive standardized work efforts to ensure efficiency and quality.

The more appropriate lesson to draw is that both the lean production system and the Uddevalla alternative have extensive room to evolve and develop. If Uddevalla had survived, it would have had to evolve in dramatically new ways to be competitive in productivity and quality. Whether it would have done so quickly enough and whether it would have retained its distinctive worker-oriented features is unclear.

In the case of the lean production system, we expect that it will evolve to be more employee oriented. In Japanese plants, managers will need to adjust to the long-term prospects of labor shortage and to changes in worker expectations as Japanese seek to enjoy more of the rewards of their extraordinary hard work. In Japanese production system plants outside Japan, the speed of this shift toward more employee orientation will depend on local factors. But the combination of standardized work and more democratic management has proven potent at NUMMI in its ability to sustain both continuous improvement and worker morale. It might well represent the model for the next generation of labor-intensive, mass-production activities.

Endnotes ————————————————————————————

Our thanks to J.D. Power and Associates for permission to reproduce copyrighted data. Their unauthorized reproduction is prohibited.

1. By contrast, there is now a rather strong consensus on the organizational designs required to support learning in more automated settings and where product designs or services change very frequently. On automated settings, see: P.S. Adler, ed., *Technology and the Future of Work* (New York: Oxford University Press, 1992). On settings where designs or services frequently change, see: S. Davis and W. Davidson, *2020 Vision* (New York; Simon & Schuster, 1991).

2. J.P. Womack, D.T. Jones, and D. Roos, *The Machine That Changed the World* (New York: Rawson, 1990).

3. See F. Naschold, *Evaluation Report Commissioned by the Board of the LOM Programme* (Berlin: Science Center, 1992), pp. 2-3; and C. Berggren, *Alternatives to Lean Production* (Ithaca, New York: ILR Press, 1992).

4. See R.R. Rehder, "Building Cars As If People Mattered," *Columbia Journal of World Business,* Summer 1992, pp. 57-70; and C. Berggren (1992).

5. J. Krafcik, "Learning from NUMMI" (Cambridge, Massachusetts: MIT Sloan School of Management, International Motor Vehicle Program, Working Paper, 1986).

6. *Power Report,* June 1992. Revised data for earlier years provided by J.D. Power and Associates.

7. "Edgar Fray on Volvo's Brave New Humanistic World," *New York*

Times, 7 July 1991, p. F5.

8. One caveat to this conclusion should be mentioned: the productivity and quality performance data are strongly influenced by the manufacturability of the respective vehicle designs. Toyota products' manufacturability has been ranked the best in the industry, whereas Volvo has been ranked fifteenth. See: J. Krafcik, "The Effect of Design Manufacturability on Productivity and Quality: An Update of the IMVP Assembly Plant Study" (Cambridge, Massachusetts: MIT Sloan School of Management, International Motor Vehicle Program, Working Paper, 1990).

9. See M. Parker and J. Slaughter, *Choosing Sides: Unions and the Team Concept* (Boston, Massachusetts: South End Press, 1988).

10. K. Dohse, U. Jurgens, and T. Malsch, "From Fordism to Toyotism? The Social Organization of the Labor Process in the Japanese Automobile Industry," *Politics and Society* 14 (1985): 115-146.

11. S. Kamata, *Japan in the Passing Lane* (New York: Random House, 1983); and J. Fucini and S. Fucini, *Working for the Japanese* (New York: Free Press, 1990).

12. Parker and Slaughter (1988).

13. R. Wokutch, *Worker Protection, Japanese Style: Occupational Safety and Health in the Auto Industry* (Ithaca, New York: ILR Press, 1992), p. 225.

14. See, for example, Fucini and Fucini (1990); and R. Cole, "Nihon kigyo yo, kokujin koyo no judaisei o shire" (Be aware of the importance of black employment in Japanese firms), *Chou Koron*, 10 October 1989.

15. R. Cole, "Racial Factors in Site Location and Employment Patterns of Japanese Auto Firms in America," *California Management Review*, Fall 1988, pp. 9-22.

16. K. Ellegard, T. Engstrom, and L. Nilsson, *Reforming Industrial Work: Principles and Reality* (Stockholm: Swedish Work Environment Fund, 1991).

17. P.S. Adler, "The Learning Bureaucracy: New United Motors Manufacturing, Inc.," in *Research in Organizational Behavior*, eds. B.M. Staw and L.L. Cummings (Greenwich, Connecticut: JAI Press, 1992).

18. K. Koike, "Learning and Incentive Systems in Japanese Industry" (Paper presented to the conference "Japan in a Global Economy: A European Perspective," held at Stockholm School of Economics, 5-6 September 1991).

19. K. Endo, "*Satei* (Personal Assessment) and Inter-Worker Competition in Japanese Firms," *Industrial Relations*, in press.

20. Koike (1991).

21. C. Brown and M. Reich, "When Does Cooperation Work? A Look at NUMMI and GM-Van Nuys," *California Management Review*, Summer 1989, pp. 26-37.

22. Adler (1992).

23. R.B. Freeman and J.L. Medoff, *What Do Unions Do?* (New York: Basic

Books, 1984).

24. R. Cole, *Work Mobility and Participation* (Berkeley: University of California Press, 1979).

25. "More Japanese Workers Demanding Shorter Hours and Less Hectic Work," *New York Times*, 3 March 1992, p. A6.

26. Ellegard et al. (1991), p. 25.

27. See P.S. Adler, "Time-and-Motion Regained," *Harvard Business Review*, January-February 1993, pp. 97-108.

28. R. Cole, "Different Quality Paradigms and Their Implications for Organizational Learning" (Paper presented to the conference "Japan in a Global Economy: A European Perspective," held at Stockholm School of Economics, 5-6 September 1991).

29. "Factory Fantasia," *Automotive News*, 13 July 1992, pp. 3, 31; and "Japan Lures Auto Workers with 'Dream' Factories," *New York Times*, 20 July 1992, pp. A1, D2.

How to Implement Total Quality Management in Strong Cultures: Alignment or Saturation?

Case 6.1
Asbjorn Osland

General Description

LITEP, Inc. is a family controlled U.S. based multinational corporation with very extensive production operations in Latin America that produce LITEP for industrialized markets, mainly North America and Europe. The company is one of the four major players in the industry. Several production divisions are located in the Central American country of Morazan. Each employs approximately 5,500 employees of whom around 500 are salaried; the rest are union members. LITEP, Inc. is the largest private employer in the country. During the 1980s the only areas of the country that developed economically, in real terms, were those located around the production divisions. LITEP, Inc. pays close to twenty million dollars each year in export and payroll taxes to the government of Morazan, a large contribution to the economy. LITEP is a labor intensive tropical export product.

The divisions are economies of scale operations. They are focused on exported volume of high quality LITEP. Quality is vital to the customer and volume is the key to lowering costs and increasing efficiency and productivity. This tension between a strategic emphasis on low-cost, commodity-like production versus maintaining market share through the sale of high quality LITEP is resolved through high volume production to dilute costs.

Historically the company provided hospitals, schools, public utilities, recreational facilities, airports, roads, and other such components of a community's infrastructure. However, the move to withdraw from the provision of infrastructure began more than 20 years ago and has continued. LITEP, Inc. has been attempting to confine itself to the production

Source: This article was written especially for this book. Reprinted by permission of the author.

of high quality LITEP and interact with the surrounding community as a production partner rather than a paternalistic total institution. However, the village-like social environments around the divisions continue to be relatively closed, comparable to those found in old logging or mining communities throughout the world. The distinction between one's work and social roles are blurred in such company towns; one's status in the community reflects one's position in the company. The company is very figural in the gestalt of workers' lives.

Adoption of Total Quality Management within LITEP, Inc. _____

Throughout the 80's and 90's a number of different measures had been taken by LITEP, Inc. to improve quality, including the following: (1) a quality coordinator was named for the region to provide consultation to troubled areas and diffuse innovations to production operations, (2) quality bonuses were awarded to reward production, engineering, and shipping personnel for desirable quality outcomes in the market, (3) quality control and production personnel were periodically rotated from the Tropics to the North American and European markets, and (4) management had been incrementally improving the processing, packaging, and shipping processes.

Still, a more comprehensive approach to quality was sought. The director of organizational development and the vice president for engineering and quality had both come to LITEP, Inc. from a major food and beverage producer that had implemented a total quality management (TQM) program. They proposed this program to the CEO of LITEP, Inc. who supported it at the corporate level.

Playa Negra, a 65 year old production division, was one of the first sites. The TQM kick-off began there in late 1991. Bocagrande, a division with a full century of history, followed in March 1992. The objectives of the training programs administered in both sites were similar, in that they were developed by the organizational development section at headquarters. The objectives were as follows: (1) become familiar with the basic elements of total quality and understand what total quality can do for the company, (2) understand the key roles in implementing the transformation to total quality and how to work within a TQM culture, and (3) learn the basic steps in beginning a total quality program. The training seminars were to build enthusiasm for the TQM process.

The transition from traditional quality inspection of the final product to continuous improvement of work processes, a critical aspect of TQM, involved the following changes: (1) include the customers, mainly internal as these were production operations, in the analysis and revision of work processes; (2) focus on the prevention of quality problems rather than inspection; (3) manage the process rather than results—managers were to work with subordinates in problem solving rather than simply revising results for variances from targets; (4) encourage employees to participate rather than waiting to be told what to do; and (5) provide tools to teams of subordinates who would analyze problem related data using simple statistical tools such as Pareto charts, "fishbone" or cause-effect diagrams, control charts, histograms, and flow charts. The culmination of the process was their presentations to managers committed to listening rather than deciding based upon some data and too much intuition, as had previously been the case. This organizational learning was to foster greater customer satisfaction in the market.

In Playa Negra, in addition to the introductory seminars given by the TQM coordinator, dozens of employees attended workshops conducted by external consultants. Topics covered included facilitation skills, leadership in participative workplaces, and statistical process control.

In Bocagrande, seminars were conducted for 140 lower level salaried employees but with the departure of the human resources manager, the seminars stopped. The regional TQM consultant and the organization development consultant from the U.S. headquarters continued to support the quality council in Bocagrande. The Bocagrande council wanted internal facilitators to be trained to lead the training effort.

The TQM program is just beginning in San Juan, another old established production division of LITEP, Inc., to which Bernal Flores has just been assigned to the position of general manager (GM). We will now become eavesdropping flies on the wall of the San Juan LITEP employee club bar.

San Juan

Bernal Flore's wife was gone for a few days—visiting her mother in the capital—and since Bernal hated eating alone, he sat munching his sandwich in the bar. He had just been transferred back to the Tropics after a six month consultation assignment as assistant to the quality manager in Northern Europe. He had been assigned back to his native country of Morazan in Central America. Bernal was familiar with San Juan; he spent his first 14 years there. His father had been the production manager. At age 14 Bernal went off to school in the U.S. and continued through college. He even did a stint in the U.S. Marine Corps. His father had retired at the time he went to boarding school but maintained contact with his former colleagues and in 1978 helped steer Bernal into the company after he finished his military service. In the company Bernal rose through the ranks in production in various countries and after 10 years became the production manager of the largest division in the company. He served in that slot from 1988 to 1992. He also had done a two-year rotation as the regional quality manager immediately before that from 1985-87.

Bernal felt qualified to handle the GM's job in spite of the ever-present problems. Like his old boss said, "Stop bitching about problems. If there weren't any, you wouldn't have a job." He knew he would face many dilemmas; for example he had to cut costs at a time when his workers were feeling the pinch of inflation. He knew that the people in headquarters were skilled professionals and astute business people but he felt they sometimes lacked understanding of the strong cultural bonds that held the production divisions together and kept commitment so high—much higher than in the U.S. People here spoke of the company as though it were one's fatherland.

He also knew he would face a great deal of upheaval as Morazan was enduring the growing pains of the political transition from a military dictatorship to a democracy. Another source of uncertainty was the devaluation. The international financial community had forced the country to float the peso. It was now officially valued at six to the dollar whereas months before it had been artificially pegged at two to one. The financial people at headquarters were ecstatic as the dollar costs had dropped dramatically; salaries to his 5,500 workers were all paid in local currency. However, Bernal knew the union would be knocking on his door very soon, given the dramatic erosion in local buying power. The company also wanted to purchase some land from the new government. The old government had adopted a very nationalistic line and refused to sell to foreign multinationals. These issues made his job exciting and he looked forward to each day. His current problem was trying to figure out what strategy to follow in implementing TQM.

The regional TQM consultant, a fellow Latino, accompanied by the American organization development consultant from headquarters, left yesterday after spending several days introducing TQM to his senior staff. These two consultants were advocating that he proceed with an alignment strategy in introducing TQM. In their report the consultants described the alignment strategy in the following terms: "Alignment refers to getting the key stakeholders to buy in before it is diffused to the lower level employees. The fundamental assumption is that department heads need to be convinced of the merits of TQM before pushing it down the hierarchy. Otherwise they will thwart the efforts of their subordinates. If we frustrate the initial efforts of the subordinates, TQM will develop a bad name and fail."

Bernal continued reading the consultants' comments. "Therefore, we want to spend 12 months preparing the foundation for TQM at the senior levels before we begin a massive training effort to diffuse the TQM message to the lower levels. The time will give the senior managers an opportunity to assimilate the new way of thinking. They need time to adjust as they are the most turf conscious of anyone within the hierarchy; they have the most to lose in yielding position power to participation. What we propose is the following: (1) participative leadership training courses for senior managers lasting four days; (2) facilitator training of one week for those middle managers and technicians chosen to eventually deliver the courses to lower level employees; (3) monthly seminars and workshops for the quality council, mainly made up of department heads; (4) name a department head as the part-time TQM coordinator; and (5) implement several quality action teams to work on priority items identified by the quality council. Only after the above is completed should training by facilitators be pushed down to lower levels.

"The regional TQM consultant will consult to the department head you name as TQM coordinator and will visit San Juan monthly. Headquarters will develop training materials for his review to make them culturally appropriate. The above approach has been used successfully in Bocagrande and we recommend it."

Bernal felt that this plan sounded reasonable. Until last night, he would have gone ahead with it. Yesterday afternoon he played a quick round of golf with Francisco, the newly assigned materials manager who, coincidentally, had been the TQM coordinator at Playa Negra, before coming to Bocagrande. Bernal beat him by three strokes but then as GM one is never sure if one wins or is allowed to win. Their subsequent conversation made Bernal wonder how to proceed with TQM implementation in San Juan.

Bernal accompanied Francisco to the club bar for a few beers as payment for the loss. On the sidewalk leading to the bar, Bernal glanced around him at the very large trees, planted close to a century ago. The huge trees, draped with Spanish moss, provided a comfortable canopy that protected them from the tropical sun—like their traditions had protected them from some of the more trendy innovations headquarters had foisted on them in the past. They entered the bar. Francisco saw his wife and excused himself saying he would be back shortly.

Bernal looked around the bar and thought of how things don't change. He felt more like a businessman now than the historical archetype of the tough man conquering the wilderness—the legendary strongman of LITEP lore. Yet on the wall of the bar, a black and white photo of a former American GM, who later became the regional VP, continued to be displayed. It was turning yellow and curling at the edges. The photo showed a man wearing two six-shooters sitting on a mule. "Such memorabilia keeps the men proud," thought Bernal. He also recalled the incident where this same GM had been rather high handed with a merchant friend of his father. The merchant had bought the first car owned by a "civilian" (i.e., non-company) in San Juan. When it was delivered on the company train, the GM in the photo had initially refused to allow it to be unloaded saying he hadn't given his authorization. Bernal flashed back to the image of the GM mentioned above. He remembered him as a portly warm man who liked his whiskey, got on well with the politicians, and who threw great Christmas parties for the children of the employees and workers. Bernal also knew that he could be tough as well.

While absorbed in his thoughts, a few subcontractors, made wealthy through their exclusive contracts with the company, entered. They had both been long term company employees who had resigned to be established in business by the company, a safe way for the company to appease the government and increase the politically required local ownership of production. One of them, a large gregarious fellow named Churrasco, was carrying a large fish by the tail. He was affectionately called "Churrasco" because he had been burned as a child and a scar covered one cheek. The name (Spanish for "broiled steak") acknowledged the scar by naming it, thereby ignoring it physically and ironically eliminating the stigma. Churrasco raised the fish with a forward motion of his arm and flopped it down on the bar. A crowd gathered around to admire his catch. "Where did you catch it?" someone asked.

"Just a few hundred yards off the coast, past the point by the mouth of the river," responded Churrasco. Several men in the group gathered around the fish, mumbled a few complimentary comments and returned to playing dominoes.

Bernal turned to Churrasco and asked, "What's the real story?"

Churrasco smiled and admitted, "I bought it from a fisherman after I returned empty handed again from a whole day of fishing. Next weekend let's watch how many boats congregate in the spot where I said I caught the fish!" Bernal smiled and shook his head.

Then the two, Churrasco and his companion, began to chide Bernal about his boat breaking down—again. Bernal's recreational boating was seemingly cursed with maintenance problems. Like everything the GM did, his mechanical difficulties were also publicly discussed. "How could you let that happen to you. That wouldn't have happened to a gringo," Churrasco teased. Pointing to the former GM in the photograph, Churrasco continued, "The old man had a boat called 'Solo Mio' (only mine). Nobody touched this boat except to keep it ready for his personal and exclusive use. That was how real GMs should behave."

Now a millionaire due to his subcontracting with the company, Churrasco was a timekeeper, one of the lowest non-union positions, when Bernal was a child. Bernal had many fond memories of Churrasco's antics. Churrasco's attention was then diverted by some former colleagues who walked in. Bernal turned and watched the show he put on for his friends. He was regaling them about how he had joined a political party composed only of rich people. He was planning on befriending the next president and felt that this party was his "ticket." The former leader of the party he previously supported was now behind bars so he had to choose another.

Churrasco changed direction like a billiard ball in his conversations. He next launched into a loud diatribe against the owners of the company and the new TQM program that he swore never to use on his production unit, the most productive in the area. He turned to Bernal and began, "They want us to fire ten hourly workers right after they give themselves huge bonuses in a year when they lost money. And now they speak of TQM." Then with a soft tone laced with false lament, he continued, "I guess it's understandable that the company wants to modernize. However, while there are a large number of administrators of the old school, the change should be slow and we should part with a smile and leave the worst of times to the best prepared."

By "best prepared" he meant professionally educated; he had risen through the ranks. The "worst of times" referred to the then looming financial crisis; the stock price had fallen to one fifth its highest value in a two year-period.

Churrasco continued, "I've seen it four times. Every time they take over they make some money for a time and then run the company into the ground. What we need is someone who is from the divisions." He meant the only people one could trust were those who had been socialized within the company. Churrasco felt that one could not simply respond to short-term financial indicators. One needed to be committed to the way of life of the divisions.

Churrasco represented the type of employee who had built the company. In LITEP, Inc. there are professional engineers, accountants, and some college educated production specialists at various levels of the hierarchy, including those of the department heads and GM. However, most supervisors and some department heads, Churrasco's last position with the company, are not college graduates but rather hard working people who had been socialized within the company during their lengthy tenures—20 years was not uncommon—with the company. Metaphorically, one could say the production, transportation, exportation, and other employees directly involved with LITEP comprised an "army of enlisted men." They were committed, loyal, and obedient members of a highly structured hierarchy and were generally not professionals. Based on their skill, hard work, and political ability (in the organizational sense), some made it to the upper levels of the hierarchy but remained relatively insular in their views due to a lack of professional association outside the company.

Bernal was aware of the importance of this socialization and his understanding of traditional factors such as this sometimes caused him to balk at projects introduced from the outside, but TQM made sense to Bernal. His dilemma was how to sell it to the staff of San Juan. Bernal hoped the insularity of his direct reports would work to his advantage since those who achieved the rank of department head were usually very skillful at organizational politics. Their processing of information would give ample consideration to what they perceived the desires of Bernal to be, given their political sensitivity and socialization.

Bernal turned to Francisco, his golf partner, who had returned to the bar after conversing with his wife. Bernal asked Francisco about his former job as the TQM coordinator in Playa Negra. Francisco related, "The idea sounded great in the beginning and I was delighted that Armando [the GM of Playa Negra] entrusted me with the job. We had consultants come in from the outside who trained us in TQM and participative leadership. A quality council was named and we got rolling. Armando sat back and allowed the council to muddle along for almost two years. Some members of the quality council did little to support me and seemed to be more concerned about their turf than anything else. However, several of them 'bought in' and were supportive. The quality manager was probably the most cooperative even though he continued to be as autocratic as a manager from the early part of the century. Several area managers in production were also very supportive but they were kicked off the council one day when they didn't go to a meeting—the council felt it had become too large.

"Subordinates were trained, named to cross-functional teams, and we got rolling. But they couldn't get much done aside from one project where they used a PC to solve a shipping box distribution problem that had plagued us for years. Aside from that initial successful effort, things did not go well in the beginning. Department heads seemed to resist giving up any autonomy. Thus Armando decided, unilaterally, as the department heads on the quality council seemed to be incapable of supporting cross-functional teams, that we would move to departmental quality action teams. I thought this was tantamount to heresy—a regression to the old idea of quality circles. TQM was based on cross-functional teams. I thought he should have pushed harder.

"Armando said, 'I could jam this down the throats of my direct reports and force them to go along. They're good soldiers and they'll do as they're told. However, I could be transferred. The new GM will come in and could throw TQM out if there is no support from the department heads. The department heads will feel no sense of ownership of TQM if I push it too hard.'

"So we went with the departmental teams. Armando wanted everybody trained in the introduction to TQM—just like he made the whole division take effective communication seminars. It took us six months of training four days per week to get through all 500 plus salaried employees with the communication seminars. It took me nearly as long to train all the salaried personnel in the introduction to TQM. We also had several very good teams working on TQM in materials and production. Only at the very end of my stint as TQM coordinator did the council come around. They named a new president, the assistant manager, who ironically initially thought that TQM was a passing fad. He finally 'bought in' and they limited council membership to supporters."

Bernal asked Francisco, "How would you assess your contribution?"

In looking back on his two years of training and working with quality action teams, Francisco related, "I made some progress although serving in a staff coordinator role was frustrating, given the strong line orientation of Playa Negra. In the end, after the initial frustration of the cross-functional quality action teams, I grew to appreciate the disciplined commitment of Armando. He 'walked the talk' and did not allow himself to get seduced into the traditional authoritarian role of the GM vis-à-vis the quality council. Armando believed he had to refrain from imposing his will on the council. He also believed that we had to simultaneously work hard at various levels of the organization to overcome the inertia. He insisted we train, train, and train some more. He also pushed me to get the quality action teams up to speed. Eventually, we found that the best way to work with the teams was to assign a quality problem to a key operations manager. He or she was then empowered to choose the members of his or her team. These people met and analyzed specific problems. Significant improvements in quality outcomes resulted. The feedback from the market has been very positive."

However, Bernal knew from attending regional meetings that concurrently with the TQM implementation, a very significant change in shipping had also occurred. Nevertheless, he understood that the participants in Playa Negra felt positive about the process and that desirable outcomes had been achieved, regardless of the causation. Bernal knew that the GM of Playa Negra, Armando, was sold on TQM. In the Fall of 1993, after several years experience with TQM, Armando enthusiastically endorsed TQM at a regional meeting. Bernal knew that Armando was political and astute. He wouldn't stand up in front of his superiors and support a "lemon." Bernal could also see how Armando had restrained himself from intervening too quickly when the council and the cross-functional teams did not generate the desired results. Instead he focused on massive training and prodding quality action teams, through Francisco, to generate results.

Francisco continued with his monologue, "In retrospect, I called this the 'saturation strategy'—we saturated the lower levels of the organization with TQM thinking and methodology, the fuel of participation! At some point, the saturated underbelly of the organization spontaneously ignited and burned the derrieres of our turf conscious department heads. Only then did we begin the transition from management by results to participative management where teams, led by supervisors, worked together to solve problems."

Bernal listened intently. This was very much at odds with what the regional TQM and the American organization development consultants were recommending. Both told him that Francisco had done a good job but had been reluctant to receive their support. Apparently Francisco wanted to do it alone. Francisco continued, "I'm glad to be in a line position again. Staff jobs—like my TQM coordinator job—are terrible in production divisions. All the power is with the line managers. I guess I'd appreciate focusing on inventories rather than TQM."

Bernal walked with Francisco to his pick-up. Francisco told Bernal to look at the results of the employee opinion survey that an external researcher doing a dissertation, with the assistance of Francisco, had completed. They had contrasted TQM participants with non-participants in Bocagrande where the alignment strategy had been pursued and TQM participants and non-participants in Playa Negra where Francisco had retroactively named their ad hoc heretical approach the "saturation strategy." Bernal took the results with him to bed and promptly dozed off.

As the steam whistle blew the next morning, Bernal was reminded of his childhood. He found it amusing that the company still woke people up but he found it absolutely hysterical that the whistle went off two more times; the next blast was to remind people that it was time to head for work and the last indicated it was time to be at work. Such throwbacks to the paternalistic era of his father were reminders that the company had been a total institution. He was surprised to hear that they still made caskets for anyone who died. This he would have to cut out as it was embarrassingly paternalistic. But he thought it quaint that the company still had a key to a gate on one of the international crossings so that the LITEP trains could pass at night. What were not so quaint were the 1,200 illegal hook-ups to the company's electrical power distribution grid—and one of these powered five of Churrasco's freezers! The company would have to continue generating electrical power for the community in addition to its operations but he'd have to talk to Churrasco soon and also get his staff to educate the others over the next few years. The company could no longer afford to present itself as a cornucopia.

Bernal left home and went to the airport to await the seven seater company plane. He was flying out that day to the capital where the three GMs would make their budget presentations to the regional VP and his finance director.

Hotel Bar in Capital City

Bernal landed at the airport and was whisked off to the budget meeting. After 12 hours of managerial "interrogation" by the regional VP, with additional clarifications sought from his finance director, the three GMs were pleased to retire to the hotel bar. Morazan produced one of those great tropical beers that was light but satisfying on a hot day. Bernal always enjoyed seeing his colleagues, Armando, the GM of Playa Negra, and Karl, the GM of Bocagrande. He had worked with them for years and had spent many hours laughing at their stories in hotel bars just like this one. They were all well into their forties now and felt foolish hanging out at discos at night. Thus, talking about TQM seemed like the appropriate alternative for middle-aged, either slightly balding or portly executives.

Bernal had once worked for Armando and knew him well. Armando was from Playa Negra. His father had been associated with the company as a professional service provider but had died in a small plane he piloted when Armando was a boy. The legend, still told by the company pilots, was that his body had been ravaged by sharks close to the wharf where LITEP was still loaded. Armando was educated in the U.S. and completed a degree in the sciences. He began working for the company in a research capacity but quickly moved to production where he has spent his entire career of more than 25 years. Bernal admired him for his highly developed political skills and charismatic leadership qualities. Bernal thought to himself, "He may be balding but he's still huge and very fit." Armando struck an imposing image as he spoke with a thundering voice and walked about with large arms waving while addressing meeting participants. He combined an engaging manner with total authority; Bernal knew one could speak frankly with him and challenge him with well founded arguments yet one remained totally cognizant of his authority.

Armando's former controller once told Bernal, "He does half the work of a controller in that he makes people follow the rules and is very cost conscious."

Like most LITEP GM's, Armando's talents were in production, including labor relations, and general leadership. He more or less left the support functions (e.g., the controller's office and materials) alone as long as policy was followed, budgets respected, and targets met. He handled the career development and succession planning for key employees himself and tended to plan and then offer options to subordinates, rather than conversing with them to ask how they saw their careers developing.

Bernal recalled how he once overheard the American HR manager suggest to Armando that he alleviate his housing shortage by moving a clerk, the wife of a transferred professional, who was still living in a large house, previously suitable for her family but too large for one person, to an apartment. Bernal remembered Armando's response, "You don't understand anything. She couldn't show her face and I have to get along with her." Later Bernal tried to explain to the American HR manager how touchy such matters were to the tight, village-like cultures created in the company towns, like San Juan, Playa Negra, and Bocagrande.

Karl, the GM of Bocagrande, held similar convictions about the importance of the strong culture within LITEP divisions. For example, an assistant controller candidate proposed by the American HR manager was rejected by Karl because the candidate's wife would not join him. This concern for the individual's family situation struck the HR manager as unusual. Bernal explained to him that what Karl seemed to have been trying to emphasize was the requisite familial commitment to the LITEP culture. It was not just a job but a lifestyle.

Bernal had trained with Karl. Karl carried a European Community passport, held a green card from the U.S., was born in the Caribbean, grew up in Central America, and was educated in Europe as a military officer and served several years in a police action in an area beset with ethnic violence. His father worked for the company and he arranged for Karl to be employed by LITEP, Inc. Karl worked his way up through the ranks of production within LITEP, Inc. and after 15 years or so with the company became a GM.

Bernal enjoyed listening to Karl's tales of crises. Karl said the only remaining disaster that had not affected Bocagrande during his tenure was a volcanic eruption. During a crisis Karl led the charge and worked day and night to get production back on track. Bernal recalled that Karl was described fondly by his subordinates with the English word "pusher," meaning one who gets things done.

Karl was also much involved in the social life of the division. His avid support of a soccer tournament left him with a severed Achilles tendon. This slowed him down for a time but he managed to hobble around the production areas on his crutches. Karl spent most of his free time with company associates.

Karl got himself into trouble from time to time with headquarters as he was more assertive than political. He was very concerned about the impact of cost cutting on the quality of life for workers. However, given the economic crisis facing the Central American LITEP industry as a whole, due to trade barriers in Europe, Karl understood the need to continue reducing costs.

Bernal began the conversation with a question, "Now that you both have gone through this TQM process, what advice would you have for me as I'm just beginning?"

Karl spoke of how difficult it was to be neutral within the quality council. "Even if I ask a question, the others are trying to guess what's on my mind." He continued by saying that he felt they had made a mistake by not working more with the department heads from the start: "We had a quality council that included several people from lower levels of the organization. Some of them objected to some of the ideas I proposed so I loaded the council with people from my office or department or section heads I could count on. The quality council became a manager's council."

Bernal knew of Karl's approach with the council. A former colleague was still in Bocagrande and told him that the council was filled with people interested in doing what the GM wanted because they were from his office and dependent on him or others who were perceived as ingratiating (the Spanish term literally translates as "sock sucker"). The council was not even relatively autonomous, as the TQM dogma prescribed.

Karl had openly stated that he didn't like it when the council objected to the projects he proposed. To keep the quality process moving in the direction he wanted, he chose to force the above change. To Karl, the TQM process was not a philosophy but rather a cafeteria of interventions from which he could select the appetizing portions (e.g., project teams, involvement of lower level employees, etc.) and pass over the less appealing items (e.g. an autonomous council).

Armando listened and indirectly countered, always sensitive to the personal dignity of those with whom he was conversing: "One has little to fear from participation. If you know the business, you can help people problem solve in a manner that enables them to develop. By giving people authority they will come to you and seek your input. This gives me more power than I would have if I simply told a passive work group what to do. I want proactive people seeking answers. However, if I already know the answer I don't ask them—I tell them what I want done."

Armando paused, took a sip from his glass, and continued. "I guess what I like most is getting a large organization to do what I want it to do. I see TQM as a chance to try something new."

Bernal thought to himself as Armando and Karl chatted with a visitor from corporate who also attended the meeting earlier that day. Bernal understood that at the conceptual level, leadership was the driving force behind the company's quality system but he didn't know whether to push for alignment, like Karl had done, to get the quality council to fall in line with how Karl perceived TQM methodology or saturate the lower levels like Armando had done in Playa Negra while waiting for the department heads in the quality council to gradually change and adopt the TQM approach.

Bernal knew that he had to be careful in pushing to overcome resistance to change with an innovation like TQM. He realized that organizational inertia was a concern but he also saw this as the continuity of a strong culture. It allowed the organization to keep on doing what it had been doing. His dilemma was to strike the appropriate balance that permitted innovation while preserving enough continuity to maintain an organizational foundation that members found motivating and meaningful. The intervention was not an isolated event; TQM was embedded in the context of a strong culture.

Armando and Karl returned to the table with Bernal and continued their discussion of TQM. Armando said, "I adopted a low key approach with the council rather than pushing it, in contrast to my standard aggressive approach to project implementation. The risk of dictating policy for the quality council was that the TQM effort could fizzle should my eventual successor not support the process. I sat and watched the council accomplish little for nearly two years. The council members eventually became frustrated with their lack of accomplishment. They changed the leadership and reduced the membership. However, when they appeared to end yet another inconclusive meeting in late July 1993, I finally intervened and ordered them to continue their meeting until they developed some direction. I didn't give them a specific direction but ordered them to find one."

As Armando and Karl excused themselves, Bernal was left with his question, "Should I pursue the alignment strategy and get the council on board first or the saturation strategy where I would work simultaneously at various levels—slowly with the council, massive training, and quality action teams?" Bernal opened his brief case and turned to the data that Francisco had given him from the surveys.

Computex Corporation

Case 6.2
Martin Hilb

Goteborg, May 30, 1985

Mr. Peter Jones
Vice President—Europe
Computex Corporation
San Francisco / USA

The writers of this letter are the headcount of the Sales Department of Computex Sweden, A.S., except for the Sales Manager.

We have decided to bring to your attention a problem which unsolved probably will lead to a situation where the majority among us will leave the company within a rather short period of time. None of us want to be in this situation, and we are approaching you purely as an attempt to save the team the benefit of ourselves as well as Computex Corporation.

We consider ourselves an experienced, professional, and sales-oriented group of people. Computex Corporation is a company which we are proud to work for. The majority among us have been employed for several years. Consequently, a great number of key customers in different areas of Sweden see us as representatives of Computex Corporation. It is correct to say that the many excellent contacts we have made have been established over years; many of them are friends of ours.

These traits give a very short background because we have never met you. What kind of problem forces us to such a serious step as to contact you?

Problems arise as a result of character traits and behavior of our General Manager, Mr. Miller.

Firstly, we are more and more convinced that we are tools that he is utilizing in order to "climb the ladder." In meetings with us individually, or as a group, he gives visions about the future, how he values us, how he wants to delegate and involve us in business, the importance of cooperation and communication, etc. When it comes to the point, these phrases turn out to be only words.

Mr. Miller loses his temper almost daily, and his outbursts and reactions are not equivalent to the possible error. His mood and views can change almost from hour to hour. This fact causes a

Source: Martin Hilb. "Computex Corporation." © 1985, University of Dallas. Reprinted by permission.

situation where we feel uncertain when facing him and consequently are reluctant to do so. Regarding human relationships,
his behavior is not acceptable, especially for a manager.

The extent of the experience of this varies within the group
due to our location. Some of us are seldom in the office.

Secondly, we have experienced clearly that he has various
means of suppressing and discouraging people within the
organization.

The new "victim" now is our Sales Manager, Mr. Johansson.
Because he is our boss, it is obvious that we regret such a situation, which to a considerable extent influences our working
conditions.

There are also other victims among us. It is indeed very difficult to carry through what is stated in our job descriptions.

We feel terribly sorry and wonder how it can be possible for
one person almost to ruin a whole organization.

If this group consisted of people less mature, many of us
would have left Computex Corporation already. So far only
one has left the company due to the above reasons.

From September 1, two new Sales Representatives are joining
the company. We regret very much that new employees get
their first contact with the company under the present circumstances. An immediate action is therefore required.

It is not our objective to get rid of Mr. Miller as General
Manager. Without going into details, we are thankful for what
he has done to the company from a business point of view. If
he could control his mood, show some respect for his colleagues, keep words, and stick to plans, we believe that we can
succeed under his leadership.

We are fully aware of the seriousness of contacting you, and
we have been in doubt whether or not to contact you directly
before talking to Mr. Miller.

After serious discussions and considerations, we have reached
the conclusion that a problem of this nature unfortunately cannot be solved without some sort of action from the superior. If
possible, direct confrontation must be avoided. It can only
make things worse.

We are hoping for a positive solution.

Six of your Sales Representatives in Sweden

Peter Jones let out a long sigh as he gazed over the letter from
Sweden. "What do I do now?" he thought, and began to reflect on the
problem. He wondered who was right and who was wrong in this
squabble, and he questioned whether he would ever get all the information necessary to make a wise decision. He didn't know much about
the Swedes, and was unsure whether this was strictly a work problem
or a "cross-cultural" problem. "How can I tease those two issues
apart?" he asked himself, as he locked his office and made his way
down the hallway to the elevator.

As Peter pulled out of the parking garage and onto the street, he began to devise a plan to deal with the problem. "This will be a test of my conflict management skills," he thought, "no doubt about it!" As he merged into the freeway traffic from the on-ramp and began his commute home, he began to wish that he had never sent Miller to Sweden in the first place. "But would Gonzalez or Harris have done any better? Would I have done any better?" Few answers seemed to come to him as he plodded along in the bumper-to-bumper traffic on Interstate 440.

Part 7

PERFORMANCE APPRAISAL
AND COMPENSATION

Continuity and Change in Japanese Management

Reading 7.1
Tomasz Mroczkowski
Masao Hanaoka

> The relationship between tradition and change in Japan has
> always been complicated by the fact that change itself is a tradition.

> —*Edward Seidensticker*

For Japan, the era of competing on the basis of being the low-cost imi-
tator of the West and of using exports to stimulate its domestic economy came to a dramatic end with the rise of the yen. Japanese companies reacted by shifting the competitive battleground to a different
plane. They have moved up-market to compete on the basis of quality,
innovation, and product leadership while defending their cost structures against NICs and Western competitors by rapid automation.
They have also sped up the process of multinationalization, moving
lower value-added production offshore and locating production facilities close to consumer markets in Europe and the U.S.

This strategy has required accelerated restructuring of the Japanese
economy, including dramatic shifts in employment. It has also required
that the Japanese management system be modified to make it more
efficient. One of the most important changes is that the "new" management system will have to encroach upon the traditional practices of
lifetime employment and seniority-based wages.

Recent economic results indicate that after the shock of the high yen
the Japanese economy has pulled off another "miracle"; and those in the
West who saw an end to Japanese competitiveness have been proven
wrong again. In 1987, Japanese industrial output was 4% higher than in
the previous year. The profits of Japanese manufacturers grew by 25-30%
in fiscal 1987 (after falling by 29% in 1986) and investment in new plants
and machinery grew by a total of 33% in real terms in 1984-86.

Remarkably, Japanese manufacturing wage costs have been kept in
check. After adding in productivity growth, Japanese firms now have
lower unit wage costs than they did a year ago (while West Germany's

have leapt by almost 5%). Japan has achieved all this while adjusting the size of its workforce, shifting manpower out of sunset industries and into new industries and the service sector, and also moving production off-shore. This remarkable achievement could not have been possible without major changes in Japanese companies' employment and reward systems—changes that many Western observers believed would be so disruptive and difficult that they would take a much longer time to implement.

This article assesses the magnitude and direction of the changes in the employment and promotion systems inside Japanese companies. An evaluation of these changes is crucial to understanding Japan's competitive strategy for the 1990s.

The Romantic Myth of Japanese Management ———————————

Almost all of the many books and articles on Japanese management published in the West have been written by non-Japanese observers. Frequently, these analyses have been used for the purpose of criticizing the shortcomings and failures of Western management. This practice has contributed to the creation of the myth of Japanese management. Until recently, this myth has gone largely unchallenged, especially in the United States.

The system of manpower management developed in the sixties and seventies that has served Japan so well is currently undergoing a gradual transformation. Even before economic and demographic conditions made it obvious, perceptive Japanese observers pointed out the inherent weaknesses of "Japanese management":

- The system of lifetime commitment and groupism encouraged employee dependency and suppressed individual creativity.

- The employment system discriminated against non-lifelong employees (temporary employees, women, part-timers, seasonal laborers and employees hired midway through their careers) and prevented the formation of a free horizontal labor market.

- The seniority-based system of rewards created a promotion gridlock for middle management and especially for the younger outstanding employee.[1]

Japanese executives have long been aware of the disadvantages of their system but believed these were outweighed by its strengths. However, by the mid-1980s many companies found themselves unable to fully maintain the "old system." The search for a new Japanese management system was assumed with a great deal of urgency.

Continuous Evolution and the Crisis of Japanese Management ——

In order to understand how it was possible to effect major changes in Japanese manpower management relatively smoothly and effectively, it is important to realize that Japanese management practices have never been static but rather have evolved through continual adjustments to new economic, social, and competitive priorities.

Prior to World War II, Japanese industry used a rigid form of status promotion (*shikaku-seido*). Employees were divided into *shokuin* (white collar) and *kòin* (blue collar) workers, with simple seniority promotion ladders within each category and no possibility of upward mobility for *kòin* workers into the *shokuin* category. After the end of World War II, during the American occupation, a number of important changes occurred. A labor standards law was introduced and labor union growth occurred. The U.S. Army introduced management training programs, and wage systems were changed as the old employee status classification system collapsed. An attempt was made to introduce an American-style job classification system. While this attempt largely failed, companies, to varying degrees, began using ability and skills instead of seniority alone as a basis for job grade assignment.

During the 1950s and 1960s, Japan experienced labor shortages due to very rapid industrial expansion. Many of the familiar features of "Japanese management" were broadly introduced at that time: by the mid-sixties more than 70% of companies used employee suggestion schemes and almost a third used regular employee morale surveys. Companies used core groups of lifetime employees who were promoted using systems of grade ladders within integrated functions. Because of the labor shortages, part-time employment of women outside the lifetime system became widespread. The actual number of hours worked was reduced while efforts were made to prolong the retirement age from 55 to 60.

Japanese management scholars regard the seventies as marking a "peak" in the development of the practices which the world learned to regard as "Japanese management." However, in the seventies there were also a number of factors that demanded modifications in Japanese human resource management practices. Economic growth rates were, on average, only half that of the previous decade. With broad introduction of automation, Japanese companies began hiring significantly fewer recruits into entry-level positions. Over the years, this caused the average age of employees moving up the seniority ladder to increase, putting pressure on average wage costs. Real opportunities for advancement became increasingly limited, and attempts to boost sagging morale brought a proliferation of new titles empty of substance.

Japanese management reacted to these problems by increasing flexibility in the employment and reward systems. Temporary transfers of surplus employees and flex-time systems were introduced. Systems of "specialist" or "expert" posts with grades similar to those for managers were created to provide ways of promoting staff workers who had already reached the highest grade and for whom managerial positions were unavailable. Efforts were made to decrease the importance of seniority as the major condition for pay raises and introduce merit components into wage and bonus systems.[2]

The early eighties saw the sharp rise in the value of the dollar, making Japanese goods very competitive in the U.S. The Japanese experienced an export boom which allowed them to postpone some of the inevitable changes in their economic policies.[3] The sharp rise of the yen in 1985 suddenly put enormous pressures on many Japanese companies. To remain competitive they had to control costs, innovate, restructure, and often move offshore. In 1986, Japan's exports declined by 15.9% and the profits of Japanese companies also declined dramatically. Because of the strong yen, the number of bankruptcies shot up (since May 1986, more than 60 companies have gone bankrupt every month) and unemployment increased.[4] Capital productivity has been decreasing in Japan in the past few years. While total factor productivity in Japan grew more rapidly than in other countries in the 1960s and 1970s, in the 1980s the growth rate leveled off. Japanese productivity specialists forecast that under these conditions it will be very difficult to continue to make the kind of productivity improvements that Japanese companies made in the past.[5] The Japanese have reached a watershed in their economic policies.

By the mid-1980s, the entire system of Japanese management faced three major challenges:

- Japanese companies have mainly relied on the variable bonus and flexible benefits to control their wage costs. After the dramatic rise in the value of the yen, the problem of cost containment became much more difficult. Average wages in Korea and Taiwan are now respectively 8 times and 6 times lower than in Japan. The challenge many Japanese companies face is how to reduce labor costs, cut capacity, and restructure without resorting to massive layoffs.

- The second major challenge Japanese management faces is how to continue to *motivate* employees and managers in a new environment in which the system of evaluation and rewards, as well as employee attitudes and expectations, is changing.

- The third challenge for Japanese management is how to redesign employment relationships in a way that would blend the advantages of the older system of dependence on the company with the necessity to promote employee self-reliance, initiative, and creativity.

The Emergence of a New Management Paradigm ——————————

Restructuring: Methods of Employment and Wage Control—For many Japanese companies, especially those in mature industries, the most immediate problem is how to achieve significant reductions in employment levels as they reduce capacity and modernize. For example, over the next three years the three biggest Japanese steel companies plan to shed 40,000 jobs without firing anyone.

This process is being carefully monitored by the Japanese Labor Ministry as well as by the Japanese Confederation of Labor, which compiled a survey of how Japanese companies carried out employment cuts and what methods they intended to use for future reductions (see Tables 1 and 2). The tables reveal the lengths to which Japanese companies will go to avoid lay-offs. All companies rely on hiring freezes and to a lesser extent on elimination of overtime. Both of these approaches are also commonly used in the West. What is peculiarly Japanese is the extensive use of job rotation and employee reassignments. In the case of larger companies (over 1,000 employees), almost half report using this as a major method of employment restructuring. Although part-time workers are indeed often laid off, firings and lay-offs of full-time employees are reported by less than 10% of the companies surveyed (with the exception of the very small companies). Interestingly, in their plans for the future, the companies intend to continue the same policies by putting even greater emphasis on job-rotation. Lay-offs of full-time employees will continue to be rare.

Some of the methods used by Japanese management to control wage and salary costs differ even more from Western practices. Wage, salary, and bonus reductions are shared by all groups in the enterprise: directors and managers as well as employees. Even when temporary or permanent layoffs *are* used, they do not have the same implications for employees as similar practices in the West. Japanese companies widely use inter-company manpower leasing and transfer. The system is run by company groups called *igyō shu kōryu*[6] and is organized on a territorial basis with local government and Chamber of Commerce support. According to a 1987 survey by the NHK (*Nippon Hosō Kyokai*, Japan Broadcasting Corporation), there are 471 local centers in which 17,000 Japanese companies participate. These centers exchange information on manpower surpluses and shortages and arrange for temporary or permanent transfers between the participating companies. They may also engage in joint new business/new product development. In effect, this system extends the lifetime employment principles while maintaining flexibility and economic rationality.

According to some Japanese HRM policy experts, Japanese companies will be moving towards more flexibility in their employment and wage policies. International and domestic competition may ultimately force companies to begin treating a larger portion of labor costs as variable costs rather than as fixed costs.[7]

Table 1. 1986 Employee Reduction (in number of companies and % of total responses)

	Size of Company (by number of employees)				
	1-99	100-299	300-999	1000-2,999	3,000 +	All Com-panies
Methods of Employment Control						
hiring freeze	54	48	57	23	21	203
	36.5%	30.8%	42.5%	54.8%	51.2%	39.0%
part-time workers terminated	36	24	22	10	14	106
	24.3%	15.4%	16.4%	23.8%	34.1%	20.3%
no overtime	23	19	21	8	6	77
	15.5%	12.2%	15.7%	19.0%	14.6%	14.8%
shortening of working day	11	12	7	2	—	32
	7.4%	7.7%	5.2%	4.8%	—	6.1%
job rotation	29	34	30	17	19	129
	19.6%	21.8%	22.4%	40.5%	46.3%	24.8%
temporary lay-offs	2	2	—	1	2	7
	1.4%	1.3%	—	2.4%	4.9%	1.3
planned employee reductions	9	3	5	2	3	22
	6.1%	1.9%	3.7%	4.8%	7.3%	4.2%
employees fired	23	12	8	3	3	49
	15.5%	7.7%	6.0%	7.1%	7.3%	9.4%
other	8	12	4	3	4	31
	5.4%	7.7%	3.0%	7.1%	9.8%	6.0%
Methods of Wage Control						
overtime pay eliminated	46	66	64	23	22	221
	31.1%	42.3%	47.8%	54.8%	53.7%	42.4%
director's/manager's pay reduced	45	32	31	6	9	123
	30.4%	20.5%	23.1%	14.3%	22.0%	23.6%
postpone increases or reduce basic pay	55	44	38	12	13	162
	37.2%	28.2%	28.4%	28.6%	31.7%	31.1%
director's bonus reduced	62	44	45	9	10	170
	41.9%	28.2%	33.6%	21.4%	24.4%	32.6%
general bonus reduced	56	45	39	11	9	160
	37.8%	28.8%	29.1%	26.2%	22.0%	30.7%
other	6	3	8	2	3	22
	41.1%	1.9%	6.0%	4.8%	7.3%	4.2%
Total Number of Companies:	148	156	134	42	41	521

Source: Susumu KoyōChousei, Ministry of Labor Employment Rationalization Survey, 1986.

Table 2. Future Reduction Forecast (in number of companies and % of total responses)

	Size of Company (by number of employees)				
	1-99	100-299	300-999	1000-2,999	3,000 +	All Companies
Methods of Employment Control						
hiring freeze	57	60	57	22	15	211
	34.8%	36.8%	40.4%	51.2%	34.1%	38.0%
part-time workers terminated	46	37	25	8	12	128
	28.0%	22.7%	17.7%	18.6%	27.3%	23.1%
no overtime	42	28	26	7	7	110
	25.6%	17.2%	18.4%	16.3%	15.9%	19.8%
shortening of working day	23	12	12	4	1	52
	14.0%	7.4%	8.5%	9.3%	2.3%	9.4%
job rotation	38	37	40	17	27	159
	23.2%	22.7%	8.4%	39.5%	61.4%	28.6%
temporary lay-offs	7	4	4	1	3	19
	4.3%	2.5%	2.8%	2.3%	6.8%	3.4%
planned employee reductions	10	7	6	4	2	29
	6.1%	4.3%	4.3%	9.3%	4.5%	5.2%
employees fired	20	8	9	2	2	41
	12.1%	4.9%	6.4%	4.7%	4.5%	7.4%
other	6	9	5	4	7	31
	3.7%	5.5%	3.5%	9.3%	15.9%	5.6%
Methods of Wage Control						
overtime pay eliminated	69	77	72	23	21	262
	42.1%	47.2%	51.1%	53.5%	47.7%	47.2%
director's/manager's pay reduced	45	28	29	8	10	120
	27.4%	17.2%	20.6%	18.6%	22.7%	21.6%
postpone increases or reduce basic pay	70	55	28	6	13	172
	42.7%	33.7%	19.9%	14.0%	29.5%	31.0%
director's bonus reduced	74	49	43	8	8	182
	45.1%	30.1%	30.5%	18.6%	18.2%	32.8%
general bonus reduced	85	70	56	12	15	238
	51.8%	42.9%	39.7%	27.9%	34.1%	42.9%
other	7	5	3	2	3	20
	4.3%	3.1%	2.1%	4.7%	6.8%	3.6%
Total Number of Companies:	164	163	141	43	44	555

Source: Susumu KoyōChousei, Ministry of Labor Employment Rationalization Survey, 1986.

The New Motivational System:
Performance-Based Evaluation and Rewards ——————————

The Changing Importance of Seniority—It is broadly believed that the principle of seniority governs the Japanese system of motivating employees, rewarding loyalty, and maintaining group harmony. In fact, the pure seniority principle has been systematically eroding in Japan, as evidenced by results of surveys carried out in Japanese companies by the *Romu Gyosei Kenkyujo* (a private research foundation). In the decade between 1978 and 1987, according to the personnel departments of the surveyed companies, the contribution of the seniority factor to pay raises systematically declined from an average of 57.9% to 46% while the contribution of the performance factor increased from 42.1% to 54% (see Table 3).

Low economic growth rates, which result in fewer recruits being hired, have made it uneconomical for companies to continue to pay ever higher wages to an increasing proportion of their senior employees. Japanese companies have reacted to this situation by remodeling the motivational system. While the retirement age in Japan has been extended, many companies are using various forms of early retirement incentives. Often, employees are finding their wage increases capped at age 44-45. In fact, in many companies average pay may drop by as much as 20% after age 50.

In order to gauge the magnitude of change taking place in the motivation systems employed by Japanese companies, it is necessary to understand the relationships between seniority and the other factors that affect employee promotion. However important, seniority has never been the only factor determining a wage or salary in a Japanese company. Assignment of an individual to a wage/salary grade depended largely on education and job-related skills. In inter-grade promotions, both of these factors also played an important part. In the process of annual within-in-grade raises and bonus awards, however, it is general company performance which is the important factor in the increment negotiations. Under

Table 3. Relative Contributions of Seniority and Merit Factors to Pay Raises

	Seniority	Ability (Merit)
1978	57.9%	42.1
1983	54.4	45.6
1984	49.0	51.0
1987	46.0	54.0

Source: Rōmu Gyōsei Kenkyūjo, July -September 11,1987 (1,900 Japanese companies surveyed).

the traditional system the final outcome in terms of a wage increment would typically incorporate a combination of the negotiated raise and seniority. The raise formula would thus look like this:

individual base x negotiated % + distribution by = raise
wage/salary   raise ("up rate")   length of service
within grade   years (expressed in
                                                     yen not as a %)

Loyalty to the company and peer pressure were judged to be sufficiently strong to motivate employees. The outstanding employee was not singled out for immediate large rewards but was kept motivated by interesting assignments, training opportunities, and eventual promotion to a higher grade or managerial position ahead of his peers.

According to a study performed by the authors at the Institute of Business Research at Daito Bunka University, this system has been undergoing substantial modifications. The HR managers from thirty large and medium-sized companies representing a cross-section of Japanese manufacturing and service sectors were surveyed and they felt without exception that the old seniority system could not be maintained without substantial change. On the other hand, only a handful of the managers wanted to abolish it completely. The majority of companies were planning and implementing gradual modification of the system allowing them to keep some of its most useful features. Modifications usually started with the introduction of merit evaluation into the promotion/reward process.

Performance Appraisal Japanese Style—The *Shikaku* (position title) classification system used to form the basis of grading, promotion, wage, and bonus decisions in Japanese companies. This gradually has been giving way to performance appraisal and merit rating systems. Rather than replacing the old system with a new one, Japanese companies grafted performance evaluation onto the old system by incorporating it as a factor in the formulas used for pay increment calculation. In companies which have embraced the individual merit rating system, the formula would typically look as follows:

individual   x average   x individual x seniority   = raise
base salary/   "up rate"   merit rating   coefficient
wage   within each
                      grade (%)

The actual impact of performance evaluations on pay varies from company to company and also depends on the position and grade of the employee. According to a 1985 study by the Japan Personnel Policy Research Institute, 35% of managerial bonus awards depended on the performance appraisal component, while for clerks this rate was only 22%.[8] Individual performance appraisal results can account for anywhere from 20% to 50% of the pay increment. The higher percentage is found in those companies that have pursued change most aggressively, including companies under Western management and joint-venture operations.

The Japanese concepts of performance and achievement are not the same as in the West and the relative importance of different components and ways of measuring and weighting them are different. The concept of personnel evaluation most widely used in Japan is the merit rating (*jinji kōka*). This concept is based on educational attainment and job ability factors such as communication skills, cooperativeness, and sense of responsibility. *Jinji kōka* is being gradually replaced by performance evaluation based on work results. The Japanese concept of performance (*gyō seki*) is distinct from the Western concept and includes not only the achievement of actual results, but the expenditure of good faith effort. New performance evaluation systems are currently being introduced in 75% of Japanese companies.[9]

Individual achievement based rewards are likely to continue to grow in importance in the motivational systems in Japanese companies. One of the factors contributing to the problems of motivating Japanese employees is the erosion of labor unions. At one time, 56% of the labor force belonged to unions. As the Japanese economy matured, labor union membership declined and union participation rates have now fallen below 28%.[10] As Japan moves out of the smokestack industries and becomes a "service" economy, further declines in union membership are expected to occur. Company and work-group loyalties are being replaced by individualism.

The trend away from seniority and towards individual performance-based pay has been documented in a survey carried out by the Social and Economic Congress of Japan which asked management and labor unions about changes in the factors that will determine Japanese wages by the year 2000 (see Table 4).

Redesigning the Employment Relationships—While maintaining considerable continuity with past practices, the system of lifetime employment is undergoing change. A 1984 survey conducted by the prime minister's office found that nearly half of all Japanese between the ages of twenty and twenty-nine expressed a preference for an "employment changing" job environment to the assurance of lifetime employment. In another survey conducted by a large job placement firm, a quarter of the college graduates interviewed had already changed jobs at least once.[11]

Most Japanese employers feel that it is advantageous to maintain the lifetime employment principle even if only in a modified form. Only a minority feel that the idea has outlived its usefulness. Most employers feel they must maintain lifetime employment for core employees in order to attract recruits of sufficient calibre. However, the group of "core" employees who enjoy lifetime employment can be quite small (it is only 10% in the fast-food industry).

Table 4. Emphasized Factors of Wage System Around in 2000 (in %)

	Management			Labor Union			Neutral			Total		
	will increase	will not change	will decrease	will increase	will not change	will decrease	will increase	will not change	will decrease	will increase	will not change	will decrease
age	6.7	21.0	69.0	15.5	26.1	57.1	5.5	21.9	71.6	8.8	22.7	66.4
service years	6.7	28.6	61.9	11.2	33.5	55.3	3.3	32.8	62.3	6.9	31.4	60.1
educational background	5.7	17.6	73.8	10.6	18.6	70.2	4.4	19.7	76.0	6.7	18.6	73.5
experience years	25.7	49.5	21.4	33.5	44.7	22.4	23.5	51.9	20.8	27.3	48.9	21.5
job, occupational category	80.0	15.7	0.5	82.6	13.7	1.9	77.0	19.1	2.7	79.8	16.2	1.6
ability for achievement	91.0	4.8	1.0	84.5	9.3	5.0	86.9	10.9	0.5	87.7	8.1	2.0
amount of work done	50.0	35.7	11.0	34.2	42.2	21.1	38.3	48.1	13.1	41.5	41.7	14.6
family size	2.4	45.7	47.1	7.5	47.8	44.1	7.7	49.7	40.4	5.6	47.7	44.0

Source: Takao Watanabe, *Demystifying Japanese Management* (Tokyo: Gakuseisha Publishing Co., Ltd., 1987), p. 195.

While most companies have postponed the retirement age (as noted earlier), employees are now obliged to consider whether they will continue to stay with the company after the age of 40 or 45 or face the possibility of being transferred to affiliated companies. Companies are also using "specialist" positions for senior employees who are either being retired from managerial posts or are not considered promotable to managerial ranks.

The lifetime employment system is also being modified through increased use of diversified hiring methods. The routine hiring of school graduates is being more and more frequently supplemented by the hiring of contract employees and part-timers.[12] Hiring on the basis of skills for a specific, narrowly defined job opening is growing. For example, in 1988 Niko Shoken (Niklko Security Co., Ltd.) started recruiting foreign exchange traders at high salaries on a contract basis. These employees in principle cannot transfer to the lifetime employment track and if their performance is below expectations their salaries may be cut or they may be fired. Similarly, Sumitomo Trust Bank has been hiring security traders and economic analysts on a contract basis. As Mr. Osamu Sakurai, President of the Bank, put it: "Under the lifetime employment system we could not offer appropriately high salaries to obtain top talent. Nor could we hire on a short-term basis."[13] With these new hiring practices, labor mobility is rising and is expected to continue to increase gradually in the future (see Table 5). Mobility among Japanese managers and professionals is also increasing. According to a study performed by Nippon Manpower, a Japanese human resource development company, 75% of those surveyed declared that they would entertain a lucrative offer from a headhunter.[14]

While Japanese management clearly wants to continue to tap the advantages of lifetime employment for selected employee groups, there is growing evidence that a partial horizontal labor market is emerging rapidly. For years, Japanese employees demonstrated a preference for security over risk and opportunity. This attitude began to change after the oil shocks.

Japanese employees realized that they could not place all their reliance on their companies and that they would have to start relying on themselves. Today, the latest catch word among personnel specialists in Japan is "employee self-reliance." It is not only that the attitudes and expectations of employees—especially younger employees—are changing, but the companies themselves are creating programs designed to promote new attitudes of self-reliance. Career development programs have been among the most popular new personnel systems adopted by Japanese companies in the past few years.[15] Today, companies like Toshiba and Yamaha use extensive career counseling to help employees develop new skills and attitudes that would enable them to survive in a horizontal labor market.

The Multi-Track Employment System

As they gradually redesign the employment and reward system in their companies, Japanese managers are trying to maintain the advantages of group harmony, employee loyalty, and cooperation (based on the lifetime employment principle) while both eliminating the burdens of employment hypertrophy and enhancing flexibility by shifting more of the risk on a greater proportion of employees. At the same time, for many companies which base their strategies on product leadership and innovations, stimulating employee initiative and creativity is a high priority.

The way Japanese management hopes to reconcile these conflicting goals is through the creation of a multi-track employment system. Employees hired for "life" enter the general track and can be moved horizontally (job rotation) as well as vertically (grade promotion). In the past, vertical promotion was often restricted by rules governing the minimum and standard "staying years" within one grade—effectively ensuring promotion by seniority. As companies relax those rules, more rapid promotion becomes possible. As job rotation and the hiring of specialists becomes more common, it becomes possible for a relatively

Table 5. The Prospect of Worker's Mobility in Future Japanese Society

	Management	Labor	Neutral	Total Polled
It will increse remarkably	3.2%	2.2%	3.3%	2.9%
It will increase a bit more or less	69.4	59.0	66.9	65.4
unchanged	17.2	19.4	9.9	15.4
it will decrease a bit	0.6	1.5	0.6	0.9
it will decrease remarkably	0.6	—	—	0.2
no answer	8.9	17.9	19.2	15.2

Source: Takao Watanabe, *Demystifying Japanese Management* (Tokyo: Gakuseisha Publishing Co., Ltd., 1987), p. 185.

junior employee to achieve a high grade. As companies choose to limit the percentage of lifetime employees, they expand hiring into the restricted tracks—which may include hiring more women, part-timers, and specialists.

As specific expertise becomes increasingly more important and seniority increasingly less, promotion grades become defined more precisely in terms of specific tasks rather than experience, general educational attainment, and general skills. Expanded flexibility can then also be applied at the higher (managerial) levels. However, promotion into these higher grades does not have to mean a managerial post. A variety of specialist positions offering high pay can be made available, which would allow for moving less-able managers into specialist positions and more-able specialists into management positions. A separate "subtrack" can be created for the failed or non-promotable. This is the well-known *taigu shoku* or "window job" track.

Compared with the grade systems that were used in the sixties and seventies, the systems emerging today offer more flexibility and more options to human resource management. Hiring methods have diversified. Today, Japanese HR departments use headhunters to fill managerial and specialist technical positions, they lease groups of needed employees from manpower agencies, they entertain "walk in" offers from candidates, and they write a variety of contracts with employees on restricted tracks—including, to a greater extent, foreigners.[16] This is indeed a far cry from the standard practices in the past of relying primarily on school and university graduates. The flexibility of the system is being continually expanded. Many high-tech companies are diversifying grade denominations and promotion rules within particular tracks—especially research and development—to stimulate employee initiative and creativity.

The Effect of the Collapse of the Bubble Economy _____

With the collapse of the bubble economy at the start of 1991, Japan is currently in the second year of an economic recession unparalleled since the recession period of 1980-1983. In order to cope with the pressures of economic turmoil, human resource management is in a process of significant adjustment.

Encouraged by the sense of economic uncertainty, several surveys which attempt to describe the direction of Japanese Human Resource Management have appeared.

A brief examination of one of these surveys by the "Japan Productivity Center" findings will illustrate some of the recent measures of adjustment.[17]

Table 6. The Shift from Japanese Seniority System to a Merit Base

Priority should be placed on merit rather than seniority when developing a rating yardstick.

	Management	Labor Union Leader
Agree	89.5	80.7
Disagree	8.0	16.7
No Response	2.5	2.7
Total	100.0	100.0
Reasons		
Companies cannot survive in an aging society if ratings are based on seniority.	17.8	9.3
If ratings are based on the employee's background, this would be in opposition to fair rating practices.	29.6	46.0
Ratings based on seniority lessen the promotion opportunities for those employees with actual ability.	38.2	22.7
Others	14.4	22.0

More than 80% of both management groups and labor unions support evaluation based on merit which reflects the decline in importance placed on seniority.

Table 7. System of Lifetime Employment

Employment should be maintained irrespective of the economic environment at the time.

	Management	Labor Union Leader
Agree	80.0	98.0
Disagree	16.0	0.7
No response	3.0	1.3
Reason		
The benefits of long-term employment outweigh that of the subsequent costs in the short-term.	28.3	23.3
There is benefit to employees by the reduction of working hours and the provision of job vitalization through rotation.	24.2	46.7
Utilization of surplus employees is an obligation of the company.	23.4	26.0
Others	24.1	4.0

Even with the pressures from fluctuations in the business environment, a clear responsibility to maintain stability is indicated. This would suggest a continuation of lifetime employment. However, such a response may only reflect a professed ideal by both management and labor union groups alike rather than a true intention or actual practice.

Media reports, for example, indicate a different reality. A growing appearance of the usage of the term *koyochosei* in printed and electronic media reveal the contradictions in management and labor purported ideals to maintain a commitment toward lifetime employment. *Koyochosei* refers to the measures taken by management to control the level of the labor force through termination of employment, lay-offs, forced early retirement, transfer to affiliated companies, hiring freeze, reduction of management positions, elimination of overtime, and reduction in the numbers of part-time workers.

The *Nihonkeizai* newspaper reported that *koyochosei* measures were implemented by 40% of the manufacturing industries during the three month period from October to December in 1986 brought out by recession due to the high value of the yen. The same period in 1992 reflects a similar implementation at a reported 39%.

Further, one of the most drastic measures of *koyochosei*, forced early retirement (unofficial termination of employment), is to be implemented by many companies. The *Nhonkeizai* newspaper reported that NTT would utilize forced early retirement effecting 10,000 employees with the same measure being applied by JVC VICTOR affecting 600 employees. Similar media reports with regard to other companies indicate the broadening appearance of such occurrences throughout Japan.

Despite management claims of support of lifetime employment as articulated by management themselves in the surveys carried out by the Japan Productivity Center, the actual realities faced by companies and their employees emphasize more of a rapid shift away to a new paradigm.

Conclusion

Many of the critical practices on which the Japanese company bases its functioning depend on the principles of lifetime employment, company loyalty, and employee commitment. The Japanese will make every effort to maintain these principles in the foreseeable future. The changes going on in employment practices and employee motivation are not designed to destroy the old system but to increase its flexibility. This is very much in keeping with the traditional Japanese approach to change; however fast and deep it is, continuity with the uniquely Japanese "essence" must be maintained. The new Japanese management paradigm will certainly be different, yet like the modern Japanese home which usually retains a Japanese style room among Western style rooms and furniture, the Japanese company will retain a core of Japanese practices.

Western assessments of Japanese capabilities tend to oscillate between total awe and serious underestimation. The difficulties in changing to a new management system should not be underestimated. Japanese company presidents find that responsibility for decisions that have to be made rapidly is being transferred to them, that they have to act boldly and quickly, and that often there is no time for gradual consensus building. Popular Japanese magazines have noted a large number of company presidents who have died in office during the past 18 months or so, blaming their untimely deaths on the pressures of diversifying, building offshore plants, cutting costs, and laying off employees. [18]

The Japanese have handled profound change in the past very well (during the Meiji era and after World War II). This suggests that they are in a good position to overcome the obstacles and difficulties. Research on the introduction of robotics and flexible manufacturing systems in Japanese and Western companies show the Japanese to have superior capabilities in effective implementation of new manufacturing technology.[19] The Japanese appear very well positioned for the age in which competitive survival will depend on the ability of human groups to manage very rapid change. After the strains and difficulties of the current transformation, Japanese companies are likely to emerge in the 1990s as even more formidable competitors than ever before.

Endnotes

1. Kunio Odaka. "Japanese Management: A Forward Looking Analysis." *Asian Productivity Organization,* Tokyo, 1986.

2. Masao Hanaoka, *Nihon no Romukanri (Personnel Management in Japan),* 2nd Edition (Tokyo: Hakuto Shobo, 1987).

3. Peter F. Drucker, "Japan's Choices," *Foreign Affairs* (1987).

4. Ministry of Foreign Affairs, "Background Statistics on the Japanese Economy," Japan, May 1987.

5. Takao Watanabe, *Demystifying Japanese Management* (Tokyo: Gakuseisha Publishing Co., Ltd., 1987).

6. *Igyōshu Kōryu* are groups or networks of small and medium-sized enterprises organized to exchange technical information, promote management development, and engage in manpower exchange.

7. Hanaoka, op. cit.

8. *Nippon Jinji Gyōsei Kenkyujo* (Japan Personnel Policy Research Institute) survey, February 8, 1985.

9. *Nihonteki Koyokanko no Henka to Tenbo* (Ministry of Labor Research Center), Tokyo, 1987.

10. "All That's Left," *The Economist,* November 28, 1987.

11. Robert C. Christopher, *Second to None: American Companies in Japan* (New York: Crown Publishers, Inc., 1986).

12. *Nikkei High Tech Report,* "Japanese Research Organizations Tap Foreign Technical Talent," April 13, 1987.

13. *Nihon Keizai Shinbun,* February 15, 1988.

14. Tomasz Mroczkowski and Masao Hanaoka, "Japan's Managers Merit More Attention," *Asian Wall Street Journal,* October 29, 1987.

15. Masao Hanaoka, "Setting Up a Hypothesis of the Characteristics of Personnel Management," Institute of Business Research, Daito Bunka University, 1986.

16. *Nikkei High Tech Report,* op. cit.

17. Japan Productivity Center, "The Second Managing Business Ethics Survey—Researching the Direction of Future Japanese Management Reconstruction," January, 1993.

18. Bernard Wysocki, "In Japan, Breaking Step Is Hard to Do," *The Wall Street Journal,* December 14, 1987.

19. Ramchandran Jaikumar. "Postindustrial Manufacturing," *Harvard Business Review* (November/December 1986).

Expatriate Performance Appraisal: Problems and Solutions

Reading 7.2
Gary Oddou
Mark Mendenhall

For more and more companies, gaining a competitive edge increasingly means making decisions that reflect an acute understanding of the global marketplace—how other countries utilize and view marketing strategies, accounting and financial systems, labor laws, leadership, communication, negotiation and decision-making styles. Gaining a knowledge of these components is most directly accomplished by sending managers to work in an overseas subsidiary and utilizing them on reentry.

Our research shows clearly that expatriates develop valuable managerial skills abroad that can be extremely useful to their development as effective senior managers. Based on current research on expatriates, including our own surveying and interviewing of more than 150 of them, probably the most significant skills expatriates develop as a result of their overseas assignments include the following:

- Being able to manage a workforce with cultural and subcultural differences

- Being able to plan for, and conceptualize, the dynamics of a complex, multinational environment

- Being more open-minded about alternative methods for solving problems

- Being more flexible in dealing with people and systems

- Understanding the interdependencies among the firm's domestic and foreign operations

These skills are the natural outgrowth of the increased autonomy and potential impact expatriates experience in their international assignment. In fact, in our study, 67 percent reported having more independence, and they also indicated they had more potential impact on the operation's performance than in their domestic position. With

---

Source: This article was written especially for this book.

increased decision-making responsibilities in a foreign environment, expatriates are subjected to a fairly intense working environment in which they must learn the ropes quickly.

The skills expatriate managers gain are obviously crucial to effectively managing any business operation, particularly at the international and multinational level. Nightmares abound in the business press of the inept decisions sometimes made by top management due to ignorance of cross-cultural differences in business practices. The ability to plan and conceptualize based on the complex interdependencies of a global market environment with significant cultural differences is required of top management in MNCs.

In short, expatriates can become a very valuable human resource for firms with international or multinational operations. However, one of the most serious stumbling blocks to expatriates' career paths is the lack of recognition of the value of expatriation and the informality with which firms accurately evaluate their expatriates' overseas performance. Although the attributes expatriates gain overseas can and do translate into concrete advantages for their firms, a quick glance at the skills previously listed indicates intangibles that are often difficult to measure and usually are not measured—or are measured inaccurately—by present performance evaluation methods. Hence, it is critical to more closely examine this potential stumbling block to expatriates' careers and to make specific recommendations to improve the process and accuracy of such reviews.

Appraising the Expatriate's Performance ——————————————————

Several problems are inherent to appraising an expatriate's performance. First, an examination of those who evaluate an expatriate's job performance is relevant. Those evaluators include the host national management and often the home office management.

Host National Management's Perceptions of Actual Job Performance

That local management evaluates the expatriate is probably necessary; however, such a process sometimes is problematic. Local management typically evaluates the expatriate's performance from its own cultural frame of reference and set of expectations. For example, one American expatriate manager we talked to used participative decision making in India but was thought of by local workers as rather incompetent because of the Indian notion that managers, partly owing to their social class level, are seen as the experts. Therefore, a manager should not have to ask subordinates for ideas. Being seen as incompetent negatively affected local management's review of this expatriate's performance, and he was denied a promotion on return to the United States. Local management's appraisal is not the only potential problem, however. In fact, based on our research with expatriates, local management's evaluation is usually perceived as being more accurate than that of the home office.

Home Office Management's Perceptions of Actual Job Performance

Because the home office management is geographically distanced from the expatriate, it is often not fully aware of what is happening overseas. As a result, for middle and upper management, home office management will often use a different set of variables than those used by local management. Typically, more visible performance criteria are used to measure the expatriate's success (for example, profits, market share, productivity levels). Such measures ignore other, less visible variables that in reality drastically affect the company's performance. Local events such as strikes, devaluation of the currency, political instability, and runaway inflation are examples of phenomena that are beyond the control of the expatriate and are sometimes "invisible" to the home office.

One expatriate executive told us that in Chile he had almost single-handedly stopped a strike that would have shut down their factory completely for months and worsened relations between the Chileans and the parent company in the United States. In a land where strikes are commonplace, such an accomplishment was quite a coup, especially for an American. The numerous meetings and talks with labor representatives, government officials, and local management required an acute understanding of their culture and a sensitivity beyond the ability of most people. However, because of exchange rate fluctuations with its primary trading partners in South America, the demand for their ore temporarily decreased by 30 percent during the expatriate's tenure. Rather than applauding the efforts this expatriate executive made to avert a strike and recognizing the superb negotiation skills he demonstrated, the home office saw the expatriate as being only somewhat better than a mediocre performer. In other words, because for home office management the most visible criterion of the expatriate's performance was somewhat negative (sales figures), it was assumed that he had not performed adequately. And though the expatriate's boss knew a strike had been averted, the bottom-line concern for sales dollars overshadowed any other significant accomplishments.

The expatriate manager must walk a tightrope. He must deal with a new cultural work group, learn the ins and outs of the new business environment, possibly determine how to work with a foreign boss, find out what foreign management expects of him, and so on. He must also understand the rules of the game on the home front. It is difficult, and sometimes impossible, to please both. Attempting to please both can result in a temporarily, or permanently, railroaded career. So it was with an individual who was considered a high potential in a semiconductor firm. He was sent to an overseas operation without the proper product knowledge preparation and barely kept his head above water because of the difficulties of cracking a nearly impossible market. On returning to the United States, he was physically and mentally exhausted from the battle. He sought a much less challenging position and got it because top management then believed they had overestimated his potential. In fact, top management never did understand what the expatriate was up against in the foreign market.

In fact, expatriates frequently indicate that headquarters does not really understand their experience—neither the difficulty of it nor the value of it. One study found that one-third of the expatriates felt that corporate headquarters did not understand the expatriate's experience at all. In a 1981 Korn/Ferry survey, 69 percent of the managers reported they felt isolated from domestic operations and their U.S. managers. It is clear from others' and our own research that most U.S. senior management does not understand the value of an international assignment or try to utilize the expatriate's skills gained abroad when they return to the home office. The underlying problem seems to be top management's ethnocentricity.

Management Ethnocentricity

Two of the most significant aspects of management's inability to understand the expatriate's experience, value it, and thereby more accurately measure his or her performance are (1) the communication gap between the expatriate and the home office and (2) the lack of domestic management's international experience.

The Communication Gap. Being physically separated by thousands of miles and in different time zones poses distinct problems of communication. Not only does the expatriate have difficulty talking directly with his manager, but usually both the U.S. manager and the expatriate executive have plenty of other responsibilities to attend to. Fixing the day-to-day problems tends to take precedence over other concerns, such as maintaining contact with one's boss (or subordinate) in order to be kept up to date on organizational changes or simply to inform him or her of what one is doing. Most of the expatriates in our research indicated they had very irregular contact with their home office and that often it was not with their immediate superior. Rarely did the boss initiate direct contact with the expatriate more than once or twice a year.

The Lack of International Experience. The old Indian expression "To walk a mile in another man's moccasins" has direct meaning here. How can one understand what another person's overseas managerial experience is like—its difficulties, challenges, stresses, and the like—without having lived and worked overseas oneself? According to one study, more than two-thirds of upper management in corporations today have never had an international assignment. If they have not lived or worked overseas, and if the expatriate and U.S. manager are not communicating regularly about the assignment, the U.S. manager cannot evaluate the expatriate's performance appropriately.

Of course, how the U.S. manager and foreign manager perceive the expatriate's performance will depend partly on the expatriate's actual performance and partly on the managers' *perceptions* of the expatriate's performance. Up to now, we have discussed the managers' perceptions of the expatriate's performance. Let's now turn our attention to what usually composes the expatriate's *actual* performance to better understand why evaluating it is problematic.

Actual Job Performance

As repeatedly mentioned by the expatriates in our study and in other research, the primary factors relating to the expatriate's actual job performance include his or her technical job know-how, personal adjustment to the culture, and various environmental factors.

Technical Job Know-How. As with all jobs, one's success overseas partly depends on one's expertise in the technical area of the job. Our research indicates that approximately 95 percent of the expatriates believe that technical competency is crucial to successful job performance. Although common sense supports this notion, research shows that technical competence is not sufficient in itself for successful job perfomance. For example, an engineer who is an expert in his or her field and who tends to ignore cultural variables that are important to job performance will likely be ineffective. He or she might be less flexible with local personnel, policies, and practices because of his or her reliance on technical know-how or because of differences in cultural views. As a result, the host nationals might become alienated by the expatriate's style and become quite resistant to his or her objectives and strategies. A less experienced engineer, with less technical competence, might be more willing to defer to the host country's employees and their procedures and customs. A shade of humility is always more likely to breed flexibility, and in the long run, the less experienced engineer might develop the trust of the foreign employees and might well be more effective than the experienced engineer.

We have been given numerous examples by expatriates, in fact, where this has been the case. One expatriate who represented a large construction firm was sent to a worksite in India. The expatriate was an expert in his field and operated in the same fashion as he did in the United States. He unintentionally ignored local work customs and became an object of hatred and distrust. The project was delayed for more than six months because of his behavior.

Adjustment to a New Culture. Just as important as the expatriate's technical expertise is his or her ability to adapt to the foreign environment, enabling him or her to deal with the indigenous people. Nearly every expatriate in our survey felt understanding the foreign culture, having an ability to communicate with the foreign nationals, and being able to reduce stress were as—if not more—important to successful job performance than was technical competence. Regardless of how much an expatriate knows, if he or she is unable to communicate with and understand the host nationals, the work will not get done.

An expatriate's adjustment overseas is also related to at least two personal variables: (1) one's marital and family status (that is, whether accompanied by a spouse and children) and (2) the executive's own personal and the family's predisposition to acculturation. Research clearly indicates that expatriates who have their family abroad are often less successful because of the stress on the family of being in a foreign environment. The stress on the spouse negatively affects the employee's concentration and job performance. With an increasing number of dual-career couples being affected by expatriation, the problems are even keener. A number of expatriates reported that their formerly career-positioned spouse suffered from depression most of the time they were overseas. Moving from experiencing the dynamics of a challenging career to having no business-world activity and being unable to communicate the most basic needs is a grueling transition for many career-oriented spouses.

Company variables affecting cultural and work adjustment also come into play. The thoroughness of the company's expatriate selection method and the type and degree of cross-cultural training will affect expatriate adjustment and performance. In other words, if the firm is not selective about the personality of the expatriate or does not appropriately prepare the employee and dependents, the firm may be building in failure before the manager ever leaves the United States.

All these factors influence the expatriate's learning curve in a foreign business environment. More time is thus required to learn the ins and outs of the job than for the expatriate's domestic counterpart who might have just taken a comparable position stateside. In fact, most expatriates say it takes three to six months to even begin to perform at the same level as in the domestic operation. Hence, *performance evaluations at the company's normal time interval may be too early to accurately and fairly reflect the expatriate's performance.*

A Summary of Factors Affecting Expatriation Performance

In summary, an expatriate's performance is based on overseas adjustment, his or her technical know-how, and various relevant environmental factors. Actual performance, however, is evaluated in terms of perceived performance, which is based on a set of fairly complex variables usually below the evaluator's level of awareness. Much of the perceived performance concerns perceptions of the expatriate and his or her situation. Depending on whether the manager assessing the expatriate's performance has had personal overseas experience or is otherwise sensitive to problems associated with overseas work, the performance appraisal will be more or less valid. *The bottom line for the expatriate is that the performance appraisal will influence the promotion potential and type of position the expatriate receives on returning to the United States.* Because expatriates generally return from their experience with valuable managerial skills, especially for firms pursuing an international or global market path, it behooves organizations to carefully review their process of appraising expatriates and the evaluation criteria themselves.

Guidelines on How to Appraise an Expatriate's Performance ——————

Human Resource Personnel: Giving Guidelines for Performance Evaluation

Human resources departments can do a couple of things to help guide the evaluator's perspective on the evaluation.

A basic breakdown of the difficulty level of the assignment should be done to properly evaluate the expatriate's performance. For example, working in Japan is generally considered more difficult than working in England or English-speaking Canada. The learning curve in Japan will take longer because of the very different ways business is conducted, the language barrier that exists, and the isolation that most Americans feel within the Japanese culture. Major variables such as the following should be considered when determining the difficulty level of the assignment:

- Operational language used in the firm

- Cultural "distance," based often on the region of the world (for example, Western Europe, Middle East, Asia)

- Stability of the factors affecting the expatriate's performance (for example, labor force, exchange rate)

Many foreigners speak English, but their proficiency does not always allow them to speak effectively or comfortably, so they rely on their native language when possible. In addition, they usually do not speak English among themselves because it is not natural. In Germany, for example, one expatriate said that while relying on English allowed a minimum level of work to be performed, the fact that he did not speak German limited his effectiveness. Secretaries, for example, had very limited English-speaking skills. German workers rarely spoke English together and therefore unknowingly excluded the expatriate from casual and often work-related conversations. And outside work, he had to spend three to four times the amount of time to accomplish the same things that he did easily in the United States. Most of the problem was because he could not speak good enough German, and many of the Germans could not speak good enough English.

Although sharing the same language facilitates effective communication, it is only the surface level of communication. More deep-rooted, cultural-based phenomena can more seriously affect an expatriate's performance.

Countries or regions where the company sends expatriates can be fairly easily divided into categories such as these: (1) somewhat more difficult than the United States, (2) more difficult than the United States, and (3) much more difficult than the United States. Plenty of information is available to help evaluate the difficulty level of assignments. The U.S. State Department and military branches have these types of ratings. In addition, feedback from a firm's own expatriates can help build the picture of the varying level of assignment difficulty.

Rather than having the manager try to subjectively build the difficulty level of the assignment into his or her performance appraisal, human resources could have a built-in, numerical difficulty factor that is multiplied times the quantity obtained by the normal evaluation process (for example, somewhat more difficult = x 1.2; more difficult = x 1.4; much more difficult = x 1.6).

Evaluator: Trying to Objectify the Evaluation

Several things can be done to try to make the evaluator's estimation more objective.

1. Most expatriates agree that it makes more sense to weight the evaluation based more on the on-site manager's appraisal than the home-site manager's notions of the employee's performance. This is the individual who has been actually working with the expatriate and who has more information to use in the evaluation. Having the on-site manager evaluate the expatriate is especially valid when the on-site manager is of the same nationality as the expatriate. This helps avoid culturally biased interpretations of the expatriate's performance.

2. In reality, however, currently the home-site manager usually performs the actual written performance evaluation after the on-site manager has given some input. When this is the case, a former expatriate from the same location should be involved in the appraisal process. This should occur particularly with evaluation dimensions where the manager is trying to evaluate the individual against criteria with which he or she is unfamiliar relative to the overseas site. For example, in South America the dynamics of the workplace can be considerably different from those of the United States. Where stability characterizes the United States, instability often characterizes much of Latin America. Labor unrest, political upheavals, different labor laws, and other elements all serve to modify the actual effects a supervisor can have on the productivity of the labor force in a company in Latin America. A manager who has not personally experienced these frustrations will not be able to evaluate an expatriate's productivity accurately. In short, if production is down while the expatriate is the supervisor, the American boss tends to believe it is because the supervisor was not effective.

3. On the other hand, when it is a foreign, on-site manager who is making the written, formal evaluation, expatriates agree that the home-site manager should be consulted before the on-site manager

completes a formal terminal evaluation. This makes sense because consulting the home-site manager can balance an otherwise hostile evaluation caused by an intercultural misunderstanding.

One expatriate we interviewed related this experience. In France, women are legally allowed to take six months off for having a baby. They are paid during that time but are not supposed to do any work related to their job. This expatriate had two of the three secretaries take maternity leave. Because they were going to be coming back, they were not replaced with temporary help. The same amount of work, however, still existed. The American expatriate asked them to do some work at home, not really understanding the legalities of such a request. The French women could be fired from their jobs for doing work at home. One of the women agreed to do it because she felt sorry for him. When the American's French boss found out one of these two secretaries was helping, he became very angry and intolerant of the American's actions. As a result, the American felt he was given a lower performance evaluation than he deserved. When the American asked his former boss to intercede and help the French boss understand his reasoning, the French boss modified the performance evaluation to something more reasonable to the American expatriate. The French manager had assumed the American should have been aware of French laws governing maternity leave.

Performance Criteria

Here again, special consideration needs to be given to the expatriate's experience. Expatriates are not only performing a specific function, as they would in their domestic operation, they are also broadening their understanding of their firm's total operations and the inherent interdependencies thereof. As a result, two recommendations are suggested.

1. Modify the normal performance criteria of the evaluation sheet for that particular position to fit the overseas position and site characteristics.

Using the Latin American example referred to before might serve to illustrate this point. In most U.S. firms, maintaining positive management-labor relations is not a primary performance evaluation criterion. Stabilizing the workforce is not highly valued because the workforce is already usually a stable entity. Instead, productivity in terms of number of units produced is a highly valued outcome. As such, motivating the workforce to work faster and harder is important. In Chile, however, the workforce is not so stable as it is in the United States. Stability is related to constant production—not necessarily to increasing production—and a stable production amount can be crucial to maintaining marketshare. In this case, if an expatriate is able to maintain positive management-labor relations such that the workforce goes on strike only two times instead of twenty-five times, the expatriate should be rewarded commensurately. In other words, while the expatriate's U.S. counterpart might be rated primarily on increases in production, the expatriate in Chile should be rated on stability of production.

How can such modifications in the normal performance criteria be determined? Ideally, returned expatriates who worked at the same site or in the same country should be involved in developing the appropriate criteria or ranking of the performance criteria or both. Only they have first-hand experience of what the possibilities and constraints are like at that site. This developmental cycle should occur approximately every five years, depending on the stability of the site—its culture, personnel, and business cycles. Reevaluating the criteria and their prioritization periodically will make sure the performance evaluation criteria remain current with the reality of the overseas situation. If expatriate availability is a problem, outside consultants who specialize in international human resource management issues can be hired to help create country-specific performance evaluation forms and criteria.

2. Include an expatriate's insights as part of the evaluation.

"Soft" criteria are difficult to measure and therefore legally difficult to support. Nevertheless, every attempt should be made to give the expatriate credit for relevant insights into the interdependencies of the domestic and foreign operations. For example, if an expatriate learns that the reason the firm's plant in India needs supplies by certain dates is to accommodate cultural norms—or even local laws—such information can be invaluable. Previously, no one at the domestic site understood why the plant in India always seemed to have such odd or erratic demands about delivery dates. And no one in India bothered to think that their U.S. supplier didn't operate the same way. If delivering supplies by specific dates asked for by their India colleagues ensures smoother production or increased sales and profits for the Indian operation, and if the expatriate is a critical link in the communication gap between the United States and India, the expatriate should be given credit for such insights. This should be reflected in his or her performance review.

To obtain this kind of information, either human resource or operational personnel should formally have a debriefing session with the expatriate on his or her return. It should be in an informal interview format so that specific and open-ended questions can be asked. Questions specific to the technical nature of the expatriate's work that relate to the firm's interdependencies should be asked. General questions concerning observations about the relationship between the two operations should also be included.

There is another, even more effective way this aspect of performance review can be handled. At regular intervals, say, every three to six months, the expatriate could be questioned by human resource or operational personnel in the domestic site about how the two operations might better work together. Doing it this way helps maximize the possibility of noting all relevant insights.

Conclusion ————————————————————————————————

With the marketplace becoming increasingly global, the firms that carefully select and manage their internationally assigned personnel will reap the benefits. Today, there is about a 20 percent turnover rate for expatriates when they return. Such a turnover rate is mostly due to firms not managing their expatriate's careers well. Firms are not prepared to appropriately reassign expatriates on their reentry. This obviously indicates that firms do not value the expatriate's experience. This further carries over into the lack of emphasis on appropriately evaluating an expatriate's performance. Appropriately evaluating an expatriate's performance is an issue of both fairness to the expatriate and competitive advantage to the firm. With the valuable experience and insights that expatriates gain, retaining them and effectively positioning them in a firm will mean the firm's business strategy will be increasingly guided by those who understand the companies' worldwide operations and markets.

International Executive Compensation

Reading 7.3
Marilyn Helms
Mark Crowder

Introduction

Few people will dispute the fact that the world is becoming smaller with the development of new technology and the globalization of business. As the old trade barriers melt away, multinational companies are extending an unparalleled sphere of influence into every corner of the world.

The next decade will be an epoch-making stage for the world economy. The North American Free Trade Agreement will undoubtedly boost the flow of goods across our borders and bring about a larger North American market in which to provide many new business opportunities for enterprising Canadian, Mexican, and U.S. entrepreneurs. The European Economic Community is proving to be a formidable competitor on the global stage despite current internal haggling over a common currency. The Pacific-Rim region, as the upstart of economic development, will continue to exert global market pressures through the 1990s as it dissolves regional trade barriers: In particular, China is reentering the global market with new technologies and foreign capital investment, not to mention one-fifth of the world population as a labor pool. Japan, long acknowledged as the world's economic powerhouse next to the United States, is using aggressive strategies to capture a larger slice of the global pie and the American domestic market; however, the new structure of global competition as evidenced by NAFTA and the EEC will force the Japanese, albeit reluctantly, to open their own markets to foreign goods.

In short, the world today is becoming a global market, just as Frank Jennings described: "World economic integration seems to be one of those unstoppable forces" (Reed, Glasgall, & Holstein, 1989). Whether or not they wish to be, all businesses in today's economy are players in the international marketing arena. Small once-domestic enterprises

Source: This article was written especially for this book. Reprinted by permission of the authors.

must now identify their advantages and weaknesses from a global standpoint; strategies for production, marketing and distribution must take advantage of worldwide economies of scale and opportunity costs.

When a company is planning to expand its operation into the international market and establish relevant strategy, it should take into account many factors which have direct and indirect impact on the success of the strategy. One of these factors is compensation for expatriates who will be sent abroad to work as representatives of the company. An effective compensation program must provide adequate incentives to encourage the right persons to accept overseas assignment and to do their best in meeting the company's strategic goals. To attract, motivate, and retain high quality expatriates, the company should make the compensation program not only equitable and compatible to domestic rates but also flexible and competitive at world market rates. For companies that are about to enter international markets, there is an urgent need to understand how we compensate our domestic executives, how other countries compensate their executives, and how to determine the appropriate compensation package for expatriates.

American Compensation ————————————————————————

Although some experts are concerned over whether the U.S. firms would lose their competitive edge and flexible responsiveness in international market competition, American chief executives are big winners in their compensation. According to *Business Week's* 1993 compensation survey of top executives, the average CEO's salary and bonus reached $984,000 in 1992, **excluding** stock options and dividend payments (Bhargava and Jesperson, 1993). In terms of total compensation, the average package for the same year was a record $3,842,247. The ten highest-paid U.S. executives averaged more than $22.8 million (Byrne, 1993).

Recent history is ripe with examples of exorbitant compensation packages for American CEOs, triggered primarily by the exercising of stock options. In 1991, Anthony O'Reilly of H.J. Heinz earned in excess of $75 million, due to the exercising of more than $70 million in options. After exercising options in 1988, Michael D. Eisner, the chairman of Walt Disney, earned over $40 million in total compensation. F. Ross Johnson, CEO of RJR Nabisco, set a record in golden parachutes in 1988 when he left the company with a package of pay, stock, and benefits that came to $53.8 million (Byrne, Grover, & Vogel, 1989). The tremendous fortune gained by American top executives eclipses their international counterparts.

Generally speaking, American executive compensation packages contain four basic components: base salary, bonus, long-term incentives, and other benefits and perks. As noted above, among the highest-paid top executives, basic salary is only a small part of total compensation.

Although there are still some arguments about whether American executives are really paid according to their performance, a more direct relationship between the performance of a company and its executive pay package has become evident in recent years. A company's profitability, far more than any other factor, determines executive paycheck. For instance, Martin J. Wygod of Medco Containment Services received an annual base salary of $459,000 in 1992, but collected more than $33 million in stock options. Wygod's total compensation is mirrored in the astronomical growth in market value of Medco stock, from $150 million in 1984 to more than $5 billion today. Charles Lazarus, the Chairman of Toys "R" Us, earned $315,000 in base salary in 1987, but his contract provided an incentive bonus of 1% of the corporate pretax profits over $18 million from which he got $3.2 million in that year (Brown, 1988). It is increasingly obvious that performance-driven systems are particularly appealing because they motivate executives to focus on specific measures of performance such as profit. The *Business Week* survey indicated that sharp performance gains had a tremendous influence on the jump in executive pay; corporation profits increased by 22% in 1992 and most companies paid their bosses accordingly (Byrne, 1993).

While company performance is certainly a relevant criterion for measuring a CEO's compensation package, many critics are voicing their displeasure. U.S. shareholders and company employees alike are viewing CEO pay with a mixture of distrust and disapproval. This sentiment is fueled by the fact that in the U.S., CEO pay averages more than 100 times that of a typical shop-floor employee (Byrne, 1992). By contrast, it is not uncommon to find Japanese CEO pay at a ratio of only 15 to 30 times that of their employees. An in-depth international comparison is detailed below.

Among long-term incentives, stock options are obviously a most important source of fortune for American executives. By exercising stock options, they are drawing and accumulating incredible wealth. In the United States, options and other types of incentives can make up to 60% of total cash compensation for chief executives of the largest U.S. corporations (Altamirano).

In addition to base salary, bonus, and long-term incentives, there are innumerable benefits and perks in American executive compensation. According to an *INC.* survey in 1988, the percentages of CEOs who enjoy different benefits and perks are as follows: company car and expenses (82%), supplemental life insurance (64%), tax return preparation (52%), club dues and expenses (43%), supplemental medical insurance (40%), personal tax and financial planning (33%), low or no-interest loan (25%), supplemental retirement benefits (15%), deferred compensation (14%), first-class air travel (11%), and moving allowance (8%) (*INC.'s* 1988 Executive Compensation Survey, 1988).

Since women are making a substantial impact on the employment market and more female executives are successfully managing their companies than ever before, women in managerial roles and their compensation have become a recent focus of research. It is estimated that among the managers and administration in the United States, 23% are women. Compared with their male counterparts, successful female executives tend to be better qualified and have greater drive. They are deeply loyal to professions and are really committed to their careers even though some of them have to cope with the conflict between the demands of home and work life. The critical problem is how to really realize equal pay for equal job. Statistics show that the earnings ratio between male and female managers and administrators rose from 1:0.51 to 1:0.67 in the past decade (Stoner & Freeman). This means although female executives have made great progress in their struggle for equal pay, they still have a long way to go. Executives like Linda J. Wachner, CEO of Warnaco Group, are breaking through the "glass ceiling": Wachner's total compensation including stock options was estimated at more than $21 million in 1991 (Crystal, 1992).

International Compensation ————————————————————

Theoretically, international executives' compensation should vary among various countries which have different economic systems and development levels, distinct political and legal institutions, and particular traditions and cultural backgrounds. It is difficult to find universally comparable measures by which we can directly compare executives' compensation throughout the world. Executive compensation in one country differs radically from that of other countries given the variables of taxable income, housing allowances, options, and other perquisites. Following is a brief review of executive compensation practices in some major countries.

European Countries

It seems that European executives are far behind their American counterparts in compensation. As described by Victor Dial, an American who is in charge of sales and marketing at Peugeot, "European managers are grossly underpaid." The disparity, however, is starting to narrow with business globalization.

It is a clear contrast between cultures that in 1988 some 300 U.S. CEOs earned at least $1 million but in Europe less than 30 CEOs could reach the $1 million mark (Altamirano). The average compensation package of $1 million for the chief executive of a billion-dollar-a-year U.S. corporation is typical, but for most of their European counterparts, it looks like a castle in the air. The CEO in a company of comparable size in France earned only $577,000 followed by the Swiss at $468,000, the West Germans at $403,000, and the British at $342,000 (Kirkpatrick, 1988). The twenty best-paid CEOs in Germany earned an estimated $1.8 million in total compensation in 1992, compared with $4.8 million for the top U.S. executives (Morais et al., 1993).

At the small company level, the compensation difference between the U.S. and Europe appeared to be slightly narrower. According to the data collected by Business International Corporation from nearly 2000 companies in the U.S. and Europe, the gross compensation of a general manager of a $30 million company in 10 different countries is provided as follows: U.S.A., $144,000; Switzerland, $140,000; West Germany, $112,000; Austria, $104,000; Netherlands, $96,000; Belgium, $95,000; Italy, $86,000; France, $82,000; Denmark, $76,000; Britain, $62,000 ("Switzerland, Germany Ahead of U.S. in Pay For Some Executives," 1987).

The reason for these discrepancies in executive compensation can be partly explained by the way executives are compensated in different countries. As we mentioned earlier, besides generous base salary, the U.S. CEOs are filling in their pockets with bonuses, stock options and other long-term incentives, while their European counterparts are still in the learning stage to introduce the American compensation system. Another reason is the effect of personal income tax rate. The U.S. executives are getting much more money at 28% tax rate after tax reform, while European executives are staggering under a heavy tax burden. The top marginal tax rate is over 80% in Sweden, 57% in France, and 45% in Britain. High tax rates produce two results; first, they dilute cash compensation, thus making large salaries less attractive than alternative compensation plans. This in turn leads executives to pursue perks or fringe benefits. Many European companies offer tax-favored perks such as company car, club memberships, augmented pensions, and entertainment and housing allowances. Perks in various forms made up 4% to 13% of compensation in most European countries, compared with 2% in the U.S. (Altamirano). "Hidden" payments, in the form of compensation in overseas subsidiaries, are not uncommon for many European companies; such payments are legal in most cases if the executive has foreign responsibilities and non-taxable when deposited in a foreign bank. It is estimated that perhaps 20% of a German CEO's compensation is taken in the form of such subsidiary payments (Morais et. al., 1993).

One trend that should be noted is the fact that in the past few years the European executive compensation structure has changed rapidly. Some compensation methods that originated in the U.S. now are introduced to Europe. Bonus and stock options are becoming more popular. As a result, the compensation difference between the U.S. and European countries is gradually narrowing.

As in the U.S. women in major European countries are playing increasingly important roles in the management field. The new generation of women is more confident and more conscious of equality than in the past. However, the barriers that prevent women from reaching the top are still manifold. For instance, in Britain, the number of female managers remains pitifully small. The quest for equal opportunity and equal pay is still a long battle.

Japan

Traditionally, Japanese compensation for both managers and workers is much less than that in other industrialized nations. Japanese CEOs in the biggest companies earn only one-third of what their American counterparts get. For example, Hiroshi Yamauchi, CEO of Nintendo, was paid an estimated $6.3 million in 1991, making him the highest-paid Japanese executive. By contrast, that same year Thomas Frist, Jr. of Hospital Corporation received $127 million, chiefly due to exercising options. This method of compensation is as yet alien to Japan (Neff, 1993). However, peculiar social and traditional ideas of value and particular corporate culture make the Japanese compensation system much different from that of other countries.

First, the Japanese compensation system is primarily based on seniority. This characteristic is a reflection of the Japanese tradition of respecting seniors. For example, the average wage of a 35-year-old worker is about 32% higher than that of a 30-year-old at one major Japanese corporation, while a 50-year-old employee receives three times that of 25-year-olds.

Secondly, the Japanese compensation system provides long-term incentives to maintain stable employment. Management advocates team spirit and encourages employees to regard themselves as part of the company, therefore establishing a sense of being the master of the company. At the same time, job security comes through the permanent employment system and companies provide a life-time income retirement program and additional retirement bonus. As a result, Japanese employees are very loyal to their company and they push themselves extremely hard to make their contribution to the company. The turnover both of managers and employees in Japan is much lower than that in other countries.

Third, skill level and performance reviews also determine a component of a compensation package which reflects the employee's competence and job performance, although this component is usually not a big part of the wage.

Finally, Japanese companies provide their employees with a variety of fringe benefits such as life insurance, accident insurance, medical insurance, and so on (Altamirano).

Traditionally Japanese women used to be housewives taking care of children and housework. New corporate Japan discovered woman power. About 50% of Japanese women hold jobs. They made up over 40% of the total labor force in 1988. The number of women holding managerial positions increased 50% between 1982 and 1987 (Solo, 1989).

Unlike American women, Japanese women take extra family responsibility and have a different viewpoint on work. Despite the passage of the Equal Employment Opportunity Law in 1986, a third of the working women have settled for a temporary job. This is partly attributed to the traditional idea that women only "want work that will not interrupt their marriage or raising their children" (Solo, 1989). Japanese companies usually demand a total commitment.

China

Before 1979, the socialist planning economy in China was basically a command economy and shortage economy. The central government controlled all natural resources and most production means, and owned most of the large- and medium-sized enterprises. The economic system was highly centralized. Under this system, the government took charge of the allocation of resources, determined the production and distribution of product, controlled money supply in circulation and price level. Employment and the wage system also were decided by government. Managers who were appointed by government had little autonomy in operating management; they were responsible for fulfilling the government plan and not caring whether or not their products would meet the needs of consumers. The managers' salary had nothing to do with their performance. It was fixed or raised by government mainly depending on seniority. At that time, egalitarianism in income was prevalent in China, and government opposed any kind of material incentive. Therefore, the compensation of managers was much lower than that in other developing countries.

Since 1979, Chinese have been carrying out economic reform and an open door policy in an attempt to incorporate market features into their planning system and to create a new system—"government controls market and market guides economic activity." Although there are many difficulties in economic reform due to political environment, ten years of reform has brought great progress. Decentralization and market-orientation provide enterprises with big drive. Competition and material incentive are encouraged. By implementing contract and leasing systems, managers have more autonomy in managing the enterprise. The salary for managers becomes more flexible; if the contract is performed well, a manager can get more bonus. Nevertheless, salary for most Chinese managers ranges from $800 to $1000 a year. But in a country with a $400 GNP per capita, that figure is pretty good. Considering the low cost of living and a variety of benefits such as company car, low rent housing (several dollars a month), and free medical care, the compensation of Chinese managers has been greatly improved in the past ten years.

Because the Chinese government adopted a policy of "extensive employment, low salary" in the past, the rate of employment for women is higher than in certain economically developed countries. Women are playing very important roles in the development of the economy. However, the negative aspect of this policy is low efficiency. "It is estimated that, nationwide, at least 20 million employees, of whom over 60 percent are women, have paid jobs but little work to do" (Lizhen, 1989). On the other hand, in recent years more and more women are emerging in the management field, where they are called strong-women. Generally speaking, equal pay for equal job is common practice, but Chinese women are still striving to gain equal opportunity.

Expatriate Compensation _____

With the development of globalization, more and more Americans will be sent to work abroad. Overseas assignment is not only a career opportunity but also a challenge, both for the company and the expatriate. From the company's standpoint, the cost of a failed assignment or early expatriate return can exceed $100,000 (Thompson, 1992; Black, Mendenhall, and Oddou, 1991). Faced with a strange culture, tradition, language, and environment, the expatriate needs extra energy to perform his or her duty. In order to induce competent persons to carry out overseas operations, the company must develop an effective expatriate compensation program which provides adequate incentive to encourage people to work outside the country and pays well enough to offset the inconvenience and hardship rising from maintaining an American standard of living in a new environment. The program should also take into consideration that the family and social needs of expatriates, such as relationship and communication with family, friends, and business associates, must be properly satisfied.

Companies use two common approaches to setting up an expatriate compensation program. One is the "international cadre" approach which is applied when the company hires expatriates from different nationalities. The purpose of this approach is to provide all expatriates with the equivalent salaries and benefits of the U.S. Another approach is the "balance sheet" approach which balances all costs of an overseas assignment and obtains an adjustment index. This index is then applied to the expatriates' base salary in order to allow them to maintain an economic status equivalent to the one they would have had if they had remained in the U.S. (Mason, 1989). In practice, the balance sheet approach is the most popular approach used by U.S. companies.

The components of a compensation program using the balance sheet approach may vary among different companies, and even within one company with multinational operations. Here, we discuss a few basic components.

The Base Salary

The principle of determining base salary is that it must be comparable with domestic rates. This means the base salary for an expatriate must be in the same range as the basic salary for a similar position in the U.S. With this base salary, the expatriate may maintain the same buying power while on overseas assignments. The base salary usually consists of the spending on goods and services, housing, savings, and tax on an annual basis. The primary difference is that expatriate salary should include some protection from exchange-rate risk (Van Pelt and Wolniansky, 1990).

The Foreign Service Premium

A foreign service premium is extra pay for working outside rather than inside the U.S. It is compensation for the inconveniences of having to live in an alien environment isolated from family and friends, for the difficulties of language and cultural barriers, for greater responsibility and reduced access to home offices resources, and for the effort needed to deal with differences in work habits. Most companies pay foreign service as a percentage of base salary ranging from 10% to 30%. This premium is usually tax-free to the expatriate (Stone, 1986).

The Hardship or Site Allowance

This allowance is paid for hardship due to bad location, extreme climate, non-availability of medical care, and so forth. It is either paid as a percentage of base salary or as a flat amount. The amount of this allowance depends on the difference in location and degree of hardship. For example, in 1986 the monthly site allowance for Hong Kong was from $0 to $200, but $500 to $900 for Beizing, China (Stone, 1986).

Cost of Living Allowance

The purpose of cost of living allowance (COLA) is to allow the expatriate to maintain the same standard of living abroad as that in the U.S. It is really a special kind of make-up because it is hard for the expatriate to find the same living environment and lifestyle in a foreign country, especially in a developing country, as in the U.S. The allowance can protect the expatriate in two ways: by protecting the expatriate's standard of living from cost of living differences in the host country, and by providing protection against exchange rate fluctuation. Typically this allowance ensures that the expatriate has reasonable spendable income for food, clothing, entertainment and the like. Cost of living allowance is normally tax-free and would be adjustable according to any changing of the living environment and the exchange rate (Stone, 1986).

Housing and Utilities Allowance

In addition to base salary, the housing allowance seems to be the biggest part of expatriate compensation. Because housing has a big influence on an expatriate's performance, companies pay ample attention to housing when they set up an expatriate compensation program. In the past few years, companies usually adopted one of three choices: (1) provided a tax-free housing allowance with a maximum limit relating to a certain percentage of base salary, (2) provided housing free of charge, or (3) made a statistical housing deduction based on home location market rate (Stone, 1986).

Although utilities are not as important as housing, this area cannot be neglected because sometimes inadequate utilities cause major dissatisfaction. Utilities are usually paid by the company or the expatriate receives a utilities allowance from the company.

Taxation

Taxation of expatriate income is a very complex problem because various foreign countries have different tax regulations and tax rates. The dilemma for the expatriate is that his or her income is dutiable to both the U.S. and the host country. To reduce the tax burden, the company usually makes up the difference in the expatriate's take-home pay when the tax rate in the host country rises. This method is called "tax protection." Another method is "tax equalization," that is, the company will pay directly to the host country any amount in excess of what the expatriate would have paid if he or she had stayed in the U.S. (Mason, 1989).

Incidental Benefits

Besides various allowances discussed above, companies provide their expatriates with medical benefits. The practice in some companies is to cover all medical expenses (except optical and dental) either in total or for the excess above that provided by medical insurance.

Some other incentives include company car or car allowance, education allowance for children, relocation allowance, rest and recreation leave, and so on.

Conclusion _____

The U.S. chief executives are drawing tremendous wealth from their compensations in base salaries, bonuses, stock options, and other long-term incentives. They also enjoy a variety of benefits and perks provided by their companies. In executive compensation, the U.S. CEOs still lead the world. Although the compensation package of CEOs in European countries is not so big and complicated as the American package, the pay gap is sharply narrowing with the application of American compensation methods in Europe. Executives in some Asian countries, in spite of being far behind the U.S. and Europe in compensation, are rising within their own peculiar corporate culture which sometimes produces an incredible drive. To maintain a competitive advantage in the world market, U.S. businesses must establish long-term strategies with a global perspective and expand the economic frontier to include the entire world. To attract and motivate high quality employees to accept overseas assignments, it is vital for a company to develop an effective expatriate compensation program that is equitable and comparative to the domestic pay rate and also competitive and flexible in the world market.

Bibliography _____

Altamirano, Brenda. "International Compensation." *Business Week*, 29(20), April 25, 1988, p. 8, 11-14, 16-19.

"Are U.S. Executives Better Off?" *Management Review*. April 1987, p. 8.

Brown, Paul B. "*INC*.s Guide to Writing Your Own Ticket," *INC.*, September 1988, p. 80.

Byrne, John A., Ronald Grover, and Todd Vogel. "Is the Boss Getting Paid Too Much?" *Business Week*, May 1, 1989, p. 46, 52.

"Executive Compensation '88. The Take At the Top," *INC.*, September 1988, p. 79,86.

Kirkpatrick, David, "Abroad, It's Another World," *Fortune*, June 6, 1988, p. 78.

Lizhen, Ma, "Women: The Debate on Jobs vs. Homemaking, *China Reconstructs*, No. 3. March 1989, p. 67.

Mason, Thoyeris, "The Expatriate Compensation Package," *Business Week*, 30(25), June 19, 1989, p. 3-5.

Mims, Robert and Ephraim Lewis. "A Portrait of the Boss," *Business Week*, October 20, 1989, p. 25.

Much, Marilyn, "How Much Are Executives Paid?" *Industry Week*, June 15, 1987, p 33.

Reed, Stanley, William Glasgall, and William J. Holstein, "Seeking Growth In a Smaller World," *Business Week*, October 16, 1989, p. 94.

Solo, Sally, "Japan Discovers Woman Power," *Fortune*, June 19, 1989, p. 153, 155.

Stone, Raymond J., "Pay and Perks For Overseas Executives," *Personnel Journal*, January 1986, p. 64, 67.

Stoner, James A. F., and R. Edward Freeman, *Management*, Fourth Edition. Prentice-Hall, Englewood Cliffs, New Jersey, 1989, p. 336.

The Road to Hell

Case 7.1
Gareth Evans

John Baker, Chief Engineer of the Caribbean Bauxite Company of Barracania in the West Indies, was making his final preparations to leave the island. His promotion to production manager of Keso Mining Corporation near Winnipeg—one of Continental Ore's fast-expanding Canadian enterprises—had been announced a month before and now everything had been tidied up except the last vital interview with his successor, the able young Barracanian, Matthew Rennalls. It was vital that this interview be a success and that Rennalls should leave his office uplifted and encouraged to face the challenge of his new job. A touch on the bell would have brought Rennalls walking into the room but Baker delayed the moment and gazed thoughtfully through the window considering just exactly what he was going to say and, more particularly, how he was going to say it.

John Baker, an English expatriate, was forty-five years old and had served his twenty-three years with Continental Ore in many different places: in the Far East; several countries of Africa; Europe; and, for the last two years, in the West Indies. He hadn't cared much for his previous assignment in Hamburg and was delighted when the West Indian appointment came through. Climate was not the only attraction. Baker had always preferred working overseas (in what were termed the developing countries) because he felt he had an innate knack—better than most other expatriates working for Continental Ore—of knowing just how to get on with regional staff. Twenty-four hours in Barracania, however, soon made him realize that he would need all of this "innate knack" if he was to deal effectively with the problems in this field that now awaited him.

At his first interview with Hutchins, the production manager, the whole problem of Rennalls and his future was discussed. There and then it was made quite clear to Baker that one of his most important tasks would be the "grooming" of Rennalls as his successor. Hutchins had pointed out that, not only was Rennalls one of the brightest Barracanian prospects on the staff of Caribbean Bauxite—at London University he had taken first-class honors in the B.Sc. Engineering Degree—but, being the son of the Minister of Finance and Economic Planning, he also had no small political pull.

Source: Gareth Evans, "Road to Hell." Intercollegiate Case Clearing House. Boston. Reprinted by permission.

The company had been particularly pleased when Rennalls decided to work for them rather than for the government in which his father had such a prominent post. They ascribed his action to the effect of their vigorous and liberal regionalization program which, since the Second World War, had produced eighteen Barracanians at mid-management level and given Caribbean Bauxite a good lead in this respect over all other international concerns operating in Barracania. The success of this timely regionalization policy has led to excellent relations with the government—a relationship that had been given an added importance when Barracania, three years later, became independent, an occasion which encouraged a critical and challenging attitude toward the role foreign interests would have to play in the new Barracania. Hutchins had therefore little difficulty in convincing Baker that the successful career development of Rennalls was of the first importance.

The interview with Hutchins was now two years old and Baker, leaning back in his office chair, reviewed just how successful he had been in the "grooming" of Rennalls. What aspects of the latter's character had helped and what had hindered? What about his own personality? How had that helped or hindered? The first item to go on the credit side would, without question, be the ability of Rennalls to master the technical aspects of his job. From the start he had shown keenness and enthusiasm and had often impressed Baker with his ability in tackling new assignments and the constructive comments he invariably made in departmental discussions. He was popular with all ranks of Barracanian staff and had an ease of manner which stood him in good stead when dealing with his expatriate seniors. These were all assets, but what about the debit side?

First and foremost, there was his racial consciousness. His four years at London University had accentuated this feeling and made him sensitive to any sign of condescension on the part of expatriates. It may have been to give expression to this sentiment that, as soon as he returned home from London, he threw himself into politics on behalf of the United Action Party who were later to win the preindependence elections and provide the country with its first Prime Minister.

The ambitions of Rennalls—and he certainly was ambitious—did not, however, lie in politics for, staunch nationalist as he was, he saw that he could serve himself and his country best (for was not bauxite responsible for nearly half the value of Barracania's export trade?) by putting his engineering talent to the best use possible. On this account, Hutchins found that he had an unexpectedly easy task in persuading Rennalls to give up his political work before entering the production department as an assistant engineer.

It was, Baker knew, Rennalls's well-repressed sense of race consciousness which had prevented their relationship from being as close as it should have been. On the surface, nothing could have seemed more agreeable. Formality between the two men was at a minimum; Baker was delighted to find that his assistant shared his own peculiar "shaggy dog" sense of humor so that jokes were continually being exchanged; they entertained each other at their houses and often played tennis together— and yet the barrier remained invisible, indefinable, but ever present. The existence of this "screen" between them was a constant source of frustration to Baker since it indicated a weakness which he was loath to accept. If successful with all other nationalities, why not with Rennalls?

But at least he had managed to "break through" to Rennalls more successfully than any other expatriate. In fact, it was the young Barracanian's attitude—sometimes overbearing, sometimes cynical—toward other company expatriates that had been one of the subjects Baker had raised last year when he discussed Rennalls's staff report with him. He knew, too, that he would have to raise the same subject again in the forthcoming interview because Jackson, the senior draftsman, had complained only yesterday about the rudeness of Rennalls. With this thought in mind, Baker leaned forward and spoke into the intercom. "Would you come in Matt, please? I'd like a word with you," and later, "Do sit down," proffering the box, "have a cigarette." He paused while he held out his lighter and then went on.

"As you know, Matt, I'll be off to Canada in a few days' time, and before I go, I thought it would be useful if we could have a final chat together. It is indeed with some deference that I suggest I can be of help. You will shortly be sitting in this chair doing the job I am now doing, but I, on the other hand, am ten years older, so perhaps you can accept the idea that I may be able to give you the benefit of my longer experience."

Baker saw Rennalls stiffen slightly in his chair as he made this point so added in explanation, "You and I have attended enough company courses to remember those repeated requests by the personnel manager to tell people how they are getting on as often as the convenient moment arises and not just the automatic 'once a year' when, by regulation, staff reports have to be discussed."

Rennalls nodded his agreement, so Baker went on. "I shall always remember the last job performance discussion I had with my previous boss back in Germany. He used what he called the 'plus and minus' technique. His firm belief was that when a senior, by discussion, seeks to improve the work performance of his staff, his prime objective should be to make sure that the latter leaves the interview encouraged and inspired to improve. Any criticism must, therefore, be constructive and helpful. He said that one very good way to encourage a person—and I fully agree with him—is to tell him about his good points—the plus factors—as well as his weak ones—the minus factors—so I thought, Matt, it would be a good idea to run our discussion along these lines."

Rennalls offered no comment, so Baker continued: "Let me say, therefore, right away, that, as far as your own work performance is concerned, the plus far outweighs the minus. I have, for instance, been most impressed with the way you have adapted your considerable theoretical knowledge to master the practical techniques of your job—that ingenious method you used to get air down to the fifth-shaft level is a sufficient case in point—and at departmental meetings I have invariably found your comments well taken and helpful. In fact, you will be interested to know that only last week I reported to Mr. Hutchins that, from the technical point of view, he could not wish for a more able man to succeed to the position of chief engineer."

"That's very good indeed of you, John," cut in Rennalls with a smile of thanks. "My only worry now is how to live up to such a high recommendation."

"Of that I am quite sure," returned Baker, "especially if you can overcome the minus factor which I would like now to discuss with you. It is one which I have talked about before so I'll come straight to the point. I have noticed that you are more friendly and get on better with your fellow Barracanians than you do with Europeans. In point of fact, I had a complaint only yesterday from Mr. Jackson, who said you had been rude to him—and not for the first time either.

"There is, Matt, I am sure, no need for me to tell you how necessary it will be for you to get on well with expatriates because until the company has trained up sufficient people of your caliber, Europeans are bound to occupy senior positions here in Barracania. All this is vital to your future interests, so can I help you in any way?"

While Baker was speaking on this theme, Rennalls had sat tensed in his chair and it was some seconds before he replied. "It is quite extraordinary, isn't it, how one can convey an impression to others so at variance with what one intends? I can only assure you once again that my disputes with Jackson—and you may remember also Godson—have had nothing at all to do with the color of their skins. I promise you that if a Barracanian had behaved in an equally peremptory manner I would have reacted in precisely the same way. And again, if I may say it within these four walls, I am sure I am not the only one who has found Jackson and Godson difficult. I could mention the names of several expatriates who have felt the same. However, I am really sorry to have created this impression of not being able to get on with Europeans—it is an entirely false one—and I quite realize that I must do all I can to correct it as quickly as possible. On your last point, regarding Europeans holding senior positions in the Company for some time to come, I quite accept the situation. I know that Caribbean Bauxite—as they have been doing for many years now—will promote Barracanians as soon as their experience warrants it. And, finally, I would like to assure you, John—and my father thinks the same too—that I am very happy in my work here and hope to stay with the company for many years to come."

Rennalls had spoken earnestly and, although not convinced by what he had heard, Baker did not think he could pursue the matter further except to say, "All right, Matt, my impression *may* be wrong, but I would like to remind you about the truth of that old saying, 'What is important is not what is true but what is believed.' Let it rest at that."

But suddenly Baker knew that he didn't want to "let it rest at that." He was disappointed once again at not being able to "break through" to Rennalls and having yet again to listen to his bland denial that there was any racial prejudice in his makeup. Baker, who had intended ending the interview at this point, decided to try another tack.

"To return for a moment to the 'plus and minus technique' I was telling you about just now, there is another plus factor I forgot to mention. I would like to congratulate you not only on the caliber of your work but also on the ability you have shown in overcoming a challenge which I, as a European, have never had to meet.

"Continental Ore is, as you know, a typical commercial enterprise—admittedly a big one—which is a product of the economic and social environment of the United States and Western Europe. My ancestors have all been brought up in this environment for the past two or three hundred years and I have, therefore, been able to live in a world in which commerce (as we know it today) has been part and parcel of my being. It has not been something revolutionary and new which has suddenly entered my life. In your case," went on Baker, "the situation is different because you and your forebears have only had some fifty or sixty years' experience of this commercial environment. You have had to face the challenge of bridging the gap between fifty and two or three hundred years. Again, Matt, let me congratulate you—and people like you—once again on having so successfully overcome this particular hurdle. It is for this very reason that I think the outlook for Barracania—and particularly Caribbean Bauxite—is so bright."

Rennalls had listened intently and when Baker finished, replied, "Well, once again, John, I have to thank you for what you have said, and, for my part, I can only say that it is gratifying to know that my own personal effort has been so much appreciated. I hope that more people will soon come to think as you do."

There was a pause and, for a moment, Baker thought hopefully that he was about to achieve his long awaited "breakthrough," but Rennalls merely smiled back. The barrier remained unbreached. There remained some five minutes' cheerful conversation about the contrast between the Caribbean and Canadian climate and whether the West Indies had any hope of beating England in the Fifth Test before Baker drew the interview to a close. Although he was as far as ever from knowing the real Rennalls, he was nevertheless glad that the interview had run along in this friendly manner and, particularly, that it had ended on such a cheerful note.

This feeling, however, lasted only until the following morning. Baker had some farewells to make, so he arrived at the office considerably later than usual. He had no sooner sat down at his desk than his secretary walked into the room with a worried frown on her face. Her words came fast. "When I arrived this morning I found Mr. Rennalls already waiting at my door. He seemed very angry and told me in quite a peremptory manner that he had a vital letter to dictate which must be sent off without any delay. He was so worked up that he couldn't keep still and kept pacing about the room, which is most unlike him. He wouldn't even wait to read what he had dictated. Just signed the page where he thought the letter would end. It has been distributed and your copy is in your 'in tray.' "

High Technology, Incorporated: The International Benefits Problem

Case 7.2
Rae Andre

At High Technology Incorporated (HTI), the benefits policy for international assignments states that:

> Wherever legally possible, HTI will attempt to provide the employee with Home Country benefits under the Life Insurance, Disability Pension and Social Security Plans during temporary international assignments.

HTI employees typically spend one to three, and sometimes as long as four years overseas. Historically, during this time, many employees have received benefits equaling or surpassing those of the home country. Recently, company policy has shifted toward equalizing benefits across countries. The system has been less than perfect, however, with some employees finding that their stay overseas has reduced their benefits. At a 1984 conference for the corporate personnel managers of local companies, Jack Cooke, HTI Corporate International Benefits Manager, commented on HTI's difficulties in fairly compensating its U.S. employees abroad. During his discussion, he made the following points.

Home Country Coverage

In 1984 HTI carried out an audit of employees and inventoried people for the purposes of determining offsets—the benefits given to overseas employees to offset loss of home country coverages for pensions, insurance, and similar benefits. The issue was to examine offsetting benefits

---

Source: Reprinted by permission of the author.

to determine (1) if there was enough funding and (2) if the funding was allocated to the appropriate areas.

HTI gathered pension and benefits data for each employee on overseas assignment. A benefits book was published for each individual. The audit revealed that there was a considerable amount of overfunding (in the plans of four countries) and some underfunding—people with no plans at all. Cooke believed that HTI was not fulfilling its promise to provide equitable contracts to employees sent overseas. The audit pointed up the fact that whereas HTI was providing adequate funding, the money was being put in the wrong buckets—it was not being well distributed among the countries and individuals who needed it.

Cooke noted that the employees' main fear concerns the security of their coverage. He vividly recalls the old saying "Don't worry . . . but don't die or get sick on assignment!" and how it applied to a Canadian employee in Scotland. The employee died on the last night of his assignment. When his wife was questioned by Scottish authorities shortly after the death, it was discovered that the man had been covered by Canadian Social Insurance (federal social security), and so was ineligible for death benefits in Scotland. The Scottish social security agency refused to pay a death benefit and returned all HTI contributions to the wife, saying the employee should not have been covered in the first place.

The Scottish case highlights the need to review the current local policy to determine when coverage should apply and what steps should be taken to ensure continuity of coverage. Currently the company does not cover the employee under foreign programs when an employee cannot be maintained in a home country plan. A lack of coverage results in one of two major ways.

First, the home country legal requirements or plan documents may not permit participation by nonresidents. For example, a citizen and resident of Country A is transferred to Country B. Country A does not provide certain coverages, retirement income coverage, for example, to its citizens if they live outside Country A. HTI does not provide this coverage either.

Second, nonnationals in the home country are not allowed to stay in home country programs. For example, a citizen of Country B is working in Country A. In Country A, he is only covered for health insurance for a specified period, after which, unless he becomes a citizen, he will not be covered. Again, HTI has no policy to cover him.

To give a real-life example: "What about my pensions in the U.K.?" is a question often asked by "permanent" British employees living in the U.S. From the company's viewpoint, it may be difficult to decide what "permanent" means. Cooke pointed out that any American citizen on a United States payroll is covered by U.S. Social Security anywhere in the world. This type of problem only arises with HTI employees from nations other than the United States.

Additional Issues ⎯⎯⎯⎯⎯⎯⎯⎯⎯⎯⎯⎯⎯⎯⎯⎯⎯⎯⎯⎯⎯⎯⎯

Cooke identified several other problems that he felt needed to be addressed. One was that the permanent relocation policy did not address past service: What happens if a person relocates permanently out of their home country? How should their benefits, especially their pension benefits, be calculated? Another problem was that the company and employee sometimes differed about how to define home country. If an employee had been in a country other than his or her country of origin for ten years or more, which was the employee's home country? Also, there were some employees with *no* evident home country.

Cooke sent questionnaires to the personnel heads in the various countries concerned, asking them to tell him what problems they would face in attempting to make the international benefits program more equitable. Three major issues were identified.

1. *Legal.* The first issue was complying with legal requirements in the various host countries. Of the three issues, this was considered to be the most serious. For example, sometimes employees found themselves involuntarily vested in host country plans by law, when HTI would have preferred them to be covered in the United States. Cooke pointed out that to date corrective action on this particular problem has involved alerting line management of the situation and developing recommendations.

   The home country law sometimes excludes nonresidents from coverage in their home country. As an example, if a U.K. (English) resident is outside the U.K. for more than three years, he or she has to leave the retirement plan. Extensions are possible, but only for the fourth year. The nonresidents can buy back into the U.K. plan later on. But in the meantime, the company has chosen to provide coverage for subsequent years.

2. *Financial.* Two issues arise here. The first is liability for past service. For example, with the case just mentioned, who pays for the uncovered years? The host country? The individual? HTI? Also, individuals may lose coverage due to local fiscal requirements. For example, a country might not have a sliding scale for social security benefits, thus putting the well-paid individual at a disadvantage relative to his home country peers.

3. *Administrative.* Not all HTI facilities even *have* pension plans. And among those that do, there are different requirements. Some have a minimum age of twenty-five, some do not. Some have a one-year waiting period for eligibility, some do not. Some have voluntary participation, some do not. And some are benefit plans, whereas some are contribution plans.

At the time of Jack Cooke's talk, these issues at HTI were far from solved. The policy was that when HTI moved someone permanently, the employee would get the sum of the benefits from the country left and the new country. However, because of high inflation in many countries, this often meant that the employee was losing money.

P A R T B

HTI: Cooke's Recommendations _____

HTI's Corporate International Benefits Manager, Jack Cooke, feels that the company's benefit policy should be revised. The problem is summarized by him as follows: "If HTI moves someone permanently, they get the sum of the parts, and the money left in the other country is often losing money for them due to inflation. This is all they get and it's not adequate." Cooke recommends that the HTI policy be revised to read:

> Assignments shall not result in loss of retirement and retirement-related benefits to the employee, whether compulsory or voluntary, calculated in accordance with the program in effect in the Home Country.

Cooke believes that for temporaries—people on international assignments of up to four years—the problem should be fixed locally. "Whatever the component—risk insurance, annuity, or pension plan—we should sit down with local counsel to provide substitute coverage that equals what they had at home." This may not lead to double coverage since HTI tries to get temporary people excluded from local plans wherever possible. Sometimes HTI chooses to live with the double coverage.

Cooke weighed the pros and cons of providing the employee with the sum of the parts earned in their different countries of employment plus vesting them and updating them in their home country. The advantages are that this policy:

- Reflects the employee's HTI career in each country
- Updates vested benefits so that total benefits are current
- Provides equitable treatment with employees in the home country
- Allows the company to retain control
- Is understood by employees
- Is simple to administer and provides more company flexibility than the alternative (i.e., moving people from country to country and changing their benefits each time, which employees resist)

The disadvantages of this policy are that it

- Is administratively complex
- May not recognize continuous service for survivorship and disability benefits
- Will be affected by exchange rates (i.e., severe inflation)
- May not achieve retirement income objectives

Cooke noted that through their research HTI found that other companies had not solved the problem either.

PART C

The Bandits _____

HTI faces an additional problem, one faced by most international companies. The problem is reclassifying people from temporary to permanent. Cooke noted, "We have thirteen to fourteen American 'bandits' living in Geneva, Switzerland. Their kids can't even speak English, and they own ski chalets. They have home leave benefits that are more generous than others. But they are 'temporary,' and they are so powerful we can't get them to change to permanent status." The same problem is found among some employees who live in the United States. Exhibit 1 indicates how many bandits of various nationalities are employed by HTI.

On the other hand, if HTI does change the bandits' designated home country, the new home country must give them benefits as if they spent their entire career there. This can be costly to the company in some instances, but it can also be an inducement: "Come over to Switzerland at age sixty-three and we'll fix you up. If the company does not do this, it reduces its flexibility to move people."

Exhibit 1. Employees on Extended Assignments

	Assignment Years				
	4-5	5-7	7-10	10 +	Total
To Switzerland	13	18	11	7	49*
To U.S.	9	18	6	1	34

*From Germany n = 11, Netherlands n = 8, U.K. n = 17, U.S. n = 13.
Source: Sample of 550 expatriates.

Part 8

LABOR RELATIONS

Strategic Management of Worker Health and Safety Issues in Mexico's Maquiladora Industry[1,2]

Reading 8.1
Mark C. Butler
Mary B. Teagarden

Mexico is a country ripe for worker health and safety abuse. Economically, the country is striving aggressively to attract investment and create jobs. Geographically, it shares a 2000 mile border with the United States, whose more stringent pollution regulations make Mexico a tempting destination for factories running away from environmental restrictions; and for manufacturers looking for a cheap, albeit illegal, toxic waste dump. In addition, stringent worker health and safety regulations in the United States "encourage" firms to flee to nearby Mexico to exploit less rigorous enforcement. Against these forces are, for example, barely 100 industrial pollution inspectors and a six-year-old law covering emissions of 12,000 substances—versus the 75,000 regulated in the United States. To compound the issue, there is the classic enforcement problem that comes with underpaid civil servants and wealthy violators: bribery. Approval of the North American Free Trade Agreement (NAFTA) between Canada, Mexico, and the U.S. intensifies the importance of these issues because it is expected to increase trade between these countries.

Differences in business practices, business standards, values and norms guiding behavior are inherent in international business. These differences are particularly evident when comparing business activities in developed and developing countries, and perhaps stand in sharpest contrast when examining issues such as worker health and safety. Internationally, multinationals (MNEs) commonly face settings where the "rules of the game" are far more ambiguous, contradictory, and dynamic than in domestic contexts. The strategies MNEs use to manage these cultural and contextual differences have a significant impact

---

Source: Reprinted by permission of the authors.

on their overall organizational effectiveness. Human resource management (HRM) practices can be used to align MNE and host country affiliate norms, values, standards, goals, and objectives. The strategic use of HRM, a view based on a long-range future, extends this alignment into the future in an effort to insure a major long-term positive impact on the host country affiliate's productivity and effectiveness.

This article begins with a discussion of strategic HRM and the benefits of reconciliation of MNE-affiliate differences in Mexico's maquiladora industry, which primarily consists of manufacturing facilities located along the Mexico-U.S. border. We provide an overview of the maquiladora industry and the North American Free Trade Agreement (NAFTA), then discuss the strategic importance of worker health and safety issues in this context. Finally, we present HRM design alternatives, and use the strategic HRM perspective to identify recommendations for managing differences and, more generally, to discuss global competitiveness.

Strategic Human Resource Management and the Maquiladora Context

Strategic human resource management is the design and implementation of human resource systems to support the firm's short- *and* long-term strategic objectives. The predominant theme in strategic HRM literature concerns the need to fit HRM strategy to the larger organizational context, specifically, to the firm's business and functional strategies. Strategic HRM is believed to promote productivity *and* overall organizational effectiveness (Devanna, Fombrun, and Tichy, 1984). This is accomplished in part by increasing worker satisfaction and investing in worker development. In contrast to the traditional view of HRM which is typically reactive, control oriented, and productivity focused, the strategic orientation is decidedly proactive in nature. Specifically, the importance of viewing traditional aspects of HRM—recruitment and selection, training, appraisal, compensation, and employee relations—from both short- and long-term perspectives affords an organization the opportunity to gain or maintain competitive advantage.

Global Competition

In the increasingly competitive global marketplace there appears to be a convergence of many manufacturing techniques, those traditional areas where competitiveness has been enhanced by increasing efficiencies. The "hard" techniques (and advantages) of Total Quality Management, Integrated Manufacturing and Design, Just-in-Time Inventory Control, Process Mapping, Benchmarking, and Best Practices are rapidly diffused internationally as compared to the "soft" techniques associated with HRM (Von Glinow and Teagarden, 1988). This diffusion has resulted in increased expectations of high quality and productivity as the new bases of competitiveness: the level of the playing field has risen for all competitors. The advent of these "hard" techniques suggest, at a minimum, the need for a more strategic focus on recruitment, selection, and training issues. However, those MNEs able to incorporate *and* move beyond the more rapidly diffused "hard" techniques to develop effective approaches for managing human resources will win future competitiveness challenges.

Strategic HRM provides a compelling rationale for reconciling MNE-affiliate differences in business practices, business standards, values and norms: from a long-term perspective strategic HRM contributes to development of a capable, effective, world-class workforce. HRM serves additional, important purposes for MNEs operating internationally. International strategic HRM practices are used to enhance MNE control in foreign affiliates, and as a mechanism for bridging cross-cultural issues that are often at the heart of MNE-affiliate differences (Milliman, Von Glinow and Nathan, 1991; Dowling and Schuler, 1990; Adler and Ghadar, 1990). Consequently, in an international setting, strategic HRM emphasizes strategic fit issues, control issues, and cross-cultural issues.

Traditionally, two generic competitive strategies have been identified: competition based on overall cost leadership, where the firm is a low cost producer; and competition based on differentiation, where the firm competes using, for example, quality, customer responsiveness, or service (Porter, 1980). Increasingly, MNEs find that remaining competitive in the global marketplace requires them to integrate these perspectives and produce high quality, low cost products with sufficient speed to meet consumer demands. As MNEs encounter these more sophisticated challenges, they find that they must shift from traditional to more strategic HRM system designs.

Maquiladoras and Global Competition

From the short term perspective, maquiladoras represent a source of "cheap labor." The "cheap labor" concept, however, deserves closer inspection. If "cheap labor" were the only criterion, then less industrialized countries like People's Republic of China (PRC), India, Thailand, or Viet Nam would offer more attractive manufacturing sites than Mexico because their wage rates are lower. Mexico offers additional benefits such as proximity to the U.S. and higher levels of productivity—in terms of output *and* quality—than these alternatives. MNEs that compete on cost, but are not sensitive to issues such as worker health and safety, run the risk of increased costs. In the short-term these costs come in the form of turnover, absenteeism, and time lost due to illness; in the long-term they risk increased regulation (cf. Barrera Bassols, 1990).

Over twenty percent of maquiladora production is done in plants using world class state-of-the-art technology that affords high quality and manufacturing flexibility. Ford, General Motors, Hewlett Packard, AT&T, and other MNEs identify Mexican plants as their highest quality producers in the world. This sentiment is echoed by Japanese MNEs such as Sony, Hitachi, and Sanyo. German MNEs like Mercedes Benz are opening Mexican operations to take advantage of high quality at a relatively low price. Even maquiladoras that use lower levels of production technology are challenged by the need to produce low cost, high quality products. The strategic challenge for MNEs is to produce relatively low cost, high quality products with sufficient speed to meet consumer demands.

Patterns of HRM in the Maquiladora Industry

To meet this global challenge well trained, loyal, committed workers are critical maquiladora resources. MNEs do not develop such workers by implementing short-term HRM thinking. This requires HRM programs that enhance individual performance through selection, training, development, and attention to culturally appropriate reward systems—all dimensions associated with strategic HRM thinking. This strategic approach can be contrasted with a more traditional approach that is encountered in maquiladoras that have a short-term, "low-cost" orientation.

Devanna, Fombrun and Tichy (1984) identify four types of assumptions about people that underlie HRM system design: (1) the nature of the employment contract; (2) the degree of participation in decision-making; (3) internal versus external labor markets; and (4) group versus individual performance. We have contrasted and extended traditional and strategic maquiladora HRM characteristics using these categories in Table 1.

As seen in Table 1, maquiladoras which embrace the strategic perspective invest in development of their human assets, workers who contribute to attainment of the firm's strategic objectives. For example, these firms implement training *and* development programs, make higher use of culturally appropriate reward systems, and develop internal labor markets. Additionally, issues regarding management of worker health and safety move to the foreground and are proactively managed when viewed through this strategic HRM lens. The next section will introduce the maquiladora industry, and identify MNE-affiliate differences relating to worker health and safety.

An Overview of the Maquiladora Industry ————————————

The Mexico-United States border is longer than any other between a developed and a developing country in the world. In 1965, Washington, D.C. and Mexico City established the Border Industrialization Program

Table 1. Dimensions of Traditional and Strategic Maquiladora HRM Systems

Characteristic	Traditional Maquiladora HRM System	Strategic Maquiladora HRM System
Time Horizon	Short-term	Long-term
Employment Contract	Work for Pay	Meaningful Work for Loyal, Committed Service
Training Objectives	Necessary Task Specific	Task Specific *and* Developmental
Decision-Making & Power	Top Down	Shared (Regarding Tasks)
Labor Market	External	Internal
Group vs. Individual Performance	Individual	Combination
Basis for Control	External, Mechanistic	Internal, Behaviorally Driven
Culturally Appropriate Rewards	Low Use	High Use
Basis for Competition	Cost	Cost *and* Differentiation

which created a free trade zone for work processing along the border. While the zone has been extended to allow location in most of Mexico, more than 80% of the maquiladoras are still located within 50 miles of the U.S. border. Maquiladoras—which are factories, assembly, or processing plants—are used to take advantage of the Border Industrialization Program. Maquiladoras are most commonly called maquilas or, less frequently, twin plants or in-bond facilities.[3] The agglomeration of maquilas are also referred to as the maquiladora industry, although they represent myriad industrial sectors.

Maquiladoras have proven attractive to foreign and Mexican investors alike, and there are now over 2,300 maquiladora facilities employing nearly 500,000 workers. They provide jobs for one tenth of Mexico's workforce, and are its most dynamic economic sector accounting for four-fifths of Mexico's manufactured exports and two-fifths of its total exports to the United States. Mexico is the U.S.'s third largest trading partner after Canada and Japan, numbers one and two respectively. With the passage of NAFTA, many economists believe that Mexico will become the U.S.'s second largest trading partner in the very near future.

The maquiladora industry is comprised of firms seeking (1) cheap, abundant labor and low costs of the other factors of production, such as manufacturing space, utilities, and so forth; (2) quick access to the U.S.

market; and (3) relaxed worker health and safety standards. These maquiladoras produce an array of goods including consumer electronics, electronic parts and assemblies, apparel, automotive equipment and accessories, furniture, toys, health care products and food. Many of the manufacturing processes use "vast quantities" of toxic materials including solvents, heavy metals, acids, resins, paints, plastics, oils, varnishes, and pesticides. The largest single maquiladora product category, electronics, often involves the use of solder flux and organic solvents that are flammable and can cause skin irritation and eye damage (Jenner, 1991).[4]

Maquiladora Worker Health and Safety

There is virtually no margin for disputes over basic rights or minimum working conditions in any organization operating in Mexico—these are prescribed and defined by Mexican Labor Law. Article 3 of the 1970 Labor Law states that employment is a right and duty of each individual, and demands liberty and dignity to those that toil. The law requires that work must be effected in a way that assures life, health, and an economic improvement for the worker and his or her family. In exchange, the worker's principle obligation is to personally execute the task contracted for under the direction and dependency of those in charge (Urbina, 1972).

Mexican Labor Law further stipulates that all employers provide employees with minimum levels of training and the formation of training committees to include management and workers. According to the law, training should allow the worker to improve skills, prepare for higher positions that may become available, improve worker productivity and general welfare, and minimize work accidents (Price, Waterhouse, 1990). Although training dictated by the law is not subsidized by the government, a tax deduction for the program costs and expenses is allowed. All training programs must be submitted to the Labor Ministry Board for approval.

Finally, labor law also requires the formation of health and security committees to insure that all companies meet the minimum requirements for health and safety on their premises. These committees are comprised of management *and* worker representatives, and work in conjunction with labor authorities to analyze and investigate causes of work-related accidents and illnesses; to develop safety practices and procedures; to communicate these to the workforce; and to oversee compliance. Both the Social Security and Labor authorities are empowered to issue safety regulations and to inspect sites to evaluate compliance with minimum work standards; to develop special standards in accordance with the type of industry or activity; and to impose sanctions for noncompliance.

In summary, existing laws, which are designed to protect Mexican workers, seem to be adequate to that purpose. In fact, such laws could be described from a generally proactive, or strategic HRM framework. Nevertheless, an interesting, but separate issue revolves around compliance with these laws. As in the U.S., organizations vary in their level of commitment to compliance with such laws, which sets the stage for creation of performance gaps such as those discussed in more detail below.

Maquiladora Workplace Conditions

Conditions relating to worker health and safety vary greatly in maquiladoras. Sklair (1989:173) cautions, "It is important to distinguish between Fortune 500-type firms—those with a corporate image they wish to protect, at least on the surface—and the mass of reasonably well run small and medium sized maquilas on one hand, and the limited group of atrocious factories that would be a scandal anywhere in the world, on the other."

Even among the best run maquilas it is possible to identify very great performance gaps between what is legally required and what actually occurs. Nevertheless, hard data on working conditions in maquilas is extremely scarce.[5] According to a report in *Technology Review*, "not only do U.S. and Mexican maquiladora managers attempt to deny access to their plants and their workers, but the Mexican government discourages inquiries and health studies" (LaDou, 1991).

What investigators have been able to piece together is that while working conditions in maquiladoras vary greatly, they are often inferior to those in the U.S. and other developed countries.[6] Many plants are inadequately ventilated, poorly lighted, and accidents resulting from inattention to safety procedures and the absence of safety equipment are frequent. According to one report, "Nogales maquiladoras reported more than 2,000 accidents in 1989—three times the accident rate of factories on the U.S. side of the border" (Satchell, 1991).

Workers in many maquilas report that sanitation is poor, production quotas are high, noise is excessive, and machinery is often unsafe. They receive few rest periods and in the electronics industry must perform long hours of microscopic assembly work. Many regularly handle hazardous materials, however the protective gloves, clothing, and other safeguards routinely required in U.S. plants are rare. To make matters worse, workers often lack safety instruction on the hazardous materials they are handling, either because they are not available or they are not written in Spanish. Many workers complain of grueling production schedules and factory fumes.

One report of interviews with dozens of employees in border communities identified complaints of headaches, vision and respiratory problems, and skin diseases caused by soldering fumes, solvents and other chemicals, particularly in the electronics assembly industry. While some plants supply protective gloves, few women wear them because they hamper dexterity and prevent workers from maintaining fast-paced production schedules (Satchell, 1991). Additionally, few men use protective gear because of "machismo"—use of such protection is not considered sufficiently masculine.

The following passage describes a worst-case example of the extent of the performance gap between what is legally required and what may occur. It is based on a study of long term effects of exposure to hazardous chemicals by Dr. Isabel de la Alonso of the Matamoros School of Special Education. The maquiladora in question is the former U.S. company, Mallory Capacitors:

> The Matamoros exposures occurred for full workdays over many months. The women often had to reach into deep vats of PCBs with no protection other than rubber gloves. Many of the workers developed the chloracne rash these chemicals normally cause. The children of these workers, however, were born with unusual characteristics that fell outside well-documented conditions such as Down's syndrome. With degrees of retardation ranging from mild to profound, these children had broad noses, bushy eyebrows, webbed and deformed hands and feet, and other distinctive birth defects. The mothers all reported that their jobs involved washing capacitors (small devices that hold electrical charges) in a chemical mixture they knew only as "electrolito." As they worked with the liquid it would cover their hands and arms and splash on their faces (Satchell, 1991).

Some of the affected mothers have filed a lawsuit against Mallory Capacitors claiming negligence. However, Mallory has changed ownership twice since the women were exposed, and the case is currently "under review" until the liable parties can be determined. Again, we reiterate that this is a worst-case example. Nevertheless, worst-case examples reflect negatively on all maquiladoras and foreign investors in general.

North American Free Trade Agreement Implications

In June 1991 the governments of the three North American nations— Canada, Mexico, and the United States—began negotiating a free trade agreement, referred to as the North American Free Trade Agreement, or NAFTA, and all three governments signed initial approval in October 1992. NAFTA is designed to reduce or eliminate barriers to trade and investment flows and went into effect on January 1, 1994. NAFTA's goal is ". . . to progressively eliminate obstacles to the flow of goods and services and to investment, provide for the protection of intellectual property rights, and establish a fair and expeditious dispute settlement mechanism" (U.S. Department of State, 1991).

Currently, both Canada and Mexico are extremely dependent on the U.S. as a trading partner—over two thirds of their trade is with the U.S.—and as a primary source of foreign investment. Some refer to the relationship as "the elephant and two ants." NAFTA will intensify the economic interaction between the U.S., Canada, and Mexico and criticism of NAFTA has come from myriad sources.[7] According to Clement and Gerber (1992) there are four basic themes in this criticism:

1. Labor and community groups in (mainly) Canada and the U.S. strongly attack the potential decline of the manufacturing

sector, loss of jobs, and deterioration of living standards that could result from freer trade and from MNCs moving to lower cost locations and the resulting disruptions to communities that would follow. In this view the NAFTA is frequently likened to a gigantic *maquiladora*.

2. Environmentalists in all countries, viewing the poor environmental enforcement record in Mexico, foresee a significant exodus of Canadian and U.S. firms to escape the stricter enforcement in their countries, aggravating both regional and global pollution.

3. Human rights groups in the three countries point to the absence of truly democratic processes and human rights violations in Mexico and advise that increasing trade links would implicitly condone such behavior.

4. In both Mexico and Canada NAFTA opponents are concerned with the potential loss of cultural identity, sovereignty and political autonomy that could result from a closer, more open relationship with their much larger and more powerful trading partner.

In light of this NAFTA-related criticism, MNE activities will be under heightened scrutiny, and MNEs will face increased pressure to respond to MNE-affiliate differences. From a reactive perspective, it is in the MNE's best interest to at least minimally comply with Mexico's worker health and safety regulations. They expose themselves to risk otherwise. From a strategic perspective, proactive management of worker health and safety issues sends an important message to employees that they are valued, and being cared for by management. Such paternalism is valued and expected by Mexican workers. A spillover benefit that accrues to MNEs through proactive management of worker health and safety issues is enhancement of their reputation in the local community and in the global marketplace.

Implications for Human Resource Executives

Mexico is currently an off-shore manufacturing "hot spot," and is expected to remain so, and grow in importance under NAFTA. Attractiveness of off-shore sites, however, shifts with changes in labor cost and availability, and other related costs. Maquiladoras, or any other off-shore manufacturing option, only remain an attractive alternative so long as they are able to help MNEs achieve or sustain global competitiveness. The recommendations offered in the following section apply as well to Thailand, Viet Nam, or Kenya as they do to Mexico.

Control-Based HRM Design

As mentioned earlier, MNEs can have a short-term productivity objective. For these MNEs, a control-based HRM design is sufficient, but not without cost. Control-based HRM strategies rely on power-coercive techniques, which are primarily based on negative reinforcement approaches such as docking pay, public chastisement, and employee termination as a solution to a variety of problems (e.g., tardiness, errors). These control-based designs are typically implemented in a relatively short time frame. They are, however, also associated with high levels of conflict, much of it rooted in cross-cultural issues. In maquiladoras this conflict results in increases in turnover and absenteeism, and higher costs associated with selection and training. It is not uncommon for MNEs to abandon their maquiladora operation due to the costs associated with an over reliance on this conflict-laden approach. For MNEs that use this HRM design and continue maquiladora operations, reports of quality and productivity deficiencies abound.

Human Relations-Based HRM Design

The longer-term human relations-based HRM design is a middle stance in which MNEs meet both increased productivity and improved worker satisfaction objectives. Human relations-based strategies rely on rational-empirical techniques, such as training or cross-training for specific tasks, and use of culturally appropriate rewards such as subsidized lunches, make-up kits, and records. These necessarily require more time to implement than do control-based HRM designs. An advantage to human relations-based designs is that they typically produce lower levels of conflict than control-based designs. Since implementation of this design typically results in productivity gains and satisfaction improvements, they are also associated with lower levels of turnover and absenteeism, and reduced selection and training costs. Given these benefits, maquiladoras that pursue this less conflict-laden design would likely emphasize both task-related and quality-focused worker training programs.

Human Resource-Based HRM Design

Finally, MNEs can simultaneously pursue productivity, satisfaction, and development objectives. In this case, a long-term human resource-based design is necessary. Such long-term HRM designs rely on normative-reeducative techniques, are process oriented, and aimed at generating improvements in worker satisfaction and development. These techniques include, for example, task specific training and cross-training *and* developmental training that could range from work-related quality or supervisory training to completion of high school education. While this design must be implemented over a longer period of time, attainment of its objectives is associated with the lowest level of conflict, and with maximum gains in productivity, levels of satisfaction, and overall employee development. Consequently, turnover and absenteeism are lower in maquiladoras using this design. However, training and selection costs, at least in the short-term, are likely be higher than those encountered in maquiladoras pursing shorter-term HRM designs. However, an emphasis on training and selection results in a workforce capable of producing world-class quality products that meet demanding customer schedules. Figure 1 illustrates the costs and results of these three HRM strategies.

We feel there is a compelling reason for MNEs to consider the strategic human resource-based HRM design outlined above: customer preferences change over time. Those who are satisfied with low cost at this point in time may well expect low cost, high quality, and rapid delivery in the future—especially if global competitors up the ante. Development of a workforce that can deliver on these more sophisticated demands takes investment in training and development, and time. MNEs that opt for strategies that yield only short term benefits place themselves at risk in the long term competitive arena where ability to compete on cost, quality-based differentiation, and speed are likely to be critical.

Figure 1. HRM Strategy Costs and Benefits

Strategies Model
Based on the following management objectives:
• Worker Productivity
• Worker Satisfaction
• Worker Development

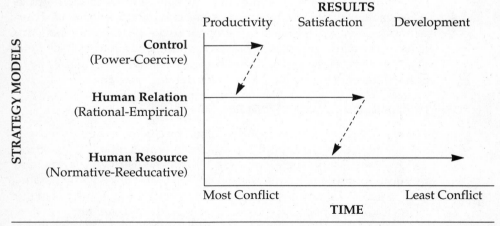

Note: From M.C. Butler and M.B. Teagarden (1993) Strategic Management of worker health, safety and envlronmental issues in Mexico's maquiladora industry. *Human Resource Management*, 32(4). Based on R. Chin & K.D. Benne (1976) General strategies for effecting change in human systems. In W.G. Bennis, K.D. Benne, R. Chin & K.E. Corey (eds.), *The Planning of Change* (3rd ed.). New York: Holt, Rinehart & Winston.

Conclusions and Future Directions ————————————————————

The foregoing discussion identifies a serious question that must be asked: How do we go about the task of solving the variety of problems identified in this article? We suggest that the strategic HRM perspective provides powerful rationale for problem solution. What we advocate is a systematic study conducted through the human resource function of organizations that currently work in the international context. In particular, those organizations that operate facilities both in the U.S. and in Mexico should be examined. While an extensive amount of anecdotal evidence exists which suggests a path that *should* be followed, such data are also somewhat insufficient for a broader range of organizational purposes.

To clarify and specifically identify the path, which would eliminate any insufficiencies in data which currently exist, a more scientifically rigorous and systematic approach is warranted. This approach must combine both quantitative and qualitative data collection methods in order to build on work that has accumulated to date. Further, the study should document (a) the extent to which the worker safety and health and environmental problems discussed earlier actually exist, (b) whether or not such occurrences vary by industry, and (c) what specific HRM strategies are currently being employed (if any) to resolve the identified problems. In short, the goal of future activity is to identify the human resource management "best practices" that can be most effectively matched to resolving the complex problems noted above. Without such a systematic approach, worker safety and health issues in the maquiladora setting will continue to go unresolved, jeopardizing countless numbers of workers as well as prospects for improved economic health between Canada or the U.S. and Mexico.

Endnotes ————————————————————————————————

1. Adapted from M.C. Butler and M.B. Teagarden (1993) Strategic management of worker health, safety and environmental issues in Mexico's maquiladora industry. *Human Resource Management*, 32(4). An earlier version of this manuscript received the Minerva Education Institute Irwin/Proctor & Gamble Award for Research Contributions to Worker Health, Safety and Environment at the 1992 National Academy of Management Meeting, Las Vegas, Nevada.

2. We would like to acknowledge the valuable contribution of two anonymous reviewers, Professor Miguel Angel Valverde of CETYS in Tijuana, Baja California, and many of our MBA graduate students and International Business and Management undergraduate students to this project. (John Hendon, Chris Feno, Marianne Sozio, Mike Adams, Jonas Almstrup, Pom Assoratgoon, Chris Barber, Al Stark, Konrad

Larson, Jeff Parkinson, John Patton, Lin Farmer, Linlee Austell, and Tehseen Lazzouni).

3. Twin plant stems from the belief that there would be similar plants on each side of the border; the U.S. side completing capital intensive functions and the Mexican side labor intensive function. In fact, less than 10% of the maquilas have a twin plant in the U.S. The in-bond term stems from the requirement that raw materials and supplies shipped to Mexico be processed and then reexported to the U.S. To guarantee reexport these inputs are bonded.

4. For a more detailed discussion of the maquiladora industry see M.B. Teagarden, M.C. Butler, and M.A. Von Glinow (1992) *Organizational Dynamics*, Winter, 20(3), 34-47.

5. Studies that address working conditions in maquilas are predominantly in Spanish. Two notable studies include *Condiciones de Trabajo en las Maquiladoras de Ciudad Juarez* [Maquiladora Work Conditions in Ciudad Juarez] by Dalia Barrera Bassols, Mexico, D.F.: Instituto Nacional de Antropologia e Historia, 1990; "La salud y la mujer obrera en las plantas maquiladoras: El caso de Tijuana," [Health and female maquiladora workers: The case of Tijuana] by Jorge Carrillo and Monica Jasis, *Enfermeria Hoy,* (June 1983), 4, 20-33. English translations of Spanish language citations are bracketed throughout the manuscript. Translations were done by M.B. Teagarden.

6. This description of working conditions is based on a synthesis of the work of Barrera Bassols (1990); Gross (1991); Jenner (1990); Kammer and Tolan (1989); LaDou (1991); "Minimal Safety Rules . . . " (1989); Moyers (1990); Pasternak (1991); Sanchez (1989); Satchell (1991); Sklair (1989); and the authors' observations.

7. There are myriad views of the costs and benefits of NAFTA. For example, see *Columbia Journal of World Business,* Summer 1991, 26(2); the *American Review of Canadian Studies,* Fall 1991, 21(2/3); NACLA (1991) The new gospel: North American Free Trade. *Report on the Americas,* 24(6); AFL-CIO (1991) Exploiting both sides: U.S.-Mexico 'Free Trade.' Washington, D.C.; and USITC (1991) *The likely impact on the United States of a Free Trade Agreement with Mexico.* Washington, D.C.: United States International Trade Commission, Publication 2353.

References

Adler, N.J. and F. Ghadar (1990) Strategic human resource management: a global perspective (pp. 235-260). In R. Piper (ed.), *Human Resource Management in International Comparison.* Berlin: de Gruyter.

Barrera Bassols, D. (1990) *Condiciones de Trabajo en las Mauiladoras de Ciudad Juarez: El Punto de Vista Obrero.* [*Work Conditions in Ciudad Juarez Maquiladoras: the Worker's Point of View.*] Mexico, D.F.: Instituto Nacional de Anthropologia e Historia.

Clement, N.C. and J. Gerber (1992) The North American Free Trade Agreement: its implications for California. Paper presented at the US/Canada/Mexico Free Trade Agreement Conference, Jesse M. Unruh Institute of Politics, University of Southern California, January 23.

Devanna, M.A., C.J. Fombrun and N.M. Tichy (1984) A framework for strategic human resource management (pp. 33-51). In C.J. Fombrun, N.M. Tichy and M.A. Devanna (eds.) *Strategic Human Resource Management*, New York: John Wiley & Sons.

Dowling, P.J. and R.S. Schuler (1990) *International Dimensions of Human Resource Management*. Boston: PWS-Kent.

Gross, G. (1991) Presto! Maquiladora toxic waste disappears. *San Diego Union*, Sunday, June 16, Al, Bl, B4-5.

Jenner, S.R. (1990) Conference offers ways to handle hazardous waste at maquiladoras. *San Diego Business Journal: Special Report Maquiladoras*, August 6, 23.

Kammer, J. and S. Tolan (1989) Toxic drums hold water for workers. *Arizona Republic*, April 19.

LaDou, J. (1991) Deadly migration: Hazardous industries' flight to the third world. *Technology Review*, July, 47-53.

Milliman, J., M.A. Von Glinow and M. Nathan (1991) Organizational life cycles and strategic international human resource management in multinational companies: implications for congruence theory. *Academy of Management Review*, 16(2), 318-339.

——— (1989) Minimal safety rules lure firms to border. *Arizona Republic*, April 17, Al.

Moyers, B. (1990) *Global Dumping Ground*. Washington: Seven Locks Press.

Pasternak, J. (1991) Firms find a haven from U.S. environmental rules. *Los Angeles Times*, Tuesday, November 19, pp. Al, A24.

Porter, M. (1980) *Competitive Strategy*. Free Press: New York.

Price-Waterhouse (1990) *Doing Business in Mexico*. New York: Price Waterhouse & Company.

Sanchez, R. (1989) Contaminacion de la industria fronteriza: riesgos para la salud y el medio ambiente [Contamination in the border industry: health and environmental risks] (pp. 155-184). In Gonzalex-Arechiga, B. and R. Barajas Escamilla (eds.), *Las Maquiladoras: Ajuste Estructural y Desarrollo Reaional*. [*The Mauiladoras: Structural Adjustment and Regional Development*.] Tijuana, B.C., Mexico: El Colegio de la Frontera Norte (COLEF).

Satchell, M. (1991) Poisoning the border: many American-owned factories in Mexico are fouling the environment and their workers aren't prospering. *U.S. News & World Report*, May 6, 32.

Sklair, L. (1989) *Assembling for Development: the Mauila Industry in Mexico and the United States*. Boston: Unwin Hyman.

Teagarden, M.B., M.C. Butler and M.A. Von Glinow (1992) Mexico's maquiladora industry: Where strategic human resource management makes a difference. *Organizational Dynamics*, Winter, 20(3), 34-47.

Urbina, A.T. (1972) *Nuevo Derecho del Trabajo—Teoria Integral [New Labor Law—Integral Theory]*. Mexico, D.F.

Von Glinow, M.A. and M.B. Teagarden (1988) The transfer of human resource management technology in Sino-US cooperative ventures. *Human Resource Management*, 27(2), 201-229.

U.S. Expatriates and the Civil Rights Act of 1991: Dissolving Boundaries

Reading 8.2
Sully Taylor
Robert W. Eder

This paper explores the impact of the extraterritoriality provision in Title VII of the 1991 Civil Rights Act on U.S. corporate international staffing policies, identifies key research questions that arise as a consequence to this U.S. law, and reveals how U.S. employment laws contribute to dissolving corporate global boundaries.

You are the director of human resources at a large southwestern teaching hospital. This hospital has a cooperative program with a major teaching hospital in Saudi Arabia. Each year several doctors from your hospital spend the year in Saudi Arabia teaching and doing research. The stay in Saudi Arabia is generally considered both lucrative as well as professionally rewarding.

This morning you had a visit from two of the doctors in the hospital who had been rejected for assignment to Saudi Arabia. They were very upset, as they are both very well qualified and ambitious. You had carefully explained to them that while the selection committee was impressed with their abilities, the fact that they are Jewish had decided the members that it would be best if they were disqualified from consideration. In spite of vigorous protest from the two doctors, you had held your ground and supported the committee's decision. However, as you sit at home reading that evening, the situation replays itself in your mind, and you think about the decision and feel a little uncertain.

Is the director of human resources correct in supporting the committee's decision? What should be the criteria used by the committee, and the director of human resources, to make a selection decision such as this? Do the doctors have any legal recourse?

Source: Sully Taylor and Robert W. Eder. "U.S. Expatriates and the Civil Rights Act of 1991: Dissolving Boundaries." *Advances in International Comparative Management* (JAI Press Inc., 1994). Reprinted by permission.

Questions like these are growing in U.S. MNCs, and gaining increasing urgency due to two trends. On the one hand, all multinational corporations (MNCs) face both the need for more top managers with an international perspective, and the need to place their best people overseas. MNCs are becoming increasingly dominant in both global and U.S. economies. The U.S. alone has more than 3,500 MNCs, 25,000 companies with overseas branches or affiliates, and around 40,000 companies doing business abroad on a sporadic basis (Prentice, 1990: 633). This has led to an increasing emphasis on international experience for senior managers (Adler and Bartholomew, 1992; Kobin, 1992; Porter, 1990). At the same time, overseas operations of MNCs represent a growing portion of the profitability of these firms (Bartlett and Ghoshal, 1991). As a consequence, there is pressure on multinationals to select their best people to manage their overseas operations.

Recent changes in the United States Civil Rights Act have important implications for the selection of U.S. expatriates. The main purpose of this article is to explore these implications. The article first places expatriate selection within the context of changing U.S. workforce demographics. Then, the legal status of the extraterritorality of U.S. employment laws is reviewed, including the Civil Rights Act of 1991. The final section of the paper explores unresolved legal issues, the likely impact of the 1991 Civil Rights Act on the international staffing policies of multinational firms, and areas in need of additional international management research.

International Selection and the Changing U.S. Workforce_____

The U.S. workforce is changing. It is becoming more demographically diverse (*Workforce 2000*). What are the consequences of these changes for international staffing?

1. Women and minorities will comprise a larger proportion of the labor pool from which to draw candidates for overseas positions. By the year 2000, only 15% of the new entrants to the U.S. labor force will be white males.

2. Women and minorities, who have been kept from top level corporate positions as well as from overseas positions ("Why Women . . .", 1990; Adler, 1984) will increasingly demand access to overseas postings as these become more and more critical to senior level executive career advancement (Adler and Batholomew, 1992).

New legal pressures from the 1991 Civil Rights Act encourage and support these two trends. U.S. EEO laws represent a formidable but as yet unrealized pressure on U.S. MNCs to increase the number of expatriates drawn from non-traditional groups. Before explaining the effect these changes in the law will have on U.S. MNCs' international staffing policies, let us first review the history of U.S. EEO laws with regard to this issue.

Brief History of Legal Decisions Regarding International Selection

Perhaps reflective of the ethnocentric mindset of the U.S. Congress when it crafted Title VII of the Civil Rights Act of 1964, the language of Title VII did not clearly indicate whether the law applied to U.S. citizens who are working abroad. Section 702 of Title VII exempts from Title VII coverage the "employment of aliens outside any State." At first, lower courts reasoned that legislative intent was to apply Title VII protections to the employment of citizens outside the U.S., though no specific language to that effect was stated in the legislation. As the following brief review illustrates, the courts later reversed themselves and withdrew that protection, leading to the necessity of an amendment to Title VII to clarify the coverage of U.S. citizens working abroad for U.S. firms.

Building the Case for Extending Civil Rights Protections to U.S. Expatriates. As summarized in the attached legal chronology exhibit (Exhibit 1), a series of court cases created the argument for the extraterritoriality of civil rights protections. In *Love v. Pullman* (1976) the court ruled that Black Pullman porters who were American citizens employed in Canada by an Illinois corporation were entitled to the full protection of Title VII, and that aliens (i.e., Canadian citizens) employed by the same U.S. firm were protected under Title VII during that portion of the workweek when the alien was working in the U.S. In *Bryant v. International Schools Services, Inc.* (1980), American citizens residing in Iran and hired by an American corporation were accorded full protection under Title VII against alleged discriminatory practices, as were American citizens hired in Frankfurt, West Germany to work for a Martin Marietta plant (*Seville v. Martin Marietta Corp.*, 1986). Also, in 1986 the Fifth Circuit Court of Appeals ruled that Jewish doctors who were refused a position in the Baylor College of Medicine's program in Saudi Arabia, allegedly because of their religion, were covered under Title VII. (*Abrams v. Baylor College of Medicine*).

In related court cases, the courts ruled in *Kern v. Dynalectron* (1984) that a BFOQ (bona fide occupational qualification) argument could be supported by a U.S. firm operating helicopter service to Mecca, Saudi Arabia to require pilots who were U.S. nationals to be Muslim, when local law punishes non-Muslims entering Mecca with death. Though U.S. non-Muslim pilots were adversely treated by the company's practice, the court used the Title VII statute with regard to BFOQ defense to rule in favor of the employer. Not all cases have been built solely around Title VII. In *EEOC v. Radio Free Europe* (1989), the court upheld

Exhibit 1. Chronology and Impact of Major Legal Decisions Affecting Overseas U.S. Employees of U.S. Corporations

Year	Case/Law	Impact
1976	*Love v. Pullman*	Upheld the extraterritoriality of Title VII, i.e., American citizens working for American firms overseas *are* protected by Title VII.
1980	*Bryant v. International Schools Services*	Upheld the extraterritoriality of Title VII, i.e., American citizens working for American firms overseas *are* protected by Title VII.
1980	*Mas Marques v. Digital Equipment Corp.*	Established that the foreign subsidiary of an American firm has to have sufficient contacts with parent firm in order for Title VII to apply. To determine whether involvement is "sufficient," a 4-part test should be applied: (1) degree of interrelated operations. (2) degree of common management. (3) centralized control of labor relations. (4) common ownership of labor relations.
1984	*Kern v. Dynalectron*	Upheld that it is a legitimate BFOQ to be a Muslim for a job in Mecca as local law punishes non-muslims entering Mecca with death.
1986	*Seville v. Martin Marietta*	Upheld the extraterritoriality of Title VII, i.e., American citizens working for American firms overseas *are* protected by Title VII.
1986	*Boureslan v. ARAMCO*	Held that Title VII does *not* apply to U.S. citizens abroad. Stated that there was no clear congressional intent for extra territoriality.
1986	*Abrams v. Baylor College of Medicine*	Held that it is *not* a legitimate BFOQ to be a non-Jew to work in Saudi Arabia as there is no explicit local law prohibiting Jews from working in the country.
1989	*EEOC v. Radio Free Europe*	Upheld the application of the Age Discrimination Act of 1964 to American workers in U.S. firms overseas, as long as local law is not violated.
1991		Supreme Court upheld *Boureslan v. ARAMCO* decision.
1991	Amendment to Title VII	Specifically states that Title VII is applicable to U.S. firms overseas. Negates *Boureslan v. ARAMCO*.

the application of the Age Discrimination Act of 1964 to U.S. workers employed by U.S. firms overseas, provided local law was not violated.

Reversing Course: Boureslan v. ARAMCO (1986). In *Boureslan v. ARAMCO* (1986), the Fifth Circuit Court ruled that Title VII does not afford extraterritorial protection to U.S. citizens and dismissed the suit. The Supreme Court upheld the ruling of the Fifth Circuit Court on March 26, 1991 by a 6-3 vote. The majority on the Supreme Court reasoned that the U.S. Congress had been silent on the geographical or transnational scope of Title VII protections and therefore, argued against extraterritorial application of Title VII statutes in the absence of "a clear congressional expression of intent to the contrary." This argument was bolstered by subsequent Supreme Court decisions (e.g., *Espinosa v. Farah Mfg. Co.*, 414 US 86 (SCt, 1973), 6 EPD 64,014.) that ruled Section 702 of Title VII covers aliens employed within the U.S., further reaffirming the "within U.S. border" interpretation of Congressional intent. Furthermore, the Supreme Court contended that requiring American employers to comply with Title VII in countries where religious and social customs are wholly at odds with U.S. civil rights protection, places American firms in the difficult position of either refusing to employ U.S. citizens abroad or discontinuing business in that country.

Ironically, it was Judge King's strong dissent in the Fifth Circuit Court of Appeals case, *Boureslan v. ARAMCO* (1986), that eventually became incorporated in Section 109 of the Civil Rights Act of 1991. Judge King argued that the rule of reasonableness should be applied to a state's attempt to apply its law in a transnational context. In accordance with international law, employers overseas could not be expected to take action that directly conflicted with the existing laws of the foreign country. Furthermore, Judge King argued that to the extent that foreign assignments were important considerations in employment advancement, the failure to extend Title VII protections to U.S. citizens abroad would constitute adverse career advancement effects for women and minorities.

Civil Rights Act of 1991. It would be left to the current U.S. Congress to clarify the extraterritoriality of Title VII, as it had with its amendment of the Age Discrimination in Employment Act (26 USC 630(f)). The Civil Rights Act of 1991 had been several years in the making, and a point of considerable partisan politics. The law was initially written to overturn a series of recent Supreme Court Cases, of which *Boureslan v. ARAMCO* was but one, that undermined the effective enforcement of Title VII statutes.

The Civil Rights Act of 1991, Section 109 (P.L. 102-199, Section 109105 STAT. 1077-1078), amended the Civil Rights Act of 1964 and the Americans with Disabilities Act of 1990 to include coverage of U.S. citizens employed in a foreign country, provided that compliance with this provision would not cause the employer to violate the law of the foreign country in which the workplace is located. To be covered under this provision the U.S. citizen must be employed overseas by a firm controlled by an American employer. Control can be determined in several ways: interrelation of operations, common management, centralized control of labor relations, or common ownership or financial control of the corporation and the employer.

Impact of the Extension of Extraterritoriality of Title VII _____

Mitsuko Hanada was frustrated and upset. She walked determinedly down the sidewalks of the fashionable Roppongi district of Tokyo, unmindful of the cold wind and rain, trying to decide what to do. If she were in the States she would know immediately!

Up until this morning Mitsuko had been pretty content in her job at Uptown KK, a large U.S. firm in the communications business. She had been hired straight out of her MBA program in the U.S., like the other five Americans in her section, because of her Japanese language ability, and given responsibilities and duties far above what a fresh MBA could expect in a first job. Moving to Tokyo one year ago, she had settled in happily, possibly because of the network of family she had from her issei parents. But today she had learned that three of the Americans who had been hired with her, all men, were receiving one-third more salary than she, and moreover getting help with apartment rent subsidies and other amenities. When she inquired about this, she was informed that their personnel affairs were being managed by the personnel manager in charge of expatriates, while she was the responsibility of the regular personnel manager, and that the differences stemmed from this administrative decision. When she had asked why males and females were being differentiated, the personnel manager had alluded vaguely to some differences in qualifications between the two groups.

Differences in qualifications!! Huh!! If there were any greater qualifications, they lay with the women, not the men!! Mitsuko gave a very American snort of disgust, startling the other pedestrians, and considered what she should do. Boy, if only she had been hired in the U.S.!!!

The impact of the extraterritoriality extension of Title VII falls into three categories: (1) the unresolved legal issues that must be clarified; (2) the effect on the policies of MNCs and their host countries; and (3) research questions that will need to be addressed. Mitsuko's situation illustrates one of the several unresolved legal issues that has not yet been resolved, as will be discussed below.

Unresolved Legal Issues

There are at least four legal questions that remain to be clarified as a result of the amendment to Title VII to cover U.S. citizens working abroad:

1. What are foreign "laws"? What is a "law"?

2. What constitutes "sufficient control" by a U.S. MNC of its overseas subsidiary?

3. Can the entire family be legally considered when an MNC makes a selection decision regarding international staffing?

    4. How can Title VII be enforced overseas? Who is going to do it?

Let's consider each of these unresolved questions in turn.

1. What are foreign "laws"?

A key issue is what constitutes a foreign law. What the U.S. defines as "civil law" may have a very different definition in a foreign country. Civil law may give deference to a particular religious doctrine, or permit localities to promulgate regulations or local conditions that have the effect of discriminating unfairly but in a manner that is consistent with the "laws" of that country. U.S. courts will have to consider what constitutes the "law" of a foreign locale and the extent to which social customs or traditions are considered inviolate. If, for example, a foreign country had such strong social taboos against women working in business that it was not uncommon for violators to be stoned, could this be regarded as a "law"? U.S. courts in employment discrimination suits have typically examined the reasonable risk of injury to the employee and whether critical tasks in the job description simply could not be performed in a specific foreign context as a basis for rejecting the employee's unfair discrimination suit. The uncertainty regarding where the courts are likely to fall within the broad continuum of options in interpreting what constitutes foreign law will likely stimulate the growth of international employment law firms in the U.S. for years to come.

Other countries show much greater deference to local custom than the U.S. when applying their equal opportunity laws. For example, Japan's Ministry of Labor in 1986 offered the following official guideline to Japanese employers as an exception to Japan's own equal opportunity requirements when employing women overseas:

> . . . where the working environment or social situation such as custom and practices of a country would make it difficult for women to realize their abilities. Here, the major reference is to working in foreign countries. This exception can severely limit the recruitment of women to jobs which would require periods of working overseas. . . . it includes not only present jobs but also jobs which, in the future, as a result of job rotation, will require overseas assignments. (MOL 1986: 49-52) (*Source:* Lam, 1992)

Clearly, Japanese MNCs are permitted to broadly include "customs and practices of a country" in disqualifying a Japanese woman not only from overseas assignment, but also from promotion considerations domestically if there is a reasonable expectation that the promotion would require future job rotation overseas to the country in question. It is difficult to envision U.S. courts interpreting foreign law as broadly as the Japanese. However, it is possible that U.S. multinational firms may claim that they suffer a global economic disadvantage given the way in which other countries apply their own EEO laws to the international situation.

2. What is "sufficient control"?

The determination of when a foreign firm is sufficiently controlled by an American firm received its initial guidelines from the 1980 court case *Mas Marques v. Digital Equipment Corp.* A key consideration is whether the U.S. firm has sufficient involvement in the foreign subsidiary's personnel policies to conclude that the U.S. parent firm is jointly responsible for the allegedly discriminatory behavior. As firms take on a more multinational structure with complex joint venture arrangements and other strategic alliances, the determination of "sufficient control" in employment policies by the U.S. firm will likely become more problematic. Is a U.S. citizen working in a joint venture abroad in which its employer controls 49% of the assets covered by Title VII? What coverage does an employee have if the joint venture is evenly split into thirds among the parent country and two foreign firms? As illustrated in the case of Mitsuko above, is a U.S. citizen recruited in the U.S. to work in Japan by the Japanese subsidiary of an American MNC covered under U.S. EEO laws? Mitsuko herself (for this is a real case) decided that she did not have any legal recourse, and reluctantly accepted the situation. Yet the area of "sufficient control" remains murky, and answers to the kinds of questions posed above are elusive and subject to court interpretation.

3. Can the family be considered in the assignment of a candidate to an overseas position?

A third issue relates to the role of the family in overseas assignments. Typically, it is the family and not the individual that is sent overseas for a two to five year assignment. Inquiries regarding one's spouse and family members have clearly been regarded as inappropriate in the U.S. in considering a person's qualifications for a position (e.g., inquiry of marital status, spouse's occupation, family plans). However, in overseas selection, it has been argued that interviews with the other members of the family unit to determine their likelihood of successful acculturation is critical to a successful overseas placement (Dowling and Schuler, 1993; Tung, 1988; Adler, 1991; Black, Gregersen and Mendenhall, 1992). Adjustment problems of spouse or children are often a key reason for overseas assignments to be prematurely ended, at considerable cost and inconvenience to the firm. However, it would seem that under the Civil Rights Act of 1991, it is now inappropriate to base an overseas selection decision on information gathered regarding the candidate's family unit.

A key legal question that arises is whether firms will be able to prove that the transfer overseas represents a clear and significantly different situation from a domestic transfer, and thus can consider the family of the candidate in their decisions. With the exception of laws in the host country that may be violated by the presence of a family member, it is difficult at this time to see whether a firm can treat the international transfer as different from the domestic transfer with regard to this issue. In fact, if U.S. MNCs are successful in making a business necessity argument based on documented costs associated with failed job placement due to family unit incompatibility with the new culture, there is no reason why such an argument couldn't be made with regard to a *domestic* transfer. As the United States becomes more regionally and ethnically diverse, concerns over the acculturation of the family unit may become more of a factor in domestic transfer success. This would be a logical development as national boundaries continue to dissolve in the global economy of the twenty-first century, as regions of one's own country become more foreign than a move overseas. For example, a Boston-based firm may have the need to transfer key executives to both domestic and international sites. For a family that has lived in the Boston metropolitan area their entire life, a potential transfer to El Paso, Texas may easily offer more of an acculturation challenge than a transfer to Toronto, Canada. Why should the issue of cross-cultural adjustment skills only be relevant for the transfer to Toronto? Are there not domestic transfers with comparable transition costs that also strain an employee's and the employee's family's ability to culturally adapt?

4. How can Title VII laws be enforced overseas?

A final legal issue involves the enforcement of U.S. EEO laws overseas. The issue of enforcement gives rise to a number of questions. Will the U.S. government be required to set up EEO offices in all the countries where U.S. MNCs are conducting business? If not, will it be a function assumed by the U.S. embassy, and if so, will embassy staff be trained in how to handle EEO complaints? Given the close relationships between the embassy and the business expatriate community in most foreign countries, will it be possible to maintain the privacy of individuals bringing a complaint overseas? Where will cases be heard and decided? If in the U.S., will this place an undue financial burden on the employee, who will have to return to the U.S. for court proceedings?

Policy Implications for International Human Resource Staffing

The extension of Title VII to overseas staffing can be expected to impact MNC policy in at least four ways. The most critical impact may be on the choice of international human resource management strategy. Other issues involve the effect of adherence to Title VII guidelines on host countries, the impact on the recruitment and selection process, and the influence on the approach to training for overseas postings. Each of these policy implications will be examined in turn.

> The meeting to select a replacement for Hal, the General Manager of the Mexican subsidiary of Tayer Manufacturing had gone much longer than anyone expected. A rather glum silence had descended on the small group appointed to select the best candidate. Finally, Sam White, the vice-president in

charge of personnel, leaned back in his chair and spoke to the group, holding Susan Troy's file in his hand as he talked.

"Look, no matter how you cut it, Susan is the best candidate. She speaks Spanish, has the technical and managerial background we need, did real well up in Canada. And she wants the job! There is really no way around it. Bill is the next best candidate, and he doesn't even come close. Heck, he doesn't even speak Spanish, and he doesn't even have a passport. I think we really have to accept the fact that Susan is the one we need to pick, no matter how difficult you think it might be for her down there. Remember, the 1991 amendment to the EEO laws simply won't let us consider the machismo aspect of all this. Besides, I think Susan can do the job."

Silence decended again. Kirk Latham, the CEO, sighed and got up and served himself another cup of coffee. Suddenly, on the way back to the table, he stopped.

"Wait a second. We've been thinking too narrowly! We have a perfect replacement for Hal, who's been sitting under our noses all this time. Gaspar Zavala could do Hal's job in a minute. He's been vice-president for operations for three years, and he runs the show every time Hal is gone, whether it's to visit up here or on annual leave. Gaspar was up here himself for three months last year, so he really knows how things are done both here and there. Gosh, why didn't I think of him before!"

As Kirk spoke the rest of the group looked up, and gradually began nodding at the saneness of the suggestion. Boy, if only they had thought of that earlier, it would have saved them several hours sitting in this windowless meeting room!

1.   Impact on international human resource management strategy.

The most serious policy implication of Title VII may be on the choice of international human resource management strategy. For firms that are aware of the extraterritoriality of the Civil Rights Act, the change in law may pressure them to take a polycentric approach to overseas staffing. The higher perceived legal liability from the enactment of this law can be minimized by switching from an ethnocentric (i.e., preferring to send U.S. citizens from American corporate headquarters to manage overseas enterprises) or geocentric (i.e., choosing the best qualified candidate for the position overseas regardless of home country, host country, or third country nationality) to a polycentric approach that searches for the best qualified host country national to fill the overseas position (Dowling and Schuler, 1993; Perlmutter, 1969). Firms may emphasize the selection of key host country hires who are temporarily transferred to the United States to receive corporate training and socialization in the firm's business philosophy. A recent example is the intensive training Disney provided hundreds of key French personnel who were to open Euro-Disney outside of Paris, which included indoctrination to the unique Disney corporate and management culture. Such a shift in overseas staffing strategy reduces the number of U.S. citizens assigned to overseas operations. Therefore, the Civil Rights Act of 1991 may actually reduce the number of opportunities U.S. citizens will have for acquiring international experience, which, as stated above, has become a necessary part of the preparation for effectively managing MNCs.

In addition to decreasing the amount of international experience among top managers in U.S. firms, a push towards polycentrism may have serious implications for both the corporate strategy and competitiveness of U.S. multinational firms. It could result in corporate reluctance to enter a relatively unfamiliar overseas market and limit the ability of the U.S. firm to react to shifting labor, resource, and customer markets worldwide (Bartlett and Ghoshal, 1989). Instead, preference may be given to entering into joint venture agreements with host country firms, or to other forms of strategic alliances that permit the U.S. firm to avoid sending U.S. expatriates abroad. In short, foreign investment decisions may become sub-optimized and result in lower firm performance and a decrease in competitiveness.

2.   Effect on host countries.

A second policy implication of the extraterritoriality of Title VII deals with its effect on host countries. For firms that choose to retain a geocentric or ethnocentric approach to international staffing, there will be the need to actively recruit women and minorities for overseas positions. But, as these firms begin to send members of these groups to their overseas subsidiaries, women and minority employees within those overseas affiliates will be exposed to managers from groups that are usually underrepresented in business in other countries. One consequence could be a change of expectations of these local employees, regarding promotions to both managerial positions and postings overseas. In order to maintain a sense of internal equity, the U.S. firm may include women and minorities employed in its overseas affiliates in the pool from which it draws its international managers. These employees may in turn be noticed by women and minorities in local firms, whose own career aspirations may be altered as a result. In short, the extraterritoriality of Title VII may lead to diffusion of U.S. social policy. This diffusion of the social effect of Title VII may, as a consequence, have policy implications for non-U.S. firms, and eventually, for employment policies in the host countries in which they operate. Whether this diffusion of U.S. social policy is beneficial or detrimental to the host country is a separate, but fascinating, issue.

3.   Impact on the recruitment and selection process.

Assuming U.S. firms continue to employ U.S. citizens abroad, even if to a lesser extent than under the Civil Rights Act of 1991, the recruitment and selection process has been made considerably more complex. First, firms will have to post available overseas positions in a more open manner, as is already required for domestic positions. The practice of a few key executives meeting behind closed doors to discuss an overseas selection, meeting with the pre-ordained choice, and quickly preparing the individual to go abroad would appear to be inconsistent with legal expectations for equal opportunity to all those able and willing to be considered. Likewise, individuals could no longer make special deals that involve explicit commitments to a particular overseas assignment as part of a career move or compensation enhancement. Furthermore, advertisements by U.S. firms for overseas assignments, regardless of where the advertisement is placed, would have to be in compliance with U.S. civil rights laws with regard to the statement of qualifications. Except where compliance with U.S. civil rights laws would cause the employer to violate the law of a foreign country in which the workplace is located, specific references to race, gender, age, or religion would be prohibited.

On the positive side, a move to a more open job posting system would require firms to integrate overseas assignments with managerial career planning, which would require a more long-term perspective to be taken in the overseas staffing decision. As employees see the postings for overseas positions, they will seek information on how to acquire experience and training that makes such assignments attainable, leading to greater career planning. Moreover, this long-term perspective could potentially reduce part of the repatriation problem, when managers return to the United States, only to find there is little thought to how their recent international experience will be valued or utilized by the firm (Adler, 1991).

4. Effect on the design of training programs.

A final policy implication of the application of Title VII to overseas assignments is the effect it will have on the design of training programs to prepare candidates for their sojourns abroad. First, there is an effect on the training process. As Black and Mendenhall (1990) observe, social learning theory states that it is desirable to have the person who models new behaviors be as similar to the trainee as possible. This implies a need for more women and minorities with overseas business experience to act as cross-cultural trainers. Regarding the content of the training, the "cultural toughness" dimension regarding women and minorities of the host culture will need to be calculated (Mendenhall and Oddou, 1985). This will influence both the behaviors and skills the candidates will have to learn, which may be different from those needed by white males. Some caution is necessary here, however. Some women and minorities may actually find discrimination against them in the foreign culture easier to deal with than their white male counterparts since they have dealt with discrimination in their own country. Interviews with black U.S. women expatriates in

Japan indicate that they perceive little or no difficulty in dealing with the slights against them as foreigners and as women because such incidents have always been part of their existence (Taylor and Napier, 1993). Finally, there may be an effect on the length and timing of the cross-cultural training, with women and minorities requiring greater training once in country as there are fewer local country nationals with whom they can identify and from whom they can learn how to manage effectively in that country.

Implications for Research in International Management

There are also implications of the extraterritoriality of Title VII for research in the field of international management. Two of the most urgent research questions are, first, the validation of selection criteria and methods for overseas assignments, and, second, determining what factors will mediate the impact of the extraterritoriality of Title VII on the international staffing behavior of U.S. MNCs.

1. Validation of selection criteria.

Previous research and practice provide guidelines regarding the selection criteria and measures that should be used. Tung (1981) identified four main groups of variables that are related to expatriate success, and hence should be used in selecting expatriates for overseas assignments: (1) technical competence; (2) personality traits or relational abilities; (3) environmental variables; and (4) family situation. With regard to the third category, environmental variables, researchers (Jones and Popper, 1972; Pinfield, 1973; Torbiorn, 1982) have found that some cultures are more difficult to adapt to than others, depending on the culture of origin for the expatriate, a dimension termed cultural toughness (Mendenhall and Oddou, 1985). Black, Gregersen and Mendenhall (1992) outline a slightly different set of factors from Tung.

In short, researchers have made some progress in identifying what makes an expatriate able to function effectively overseas, and therefore what criteria should be utilized in the selection decision. However, validation of the suggested criteria has not been undertaken in separate studies, creating a gap in our research knowledge that must be addressed given the increased political risk facing U.S. MNCs. Both construct and criterion related research is required to establish the predictive and incremental validities of each of the selection criteria currently in use. In Exhibit 2, Black et al. (1992) recommend which selection methods are most relevant for each selection criterion. However, these recommendations must be tested before they can provide the sort of validity that can withstand the legal scrutiny of the courts. As Black et al. point out, there is little academic or practitioner consensus with regard to which selection criteria should be used to identify highly qualified expatriates. Criteria receiving widely variant opinions with regard to importance include foreign language proficiency, family support, and prior overseas experience.

There has also been little research with regard to the relative weight that should be given each category of selection criteria. In one study, Tung found that the fourth category, family situation, was the primary reason for failure among expatriates (Tung, 1982), and recommended that firms include the spouse and family in making selection decisions. As noted above, this is a recommendation which if followed may create some legal risk. The weights may also be partially determined by the national origin of the firm. Recent research indicates that the national origin of a firm influences which variables will be emphasized in the selection decision (Stone, 1991), which could indicate either a cultural belief in the importance of some variables over others, or that cultures vary in the way they define the roles of an expatriate. Finally, Black et al. (1992) recommended that the firm determine which factors are most important for a particular assignment. In sum, a key part of validating the selection criteria will be determining how much weight to give each selection criterion within the decision model the firm chooses to use. The utility of this selection model for the firm will be a function of, not only the validity coefficient (i.e., multiple R) for the battery of tests, but also the adequacy of an applicant pool from which an overseas assignment is made, the historical pattern of success or failure in past similar selections, and the overall cost of the selection procedures that are used.

A second major area that will need to be addressed is the validation of different methods of selection. Black et al. (1992) noted that the variety of methods available to firms is much greater than what is actually utilized, and includes such approaches as assessment centers, work samples, biographical and background data, standardized tests, interviews and references. At present firms tend to underutilize the range of both criteria and selection methods available to them: ". . . the short-term approach of most multinational firms leads them to rely on . . . the least reliable and valid selection methods (interviews and references)" (Black et al., 1992: 73-74).

Before leaving this section, it should be noted that even if researchers are successful in validating expatriate selection criteria, past research indicates that firms ignore the recommendations of researchers concerning international selection. The actual overseas selection practice of MNCs does not utilize accumulated selection validation research. Some research has indicated that technical expertise is used as the primary selection criterion by U.S. MNCs (Baker and Ivancevich, 1971; Miller, 1973; Tung, 1981), ignoring the other categories of criteria because technical expertise is so much easier to determine than other factors. However, as Black et al. (1992:56) note, ". . . (the) people with the best technical skills are not necessarily those with the best cross-cultural adjustment skills. In fact, a global assignment failure (poor performance or premature return) is generally the result of ineffective cross-cultural adjustment by expatriates and their families, rather than the outcome of inadequate technical or professional skills." Firms also apparently avoid even attempting to measure non-technical, human relations skills. In her study, Tung (1981) found that only five percent of firms formally assess a candidate's relational ability, even though the relationship abilities of expatriates have been identified as important to overseas success. Finally, only between 40% and 50% of all firms interview both candidate and spouse for an overseas position, even though the family has been shown to be an important determinant of overseas success (Tung, 1981). While the extension of Title VII to the overseas assignment makes it legally risky to consider the family as part of the selection decision, it is still noteworthy that most U.S. MNCs have been ignoring the considerable research evidence that suggests this as an important selection criterion. In sum, researchers will also have to determine, as part of their validation of selection criteria and methods, the factors that inhibit firms from utilizing the findings concerning how to successfully select candidates for overseas.

2. Factors that will mediate the impact of the extraterritoriality of Title VII.

A second major research question that arises from the extension of Title VII to the international arena is what factors will influence its impact on firm behavior. Two obvious factors that will be important are the risk averseness of the firm, and its stance regarding multiculturalism. Risk averseness is the probability that the firm could face discrimination lawsuits from the extraterritoriality of Title VII, and the potential magnitude of the settlements. It is probably a function of the firm's history of past lawsuits, as well as its risk minimization stance due to its industry. Banks, for example, will tend to be more risk averse because of the large role government plays in overseeing the industry, and the consequent necessity of justifying actions to regulating authorities.

Multiculturalism is the degree to which the firm is proactive in encouraging diversity in its workforce, both domestic and international. This may be a function of top management philosophy and the percentage of the workforce overseas. These two dimensions have been mapped against each other in Figure 1, resulting in four quadrants that give some indication of the potential effects on the behavior of the firm.

Figure 1. Differential Impact on Expatriate Selection of Women and Minorities in Response to 1991 Civil Rights Act

		Commitment to Multiculturalism	
		Low	High
Risk	Low	Minimal Effect On Firm (1)	Proactive Assignment of Women/Minorities Overseas (3)
Averseness	High	Minimize Expatriates/ Polycentric Strategy (2)	Calculative Response/ Validate Process First (4)

Firms in quadrant 1 are not proactive with regard to multicultural-ism in their workforce, and hence do not have in place many mecha-nisms for increasing the number of women and minorities at different levels of the organization. With regard to risk averseness, these firms do not perceive that there is much legal risk from lawsuits, perhaps because they have not been the target of them in the past, either for size or geographic location reasons. For these firms, it is proposed that the effect of the extraterritoriality of Title VII will be relatively minimal. Firm behavior will not likely change; there will be little interest in pro-moting expatriate selection.

Firms in quadrant 2 are risk averse, and will avoid putting them-selves in a position that might increase the probability of lawsuits. At the same time, these firms have traditionally not been at the forefront of nurturing cultural diversity in their workforces. These firms will be dis-couraged from utilizing expatriates due to the extraterritoriality of Title VII. For these firms, a polycentric approach may replace an ethnocentric approach, or the firm may emphasize the use of third country nationals if there is an insufficient supply of capable host country nationals. Another possibility is that firms in this quadrant may attempt to dis-tance themselves legally as much as possible by changing their overseas investments to joint ventures or through subcontracting operations. Obviously the industry of the firm also influences the degree to which it can move in such a direction. This approach is most likely to be effec-tive when the firm's production can be undertaken outside of the firm, or when there are sufficient legal protections of its distinctive technolo-gy or trademark to make alliances safe alternatives.

The third quadrant consists of firms who perceive low legal risk and have a proactive approach to multiculturalism in the firm. Many of these firms have a history of avoiding discrimination lawsuits by actively promoting women and minorities. These firms will be proac-tive in inducing members of these two groups to work overseas as a consequence of Title VII. Moreover, the 1991 Title VII law can help them persuade such candidates to undertake an overseas assignment because now the law clearly states that they will be protected even while working overseas.

Finally, in quadrant four are those firms who see a high legal risk from lawsuits, probably from having experienced a number of such suits in the past. These firms tend to be perceived as having deep pockets and thus are often targets of discrimination suits. At the same time, these firms cannot avoid going overseas. Compared to firms in quadrant three, companies in this group are as publicly committed to multicultur-ism, but must be more careful in proceeding in a manner that does not unreasonably increase legal risks. Firms in the steel and transportation industries would fit this profile, as would law firms. For these compa-nies, overseas investments are usually direct and wholly owned. It is predicted that these firms will, as a consequence of the extraterritoriality of Title VII, take a more calculative response with regard to assigning women and minorities overseas, complying with the legal requirement to change recruitment and selection approaches, validating selection criteria and processes, but not taking an unrestrained proactive approach to inducing women and minorities to go overseas.

Conclusions _____

By establishing the extraterritoriality of Title VII, the 1991 Congress clearly signaled that U.S. MNCs have an obligation to follow the strictures laid out by U.S. society wherever they are operating, abroad or at home. The law has removed the ambiguity that existed concerning whether U.S. citizens can rightfully claim civil rights protection while serving their companies abroad, although as was discussed above, some legal issues remain to be resolved, and are subject to further court interpretation.

Possibly the most interesting aspect of the establishment of the extraterritoriality of Title VII is that it is yet another signal of the degree to which nation states are becoming superseded by the economic interdependence of the world. By requiring U.S. MNCs, which together hold the largest investment overseas, to adhere to the same legal and social standards as they do at home, there is in effect a diffusion of American social mores and cultural values to other countries. Again, our point is not to debate whether the U.S. stance on promoting women and minority rights in the workplace is socially or morally superior to that in other countries. The fact is that countries which have put less emphasis on equal employment opportunity for all their citizens, and that have not enacted laws to support it as a consequence, will find within their borders firms with a proactive stance with regard to the hiring and promotion of women and minorities. While this staffing policy may initially impact only foreign workers, the necessity of maintaining internal equity in an overseas subsidiary may lead the firm to extend equal employment opportunity practices to host country nationals. Thus while certain countries may not wish to promote equal opportunity for either social or religious reasons, they may find within their midst a modern Trojan horse from which spills out agents of change created by the extraterritoriality of Title VII.

As a side issue, it is ironic that at a time when U.S. MNCs are required to extend civil rights protection to U.S. citizens working abroad, foreign firms operating in the U.S. are often permitted to prefer home country nationals over host country U.S. citizens for key managerial positions, in accordance with a mosaic of Friendship, Commerce, and Navigation treaties. For example, the Seventh Circuit Court of Appeals ruled that Japanese subsidiaries operating in the U.S. may legally prefer Japanese citizens over U.S. citizens and that Title VII prohibitions against discrimination on the basis of national origin do not apply (*Fortino v.*

Quasar Co., 1992). In effect, a "glass ceiling" for all U.S. employees working in Japanese-owned firms is in effect. In some industries (e.g., microelectronics) a U.S. manager may have more career opportunity and more U.S. Civil Rights protections working for a U.S. MNC overseas than for a foreign-owned MNC operating in the manager's own home country.

U.S. MNCs face a number of challenges in making the transition to a world in which their overseas staffing is covered by Title VII. The greatest challenge is to re-examine their recruitment and selection of candidates for overseas positions, and bring these procedures up to a standard of validation commensurate with procedures used for domestic hires. As mentioned previously, there is also the necessity of changing the training and career planning procedures to facilitate utilization of women and minorities in overseas positions. While some firms will be more proactive than others in trying to achieve these goals, and some will try to avoid the question entirely through alternative foreign investments, there is no doubt that on the whole the extraterritoriality of Title VII represents a significant challenge for U.S. MNCs with regard to international human resource management.

References _____

Adler, N. J., and Bartholomew, S. (1992). Managing globally competent people. *Academy of Management Executive,* 6(3):52-65.

Adler, N. J. (1991). *International Dimensions of Organizational Behavior.* Boston: PWS-Kent.

Adler, N. J. (1984). Expecting international success: Female managers overseas. *Columbia Journal of World Business,* 19 (3), Fall, 79-85.

Adler, N. J. (1984). Women in international management: Where are they? *California Management Review,* 26(4), Summer, 78-89.

Baker, J. C. and Ivancevich, J. M. (1971). The assignment of American executives abroad: Systematic, haphazard, or chaotic? *California Management Review,* 13(3): 39-41.

Bartlett, C. and Ghoshal, S. (1989). *Managing Across Borders.* Boston: Harvard University Press.

Black, S. and Mendenhall, M. (1990). Cross-cultural training effectiveness: A review and a theoretical framework for future research. *Academy of Management Review,* 15(1): 113-136.

Benson, P. G. (1978). Measuring cross-cultural adjustment: The problem of criteria. *International Journal of Intercultural Relations.* Spring, 21-37.

Business Week, (1991). Were Civil Rights Laws Meant to Travel? January 21, page 36.

Coulter, T.A. (1990). Testing the United States' commitment to international law: The conflict between Title VII and treaties of friendship, commerce, and navigation. *Wake Forest Law Review,* 25: 287-313.

Dowling, P. J. and Schuler, R. S. (1993). *International Dimensions of Human Resource Management* (2nd ed.). Boston, MA: PWS-Kent.

Dowling, P. J. and Welch, D. (1988). International human resource management: An Australian perspective, *Asia-Pacific Journal of Management* 6(1): 39-45.

Doz, Y. (1991). Ciba-geigy-management development, in M. Mendenhall and G. Oddou (eds.), *International Human Resource Management.* Boston: PWS-Kent.

Jones, R.R. and Popper, R. (1972). Characteristics of peace corps host countries and the behavior of volunteers. *Journal of Cross-cultural Psychology,* 3: 233-245.

Kobrin, (1992). Multinational strategy and international human resource management policy. *Wharton WP,* 92-14.

Lam, A. C. L., (1992). *Women and Japanese Management,* London, Routledge, Chapman and Hall, Inc.

Mendenhall, M. and G. Oddou. (1985). The dimensions of expatriate acculturation: A review, *Academy of Management Review,* 10(1): 39-47.

Miller, E. L. (1973). The international selection decision: A study of some dimensions of managerial behavior in the selection decision process. *Academy of Management Journal,* 16: 239-252.

Perlmutter, H. V. (1969). The tortuous evolution of the multinational corporation. *Columbia Journal of World Business,* 4, Jan.-Feb., 9-18.

Pinfield, L. T. (1973). Sociocultural factors and inter-organizational relations. *Academy of Management Proceedings,* 33rd Annual Meeting, Boston.

Porter, M. E. (1990). *The Competitive Advantage of Nations.* New York: The Free Press.

Prentice, R. (1990). The muddled state of Title VII's application abroad. *Labor Law Journal,* Sept., 633-640.

Ronen, S. (1989). Training the international assignee, in I. Goldstein (ed.), *Training and Career Development.* San Francisco: Jossey-Bass.

Silver, G. D. (1989). Friendship, commerce and navigation treaties and United States discrimination law: The right of branches of foreign companies to hire executives "of their choice." *Fordham Law Review,* 57: 765-784.

Simon, H.A., and Brown, F. (1991). International enforcement of Title VII: A small world after all? *Employee Relations Law Journal,* 281-300.

Stone, R. J. (1991). Expatriate selection and failure. *Human Resource Planning,* 14(1): 9-18.

Taylor, S., and Napier, N. (1993). Successful women expatriates: The case of Japan. Paper presented at the Academy of International Business, Hawaii, October 22.

Torbiorn, I. (1982). *Living Abroad: Personal Adjustment and Personnel Policy in the Overseas Setting.* New York: Wiley.

Tung, R. (1988). *The New Expatriates: Managing Human Resources Abroad.* Cambridge, MA: Ballinger.

Tung, R. L. (1981). Selection and training of personnel for overseas assignments. *Columbia Journal of World Business,* 6(1): 66-78.

Tung, R. L. (1982). Selection and training procedures of U.S., European, and Japanese multinationals. *California Management Review,* 25(1):57-71.

Workforce 2000. (1987). Indianapolis: Hudson Institute.

"Why Women Still Aren't Getting to the Top." (1990). *Fortune,* July 30, pp. 40-62.

Cashbuild

Case 8.1
Alan Bernstein
Susan Schneider

Albert Koopman, managing director of Cashbuild, left the company's April 1983 conference deeply concerned. Despite a booming South African economy and a year in which sales revenue had grown by over 60 percent, earnings growth had slowed to a mere 6 percent. Of far deeper concern to Koopman, however, was that signs of severe organizational and motivational strain had begun to emerge. Results of the company's corporate culture survey showed a slip in procompany feeling among managers, from 89 percent in 1982 to 74 percent in 1983. More fundamentally, staff turnover had risen to 120 percent a year on average, and stock shrinkage had reached record levels.

Origins

Cashbuild started operations in July 1978 as a wholly owned subsidiary of Metro Cash & Carry, South Africa's largest wholesaler of consumer goods. Metro Cash & Carry, as its name implies, provides a wholesale service to retailers through vast warehouses countrywide. Cashbuild's formation resulted from Metro's need to diversify into new avenues of business, one of which was building materials.

Koopman and a colleague at Metro, Gerald Haumant, were given $500,000 and six months in which to start the new business. Their intention was to provide a wholesale cash and carry service, stocking primarily a range of heavy building materials, door frames, steel windows, corrugated iron, and cement. Cashbuild's initial target market was the small builder and shopkeeper, not the man in the street. The specific focus was on black housing—builders and shopkeepers in rural, underdeveloped areas.

The initial idea was to set up many stores in rural areas, but the company's choice of start-up locations was limited by the parent company. According to Haumant, "Where we could enter at the lowest cost, for example, where Metro had a vacant piece of land, we put up stores." This may, however, have been an advantage in that it allowed the market to be tested nationally .

Source: Alan Bernstein and Susan Schneider. "Cashbuild." © 1988 INSEAD. All rights reserved.

The first branch was opened in King Williams Town (200 km inland from Port Elizabeth) in December 1978, followed in 1979 by branches in Vryburg (300 km inland from Durban), Louis Trichardt, and Pietersburg (400 km and 300 km north of Johannesburg, respectively).

In South Africa, country towns like these are typical of the extremely conservative, nationalistic character of white Afrikaaner politics. They form the core electoral base of South Africa's ruling National Party on the one hand, but also reflect a striking contrast between white (First World Culture) and black (Third World Culture).

By the 1979 financial year end, the first stores were already operating on a profitable basis, and another four were under construction. Pretax profits rose from $20,000 in 1979 to $350,000 in 1981, and the number of stores had increased to twelve, with another five under construction.

Wholesaling is a low-margin, high-volume business, and Cashbuild's initial strategy had paid off. The company's limited range of about 2,000 line items had helped achieve the required stockturns. Emphasis had been placed on developing stringent control procedures and focusing carefully on merchandise mix. According to Haumant,

> We were very disciplined from the word go, in terms of positioning. We wanted to prove that the cash and carry market for building materials was big enough to support a multistore operation and that it could switch a portion of the credit market over to cash and carry. Traditionally, the building industry is undercapitalized and the nature of the materials, their weight and bulk, were not thought to lend themselves to cash and carry selling.

One consequence of Cashbuild's business strategy was that a traditional organizational structure and corporate culture had emerged. Staff members were assigned line functions on a strictly hierarchical basis. Job descriptions were rigidly defined in terms of this hierarchy, and an individual's ability to advance through the organization was almost entirely determined by the level at which he entered. This, in turn, was a function of his level of skills, qualifications, and experience at the time of joining the company.

This created problems for black employees. Generations of inferior education and racial prejudice meant that the majority of black workers entered the company at a very low level (general laborers, floor sweepers, goods-receiving clerks, etc.). Their limited prospects for promotion and their rigidly defined areas of responsibility served to demotivate these employees.

Koopman and his executive team had developed the company's original philosophy from their First World perspective. They had thought that they would build a successful organization if they concentrated on just three aspects of their business:

- Give value to the customer
- Innovation and adaptability

- Total commitment to the business and to efficient organizational structures and procedure

As Koopman explains it:

The way it worked was simple and straightforward. Point number one was easy: In the early days of any business, the one and only thing you understand is that the customer is king. The person who knows all there is to know about the customer is the boss. Point number two is just as easy: The boss knows the market, determines the merchandise mix, refines and implements control systems, even if he doesn't work in them himself. Commitment, of course, is beyond debate. If the boss is 100 percent committed, why shouldn't everyone else be. After all, if business is successful, there will be pay increases, bonuses, better conditions—surely all employees would be committed. As for organizational matters, what would the average worker know about such things?

Cashbuild's management began to understand that the company's traditional organizational structure and autocratic management style had resulted in "corporate rigor mortis." The organization had lost the single-mindedness of its early days. The consequence of management's adherence to a hierarchical organizational chart (prominently displayed at Cashbuild's head office) was that individual goals and values were no longer congruent with management's goals and values, and neither of the two was in keeping with the company's philosophy.

Organizational Crisis ———————————————————————————

Koopman and his team had been monitoring Cashbuild's slipping performance for almost a year. With margins down, profits falling, and an unmotivated staff, Cashbuild had lost direction. Koopman, a restless and inquisitive character with an eclectic appetite for inspiration from sources as diverse as Marx and Sartre to Alvin Tofler's *Future Shock* and Schumacher's *Small is Beautiful*, set out to question his white managers about the company's poor state. "I went round all the branches and asked a thousand questions," says Koopman. "I found that most of my managers blamed their black force for being indolent, not interested, and unmotivated." When he probed further into their perceptions of his own management style, the response was that they found him to be "pompous, egocentric, dictatorial, and authoritarian."

Koopman recognized that these were precisely the kind of attributes inculcated by the system under which most whites are educated and brought up in South Africa. But what most concerned Koopman after this sobering experience was the thought that if his white lieutenants had these perceptions, what were black workers' attitudes?

One of the questions he asked black workers on his systematic tour of Cashbuild's then eighteen branches, was "How does Cashbuild make its money? How do you make yours?" The standard reply went something like this, "My wages come from the boss. He gets the money from the tin boxes delivered by a green van (Fidelity Guards) which comes round on Fridays. He buys stocks, and these get rung up on the till. Every night he takes the money home, works out what he owes us, and pays our wages." For Koopman, this represented a perfect description of how it happened but revealed total ignorance of how money was earned at Cashbuild.

Koopman became increasingly aware that the company's organizational and motivational crisis was rooted in South Africa's complex social and economic structures, which were then so intrinsically part of Cashbuild's corporate culture. Black workers viewed their jobs from a perspective of generations of educational disadvantage and racial prejudice. As a result of being denied the rewards of "free enterprise" in terms of land and business ownership, black workers' expectations were restricted to short-term needs. All too often, a job became simply a means to earn enough money to survive on a day-to-day basis. White workers, by contrast, viewed their jobs from the perspective of long-term career planning. With the advantage of superior education and access to the rewards of the capitalist system, their expectations tended to relate to the accumulation of wealth and personal status.

Cashbuild's Transformation

Koopman embarked on a process of organizational change by conducting three regional workshops with managers, regional managers, and head office teams. Each workshop dealt with questions such as:

- What do you think of the CEO as a leader?
- How do you rate your regional manager?
- How effective are our marketing strategies?
- What about black advancement?
- How do we cope with environmental change?
- Is our internal communication effective?
- How do you view union activities?
- How are we going to break across cultural lines?

According to the managers taking part in the workshops, black employees were just not motivated. With disturbing consistency, managers responded that blacks "don't care for the company," "are badly educated and don't understand the business," or "won't talk or open up."

Koopman concluded that employee demotivation could stem only from inappropriate management practices. The Cashbuild culture with its boxed hierarchy was meaningless to them. Workers could not see the connection between their worth and the company's efforts. With this conclusion came the general realization that, in South Africa, managers have separated the social man from the productive man who is paid for his capacity as a productive unit rather than for his pride in his labor. Further, most South African managers judge and reward their labor force by means of rank and status—something the Cashbuild workers said they despised. An individual had to "earn the right" to be a leader before he could step out ahead of the team, and the workers preferred the security of the team to individual treatment.

Finally, Koopman's perceptions of the cause of Cashbuild's organizational crises led to his understanding that any successful restructuring had to deal with two central issues:

1. Black workers would not relate to the business and its functions until they obtain full participation, with an accompanying right to benefit both materially and spiritually.

2. A hopelessly inadequate educational system leaves black job entrants at a considerable disadvantage to their counterparts, not only in knowledge and skills but in overall perception of business.

The three regional workshops served as precursors to many more formal and informal sessions that cut across every level of the company's structure. Koopman understood the level of risk that he was taking in search of appropriate management solutions. He nevertheless recognized that having decided to ensure survival by implementing a philosophy of worker participation, he had to be seen as taking action. Cashbuild called the process MBFA, Management By Fumbling Around. Koopman was convinced the process of discussion and "value-trading" at every level of the company was the key to the successful redirection of Cashbuild.

Throughout the process, Cashbuild's management attempted to categorize the issues that were raised, and five key elements came up repeatedly: the customer, the employee, the company, the competitor/supplier, and motivation.

We realized that these five elements could give us our starting point. I started to see that our five key elements were interdependent, and at the same time, our marketing, sales—in fact, our whole business—revolved around each employee. The importance of the team started to mean something tangible to me—there could be no distinction in color, sex, class, or *job classification*. When you've heard a man's heartbeat, you can never think him into a rigid hierarchical box.

Cashbuild's first step in implementing participative management was to create a new "holistic" organizational structure, which redefined corporate objectives .

Participative Management: The Care Philosophy_____

Koopman's views on participative management developed from the notion that Cashbuild's managers could no longer be seen as an extension of capitalist ownership. Since capital and land are out of reach for most black people in South Africa, either through lack of resources or simply through legislation, their only access to direct control is through the enterprise itself (policy and decision making) and through labor. By giving every employee a say in the policy and decision-making process, a sense of vested interest could be created. As a matter of necessity rather than ideology, participative management meant a move to communal ownership of Cashbuild's means of production. In late 1983, five years was envisioned to build a workable system.

Says Koopman:

> It's difficult now to reconstruct how the philosophy evolved. By no means was it a tidy sequence of events! We went into the whole process of change without any prerequisites or preconceptions. It was an article of faith that it should be an open-ended process. There was constant discussion. Management would come up with ideas, and we'd talk to workers about them—and they would respond with more ideals, suggestions, demands. So it went.

One of the enormous problems to be overcome was the immense communication gap that existed between black and white employees. Koopman was made especially aware of this gap when a puzzled black employee asked, "Why are you angry with me, Mr. Koopman?" When this was met with an equally puzzled expression from Koopman, the employee went on to say, "You must shake hands like this," serving him a limp handshake. To the employee, a firm handshake signaled anger.

Since 1983, Cashbuild had been developing a company philosophy and organizational environment that aimed at ensuring total commitment by all employees. A system of CARE groups had been embarked on in 1984 in an attempt to build team cohesion. Modeled on deeply rooted feelings of team, family, and nation cohesion in black African culture, the CARE group philosophy was based on the idea that "the company cares about its people, and the people must care about the company."

The CARE group concept evolved as a means of bridging this cultural gap. The groups were intended to provide a platform for participation in company affairs by all staff members. They were also intended to start the formation of an internal power base for staff. Cashbuild's employees were broken down into five main groups:

CARE group 1: Caddies, sweepers, and general laborers

CARE group 2: Goods-receiving clerks, cashiers, receptionists, and other semiskilled tasks

CARE group 3: Managers, trainers, and long-term advancement trainees

CARE group 4: Administrators, bookkeepers, and regional managers

CARE group 5: CEO, operations manager, buyer, finance manager, and personnel manager

A president was elected for each group by a majority vote. The president's function was to interface with management on issues of common concern. Meetings were to be held each month with members of the next level of CARE group present so that issues between the different levels could be confronted. One of the first tasks of the CARE groups was to design a "statement of company policy." The resulting booklet was translated into nine languages, and all staff members—from CEO to tea person—could be reprimanded by anyone else for violation of the company philosophy.

Labor Relations at EuroDisneyland*

Case 8.2
J. Stewart Black
Hal B. Gregersen

Only one year after the grand opening of EuroDisneyland, Robert Fitzpatrick left his position as EuroDisney's chairperson, citing a desire to start his own consulting firm. In April, 1993, Philippe Bourguignon took over the helm of EuroDisney, thought by some to be a sinking ship. EuroDisney faced a net loss of FFr188mm for the fiscal year ending September, 1992.[1] The European park also fell 1mm visitors short of its goal for the first year of operation, with the French comprising only 29% of the park's total visitors between April and September, 1992—a far cry from the predicted 50%.[2]

In addition to the financial woes weighing down on Bourguignon, he was also expected to stem the flow of bad publicity which EuroDisney had experienced from its inception. Phase Two development at EuroDisneyland was slated to start in September, 1993, but in light of their drained cash reserves (FFr1.1bn in May, 1993)[3], and monstrous debts (estimated at FFr21bn)[4], it was unclear as to how the estimated FFr8-10bn Phase Two project would be financed.

Despite this bleak picture, Michael Eisner, CEO of Walt Disney Co., remained optimistic about the venture: "Instant hits are things that go away quickly, and things that grow slowly and are part of the culture are what we look for. What we created in France is the biggest private investment in a foreign country by an American company ever. And it's gonna pay off."[5]

Source: Reprinted by permission of the authors.

This case was adapted for use in this book by Mark Mendenhall, 1994, with permission of the authors.

*This case was written by Research Assistant Tanya M. Spyridakis under the direction of Associate Professor J. Stewart Black, with the assistance of Associate Professor Hal Gregersen and Research Assistant Sonali Krishna as the basis for class discussion; it is not meant to illustrate the effective or ineffective handling of an administrative situation.

History

On March 24, 1987, Michael Eisner and Jacques Chirac, then the French Prime Minister, signed a contract for the building of a Disney theme park at Marne-la-Vallee. At the signing, Robert Fitzpatrick, fluent in French, recipient of two awards from the French government, and married to French national Sylvie Blondet, was introduced as the president of EuroDisneyland. Fitzpatrick was expected to be a key player in wooing support for the theme park from the French establishment.

Explanations for location choice included Marne-la-Vallee's close proximity to one of the world's tourism capitals (it is 20 miles from Paris), and approximately 300 mm people throughout France, Belgium, England, and Germany are within a day's drive or highspeed train ride. Good transportation was another advantage mentioned; one of the train/RER lines of the Paris Metro subway runs to Torcy, located in the center of Marne-la-Vallee. In addition, the French government promised to extend this line to the actual site of the park. The park is also served by A-4, a modern highway that runs from Paris to the German border, as well as a freeway that runs to Charles de Gaulle airport. Finally, the "chunnel" between France and England was expected to be completed near the time of EuroDisney's opening.

With a signed letter of intent in hand, Disney knew that the French government had too much at stake to let the project fail. This knowledge was enough to allow the company to hold out for concession after concession: the normal 18.6% VAT (Value Added Tax) on ticket sales was reduced to only 7%;[6] subsidized loans were secured to fund one-fourth of the building costs; contractual disputes would be settled by a special international panel of arbitrators, rather than by the French courts. Disney, however, did have to make a concession: it would respect and utilize French culture in its themes.

The park's development was to consist of two major phases. Phase One of the park would be a theme park as well as a complex of hotels, golf courses, and an aquatic park. Phase Two, slated to begin construction after the gates opened in 1992, entailed a community to be built around the park, including a sports complex, a technology park, a conference center, a theatre, a shopping mall, a university campus, villas, and condominiums.

In total, EuroDisney had 5,000 acres to play with. The theme park itself would initially occupy about 200 acres; totaling 730 acres by 1995.[7] Opening was set for early 1992, with a predicted attendance level of 11 mm visitors annually, and an estimated break-even point somewhere between 7 and 8 mm. Phase One's preliminary estimations on cost were $1 bn. This venture represented the largest single foreign investment ever in France. A French "pivot" company was formed to build the park with starting capital of FFr3bn, split 60% French, and 40% foreign.

Disney invested $160 mm directly into the project; a total of $600 mm in foreign investment was expected to flow into France each year.

At this point no definite plans for Phase Two had been laid out, making it difficult to do more than guess about the final size of the park. Costs, however, were expected to surpass the price tag of the first phase. In addition, in November, 1989, Fitzpatrick announced plans for a European version of the Disney-MGM studios, based on the original located at Disney World in Orlando, Florida. The studios would increase Disney's production of live action and animated filmed entertainment in Europe for both the European and world markets. Opening was projected for sometime in 1996.

Optimism was at an all time high; individuals and businesses alike raced to become part of the "Mickey Mouse money machine." "The phone's been ringing here ever since the announcement," said Marc Berthod of EpaMarne, the government body that oversees the Marne-la-Vallee region. "We've gotten calls from hotel chains to language interpreters—all asking for details on EuroDisneyland. And the individual mayors of the villages around here have been swamped with calls from people looking for jobs," he added.[8]

It was hoped that EuroDisney would provide the region some relief to their unemployment rate, which had hovered at 10% plus for the past several years. EuroDisney expected to generate as many as 28,000 plus jobs, from permanent park employees, to construction workers; a new laundry facility alone would employ 400 outside workers, just to wash the fifty tons of laundry expected to be generated per day by EuroDisneyland's 14,000 employees.

Cultural Chernobyl? _____

The "deal of the century" as many called EuroDisney, came under protests from all sides. Communists and intellectuals protested heavily. Ariane Mnouchkine, a theatre director, described it as a "cultural Chernobyl." "I wish with all my heart that the rebels would set fire to Disneyland," thundered one intellectual in the French newspaper *Le Figaro*. "Mickey Mouse," sniffed another, "is stifling individualism and transforming children into consumers." Other criticisms of the park cited the project as another attack on France's cultural landscape, already under siege from American movies and music. The theme park was damned as an example of American "neoprovincialism."[9]

Never ones to suppress their emotions, the farmers of the Marne-la-Vallee region manned protests of their own. Incited over terms of the government's contract with Disney, in which the French government would expropriate the necessary land and sell it without profit to EuroDisneyland development company, farmers lined the roadside with signs such as "Disney go home," "Stop the massacre," and "Don't gnaw away our national wealth." Local officials, though sympathetic to the plight of the farmers, were unwilling to let their predicament interfere with the Disney deal. "For many years these farmers have had the fortune to cultivate what is considered some of the richest land in France," said Berthod. "Now they'll have to find another occupation."[10]

One other front to be contended with by Disney was the communist dominated labor federation—the Confederation Generale du Travail (CGT). The CGT was skeptical of Disney's job creation claims. The CGT fought against the passage of a bill which would give managers the right to establish flexible work hours. This was believed to be essential for the profitable operation of EuroDisney, especially with its seasonal attendance variations.

Working to allay fears of traffic congestion, noise, pollution, etc.—all stemming from the project—Disney launched an aggressive community relations program. Efforts included: inviting local children to a birthday party for Mickey Mouse, sending Mickey to area hospitals, and hosting free trips to Disney World in Florida for dozens of local children and officials. This type of public relations is a rarity in France; businesses make little effort to establish good relations with local residents.

Dress and Indoctrination at Disney _____

Creating a fantasy worthy of the Magic Kingdom required more than just buildings and technology; it required people—a lot of people. Disney needed 12,000 plus employees for the theme park alone. Unlike either of the two U.S. theme parks, which have many seasonal and temporary, part-time college workers, these employees would be permanent cast members on the EuroDisney stage. "Casting centers" were set up in Paris, London, Amsterdam, and Frankfurt, in a drive to mirror the multicountry make-up/aspect of EuroDisney's visitors with the composition of the employees. It was nonetheless understood between the French government and Disney that a concentrated effort would be made to tap into the local French labor market. Overall, Disney was looking for workers with communications skills, spoke two European languages (French and one other), were outgoing, and liked to be around people.

As with all the parks, EuroDisney has its own "Disney University." Not being known for having the same definition of service, speculation abounded as to whether or not Disney would find enough Europeans with the right attitude for the job. However, with 24,000 applicants by November, 1991, this proved not to be a problem. "A lot of people made assumptions about France and Europe that have not turned out to be true. We find that we are attracting the same kind of people we did in the U.S.," said Thor Degelmann, a native Californian who has been with Disney for more than 25 years, and is EuroDisney's personnel director.[11]

Controversy did arise over Disney's strict appearance code, enforced in all of its parks. The rules are spelled out in a video presentation and in a guide book, given to all new cast members. The guide book details the requirements for just about everything one could imagine. Mens' hair must be cut above the collar and ears; no beards or mustaches allowed; all tatoos must be covered. Women must keep their hair in one "natural color," no frosting or streaking. Use of make-up is limited. False eyelashes, eyeliner, and eye pencil are completely off limits. Fingernails are not allowed to pass one's fingertips. Jewelry is allowed at an absolute minimum: Women can wear only one earring in each ear, but the earring must not go beyond the specified three-quarters of an inch diameter limit. Men and women alike are restricted to one ring per hand. In addition, women must wear the appropriate undergarments, and only transparent pantyhose are permitted. Cast members were also informed that they were expected to show up "fresh and clean" each day. A related training video contained a shower scene, indirectly saying that a daily bath was required.

French labor unions mounted protests against the appearance code, which they saw as "an attack on individual liberty." Others criticized Disney as being insensitive to French culture, individualism, and privacy, because restrictions on individual and collective liberties are illegal under French law, unless it can be demonstrated that the restrictions are requisite to the job and do not exceed what is necessary. Disney countered by saying that a ruling that barred them from imposing a squeaky-clean employment standard could threaten the image and long-term success of the park. "For us, the appearance code has a great effect from a product identification standpoint," said Degelmann. "Without it we wouldn't be presenting the Disney product that people would be expecting."[12] Degelmann also pointed out that many other companies, particularly airlines, had appearance codes just as strict, Disney's just happened to be written down. Aware of cultural differences, the company, according to Degelmann, had toned down the wording from the original American version. According to Degelmann no more than 5% of all applicants interviewed and provided the initial orientation, decided against working at EuroDisneyland.

EuroDisney also faced the challenge of getting the new cast members used to smiling and being polite to park guests on a consistent basis. Responding to a criticism of Disney's indoctrinating people, Degelmann stated, "You can't *make* someone be sincere all day. We select people who want to work here and are predisposed to do well in this environment. We don't try to change people, we arm them with the tools and motivation to perform."[13]

EuroDisneyland's Grand Opening

April 12, 1992. *France-Soir* enthusiastically predicted Disney dementia. "Mickey! It's madness," read its front page headline. Would-be visitors were warned of chaos on the roads. A government survey indicated half a million people carried by 90,000 cars might try to get in. Would people be turned away? French radio warned traffic to avoid the area.

By lunchtime the parking lot was less than half-full, suggesting an attendance level below 25,000. Speculative explanations ranged from people heeding the advice to stay away, to the more likely one-day strike that cut the direct rail link to EuroDisney from the center of Paris.

Queues for the main rides such as Pirates of the Caribbean and Big Thunder Mountain, were averaging around 15 minutes less than for an ordinary day at Disney World in Florida. Despite this fact, English visitors found the French reluctant to stand in line and wait. "The French seem to think that if God had meant them to queue, He wouldn't have given them elbows," commented one.[14] Different cultures have varying definitions of personal space. EuroDisney guests' problems ranged from people who either got too close or who left too much space between themselves and the person in front of them.

Other Problems Along the Way

Disney's first ads for work bids were all placed in English, which left small and medium-sized French firms feeling like foreigners in their own land. A data bank was eventually set up with information on over 20,000 French and European firms looking for work. The Chamber of Commerce, with the aid of Disney, developed a video text information bank that the smaller companies would be able to tap into. Local companies were told they would get work, but had to compete for it.

The building of EuroDisneyland was plagued by construction delays and modifications. All facades were given six coats of paint versus the standard one coat in the two U.S. parks. *Le Visionarium*, a 360-degree Circle-Vision screen movie, finished construction with $8-10 mm in extras. At one point Eisner ordered a $200,000 staircase be removed because it blocked a view of the Star Tours ride. This further hiked-up the EuroDisney bill, which already had to deal with construction costs being, on average, 20% higher than for similar jobs in the U.S. Another set back occurred when a fire, sparked by a short circuit, caused minor damage to the Sequoia Lodge while it was under construction.

Subcontractors also created headaches for Disney. Though already paid by Disney, the Gabot-Eremco construction contracting group had been unable to meet all of its obligations to the subcontractors it used on the EuroDisney project. Many of these subcontractors feared bankruptcy if not paid for their work in the park. Disney agreed to pay some of the money owed. Demands totaled $157 mm, stemming from work added to the project after the initial contracts had been signed; Disney conceded to about $20.3 mm.

Exhibit 1: Mickey Goes to France: The EuroDisney Deal

1984-1985 Disney negotiates with Spain and France for site of European Disneyland; France is chosen; protocol letter is signed by Eisner and Laurent Fabius, French Prime Minister.

1986 Farmers protest against government plan to expropriate necessary land.

1987 Disney and Jaques Chirac, French Prime Minister, sign letter of intent.

1988 Selects lead commercial bank lenders for the senior portion of the project. Forms the Societe en Nom Collectif (SNC). Begins planning for the equity offering of 51% of EuroDisneyland as required in the letter of intent. Disney and Michel Rocard, French Prime Minister, sign a rider to give Disney rights to the land immediately instead of 1989, as originally planned; construction begins.

1989 European press and stock analysts visit Walt Disney World in Orlando. Begin extensive news and television campaign. Stock starts trading at 20% to 25% premium from the issue price. Disney announces plans for a European version of the Disney-MGM Studios with a projected opening in 1996.

1991 Disney sets up "casting centers" in Paris, London, Amsterdam, and Frankfurt. Controversy erupts over dress codes.

1992 Disney bails out subcontractors. Pre-Opening party held at Buffalo Bill's Wild West Show; Threat of strike hangs over EuroDisneyland's Grand Opening. Grand Opening—April 12, 1992.

1993 Phillipe Bourguignon replaces Robert Fitzpatrick.

Source: *L'Expansion,* January, 1994.

It was thought that competition from French theme parks, which had significantly lower admission costs, might be a concern. However, Fitzpatrick did not appear to be daunted: "We are spending 22 billion French francs before we open the door, while the other places spent 700 million," he said. "This means we can pay infinitely more attention to details—to costumes, hotels, shops, trash baskets—to create a fantastic place. There's just too great a response to Disney for us to fail."[15]

With these bold predictions of his predecessor echoing in his ears, Bourguignon stared at his desk. Surrounding him were piles of financial statements drowning in red ink (to the tune of $500 mm), stock market reports chronicling EuroDisney's falling price from FFr166 on opening day to approximately FFr65, and newspapers full of stories of EuroDisneyland's cultural blunders. He wondered where he would find the magic to turn this kingdom around.

Endnotes

1. David Jefferson. "American Quits Chairman Post at EuroDisney." *The Wall Street Journal* (January 18, 1993): pp B1.
2. Ibid.
3. "Euro Disney: Waiting For Dumbo." *The Economist* (May 1, 1993): pp 74.
4. Peter Gumbel and Richard Turner. "Blundering Mouse: Fans Like EuroDisney But Its Parents' Goofs Weigh the Park Down." *The Wall Street Journal* (March 10, 1994): pp A12.
5. David Jefferson. "American Quits Chairman Post at Euro Disney." *The Wall Street Journal* (January 18, 1993): pp B1.
6. "Euro Disneyland: Mickey Hops the Pond." *The Economist* (March 28, 1987): pp 85.
7. "France, Disney Ink $2-Bil Contract to Construct Euroland." *Variety* (March 25, 1987).
8. Jaques Neher. "Mickey and Money for France." *The Journal of Commerce* (February 26, 1986): pp 1.
9. Richard Turner and Peter Gumbel. "Major Attraction: As Euro Disney Braces for its Grand Opening, the French Go Goofy." *The Wall Street Journal* (April 10, 1992): pp A1.
10. Jaques Neher. "Mickey and Money for France." *The Journal of Commerce* (February 26, 1986): pp 1.
11. Rone Tempest. "Challenging Casting Call For Disney; Help Wanted: Native American Indian, French-Speaking Preferred, To Play Sitting Bull in Wild West Show . . ." *Los Angeles Times* (November 8, 1991): pp A5.
12. "A Disney Dress Code Chafes in the Land of Haute Couture." *New York Times* (December 25, 1991): pp 1.
13. Anne Ferguson. "Maximising the Mouse." *Management Today* (September, 1989): pp 60.
14. Frank Barrett. "French Play Cat and Mouse with Mickey." *The Independent* (April 13, 1992): pp 10.
15. Steven Greenhouse. "Playing Disney in the Parisian Fields." *The New York Times* (February 17, 1991): pp C1.

Bibliography

Richard Turner and Peter Gumbel. "Major Attraction: As Euro Disney Braces for its Grand Opening, the French Go Goofy." *The Wall Street Journal* (April 10, 1992): pp A1.

David Jefferson. "An American Quits Chairman Post at Disney." *The Wall Street Journal* (January 18, 1993): pp B1.

Frank Barrett. "French Play Cat and Mouse with Mickey." *The Independent* (April 13, 1992): pp 10.

Joan Bakos. "Allons Enfants au Euro Disneyland!" *Restaurant Business* (April 10, 1991): pp 96-101.

"A Disney Dress Code Chafes in the Land of Haute Couture." *New York Times* (December 25, 1991): pp 1.

Robert Neff. "An American in Paris." *Business Week*. (March 12, 1990): pp 60-64.

Linda Bernier, Susan Roberts, and Elizabeth Ames. "Monsieur Mickey or Senor Miqui? Disney Seeks a European Site." *Business Week* (July 15, 1985): pp 48.

Mary Ann Galante. "Disney's Ambassador Guides Foreign Policy for a Magic Kingdom." *The Los Angeles Times* (May 27, 1987): pp 1.

Christopher Knowlton. "How Disney Keeps the Magic Going." *Fortune* (December 4, 1989): pp 111-132.

Jaques Neher. "Mickey and Money for France." *The Journal of Commerce* (February 26, 1986): pp 1.

"Can Disney Do it Again?" *Dun's Review* (June 1981): pp 80-82.

Irwin Ross. "Disney Gambles on Tomorrow." *Fortune* (October 4, 1982): 63-68.

Nigel Andrews. "Euro Disney and the Mouse that Soared." *The Financial Times* (April 11, 1991).

Myron Magnet. "The Mouse at Disney." *Fortune* (December 10, 1984): pp 57-64.

Stephen Koepp. "Do You Believe in Magic?" *Time* (April 25, 1988): 66-73.

Charles Leerhsen and Diona Gleizes. "And Now, Goofy Goes Gallic: A Little Bit of Orlando in Central France." *Newsweek* (April 13, 1992): pp 67.

Judson Green. "Brought to Account: Not a Mickey Mouse Organization." *Accountancy* (November, 1989): pp 16.

"Euro Disney: Waiting for Dumbo." *The Economist* (May 1, 1993): pp 74.

Roger Cohen. "Threat of Strike in Euro Disney Debut." *The New York Times* (April 10, 1992): pp 20.

Stanley Meisler. "Mickey, Minnie, and Cohorts Have a New Home in France." *The Los Angeles Times* (March 25, 1987): pp 1.

"Euro Disneyland: Mickey Hops the Pond." *The Economist* (March 28, 1987): pp 85.

Awata Fusaho. "Disneyland's Dreamlike Success." *Japan Quarterly* (January-March, 1988): pp 58-62.

Ellen Paris. "A Yen for Fun." *Forbes* (July 11, 1988): pp 38-39.

Hiroko Katayama. "Mouse Madness." *Forbes* (February 8, 1988): pp 152.

Tracy Dahlby. "Magic Kingdom East: Tokyo Disneyland Bets on Mikki Mausu." *The Washington Post* (April 10, 1983): pp F1.

Gale Eisenstodt and Hiroko Katayama. "Mickey Does Tokyo." *Forbes* (September 16, 1991): pp 16.

Hokaji Mino. "Tokyo Disneyland Inspires New Leisure Parks." *Business Japan* (July, 1988) pp 47-49.

Robert Wrubel. "Le Defi Mickey Mouse." *Financial World* (October 17, 1989): pp 18-21.

Rone Tempest. "Challenging Casting Call For Disney; Help Wanted: Native American Indian, French-Speaking Preferred, To Play Sitting Bull in Wild West Show . . ." *Los Angeles Times* (November 8, 1991): pp A5.

Jaques Neher. "Putting On a Show For the French; Disney Woos Europeans For Latest Theme Park." *The Washington Post* (April 2, 1989): pp H2.

"Euro Disney to Bail Out 40 Subcontractors;" *Los Angeles Times* (February 12, 1992): pp D5.

"New Disney Deal." *The New York Times* (March 12, 1992): pp D4.

Anne Ferguson. "Maximising the Mouse." *Management Today* (September, 1989): pp 57-62.

Cindy Gurlay. "Disney keeps O&M on tight rein in Europe; Ogilvy & Mather Intl.'s advertising contract with EuroDisneyland." *Information Access Company; Haymarket Publications Ltd. 1991* (March 28, 1991): pp 8.

Steven Greenhouse. "Playing Disney in the Parisian Fields." *The New York Times* (February 17, 1991): pp C1.

Peter Gumbel and Richard Turner. "Blundering Mouse: Fans Like Euro Disney But Its Parents' Goofs Weigh the Park Down." *The Wall Street Journal* (March 10, 1994): pp A1 & A12.

"Magic of the Magic Kingdom." *Los Angeles Times* (July 31, 1978): pp 1.

"Disney Magic Spreads Across the Atlantic; Popular U.S. Theme Park Prepares For Opening of Euro Disneyland Resort Near Paris in April, 1992." *Nation's Restaurant News* (October 28, 1991): pp 3.

Jane Sassen. "MICKEYMANIA" *International Management* (November, 1989): pp 32-34.

"France, Disney Ink $2-Bil Contract to Construct Euroland." *Variety* (March 25, 1987).

Suzanne Stephens. "That's Entertainment." *Architectural Record* (August, 1990): pp 72-79.

Judson Gooding. "Of Mice and Men." *Across the Board* (March, 1992): pp 40-44.

Chris Baum. "Euro Disney Awaits Mickey's Fans." *HOTELS* (October, 1991): pp 29-30.

Alan Riding. "Near Paris, Disney's Next Park." *The New York Times* (October 20, 1991): pp E6.

Robert Neff. "In Japan They're Goofy about Disney." *Business Week* (March 12, 1990).

Index